Readings in Certified Quantitative Risk Management (CQRM)

Applying Monte Carlo Risk Simulation,
Strategic Real Options, Stochastic Forecasting,
Portfolio Optimization, Data Analytics,
Business Intelligence, and Decision Modeling

Press

Johnathan Mun, Ph.D.
California, USA

For Jayden, Emma, and Penny.

In a world where risk and uncertainty abound,
you are the only constants in my life.

Dedicated in loving memory of my mom.

*Delight yourself in the Lord and He will
give you the desires of your heart.*

Psalm 37:4

INTRODUCTION

This readings book was created specifically to cover the areas tested in the Certified Quantitative Risk Management (CQRM) program, and is based on one of the author's book, *Modeling Risk* (Third Edition): *Applying Monte Carlo Risk Simulation, Strategic Real Options, Stochastic Forecasting, Portfolio Optimization, Data Analytics, Business Intelligence, and Decision Modeling* (2015). This current readings book mirrors the contents of the *Modeling Risk* book with the exception of the three chapters on Excel modeling and 21 applied business cases available only in *Modeling Risk*.

We live in an environment fraught with risk and operate our businesses in a risky world, as higher rewards only come with risks. It is unimaginable if the element of risk is not considered when corporate strategy is framed and when tactical projects are implemented. *Modeling Risk* provides a novel view of evaluating business decisions, projects, and strategies by taking into consideration a unified strategic portfolio analytical process. The book provides a qualitative and quantitative description of risk, as well as introductions to the Integrated Risk Management methods used in identifying, quantifying, applying, predicting, valuing, hedging, diversifying, and managing risk, through rigorous examples of the methods' applicability in the decision-making process.

Pragmatic applications are emphasized in order to demystify the many elements inherent in risk analysis. A black box will remain a black box if no one can understand the concepts despite its power and applicability. It is only when the black box becomes transparent so that analysts can understand, apply, and convince others of its results, value-add, and applicability, that the approach will receive widespread influence. This is done through step-by-step applications of risk analysis as well as presenting multiple cases and discussing real-life applications.

This book is targeted at the CQRM certification program but can also be used by the uninitiated professional as well as those well-versed in risk analysis—there is something for everyone. It is also applicable for use as a second-year M.B.A. level or introductory Ph.D. textbook.

Additional information on the CQRM program can be obtained at:

www.iiper.org and *www.realoptionsvaluation.com* or *www.rovusa.com*

ABOUT THE AUTHOR

 Dr. Johnathan C. Mun is the founder, chairman, and CEO of Real Options Valuation, Inc. (ROV), a consulting, training, and software development firm specializing in strategic real options, financial valuation, Monte Carlo risk simulation, stochastic forecasting, optimization, decision analytics, business intelligence, healthcare analytics, enterprise risk management, project risk management, and risk analysis located in northern Silicon Valley, California. ROV has partners around the world including Argentina, Beijing, Chicago, China, Colombia, Hong Kong, India, Italy, Japan, Malaysia, Mexico City, New York, Nigeria, Peru, Puerto Rico, Russia, Saudi Arabia, Shanghai, Singapore, Slovenia, South Korea, Spain, Venezuela, Zurich, and others. ROV also has a local office in Shanghai.

Dr. Mun is also the chairman of the International Institute of Professional Education and Research (IIPER), an accredited global organization staffed by professors from named universities from around the world that provides the Certified Quantitative Risk Management (CQRM) designation, among others. He is the creator of many different powerful software tools including Risk Simulator, Real Options SLS Super Lattice Solver, Modeling Toolkit, Project Economics Analysis Tool (PEAT), Credit Market Operational Liquidity Risk (CMOL), Employee Stock Options Valuation, ROV BizStats, ROV Modeler Suite (Basel Credit Modeler, Risk Modeler, Optimizer, and Valuator), ROV Compiler, ROV Extractor and Evaluator, ROV Dashboard, ROV Quantitative Data Miner, and other software applications, as well as the risk-analysis training DVD. He holds public seminars on risk analysis and CQRM programs. He has over 21 registered patents and patents pending globally. He has authored 26 books published by John Wiley & Sons, Elsevier Science, and ROV Press, including *Modeling Risk: Applying Monte Carlo Simulation, Real Options, Optimization, and Forecasting,* First Edition (Wiley, 2006), Second Edition (Wiley, 2010), and Third Edition (ROV Press, 2015); *The Banker's Handbook on Credit Risk* (2008); *Advanced Analytical Models: 250 Applications from Basel II Accord to Wall Street and Beyond* (2008); *Real Options Analysis: Tools and Techniques,* First Edition (2003) and Second Edition (2005); *Real Options Analysis Course: Business Cases* (2003); *Applied Risk Analysis: Moving Beyond Uncertainty* (2003); and *Valuing Employee Stock Options* (2004). His books and software are being used at over 350 top universities around the world, including the Bern Institute in Germany, Chung-Ang University in South Korea, Georgetown University, ITESM in Mexico, Massachusetts Institute of Technology, U.S. Naval Postgraduate School, New York University, Stockholm University in Sweden, University of the Andes in Chile, University of Chile, University of Pennsylvania Wharton School, University of York in the United Kingdom, and Edinburgh University in Scotland, among others.

Currently a risk, finance, and economics professor, Dr. Mun has taught courses in financial management, investments, real options, economics, and statistics at the undergraduate and the graduate MBA levels. He teaches and has taught at universities all over the world, from the U.S. Naval Postgraduate School (Monterey, California) and University of Applied Sciences (Switzerland and Germany) as full professor, to Golden Gate University (California) and St. Mary's College (California), and has chaired many graduate research MBA thesis and Ph.D. dissertation committees. He also teaches weeklong Risk Analysis, Real Options Analysis, and Risk Analysis for Managers public courses where participants can obtain the CRM and CQRM designations on completion. He is a senior fellow at the Magellan Center and sits on the board of standards at the American Academy of Financial Management.

He was formerly the Vice President of Analytics at Decisioneering, Inc., where he headed the development of options and financial analytics software products, analytical consulting, training, and technical support, and where he was the creator of the Real Options Analysis Toolkit software, the older and much less powerful predecessor of the Real Options Super Lattice software. Prior to joining Decisioneering, he was a Consulting Manager and Financial Economist in the Valuation Services and Global Financial Services practice of KPMG Consulting and a Manager with the Economic Consulting Services practice at KPMG LLP.

He has extensive experience in econometric modeling, financial analysis, real options, economic analysis, and statistics. During his tenure at Real Options Valuation, Inc., Decisioneering, and KPMG Consulting, he taught and consulted on a variety of real options, risk analysis, financial forecasting, project management, and financial valuation issues for more than 100 multinational firms (current and former clients include 3M, Airbus, Boeing, BP, Chevron Texaco, Financial Accounting Standards Board, Fujitsu, GE, Goodyear, Microsoft, Motorola, Pfizer, Timken, U.S. Department of Defense, U.S. Navy, Veritas, and many others). His experience prior to joining KPMG included being department head of financial planning and analysis at Viking Inc. of FedEx, performing financial forecasting, economic analysis, and market research. Prior to that, he did financial planning and freelance financial consulting work.

Dr. Mun received a Ph.D. in finance and economics from Lehigh University, where his research and academic interests were in the areas of investment finance, econometric modeling, financial options, corporate finance, and microeconomic theory. He also has an MBA in business administration, an MS in management science, and a BS in biology and physics. He is Certified in Financial Risk Management, Certified in Financial Consulting, and Certified in Risk Management. He is a member of the American Mensa, Phi Beta Kappa Honor Society, and Golden Key Honor Society as well as several other professional organizations, including the Eastern and Southern Finance Associations, American Economic Association, and Global Association of Risk Professionals.

In addition, he has written many academic articles published in the *Journal of Expert Systems with Applications; Defense Acquisition Research Journal; American Institute of Physics Proceedings; Acquisitions Research (U.S. Department of Defense); Journal of the Advances in Quantitative Accounting and Finance; Global Finance Journal; International Financial Review; Journal of Financial Analysis; Journal of Applied Financial Economics; Journal of International Financial Markets, Institutions and Money; Financial Engineering News;* and *Journal of the Society of Petroleum Engineers.* Finally, he has contributed chapters in dozens of books and written over a hundred technical whitepapers, newsletters, case studies, and research papers for Real Options Valuation, Inc.

JohnathanMun@cs.com
San Francisco, California
Amazon Author Site: *https://www.amazon.com/author/johnathanmun*
Google Scholar: *https://scholar.google.com/citations?hl=en&user=RdhYvvcAAAAJ*
Research Net: *https://www.researchgate.net/profile/Johnathan_Mun/research*
Linked In: *https://www.linkedin.com/in/drjohnathanmun*

SUMMARY PRAISES FOR *MODELING RISK*

... powerful toolset for portfolio/program managers to make rational choices among alternatives...
Rear Admiral James Greene (Ret.), Naval Postgraduate School, Acquisitions Chair (USA)

...unavoidable for any professional...logical, concrete and conclusive approach...
Jean Louis Vaysse, Vice President, Airbus (France)

...proven, revolutionary approach to quantifying risks and opportunities in an uncertain world...
Mike Twyman, Executive Vice President, Cubic Global Defense, Inc. (USA)

...must read for anyone running investment economics...best way to quantify risk and strategic options...
Mubarak A. Alkhater, Executive Director, New Business, Saudi Electric Co. (Saudi Arabia)

... pragmatic powerful risk techniques, valuable theoretical insights and analytics useful in any industry...
Dr. Robert S. Finocchiaro, Director, Corporate R&D Services, 3M (USA)

...most important risk tools in one volume, definitive source on risk management with vivid examples...
Dr. Ricardo Valerdi, Engineering Systems, Massachusetts Institute of Technology (USA)

...step-by-step complex concepts with unmatched ease and clarity...a "must read" for all professionals...
Dr. Hans Weber, Product Development Leader, Syngenta AG (Switzerland)

...clear step-by-step approach...latest technology in decision making for real-world business...
Dr. Paul W. Finnegan, Vice President, Alexion Pharmaceuticals (USA)

...clear roadmap and breadth of topics to create dynamic risk-adjusted strategies and options...
Jeffrey A. Clark, Vice President Strategic Planning, The Timken Company (USA)

...clearly organized and tool-supported exploration of real-life business risks, options, strategy...
Robert Mack, Vice President, Distinguished Analyst, Gartner Group (USA)

…full range of methodologies for quantifying and mitigating risk for effective enterprise management…

Raymond Heika, Director of Strategic Planning, Northrop Grumman Corporation (USA)

…a must-read for product portfolio managers…captures risk exposure of strategic investments…

Rafael Gutierrez, Executive Director Strategic Marketing Planning, Seagate Tech. (USA)

…complex topics exceptionally explained…can understand and practice…

Agustín Velázquez, Senior Economist, Venezuela Central Bank (Venezuela)

…constant source of practical applications with risk management theory…simply excellent!

Alfredo Roisenzvit, Executive Director/Professor, Risk-Business Latin America (Argentina)

…the best risk modeling book is now better…required reading by all executives…

David Mercier, Vice President Corporate Dev., Bonanza Creek Energy [Oil & Gas] (USA)

…bridge of theory and practice, intuitive, understandable interpretations…

Luis Melo, Senior Econometrician, Colombia Central Bank (Colombia)

…valuable tools for corporations to deliver value to shareholders and society even in rough times…

Dr. Markus Götz Junginger, Lead Partner, Gallup (Germany)

…innovative approach bridging the gap between theory and practice…

Dr. Richard J. Kish, Chair and Professor of Finance, Lehigh University (USA)

…absolutely the best book in risk…allows even mere mortals to do it…useful in all industries…

Dr. Thomas Housel, Professor, U.S. Naval Postgraduate School (USA)

…best theoretical and practical support for risk managers in all industries facing today's complex risks…

Dr. Timotej Jagric, Professor/Head, Finance and Banking, University of Maribor (Slovenia)

CONTENTS

CHAPTER SUMMARIES

This book is divided into eleven sections starting from a discussion of what risk is and how it is quantified, to how risk can be predicted, diversified, taken advantage of, hedged, and managed. The first section deals with *risk identification* where the different aspects of business risks are identified, including a brief historical view of how risk was evaluated in the past. The second section deals with *risk evaluation* explaining why disastrous ramifications may result if risk is not considered in business decisions. Section three pertains to *risk quantification* and details how risk can be captured quantitatively through step-by-step applications of Monte Carlo simulation. Section four pertains to *risk prediction* where the uncertain and risky future is predicted using analytical time-series methods. Section five deals with how *risk diversification* works when multiple projects exist in a portfolio. Section six's *risk mitigation* discussion deals with how a firm or management can take advantage of risk and uncertainty by implementing and maintaining flexibility in projects. Section seven provides a capstone discussion of applying *risk management* in companies, including how to obtain senior management's buy-in and implementing a change of perspective in corporate culture as it applies to risk analysis. This section also discusses the more traditional qualitative approach of Enterprise Risk Management and how it can be adapted to incorporate quantitative methods. Section eight presents a series of technical notes and section nine provides a quick reference guide to the analytics used throughout the book. Following is a synopsis of the material covered in each chapter of the book.

SECTION ONE–RISK IDENTIFICATION

Chapter 1–Moving Beyond Uncertainty

To the people who lived centuries ago, risk was simply the inevitability of chance occurrence beyond the realm of human control. We have been struggling with risk our entire existence, but, through trial and error and through the evolution of human knowledge and thought, have devised ways to describe and quantify risk. Risk assessment should be an important part of the decision-making process otherwise bad decisions may be made. Chapter 1 explores the different facets of risk within the realms of applied business risk analysis, providing an intuitive feel of what risk looks like.

SECTION TWO–RISK EVALUATION

Chapter 2–From Risk to Riches

The concepts of risk and return are detailed in Chapter 2, illustrating their relationships in the financial world, where a higher-risk project necessitates a higher expected return. How are uncertainties estimated and risk calculated? How do you convert a measure of uncertainty into a measure of risk? These are the topics covered in this chapter, starting from the basics of statistics to applying them in risk analysis, and including a discussion of the different measures of risk.

SECTION THREE—RISK QUANTIFICATION

Chapter 3—On the Shores of Monaco

Monte Carlo simulation in its simplest form is just a random number generator useful for forecasting, estimation, and risk analysis. A simulation calculates numerous scenarios of a model by repeatedly picking values from the probability distribution for the uncertain variables and using those values for the event—events such as totals, net profit, or gross expenses. Simplistically, think of the Monte Carlo simulation approach as repeatedly picking golf balls out of a large basket. Chapter 3 illustrates why simulation is important through the flaw of averages example. Excel is used to perform rudimentary simulations, and simulation is shown as a logical next-step extension to traditional approaches used in risk analysis.

Chapter 4—Test Driving Risk Simulator

Chapter 4 guides the user through applying the world's premier risk analysis and simulation software: *Risk Simulator*. With a few simple mouse clicks, the reader will be on his or her way to running sophisticated Monte Carlo simulation analysis to capture both uncertainty and risks using the Risk Simulator software. In addition, the interpretation of said analysis is also very important. The best analysis in the world is only as good as the analyst's ability to understand, utilize, present, report, and convince management or clients of the results.

Chapter 5—Pandora's Toolbox

Powerful simulation-related tools such as bootstrapping, distributional fitting, hypothesis test, correlated simulation, multidimensional simulation, tornado charts, and sensitivity charts are discussed in detail in Chapter 5, complete with step-by-step illustrations. These tools are extremely valuable to analysts working in the realm of risk analysis. The applicability of each tool is discussed in detail. For example, the use of nonparametric bootstrapping simulation as opposed to parametric Monte Carlo simulation approaches is discussed.

SECTION FOUR—RISK PREDICTION

Chapter 6—Tomorrow's Forecast Today

Chapter 6 focuses on applying Risk Simulator to run time-series forecasting methods, multivariate regressions, nonlinear extrapolation, stochastic processes, and Box–Jenkins ARIMA. In addition, the issues of seasonality and trend are discussed, together with the eight time-series models most commonly used by analysts to forecast future events given historical data. The software applications of each method are discussed in detail, complete with their associated measures of forecast errors and potential pitfalls.

Chapter 7—Using the Past to Predict the Future

The main thrust of Chapter 7 is time-series and regression analysis made easy. Starting with some basic time-series decomposition models, including exponential smoothing and moving averages, and moving onto more complex models, such as the Holt–Winters additive and multiplicative models, the reader will very easily manage to navigate through the maze of time-series analysis. The basics of regression analysis are also discussed, complete with pragmatic discussions of statistical validity tests as well as the pitfalls of regression analysis, including how to identify and fix heteroskedasticity, autocorrelation, and multicollinearity.

SECTION FIVE–RISK DIVERSIFICATION

Chapter 8–The Search for the Optimal Decision

In most business or analytical models, there are variables over which you have control, such as how much to charge for a product or how much to invest in a project. These controlled variables are called *decision variables*. Finding the optimal values for decision variables can make the difference between reaching an important goal and missing that goal. Chapter 8 details the optimization process at a high level, with illustrations on solving deterministic optimization problems manually, using graphs, and applying Excel's Solver add-in. Chapter 9 illustrates the solution to optimization problems under uncertainty, mirroring more closely real-life business conditions.

Chapter 9–Optimization under Uncertainty

Chapter 9 illustrates two optimization models with step-by-step details. The first model is a discrete portfolio optimization of projects under uncertainty. Given a set of 12 potential projects, the model evaluates all possible discrete combinations of projects on a "go" or "no-go" basis such that a budget constraint is satisfied, while simultaneously providing the best level of returns subject to uncertainty. The best projects will then be chosen based on these criteria. The second model evaluates a financial portfolio's continuous allocation of different asset classes with different levels of risks and returns. The objective of this model is to find the optimal allocation of assets subject to a 100 percent allocation constraint that still maximizes the Sharpe ratio, or the portfolio's *return to risk* ratio. This ratio will maximize the portfolio's return subject to the minimum risks possible while accounting for the cross-correlation diversification effects of the asset classes in a portfolio.

SECTION SIX–RISK MITIGATION

Chapter 10–What's So Real about Real Options, and Why Are They Optional?

Chapter 10 describes what real options analysis is, who has used the approach, how companies are using it, and what some of the characteristics of real options are. The chapter describes real options analysis in a nutshell, providing the reader with a solid introduction to their concepts without the need for their theoretical underpinnings. Real options are applicable if the following requirements are met: traditional financial analysis can be performed and models can be built; uncertainty exists; the same uncertainty drives value; management or the project has strategic options or flexibility to either take advantage of these uncertainties or to hedge them; and management must be credible to execute the relevant strategic options when they become optimal to do so.

Chapter 11–The Black Box Made Transparent: Real Options SLS

Chapter 11 introduces the readers to the world's first true real options software applicable across all industries. The chapter illustrates how a user can get started with the software in a few short moments after it has been installed. The reader is provided with hands-on experience with the *Real Options Super Lattice Solver* to obtain immediate results—a true test when the rubber meets the road.

SECTION SEVEN–RISK MANAGEMENT

Chapter 12–The Warning Signs

The risk analysis software applications illustrated in this book are extremely powerful tools and could prove detrimental in the hands of untrained and unlearned novices. Management, the end user of the results from said tools, must be able to discern if quality analysis has been performed. Chapter 12 delves into the thirty-some problematic issues most commonly encountered by analysts applying risk analysis techniques, and how management can spot these mistakes. While it might be the job of the analyst to create the models and use the fancy analytics, it is senior management's job to challenge the assumptions and results obtained from the analysis. Model errors, assumption and input errors, analytical errors, user errors, and interpretation errors are some of the issues discussed in this chapter. Some of the issues and concerns raised for management's consideration in performing due diligence include challenging distributional assumptions, critical success factors, impact drivers, truncation, forecast validity, endpoints, extreme values, structural breaks, values at risk, a priori expectations, backcasting, statistical validity, specification errors, out of range forecasts, heteroskedasticity, multicollinearity, omitted variables, spurious relationships, causality and correlation, autoregressive processes, seasonality, random walks, and stochastic processes.

Chapter 13–Enterprise Risk Management

This chapter delves into Enterprise Risk Management (ERM) in an organization, which by definition includes the business processes and methods used to identify and manage risks as well as seize upside opportunities to achieve its objectives. ERM, therefore, provides a methodological framework in risk management for identifying risky events or conditions relevant to the organization's objectives, risks, and opportunities, identifying and assessing these conditions in terms of *likelihood* or frequency of occurrence as well as the risk condition's magnitude or *impact*, determining risk mitigation and postrisk response strategy, and monitoring the progress of these risk controls. ERM applies to a broad spectrum of risks facing an organization to ensure that these risks are properly identified and managed. Investors, government regulators, banks, and debt rating agencies, among others, tend to scrutinize the risk-management processes of an organization as a key metric to its potential success. In addition, ERM is also described as a risk-based approach to strategic planning as well as for managing an organization by integrating internal risk controls and external risk-compliance requirements. This chapter explains how the Project Economics Analysis Tool (PEAT) utility's ERM module enhances qualitative risk management with advanced analytics in Integrated Risk Management® (IRM), and concludes with global risk compliance issues such as COSO, ISO 31000:2009, Basel III, and the Sarbanes–Oxley Act.

Chapter 14–Changing a Corporate Culture

Advanced analytics is hard to explain to management. So, how do you get risk analysis accepted as the norm into a corporation, especially if your industry is highly conservative? It is a guarantee in companies like these that an analyst showing senior management a series of fancy and mathematically sophisticated models will be thrown out of the office together with his or her results, and have the door slammed shut. Change management is the topic of discussion in Chapter 14. Explaining the results and convincing management appropriately go hand in hand with the characteristics of the analytical tools, which, if they satisfy certain change management requisites, can make acceptance easier. The approach that guarantees acceptance has to be three pronged: top, middle, and junior levels must all get in on the action. Change management specialists underscore that change comes more easily if the methodologies to be accepted are applicable to the problems at hand, are accurate and consistent, provide value-added propositions, are easy to explain, have comparative advantage over traditional approaches, are compatible with the old, have modeling flexibility, are backed by executive sponsorship, and are influenced and championed by external parties including competitors, customers, counterparties and vendors.

Chapter 15–Putting It All Together: Integrated Risk Management with PEAT

As the name implies, this chapter provides a capstone case application and completes the circle in terms of IRM steps introduced throughout the book, starting in Chapter 1 by methodically solving a portfolio of risk-based projects. The chapter starts off with a quick review of the IRM process and continues with the introduction of the PEAT utility to value the multiple projects, compare them as a portfolio of analysis of alternatives, run tornado, scenario, sensitivity, risk simulations, and portfolio optimization on the static results.

SECTION EIGHT–TECHNICAL NOTES

Technical Notes 1–8

This section includes several technical notes on interpreting PDF, CDF, and ICDF; explanations of convolution theory and copulas; comparing Pareto charts with sensitivity charts; probability distribution charts analysis and comparisons; fitting distributions using percentiles; dynamic project management with cost and schedule risk; and an introduction to ROV BizStats for running business statistics analysis.

SECTION NINE–VISUAL GUIDES AND SUMMARIES

Visual Guides

Multiple visual guides summarizing the key contents of the book are provided in a convenient all-in-one location.

Quick Reference: Analytics Summary

This subsection provides a quick reference guide to all the analytics presented in this book in one convenient list.

Tables You Really Need

Multiple tables are included in the back of the book covering various aspects of probability distributions and strategic real options valuation multiples.

SECTION ONE –
RISK IDENTIFICATION

CHAPTER 1 – MOVING BEYOND UNCERTAINTY

A BRIEF HISTORY OF RISK:
WHAT EXACTLY IS RISK?

Since the beginning of recorded history, games of chance have been a popular pastime. Even in Biblical accounts, Roman soldiers cast lots for Christ's robes. In earlier times, chance was something that occurred in nature, and humans were simply subjected to it as a ship is to the capricious tosses of the waves in an ocean. Even up to the time of the Renaissance, the future was thought to be simply a chance occurrence of completely random events and beyond the control of humans. However, with the advent of games of chance, human greed has propelled the study of risk and chance to ever more closely mirror real-life events. Although these games were initially played with great enthusiasm, no one actually sat down and figured out the odds. Of course, the individual who understood and mastered the concept of chance was bound to be in a better position to profit from such games of chance. It was not until the mid-1600s that the concept of chance was properly studied, and the first such serious endeavor can be credited to Blaise Pascal, one of the fathers of modern choice, chance, and probability.[1] Fortunately for us, after many centuries of mathematical and statistical innovations from pioneers such as Pascal, Bernoulli, Bayes, Gauss, LaPlace, and Fermat, our modern world of uncertainty can be explained with much more elegance through methodological applications of risk and uncertainty management techniques.

To the people who lived centuries ago, risk was simply the inevitability of chance occurrence beyond the realm of human control. Albeit many phony soothsayers profited from their ability to convincingly profess their clairvoyance by simply stating the obvious or reading the victims' body language and telling them what they wanted to hear. We modern-day humans, ignoring for the moment the occasional seers among us, with our fancy technological achievements, are still susceptible to risk and uncertainty. We may be able to predict the orbital paths of planets in our solar system with astounding accuracy or the escape velocity required to shoot a man from the Earth to the Moon, but when it comes to predicting a firm's revenues the following year, we are at a loss. Humans have been struggling with risk our entire existence, but through trial and error, and through the evolution of human knowledge and thought, have devised ways to describe, quantify, hedge, and take advantage of risk.

Clearly the entire realm of risk analysis is great and would most probably be intractable within the few chapters of a book. Therefore, this book is concerned with only a small niche of risk, namely, *applied business risk modeling and analysis*. Even in the areas of applied business risk analysis, the diversity is great. For instance, business risk can be roughly divided into the areas of operational risk management and financial risk management. In financial risk, one can look at market risk, private risk, credit risk, default risk, maturity risk, liquidity risk, inflationary risk, interest rate risk, country risk, and so forth. This book focuses on the application of risk analysis in the sense of how to adequately apply the tools to identify, understand, quantify, and diversify risk such that it can be hedged and managed more effectively. These tools are generic enough that they can be applied across a whole spectrum of business conditions, industries, and needs. Finally, understanding this text, together with *Real Options Analysis,* Second Edition (Wiley 2005), and the associated Risk Simulator and Real Options SLS software, are required for the Certified Quantitative Risk Management or CQRM certification program (see www.realoptionsvaluation.com for more details).

UNCERTAINTY VERSUS RISK

Risk and uncertainty are very different-looking animals but they are of the same species; however, the lines of demarcation are often blurred. A distinction is critical at this juncture before proceeding and worthy of segue. Suppose I am senseless enough to take a sky-diving trip with a good friend and we board a plane headed for the Palm Springs desert. While airborne at 10,000 feet and watching our lives flash before our eyes, we realize that in our haste we forgot to pack our parachutes on board. However, there is an old, dusty, and dilapidated emergency parachute on the plane. At that point, both my friend and I have the same level of uncertainty—the uncertainty of whether the old parachute will open and if it does not, whether we will fall to our deaths. However, being the risk-adverse, nice guy I am, I decide to let my buddy take the plunge. Clearly, he is the one taking the plunge and the same person taking the risk. I bear no risk at this time while my friend bears all the risk.[2] However, we both have the same level of uncertainty as to whether the parachute will actually fail. In fact, we both have the same level of uncertainty as to the outcome of the day's trading on the New York Stock Exchange—which has absolutely no impact on whether we live or die that day. Only when he jumps and the parachute opens will the uncertainty become resolved through the passage of time, action, and events. However, even when the uncertainty is resolved with the opening of the parachute, the risk still exists as to whether he will land safely on the ground below.

Therefore, risk is something one bears and is the outcome of uncertainty. Just because there is uncertainty, there could very well be no risk. If the only thing that bothers a U.S.-based firm's CEO is the fluctuation in the foreign exchange market of the Zambian kwacha, then I might suggest shorting some kwachas and shifting his portfolio to U.S.-based debt. This uncertainty if it does not affect the firm's bottom line in any way is only uncertainty and not risk. This book is concerned with risk by performing uncertainty analysis—the same uncertainty that brings about risk by its mere existence as it impacts the value of a particular project. It is further assumed that the end user of this uncertainty analysis uses the results appropriately, whether the analysis is for identifying, adjusting, or selecting projects with respect to their risks, and so forth. Otherwise, running millions of fancy simulation trials and letting the results "marinate" will be useless. By running simulations on the foreign exchange market of the Zambian kwacha, an analyst sitting in a cubicle somewhere in downtown San Francisco will in no way reduce the risk of the kwacha in the market or the firm's exposure to the same. Only by using the results from an uncertainty simulation analysis and finding ways to hedge or mitigate the quantified fluctuation and downside risks of the firm's foreign exchange exposure through the derivatives market could the analyst be construed as having performed risk analysis and risk management.

To further illustrate the differences between risk and uncertainty, suppose we are attempting to forecast the stock price of Microsoft (MSFT). Suppose MSFT is currently priced at $25 per share, and historical prices place the stock at 21.89% volatility. Now suppose that for the next 5 years, MSFT does not engage in any risky ventures and stays exactly the way it is, and further suppose that the entire economic and financial world remains constant. This means that *risk* is fixed and unchanging, that is, volatility is unchanging for the next 5 years. However, the price uncertainty still increases over time. That is, the width of the forecast intervals will still increase over time. For instance, Year 0's forecast is known and is $25. However, as we progress one day, MSFT will most probably vary between $24 and $26. One year later, the uncertainty bounds may be between $20 and $30. Five years into the future, the boundaries might be between $10 and $50. So, in this example, *uncertainties increase* while *risks remain the same*. Therefore, risk is not equal to uncertainty. This idea is, of course, applicable to any forecasting approach whereby it becomes more and more difficult to forecast the future even though the risk remains the same. Now, if risk changes over time, the bounds of uncertainty get more complicated (e.g., uncertainty bounds of sinusoidal waves with discrete event jumps).

In other instances, risk and uncertainty are used interchangeably. For instance, suppose you play a coin-toss game—bet $0.50 and if heads come up you win $1 but you lose everything if tails appear. The risk here is you lose everything because the risk is that tails may appear. The uncertainty here is that tails may appear. Given that tails appear, you lose everything; hence, uncertainty brings with it risk. Uncertainty is the possibility of an event occurring, and risk is the ramification of such an event occurring. People tend to use these two terms interchangeably.

In discussing uncertainty, there are three levels of uncertainties in the world: the *known*, the *unknown*, and the *unknowable*. The known is, of course, what we know will occur and are certain of its occurrence (contractual obligations or a guaranteed event); the unknown is what we do not know and can be simulated. These events will become known through the passage of time, events, and action (the uncertainty of whether a new drug or technology can be developed successfully will become known after spending years and millions on research programs—it will either work or not, and we will know this in the future), and these events carry with them risks but these risks will be reduced or eliminated over time. However, unknowable events carry both uncertainty and risk such that the totality of the risk and uncertainty may not change through the passage of time, events, or actions. These are events such as when the next tsunami or earthquake will hit, or when another act of terrorism will occur around the world. When an event occurs, uncertainty becomes resolved but risk still remains (another one may or may not hit tomorrow). In traditional analysis, we care about the known factors. In risk analysis, we care about the unknown and unknowable factors. The unknowable factors are easy to hedge—get the appropriate insurance! That is, do not do business in a war-torn country, get away from politically unstable economies, buy hazard and business interruption insurance, and so forth. It is the unknown factors that risk analysis will provide the most significant amount of value.

WHY IS RISK IMPORTANT IN MAKING DECISIONS?

Risk should be an important part of the decision-making process; otherwise bad decisions may be made without an assessment of risk. For instance, suppose projects are chosen based simply on an evaluation of returns; clearly the highest-return project will be chosen over lower-return projects. In financial theory, projects with higher returns will in most cases bear higher risks.[3] Therefore, instead of relying purely on bottom-line profits, a project should be evaluated based on its returns as well as its risks. Figures 1.1 and 1.2 illustrate the errors in judgment when risks are ignored.

> The concepts of risk and uncertainty are related but different. Uncertainty involves variables that are unknown and changing, but uncertainty will be become known and resolved through the passage of time, events, and action. Risk is something one bears and is the outcome of uncertainty. Sometimes, risk may remain constant while uncertainty increases over time.

Figure 1.1 lists three *mutually exclusive* projects with their respective costs to implement, expected net returns (net of the costs to implement), and risk levels (all in present values).[4] Clearly, for the budget-constrained manager, the cheaper the project the better, resulting in the selection of Project X.[5] The returns-driven manager will choose Project Y with the highest returns, assuming that budget is not an issue. Project Z will be chosen by the risk-averse manager as it provides the least amount of risk while providing a positive net return. The upshot is that, with three different projects and three different managers, three different decisions will be made. Which manager is correct and why?

Why is Risk Important?

Name of Project	Cost	Returns	Risk
Project X	$50	$50	$25
Project Y	$250	$200	$200
Project Z	$100	$100	$10

Project X for the cost and budget-constrained manager

Project Y for the returns driven and nonresource-constrained manager

Project Z for the risk-adverse manager

Project Z for the smart manager

Figure 1.1: Deciding Among Different Projects

Figure 1.2 shows that Project Z should be chosen. For illustration purposes, suppose all three projects are independent and mutually exclusive,[6] and that an unlimited number of projects from each category can be chosen but the budget is constrained at $1,000. Therefore, with this $1,000 budget, 20 Project Xs can be chosen, yielding $1,000 in net returns and $500 risks, and so forth. It is clear from Figure 1.2 that Project Z is the best project as for the same level of net returns ($1,000), the least amount of risk is undertaken ($100). Another way of viewing this selection is that for each $1 of returns obtained, only $0.1 amount of risk is involved on average, or that for each $1 of risk, $10 in returns are obtained on average. This example illustrates the concept of *bang for the buck* or getting the best value with the least amount of risk. An even more blatant example is if there are several different projects with identical single-point average net returns of $10 million each. Without risk analysis, a manager should in theory be indifferent in choosing any of the projects.[7] However, with risk analysis, a better decision can be made—for instance, suppose the first project has a 10 percent chance of exceeding $10 million, the second a 15 percent chance, and the third a 55 percent chance, which means that the third project is the best bet.

This approach of bang for the buck, or returns to risk ratio, is the cornerstone of the Markowitz efficient frontier in modern portfolio theory. That is, if we constrained the total portfolio risk level and successively allowed it to increase over time, we will obtain several efficient portfolio allocations for different risk characteristics. Thus, different efficient portfolio allocations can be obtained for different individuals with different risk preferences.

At the bottom of Figure 1.2, we see a sample Markowitz efficient frontier. In Chapter 9, we revisit this topic in more detail through the use of an example of portfolio optimization of various investment decisions as well as a military portfolio example, to determine the optimal or best allocation of assets and investments or project selection within the context of a portfolio (maximizing a certain objective such as profits or bang-for-the-buck Sharpe ratio subject to certain constraints such as time, budget, cost, risk, and so forth). But briefly, in the chart in Figure 1.2, each dot represents a *portfolio* of multiple projects, projected in a two-dimensional plot of returns (y-axis) and risk (x-axis). If you compare portfolios A and B, a rational decision maker will choose portfolio A because it has a higher return with the same amount of risk as B. In addition, the same decision maker will choose portfolio A over portfolio C because for the same returns, A has a lower risk. For similar reasons, D will be chosen over C.

Looking at bang for the buck, X (2), Y (1), Z (10), Project Z should be chosen--with a $1,000 budget, the following can be obtained:

Project X: 20 Project Xs returning $1,000, with $500 risk
Project Y: 4 Project Xs returning $800, with $800 risk
Project Z: 10 Project Xs returning $1,000, with $100 risk

Project X: For each $1 return, $0.5 risk is taken
Project Y: For each $1 return, $1.0 risk is taken
Project Z: For each $1 return, $0.1 risk is taken

Project X: For each $1 of risk taken, $2 return is obtained
Project Y: For each $1 of risk taken, $1 return is obtained
Project Z: For each $1 of risk taken, $10 return is obtained

Conclusion: Risk is important. Forgoing risks results in making the wrong decision.

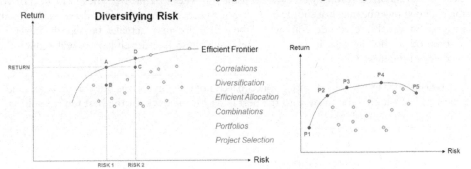

Figure 1.2: Adding an Element of Risk

In other words, there are multiple combinations of portfolios that can be developed, but there is an extreme set of portfolios that will yield the highest returns subject to the least amount of risk or the best bang for the buck, and these portfolios lie on the upper end of the curve, named the efficient frontier. We can obtain these portfolio points by running an optimization. *Each point on this graph is an optimization run, and the efficient frontier is simply multiple optimization runs across different and changing constraints.* This approach allows the decision maker flexibility or to have a portfolio of options, an important topic discussed in more detail later (Chapters 10 and 11), rather than be fixed with only a single decision point. In fact, if going from one portfolio to another lies in a steep upward sloping curve (going from P1 to P2 in Figure 1.2), then it is a good idea to move up to the next portfolio, assuming the new portfolio's constraints are acceptable. In other words, a steep positive slope means that for the same amount of risk, the amount of returns you obtain is significantly higher to compensate for the additional resources and risk. In contrast, if the slope is relatively flat (going from P3 to P4), going to the next portfolio on the curve is, perhaps, not such a good idea as only a little marginal return is obtained for a significantly higher risk. However, if additional resources are available and there are no better alternatives, and if the decision maker is willing to take the higher risk for a slight gain, then the next portfolio might still be advisable. At the point where the frontier curves downward (going from P4 to P5), it is no longer efficient and definitely not advisable because for the additional resource constraints required, the risk increases but returns actually decrease, indicating not only diminishing marginal returns, but completely negative marginal returns. So, when presented with such an analysis, the decision maker can decide which portfolio to undertake, what the resources required will be, and what the projected returns and risks will be.

DEALING WITH RISK THE OLD-FASHIONED WAY

Businesses have been dealing with risk since the beginning of the history of commerce. In most cases, managers have looked at the risks of a particular project, acknowledged their existence, and moved on. Little quantification was performed in the past. In fact, most decision makers look only to single-point estimates of a project's profitability. Figure 1.3 shows an example of a single-point estimate. The estimated net revenue of $30 is simply that, a single point whose probability of occurrence is close to zero.[8] Even in the simple model shown in Figure 1.3, the effects of interdependencies are ignored, and in traditional modeling jargon, we have the problem of *garbage-in, garbage-out* (GIGO). As an example of interdependencies, the units sold are probably negatively correlated to the price of the product,[9] and positively correlated to the average variable cost,[10] ignoring these effects in a single-point estimate will yield grossly incorrect results. For instance, if the unit sales variable becomes 11 instead of 10, the resulting revenue may not simply be $35. The net revenue may actually decrease due to an increase in variable cost per unit, while the sale price may actually be slightly lower to accommodate this increase in unit sales. Ignoring these interdependencies will reduce the accuracy of the model.

> A rational manager would choose projects based not only on returns but also on risks. The best projects tend to be those with the best bang for the buck, or the best returns subject to some specified risks.

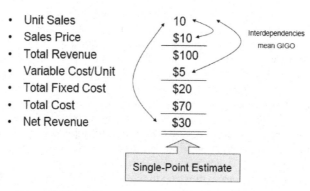

How confident are you of the analysis outcome?
This may be dead wrong!

Figure 1.3: Single-point Estimates

One approach used to deal with risk and uncertainty is the application of scenario analysis, as seen in Figure 1.4. Suppose the worst-case, nominal-case, and best-case scenarios are applied to the unit sales; the resulting three scenarios' net revenues are obtained. As earlier, the problems of interdependencies are not addressed. The net revenues obtained are simply too variable, ranging from $5 to $55. Not much can be determined from this analysis.

Scenario Analysis

• Unit Sales	10	Best Case: 15
• Sales Price	$10	Most Likely: 10
• Total Revenue	$100	Worst Case: 5
• Variable Cost/Unit	$5	
• Total Fixed Cost	$20	
• Total Cost	$70	Best Case: $55
• Net Revenue	$30	Most Likely: $30
		Worst Case: $5

Outcomes are too variable–which will occur?

The best, most likely, and worst-case scenarios are
usually simply wild guesses!

Figure 1.4: Scenario Analysis

A related approach is to perform *what-if* or *sensitivity* analysis as seen in Figure 1.5. Each variable is perturbed a prespecified amount and the resulting change in net revenues is captured. This approach is great for understanding which variables drive or impact the bottom line the most. A related approach is the use of tornado and sensitivity charts as detailed in Chapter 5, Pandora's Toolbox, which looks at a series of simulation tools. These approaches were usually the extent to which risk and uncertainty analysis were traditionally performed. Clearly, a better and more robust approach is required.

What-If Analysis

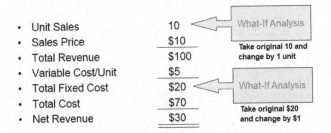

• Unit Sales	10	What-If Analysis
• Sales Price	$10	
• Total Revenue	$100	Take original 10 and change by 1 unit
• Variable Cost/Unit	$5	
• Total Fixed Cost	$20	What-If Analysis
• Total Cost	$70	
• Net Revenue	$30	Take original $20 and change by $1

Captures the marginal impacts, but which
condition will really occur?

Great in capturing sensitivities!

Figure 1.5: What-If Sensitivity Analysis

This is the point where simulation comes in. Figure 1.6 shows how simulation can be viewed as simply an extension of the traditional approaches of sensitivity and scenario testing. The critical success drivers or the variables that affect the bottom-line net-revenue variable the most, which at the same time are uncertain, are simulated. In simulation, the interdependencies are accounted for by using correlations. The uncertain variables are then simulated thousands of times to emulate all potential permutations and combinations of outcomes. The resulting net revenues from these simulated potential outcomes are tabulated and analyzed. In essence, in its most basic form, simulation is simply an enhanced version of traditional approaches such as sensitivity and scenario analysis but automatically performed for thousands of times while accounting for all the dynamic interactions between the simulated variables. The resulting net revenues from simulation, as seen in Figure 1.7, show that there is a 90 percent probability that the net revenues will fall between $20.15 and $39.85, with a 5 percent worst-case scenario of net revenues falling below $20.15. Rather than having only three scenarios, simulation created 10,000 scenarios, or trials, where multiple variables are simulated and changing simultaneously (unit sales, sale price, and variable cost per unit), while their respective relationships or correlations are maintained.

Simulation Approach

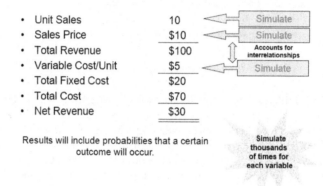

Figure 1.6: Monte Carlo Simulation Approach

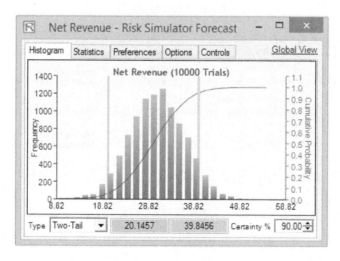

Figure 1.7: Simulation Results

THE LOOK AND FEEL OF
RISK AND UNCERTAINTY

In most financial risk analyses, the first step is to create a series of free cash flows (FCF) discounted at the weighted average cost of capital (WACC),[11] which can take the shape of an income statement or discounted cash-flow (DCF) model. The resulting deterministic free cash flows are depicted on a time line, akin to that shown in Figure 1.8. These cash-flow figures are in most cases forecasts of the unknown future. In this simple example, the cash flows are assumed to follow a straight-line growth curve (of course, other shaped curves also can be constructed). Similar forecasts can be constructed using historical data and fitting these data to a time-series model or a regression analysis.[12] Whatever the method of obtaining said forecasts or the shape of the growth curve, these are point estimates of the unknown future. Performing a financial analysis on these static cash flows provides an accurate value of the project if and only if all the future cash flows are known with certainty—that is, no uncertainty exists.

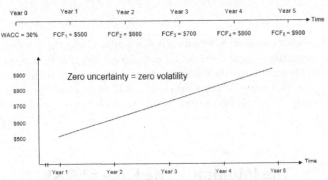

The Intuition – Deterministic Analysis

This straight-line cash-flow projection is the basics of DCF analysis.
This assumes a static and known set of future cash flows.

Figure 1.8: The Intuition of Risk—Deterministic Analysis [13]

However, in reality, business conditions are hard to forecast. Uncertainty exists, and the actual levels of future cash flows may look more like those in Figure 1.9; that is, at certain time periods, actual cash flows may be above, below, or at the forecast levels. For instance, at any time period, the actual cash flow may fall within a range of figures with a certain percent probability. As an example, the first year's cash flow may fall anywhere between $480 and $520. The actual values are shown to fluctuate around the forecast values at an average volatility of 20 percent.[14] (We use volatility here as a measure of uncertainty, i.e., the higher the volatility, the higher the level of uncertainty, where at zero uncertainty, the outcomes are 100 percent certain.[15]) This example definitely provides a much more accurate view of the true nature of business conditions, which are fairly difficult to predict with any amount of certainty.

The Intuition – Monte Carlo Simulation

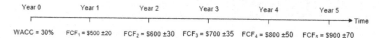

This graph shows that in reality, at different times, actual cash flows may be above, below, or at the forecast value line due to uncertainty and risk.

Figure 1.9: The Intuition of Risk

Figure 1.10 shows two sample actual cash flows around the straight-line forecast value. The higher the uncertainty around the actual cash-flow levels, the higher the volatility. The darker line with 20 percent volatility fluctuates more wildly around the forecast values. These values can be quantified using Monte Carlo simulation fairly easily but cannot be properly accounted for using more simplistic traditional methods such as sensitivity or scenario analyses.

The Intuition – The Face of Risk

The higher the risk, the higher the volatility and the higher the fluctuation of actual cash flows around the forecast value. When volatility is zero, the values collapse to the forecast straight-line static value.

Figure 1.10: A Visualization of Risk

INTEGRATED RISK MANAGEMENT (IRM)®

Before diving into the different risk analysis methods in the remaining chapters of the book, it is important to first understand the *Integrated Risk Management* and how these different techniques are related in a risk analysis and risk management context. This framework comprises eight distinct phases of a successful and comprehensive risk analysis implementation, going from a qualitative management screening process to creating clear and concise reports for management. The process was developed by the author based on previous successful implementations of risk analysis, forecasting, real options, valuation, and optimization projects both in the consulting arena and in industry-specific problems. These phases can be performed either in isolation or together in sequence for a more robust integrated analysis.

Figure 1.11 shows the Integrated Risk Management process up close. We can segregate the process into the following eight simple steps:

1. Qualitative Management Screening.

2. Forecast Predictive Modeling.

3. Base Case Static Model.

4. Monte Carlo Risk Simulation.

5. Real Options Problem Framing.

6. Real Options Valuation and Modeling.

7. Portfolio and Resource Optimization.

8. Reporting, Presentation, and Update Analysis.

1. Qualitative Management Screening

Qualitative management screening is the first step in any Integrated Risk Management process. Management has to decide which projects, assets, initiatives, or strategies are viable for further analysis, in accordance with the firm's mission, vision, goal, or overall business strategy. The firm's mission, vision, goal, or overall business strategy may include market penetration strategies, competitive advantage, technical, acquisition, growth, synergistic, or globalization issues. That is, the initial list of projects should be qualified in terms of meeting management's agenda. Often the most valuable insight is created as management frames the complete problem to be resolved. This is where the various risks to the firm are identified and flushed out.

2. Forecast Predictive Modeling

The future is then forecasted using time-series analysis or multivariate regression analysis if historical or comparable data exist. Otherwise, other qualitative forecasting methods may be used (subjective guesses, growth rate assumptions, expert opinions, Delphi method, and so forth). In a financial context, this is the step where future revenues, sale price, quantity sold, volume, production, and other key revenue and cost drivers are forecasted. See Chapters 6 and 7 for details on forecasting and using the author's *Risk Simulator* software to run time-series, nonlinear extrapolation, stochastic process, ARIMA, multivariate regression forecasts, fuzzy logic, neural networks, econometric models, GARCH, etc.

3. Base Case Static Model

For each project that passes the initial qualitative screens a discounted cash-flow model is created. This model serves as the base case analysis where a net present value is calculated for each project, using the forecasted values in the previous step. This step also applies if only a single project is under evaluation. This net present value is calculated using the traditional approach of modeling and forecasting revenues and costs, and discounting the net of these revenues and costs at an appropriate risk-adjusted rate. The return on investment and other profitability, cost-benefit, and productivity metrics are generated here.

4. Monte Carlo Risk Simulation

Because the static discounted cash flow produces only a single-point estimate result, there is oftentimes little confidence in its accuracy given that future events that affect forecast cash flows are highly uncertain. To better estimate the actual value of a particular project, Monte Carlo risk simulation should be employed next. (See Chapters 3 and 4 for details on running Monte Carlo risk simulation using the author's *Risk Simulator* software.) Usually, a sensitivity analysis is first performed on the discounted cash-flow model; that is, setting the net present value as the resulting variable, we can change each of its precedent variables and note the change in the resulting variable. Precedent variables include revenues, costs, tax rates, discount rates, capital expenditures, depreciation, and so forth, which ultimately flow through the model to affect the net present value figure. By tracing back all these precedent variables, we can change each one by a preset amount and see the effect on the resulting net present value. A graphical representation can then be created, which is oftentimes called a tornado chart (see Chapter 5 on using Risk Simulator's simulation analysis tools like tornado charts, spider charts, and sensitivity charts) because of its shape, where the most sensitive precedent variables are listed first, in descending order of magnitude. Armed with this information, the analyst can then decide which key variables are highly uncertain in the future and which are deterministic. The uncertain key variables that drive the net present value and hence, the decision are called *critical success drivers*. These critical success drivers are prime candidates for Monte Carlo simulation. Because some of these critical success drivers may be correlated—for example, operating costs may increase in proportion to quantity sold of a particular product, or prices may be inversely correlated to quantity sold—a correlated Monte Carlo simulation may be required. Typically, these correlations can be obtained through historical data. Running correlated simulations provides a much closer approximation to the variables' real-life behaviors.

5. Real Options Problem Framing

After quantifying risks in the previous step, the question now is, what's next? The risk information obtained somehow needs to be converted into *actionable intelligence*. Just because risk has been quantified to be such and such using Monte Carlo simulation, so what and what do we do about it? The answer is to use real options analysis to hedge these risks, to value these risks, and to position yourself to take advantage of the risks. The first step in real options is to generate a strategic map through the process of framing the problem. Based on the overall problem identification occurring during the initial qualitative management screening process, certain strategic optionalities would have become apparent for each particular project. The strategic optionalities may include among other things, the option to expand, contract, abandon, switch, choose, and so forth. Based on the identification of strategic optionalities that exist for each project or at each stage of the project, the analyst can then choose from a list of options to analyze in more detail. Real options are added to the projects to hedge downside risks and to take advantage of upside swings.

6. Real Options Valuation and Modeling

Through the use of Monte Carlo risk simulation, the resulting stochastic discounted cash-flow model will have a distribution of values. Thus, simulation models, analyzes, and quantifies the various risks and uncertainties of each project. The result is a distribution of the NPVs and the project's volatility. In real options, we assume that the underlying variable is the future profitability of the project, which is the future cash-flow series. An implied volatility of the future free cash flow or underlying variable can be calculated through the results of a Monte Carlo simulation previously performed. Usually, the volatility is measured as the standard deviation of the logarithmic returns on the free cash-flow stream (other approaches include running GARCH models and using simulated coefficients of variation as proxies). In addition, the present value of future cash flows for the base case discounted cash-flow model is used as the initial underlying asset value in real options modeling. Using these inputs, real options analysis is performed to obtain the projects' strategic option values—see Chapters 10 and 11 for details on understanding the basics of real options and on using the Real Options Super Lattice Solver software.

7. Portfolio and Resource Optimization

Portfolio optimization is an optional step in the analysis. If the analysis is done on multiple projects, management should view the results as a portfolio of rolled-up projects because the projects are in most cases correlated with one another, and viewing them individually will not present the true picture. As firms do not only have single projects, portfolio optimization is crucial. Given that certain projects are related to others, there are opportunities for hedging and diversifying risks through a portfolio. Because firms have limited budgets, as well as time and resource constraints, while at the same time have requirements for certain overall levels of returns, risk tolerances, and so forth, portfolio optimization takes into account all these to create an optimal portfolio mix. The analysis will provide the optimal allocation of investments across multiple projects—see Chapters 8 and 9 for details on using Risk Simulator to perform portfolio optimization.

8. Reporting, Presentation, and Update Analysis

The analysis is not complete until reports can be generated. Not only are results presented, but the process should also be shown. Clear, concise, and precise explanations transform a difficult black-box set of analytics into transparent steps. Management will never accept results coming from black boxes if they do not understand where the assumptions or data originate and what types of mathematical or financial massaging takes place. Risk analysis assumes that the future is uncertain and that management has the right to make midcourse corrections when these uncertainties become resolved or risks become known; the analysis is usually done ahead of time and thus, ahead of such uncertainty and risks. Therefore, when these risks become known, the analysis should be revisited to incorporate the decisions made or revising any input assumptions. Sometimes, for long-horizon projects, several iterations of the real options analysis should be performed, where future iterations are updated with the latest data and assumptions. Understanding the steps required to undertake an Integrated Risk Management is important because it provides insight not only into the methodology itself but also into how it evolves from traditional analyses, showing where the traditional approach ends and where the new analytics start.

This entire book is dedicated to exploring the IRM steps and methods, and ends with Chapter 15 showcasing how the IRM process can be seamlessly integrated into a risk-based decision analytics model involving multiple risky projects in a portfolio.

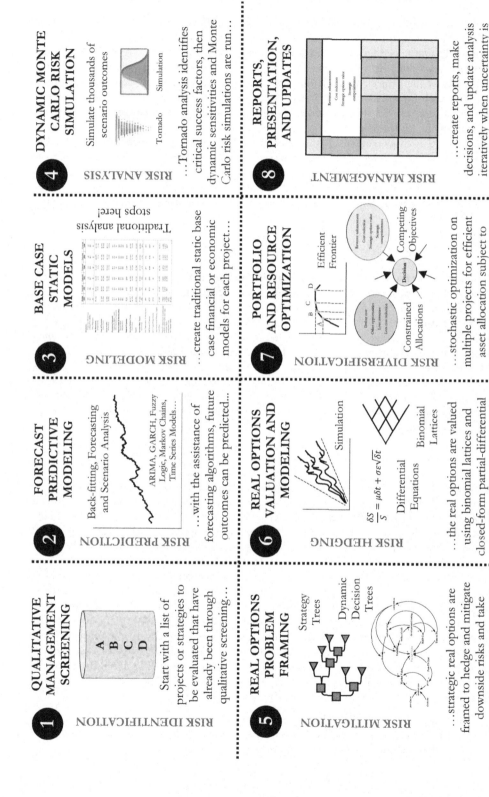

1 RISK IDENTIFICATION

QUALITATIVE MANAGEMENT SCREENING

A
B
C
D

Start with a list of projects or strategies to be evaluated that have already been through qualitative screening…

2 RISK PREDICTION

FORECAST PREDICTIVE MODELING

Back-fitting, Forecasting and Scenario Analysis

ARIMA, GARCH, Fuzzy Logic, Markov Chains, Time Series Models…

…with the assistance of forecasting algorithms, future outcomes can be predicted…

3 RISK MODELING

BASE CASE STATIC MODELS

Traditional analysis stops here!

…create traditional static base case financial or economic models for each project…

4 RISK ANALYSIS

DYNAMIC MONTE CARLO RISK SIMULATION

Simulate thousands of scenario outcomes

Tornado   Simulation

…Tornado analysis identifies critical success factors, then dynamic sensitivities and Monte Carlo risk simulations are run…

5 RISK MITIGATION

REAL OPTIONS PROBLEM FRAMING

Strategy Trees

Dynamic Decision Trees

…strategic real options are framed to hedge and mitigate downside risks and take advantage of upside potential…

6 RISK HEDGING

REAL OPTIONS VALUATION AND MODELING

Simulation

$$\frac{\delta S}{S} = \mu \delta t + \sigma v \sqrt{\delta t}$$

Differential Equations   Binomial Lattices

…the real options are valued using binomial lattices and closed-form partial-differential models with simulation…

7 RISK DIVERSIFICATION

PORTFOLIO AND RESOURCE OPTIMIZATION

Efficient Frontier

Constrained Allocations

Competing Objectives

Decision

…stochastic optimization on multiple projects for efficient asset allocation subject to resource constraints…

8 RISK MANAGEMENT

REPORTS, PRESENTATION, AND UPDATES

…create reports, make decisions, and update analysis iteratively when uncertainty is resolved over time…

Figure 1.11: Visual Representation of the Integrated Risk Management Process

Questions

1. Why is risk important in making decisions?

2. Describe the concept of bang for the buck.

3. Compare and contrast between risk and uncertainty.

SECTION TWO –
RISK EVALUATION

CHAPTER 2 – FROM RISK TO RICHES

TAMING THE BEAST

Risky ventures are the norm in the daily business world. The mere mention of names such as George Soros, John Meriweather, Paul Reichmann, Nicholas Leeson, or firms such as Long Term Capital Management, Metallgesellschaft, Barings Bank, Bankers Trust, Daiwa Bank, Sumimoto Corporation, WorldCom, Tyco, Enron, Merrill Lynch and Citibank brings a shrug of disbelief and fear. These names are some of the biggest in the world of business and finance. Their claim to fame is not simply for being the best and brightest individuals nor being the largest and most respected firms, but for bearing the stigma of being involved in highly risky ventures that turned sour almost overnight.[16]

George Soros was and still is one of the most respected names in high finance; he is known globally for his brilliance and exploits. Paul Reichmann was a reputable and brilliant real estate and property tycoon. Between the two of them, nothing was impossible, but when they ventured into investments in Mexican real estate, the wild fluctuations of the peso in the foreign exchange market was nothing short of a disaster. During late 1994 and early 1995, the peso hit an all-time low and their ventures went from bad to worse, but the one thing that they did not expect was that the situation would become a lot worse before it was all over and billions would be lost as a consequence.

Long Term Capital Management was headed by Meriweather, one of the rising stars in Wall Street, with a slew of superstars on its management team, including Nobel laureates in finance and economics (Robert Merton and Myron Scholes). The firm was also backed by giant investment banks. A firm that seemed indestructible literally blew up with billions of dollars in the red, shaking the international investment community with repercussions throughout Wall Street as individual investors started to lose faith in large hedge funds and wealth-management firms, forcing the eventual massive Federal Reserve bailout.

Barings was one of the oldest banks in England. They were so respected that even Queen Elizabeth II herself held a private account with them. This multibillion-dollar institution was brought down single-handedly by Nicholas Leeson, an employee halfway around the world. Leeson was a young and brilliant investment banker who headed up Barings' Singapore branch. His illegally doctored track record showed significant investment profits which gave him more leeway and trust from the home office over time. He was able to cover his losses through fancy accounting and by taking significant amounts of risk. His speculations in the Japanese yen went south and he took Barings down with him and the top echelon in London never knew what hit them.

Had any of the managers in the boardrooms at their respective headquarters bothered to look at the risk profile of their investments or engaged in proper risk management practices, they would surely have made a very different decision much earlier on, preventing what became major embarrassments in the global investment community. If the projected returns are adjusted for risks, that is, finding what levels of risks are required to attain such seemingly extravagant returns, it would be sensible not to proceed.

Risks occur in everyday life that do not require investments in the multimillions. For instance, when would one purchase a house in a fluctuating housing market? When would it be more profitable to lock in a fixed-rate mortgage rate rather than keep a floating variable rate? What are the chances that there will be insufficient funds at retirement? What about the potential personal property losses when a hurricane hits? How much accident insurance is considered sufficient? How much is a lottery ticket actually worth?

Risk permeates all aspects of life and one can never avoid taking or facing risks. What we can do is to understand risks better through a systematic assessment of their impacts and repercussions. This assessment framework must also be capable of measuring, monitoring, and managing risks, otherwise, simply noting that risks exist and moving on is not optimal. This book provides the tools and framework necessary to tackle risks head-on. Only with the added insights gained through a rigorous assessment of risk can one actively manage and monitor risk.

> Risks permeate every aspect of business but we do not have to be passive participants. What we can do is develop a framework to better understand risks through a systematic assessment of their impacts and repercussions. This framework must be capable of measuring, monitoring and managing risks.

THE BASICS OF RISK

Risk can be simply defined as any uncertainty that affects a system in an unknown fashion whereby the ramifications are also unknown but bear with them great fluctuation in value and outcome. In every instance, for risk to be evident, the following generalities must exist:

- Uncertainties and risks have a time horizon.

- Uncertainties exist in the future and will evolve over time.

- Uncertainties become risks if they affect the outcomes and scenarios of the system.

- These changing scenarios' effects on the system can be measured.

- The measurement has to be set against a benchmark.

Risk is never instantaneous. It has a time horizon. For instance, a firm engaged in a risky research and development venture will face significant amounts of risk but only until the product is fully developed or has proven itself in the market. These risks are caused by uncertainties in the technology of the product under research, uncertainties about the potential market, uncertainties about the level of competitive threats and substitutes, and so forth. These uncertainties will change over the course of the company's research and marketing activities——some uncertainties will increase while others will most likely decrease through the passage of time, actions and events. However, only the uncertainties that affect the product directly will have any bearing on the risks of the product being successful. That is, only uncertainties that change the possible scenario outcomes will make the product risky (e.g., market and economic conditions). Finally, risk exists if it can be measured and compared against a benchmark. If no benchmark exists, then perhaps the conditions just described are the norm for research and development activities, and thus the negative results are to be expected. These benchmarks have to be measurable and tangible, for example, gross profits, success rates, market share, time to implementation, and so forth.

> Risk is any uncertainty that affects a system in an unknown fashion with unknown ramifications, but it brings great fluctuation in value and outcome. Risk has a time horizon, meaning that uncertainty evolves over time, which affects measurable future outcomes and scenarios with respect to a benchmark.

THE NATURE OF RISK AND RETURN

Nobel Laureate Harry Markowitz's groundbreaking research into the nature of risk and return has revolutionized the world of finance. His seminal work, which is now known all over the world as the *Markowitz Efficient Frontier*, looks at the nature of risk and return. Markowitz did not look at risk as the enemy but as a condition that should be embraced and balanced out through its expected returns. The concept of risk and return was then refined through later works by William Sharpe and others who stated that a heightened risk necessitates a higher return, as elegantly expressed through the *capital asset pricing model (CAPM)*, where the required rate of return on a marketable risky equity is commensurate with the return on an equivalent riskless asset plus a beta systematic and undiversifiable risk measure multiplied by the market risk's return premium. In essence, a higher risk asset requires a higher return. In Markowitz's model, one could strike a balance between risk and return. Depending on the risk appetite of an investor, the optimal or best-case returns can be obtained through the *efficient frontier*. Should the investor require a higher level of returns, he or she would have to face a higher level of risk. Markowitz's work carried over to finding combinations of individual projects or assets in a portfolio that would provide the best *bang for the buck*, striking an elegant balance between risk and return. In order to better understand this balance, also known as risk-adjustment in modern risk analysis language, risks must first be measured and understood. The following sections illustrate how risk can be measured.

THE STATISTICS OF RISK

The study of statistics refers to the collection, presentation, analysis, and utilization of numerical data to infer and make decisions in the face of uncertainty, where the actual population data is unknown. There are two branches in the study of statistics: descriptive statistics, where data is summarized and described, and inferential statistics, where the *population* is generalized through a small random sample such that the *sample* becomes useful for making predictions or decisions when the population characteristics are unknown.

A sample can be defined as a subset of the population being measured, whereas the population can be defined as all possible observations of interest of a variable. For instance, if one is interested in the voting practices of all U.S. registered voters, the entire pool of a hundred million registered voters is considered the population, whereas a small survey of one thousand registered voters taken from several small towns across the nation is the sample. The calculated characteristics of the sample (e.g., mean, median, standard deviation) are termed *statistics*, while *parameters* imply that the entire population has been surveyed and the results tabulated. Thus, in decision making, the statistic is of vital importance, seeing that sometimes the entire population is yet unknown (e.g., who are all your customers, what is the total market share, etc.) or it is very difficult to obtain all relevant information on the population seeing that it would be too time- or resource-consuming. In inferential statistics, the usual steps undertaken include:

- Designing the experiment—this phase includes designing the ways to collect all possible and relevant data.

- Collection of sample data—data is gathered and tabulated.

- Analysis of data—statistical analysis is performed.

- Estimation or prediction—inferences are made based on the statistics obtained.

- Hypothesis testing—decisions are tested against the data to see the outcomes.

- Goodness-of-fit—actual data is compared to historical data to see the accuracy, validity, and reliability of the inference.

- Decision making—decisions are made based on the outcome of the inference.

MEASURING THE CENTER OF THE DISTRIBUTION—FIRST MOMENT

The first moment of a distribution measures the *expected rate of return* on a particular project. It measures the central tendency and location of the project's scenarios and possible outcomes on average. The common statistics for the first moment include the mean (average), median (center of a distribution or fiftieth percentile), and mode (most commonly occurring value). Figure 2.1 illustrates the first moment—where, in this case, the first moment of this distribution is measured by the mean (μ) or average value.

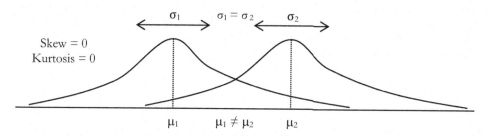

Figure 2.1: First Moment

MEASURING THE SPREAD OF THE DISTRIBUTION—SECOND MOMENT

The second moment measures the spread of a distribution, which is a measure of *risk*. The spread or width of a distribution measures the variability of a variable, that is, the potential that the variable can fall into different regions of the distribution—in other words, the potential scenarios of outcomes. Figure 2.2 illustrates two distributions with identical first moments (identical means) but very different second moments or risks. The visualization becomes clearer in Figure 2.3. As an example, suppose there are two stocks and the first stock's movements (illustrated by the dotted line) with the smaller fluctuation is compared against the second stock's movements (illustrated by the darker line) with a much higher price fluctuation. Clearly an investor would view the stock with the wilder fluctuation as riskier because the outcomes of the riskier stock are relatively more unknown than the less risky stock. The vertical axis in Figure 2.3 measures the stock prices, thus, the riskier stock has a wider range of potential outcomes. This range is translated into a distribution's width (the horizontal axis) in Figure 2.2, where the wider distribution represents the riskier asset. Hence, width or spread of a distribution measures a variable's risks.

Notice that in Figure 2.2, both distributions have identical first moments or central tendencies but clearly the distributions are very different. This difference in the distributional width is measurable. Mathematically and statistically, the width or risk of a variable can be measured through several different statistics, including the range, standard deviation (σ), variance, coefficient of variation, volatility, confidence interval, and interquartile range.

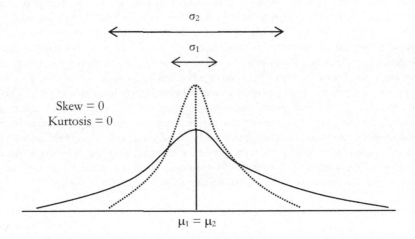

Figure 2.2: Second Moment

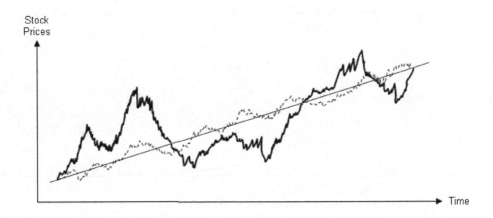

Figure 2.3: Stock Price Fluctuations

MEASURING THE SKEW OF THE DISTRIBUTION—THIRD MOMENT

The third moment measures a distribution's *skewness*, that is, how the distribution is pulled to one side or the other. Figure 2.4 illustrates a negative or left skew (the tail of the distribution points to the left), and Figure 2.5 illustrates a positive or right skew (the tail of the distribution points to the right). The mean is always skewed toward the tail of the distribution while the median remains constant (e.g., in Figure 2.4, μ_2 is the mean and median of the symmetrical distribution, whereas μ_1 is the mean and μ_2 is the median of the negatively skewed distribution). Another way of seeing this is that the mean moves with the tail of a distribution but the median may remain relatively stable. If the third moment is not considered, then looking only at the expected returns (e.g., mean) and risk (e.g., standard deviation), a positively skewed project might be incorrectly chosen. For example, if the horizontal x-axis represents the net profits of a project, then clearly a left or negatively skewed distribution might be preferred as there is a higher probability of greater net returns (Figure 2.4) as compared to a higher probability for a lower level of net returns (Figure 2.5). Thus, in a skewed distribution, the median is a better measure of returns, as the medians for both Figures 2.4 and 2.5 are identical, risks are identical, and hence, a project with a negatively skewed distribution of net profits is a better choice. Conversely, if the x-axis measures risks, costs, or schedule (risks, costs or time to complete development of a project) then a positively skewed distribution is more favorable. Failure to account for a project's distributional skewness may mean that the incorrect project may be chosen (e.g., two projects may have identical first and second moments, that is, they both have identical returns and risk profiles, but their distributional skews may be very different). Finally, note that a distribution with zero skew implies symmetry, and may not imply normality (normality implies symmetry but symmetry by itself does not imply normality as there are other distributions that are symmetrical such as uniform, triangular, t, and so forth).

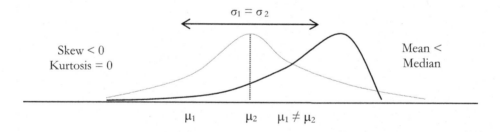

Figure 2.4: Third Moment (Left Skew)

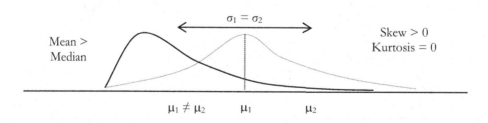

Figure 2.5: Third Moment (Right Skew)

MEASURING THE CATASTROPHIC TAIL EVENTS
OF THE DISTRIBUTION—FOURTH MOMENT

The fourth moment or kurtosis, measures the *peakedness* of a distribution. Figure 2.6 illustrates this effect. The background (denoted by the dotted line) is a normal distribution with an excess kurtosis of 0. The new distribution has a higher kurtosis, thus the area under the curve is thicker at the tails with less area in the central body. This condition has major impacts on risk analysis such as for the two distributions in Figure 2.6, where the first three moments (mean, standard deviation, and skewness) can be identical but the fourth moment (kurtosis) is different. This condition means that, although the returns and risks are identical, the probabilities of extreme and catastrophic events (potential large losses or large gains) occurring are higher for a high kurtosis distribution (e.g., stock market returns are leptokurtic or have high kurtosis). Ignoring a project's return's kurtosis may be detrimental. Note that sometimes a normal kurtosis is denoted as 3.0, but in this book we use the measure of excess kurtosis, henceforth simply known as kurtosis. In other words, a kurtosis of 3.5 is also known as an excess kurtosis of 0.5, indicating that the distribution has 0.5 additional kurtosis above the normal distribution. The use of excess kurtosis is more prevalent in academic literature and is, hence, used here. Finally, the normalization of kurtosis to a base of 0 makes for easier interpretation of the statistic (e.g., a positive kurtosis indicates fatter-tailed distribution while negative kurtosis indicates thinner-tailed distributions or no long tails where the endpoints are truncated at some minimum or maximum value).

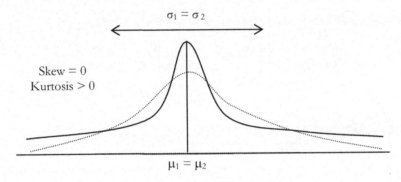

Figure 2.6: Fourth Moment

Most distributions of data can be defined up to four moments. The first moment describes its location or central tendency (expected returns), the second moment describes its width or spread (risks), the third moment its directional skew (most probable events), and the fourth moment its peakedness or thickness in the tails (catastrophic losses or gains). All four moments should be calculated and interpreted to provide a more comprehensive risk profile of the project under analysis.

THE FUNCTIONS OF MOMENTS

Ever wonder why these risk statistics are called "moments"? In mathematical vernacular, "moment" means *raised to the power of some value*. In other words, the third moment implies that in an equation, three is most probably the highest power. In fact, the equations that follow illustrate the mathematical functions and applications of some moments for a sample statistic. For example, notice that the highest power for the first moment (average) is one; for the second moment (standard deviation), it is two; for the third moment (skew), it is three, and the highest power for the fourth moment (kurtosis) is four.

First Moment: Average or Mean (the Excel equivalent function is AVERAGE)

$$\bar{x} = \frac{\sum_{i=1}^{n} x_i}{n}$$

Second Moment: Standard Deviation (Sample)

The Excel equivalent function is STDEV for a sample standard deviation

The Excel equivalent function is STDEVP for a population standard deviation

$$s = \sqrt{\frac{\sum_{i=1}^{n} (x_i - \bar{x})^2}{n-1}}$$

Third Moment: Skew (the Excel equivalent function is SKEW)

$$skew = \frac{n}{(n-1)(n-2)} \sum_{i=1}^{n} \left[\frac{x_i - \bar{x}}{s} \right]^3$$

Fourth Moment: Kurtosis (the Excel equivalent function is KURT)

$$kurtosis = \frac{n(n+1)}{(n-1)(n-2)(n-3)} \sum_{i=1}^{n} \left[\frac{(x_i - \bar{x})}{s} \right]^4 - \frac{3(n-1)^2}{(n-2)(n-3)}$$

THE MEASUREMENTS OF RISK

There are multiple ways to measure risk in projects. This section summarizes some of the more common measures of risk and lists their potential benefits and pitfalls. The chapter Appendix illustrates step-by-step example calculations of some of the more common measurements of risk, which are also briefly defined next:

- Probability of Occurrence

This approach is simplistic yet effective. As an example, there is a 10 percent probability that a project will not break even (it will return a negative net present value indicating losses) within the next 5 years. Further, suppose two similar projects have identical implementation costs and expected returns. Based on a single-point estimate, management should be indifferent between them. However, if risk analysis such as Monte Carlo simulation is performed, the first project might reveal a 70 percent probability of losses compared to only a 5 percent probability of losses on the second project. Clearly, the second project is better when risks are analyzed.

- Standard Deviation and Variance

Standard deviation is a measure of the average of each data point's deviation from the mean.[17] This is the most popular measure of risk, where a higher standard deviation implies a wider distributional width and, thus, a higher risk. The drawback of this measure is that both the upside and downside variations are included in the computation of the standard deviation.

Some analysts define risks as the potential losses or downside; thus, standard deviation and variance will penalize upswings as well as downsides.

- Semi-Standard Deviation

The semi-standard deviation only measures the standard deviation of the downside risks and ignores the upside fluctuations. Modifications of the semi-standard deviation include calculating only the values below the mean, or values below a threshold (e.g., negative profits or negative cash flows). This provides a better picture of downside risk but is more difficult to estimate.

- Volatility

The concept of volatility is widely used in the applications of real options and can be defined briefly as a measure of uncertainty and risks.[18] Volatility can be estimated using multiple methods, including simulation of the uncertain variables impacting a particular project and estimating the standard deviation of the resulting asset's logarithmic returns over time. This concept is more difficult to define and estimate but more powerful than most other risk measures in that this single value incorporates all sources of uncertainty rolled into one value.

- Beta

Beta is another common measure of risk in the investment finance arena. Beta can be defined simply as the undiversifiable, systematic risk of a financial asset. This concept is made famous through the CAPM, where a higher beta means a higher risk, which in turn requires a higher expected return on the asset.

- Coefficient of Variation

The coefficient of variation is simply defined as the ratio of standard deviation to the mean, where risks are common-sized. For example, a distribution of a group of students' heights (measured in meters) can be compared to the distribution of the students' weights (measured in kilograms).[19] This measure of risk or dispersion is applicable when the variables' estimates, measures, magnitudes, or units differ.

- Value at Risk (VaR)

Value at Risk was made famous by J. P. Morgan in the mid-1990s through the introduction of their *RiskMetrics* approach, and has been sanctioned by bank governing bodies around the world. Briefly, it measures the amount of capital reserves at risk given a particular holding period at a particular probability of loss. This measurement can be modified to risk applications by stating, for example, the amount of potential losses a certain percentage of the time during the period of the economic life of the project—clearly, a project with a smaller VaR is better.

- Worst-Case Scenario and Regret

Another simple measure is the value of the worst-case scenario given catastrophic losses. Another definition is regret. That is, if a decision is made to pursue a particular project, but if the project becomes unprofitable and suffers a loss, the level of regret is simply the difference between the actual losses compared to doing nothing at all.

- Risk-Adjusted Return on Capital

Risk-adjusted return on capital (RAROC) takes the ratio of the difference between the fiftieth percentile (median) return and the fifth percentile return on a project to its standard deviation. This approach is used mostly by banks to estimate returns subject to their risks by measuring only the potential downside effects and ignoring the positive upswings.

APPENDIX—COMPUTING RISK

This appendix illustrates how some of the more common measures of risk are computed. Each risk measurement has its own computations and uses. For example, certain risk measures are applicable only on time-series data (e.g., volatility) while others are applicable in both cross-sectional and time-series data (e.g., variance, standard deviation, and covariance), while yet others require a consistent holding period (e.g., Value at Risk) or a market comparable or benchmark (e.g., beta coefficient).

Probability of Occurrence

This approach is simplistic and yet effective. The probability of success or failure can be determined several ways. The first is through management expectations and assumptions, also known as expert opinion, based on historical occurrences or experience of the expert. Another approach is simply to gather available historical or comparable data, industry averages, academic research, or other third-party sources, indicating the historical probabilities of success or failure (e.g., pharmaceutical R&D's probability of technical success based on various drug indications can be obtained from external research consulting groups). Finally, Monte Carlo simulation can be run on a model with multiple interacting input assumptions and the output of interest (e.g., net present value, gross margin, tolerance ratios, and development success rates) can be captured as a simulation forecast and the relevant probabilities can be obtained, such as the probability of breaking even, probability of failure, probability of making a profit, and so forth. See Chapter 4 for step-by-step instructions on running and interpreting simulations and probabilities.

Standard Deviation and Variance

Standard deviation is a measure of the average of each data point's deviation from the mean. A higher standard deviation or variance implies a wider distributional width and, thus, a higher risk.

The standard deviation can be measured in terms of the population or sample, and for illustration purposes, is shown as the following list, where we define x_i as the individual data points, μ as the population mean, N as the population size, $\bar{x}$ as the sample mean, and n as the sample size:

Population standard deviation: $\sigma = \sqrt{\dfrac{\sum_{i=1}^{n}(x-\mu)^2}{N}}$ and population variance is simply the square of the standard deviation or σ^2. Alternatively, use Excel's *STDEVP* and *VARP* functions for the population standard deviation and variance, respectively.

Sample standard deviation: $s = \sqrt{\dfrac{\sum_{i=1}^{n}(x-\bar{x})^2}{n-1}}$ and sample variance is similarly the square of the standard deviation or s^2. Alternatively, use Excel's *STDEV* and *VAR* functions for the sample standard deviation and variance, respectively. Figure 2.7 shows the step-by-step computations.

Standard Deviation and Variance Computation

X	X - Mean	Square of (X - Mean)
-10.50	-9.07	82.2908
12.25	13.68	187.1033
-11.50	-10.07	101.4337
13.25	14.68	215.4605
-14.65	-13.22	174.8062
15.65	17.08	291.6776
-14.50	-13.07	170.8622
Sum	-10.00	
Mean	-1.43	

Population Standard Deviation and Variance

Sum of Square (X - Mean)	1223.6343
Variance = Sum of Square (X - Mean) / N	174.8049
Using Excel's VARP function:	174.8049
Standard Deviation = Square Root of (Sum of Square (X - Mean) / N)	13.2214
Using Excel's STDEVP function:	13.2214

Sample Standard Deviation and Variance

Sum of Square (X - Mean)	1223.6343
Variance = Sum of Square (X - Mean) / (N - 1)	203.9390
Using Excel's VAR function:	203.9390
Standard Deviation = Square Root of (Sum of Square (X - Mean) / (N-1))	14.2807
Using Excel's STDEV function:	14.2807

Figure 2.7: Standard Deviations and Variances

The drawbacks of this measure are that both the upside and downside variations are included in the computation of the standard deviation, and its dependence on the units (e.g., values of x in thousands of dollars versus millions of dollars are not comparable). Some analysts define risks as the potential losses or downside; thus, standard deviation and variance penalize upswings as well as downsides. An alternative is the semi-standard deviation.

Semi-Standard Deviation

The semi-standard deviation only measures the standard deviation of the downside risks and ignores the upside fluctuations. Modifications of the semi-standard deviation include calculating only the values below the mean, or values below a threshold (e.g., negative profits or negative cash flows). This approach provides a better picture of downside risk but is more difficult to estimate. Figure 2.8 shows how a sample semi-standard deviation and semi-variance are computed. Note that the computation must be performed manually.

Volatility

The concept of volatility is widely used in the applications of real options and can be defined briefly as a measure of uncertainty and risks. Volatility can be estimated using multiple methods, including simulation of the uncertain variables impacting a particular project and estimating the standard deviation of the resulting asset's logarithmic returns over time. This concept is more difficult to define and estimate but is more powerful than most other risk measures in that this single value incorporates all sources of uncertainty rolled into one value. Figure 2.9 illustrates the computation of an annualized volatility. Volatility is typically computed for time-series data only (i.e., data that follows a time-series such as stock price, price of oil, interest rates, and so forth). The first step is to determine the relative returns from period to period, take their natural logarithms (*ln*) and then compute the sample standard deviation of these logged values. The result is the periodic volatility. Then, annualize the volatility by multiplying this periodic volatility by the square root of the number of periods in a year (e.g., 1 if annual data, 4 if quarterly data, and 12 if monthly data are used).

For a more detailed discussion of volatility computation as well as other methods for computing volatility such as using the logarithmic present value approach, management assumptions and GARCH or generalized autoregressive conditional heteroskedasticity models and how a discount rate can be determined from volatility, see *Real Options Analysis,* Second Edition, by Johnathan Mun (Wiley 2005).

Semi-Standard Deviation and Variance Computation

X	X - Mean	Square of (X - Mean)	
-10.50	2.29	5.2327	
12.25	Ignore		(Ignore the positive values)
-11.50	1.29	1.6577	
13.25	Ignore		(Ignore the positive values)
-14.65	-1.86	3.4689	
15.65	Ignore		(Ignore the positive values)
-14.50	-1.71	2.9327	
Sum		-51.15	
Mean		-12.79	

Population Standard Deviation and Variance

Sum of Square (X - Mean)	13.2919
Variance = Sum of Square (X - Mean) / N	3.3230
Using Excel's VARP function:	3.3230
Standard Deviation = Square Root of (Sum of Square (X - Mean) / N)	1.8229
Using Excel's STDEVP function:	1.8229

Sample Standard Deviation and Variance

Sum of Square (X - Mean)	13.2919
Variance = Sum of Square (X - Mean) / (N - 1)	4.4306
Using Excel's VAR function:	4.4306
Standard Deviation = Square Root of (Sum of Square (X - Mean) / (N-1))	2.1049
Using Excel's STDEV function:	2.1049

Figure 2.8: Semi-Standard Deviations and Variances

Volatility

Months	X	Relative Returns	LN (Relative Returns)	Square of (LN Relative Returns - Average)
0	10.50			
1	12.25	1.17	0.1542	0.0101
2	11.50	0.94	-0.0632	0.0137
3	13.25	1.15	0.1417	0.0077
4	14.65	1.11	0.1004	0.0022
5	15.65	1.07	0.0660	0.0001
6	14.50	0.93	-0.0763	0.0169
Sum			0.3228	
Average			0.0538	

Sample Standard Deviation and Variance

Sum of Square (LN Relative Returns - Average)	0.0507
Volatility = Square Root of (Sum of Square (LN Relative Returns - Average))	**10.07%**
Using Excel's STDEV function on LN(Relative Returns):	**10.07%**
Annualized Volatility (Periodic Volatility x Square Root (Periods in a Year))	**34.89%**

Figure 2.9: Volatility Computation

Beta

Beta is another common measure of risk in the investment finance arena. Beta can be defined simply as the undiversifiable, systematic risk of a financial asset. This concept is made famous through the CAPM, where a higher beta means a higher risk, which in turn requires a higher expected return on the asset. The beta coefficient measures the relative movements of one asset value to a comparable benchmark or market portfolio; that is, we define the beta coefficient as:

$$\beta = \frac{Cov(x,m)}{Var(m)} = \frac{\rho_{x,m}\sigma_x\sigma_m}{\sigma_m^2}$$

where $Cov(x,m)$ is the population covariance between the asset x and the market or comparable benchmark m, and $Var(m)$ is the population variance of m, where both can be computed in Excel using the $COVAR$ and $VARP$ functions. The computed beta will be for the population. In contrast, the sample beta coefficient is computed using the correlation coefficient between x and m or ρ_{xm} and the sample standard deviations of x and m or s_x and s_m instead of σ_x and σ_m.

A beta of 1.0 implies that the relative movements or risk of x is identical to the relative movements of the benchmark (see Figure 2.10's Example 1 where the asset x is simply one unit less than the market asset m but they both fluctuate at the same levels). Similarly, a beta of 0.5 implies that the relative movements or risk of x is half of the relative movements of the benchmark (see Figure 2.10's Example 2 where the asset x is simply half the market's fluctuations m). Therefore, beta is a powerful measure but requires a comparable asset to benchmark its fluctuations.

Beta Coefficient		
Example 1: Similar fluctuations with the market		
		Market
Months	X	Comparable
		M
0	10.50	11.50
1	12.25	13.25
2	11.50	12.50
3	13.25	14.25
4	14.65	15.65
5	15.65	16.65
6	14.50	15.50

Sample Beta
Correlation Between X and M using Excel's CORREL:	1.0000
Standard Deviation of X using Excel's STDEV:	1.8654
Standard Deviation of M using Excel's STDEV:	1.8654
Beta Coefficient	*1.0000*
(Correlation X and M * Stdev X * Stdev M)/(Stdev M * Stdev M)	

Population Beta
Covariance Population using Excel's COVAR:	2.9827
Variance of M using Excel's VARP:	2.9827
Population Beta	*1.0000*
(Covariance Population (X, M) /Variance (M))	

Beta Coefficient		
Example 2: Half the fluctuations of the market		
		Market
Months	X	Comparable
		M
0	10.50	21.00
1	12.25	24.50
2	11.50	23.00
3	13.25	26.50
4	14.65	29.30
5	15.65	31.30
6	14.50	29.00

Sample Beta
Correlation Between X and M using Excel's CORREL:	1.0000
Standard Deviation of X using Excel's STDEV:	1.8654
Standard Deviation of M using Excel's STDEV:	3.7308
Beta Coefficient	*0.5000*
(Correlation X and M * Stdev X * Stdev M)/(Stdev M * Stdev M)	

Population Beta
Covariance Population using Excel's COVAR:	5.9653
Variance of M using Excel's VARP:	11.9306
Population Beta	*0.5000*
(Covariance Population (X, M) /Variance (M))	

Figure 2.10: Beta Coefficient Computation

Coefficient of Variation

The coefficient of variation (CV) is simply defined as the ratio of standard deviation to the mean, where the risks are *common-sized* and *relativized*. For example, a distribution of a group of students' heights (measured in meters) can be compared to the distribution of the students' weights (measured in kilograms). This measure of risk or dispersion is applicable when the variables' estimates, measures, magnitudes, or units differ.

In risk analysis, CV is used in a variety of ways, including risk comparisons and optimization. For instance, suppose you have a portfolio of projects as follows:

	Analyst 1 ($M)	Analyst 2 ($K)	Analyst 3 ($)
Project A	$10.25	$10,250	$10,250,000
Project B	$11.55	$11,550	$11,550,000
Project C	$12.79	$12,790	$12,790,000
Project D	$9.57	$9,570	$9,570,000
Project E	$16.25	$16,250	$16,250,000
Average	$12.08	$12,082	$12,082,000
Standard Deviation	$2.64	$2,637	$2,637,370
Coefficient of Variation	21.83%	21.83%	21.83%

The same portfolio of projects was computed by three different analysts; one uses millions of dollars, another denominates the values as thousands of dollars, and the third simply uses dollars. It is the same portfolio of projects, but if we relied solely on standard deviation as the measure of risk, then Analyst 3 would say that the portfolio has a much higher risk than Analyst 2 or 1 would (the standard deviation of Analyst 3 is the highest). So, standard deviation is a good measure of absolute risk levels, especially when analyzing values denominated in similar units (i.e., useful when comparing projects or assets within similar magnitudes). However, in contrast, notice that the CV yields exactly the same value for all three analysts because CV takes the standard deviation and normalizes it (i.e., divides it) by the mean, generating a relative percentage value.

Coefficient of variation is a good measure of *relative risk*. In fact, you can now use CV to compare the relative risk across multiple projects of different types and magnitude (e.g., compare a multibillion-dollar's relative risk to a multithousand-dollar project). Also, standard deviations and averages are denominated in the original units in which the values were measured (if the original project was measured in dollars, then average and standard deviation are denominated in dollars), whereas CV is a relative measure and is unitless (standard deviation divided by average where we have dollar unit divided by dollar unit making the new variable unitless). That is, CV can be written as a decimal or percentage, allowing it to be comparable across multiple types of projects (e.g., comparing a U.S. dollar-denominated project in billions of dollars to a Euro-denominated multimillion-dollar project).

Finally, CV is the second moment divided by the first moment, or standard deviation divided by the mean, which can be loosely described as buck for the bang. Take the inverse of CV and you have bang for the buck. In fact, the Sharpe ratio that is often used in portfolio optimization is the inverse of CV. The Sharpe ratio is $S = \dfrac{E[R] - R_{rf}}{\sigma}$, which is the expected return $E[R]$ or sometimes written as average return μ, less some benchmark returns such as the risk-free rate R_{rf}, divided by the standard deviation or risk σ. Sometimes, the benchmark is set to zero for simplicity, and we then have $S = \dfrac{\mu}{\sigma}$, which is nothing but the inverse of the CV.

Due to its relative characteristic, the Sharpe ratio or return to risk ratio, and, by extension, the CV or risk to return ratio are used in portfolio optimization to determine the best bang for the buck to reconstruct the efficient frontier as described in Chapter 1, which, again, was simply the optimal portfolio allocation given the risk-return levels of all possible combinations in a portfolio.

CV works in most cases except when expected value (mean) is negative, which means CV is negative. In this situation, take its absolute value to solve the problem. Another issue is when the expected returns (mean) is very small (e.g., 0.1 or 0.001), which will artificially inflate CV to many orders of magnitude. In such cases, simply change the units of measurement to solve this problem (i.e., change $0.1 million to $100 thousand).

Value at Risk (Value at Stake)

Value at Risk (VaR) was made famous by J. P. Morgan in the mid-1990s through the introduction of its *RiskMetrics* approach, and has thus far been sanctioned by bank-governing bodies around the world. Briefly, it measures the amount of capital reserves at risk given a particular holding period at a particular probability of loss. This measurement can be modified to risk applications by stating, for example, the amount of potential losses a certain percentage of the time during the period of the economic life of the project.

Economic capital is critical to a bank as it links a bank's earnings and returns to risks that are specific to a business line or business opportunity. In addition, these economic capital measurements can be aggregated into a portfolio of holdings. In such situations, VaR is used in trying to understand how the entire organization is affected by the various risks of each holding as aggregated into a portfolio, after accounting for cross-correlations among various holdings. VaR measures the maximum possible loss given some predefined probability level (e.g., 99.90 percent) over some holding period or time horizon (e.g., 10 days). Senior management at the bank usually selects the probability or confidence interval, which is typically a decision made by senior management that reflects the board's risk appetite. Stated another way, we can define the probability level as the bank's desired probability of surviving per year. In addition, the holding period is usually chosen such that it coincides with the time period it takes to liquidate a loss position.

VaR can be computed several ways. Two main families of approaches exist: structural closed-form models and Monte Carlo risk simulation. The latter is a much more powerful approach. Instead of simply correlating individual business lines or assets, Monte Carlo risk simulation can correlate entire probability distributions using mathematical copulas and simulation algorithms, by using Risk Simulator. In addition, tens to hundreds of thousands of scenarios can be generated using simulation, providing a very powerful stress testing mechanism for valuing VaR. Distributional fitting methods are applied to reduce the thousands of data points into their appropriate probability distributions, allowing their modeling to be handled with greater ease.

For our purposes, we can loosely define VaR as the left-tail or the right-tail values given some probability. Figure 2.11 illustrates the right-tail VaR and left-tail VaR as used in risk analysis for projects and portfolios. For instance, if we say there is a *right-tail* VaR$_{10\%}$ of *$X,* we simply mean that there is a 90 percent probability that you will get less than or equal to *$X,* and a 10 percent chance you will get more than *$X.* The inverse is true for the left-tail VaR. And it really depends what variable you are looking at before you can determine if a high or low VaR is desirable. For instance, if you are modeling returns or profits, a *higher* right-tail *$X* VaR value is more desirable than a lower VaR, and a *higher $X* left-tail VaR is better than a low left-tail VaR (e.g., I have a 90 percent chance of making at least $10M as compared to $1M). So, this analysis means that the value at "risk" should be higher. The opposite is true if you are modeling cost, losses, or risk of a project, where you would and should prefer a *lower* VaR (e.g., would you prefer to have a project with a 90 percent chance of exceeding $10M in cost and losses, or $1M in cost and losses?), and in this case, the value at "risk" should be lower. In fact, banks use the latter definition of VaR (i.e., a lower VaR portfolio indicates a lower potential catastrophic loss under the worst-case scenario). Think about it carefully and draw the pictures to convince yourself.

Finally, if you are using VaR as a measure of the width of the distribution and, by extension, the second moment and the uncertainty of the project, a lower left-tail VaR or higher right-tail VaR implies a wider distribution and, hence, a higher level of *uncertainty* (but the risks may not be equally distributed, so we use the term *uncertainty* in this context).

For more technical details on modeling VaR in a banking environment, see my other books, including *Advanced Analytical Models: 800 Functions and 300 Models from Basel II to Wall Street and Beyond* (Wiley Finance 2008). In Chapters 95 and 160 through 164 of that book, you will find detailed VaR analysis including applications of static covariance, simulation, and optimization models to minimize VaR for a bank's economic capital requirements.

Worst-Case Scenario and Regret

Another simple measure is the value of the worst-case scenario given catastrophic losses. An additional definition is regret; that is, if a decision is made to pursue a particular project, but if the project becomes unprofitable and suffers a loss, the level of regret is simply the difference between the actual losses compared to doing nothing at all. This analysis is very similar to the VaR but is not time dependent. For instance, a financial return on investment model can be created and a simulation is run. The 5% worst-case scenario can be read directly from the forecast chart in Risk Simulator.

Risk-Adjusted Return on Capital

Risk-adjusted return on capital (RAROC) takes the ratio of the difference between the fiftieth percentile P_{50} or its median return and the fifth percentile P_5 return on a project to its standard deviation σ written as:

$$RAROC = \frac{P_{50} - P_5}{\sigma}$$

This approach is used mostly by banks to estimate returns subject to their risks by measuring only the potential downside effects and truncating the distribution to the worst-case 5% of the time, ignoring the positive upswings, while at the same time common-sizing to the risk measure of standard deviation. Thus, RAROC can be seen as a measure that combines standard deviation, CV, semi-standard deviation, and worst-case scenario analysis. This measure is useful when applied with Monte Carlo simulation, where the percentiles and standard deviation measurements required can be obtained through the forecast chart's statistics view in Risk Simulator.

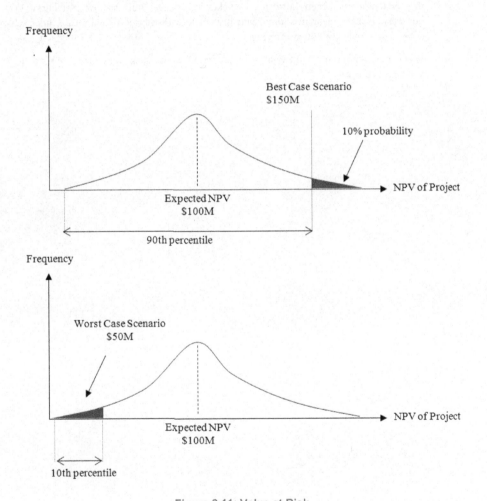

Figure 2.11: Value at Risk

Questions

1. What is the efficient frontier and when is it used?

2. What are inferential statistics and what steps are required in making inferences?

3. When is using standard deviation less desirable than using semi-standard deviation as a measure of risk?

4. If comparing three projects' net profitability or returns with similar first, second, and fourth moments, would you prefer a project that has no skew, a positive skew, or a negative skew?

5. If comparing three projects with similar first to third moments, would you prefer a project that is leptokurtic (high kurtosis), mesokurtic (average kurtosis) or platykurtic (low kurtosis)? Explain your reasoning with respect to a distribution's tail area. Under what conditions would your answer change?

6. What are the differences and similarities between Value at Risk and worst-case scenario as a measure of risk?

SECTION THREE –
RISK QUANTIFICATION

CHAPTER 3 – ON THE SHORES OF MONACO

Monte Carlo simulation, named for the famous gambling capital of Monaco, is a very potent methodology. For the practitioner, simulation opens the door for solving difficult and complex but practical problems with great ease. Perhaps the most famous early use of Monte Carlo simulation was by the Nobel physicist Enrico Fermi (sometimes referred to as the father of the atomic bomb) in 1930, when he used a random method to calculate the properties of the newly discovered neutron. Monte Carlo methods were central to the simulations required for the Manhattan Project, where in the 1950s Monte Carlo simulation was used at Los Alamos for early work relating to the development of the hydrogen bomb, and became popularized in the fields of physics and operations research. The RAND Corporation and the U.S. Air Force were two of the major organizations responsible for funding and disseminating information on Monte Carlo methods during this time, and today there is a wide application of Monte Carlo simulation in many different fields including engineering, physics, research and development, business, and finance.

Simplistically, Monte Carlo simulation creates artificial futures by generating thousands and even hundreds of thousands of sample paths of outcomes and analyzes their prevalent characteristics. In practice, Monte Carlo simulation methods are used for risk analysis, risk quantification, sensitivity analysis, and prediction. An alternative to simulation is the use of highly complex stochastic closed-form mathematical models. For analysts in a company, taking graduate level advanced math and statistics courses is just not logical or practical. A brilliant analyst would use all available tools at his or her disposal to obtain the same answer the easiest and most practical way possible. And in all cases, when modeled correctly, Monte Carlo simulation provides similar answers to the more mathematically elegant methods. In addition, there are many real-life applications where closed-form models do not exist and the only recourse is to apply simulation methods. So, what exactly is Monte Carlo simulation and how does it work?

WHAT IS MONTE CARLO SIMULATION?

Today, fast computers have made possible many complex computations that were seemingly intractable in past years. For scientists, engineers, statisticians, managers, business analysts, and others, computers have made it possible to create models that simulate reality and aid in making predictions, one of which is used in simulating real systems by accounting for randomness and future uncertainties through investigating hundreds and even thousands of different scenarios. The results are then compiled and used to make decisions. This is what Monte Carlo simulation is all about.

Monte Carlo simulation in its simplest form is a random number generator that is useful for forecasting, estimation, and risk analysis. A simulation calculates numerous scenarios of a model by repeatedly picking values from a user-predefined *probability distribution* for the uncertain variables and using those values for the model. As all those scenarios produce associated results in a model, each scenario can have a forecast. Forecasts are events (usually with formulas or functions) that you define as important outputs of the model.

Think of the Monte Carlo simulation approach as picking golf balls out of a large basket repeatedly with replacement. The size and shape of the basket depend on the distributional *Input Assumption* (e.g., a normal distribution with a mean of 100 and a standard deviation of 10, versus a uniform distribution or a triangular distribution) where some baskets are deeper or more symmetrical than others, allowing certain balls to be pulled out more frequently than others. The number of balls pulled repeatedly depends on the number of *Trials* simulated. For a large model with multiple related assumptions, imagine the large model as a very large basket, where many baby baskets reside. Each baby basket has its own set of colored golf balls that are bouncing around. Sometimes these baby baskets are linked with each other (if there is a *Correlation* between the variables), forcing the golf balls to bounce in tandem whereas in other uncorrelated cases, the balls are bouncing independently of one another. The balls that are picked each time from these interactions within the model (the large basket) are tabulated and recorded, providing a *Forecast Output* result of the simulation.

WHY ARE SIMULATIONS IMPORTANT?

An example of why simulation is important can be seen in the case illustration in Figures 3.1 and 3.2, termed the Flaw of Averages.[21] The example is most certainly worthy of more detailed study. It shows how an analyst may be misled into making the wrong decisions without the use of simulation. Suppose you are the owner of a shop that sells perishable goods and you need to make a decision on the optimal inventory to have on hand. Your new-hire analyst was successful in downloading 5-years' worth of monthly historical sales levels and she estimates the average to be five units. You then make the decision that the optimal inventory to have on hand is five units. You have just committed the flaw of averages. As the example shows, the obvious reason why this error occurs is that the distribution of historical demand is highly skewed while the cost structure is asymmetrical. For example, suppose you are in a meeting, and your boss asks what everyone made last year. You take a quick poll and realize that the salaries range from $60,000 to $150,000. You perform a quick calculation and find the average to be $100,000. Then, your boss tells you that he made $20 million last year! Suddenly, the average for the group becomes $1.5 million. This value of $1.5 million clearly in no way represents how much each of your peers made last year. In this case, the median may be more appropriate. Here you see that simply using the average will provide highly misleading results.[22]

Continuing with the example, Figure 3.2 shows how the right inventory level is calculated using simulation. The approach used here is called *nonparametric* bootstrap simulation. It is nonparametric because in this simulation approach, no distributional parameters are assigned. Instead of assuming some preset distribution (normal, triangular, lognormal, or the like) and its required parameters (mean, standard deviation, and so forth) as required in a Monte Carlo *parametric* simulation, nonparametric simulation uses the data themselves to tell the story.

Imagine that you collect 5-years' worth of historical demand levels and write down the demand quantity on a golf ball for each month. Throw all 60 golf balls into a large basket and mix the basket randomly. Pick a golf ball out at random and write down its value on a piece of paper, then replace the ball in the basket and mix the basket again. Do this 60 times, and calculate the average. This process is a single grouped trial. Perform this entire process several thousand times, with replacement. The distribution of these thousands of averages represents the outcome of the simulation forecast. The expected value of the simulation is simply the average value of these thousands of averages. Figure 3.2 shows an example of the distribution stemming from a nonparametric simulation. As you can see, the optimal inventory rate that minimizes carrying costs is nine units, far from the average value of five units previously calculated in Figure 3.1.

The Flaw of Averages

Actual	5		Average	5.00
Inventory Held	6			

		Historical Data (5 Yr)	
Perishable Cost	$100	Month	Actual
Fed Ex Cost	$175	1	12
		2	11
Total Cost	$100	3	7
		4	0

Your company is a retailer in perishable goods and	5 0
you were tasked with finding the optimal level of	6 2
inventory to have on hand. If your inventory exceeds	7 7
actual demand, there is a $100 perishable cost	8 0
while a $175 Fed Ex cost is incurred if your inventory	9 11
is insufficient to cover the actual level of demand.	10 12
These costs are on a per unit basis. Your first	11 0
inclination is to collect historical demand data as	12 9
seen on the right, for the past 60 months. You then	13 3
take a simple average which was found to be 5	14 5
units. Hence, you select 5 units as the optimal	15 0
inventory level. You have just committed a major	16 2
mistake called the Flaw of Averages!	17 1
	18 10

Your company is a retailer in perishable goods and you were tasked with finding the optimal level of inventory to have on hand. If your inventory exceeds actual demand, there is a $100 perishable cost while a $175 Fed Ex cost is incurred if your inventory is insufficient to cover the actual level of demand. These costs are on a per unit basis. Your first inclination is to collect historical demand data as seen on the right, for the past 60 months. You then take a simple average which was found to be 5 units. Hence, you select 5 units as the optimal inventory level. You have just committed a major mistake called the Flaw of Averages!

The actual demand data are shown here on the right. Rows 19 through 57 are hidden to conserve space. Being the analyst, what must you then do?

Month	Actual
58	3
59	2
60	17

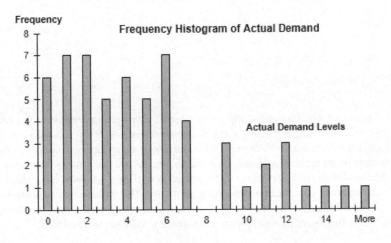

Figure 3.1: Illustrating the Flaw of Averages

Clearly, each approach has its merits and disadvantages. Nonparametric simulation, which can be easily applied using Risk Simulator's nonparametric custom distribution,[23] uses historical data to tell the story and to predict the future. Parametric simulation, however, forces the simulated outcomes to follow well-behaving distributions, which is desirable in most cases. Instead of having to worry about cleaning up any messy data (e.g., outliers and nonsensical values) as is required for nonparametric simulation, parametric simulation starts fresh every time.

> Monte Carlo simulation is a type of parametric simulation, where specific distributional parameters are required before a simulation can begin. The alternative approach is nonparametric simulation (also known as historical simulation) where the raw historical data is used and no distributional parameters are required for the simulation to run.

Fixing the Law of Averages with Simulation

Simulated Average Actual Demand	8.53	Simulated Demand Range	From 7.21 and 9.85
Inventory Held	9.00	Simulated Cost Range	From 178.91 to 149

Perishable Cost	$100
Fed Ex Cost	$175
Total Cost	$46.88

The best method is to perform a nonparametric simulation where we use the actual historical demand levels as inputs to simulate the most probable level of demand going forward which we found as 8.53 units. Given this demand, the lowest cost is obtained through a trial inventory of 9 units, a far cry from the original Flaw of Averages estimate of 5 units.

Trial Inventory	Total Cost
1.00	$1,318
2.00	$1,143
3.00	$968
4.00	$793
5.00	$618
6.00	$443
7.00	$268
8.00	$93
9.00	$47
10.00	$147
11.00	$247
12.00	$347
13.00	$447
14.00	$547
15.00	$647
16.00	$747

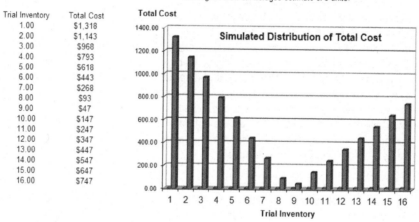

Figure 3.2: A Fix for the Flaw of Averages

COMPARING SIMULATION WITH TRADITIONAL ANALYSES

Figure 3.3 illustrates some traditional approaches used to deal with uncertainty and risk. The methods include performing sensitivity analysis, scenario analysis, and probabilistic scenarios. The next step is the application of Monte Carlo simulation, which can be seen as an extension to the next step in uncertainty and risk analysis. Figure 3.4 shows a more advanced use of Monte Carlo simulation for forecasting.[24] The examples in Figure 3.4 show how Monte Carlo simulation can be really complicated depending on its use. The Risk Simulator software has a stochastic process module that apply some of these more complex stochastic forecasting models, including Brownian motion, mean-reversion, and random walk models.

Point Estimates, Sensitivity Analysis, Scenario Analysis, Probabilistic Scenarios and Simulations

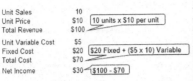

Unit Sales	10
Unit Price	$10 [10 units x $10 per unit]
Total Revenue	$100
Unit Variable Cost	$5
Fixed Cost	$20 [$20 Fixed + ($5 x 10) Variable]
Total Cost	$70
Net Income	$30 [$100 - $70]

Point Estimates

This is a simple example of a Point Estimate approach. The issues that arise may include the risk of how confident you are in the unit sales projections, the sales price and variable unit cost.

Since the bottom line Net Income is the key financial performance indicator here, an uncertainty in future sales volume will be impounded into the Net Income calculation. How much faith do you have on your calculation based on a simple point estimate?

Recall the Flaw of Average example where a simple point estimate could yield disastrous conclusions.

Sensitivity Analysis

Here, we can make unit changes to the variables in our simple model to see the final effects of such a change. Looking at the simple example, we know that only Unit Sales, Unit Price and Unit Variable Cost can change. This is since Total Revenues, Total Costs and Net Income are calculated values while Fixed Cost is assumed to be fixed and unchanging, regardless of the amount of sales units or sales price. Changing these three variables by one unit shows that from the original $40, Net Income has now increased $5 for Unit Sales, increased $10 for Unit Price and decreased $10 for Unit Variable Cost.

Unit Sales	11		Unit Sales	10		Unit Sales		10
Unit Price	$10 [Change 1 unit]		Unit Price	$11		Unit Price		$10
Total Revenue	$110		Total Revenue	$110 [Change 1 unit]		Total Revenue		$100
Unit Variable Cost	$5		Unit Variable Cost	$5		Unit Variable Cost		$6
Fixed Cost	$20		Fixed Cost	$20		Fixed Cost		$20
Total Cost	$75		Total Cost	$70	[Change 1 unit]	Total Cost		$80
Net Income	$35 [Up $5] [Up $10]		Net Income	$40	[Down $10]	Net Income		$20

Hence, we know that Unit Price has the most positive impact on the Net Income bottom line and Unit Variable Cost the most negative impact. In terms of making assumptions, we know that additional care must be taken when forecasting and estimating these variables. However, we still are in the dark concerning which sensitivity set of results we should be looking at or using.

Scenario Analysis

In order to provide an added element of variability, using the simple example above, you can perform a Scenario Analysis, where you would change values of key variables by certain units given certain assumed scenarios. For instance, you may assume three economic scenarios where unit sales and unit sale prices will vary. Under a good economic condition, unit sales go up to 14 at $11 per unit. Under a nominal economic scenario, units sales will be 10 units at $10 per unit. Under a bleak economic scenario, unit sales decrease to 8 units but prices per unit stays at $10.

Unit Sales	14 [Good Economy]		Unit Sales	10 [Average Economy]		Unit Sales	8
Unit Price	$11		Unit Price	$10		Unit Price	$10
Total Revenue	$154		Total Revenue	$100		Total Revenue	$80
Unit Variable Cost	$5		Unit Variable Cost	$5		Unit Variable Cost	$5
Fixed Cost	$20		Fixed Cost	$20 [Bad Economy]		Fixed Cost	$20
Total Cost	$90		Total Cost	$70		Total Cost	$60
Net Income	$64		Net Income	$30		Net Income	$20

Looking at the Net Income results, we have $64, $30 and $20. The problem here is, the variation is too large. Which condition do I think will most likely occur and which result do I use in my budget forecast for the firm? Although Scenario Analysis is useful in ascertaining the impact of different conditions, both advantageous and adverse, the analysis provides little insight to which result to use.

Probabilistic Scenario Analysis

	Probability	Net Income
Good Economy	35%	$64.00
Average Economy	40%	$30.00
Bad Economy	25%	$20.00
EMV		$39.40

We can always assign probabilities that each scenario will occur, creating a Probabilistic Scenario Analysis and simply calculate the Expected Monetary Value (EMV) of the forecasts. The results here are more robust and reliable than a simple scenario analysis since we have collapsed the entire range of potential outcomes of $64, $30 and $20 into a single expected value. This value is what you would expect to get on average.

Simulation Analysis

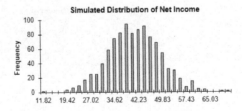

Unit Sales	10
Unit Price	$10
Total Revenue	$100
Unit Variable Cost	$5
Fixed Cost	$20
Total Cost	$70
Net Income	$30

Looking at the original model, we know that through Sensitivity Analysis, Unit Sales, Unit Price and Unit Variable Cost are three highly uncertain variables. We can then very easily simulate these three unknowns thousands of times (based on certain distributional assumptions) to see what the final Net Income value looks like.

By performing the simulation thousands of times, we essentially perform thousands of sensitivity analysis and scenario analysis given different sets of probabilities. These are all set in the original simulation assumptions (types of probability distributions, the parameters of the distributions and which variables to simulate).

Simulated Distribution of Net Income

(histogram with y-axis "Frequency" ranging 0 to 100, x-axis values 11.82, 19.42, 27.02, 34.62, 42.23, 49.83, 57.43, 65.03)

Figure 3.3: Point Estimates, Sensitivity Analysis, Scenario Analysis, and Simulations

Conceptualizing the Lognormal Distribution

A Simple Simulation Example
We need to perform many simulations to obtain a valid distribution

Mean	15%	
Sigma	30%	
Timing	Daily ▼	
Starting Value	100	

Here we see the effects of performing a simulation of stock price paths following a Geometric Brownian Motion model for daily closing prices. Three sample paths are seen here. In reality, thousands of simulations are performed and their distributional properties are analyzed. Frequently, the average closing prices of these thousands of simulations are analyzed, based on these simulated price paths.

time days	normal deviates	value simulated
0	NA	100.0000
1	0.0873	100.2259
2	-0.4320	99.4675
3	-0.1389	99.2652
4	-0.4583	98.4649
5	1.7807	101.9095
6	-1.4406	99.2212
7	-0.5577	98.2357
8	0.5277	99.2838
9	-0.4844	98.4345
10	-0.2307	98.0634
11	0.8688	99.7532
12	2.1195	83.9088
13	-1.9756	100.1461
14	1.3734	102.8517
15	-0.8790	101.2112
16	-0.7610	99.8203
17	0.3168	100.4824
18	-0.0511	100.4452
19	0.0653	100.6301
20	-0.6073	99.5368
21	0.6900	100.9091
22	-0.7012	99.6353
23	1.4784	102.5312
24	-0.9195	100.8184
25	-0.3343	100.2411
26	-2.3395	95.9465
27	-1.7831	92.8103
28	-0.3247	92.2958
29	0.5053	93.2409
30	0.0386	93.3652
250	0.0451	100.0978

Rows 31 through 249 have been hidden to conserve space.

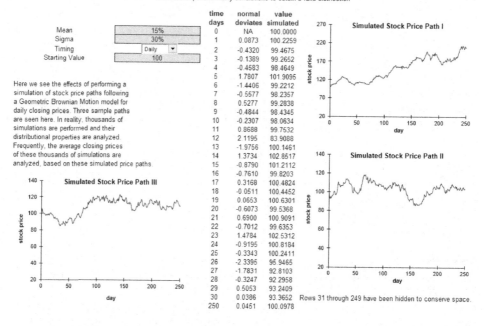

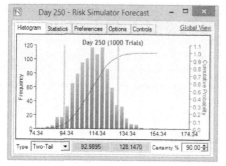

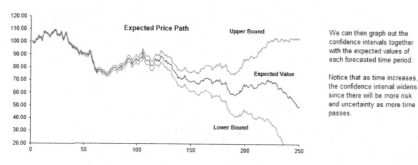

The thousands of simulated price paths are then tabulated into probability distributions. Here is a sample price path at period 250.

We can also analyze each of these time-specific probability distribution and calculate relevant statistically valid confidence intervals for decision-making purposes.

We can then graph out the confidence intervals together with the expected values of each forecasted time period.

Notice that as time increases, the confidence interval widens since there will be more risk and uncertainty as more time passes.

Figure 3.4: Conceptualizing the Lognormal Distribution

USING RISK SIMULATOR AND
EXCEL TO PERFORM SIMULATIONS

Basic simulations can be performed using Excel. However, more advanced simulation packages such as Risk Simulator perform the task more efficiently, in addition to having additional features preset in each simulation. We now present both Monte Carlo parametric simulation and nonparametric bootstrap simulation using Excel and Risk Simulator.

The examples in Figures 3.5 and 3.6 are created using Excel to perform a limited number of simulations on a set of probabilistic assumptions. We assume that having performed a series of scenario analyses, we obtain a set of nine resulting values, complete with their respective probabilities of occurrence. The first step in setting up a simulation in Excel for such a scenario analysis is to understand the function *"RAND()"* within Excel. This function is simply a random number generator Excel uses to create random numbers from a uniform distribution between 0 and 1. Then it translates this 0 to 1 range using the assigned probabilities in our assumption into ranges or bins. For instance, if the value $362,995 occurs with a 55 percent probability, we can create a bin with a range of 0.00 to 0.55. Similarly, we can create a bin range of 0.56 to 0.65 for the next value of $363,522 which occurs 10 percent of the time, and so forth. Based on these ranges and bins, the nonparametric simulation can now be set up.

Figure 3.5 illustrates an example with 5,000 sets of trials. Each set of trials is simulated 100 times; that is, in each simulation trial set, the original numbers are picked randomly with replacement by using the Excel formula *"VLOOKUP(RAND(), $D$16:$F$24, 3)"* which picks up the third column of data from the D16 to F24 area by matching the results from the *RAND()* function and data from the first column.

The average of the data sampled is then calculated for each trial set. The distribution of these 5,000 trial sets' averages is obtained and the frequency distribution is shown at the bottom of Figure 3.5. According to the Central Limit Theorem, the average of these sample averages will approach the real true mean of the population at the limit. In addition, the distribution will most likely approach normality when a sufficient set of trials is performed. Clearly running this nonparametric simulation manually in Excel is fairly tedious. An alternative is to use Risk Simulator's custom distribution, which does the same thing but in an infinitely faster and more efficient fashion. Chapter 5, Pandora's Toolbox, illustrates some of these simulation tools in more detail.

Nonparametric simulation is a very powerful tool but it is only applicable if data are available. Clearly, the more data there are, the higher the level of precision and confidence in the simulation results. However, when no data exist or when a valid systematic process underlies the dataset (e.g., physics, engineering, economic relationship, and so forth) parametric simulation may be more appropriate, where exact probabilistic distributions are used.

Using Excel to perform simulations is easy and effective for simple problems. However, when more complicated problems or requirements arise (e.g., correlations exist among input variables, dynamic sensitivities, reports and charts, simulation statistics, portfolio optimization, predictive modeling, stochastic processes, and many other such issues), the use of more specialized simulation packages is warranted. Risk Simulator is such a simulation package. In the example shown in Figure 3.7, the green-colored cells (Revenues, Opex, FCF/EBITDA) are the assumption cells, where we enter our distributional input assumptions, such as the type of distribution the variable follows and what the parameters are. For instance, we can say that revenues follow a normal distribution with a mean of $1,010 and a standard deviation of $100, based on analyzing historical revenue data for the firm. The net present value (NPV) cells are the forecast output cells, that is, the results of these cells are the results we ultimately wish to analyze. Refer to Chapter 4, Test Driving Risk Simulator, for details on setting up and getting started with using the Risk Simulator software. The rest of this book is dedicated to modeling more complex requirements using the software.

Simulation (Probability Assumptions)

	Value	Probability	
Step 1:	362995	55%	Here are the assumed values and their corresponding probabilities of
The Assumptions	363522	10%	occurrence. The sum of the probabilities have to add up to 100%.
	252094	10%	
	122922	10%	We then translate the assumed values into a set of
	23572	3%	random numbers bounded by [0,1]. For instance, for
	305721	3%	a normal distribution, the probability of getting a number
	61877	3%	between 0.00 and 0.55 is 55% and between 0.56 and
	147322	3%	0.65 is 10% and so forth. This is done in Step 2 below.
	179360	3%	

CELLS $D$15:$F$23

	Minimum	Maximum	Implied	
Step 2:	0.00	0.55	362994.83	Simulate this for 100 trials and take the average. Then,
The Table Setup	0.56	0.65	363522.33	repeat this for several thousand sets, taking the average
	0.66	0.75	252094	on every set. Then, using these thousands of simulated
	0.76	0.85	122922.05	sets, create a probability distribution and calculate its
	0.86	0.88	23572.39	corresponding descriptive statistics (mean, standard
	0.89	0.91	305721.43	deviation, confidence intervals, probabilities, et cetera).
	0.92	0.94	61876.66	
	0.95	0.97	147322.19	VLOOKUP(RAND(),$D$15:$F$23,3)
	0.98	1.00	179359.73	

Average 297185
90th% 310390

Step 3:	Trials	Set 1	Set 2	Set 3	Set 4	Set 5	Set 100	Set 1000	Set 1500	Set 2000	Set 5000
Simulate	1	147322	122922	252094	362995	362995	362995	252094	362995	61877	363522
	2	362995	362995	362995	362995	147322	61877	61877	362995	122922	179360
	3	252094	362995	362996	122922	362995	252094	61877	362995	362995	362995
	4	362995	362995	252094	362995	362995	362995	61877	179360	179360	122922
	5	252094	362995	363522	362995	363522	122922	363522	252094	147322	362995
	6	362995	362995	363522	122922	252094	363522	362995	179360	122922	179360
	7	122922	362995	363522	362995	362995	122922	122922	252094	61877	122922
	8	363522	362995	362996	122922	362995	122922	122922	122922	362995	61877
	9	362995	362995	362996	252094	252094	362995	362995	362995	179360	363522
	10	122922	122922	363522	362995	305721	362995	252094	61877	362995	362995
	11	305721	362995	362995	362995	252094	362995	252094	363522	362995	362995
	12	362995	362995	362995	362995	252094	362995	362995	252094	362995	122922
Rows 13	95	252094	362995	362995	363522	362995	122922	362995	362995	252094	61877
to 94 have	96	252094	252094	61877	362995	363522	122922	23572	122922	305721	362995
been hidden	97	362995	23572	362996	362995	122922	305721	362995	362995	23572	362995
to conserve	98	362995	362995	362995	147322	362995	252094	362995	362995	362995	252094
space.	99	122922	362995	362995	362995	362995	362995	362995	147322	362995	252094
	100	363522	252094	362995	362995	362995	362995	362995	362995	362995	362995
	Average	275763	282681	318044	292146	300325	299948	298498	302302	296806	294590

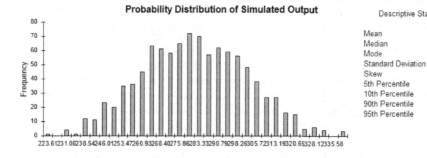

Probability Distribution of Simulated Output

Descriptive Statistics

Mean	279.50
Median	279.34
Mode	313.66
Standard Deviation	20.42
Skew	0.05
5th Percentile	245.34
10th Percentile	253.16
90th Percentile	306.00
95th Percentile	312.71

Figure 3.5: Simulation Using Excel I

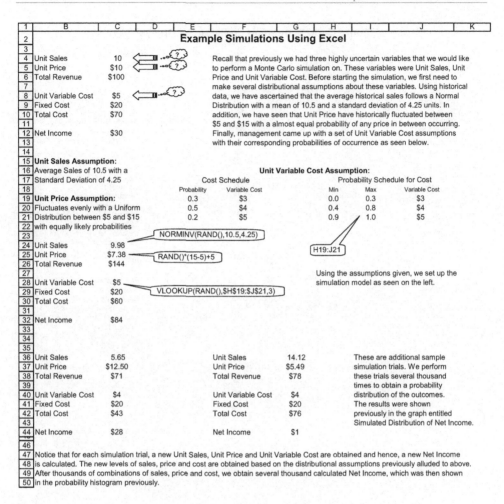

Figure 3.6: Simulation Using Excel II

The "RAND()" function in Excel is used to generate random numbers for a uniform distribution between 0 and 1. "RAND()*(B-A)+A" is used to generate random numbers for a uniform distribution between A and B. "NORMSINV(RAND())" generates random numbers from a standard-normal distribution with mean of zero and variance of one or Normal (0,1).

Monte Carlo Simulation on Financial Analysis

Project A

		2001	2002	2003	2004	2005		NPV	$126
Revenues		$1,010	$1,111	$1,233	$1,384	$1,573		IRR	15.68%
Opex/Revenue Multiple		0.09	0.10	0.11	0.12	0.13		Risk Adjusted Discount Rate	12.00%
Operating Expenses		$91	$109	$133	$165	$210		Growth Rate	3.00%
EBITDA		$919	$1,002	$1,100	$1,219	$1,363		Terminal Value	$8,692
FCF/EBITDA Multiple		0.20	0.25	0.31	0.40	0.56		Terminal Risk Adjustment	30.00%
Free Cash Flows	($1,200)	$187	$246	$336	$486	$760		Discounted Terminal Value	$2,341
Initial Investment	($1,200)							Terminal to NPV Ratio	18.52
Revenue Growth Rates		10.00%	11.00%	12.21%	13.70%	15.58%		Payback Period	3.89
								Simulated Risk Value	$390

Project B

		2001	2002	2003	2004	2005		NPV	$149
Revenues		$1,200	$1,404	$1,683	$2,085	$2,700		IRR	33.74%
Opex/Revenue Multiple		0.09	0.10	0.11	0.12	0.13		Risk Adjusted Discount Rate	19.00%
Operating Expenses		$108	$138	$181	$249	$361		Growth Rate	3.75%
EBITDA		$1,092	$1,266	$1,502	$1,836	$2,340		Terminal Value	$2,480
FCF/EBITDA Multiple		0.10	0.11	0.12	0.14	0.16		Terminal Risk Adjustment	30.00%
Free Cash Flows	($400)	$109	$139	$183	$252	$364		Discounted Terminal Value	$668
Initial Investment	($400)							Terminal to NPV Ratio	4.49
Revenue Growth Rates		17.00%	19.89%	23.85%	29.53%	38.25%		Payback Period	2.83
								Simulated Risk Value	$122

Project C

		2001	2002	2003	2004	2005		NPV	$29
Revenues		$950	$1,069	$1,219	$1,415	$1,678		IRR	15.99%
Opex/Revenue Multiple		0.13	0.15	0.17	0.20	0.24		Risk Adjusted Discount Rate	15.00%
Operating Expenses		$124	$157	$205	$278	$395		Growth Rate	5.50%
EBITDA		$827	$912	$1,014	$1,136	$1,283		Terminal Value	$7,935
FCF/EBITDA Multiple		0.20	0.25	0.31	0.40	0.56		Terminal Risk Adjustment	30.00%
Free Cash Flows	($1,100)	$168	$224	$309	$453	$715		Discounted Terminal Value	$2,137
Initial Investment	($1,100)							Terminal to NPV Ratio	74.73
Revenue Growth Rates		12.50%	14.06%	16.04%	18.61%	22.08%		Payback Period	3.88
								Simulated Risk Value	$53

	Implementation Cost	Sharpe Ratio	Weight	Project Cost	Project NPV	Risk Parameter	Payback Period	Technology Level	Tech Mix
Project A	$1,200	0.02	5.14%	$62	$6	29%	3.89	5	0.26
Project B	$400	0.31	25.27%	$101	$38	15%	2.83	3	0.76
Project C	$1,100	0.19	34.59%	$380	$10	21%	3.88	2	0.69
Total	$3,450	0.17	100.00%	$806	$63	28%	3.49	3.5	3.11

Figure 3.7: Simulation Using Risk Simulator

Questions

1. Compare and contrast parametric and nonparametric simulation.

2. What is a stochastic process (e.g., Brownian motion)?

3. What does the "RAND( )" function do in Excel?

4. What does the "NORMSINV( )" function do in Excel?

5. What happens when both functions are used together, i.e., "NORMSINV(RAND( ))"?

6. For modeling each of the following, determine which distribution(s) is/are most applicable and explain why. (Refer to the Appendix in Chapter 4 for the different distributions.)

   a. Number of phone calls a minute or number of errors in a page.

   b. Number of defective items in a batch of 100 items.

   c. Real estate prices and stock prices.

   d. Measuring earthquakes and rainfall frequency.

   e. Number of sales calls required to get to the 10th successful sale.

   f. Height, weight, and IQ of individuals.

   g. Conditions with min and max limits, with most likely values in between.

   h. Number of people in line at a bank within a specified time period.

   i. Stock returns.

CHAPTER 4 – TEST DRIVING RISK SIMULATOR

This chapter provides the novice risk analyst an introduction to the Risk Simulator software for performing Monte Carlo simulation, a trial version of which is included in the book. The chapter starts off by illustrating what Risk Simulator does and what steps are taken in a Monte Carlo simulation, as well as some of the more basic elements in a simulation analysis. The chapter then continues with how to interpret the results from a simulation and ends with a discussion of correlating variables in a simulation as well as applying precision and error control. As software versions with new enhancements are continually released, be sure to review the software's user manual for more up-to-date details on using the latest version of the software.

GETTING STARTED WITH RISK SIMULATOR

Risk Simulator is a Monte Carlo simulation, forecasting, optimization, and risk analytics software. It is written in Microsoft .NET C# and functions together with Excel as an add-in. When you have the software installed, simply start Excel and you will see a new menu item called Risk Simulator. If you are using Excel 2010 or Excel 2013, you will see a new tab called Risk Simulator as well as some large icons that you can access. The examples referenced throughout this book use Risk Simulator version 2014 or later, with the following languages: English, Arabic, Chinese (Simplified), Chinese (Traditional), French, German, Italian, Japanese, Korean, Portuguese, Russian, and Spanish.

This software is also compatible and often used with the Real Options SLS (Super Lattice Solver) software (see Chapters 10 and 11), both developed by the author. The different functions or modules in both software applications are briefly described in the list that follows. Note that there are other software applications such as the ROV Modeling Toolkit, Project Economics Analysis Toolkit (PEAT), ROV Employee Stock Options Valuation Toolkit, ROV Compiler, ROV Risk Extractor and Evaluator, ROV BizStats, ROV Modeler, ROV Valuator, ROV Dashboard, and others, also created by the same company that developed Risk Simulator, and introduced in this book. You can get more information on these tools by visiting *www.realoptionsvaluation.com* and clicking on the *Downloads* tab, where you can also view some getting started videos and obtain whitepapers, case studies, and other free models.

The following lists the modules available in the Risk Simulator software. This chapter covers the simulation module, while Chapter 5 reviews the analytical tools module; Chapters 6–7 illustrate the forecasting module; Chapters 8–9 dive into the optimization module; Chapters 10–11 explain the use of the real options SLS and dynamic decision tree modules; and Technical Note 8 covers the basics of the ROV BizStats module.

- The *Monte Carlo Simulation* module allows you to run simulations in your existing Excel-based models, generate and extract simulation forecasts (distributions of results), perform distributional fitting (automatically finding the best-fitting statistical distribution), compute correlations (maintain relationships among simulated random variables), identify sensitivities (creating tornado and sensitivity charts), test statistical hypotheses (finding statistical differences between pairs of forecasts), run bootstrap simulation (testing the robustness of result statistics), and run custom and nonparametric simulations (simulations using historical data without specifying any distributions or their parameters for forecasting without data or applying expert opinion forecasts).

- The *Analytical Tools* module allows you to run segmentation clustering, hypothesis testing, statistical tests of raw data, data diagnostics of technical forecasting assumptions (e.g., heteroskedasticity, multicollinearity, and the like), sensitivity and scenario analyses, overlay chart analysis, spider charts, tornado charts, and many other powerful tools.

- The *Forecasting* module can be used to generate automatic time-series forecasts (with and without seasonality and trend), multivariate regressions (modeling relationships among variables), nonlinear extrapolations (curve fitting), stochastic processes (random walk, mean-reversion, jump-diffusion, and mixed processes), Box–Jenkins ARIMA (econometric forecasts), Auto ARIMA, basic econometrics and auto-econometrics (modeling relationships and generating forecasts), exponential J-curves, logistic S-curves, GARCH models and its multiple variations (modeling and forecasting volatility), maximum likelihood models for limited dependent variables (Logit, Tobit, and Probit models), Markov chains, trendlines, spline curves, and others.

- The *Optimization* module is used for optimizing multiple decision variables subject to constraints to maximize or minimize an objective, and can be run either as a static optimization, as dynamic and stochastic optimization under uncertainty together with Monte Carlo simulation, or as a stochastic optimization with super speed simulations. The software can handle linear and nonlinear optimizations with binary, integer, and continuous variables, as well as generate Markowitz efficient frontiers.

- The *Real Options Super Lattice Solver (SLS)* module is another standalone software complementing Risk Simulator, for solving simple to complex strategic real options problems, financial options, exotic options, employee stock options, and other options-embedded investment vehicles and contracts.

- The *Dynamic Decision Tree* module allows users to create and model traditional decision trees, coupled with more advanced analytics including running dynamic simulations, scenarios, sensitivities, minimax computations, risk-based utility functions, and Bayesian analysis.

- The *ROV BizStats* module covers applied business statistics and business intelligence analysis, from forecasting and data mining to parametric and nonparametric models.

The following sections walk you through the basics of the *Simulation Module* in Risk Simulator, while subsequent chapters provide more details on the applications of other modules. To follow along, make sure you have Risk Simulator installed on your computer to proceed. Be sure to see *Software Download and Install* section at the end of this book for directions on installing your 30-day trial software. Also note that there are additional hands-on exercises available at the end of certain chapters in which you can get step-by-step instructions on running sample models using Risk Simulator.

RUNNING A MONTE CARLO SIMULATION

Typically, to run a simulation in your existing Excel model, the following steps have to be performed:

1. Start a new simulation profile or open an existing profile.

2. Define input assumptions in the relevant cells.

3. Define output forecasts in the relevant cells.

4. Run simulation.

5. Interpret the results.

If desired, and for practice, open the example file called *Basic Simulation Model* and follow along with the examples provided here on creating a simulation. The example file can be found by first starting Excel, and then clicking on *Risk Simulator | Example Models | 02 Basic Simulation Model*.

1. Start a New Simulation Profile

To start a new simulation, you must first create a simulation profile (Figure 4.1). A simulation profile contains a complete set of instructions on how you would like to run a simulation (i.e., all the assumptions, forecasts, run preferences, and so forth). Having profiles facilitates creating multiple scenarios of simulations. That is, using the same exact model, several profiles can be created, each with its own specific simulation properties and requirements. The same person can create different test scenarios using different distributional assumptions and inputs, or multiple persons can test their own assumptions and inputs on the same model.

- Start Excel and create a new or open an existing model (you can use the Basic Simulation Model example to follow along).

- Click on *Risk Simulator | New Simulation Profile*.

- Specify a title for your simulation as well as all other pertinent information.

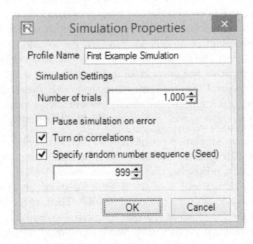

Figure 4.1: New Simulation Profile

The following explains the user input requirements in Figure 4.1:

- *Title.* Specifying a simulation title allows you to create multiple simulation profiles in a single Excel model. Using a title means that you can now save different simulation scenario profiles within the same model without having to delete existing assumptions and changing them each time a new simulation scenario is required. You can always change the profile's name later (*Risk Simulator | Edit Profile*).

- *Number of Trials.* This is where the number of simulation trials required is entered. That is, running 1,000 trials means that 1,000 different iterations of outcomes based on the input assumptions will be generated. You can change this as desired, but the input has to be positive integers. The default number of runs is 1,000 trials. You can use precision and error control to automatically help determine how many simulation trials to run (see the section on precision and error control later in this chapter for details).

- *Pause Simulation on Error.* If checked, the simulation stops every time an error is encountered in the Excel model. That is, if your model encounters a computation error (e.g., some input values generated in a simulation trial may yield a divide by zero error in one of your spreadsheet cells), the simulation stops. This feature is important to help audit your model to make sure there are no computational errors in your Excel model. However, if you are sure the model works, then there is no need for this preference to be checked.

- *Turn On Correlations.* If checked, correlations between paired input assumptions will be computed. Otherwise, correlations will all be set to zero and a simulation is run assuming no cross-correlations between input assumptions. As an example, applying correlations will yield more accurate results if indeed correlations exist and will tend to yield a lower forecast confidence if negative correlations exist. After turning on correlations here, you can later set the relevant correlation coefficients on each assumption generated (see the section on correlations and precision control later in this chapter for more details).

- *Specify Random Number Sequence.* Simulation, by definition, will yield slightly different results every time a simulation is run. Different results occur by virtue of the random number generation routine in Monte Carlo simulation; this characteristic is a theoretical fact in all random number generators. However, when making presentations, if you require the same results (especially if you have already run a simulation and generated a report to present a set of results, and you would like to show the same results being generated in a live presentation; or when you are sharing models with others and would like the same results to be obtained every time), then check this preference and enter in an initial seed number. The seed number can be any positive integer. Using the same initial seed value, the same number of trials, and the same input assumptions, the simulation will always yield the same sequence of random numbers, guaranteeing the same final set of results.

Note that once a new simulation profile has been created, you can come back later and modify these selections. In order to do this, make sure that the current active profile is the profile you wish to modify, otherwise, click on *Risk Simulator | Change Simulation Profile*, select the profile you wish to change and click *OK* (Figure 4.2 shows an example where there are multiple profiles and how to activate a selected profile). Then, click on *Risk Simulator | Edit Simulation Profile* and make the required changes. You can also duplicate or rename an existing profile. When creating multiple profiles in the same Excel model, make sure to provide each profile a unique name so you can tell them apart later on. Also, these profiles are stored inside hidden sectors of the Excel *.xlsx file and you do not have to save any additional files. The profiles and their contents (assumptions, forecasts, etc.) are automatically saved when you save the Excel file. Finally, the last profile that is active when you exit and save the Excel file will be the one that is opened the next time the Excel file is accessed.

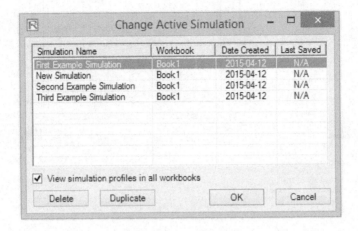

Figure 4.2: Change Active Simulation

2. Define Input Assumptions

The next step is to set input assumptions in your model. Note that assumptions can only be assigned to cells without any equations or functions (i.e., typed-in numerical values that are inputs in a model), whereas output forecasts can only be assigned to cells with equations and functions (i.e., outputs of a model). Recall that assumptions and forecasts cannot be set unless a simulation profile already exists. Do the following to set new input assumptions in your model:

1. Make sure a Simulation Profile exists, open an existing profile, or start a new profile (*Risk Simulator | New Simulation Profile*).

2. Select the cell you wish to set an assumption on (e.g., cell G8 in the Basic Simulation Model example).

3. Click on *Risk Simulator | Set Input Assumption* or click on the set input assumption icon in the Risk Simulator icon toolbar.

4. Select the relevant distribution you want, enter the relevant distribution parameters (e.g., select *Triangular* distribution and use 1, 2, and 2.5 as the minimum, most likely and maximum values), and hit *OK* to insert the input assumption into your model (Figure 4.3).

Note that you can also set assumptions by selecting the cell you wish to set the assumption on and, using the mouse right-click, access the shortcut Risk Simulator menu to set an input assumption.

In addition, for expert users, you can set input assumptions using the Risk Simulator *RS Functions*: select the cell of choice, click on Excel's *Insert, Function*, and select the *All Category*, and scroll down to the *RS* functions list (we do not recommend using RS functions unless you are an expert user). For the examples going forward, we suggest following the basic instructions in accessing menus and icons.

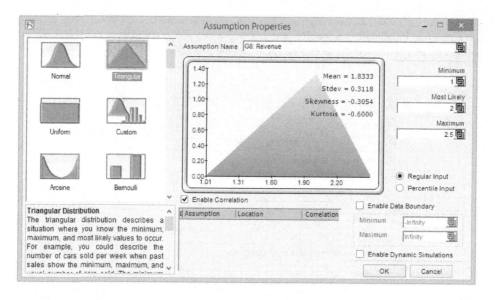

Figure 4.3: Setting an Input Assumption

Notice that in the Assumption Properties, there are several key areas worthy of mention. Figure 4.4 shows the different areas:

- *Assumption Name.* This is an optional area that allows you to enter in unique names for the assumptions to help track what each of the assumptions represent. Good modeling practice is to use short but precise assumption names.

- *Distribution Gallery.* This area to the left shows the 50 different probability distributions available in the software. To change the views, right click anywhere in the gallery and select large icons, small icons, or list.

- *Input Parameters.* Depending on the distribution selected, the required relevant parameters are shown. You may either enter the parameters directly or link them to specific cells in your worksheet. Hard coding or typing the parameters is useful when the assumption parameters are assumed not to change. Linking to worksheet cells is useful when the input parameters need to be visible or are allowed to be changed (click on the link icon to link an input parameter to a worksheet cell).

- *Enable Data Boundary.* This feature is typically not used by the average analyst but exists for truncating the distributional assumptions. For instance, if a normal distribution is selected, the theoretical boundaries are between negative infinity and positive infinity. However, in practice, the simulated variable exists only within some smaller range, and this range can then be entered to truncate the distribution appropriately.

- *Correlations.* Pairwise correlations can be assigned to input assumptions here. If correlations are required in the simulation model, remember to check the *Turn on Correlations* preference by clicking on *Risk Simulator | Edit Simulation Profile.* See the discussion on correlations later in this chapter for more details about assigning correlations and the effects correlations have on a model. Notice that you can either truncate a distribution or correlate it to another assumption but not both.

- *Short Descriptions.* These exist for each of the distributions in the gallery. The short descriptions explain when a certain distribution is used as well as the input parameter requirements. See the appendix on Understanding Probability Distributions for details on running Monte Carlo simulations on each distribution type in the software.

- *Regular Input and Percentile Input.* This option allows the user to perform a quick due diligence test of the input assumption. For instance, if setting a normal distribution with some mean and standard deviation inputs, you can click on the percentile input to see what the corresponding 10th and 90th percentiles are.

- *Enable Dynamic Simulations.* This option is unchecked by default, but if you wish to run a multidimensional simulation (i.e., if you link the input parameters of the assumption to another cell that is itself an assumption, you are simulating the inputs, or simulating the simulation), then remember to check this option. Dynamic simulation will not work unless the inputs are linked to other changing input assumptions.

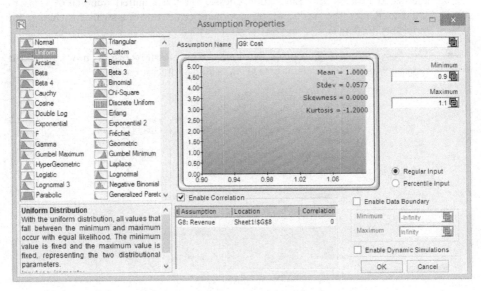

Figure 4.4: Assumption Properties

Note: If you are following along with the example, continue by setting another assumption on cell G9. This time use the *Uniform* distribution with a minimum value of 0.9 and a maximum value of 1.1. Then, proceed to defining the output forecasts in the next step.

3. Define Output Forecasts

The next step is to define output forecasts in the model. Forecasts can only be defined on output cells with equations or functions. The following describes the set forecast process:

1. Select the cell you wish to set an assumption on (e.g., cell G10 in the Basic Simulation Model example).

2. Click on *Risk Simulator | Set Output Forecast* or click on the set output forecast icon on the Risk Simulator icon toolbar.

3. Enter the relevant information and click *OK.*

Note that you can also set output forecasts by selecting the cell you wish to set the assumption on and, using the mouse right-click, access the shortcut Risk Simulator menu to set an output forecast.

Figure 4.5 illustrates the set forecast properties:

- *Forecast Name.* Specify the name of the forecast cell. This is important because when you have a large model with multiple forecast cells, naming the forecast cells individually allows you to access the right results quickly. Do not underestimate the importance of this simple step. Good modeling practice is to use short but precise assumption names.

- *Forecast Precision.* Instead of relying on a guesstimate of how many trials to run in your simulation, you can set up precision and error controls. When an error-precision combination has been achieved in the simulation, the simulation will pause and inform you of the precision achieved, making the number of simulation trials an automated process and eliminating guesses on the required number of trials to simulate. Review the section on precision and error control later in this chapter for more specific details.

- *Show Forecast Window.* This property allows the user to show or not show a particular forecast window. The default is to always show a forecast chart.

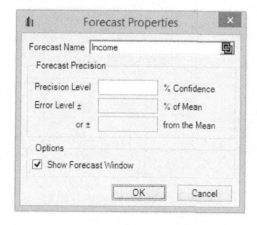

Figure 4.5: Set Output Forecast

4. Run Simulation

If everything looks right, simply click on *Risk Simulator | Run Simulation* or click on the *Run* icon on the Risk Simulator toolbar and the simulation will proceed. You may also reset a simulation after it has run to rerun it (*Risk Simulator | Reset Simulation* or the reset simulation icon on the toolbar) or to pause it during a run. Also, the *step* function (*Risk Simulator | Step Simulation* or the step simulation icon on the toolbar) allows you to simulate a single trial, one at a time, useful for educating others on simulation (i.e., you can show that at each trial, all the values in the assumption cells are being replaced and the entire model is recalculated each time). You can also access the run simulation menu by right-clicking anywhere in the model and selecting *Run Simulation*.

Risk Simulator also allows you to run the simulation at extremely fast speed, called Super Speed. To do this, click on *Risk Simulator | Run Super Speed Simulation* or use the run super speed icon. Notice how much faster the super speed simulation runs. In fact, for practice, click on *Reset Simulation* and then *Edit Simulation Profile*, change the *Number of Trials* to *100,000*, and click on *Run Super Speed*. It should only take a few seconds to run. However, be aware that super speed simulation will not run if the model has errors, VBA (Visual Basic for Applications), or links to external data sources or applications. In such situations, you will be notified and the regular speed simulation will be run instead. Regular speed simulations are always able to run even with errors, VBA, or external links.

5. Interpret the Forecast Results

The final step in Monte Carlo simulation is to interpret the resulting forecast charts. Figures 4.6 to 4.13 show the forecast chart and the corresponding statistics generated after running the simulation. Typically, the following features are important in interpreting the results of a simulation:

- *Forecast Chart*. The forecast chart shown in Figure 4.6 is a probability histogram that shows the frequency counts of values occurring in the total number of trials simulated. The vertical bars show the frequency of a particular x value occurring out of the total number of trials, while the cumulative frequency (smooth line) shows the total probabilities of all values at and below x occurring in the forecast.

- *Forecast Statistics*. The forecast statistics shown in Figure 4.7 summarize the distribution of the forecast values in terms of the four moments of a distribution. See the section on understanding the forecast statistics in Chapter 2 for more details on what some of these statistics mean. You can rotate between the histogram and statistics tab by depressing the space bar.

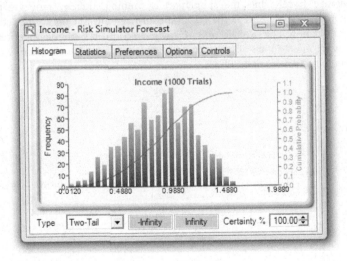

Figure 4.6: Forecast Chart

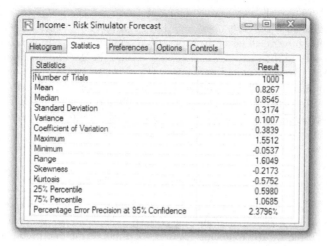

Figure 4.7: Forecast Statistics

- *Preferences.* The preferences tab in the forecast chart (Figure 4.8) allows you to change the look and feel of the charts. For instance, if *Always Show Window on Top* is selected, the forecast charts will always be visible regardless of what other software are running on your computer. *Histogram Resolution* allows you to change the number of bins of the histogram, anywhere from 5 bins to 100 bins. Also, the *Data Update Interval* section allows you to control how fast the simulation runs versus how often the forecast chart is updated. That is, if you wish to see the forecast chart updated at almost every trial, this feature will slow down the simulation as more memory is being allocated to updating the chart versus running the simulation. This option is merely a user preference and in no way changes the results of the simulation, just the speed of completing the simulation. To further increase the speed of the simulation, you can minimize Excel while the simulation is running, thereby reducing the memory required to visibly update the Excel spreadsheet and freeing up the memory to run the simulation. The *Close All* and *Minimize All* controls both the open forecast charts, and *Copy Chart* allows you to copy the histogram into the clipboard where you can paste it into other applications.

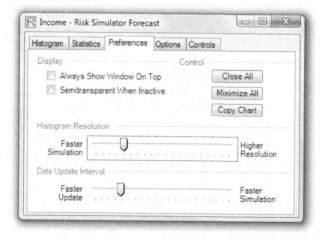

Figure 4.8: Forecast Chart Preferences

- *Options.* This forecast chart option (Figure 4.9, top) allows you to show all the forecast data or to filter in/out values that fall within some specified interval you choose, or within some standard deviation you choose. Also, the precision level can be set here for this specific forecast to show the error levels in the statistics view. See the section on precision and error control later in this chapter for more details. *Show the Following Statistic on Histogram* is a user preference if the mean, median, first quartile, and fourth quartile lines (25th and 75th percentiles) should be displayed on the forecast chart. Preferences on the number of decimals to show in the chart, confidence intervals, and simulation statistics, can also be set here.

- *Controls.* This tab (Figure 4.9, bottom) has all the functionalities in allowing you to change the type, color, size, zoom, tilt, 3D, and other things in the forecast chart, as well as providing overlay charts (PDF, CDF) and running distributional fitting on your forecast data (see the Data Fitting sections in Chapter 5 for more details on this methodology).

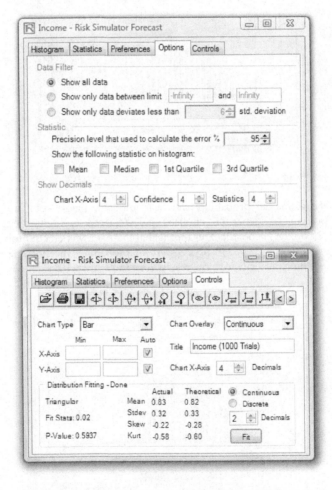

Figure 4.9: Forecast Chart Options and Control

USING FORECAST CHARTS AND CONFIDENCE INTERVALS

In forecast charts, you can determine the probability of occurrence called *confidence intervals*. That is, given two values, what are the chances that the outcome will fall between these two values? Figure 4.10 illustrates that there is a 90 percent probability that the final outcome (in this case, the level of income) will be between $0.2653 and $1.3230. The two-tailed confidence interval can be obtained by first selecting *Two-Tail* as the type, entering the desired certainty value (e.g., 90) and hitting *TAB* on the keyboard. The two computed values corresponding to the certainty value will then be displayed. In this example, there is a 5 percent probability that income will be below $0.2653 and another 5 percent probability that income will be above $1.3230. That is, the two-tailed confidence interval is a symmetrical interval centered on the median or 50th percentile value. Thus, both tails will have the same probability.

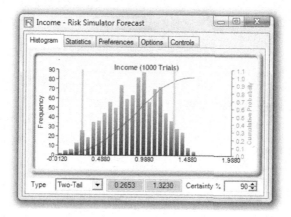

Figure 4.10: Forecast Chart Two-Tail Confidence Interval

Alternatively, a one-tail probability can be computed. Figure 4.11 shows a *Left-Tail* selection at 95 percent confidence (i.e., choose *Left-Tail* ≤ as the type, enter 95 as the certainty level, and hit *TAB* on the keyboard). This means that there is a 95 percent probability that the income will be at or below $1.3230 or a 5 percent probability that income will be above $1.3230, corresponding perfectly with the results seen in Figure 4.10.

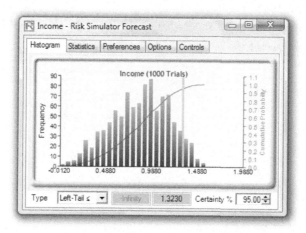

Figure 4.11: Forecast Chart One-Tail Confidence Interval

In addition to evaluating what the confidence interval is (i.e., given a probability level and finding the relevant income values), you can determine the probability of a given income value (Figure 4.12). For instance, what is the probability that income will be less than or equal to $1? To do this, select the *Left-Tail* ≤ probability type, enter 1 into the value input box, and hit *TAB*. The corresponding certainty will then be computed (in this case, there is a 67.70 percent probability income will be at or below $1).

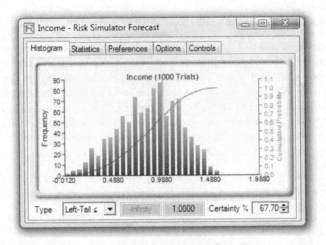

Figure 4.12: Forecast Chart Probability Evaluation (Left-tail)

For the sake of completeness, you can select the *Right-Tail* > probability type and enter the value 1 in the value input box, and hit *TAB* (Figure 4.13). The resulting probability indicates the right-tail probability past the value 1, that is, the probability of income exceeding $1 (in this case, we see that there is a 32.30 percent probability of income exceeding $1). The sum of 32.30 percent and 67.70 percent is, of course 100 percent, the total probability under the curve.

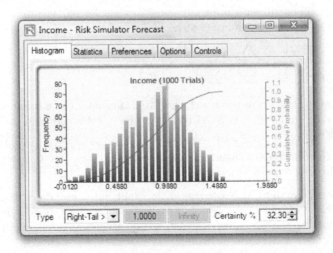

Figure 4.13: Forecast Chart Probability Evaluation (Right-tail)

Additional Tips

- The forecast window is resizable by clicking on and dragging the bottom right corner of the forecast window. It is always advisable that before rerunning a simulation, the current simulation should be reset (*Risk Simulator | Reset Simulation*).

- Remember that you will need to hit *TAB* on the keyboard to update the chart and results when you type in the certainty values or right- and left-tail values.

- You can also hit the *Spacebar* on the keyboard repeatedly to cycle among the histogram, statistics, preferences, options, and control tabs.

- In addition, if you click on *Risk Simulator | Options,* you can access several different options for Risk Simulator, including allowing Risk Simulator to start each time Excel starts or to only start when you want it to (by double clicking on the *Risk Simulator* icon on the desktop), change the *cell colors* of assumptions and forecasts, as well as turn *cell comments* on and off (cell comments will allow you to see which cells are input assumptions and which are output forecasts as well as their respective input parameters and names). Do spend some time experimenting with the forecast chart outputs and various bells and whistles, especially the *Controls* tab.

- You can also click on the *Global View* (top right corner of the forecast charts) to view all the tabs in a single comprehensive interface, and return to the regular view by clicking on the *Normal View* link.

CORRELATIONS AND PRECISION CONTROL

The Basics of Correlations

The correlation coefficient is a measure of the strength and direction of the relationship between two variables, and it can take on any values between −1.0 and +1.0. That is, the correlation coefficient can be decomposed into its sign (positive or negative relationship between two variables) and the magnitude or strength of the relationship (the higher the absolute value of the correlation coefficient, the stronger the relationship).

The correlation coefficient can be computed in several ways. The first approach is to manually compute the correlation r of two variables x and y using:

$$r_{x,y} = \frac{n\sum x_i y_i - \sum x_i \sum y_i}{\sqrt{n\sum x_i^2 - \left(\sum x_i\right)^2} \sqrt{n\sum y_i^2 - \left(\sum y_i\right)^2}}$$

The second approach is to use Excel's *CORREL* function. For instance, if the 10 data points for x and y are listed in cells A1:B10, then the Excel function to use is *CORREL (A1:A10, B1:B10).*

The third approach is to run Risk Simulator's *Analytical Tools | Distributional Fitting | Multi-Variable,* and the resulting correlation matrix will be computed and displayed.

It is important to note that correlation does not imply causation. Two completely unrelated random variables might display some correlation, but this does not imply any causation between the two (e.g., sunspot activity and events in the stock market are correlated, but there is no causation between the two).

There are two general types of correlations: parametric and nonparametric correlations. Pearson's product moment correlation coefficient is the most common correlation measure, and is usually referred to simply as the correlation coefficient. However, Pearson's correlation is a parametric measure, which means that it requires both correlated variables to have an underlying normal distribution and that the relationship between the variables is linear.[25] When these conditions are violated, which is often the case in Monte Carlo simulation, the nonparametric counterparts become more important. Spearman's rank correlation and Kendall's tau are the two nonparametric alternatives. The Spearman correlation is most commonly used and is most appropriate when applied in the context of Monte Carlo simulation—there is no dependence on normal distributions or linearity, meaning that correlations between different variables with different distributions can be applied. In order to compute the Spearman correlation, first rank all the x and y variable values and then apply the Pearson's correlation computation.

In the case of Risk Simulator, the correlation used is the more robust nonparametric Spearman's rank correlation. However, to simplify the simulation process, and to be consistent with Excel's correlation function, the correlation inputs required are the Pearson's correlation coefficient. Risk Simulator will then apply its own algorithms to convert them into Spearman's rank correlation, thereby simplifying the process. However, to simplify the user interface, we allow users to enter the more common Pearson's product-moment correlation (e.g., computed using Excel's *CORREL* function), while in the mathematical codes, we convert these simple correlations into Spearman's rank-based correlations for distributional simulations.

Applying Correlations in Risk Simulator

Correlations can be applied in Risk Simulator in several ways:

- When defining assumptions (*Risk Simulator | Set Input Assumption*), simply enter the correlations into the correlation matrix grid in the Distribution Gallery of existing assumptions already setup.

- With existing data, run the Multi-Fit tool (*Risk Simulator | Analytical Tools | Distributional Fitting | Multiple Variables*) to perform distributional fitting and to obtain the correlation matrix between pairwise variables. If a simulation profile exists, the assumptions fitted will automatically contain the relevant correlation values.

- With existing assumptions already setup, you can click on *Risk Simulator | Analytical Tools | Edit Correlations* to enter the pairwise correlations of all the assumptions directly in one user interface.

Note that the correlation matrix must be positive definite. That is, the correlation must be mathematically valid. For instance, suppose you are trying to correlate three variables: grades of graduate students in a particular year, the number of beers they consume a week, and the number of hours they study a week. One would assume the following relationships:

Grades and Beer: −   *The more they drink, the lower the grades (no show on exams)*

Grades and Study: +   *The more they study, the higher the grades*

Beer and Study: −   *The more they drink, the less they study (drunk and partying all the time)*

However, if you input a negative correlation between Grades and Study, and assuming that the correlation coefficients have high magnitudes, the correlation matrix will be nonpositive definite. It would defy logic, correlation requirements, and matrix mathematics. However, smaller coefficients can sometimes still work even with the bad logic. When a nonpositive or bad correlation matrix is entered, Risk Simulator will automatically inform you and adjust these correlations to something that is semi-positive definite while still maintaining the overall structure of the correlation relationship (same signs and relative strengths).

The Effects of Correlations in Monte Carlo Simulation

Although the computations required to correlate variables in a simulation is complex, the resulting effects are fairly clear. Figure 4.14 shows a simple correlation model (*Risk Simulator | Example Models | Correlation Effects Model*). The calculation for revenue is simply price multiplied by quantity. The same model is replicated for no correlations, positive correlation (+0.8), and negative correlation (–0.8) between price and quantity.

Correlation Model

	Without Correlation	Positive Correlation	Negative Correlation
Price	$2.00	$2.00	$2.00
Quantity	1.00	1.00	1.00
Revenue	$2.00	$2.00	$2.00

Figure 4.14: Example of a Simple Correlation Model

The resulting statistics are shown in Figure 4.15. Notice that the standard deviation of the model without correlations is 0.1450, compared to 0.1886 for the positive correlation, and 0.0717 for the negative correlation. That is, for simple models, negative correlations tend to reduce the average spread of the distribution and create a tighter and more concentrated forecast distribution as compared to positive correlations with larger average spreads. However, the mean remains relatively stable. This result implies that correlations do little to change the expected value of projects but can reduce or increase a project's risk.

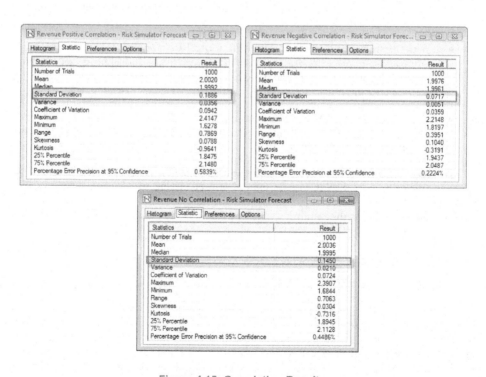

Figure 4.15: Correlation Results

Figure 4.16 illustrates the results after running a simulation, extracting the raw data of the assumptions, and computing the correlations between the variables. The figure shows that the input assumptions are recovered in the simulation. That is, you enter +0.8 and –0.8 correlations, and the resulting simulated values have the same correlations.

Price Positive Correlation	Quantity Positive Correlation		Price Negative Correlation	Quantity Negative Correlation	
1.95	0.91		1.89	1.06	
1.92	0.95		1.98	1.05	
2.02	1.04	Pearson's Correlation:	1.89	1.09	Pearson's Correlation:
2.04	1.03		1.88	1.04	
1.89	0.91	**0.80**	1.96	0.93	**-0.80**
1.98	1.05		2.02	0.93	
2.05	1.03		2.00	1.02	
1.87	0.91		1.86	1.04	
1.84	0.91		1.96	1.02	
2.06	1.03		1.90	1.02	
1.98	1.01		1.92	1.10	
1.99	0.96		2.00	1.02	
1.93	1.01		1.84	1.10	
2.01	1.02		1.83	1.09	

Figure 4.16: Correlations Recovered

Key Correlation Details

The following lists some key correlation effects and details that will be helpful in modeling:

- Correlation coefficients range from –1.00 to +1.00, with 0.00 as a possible value.

- The correlation coefficient has two parts: a sign and a value. The sign shows the directional relationship whereas value shows the magnitude of the effect (the higher the value, the higher the magnitude, while zero values imply no relationship). Another way to think of a correlation's magnitude is the inverse of noise (the lower the value, the higher the noise).

- Correlation implies dependence and not causality. In other words, if two variables are correlated, it simply means both variables move together in the same or opposite direction (positive versus negative correlations) with some strength of co-movements. It does not, however, imply that one variable causes another. In addition, one cannot determine the exact impact or how much one variable *causes* another to move.

- If two variables are independent of one another, correlation will be, by definition, zero. However, a zero correlation may not imply independence (because there might be some nonlinear relationships).

- Correlations can be visually approximated on an X-Y plot (see Figures 4E2.I and 4E2.J in this chapter's Exercises for some examples). If we generate an X-Y plot and the line is flat, the correlation is close to or equal to zero; if the slope is positive (data slopes upward), then the correlation is positive; if the slope is negative (data slopes downward), then the correlation is negative; the closer the scatter plot's data points are to a straight line, the higher the linear correlation value.

- The population correlation coefficient (ρ) can be defined as the standardized covariance:

  - $\rho_{x,y} = corr(X,Y) = \dfrac{\text{cov}(X,Y)}{\sigma_X \sigma_Y} = \dfrac{E\left[(X - \mu_X)(Y - \mu_Y)\right]}{\sigma_X \sigma_Y}$ where X and Y are the data

    from two variables' population. The covariance measures the average or expectation (E) of the co-movements of all X values from its mean (μ_X) multiplied by the co-movements of all Y values from its population mean (μ_Y). The value of covariance is between negative and positive infinity, making its interpretation fairly difficult. However, by standardizing the covariance through dividing it by the population standard deviation (σ) of X and Y, we obtain the correlation coefficient, which is bounded between −1.00 and +1.00.

- However, in practice, we typically only have access to sample data and the sample correlation coefficient (r) can be determined using the sample data from two variables x and y, their averages ($\bar{x}, \bar{y}$), their standard deviations (s_x, s_y), and the count (n) of x and y data pairs:

$$r_{x,y} = \frac{\sum_{i=1}^{n} x_i y_i - n\bar{x}\bar{y}}{(n-1)s_x s_y} = \frac{\sum_{i=1}^{n}(x_i - \bar{x})(y_i - \bar{y})}{(n-1)s_x s_y}$$

$$r_{x,y} = \frac{\sum_{i=1}^{n}(x_i - \bar{x})(y_i - \bar{y})}{\sqrt{\sum_{i=1}^{n}(x_i - \bar{x})^2 \sum_{i=1}^{n}(y_i - \bar{y})^2}}$$

$$r_{x,y} = \frac{n\sum_{i=1}^{n} x_i y_i - \sum_{i=1}^{n} x_i \sum_{i=1}^{n} y_i}{\sqrt{n\sum_{i=1}^{n} x_i^2 - \left(\sum_{i=1}^{n} x_i\right)^2} \sqrt{n\sum_{i=1}^{n} y_i^2 - \left(\sum_{i=1}^{n} y_i\right)^2}}$$

- Correlations are symmetrical. In other words, the $r_{A,B} = r_{B,A}$. Therefore, we sometimes call correlation coefficients *pairwise* correlations.

- If there are n variables, the number of total pairwise correlation is $C_x^n = \dfrac{n!}{x!(n-x)!}$. For example, if there are $n = 3$ variables, A, B, C, the number of pairwise ($x = 2$, or two items are chosen at a time) combinations total $C_2^3 = \dfrac{3!}{2!(3-2)!} = \dfrac{3!}{2!1!} = 3$ correlation pairs: $r_{A,B}$, $r_{A,C}$ and $r_{B,C}$.

- Correlations can be linear or nonlinear. Pearson's product moment correlation coefficient is used to model linear correlations and Spearman's rank-based correlation is used to model nonlinear correlations. For more details, see this chapter's Exercise 2.

- Linear correlations (also known as the Pearson's R) can be computed using Excel's CORREL function or using the equations described previously.

- Nonlinear correlations are computed by first ranking the nonlinear raw data, and then applying the linear Pearson's correlation. The result is a nonlinear rank correlation or Spearman's R. Use the correlation version (linear or nonlinear) that has a higher absolute value.

- Pearson's linear correlation is also a parametric correlation, with the implicit underlying assumption that the data is linear and close to being normally distributed. Spearman's rank correlation is nonparametric and has no dependence on the underlying data being normal.

- The square of the correlation coefficient (R) is called the coefficient of determination or R-squared. This is the same R-squared used in regression modeling, and it indicates the percentage variation in the dependent variable that is explained given the variation in the independent variable(s).

- R-squared is limited to be between 0.00 and 1.00, and is usually shown as a percent. Specifically, as R has a domain between −1.00 and +1.00, squaring either a positive or negative R value will always yield a positive R-squared value, and squaring any R value between 0.00 and 1.00 will always yield an R-squared result between 0.00 and 1.00. This means that R-squared is localized to between 0% and 100% by construction.

- In a simple positively related model, negative correlations reduce total portfolio risk, whereas positive correlations increase total portfolio risk. Conversely, in a simple negatively related model, negative correlations increase total portfolio risk, whereas positive correlations decrease total portfolio risk.

  - Positive Model (+) with Positive Correlation (+) = Higher Risk (+).

  - Positive Model (+) with Negative Correlation (−) = Lower Risk (−).

  - Negative Model (−) with Positive Correlation (+) = Lower Risk (−).

  - Negative Model (−) with Negative Correlation (−) = Higher Risk (+).

- Portfolio Diversification typically implies the following condition: Positive Model (+) with Negative Correlation (−) = Lower Risk (−). For example, the portfolio level's (p) diversified risk is computed by taking $\sigma_P = \sqrt{\sum_{i=1}^{n} \omega_i^2 \sigma_i^2 + \sum_{i=1}^{n} \sum_{j=1}^{m} 2\omega_i \omega_j \rho_{i,j} \sigma_i \sigma_j}$ where $\omega_{i,j}$ are the respective weights or capital allocation across each project; $\rho_{i,j}$ are the respective cross-correlations between the assets, and $\sigma_{i,j}$ are the volatility risks. Hence, if the cross-correlations are negative, there are risk diversification effects, and the portfolio risk decreases.

- Examples of a simple positively related model are an investment portfolio (the total of the returns in a portfolio is the sum of each individual asset's returns, i.e., A + B + C = D, therefore, increase A or B or C, and the resulting D will increase as well, indicating a positive directional relationship) or the total of the revenues of a company is the sum of all the individual products' revenues. Negative correlations in such models mean that if one asset's returns decrease (losses), another asset's returns would increase (profits). The spread or distribution of the total net returns for the entire portfolio would decrease (lower risk). The negative correlation would, therefore, *diversify* the portfolio risk.

- Alternatively, an example of a simple negatively related model is revenue less cost equals net income (i.e., A − B = C, which means that as B increases, C would decrease, indicating a negative relationship). Negatively correlated variables in such a model would increase the total spread of the net income distribution.

- In more complex or larger models where the relationship is difficult to determine (e.g., in a discounted cash flow model where we have revenues of one product being added to revenues of other products but less costs to obtain the gross profits, and where depreciation is used as tax shields, then taxes are deducted, etc.), and both positive and negative correlations may exist between the various revenues (e.g., similar product lines versus competing product lines cannibalizing each other's revenues), the only way to determine the final effect is through simulations.

- Correlations typically affect only the second moment (risk) of the distribution, leaving the first moment (mean or expected returns) relatively stable. There is an unknown effect on the third and fourth moments (skew and kurtosis), and only after a simulation is run can the outcomes be empirically determined because the effects are wholly dependent on the distributions' type, skew, kurtosis, and shape. Therefore, in traditional single-point estimates where only the first moment is determined, correlations will not affect the results. When simulation models are used, the entire probability distribution of the results are obtained and, hence, correlations are critical.

- Correlations should be used in a simulation if there are historical data to compute its value. Even in situations without historical data but with clear theoretical justifications for correlations, one should still input them. Otherwise the distributional spreads would not be accurate. For instance, a demand curve is theoretically negatively sloped (negatively correlated), where the higher the price, the lower the quantity demanded (due to income and substitution effects) and vice versa. Therefore, if no correlations are entered in the model, the simulation results may randomly generate high prices with high quantity demanded, creating extreme high revenues, as well as low prices and low quantity demanded, creating extreme low revenues. The simulated probability distribution of revenues would, hence, have wider spreads into the left and right tails. These wider spreads are not representative of the true nature of the distribution. Nonetheless, the mean or expected value of the distribution remains relatively stable. It is only the percentiles and confidence intervals that get biased in the model.

- Therefore, even without historical data, if we know that correlations do exist through experimentation, widely accepted theory, or even simply by logic and guesstimates, one should still input approximate correlations into the simulation model. This approach is acceptable because the first moment or expected values of the final results will remain unaffected (only the risks will be affected as discussed). Typically, the following approximate correlations can be applied even without historical data:

    o Use 0.00 if there are no correlations between variables.

    o Use ±0.25 for weak correlations (use the appropriate sign).

    o Use ±0.50 for medium correlations (use the appropriate sign).

    o Use ±0.75 for strong correlations (use the appropriate sign).

- It is theoretically very difficult, if not impossible, to have large sets of empirical data from real-life variables that are perfectly uncorrelated (i.e., a correlation of 0.0000000... and so forth). Therefore, given any random data, adding additional variables will typically increase the total absolute values of correlation coefficients in a portfolio (R-squared always increases, which is why in Chapters 6 and 7 we introduce the concept of Adjusted R-squared, which accounts for the marginal increase in total correlation compared against the number of variables; think of Adjusted R-squared for now as the adjustment to R-squared by taking into account garbage correlations). Therefore, it is usually important to perform statistical tests on correlation coefficients to see if they are statistically significant or their values can be considered random and insignificant. For example, we know that a correlation of 0.9 is probably significant, but what about 0.8, or 0.7, or 0.3, and so forth? That is, at what point can we statistically state that a correlation is insignificantly different from zero; would 0.10 qualify, or 0.05, or 0.03, and so forth?

- The t-test with $n - 2$ degrees of freedom hypothesis test can be computed by taking $t = r\sqrt{\dfrac{n-2}{1-r^2}}$. The null hypothesis is such that the population correlation $\rho = 0$.

- There are other measures of dependence such as Kendall's τ, Brownian correlation, Randomized Dependence Coefficient (RDC), entropy correlation, polychoric correlation, canonical correlation, and copula-based dependence measures. These are less applicable in most empirical data and are not as popular or applicable in most situations.

- Finally, here are some notes in applying and analyzing correlations in Risk Simulator:

    o Risk Simulator uses the Normal, T, and Quasi-Normal Copula methods to simulate correlated variable assumptions. The default is the Normal Copula, and it can be changed within the *Risk Simulator | Options* menu item. The T Copula is similar to the Normal Copula but allows for extreme values in the tails (higher kurtosis events), and the Quasi-Normal Copula simulates correlated values between the Normal and T Copulas.

    o After setting up at least two or more assumptions, you can set correlations between pairwise variables by selecting an existing assumption and using the *Risk Simulator | Set Input Assumption* dialog.

    o Alternatively, the *Risk Simulator | Analytical Tools | Edit Correlations* menu item can be used to enter multiple correlations using a correlation matrix.

    o If historical data from multiple variables exist, by performing a distributional fitting using *Risk Simulator | Analytical Tools | Distributional Fitting (Multi-Variable)*, the report will automatically generate the best-fitting distributions with their pairwise correlations computed and entered as simulation assumptions. In addition, this tool allows you to identify and isolate correlations that are deemed statistically insignificant using a two-sample t-test.

PRECISION AND ERROR CONTROL

One very powerful tool in Monte Carlo simulation is that of precision control. For instance, how many trials are considered sufficient to run in a complex model? Precision control takes the guesswork out of estimating the relevant number of trials by allowing the simulation to stop if the level of prespecified precision is reached.

The precision control functionality lets you set how precise you want your forecast to be. Generally speaking, as more trials are calculated, the confidence interval narrows and the statistics become more accurate. The precision control feature in Risk Simulator uses the characteristic of confidence intervals to determine when a specified accuracy of a statistic has been reached. For each forecast, you can specify the specific confidence interval for the precision level (Figure 4.17). If the error precision is achieved within the number of trials you set, the simulation will run as usual, otherwise, you will be informed that additional simulation trials are required to meet the more stringent required error precision.

Make sure that you do not confuse three very different terms: error, precision, and confidence. Although they sound similar, the concepts are significantly different from one another. A simple illustration is in order. Suppose you are a taco shell manufacturer and are interested in finding out how many broken taco shells there are on average in a box of 100 shells. One way to do this is to collect a sample of prepackaged boxes of 100 taco shells, open them, and count how many of them are actually broken. You manufacture 1 million boxes a year (this is your *population*), but you randomly open only 10 boxes (this is your *sample* size, also known as your number of *trials* in a simulation). The number of broken shells in each box is as follows: 24, 22, 4, 15, 33, 32, 4, 1, 45, and 2. The calculated average number of broken shells is 18.2. Based on these 10 samples or trials, the average is 18.2 units, while based on the sample, the 80 percent confidence interval is between 2 and 33 units (that is, 80 percent of the time, the number of broken shells is between 2 and 33 *based on this sample size or number of trials run*). However, how sure are you that 18.2 is the correct average? Are 10 trials sufficient to establish this?

The confidence interval between 2 and 33 is too wide and too variable. Suppose you require a more accurate average value where the error is ±2 taco shells 90 percent of the time——this means that if you open *all* 1 million boxes manufactured in a year, 900,000 of these boxes will have broken taco shells on average at some mean unit ±2 tacos. How many more taco shell boxes would you then need to sample (or trials run) to obtain this level of precision? Here, the 2 tacos is the error level while the 90 percent is the level of precision. If sufficient numbers of trials are run, then the 90 percent confidence interval will be identical to the 90 percent precision level, where a more precise measure of the average is obtained such that 90 percent of the time, the error, and, hence, the confidence will be ±2 tacos. As an example, say the average is 20 units, then the 90 percent confidence interval will be between 18 and 22 units, where this interval is precise 90 percent of the time, where in opening all 1 million boxes, 900,000 of them will have between 18 and 22 broken tacos. The number of trials required to hit this precision is based on the sampling error equation of

$$\bar{x} \pm Z \frac{s}{\sqrt{n}}$$

where

$$Z \frac{s}{\sqrt{n}}$$

is the error of 2 tacos, $\bar{x}$ is the sample average, Z is the standard-normal Z-score obtained from the 90 percent precision level, s is the sample standard deviation, and n is the number of trials required to hit this level of error with the specified precision.

Figures 4.17 and 4.18 illustrate how precision control can be performed on multiple simulated forecasts in Risk Simulator. This feature prevents the user from having to decide how many trials to run in a simulation and eliminates all possibilities of guesswork. Figure 4.17 illustrates the set forecast user interface with a 95 percent precision level set. The calculated error precision levels of the simulation will be reflected in the last line of the *Statistics* tab as shown in Figure 4.18.

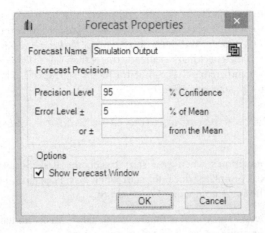

Figure 4.17: Setting the Forecast's Precision Level

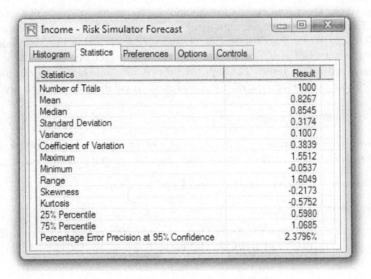

Figure 4.18: Computing the Error

TROUBLESHOOTING AND RISK SIMULATOR TIPS

You may encounter some trouble while using Risk Simulator. This section explains some of the most commonly encountered issues, their symptoms, and how to solve them.

1. Missing Risk Simulator ribbon when Excel starts.

- Symptom: Sometimes when you start Excel, the Risk Simulator icon ribbon is missing or Risk Simulator does not start when Excel opens.

- Diagnosis: This happens because Excel sometimes goes into Safe Mode when something adverse occurs (e.g., electrical power failure, force-closing Excel, Ctrl + Alt + Delete, Trojan virus, etc.) that may interrupt an existing Excel system process.

- Solution: There is an easy fix for this and you do not have to reinstall Risk Simulator. In Excel 2010 or 2013, click on *File | Options | Add-Ins* and at the *Manage* drop-down list, select *COM Add-Ins* and make sure to put a *checkmark on Risk Simulator* and then restart Excel. If the checkmark is already there, then select *Disabled Items* in the *Manage* drop-down list and enable Risk Simulator then restart Excel. These steps will restore Risk Simulator to start with Excel.

2. There might be other competing Excel add-ins interfering with Risk Simulator.

- Symptom: Sometimes when you start Excel, the Risk Simulator icon ribbon is missing or Risk Simulator does not start when Excel opens and the suspicion is that there might be some competing Excel add-in.

- Diagnosis: Before some new software was installed, Risk Simulator and other Excel-based software worked well, but they are not starting correctly with Excel after installing this new software.

- Solution: There is an easy fix for this and you do not have to reinstall Risk Simulator. Check to see if there are competing and incompatible Excel add-ins installed. In Excel 2010 or 2013, click on *File | Options | Add-Ins* and in the *Manage* drop-down list, select *COM Add-Ins* and then manually disable each one of the add-ins one at a time and restart Excel. Through the process of elimination, you can identify the offending culprit and decide if you wish to uninstall the problem software.

3. Risk Simulator Profiles are missing.

- Symptom: Sometimes when someone e-mails you an Excel model with Risk Simulator profiles, some of the profiles might be missing or do not come up and run.

- Diagnosis: You have Excel's *Protected View* turned on.

- Solutions:

  o Either copy the Excel file to your desktop/folder and then open it from there instead of double-clicking and opening the Excel model directly from the e-mail or:

  o Turn off Protected View: In Excel 2010 or 2013, click on *File | Options | Trust Center | Trust Center Settings | Protected View*. Then *uncheck* the *Enable Protected View for Outlook Attachments*. Then *restart Excel* and try again.

4. What version of Risk Simulator do I install (32 bit or 64 bit)?

- Symptom: Which of the two versions of Risk Simulator (x32 and x64) do I install? Or, when I installed Risk Simulator (x32), I cannot launch it in Excel 2013 (64 bit).

- Diagnosis: You may have installed the wrong version of Risk Simulator.

- Solution: Check your Excel's bit version and uninstall/reinstall the correct version of Risk Simulator.

- Explanations: Risk Simulator 2014 works on Windows XP, Vista, 7, 8, 10 (32 & 64 bits) with Excel 2007, 2010, 2013 (32 & 64 bits). Install the most common 32-bit version of Risk Simulator if Excel 32 bit is installed (regardless of Windows 64 or 32 bit), but install Risk Simulator 64 bit if you have a 64-bit Excel.

- Note: there is the Microsoft Windows operating system bitness and then there is the Microsoft Office bitness. These two bitness levels can be the same or different. What is important here is the Office/Excel bit level. If Excel 32 bit is installed, then make sure the regular Risk Simulator x32 is downloaded and installed. If 64 bit is listed, uninstall any old versions, and redownload and install Risk Simulator x64.

- To identify the Excel bit level, follow the steps below:

  o If you have Excel 2013, start Excel and click on *File | Account | About Excel,* and take note of the bit settings on the pop-up *About* screen. The bitness is shown on the first line of the pop-up (e.g., it might say something like "Microsoft Excel 2013 (15.0.X.X) MSO (15.0.X.X) 32 bit").

  o If you have Excel 2010, to check the bitness of Excel: Start Excel, click on *File | Help* and take note of the bit settings under the *About Microsoft Excel* header (e.g., it might say something like "Version 14.0.X.X [32 bit]").

HELPFUL TIPS AND TECHNIQUES
IN RISK SIMULATOR

The following are some quick helpful tips and shortcut techniques for advanced users of Risk Simulator. For technical and application details on using specific tools, refer to the relevant sections in the book.

TIPS: Assumptions (Set Input Assumption User Interface)

- Quick Jump—select any distribution and type in any letter and it will jump to the first distribution starting with that letter (e.g., *click on normal distribution* and *type in W* and it will take you to the Weibull distribution).

- Right-Click Views—select any distribution, right-click, and select the different views of the distributions (large icons, small icons, list).

- Tab to Update Charts—after entering some new input parameters (e.g., you type in a new mean or standard deviation value), hit *TAB* on the keyboard or click anywhere on the user interface away from the input box to see the distributional chart automatically update.

- Enter Correlations—enter pairwise correlations directly here (the columns are resizable as needed), use the multiple distributional fitting tool to automatically compute and enter all pairwise correlations, or, after setting some assumptions, use the edit correlation tool to enter your correlation matrix.

- Equations in an Assumption Cell—only empty cells or cells with static values can be set as assumptions; however, there might be times when a function or equation is required in an assumption cell. To use a function or equation, first set the input assumption in the cell and then type in the equation or function (when the simulation is being run, the simulated values will replace the function, and after the simulation completes, the function or equation is again shown).

TIPS: Copy and Paste

- Copy and Paste on Multiple Cells—select multiple cells for copy and paste (with contiguous and noncontiguous assumptions).

TIPS: Correlations

- Set Assumption—set pairwise correlations using the set input assumption dialog (ideal for entering only several correlations).

- Edit Correlations—set up a correlation matrix by manually entering or pasting from Windows clipboard (ideal for large correlation matrices and multiple correlations).

- Multiple Distributional Fitting—automatically computes and enters pairwise correlations (ideal when performing multiple variable fitting to automatically compute the correlations for deciding what constitutes a statistically significant correlation).

TIPS: Data Diagnostics and Statistical Analysis

- Stochastic Parameter Estimation—in the Statistical Analysis and Data Diagnostic reports, there is a tab on stochastic parameter estimations that estimates the volatility, drift, mean-reversion rate, and jump-diffusion rates based on historical data. Be aware that these parameter results are based solely on historical data used, and the parameters may change over time and depending on the amount of fitted historical data. Further, the analysis results show all parameters and do not imply which stochastic process model (e.g., Brownian motion, mean-reversion, jump-diffusion, or mixed process) is the best fit. It is up to the user to make this determination depending on the time-series variable to be forecasted. The analysis cannot determine which process is best; only the user can do this (e.g., Brownian motion process is best for modeling stock prices, but the analysis cannot determine that the historical data analyzed is from a stock or some other variable, and only the user will know this). Finally, a good hint is that if a certain parameter is out of the normal range, the process requiring this input parameter is most probably not the correct process (e.g., if the mean-reversion rate is 110%, chances are, mean-reversion is not the correct process).

TIPS: Distributional Analysis, Charts and Probability Tables

- Distributional Analysis—used to quickly compute the PDF, CDF, and ICDF of the 50 probability distributions available in Risk Simulator, and to return a table of these values.

- Distributional Charts and Tables—used to compare different parameters of the same distribution (e.g., takes the shapes and PDF, CDF, ICDF values of a Weibull distribution with Alpha and Beta of [2, 2], [3, 5], and [3.5, 8] and overlays them on top of one another).

- Overlay Charts—used to compare different distributions (theoretical input assumptions and empirically simulated output forecasts) and overlay them on top of one another for a visual comparison.

TIPS: Efficient Frontier

- Efficient Frontier Variables—to access the frontier variables, first set the model's Constraints before setting efficient frontier variables.

TIPS: Forecast Cells

- Forecast Cells with No Equations—you can set output forecasts on cells without any equations or values (simply ignore the warning message) but be aware that the resulting forecast chart will be empty. Output forecasts are typically set on empty cells when there are macros that are being computed and the cell will be continually updated by the VBA macro.

TIPS: Forecast Charts

- TAB versus Spacebar—hit *TAB* on the keyboard to update the forecast chart and to obtain the percentile and confidence values after you enter some inputs, and hit the *Spacebar* to rotate among the various tabs in the forecast chart.

- Normal versus Global View—click on these views to rotate between a tabbed interface and a global interface where all elements of the forecast charts are visible.

- Copy—copies the forecast chart or the entire global view depending on whether you are in the normal or global view.

- Click on the *Excel button* in the *Options* tab to generate live charts in Excel.

TIPS: Forecasting

- Cell Link Address—if you first select the data in the spreadsheet and then run a forecasting tool, the cell address of the selected data will be automatically entered into the user interface. Otherwise, you will have to manually enter in the cell address or use the link icon to link to the relevant data location.

- Forecast RMSE—use as the universal error measure on multiple forecast models for direct comparisons of the accuracy of each model.

TIPS: Forecasting—ARIMA

- Forecast Periods—the number of exogenous data rows has to exceed the time-series data rows by at least the desired forecast periods (e.g., if you wish to forecast 5 periods into the future and have 100 time-series data points, you will need to have at least 105 or more data points on the exogenous variable). Otherwise, just run ARIMA without the exogenous variable to forecast as many periods as you wish without any limitations.

- ARIMA can use only its own time-series data for running forecasts, or add external exogenous explanatory independent variables just like in a multiple regression model.

TIPS: Forecasting—Basic Econometrics

- Variable Separation with Semicolons—separate independent variables using a semicolon.

TIPS: Forecasting—Logit, Probit, and Tobit

- Data Requirements—the dependent variables for running logit and Probit models must be binary only (0 and 1), whereas the Tobit model can take binary and other numerical decimal values. The independent variables for all three models can take any numerical value.

TIPS: Forecasting—Stochastic Processes

- Default Sample Inputs—when in doubt, use the default inputs as a starting point to develop your own model.

- Statistical Analysis Tool for Parameter Estimation—use this tool to calibrate the input parameters into the stochastic process models by estimating them from your raw data.

- Stochastic Process Model—sometimes if the stochastic process user interface hangs for a long time, chances are your inputs are incorrect and the model is not correctly specified (e.g., if the mean-reversion rate is 110%, mean-reversion is probably not the correct process). Try with different inputs or use a different model.

TIPS: Forecasting—Trendlines

- Forecast Results—scroll to the bottom of the report to see the forecasted values.

TIPS: Function Calls

- RS Functions—there are functions that you can use inside your Excel spreadsheet to set input assumption and get forecast statistics. To use these functions, you need to first install RS Functions (which include *Start | Programs | Real Options Valuation | Risk Simulator | Analytical Tools | Install Functions*) and then run a simulation before setting the RS functions inside Excel. Refer to the example model 24 in Risk Simulator for examples on how to use these functions. In Windows 8 or 10, you can also click on the *Windows button + C*, then select *Search* and enter *Install Functions* as the search term.

TIPS: Getting Started Exercises and Getting Started Videos

- Getting Started Exercises—there are multiple step-by-step hands-on examples and results interpretation exercises available in the *Risk Simulator | Example Models* shortcut location. These exercises are meant to quickly get you up to speed with the use of the software. In Windows 8 or 10, you can also click on the *Windows button + C*, then select *Search* and enter *Detailed Exercises* as the search term.

- Getting Started Videos—these are all available for free on our website: www.realoptionsvaluation.com/download.html or www.rovusa.com/download.html.

TIPS: Hardware ID (HWID)

- Start Risk Simulator and click on *Risk Simulator | License*. In the pop-up screen, right-click on the HWID and *Copy*—in the Install License user interface, select or double-click on the HWID to select its value, right-click to copy or click on the *E-mail HWID* link to generate an e-mail with the HWID.

- Troubleshooter—run the Troubleshooter from the *Start | Programs | Real Options Valuation | Risk Simulator* folder, and run the Get HWID tool to obtain your computer's HWID. In Windows 8 or 10, you can also click on the *Windows button + C*, then select *Search* and enter *ROV Troubleshooter* as the search term.

TIPS: Latin Hypercube Sampling (LHS) vs. Monte Carlo Simulation (MCS)

- Correlations—when setting pairwise correlations among input assumptions, we recommend using the *Monte Carlo* setting in the Risk Simulator *Options* menu. *Latin Hypercube Sampling* is not compatible with the correlated copula method for simulation.

- LHS Bins—a larger number of bins will slow down the simulation while providing a more uniform set of simulation results.

- Randomness—all of the random simulation techniques in the *Options* menu have been tested and are all good simulators and approach the same levels of randomness when larger number of trials are run.

TIPS: Online Resources

- Books, Getting Started Videos, Models, White Papers—resources available on our website: www.realoptionsvaluation.com/download.html   or www.rovdownloads.com/download.html.

TIPS: Optimization

- Infeasible Results—if the optimization run returns infeasible results, you can change the constraints from an Equal (=) to an Inequality (≥ or ≤) and try again. This also applies when you are running an efficient frontier analysis.

TIPS: Profiles

- Multiple Profiles—create and switch among multiple profiles in a single model. This allows you to run scenarios on simulation by being able to change input parameters or distribution types in your model to see the effects on the results.

- Profile Required—Assumptions, Forecasts, or Decision Variables cannot be created if there is no active profile. However, once you have a profile, you no longer have to keep creating new profiles each time. In fact, if you wish to run a simulation model by adding additional assumptions or forecasts, you should keep the same profile.

- Active Profile—the last profile used when you save Excel will be automatically opened the next time the Excel file is opened.

- Multiple Excel Files—when switching between several opened Excel models, the active profile will be from the current and active Excel model.

- Cross Workbook Profiles—be careful when you have multiple Excel files open because if only one of the Excel files has an active profile and you accidentally switch to another Excel file and set assumptions and forecasts on this file, the assumptions and forecast will not run and will be invalid.

- Deleting Profiles—you can clone existing profiles and delete existing profiles, but note that at least one profile must exist in the Excel file if you delete profiles.

- Profile Location—the profiles you create (containing the assumptions, forecasts, decision variables, objectives, constraints, etc.) are saved as an encrypted hidden worksheet. This is why the profile is automatically saved when you save the Excel workbook file.

TIPS: Right-Click Shortcut and Other Shortcut Keys

- Right-Click—you can open the Risk Simulator shortcut menu by right-clicking on a cell anywhere in Excel.

TIPS: Save

- Saving the Excel File—saves the profile settings, assumptions, forecasts, decision variables, and your Excel model (including any Risk Simulator reports, charts, and data extracted). Click on *File | Save* in Excel.

- Saving the Chart Settings—saves the forecast chart settings such that the same settings can be recovered and applied to future forecast charts (use the save and open icons in the forecast charts). *Run the simulation*, then in the *forecast chart*, click on *Global View | Save* or *Open* icons above the simulation charts.

- Saving and Extracting Simulated Data in Excel—extracts a simulated run's assumptions and forecasts; the Excel file itself will still have to be saved in order to save the data for retrieval later. *Run the simulation*, then click on *Risk Simulator | Analytical Tools | Data Extraction | New Excel Worksheet.*

- Saving Simulated Data and Charts in Risk Simulator—using the Risk Simulator *Data Extract* and saving to a *.RiskSim* file will allow you to reopen the dynamic and live forecast chart with the same data in the future without having to rerun the simulation. *Run the simulation*, then click on *Risk Simulator | Analytical Tools | Data Extraction | Risk Simulator Data File (*.RiskSim).*

- Saving and Generating Reports—simulation reports and other analytical reports are extracted as separate worksheets in your workbook, and the entire Excel file will have to be saved in order to save the data for future retrieval later. *Run the simulation*, then click on *Risk Simulator | Analytical Tools | Create Report.*

- Save As Live Excel Charts—after running simulations, tornado, and scenario analysis, you can save the charts as live editable Excel charts. *Run the simulation*, then in the forecast chart, click on *Global View | Excel* button. *Run a tornado analysis*, then in the user interface, click on the *Excel* button to create a live editable tornado chart in Excel.

TIPS: Sampling and Simulation Techniques

- Random Number Generator—there are six supported random number generators (see the user manual for details) and, in general, the *ROV Risk Simulator* default method and the *Advanced Subtractive Random Shuffle* method are the two recommended approaches to use. Do not apply the other methods unless your model or analytics specifically calls for their uses, and, even then, we recommended testing the results against these two recommended approaches.

TIPS: Software Development Kit (SDK) and DLL Libraries

- SDK, DLL, and OEM—all of the analytics in Risk Simulator can be called outside of this software and integrated into any user proprietary software. Contact admin@realoptionsvaluation.com for details on using our Software Development Kit to access the Dynamic Link Library (DLL) analytics files.

TIPS: Starting Risk Simulator with Excel

- ROV Troubleshooter—run this troubleshooter to obtain your computer's HWID for licensing purposes, to view your computer settings and prerequisites, and to re-enable Risk Simulator if it has been accidentally disabled.

- Start Risk Simulator when Excel Starts—you can let Risk Simulator start automatically when Excel starts each time or start it manually from the *Start | Programs | Real Options Valuation | Risk Simulator* shortcut or double click on the Risk Simulator *desktop icon*. In Windows 8 or 10, you can also click on the *Windows button + C*, then select *Search* and enter *Risk Simulator* as the search term. This preference can be set in the Risk Simulator, *Options* menu.

TIPS: Super Speed Simulation

- Model Development—if you wish to run super speed in your model, test run a few super speed simulations while the model is being constructed to make sure that the final product will run the super speed simulation. Do not wait until the final model is complete before testing super speed to avoid having to backtrack to identify where any broken links or incompatible functions exist.

- Regular Speed—when in doubt, regular speed simulation always works.

TIPS: Tornado Analysis

- Tornado Analysis—the tornado analysis should never be run just once. It is meant as a model diagnostic tool, which means that it should ideally be run several times on the same model. For instance, in a large model, tornado analysis can be run the first time using all of the default settings and all precedents should be shown (select *Show All Variables*). This single analysis may result in a large report and long (and potentially unsightly) tornado charts. Nonetheless, it provides a great starting point to determine how many of the precedents are considered critical success factors. For example, the tornado chart may show that the first 5 variables have high impact on the output, while the remaining 200 variables have little to no impact, in which case, a second tornado analysis is run showing fewer variables. For the second run, select *Show Top 10 Variables* if the first 5 are critical, thereby creating a more concise report and a tornado chart that shows a contrast between the key factors and less critical factors. (You should never show a tornado chart with only the key variables without showing some less critical variables as a contrast to their effects on the output.)

- Default Values—the default testing points can be increased from the ±10% value to some larger value to test for nonlinearities (the Spider chart will show nonlinear lines and tornado charts will be skewed to one side if the precedent effects are nonlinear).

- Zero Values and Integers—inputs with zero or integer values only should be deselected in the tornado analysis before it is run. Otherwise, the percentage perturbation may invalidate your model (e.g., if your model uses a lookup table where Jan = 1, Feb = 2, Mar = 3, etc., perturbing the value 1 at a ±10% value yields 0.9 and 1.1, which makes no sense to the model).

- Chart Options—try various chart options to find the best options to turn on or off for your model.

Questions

1. Why do you need to have profiles in a simulation?

2. Explain the differences between Pearson's product moment correlation coefficient and Spearman's rank-based correlation.

3. Will more or fewer trials be required to obtain higher error levels, higher precision levels, and a wider confidence interval?

4. Explain the differences between error and precision and how these two concepts are linked.

5. If you know that two simulated variables are correlated but do not have the relevant correlation value, should you still go ahead and correlate them in a simulation?

After the appendices are some hands-on exercises using Risk Simulator. The example files are located at *Risk Simulator | Example Models* or you can manually find them in the software installation path's Examples folder (e.g., *C:\Program Files (x86)\Real Options Valuation\Risk Simulator\Examples*).

APPENDIX—UNDERSTANDING PROBABILITY DISTRIBUTIONS

This appendix demonstrates the power of Monte Carlo risk simulation but in order to get started with simulation, one first needs to understand the concept of probability distributions. This appendix continues with the use of the author's *Risk Simulator* software and shows how simulation can be very easily and effortlessly implemented in an existing Excel model. A limited trial version of the *Risk Simulator* software (to obtain a permanent version, please visit the author's website at *www.realoptionsvaluation.com*). Professors can obtain free semester-long computer lab licenses for their students and themselves if this book and the simulation/options valuation software are used and taught in an entire class.

To begin to understand probability, consider this example: You want to look at the distribution of nonexempt wages within one department of a large company. First, you gather raw data—in this case, the wages of each nonexempt employee in the department. Second, you organize the data into a meaningful format and plot the data as a frequency distribution on a chart. To create a frequency distribution, you divide the wages into group intervals and list these intervals on the chart's horizontal axis. Then you list the number or frequency of employees in each interval on the chart's vertical axis. Now you can easily see the distribution of nonexempt wages within the department.

A glance at the chart illustrated in Figure 4A.1 reveals that the employees earn from $7.00 to $9.00 per hour. You can chart this data as a probability distribution. A probability distribution shows the number of employees in each interval as a fraction of the total number of employees. To create a probability distribution, you divide the number of employees in each interval by the total number of employees and list the results on the chart's vertical axis.

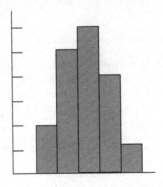

Figure 4A.1: Frequency Histogram I

The chart in Figure 4A.2 shows the number of employees in each wage group as a fraction of all employees; you can estimate the likelihood or probability that an employee drawn at random from the whole group earns a wage within a given interval. For example, assuming the same conditions exist at the time the sample was taken, the probability is 0.20 (a one in five chance) that an employee drawn at random from the whole group earns $8.50 an hour.

Probability distributions are either discrete or continuous. *Discrete probability distributions* describe distinct values, usually integers, with no intermediate values and are shown as a series of vertical bars. A discrete distribution, for example, might describe the number of heads in four flips of a coin as 0, 1, 2, 3, or 4. *Continuous probability distributions* are actually mathematical abstractions because they assume the existence of every possible intermediate value between two numbers; that is, a continuous distribution assumes there is an infinite number of values between any two points in the distribution. However, in many situations, you can effectively use a continuous distribution to approximate a discrete distribution even though the continuous model does not necessarily describe the situation exactly.

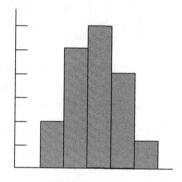

Figure 4A.2: Frequency Histogram II

Selecting a Probability Distribution

Plotting data is one method for selecting a probability distribution. The following steps provide another process for selecting probability distributions that best describe the uncertain variables in your spreadsheets.

To select the correct probability distribution, use the following steps:

- Look at the variable in question. List everything you know about the conditions surrounding this variable. You might be able to gather valuable information about the uncertain variable from historical data. If historical data are not available, use your own judgment, based on experience, listing everything you know about the uncertain variable.

- Review the descriptions of the probability distributions.

- Select the distribution that characterizes this variable. A distribution characterizes a variable when the conditions of the distribution match those of the variable.

Alternatively, if you have historical, comparable, contemporaneous, or forecast data, you can use *Risk Simulator's* distributional fitting modules to find the best statistical fit for your existing data. This fitting process will apply some advanced statistical techniques to find the best distribution and its relevant parameters that describe the data.

Probability Density Functions, Cumulative Distribution Functions, and Probability Mass Functions

In mathematics and Monte Carlo simulation, a probability density function (PDF) represents a *continuous* probability distribution in terms of integrals. If a probability distribution has a density of $f(x)$, then intuitively the infinitesimal interval of $[x, x + dx]$ has a probability of $f(x)$ dx. The PDF therefore can be seen as a smoothed version of a probability histogram; that is, by providing an empirically large sample of a continuous random variable repeatedly, the histogram using very narrow ranges will resemble the random variable's PDF. The probability of the interval between [a, b] is given by $\int_a^b f(x)dx$, which means that the total integral of the function f must be 1.0. *It is a common mistake to think of f(a) as the probability of a.* This is incorrect. In fact, *f(a)* can sometimes be larger than 1—consider a uniform distribution between 0.0 and 0.5. The random variable *x* within this distribution will have *f(x)* greater than 1. The probability, in reality, is the function *f(x)dx* discussed previously, where *dx* is an infinitesimal amount.

The cumulative distribution function (CDF) is denoted as $F(x) = P(X \leq x)$ indicating the probability of X taking on a less than or equal value to x. Every CDF is monotonically increasing, is continuous from the right, and at the limits, has the following properties: $\lim_{x \to -\infty} F(x) = 0$ and $\lim_{x \to +\infty} F(x) = 1$. Further, the CDF is related to the PDF by

$$F(b) - F(a) = P(a \leq X \leq b) = \int_a^b f(x)dx,$$ where the PDF function f is the derivative of the CDF function F.

In probability theory, a probability mass function, or PMF, gives the probability that a *discrete* random variable is exactly equal to some value. The PMF differs from the PDF in that the values of the latter, defined only for continuous random variables, are not probabilities; rather, its integral over a set of possible values of the random variable is a probability. A random variable is discrete if its probability distribution is discrete and can be characterized by a PMF. Therefore, X is a discrete random variable if $\sum_u P(X = u) = 1$ as u runs through all possible values of the random variable X.

APPENDIX—DISCRETE DISTRIBUTIONS

Following is a detailed listing of the different types of discrete probability distributions that can be used in Monte Carlo simulation. This listing is included in the current appendix for the reader's reference.

Bernoulli or Yes/No Distribution

The Bernoulli distribution is a discrete distribution with two outcomes (e.g., head or tails, success or failure, 0 or 1). The Bernoulli distribution is the binomial distribution with one trial and can be used to simulate Yes/No or Success/Failure conditions. This distribution is the fundamental building block of other more complex distributions. For instance:

- Binomial distribution: Bernoulli distribution with higher number of *n* total trials and computes the probability of *x* successes within this total number of trials.

- Geometric distribution: Bernoulli distribution with higher number of trials and computes the number of failures required before the first success occurs.

- Negative binomial distribution: Bernoulli distribution with higher number of trials and computes the number of failures before the *x*th success occurs.

The mathematical constructs for the Bernoulli distribution are as follows:

$$P(x) = \begin{cases} 1-p & for\ x=0 \\ p & for\ x=1 \end{cases}$$

or

$$P(x) = p^x(1-p)^{1-x}$$

Mean $= p$

Standard Deviation $= \sqrt{p(1-p)}$

Skewness $= \dfrac{1-2p}{\sqrt{p(1-p)}}$

Excess Kurtosis $= \dfrac{6p^2-6p+1}{p(1-p)}$

The probability of success (p) is the only distributional parameter. Also, it is important to note that there is only one trial in the Bernoulli distribution, and the resulting simulated value is either 0 or 1.

Input requirements: Probability of success > 0 and < 1 (that is, $0.0001 \le p \le 0.9999$)

Binomial Distribution

The binomial distribution describes the number of times a particular event occurs in a fixed number of trials, such as the number of heads in 10 flips of a coin or the number of defective items out of 50 items chosen.

The three conditions underlying the binomial distribution are:

- For each trial, only two outcomes are possible that are mutually exclusive.

- The trials are independent—what happens in the first trial does not affect the next trial.

- The probability of an event occurring remains the same from trial to trial.

The mathematical constructs for the binomial distribution are as follows:

$$P(x) = \frac{n!}{x!(n-x)!}p^x(1-p)^{(n-x)} \quad for\ n>0;\ x=0,\ 1,\ 2,\ \ldots\ n,\ and\ 0<p<1$$

Mean $= np$

Standard Deviation $= \sqrt{np(1-p)}$

Skewness $= \dfrac{1-2p}{\sqrt{np(1-p)}}$

Excess Kurtosis $= \dfrac{6p^2-6p+1}{np(1-p)}$

The probability of success (p) and the integer number of total trials (n) are the distributional parameters. The number of successful trials is denoted x. It is important to note that probability of success (p) of 0 or 1 are trivial conditions and do not require any simulations, and hence, are not allowed in the software.

Input requirements:

Probability of success > 0 and < 1 (that is, $0.0001 \leq p \leq 0.9999$)

Number of trials ≥ 1 or positive integers and ≤ 1000 (for larger trials, use the normal distribution with the relevant computed binomial mean and standard deviation as the normal distribution's parameters).

Discrete Uniform Distribution

The discrete uniform distribution is also known as the *equally likely outcomes* distribution, where the distribution has a set of N elements, and each element has the same probability. This distribution is related to the uniform distribution but its elements are discrete and not continuous.

The mathematical constructs for the discrete uniform distribution are as follows:

$$P(x) = \frac{1}{N}$$

$$Mean = \frac{N+1}{2} \text{ ranked value}$$

$$Standard\ Deviation = \sqrt{\frac{(N-1)(N+1)}{12}} \text{ ranked value}$$

Skewness = 0 (that is, the distribution is perfectly symmetrical)

$$Excess\ Kurtosis = \frac{-6(N^2+1)}{5(N-1)(N+1)} \text{ ranked value}$$

Input requirements: Minimum < Maximum and both must be integers (negative integers and zero are allowed)

Geometric Distribution

The geometric distribution describes the number of trials until the first successful occurrence, such as the number of times you need to spin a roulette wheel before you win.

The three conditions underlying the geometric distribution are:

- The number of trials is not fixed.

- The trials continue until the first success.

- The probability of success is the same from trial to trial.

The mathematical constructs for the geometric distribution are as follows:

$$P(x) = p(1-p)^{x-1} \ \ for\ 0 < p < 1\ and\ x = 1,\ 2,\ ...,\ n$$

$$Mean = \frac{1}{p} - 1$$

$$Standard\ Deviation = \sqrt{\frac{1-p}{p^2}}$$

$$Skewness = \frac{2-p}{\sqrt{1-p}}$$

$$Excess\ Kurtosis = \frac{p^2 - 6p + 6}{1-p}$$

The probability of success (p) is the only distributional parameter. The number of successful trials simulated is denoted x, which can only take on positive integers.

Input requirements: Probability of success > 0 and < 1 (that is, $0.0001 \leq p \leq 0.9999$). It is important to note that probability of success (p) of 0 or 1 are trivial conditions and do not require any simulations, and hence, are not allowed in the software.

Hypergeometric Distribution

The hypergeometric distribution is similar to the binomial distribution in that both describe the number of times a particular event occurs in a fixed number of trials. The difference is that binomial distribution trials are independent, whereas hypergeometric distribution trials change the probability for each subsequent trial and are called *trials without replacement*. For example, suppose a box of manufactured parts is known to contain some defective parts. You choose a part from the box, find it is defective, and remove the part from the box. If you choose another part from the box, the probability that it is defective is somewhat lower than for the first part because you have removed a defective part. If you had replaced the defective part, the probabilities would have remained the same, and the process would have satisfied the conditions for a binomial distribution.

The three conditions underlying the hypergeometric distribution are:

- The total number of items or elements (the population size) is a fixed number, a finite population. The population size must be less than or equal to 1,750.

- The sample size (the number of trials) represents a portion of the population.

- The known initial probability of success in the population changes after each trial.

The mathematical constructs for the hypergeometric distribution are as follows:

$$P(x) = \frac{\dfrac{(N_x)!}{x!(N_x - x)!}\dfrac{(N - N_x)!}{(n-x)!(N - N_x - n + x)!}}{\dfrac{N!}{n!(N-n)!}}\quad for\ x = Max(n - (N - N_x), 0),\ ...,\ Min(n, N_x)$$

$$Mean = \frac{N_x n}{N}$$

$$Standard\ Deviation = \sqrt{\frac{(N - N_x)N_x n(N - n)}{N^2(N - 1)}}$$

$$Skewness = \frac{(N - 2N_x)(N - 2n)}{N - 2}\sqrt{\frac{N - 1}{(N - N_x)N_x n(N - n)}}$$

$$Excess\ Kurtosis = \frac{V(N, N_x, n)}{(N - N_x)\ N_x n(-3 + N)(-2 + N)(-N + n)}\quad where$$

$$V(N, N_x, n) = (N - N_x)^3 - (N - N_x)^5 + 3(N - N_x)^2 N_x - 6(N - N_x)^3 N_x$$
$$+ (N - N_x)^4 N_x + 3(N - N_x) N_x^2 - 12(N - N_x)^2 N_x^2 + 8(N - N_x)^3 N_x^2 + N_x^3$$
$$- 6(N - N_x) N_x^3 + 8(N - N_x)^2 N_x^3 + (N - N_x) N_x^4 - N_x^5 - 6(N - N_x)^3 N_x$$
$$+ 6(N - N_x)^4 N_x + 18(N - N_x)^2 N_x n - 6(N - N_x)^3 N_x n + 18(N - N_x) N_x^2 n$$
$$- 24(N - N_x)^2 N_x^2 n - 6(N - N_x)^3 n - 6(N - N_x) N_x^3 n + 6N_x^4 n + 6(N - N_x)^2 n^2$$
$$- 6(N - N_x)^3 n^2 - 24(N - N_x) N_x n^2 + 12(N - N_x)^2 N_x n^2 + 6N_x^2 n^2$$
$$+ 12(N - N_x) N_x^2 n^2 - 6N_x^3 n^2$$

The number of items in the population (N), trials sampled (n), and number of items in the population that have the successful trait (N_x) are the distributional parameters. The number of successful trials is denoted x.

Input requirements:

Population $\geq$ 2 and integer

Trials $>$ 0 and integer

Successes $>$ 0 and integer

Population $>$ Successes

Trials $<$ Population

Population $<$ 1750

Negative Binomial Distribution

The negative binomial distribution is useful for modeling the distribution of the number of trials until the rth successful occurrence, such as the number of sales calls you need to make to close a total of 10 orders. It is essentially a *superdistribution* of the geometric distribution. This distribution shows the probabilities of each number of trials in excess of r to produce the required success r.

The three conditions underlying the negative binomial distribution are:

- The number of trials is not fixed.

- The trials continue until the rth success.

- The probability of success is the same from trial to trial.

The mathematical constructs for the negative binomial distribution are as follows:

$$P(x) = \frac{(x + r - 1)!}{(r - 1)! x!} p^r (1 - p)^x \quad for \ x = r, \ r + 1, \ ...; \ and \ 0 < p < 1$$

$$Mean = \frac{r(1 - p)}{p}$$

$$Standard \ Deviation = \sqrt{\frac{r(1 - p)}{p^2}}$$

$$Skewness = \frac{2 - p}{\sqrt{r(1 - p)}}$$

$$Excess\ Kurtosis = \frac{p^2 - 6p + 6}{r(1-p)}$$

Probability of success (p) and required successes (r) are the distributional parameters.

Input requirements:

Successes required must be positive integers > 0 and < 8000

Probability of success > 0 and < 1 (that is, $0.0001 \le p \le 0.9999$)

It is important to note that probability of success (p) of 0 or 1 are trivial conditions and do not require any simulations, and hence, are not allowed in the software.

Pascal Distribution

The Pascal distribution is useful for modeling the distribution of the number of total trials needed to obtain the number of successful occurrences required. For instance, to close a total of 10 sales opportunities, how many total sales calls would you need to make given some probability of success in each call? The x-axis shows the total number of calls required, which includes successful and failed calls. The number of trials is not fixed, the trials continue until the Rth success, and the probability of success is the same from trial to trial. Pascal distribution is related to the negative binomial distribution. Negative binomial distribution computes the number of events needed in addition to the number of successes required given some probability (in other words, the total failures), whereas the Pascal distribution computes the total number of events needed (in other words, the sum of failures and successes) to achieve the successes required given some probability. Successes required and probability are the two distributional parameters.

The mathematical constructs for the Pascal distribution are shown below:

$$f(x) = \begin{cases} \dfrac{(x-1)!}{(x-s)!(s-1)!} p^s (1-p)^{x-s} & \textit{for all } x \ge s \\ 0 \ \textit{otherwise} \end{cases}$$

$$F(x) = \begin{cases} \displaystyle\sum_{x=1}^{k} \dfrac{(x-1)!}{(x-s)!(s-1)!} p^s (1-p)^{x-s} & \textit{for all } x \ge s \\ 0 \ \textit{otherwise} \end{cases}$$

$$Mean = \frac{s}{p}$$

$$Standard\ Deviation = \sqrt{s(1-p)p^2}$$

$$Skewness = \frac{2-p}{\sqrt{r(1-p)}}$$

$$Excess\ Kurtosis = \frac{p^2 - 6p + 6}{r(1-p)}$$

The three conditions underlying the Pascal as well as negative binomial distribution are:

- The number of trials is not fixed.

- The trials continue until the Rth success.

- The probability of success is the same from trial to trial.

Successes Required and Probability are the distributional parameters.

Input requirements:

Successes required > 0 and is an integer

$0 \leq$ Probability ≤ 1

Poisson Distribution

The Poisson distribution describes the number of times an event occurs in a given interval, such as the number of telephone calls per minute or the number of errors per page in a document.

The three conditions underlying the Poisson distribution are:

- The number of possible occurrences in any interval is unlimited.

- The occurrences are independent. The number of occurrences in one interval does not affect the number of occurrences in other intervals.

- The average number of occurrences must remain the same from interval to interval.

The mathematical constructs for the Poisson are as follows:

$$P(x) = \frac{e^{-\lambda}\lambda^x}{x!} \; for \; x \; and \; \lambda > 0$$

$Mean = \lambda$

$Standard \; Deviation = \sqrt{\lambda}$

$Skewness = \dfrac{1}{\sqrt{\lambda}}$

$Excess \; Kurtosis = \dfrac{1}{\lambda}$

Rate (λ) is the only distributional parameter.

Input requirements: Rate > 0 and ≤ 1000 (that is, $0.0001 \leq$ rate ≤ 1000)

APPENDIX—CONTINUOUS DISTRIBUTIONS

Following is a detailed listing of the different types of continuous probability distributions that can be used in Monte Carlo simulation.

Arcsine Distribution

The arcsine distribution is U-shaped and is a special case of the beta distribution when both shape and scale are equal to 0.5. Values close to the minimum and maximum have high probabilities of occurrence whereas values between these two extremes have very small probabilities of occurrence. Minimum and maximum are the distributional parameters.

The mathematical constructs for the arcsine distribution are shown below. The probability density function (PDF) is denoted $f(x)$ and the cumulative distribution function (CDF) is denoted $F(x)$.

$$f(x) = \begin{cases} \dfrac{1}{\pi\sqrt{x(1-x)}} & \text{for } 0 \le x \le 1 \\ 0 & \text{otherwise} \end{cases}$$

$$F(x) = \begin{cases} 0 & x < 0 \\ \dfrac{2}{\pi}\sin^{-1}(\sqrt{x}) & \text{for } 0 \le x \le 1 \\ 1 & x > 1 \end{cases}$$

$$Mean = \frac{Min + Max}{2}$$

$$Standard\ Deviation = \sqrt{\frac{(Max - Min)^2}{8}}$$

Skewness = 0 for all inputs

Excess Kurtosis = 1.5 for all inputs

Minimum and maximum are the distributional parameters.

Input requirements: Max > Min (either input can be positive, negative, or zero)

Beta Distribution

The beta distribution is very flexible and is commonly used to represent variability over a fixed range. One of the more important applications of the beta distribution is its use as a conjugate distribution for the parameter of a Bernoulli distribution. In this application, the beta distribution is used to represent the uncertainty in the probability of occurrence of an event. It is also used to describe empirical data and predict the random behavior of percentages and fractions, as the range of outcomes is typically between 0 and 1.

The value of the beta distribution lies in the wide variety of shapes it can assume when you vary the two parameters, alpha and beta. If the parameters are equal, the distribution is symmetrical. If either parameter is 1 and the other parameter is greater than 1, the distribution is J-shaped. If alpha is less than beta, the distribution is said to be positively skewed (most of the values are near the minimum value). If alpha is greater than beta, the distribution is negatively skewed (most of the values are near the maximum value).

The mathematical constructs for the beta distribution are as follows:

$$f(x) = \frac{(x)^{(\alpha-1)}(1-x)^{(\beta-1)}}{\left[\frac{\Gamma(\alpha)\Gamma(\beta)}{\Gamma(\alpha+\beta)}\right]} \quad for \; \alpha > 0; \; \beta > 0; \; x > 0$$

$$Mean = \frac{\alpha}{\alpha + \beta}$$

$$Standard \; Deviation = \sqrt{\frac{\alpha\beta}{(\alpha+\beta)^2(1+\alpha+\beta)}}$$

$$Skewness = \frac{2(\beta-\alpha)\sqrt{1+\alpha+\beta}}{(2+\alpha+\beta)\sqrt{\alpha\beta}}$$

$$Excess \; Kurtosis = \frac{3(\alpha+\beta+1)[\alpha\beta(\alpha+\beta-6)+2(\alpha+\beta)^2]}{\alpha\beta(\alpha+\beta+2)(\alpha+\beta+3)} - 3$$

Alpha (α) and beta (β) are the two distributional shape parameters, and Γ is the gamma function. The two conditions underlying the beta distribution are:

- The uncertain variable is a random value between 0 and a positive value.

- The shape of the distribution can be specified using two positive values.

Input requirements: Alpha and beta > 0 and can be any positive value

Beta 3 and Beta 4 Distributions

The original beta distribution only takes two inputs, alpha and beta shape parameters. However, the output of the simulated value is between 0 and 1. In the beta 3 distribution, we add an extra parameter called location or shift, where we are not free to move away from this 0 to 1 output limitation, therefore the beta 3 distribution is also known as a shifted beta distribution. Similarly, the beta 4 distribution adds two input parameters, location, or shift, and factor. The original beta distribution is multiplied by the factor and shifted by the location, and, therefore the beta 4 is also known as the multiplicative shifted beta distribution.

The mathematical constructs for the beta 3 and beta 4 distributions are based on those in the beta distribution, with the relevant shifts and factorial multiplication (e.g., the PDF and CDF will be adjusted by the shift and factor, and some of the moments, such as the mean, will similarly be affected; the standard deviation, in contrast, is only affected by the factorial multiplication, whereas the remaining moments are not affected at all).

Input requirements:

Location can take on any positive or negative value including zero

Factor > 0

Cauchy Distribution or Lorentzian Distribution or Breit–Wigner Distribution

The Cauchy distribution, also called the Lorentzian distribution or Breit–Wigner distribution, is a continuous distribution describing resonance behavior. It also describes the distribution of horizontal distances at which a line segment tilted at a random angle cuts the x-axis.

The mathematical constructs for the Cauchy or Lorentzian distribution are as follows:

$$f(x) = \frac{1}{\pi} \frac{\gamma/2}{(x-m)^2 + \gamma^2/4}$$

The Cauchy distribution is a special case where it does not have any theoretical moments (mean, standard deviation, skewness, and kurtosis) as they are all undefined.

Mode location (m) and scale (γ) are the only two parameters in this distribution. The location parameter specifies the peak or mode of the distribution while the scale parameter specifies the half-width at half-maximum of the distribution. In addition, the mean and variance of a Cauchy or Lorentzian distribution are undefined.

In addition, the Cauchy distribution is the Student's t-distribution with only 1 degree of freedom. This distribution is also constructed by taking the ratio of two standard-normal distributions (normal distributions with a mean of zero and a variance of one) that are independent of one another.

Input requirements:

Location can be any value

Scale > 0 and can be any positive value

Chi-Square Distribution

The chi-square distribution is a probability distribution used predominantly in hypothesis testing, and it is related to the gamma distribution and the standard-normal distribution. For instance, the sums of independent normal distributions are distributed as a chi-square (χ^2) with k degrees of freedom:

$$Z_1^2 + Z_2^2 + \ldots + Z_k^2 \overset{d}{\sim} \chi_k^2$$

The mathematical constructs for the chi-square distribution are as follows:

$$f(x) = \frac{2^{-k/2}}{\Gamma(k/2)} x^{k/2-1} e^{-x/2} \text{ for all } x > 0$$

$Mean = k$

$Standard\ Deviation = \sqrt{2k}$

$Skewness = 2\sqrt{\dfrac{2}{k}}$

$Excess\ Kurtosis = \dfrac{12}{k}$

Γ is the gamma function. Degrees of freedom k is the only distributional parameter.

The chi-square distribution can also be modeled using a gamma distribution by setting the shape parameter $= \frac{k}{2}$ and scale $= 2S^2$ where S is the scale.

Input requirements: Degrees of freedom > 1 and must be an integer < 1000

Cosine Distribution

The cosine distribution looks like a logistic distribution where the median value between the minimum and maximum have the highest peak or mode, carrying the maximum probability of occurrence, while the extreme tails close to the minimum and maximum values have lower probabilities. Minimum and maximum are the distributional parameters.

The mathematical constructs for the cosine distribution are shown below:

$$f(x) = \begin{cases} \dfrac{1}{2b} Cos\left[\dfrac{x-a}{b}\right] & for\ Min \le x \le Max \\ 0 & otherwise \end{cases}$$

$$where\ a = \frac{Min + Max}{2}\ and\ b = \frac{Max - Min}{\pi}$$

$$F(x) = \begin{cases} \dfrac{1}{2}\left[1 + Sin\left(\dfrac{x-a}{b}\right)\right] & for\ Min \le x \le Max \\ 1 & for\ x > Max \end{cases}$$

$$Mean = \frac{Min + Max}{2}$$

$$Standard\ Deviation = \sqrt{\frac{(Max - Min)^2(\pi^2 - 8)}{4\pi^2}}$$

$$Skewness\ is\ always\ equal\ to\ 0$$

$$Excess\ Kurtosis = \frac{6(90 - \pi^4)}{5(\pi^2 - 6)^2}$$

Minimum and maximum are the distributional parameters.

Input requirements: Maximum $>$ minimum (either input parameter can be positive, negative, or zero)

Double Log Distribution

The double log distribution looks like the Cauchy distribution where the central tendency is peaked and carries the maximum value probability density but declines faster the further away from the center it gets, creating a symmetrical distribution with an extreme peak in between the minimum and maximum values. Minimum and maximum are the distributional parameters.

The mathematical constructs for the double log distribution are shown below:

$$f(x) = \begin{cases} \dfrac{-1}{2b} \ln\left(\dfrac{|x-a|}{b} \right) & \text{for } Min \leq x \leq Max \\ 0 & \text{otherwise} \end{cases}$$

$$\text{where } a = \frac{Min + Max}{2} \text{ and } b = \frac{Max - Min}{2}$$

$$F(x) = \begin{cases} \dfrac{1}{2} - \left(\dfrac{|x-a|}{2b} \right)\left[1 - \ln\left(\dfrac{|x-a|}{b} \right) \right] & \text{for } Min \leq x \leq a \\ \dfrac{1}{2} + \left(\dfrac{|x-a|}{2b} \right)\left[1 - \ln\left(\dfrac{|x-a|}{b} \right) \right] & \text{for } a \leq x \leq Max \end{cases}$$

$$Mean = \frac{Min + Max}{2}$$

$$Standard\ Deviation = \sqrt{\frac{(Max - Min)^2}{36}}$$

Skewness is always equal to 0

Excess Kurtosis is a complex function and not easily represented

Minimum and maximum are the distributional parameters.

Input requirements: Maximum > minimum (either input parameter can be positive, negative, or zero)

Erlang Distribution

The Erlang distribution is the same as the gamma distribution with the requirement that the alpha or shape parameter must be a positive integer. An example application of the Erlang distribution is the calibration of the rate of transition of elements through a system of compartments. Such systems are widely used in biology and ecology (e.g., in epidemiology, an individual may progress at an exponential rate from being healthy to becoming a disease carrier, and continue exponentially from being a carrier to being infectious). Alpha (also known as shape) and beta (also known as scale) are the distributional parameters.

The mathematical constructs for the Erlang distribution are shown below:

$$f(x) = \begin{cases} \dfrac{\left(\dfrac{x}{\beta} \right)^{\alpha-1} e^{-x/\beta}}{\beta(\alpha - 1)} & \text{for } x \geq 0 \\ 0 & \text{otherwise} \end{cases}$$

$$F(x) = \begin{cases} 1 - e^{-x/\beta} \sum_{i=0}^{\alpha-1} \dfrac{(x/\beta)^i}{i!} & \text{for } x \geq 0 \\ 0 & \text{otherwise} \end{cases}$$

$$Mean = \alpha\beta$$

$$Standard\ Deviation = \sqrt{\alpha \beta^2}$$

$$Skew = \frac{2}{\sqrt{\alpha}}$$

$$Excess\ Kurtosis = \frac{6}{\alpha} - 3$$

Alpha and beta are the distributional parameters.

Input requirements: Alpha (shape) > 0 and is an integer and Beta (scale) > 0

Exponential Distribution

The exponential distribution is widely used to describe events recurring at random points in time, such as the time between failures of electronic equipment or the time between arrivals at a service booth. It is related to the Poisson distribution, which describes the number of occurrences of an event in a given interval of time. An important characteristic of the exponential distribution is the "memoryless" property, which means that the future lifetime of a given object has the same distribution, regardless of the time it existed. In other words, time has no effect on future outcomes.

The mathematical constructs for the exponential distribution are as follows:

$$f(x) = \lambda e^{-\lambda x} \quad for\ x \geq 0;\ \lambda > 0$$

$$Mean = \frac{1}{\lambda}$$

$$Standard\ Deviation = \frac{1}{\lambda}$$

Skewness = 2 (this value applies to all success rate λ inputs)

Excess Kurtosis = 6 (this value applies to all success rate λ inputs)

Success rate (λ) is the only distributional parameter. The number of successful trials is denoted x. The condition underlying the exponential distribution is:

The exponential distribution describes the amount of time between occurrences.

Input requirements: Rate > 0 and ≤ 300

Exponential 2 Distribution

The exponential 2 distribution uses the same constructs as the original exponential distribution but adds a location or shift parameter. The exponential distribution starts from a minimum value of 0, whereas this exponential 2, or shifted exponential, distribution shifts the starting location to any other value.

Rate, or lambda, and location, or shift, are the distributional parameters.

Input requirements:

Rate (lambda) > 0

Location can be any positive or negative value including zero

Extreme Value Distribution or Gumbel Distribution

The extreme value distribution (Type 1) is commonly used to describe the largest value of a response over a period of time, for example, extreme losses in investment portfolios, extreme stock price movements, flood flows, rainfall, and earthquakes. Other applications include the breaking strengths of materials, construction design, and aircraft loads and tolerances. The extreme value distribution is also known as the Gumbel distribution.

The mathematical constructs for the extreme value distribution are as follows:

$$f(x) = \frac{1}{\beta} z e^{-z} \text{ where } z = e^{\frac{x-m}{\beta}} \text{ for } \beta > 0; \text{ and any value of } x \text{ and } m$$

$$Mean = m + 0.577215\beta$$

$$Standard\ Deviation = \sqrt{\frac{1}{6}\pi^2\beta^2}$$

$$Skewness = \frac{12\sqrt{6}(1.2020569)}{\pi^3} = 1.13955 \text{ (this applies for all values of mode and scale)}$$

$$Excess\ Kurtosis = 5.4 \text{ (this applies for all values of mode and scale)}$$

Mode (m) and scale (β) are the distributional parameters.

There are two standard parameters for the extreme value distribution: mode and scale. The mode parameter is the most likely value for the variable (the highest point on the probability distribution). The scale parameter is a number greater than 0. The larger the scale parameter, the greater the variance.

Input requirements: Mode can be any value and Scale > 0

F-Distribution or Fisher–Snedecor Distribution

The F-distribution, also known as the Fisher–Snedecor distribution, is another continuous distribution used most frequently for hypothesis testing. Specifically, it is used to test the statistical difference between two variances in analysis of variance tests and likelihood ratio tests. The F-distribution with the numerator degree of freedom n and denominator degree of freedom m is related to the chi-square distribution in that:

$$\frac{\chi_n^2/n}{\chi_m^2/m} \overset{d}{\sim} F_{n,m} \text{ or } f(x) = \frac{\Gamma\left(\frac{n+m}{2}\right)\left(\frac{n}{m}\right)^{n/2} x^{n/2-1}}{\Gamma\left(\frac{n}{2}\right)\Gamma\left(\frac{m}{2}\right)\left[x\left(\frac{n}{m}\right)+1\right]^{(n+m)/2}}$$

$$Mean = \frac{m}{m-2}$$

$$Standard\ Deviation = \frac{2m^2(m+n-2)}{n(m-2)^2(m-4)} \text{ for all } m > 4$$

$$Skewness = \frac{2(m+2n-2)}{m-6}\sqrt{\frac{2(m-4)}{n(m+n-2)}}$$

$$Excess\ Kurtosis = \frac{12(-16+20m-8m^2+m^3+44n-32mn+5m^2n-22n^2+5mn^2)}{n(m-6)(m-8)(n+m-2)}$$

The numerator degree of freedom n and denominator degree of freedom m are the only distributional parameters.

Input requirements: Degrees of freedom numerator and degrees of freedom denominator both > 0 integers

Gamma Distribution (Erlang Distribution)

The gamma distribution applies to a wide range of physical quantities and is related to other distributions: lognormal, exponential, Pascal, Erlang, Poisson, and Chi-Square. It is used in meteorological processes to represent pollutant concentrations and precipitation quantities. The gamma distribution is also used to measure the time between the occurrences of events when the event process is not completely random. Other applications of the gamma distribution include inventory control, economic theory, and insurance risk theory.

The gamma distribution is most often used as the distribution of the amount of time until the rth occurrence of an event in a Poisson process. When used in this fashion, the three conditions underlying the gamma distribution are:

- The number of possible occurrences in any unit of measurement is not limited to a fixed number.

- The occurrences are independent. The number of occurrences in one unit of measurement does not affect the number of occurrences in other units.

- The average number of occurrences must remain the same from unit to unit.

The mathematical constructs for the gamma distribution are as follows:

$$f(x) = \frac{\left(\frac{x}{\beta}\right)^{\alpha-1} e^{-\frac{x}{\beta}}}{\Gamma(\alpha)\beta} \quad with\ any\ value\ of\ \alpha > 0\ and\ \beta > 0$$

$Mean = \alpha\beta$

$Standard\ Deviation = \sqrt{\alpha\beta^2}$

$Skewness = \dfrac{2}{\sqrt{\alpha}}$

$Excess\ Kurtosis = \dfrac{6}{\alpha}$

Shape parameter alpha (α) and scale parameter beta (β) are the distributional parameters, and Γ is the gamma function. When the alpha parameter is a positive integer, the gamma distribution is called the Erlang distribution, used to predict waiting times in queuing systems, where the Erlang distribution is the sum of independent and identically distributed random variables each having a memoryless exponential distribution. Setting n as the number of these random variables, the mathematical construct of the Erlang distribution is:

$$f(x) = \frac{x^{n-1}e^{-x}}{(n-1)!} \text{ for all } x > 0 \text{ and all positive integers of } n$$

Input requirements:

Scale beta > 0 and can be any positive value

Shape alpha ≥ 0.05 and any positive value

Location can be any value

Laplace Distribution

The Laplace distribution is also sometimes called the double exponential distribution because it can be constructed with two exponential distributions (with an additional location parameter) spliced together back-to-back, creating an unusual peak in the middle. The probability density function of the Laplace distribution is reminiscent of the normal distribution. However, whereas the normal distribution is expressed in terms of the squared difference from the mean, the Laplace density is expressed in terms of the absolute difference from the mean, making the Laplace distribution's tails fatter than those of the normal distribution. When the location parameter is set to zero, the Laplace distribution's random variable is exponentially distributed with an inverse of the scale parameter. Alpha (also known as location) and beta (also known as scale) are the distributional parameters.

The mathematical constructs for the Laplace distribution are shown below:

$$f(x) = \frac{1}{2\beta} \exp\left(-\frac{|x-\alpha|}{\beta} \right)$$

$$F(x) = \begin{cases} \frac{1}{2} \exp\left[\frac{x-\alpha}{\beta} \right] & \text{when } x < \alpha \\ 1 - \frac{1}{2} \exp\left[-\frac{x-\alpha}{\beta} \right] & \text{when } x \geq \alpha \end{cases}$$

Mean = α

Standard Deviation = 1.4142β

Skewness is always equal to 0 as it is a symmetrical distribution

Excess Kurtosis is always equal to 3

Input requirements:

Alpha (location) can take on any positive or negative value including zero

Beta (scale) > 0

Logistic Distribution

The logistic distribution is commonly used to describe growth, that is, the size of a population expressed as a function of a time variable. It also can be used to describe chemical reactions and the course of growth for a population or individual.

The mathematical constructs for the logistic distribution are as follows:

$$f(x) = \frac{e^{\frac{\mu - x}{\alpha}}}{\alpha \left[1 + e^{\frac{\mu - x}{\alpha}} \right]^2} \quad \text{for any value of } \alpha \text{ and } \mu$$

Mean $= \mu$

Standard Deviation $= \sqrt{\frac{1}{3} \pi^2 \alpha^2}$

Skewness $= 0$ (this applies to all mean and scale inputs)

Excess Kurtosis $= 1.2$ (this applies to all mean and scale inputs)

Mean (μ) and scale (α) are the distributional parameters.

There are two standard parameters for the logistic distribution: mean and scale. The mean parameter is the average value, which for this distribution is the same as the mode, because this distribution is symmetrical. The scale parameter is a number greater than 0. The larger the scale parameter, the greater the variance.

Input requirements:

Scale > 0 and can be any positive value

Mean can be any value

Lognormal Distribution

The lognormal distribution is widely used in situations where values are positively skewed, for example, in financial analysis for security valuation or in real estate for property valuation, and where values cannot fall below zero.

Stock prices are usually positively skewed rather than normally (symmetrically) distributed. Stock prices exhibit this trend because they cannot fall below the lower limit of zero but might increase to any price without limit. Similarly, real estate prices illustrate positive skewness and are lognormally distributed as property values cannot become negative.

The three conditions underlying the lognormal distribution are:

The uncertain variable can increase without limits but cannot fall below zero.

The uncertain variable is positively skewed, with most of the values near the lower limit.

The natural logarithm of the uncertain variable yields a normal distribution.

Generally, if the coefficient of variability is greater than 30%, use a lognormal distribution. Otherwise, use the normal distribution.

The mathematical constructs for the lognormal distribution are as follows:

$$f(x) = \frac{1}{x\sqrt{2\pi}\ln(\sigma)} e^{\frac{-[\ln(x)-\ln(\mu)]^2}{2[\ln(\sigma)]^2}} \quad for\ x > 0;\ \mu > 0\ and\ \sigma > 0$$

$$Mean = \exp\left(\mu + \frac{\sigma^2}{2}\right)$$

$$Standard\ Deviation = \sqrt{\exp\left(\sigma^2 + 2\mu\right)\left[\exp\left(\sigma^2\right) - 1\right]}$$

$$Skewness = \left[\sqrt{\exp\left(\sigma^2\right) - 1}\right](2 + \exp(\sigma^2))$$

$$Excess\ Kurtosis = \exp\left(4\sigma^2\right) + 2\exp\left(3\sigma^2\right) + 3\exp\left(2\sigma^2\right) - 6$$

Mean (μ) and standard deviation (σ) are the distributional parameters.

Input requirements: Mean and standard deviation both > 0 and can be any positive value

Lognormal Parameter Sets: By default, the lognormal distribution uses the arithmetic mean and standard deviation. For applications for which historical data are available, it is more appropriate to use either the logarithmic mean and standard deviation, or the geometric mean and standard deviation.

Lognormal 3 Distribution

The lognormal 3 distribution uses the same constructs as the original lognormal distribution but adds a location, or shift, parameter. The lognormal distribution starts from a minimum value of 0, whereas this lognormal 3, or shifted lognormal, distribution shifts the starting location to any other value.

Mean, standard deviation, and location (shift) are the distributional parameters.

Input requirements:

Mean > 0 and Standard Deviation > 0

Location can be any positive or negative value including zero

Normal Distribution

The normal distribution is the most important distribution in probability theory because it describes many natural phenomena, such as people's IQs or heights. Decision makers can use the normal distribution to describe uncertain variables such as the inflation rate or the future price of gasoline.

The three conditions underlying the normal distribution are:

- Some value of the uncertain variable is the most likely (the mean of the distribution).

- The uncertain variable could as likely be above the mean as it could be below the mean (symmetrical about the mean).

- The uncertain variable is more likely in the vicinity of the mean than further away.

The mathematical constructs for the normal distribution are as follows:

$$f(x) = \frac{1}{\sqrt{2\pi}\sigma} e^{\frac{-(x-\mu)^2}{2\sigma^2}} \quad \text{for all values of } x \text{ and } \mu; \text{ while } \sigma > 0$$

Mean $= \mu$

Standard Deviation $= \sigma$

Skewness $= 0$ (this applies to all inputs of mean and standard deviation)

Excess Kurtosis $= 0$ (this applies to all inputs of mean and standard deviation)

Mean (μ) and standard deviation (σ) are the distributional parameters.

Input requirements: Standard deviation > 0 and can be any positive value whereas mean can be any value

Parabolic Distribution

The parabolic distribution is a special case of the beta distribution when *Shape* = *Scale* = 2. Values close to the minimum and maximum have low probabilities of occurrence, whereas values between these two extremes have higher probabilities or occurrence. Minimum and maximum are the distributional parameters.

The mathematical constructs for the parabolic distribution are shown below:

$$f(x) = \frac{(x)^{(\alpha-1)}(1-x)^{(\beta-1)}}{\left[\frac{\Gamma(\alpha)\Gamma(\beta)}{\Gamma(\alpha+\beta)}\right]} \quad \text{for } \alpha > 0; \beta > 0; x > 0$$

Whereas the functional form above is for a beta distribution, for a parabolic function, we set alpha = beta = 2 and a shift of location in minimum, with a multiplicative factor of (Max – Min).

Mean $= \dfrac{Min + Max}{2}$

Standard Deviation $= \sqrt{\dfrac{(Max - Min)^2}{20}}$

Skewness $= 0$

Excess Kurtosis $= -0.8571$

Minimum and maximum are the distributional parameters.

Input requirements: Maximum > minimum (either can be positive, negative, or zero)

Pareto Distribution

The Pareto distribution is widely used for the investigation of distributions associated with such empirical phenomena as city population sizes, the occurrence of natural resources, the size of companies, personal incomes, stock price fluctuations, and error clustering in communication circuits.

The mathematical constructs for the Pareto are as follows:

$$f(x) = \frac{\beta L^{\beta}}{x^{(1+\beta)}} \quad for \; x > L$$

$$Mean = \frac{\beta L}{\beta - 1}$$

$$Standard \; Deviation = \sqrt{\frac{\beta L^{2}}{(\beta - 1)^{2}(\beta - 2)}}$$

$$Skewness = \sqrt{\frac{\beta - 2}{\beta}} \left[\frac{2(\beta + 1)}{\beta - 3} \right]$$

$$Excess \; Kurtosis = \frac{6(\beta^{3} + \beta^{2} - 6\beta - 2)}{\beta(\beta - 3)(\beta - 4)}$$

Location (L) and shape (β) are the distributional parameters.

There are two standard parameters for the Pareto distribution: location and shape. The location parameter is the lower bound for the variable. After you select the location parameter, you can estimate the shape parameter. The shape parameter is a number greater than 0, usually greater than 1. The larger the shape parameter, the smaller the variance and the thicker the right tail of the distribution.

Input requirements:

Location > 0 and can be any positive value

Shape ≥ 0.05

Pearson V Distribution

The Pearson V distribution is related to the inverse gamma distribution, where it is the reciprocal of the variable distributed according to the gamma distribution. Pearson V distribution is also used to model time delays where there is almost certainty of some minimum delay and the maximum delay is unbounded; for example, delay in arrival of emergency services and time to repair a machine. Alpha (also known as shape) and beta (also known as scale) are the distributional parameters.

The mathematical constructs for the Pearson V distribution are shown below:

$$f(x) = \frac{x^{-(\alpha+1)} e^{-\beta/x}}{\beta^{-\alpha} \Gamma(\alpha)}$$

$$F(x) = \frac{\Gamma(\alpha, \beta/x)}{\Gamma(\alpha)}$$

$$Mean = \frac{\beta}{\alpha - 1}$$

$$Standard \; Deviation = \sqrt{\frac{\beta^{2}}{(\alpha - 1)^{2}(\alpha - 2)}}$$

$$Skew = \frac{4\sqrt{\alpha - 2}}{\alpha - 3}$$

$$Excess\ Kurtosis = \frac{30\alpha - 66}{(\alpha-3)(\alpha-4)} - 3$$

Input requirements: Alpha (shape) > 0 and Beta (scale) > 0

Pearson VI Distribution

The Pearson VI distribution is related to the gamma distribution, where it is the rational function of two variables distributed according to two gamma distributions. Alpha 1 (also known as shape 1), alpha 2 (also known as shape 2), and beta (also known as scale) are the distributional parameters. The mathematical constructs for the Pearson VI distribution are shown below:

$$f(x) = \frac{(x/\beta)^{\alpha_1 - 1}}{\beta\ B(\alpha_1, \alpha_2)[1 + (x/\beta)]^{\alpha_1 + \alpha_2}}$$

$$F(x) = F_B\left(\frac{x}{x+\beta}\right)$$

$$Mean = \frac{\beta\alpha_1}{\alpha_2 - 1}$$

$$Standard\ Deviation = \sqrt{\frac{\beta^2\alpha_1(\alpha_1 + \alpha_2 - 1)}{(\alpha_2 - 1)^2(\alpha_2 - 2)}}$$

$$Skew = 2\sqrt{\frac{\alpha_2 - 2}{\alpha_1(\alpha_1 + \alpha_2 - 1)}}\left[\frac{2\alpha_1 + \alpha_2 - 1}{\alpha_2 - 3}\right]$$

$$Excess\ Kurtosis = \frac{3(\alpha_2 - 2)}{(\alpha_2 - 3)(\alpha_2 - 4)}\left[\frac{2(\alpha_2 - 1)^2}{\alpha_1(\alpha_1 + \alpha_2 - 1)} + (\alpha_2 + 5)\right] - 3$$

Input requirements: Alpha 1 (shape 1) > 0; Alpha 2 (shape 2) > 0; and Beta (scale) > 0

PERT Distribution

The PERT distribution is widely used in project and program management to define the worst-case, nominal-case, and best-case scenarios of project completion time. It is related to the beta and triangular distributions. PERT distribution can be used to identify risks in project and cost models based on the likelihood of meeting targets and goals across any number of project components using minimum, most likely, and maximum values, but it is designed to generate a distribution that more closely resembles realistic probability distributions. The PERT distribution can provide a close fit to the normal or lognormal distributions. Like the triangular distribution, the PERT distribution emphasizes the *most likely* value over the minimum and maximum estimates. However, unlike the triangular distribution, the PERT distribution constructs a smooth curve that places progressively more emphasis on values around (near) the most likely value, in favor of values around the edges. In practice, this means that we *trust* the estimate for the most likely value, and we believe that even if it is not exactly accurate (as estimates seldom are), we have an expectation that the resulting value will be close to that estimate. Assuming that many real-world phenomena are normally distributed, the appeal of the PERT distribution is that it produces a curve similar to the normal curve in shape, without knowing the precise parameters of the related normal curve. Minimum, most likely, and maximum are the distributional parameters.

The mathematical constructs for the PERT distribution are shown below:

$$f(x) = \frac{(x - Min)^{A1-1}(Max - x)^{A2-1}}{B(A1, A2)(Max - Min)^{A1+A2-1}}$$

where $A1 = 6\left[\dfrac{\dfrac{Min + 4(Likely) + Max}{6} - Min}{Max - Min}\right]$ and $A2 = 6\left[\dfrac{Max - \dfrac{Min + 4(Likely) + Max}{6}}{Max - Min}\right]$

and B is the Beta function

$$Mean = \frac{Min + 4\,Mode + Max}{6}$$

$$Standard\ Deviation = \sqrt{\frac{(\mu - Min)(Max - \mu)}{7}}$$

$$Skew = \sqrt{\frac{7}{(\mu - Min)(Max - \mu)}}\left(\frac{Min + Max - 2\mu}{4}\right)$$

Excess Kurtosis is a complex function and cannot be readily computed

Input requirements: Min $\leq$ Most Likely $\leq$ Max and can be positive, negative, or zero

Power Distribution

The power distribution is related to the exponential distribution in that the probability of small outcomes is large but exponentially decreases as the outcome value increases. Alpha (also known as shape) is the only distributional parameter. The mathematical constructs for the power distribution are shown below:

$$f(x) = \alpha x^{\alpha-1}$$
$$F(x) = x^{\alpha}$$

$$Mean = \frac{\alpha}{1 + \alpha}$$

$$Standard\ Deviation = \sqrt{\frac{\alpha}{(1+\alpha)^2(2+\alpha)}}$$

$$Skew = \sqrt{\frac{\alpha+2}{\alpha}}\left(\frac{2(\alpha-1)}{\alpha+3}\right)$$

Excess Kurtosis is a complex function and cannot be readily computed

Input requirements: Alpha > 0

Power 3 Distribution

The power 3 distribution uses the same constructs as the original power distribution but adds a location, or shift, parameter, and a multiplicative factor parameter. The power distribution starts from a minimum value of 0, whereas this power 3, or shifted multiplicative power, distribution shifts the starting location to any other value.

Alpha, location or shift, and factor are the distributional parameters.

Input requirements:

Alpha > 0.05

Location, or shift, can be any positive or negative value including zero

Factor > 0

Student's t-Distribution

The Student's t-distribution is the most widely used distribution in hypothesis test. This distribution is used to estimate the mean of a normally distributed population when the sample size is small, and is used to test the statistical significance of the difference between two sample means or confidence intervals for small sample sizes.

The mathematical constructs for the t-distribution are as follows:

$$f(t) = \frac{\Gamma[(r+1)/2]}{\sqrt{r\pi}\,\Gamma[r/2]} (1 + t^2/r)^{-(r+1)/2}$$

Mean = 0 (all degrees of freedom *r* except if the distribution is shifted to another nonzero central location)

Standard Deviation $= \sqrt{\dfrac{r}{r-2}}$

Skewness = 0 (this applies to all degrees of freedom *r*)

Excess Kurtosis $= \dfrac{6}{r-4}$ for all $r > 4$ where $t = \dfrac{x - \bar{x}}{s}$ and Γ is the gamma function.

Degree of freedom *r* is the only distributional parameter.

The t-distribution is related to the F-distribution as follows: the square of a value of t with r degrees of freedom is distributed as F with 1 and r degrees of freedom. The overall shape of the probability density function of the t-distribution also resembles the bell shape of a normally distributed variable with mean 0 and variance 1, except that it is a bit lower and wider or is leptokurtic (fat tails at the ends and peaked center). As the number of degrees of freedom grows (say, above 30), the t-distribution approaches the normal distribution with mean 0 and variance 1.

Input requirements: Degrees of freedom ≥ 1 and must be an integer

Triangular Distribution

The triangular distribution describes a situation where you know the minimum, maximum, and most likely values to occur. For example, you could describe the number of cars sold per week when past sales show the minimum, maximum, and usual number of cars sold.

The three conditions underlying the triangular distribution are:

- The minimum number of items is fixed.

- The maximum number of items is fixed.

- The most likely number of items falls between the minimum and maximum values, forming a triangular-shaped distribution, which shows that values near the minimum and maximum are less likely to occur than those near the most-likely value.

The mathematical constructs for the triangular distribution are as follows:

$$f(x) = \begin{cases} \dfrac{2(x - Min)}{(Max - Min)(Likely - min)} & \text{for } Min < x < Likely \\[2em] \dfrac{2(Max - x)}{(Max - Min)(Max - Likely)} & \text{for } Likely < x < Max \end{cases}$$

$$Mean = \frac{1}{3}(Min + Likely + Max)$$

$$Standard\ Deviation = \sqrt{\frac{1}{18}(Min^2 + Likely^2 + Max^2 - Min\,Max - Min\,Likely - Max\,Likely)}$$

$$Skewness = \frac{\sqrt{2}(Min + Max - 2Likely)(2Min - Max - Likely)(Min - 2Max + Likely)}{5(Min^2 + Max^2 + Likely^2 - MinMax - MinLikely - MaxLikely)^{3/2}}$$

Excess Kurtosis = −0.6 (this applies to all inputs of Min, Max, and Likely)

Minimum (Min), most likely (Likely) and maximum (Max) are the parameters.

Input requirements:

Min ≤ Most Likely ≤ Max and can take any value

However, Min < Max and can take any value

Uniform Distribution

With the uniform distribution, all values fall between the minimum and maximum and occur with equal likelihood.

The three conditions underlying the uniform distribution are:

- The minimum value is fixed.

- The maximum value is fixed.

- All values between the minimum and maximum occur with equal likelihood.

The mathematical constructs for the uniform distribution are as follows:

$$f(x) = \frac{1}{Max - Min} \quad \text{for all values such that } Min < Max$$

$$Mean = \frac{Min + Max}{2}$$

$$Standard\ Deviation = \sqrt{\frac{(Max - Min)^2}{12}}$$

Skewness = 0 (this applies to all inputs of Min and Max)

Excess Kurtosis = −1.2 (this applies to all inputs of Min and Max)

Maximum value (*Max*) and minimum value (*Min*) are the distributional parameters.

Input requirements: Min < Max and can take any value

Weibull Distribution (Rayleigh Distribution)

The Weibull distribution describes data resulting from life and fatigue tests. It is commonly used to describe failure time in reliability studies as well as the breaking strengths of materials in reliability and quality control tests. Weibull distributions are also used to represent various physical quantities, such as wind speed.

The Weibull distribution is a family of distributions that can assume the properties of several other distributions. For example, depending on the shape parameter you define, the Weibull distribution can be used to model the exponential and Rayleigh distributions, among others. The Weibull distribution is very flexible. When the Weibull shape parameter is equal to 1.0, the Weibull distribution is identical to the exponential distribution. The Weibull location parameter lets you set up an exponential distribution to start at a location other than 0.0. When the shape parameter is less than 1.0, the Weibull distribution becomes a steeply declining curve. A manufacturer might find this effect useful in describing part failures during a burn-in period.

The mathematical constructs for the Weibull distribution are as follows:

$$f(x) = \frac{\alpha}{\beta}\left[\frac{x}{\beta}\right]^{\alpha-1} e^{-\left(\frac{x}{\beta}\right)^{\alpha}}$$

$$Mean = \beta \Gamma(1 + \alpha^{-1})$$

$$Standard\ Deviation = \beta^2 \left[\Gamma(1 + 2\alpha^{-1}) - \Gamma^2(1 + \alpha^{-1})\right]$$

$$Skewness = \frac{2\Gamma^3(1 + \beta^{-1}) - 3\Gamma(1 + \beta^{-1})\Gamma(1 + 2\beta^{-1}) + \Gamma(1 + 3\beta^{-1})}{\left[\Gamma(1 + 2\beta^{-1}) - \Gamma^2(1 + \beta^{-1})\right]^{3/2}}$$

$$Excess\ Kurtosis =$$

$$\frac{-6\Gamma^4(1 + \beta^{-1}) + 12\Gamma^2(1 + \beta^{-1})\Gamma(1 + 2\beta^{-1}) - 3\Gamma^2(1 + 2\beta^{-1}) - 4\Gamma(1 + \beta^{-1})\Gamma(1 + 3\beta^{-1}) + \Gamma(1 + 4\beta^{-1})}{\left[\Gamma(1 + 2\beta^{-1}) - \Gamma^2(1 + \beta^{-1})\right]^2}$$

Location (*L*), shape (α) and scale (β) are the distributional parameters, and Γ is the Gamma function.

Input requirements:

Scale > 0 and can be any positive value

Shape ≥ 0.05

Location can take on any value

Weibull 3 Distribution

The Weibull 3 distribution uses the same constructs as the original Weibull distribution but adds a location, or shift, parameter. The Weibull distribution starts from a minimum value of 0, whereas this Weibull 3, or shifted Weibull, distribution shifts the starting location to any other value.

Alpha, beta, and location or shift are the distributional parameters.

Input requirements:

Alpha (shape) ≥ 0.05.

Beta (central location scale) > 0 and can be any positive value.

Location can be any positive or negative value including zero.

RELATIONSHIPS AMONG PROBABILITY DISTRIBUTIONS

Figure 4A.3 illustrates the complex interrelationships among the various distributions described above. Some distributions are simply special cases of other distributions (e.g., standard-normal distribution is a special case of the normal distribution), limiting cases (e.g., the t-distribution approaches the normal distribution at the limit), modifications of others (e.g., power 3 is a modification of the power distribution by adding a location and multiplicative factor parameter), and mathematical transformations (e.g., log gamma is a logarithmic transformation of the gamma distribution). In other cases, some distributions can be obtained through a mathematical convolution of multiple identical distributions (e.g., the sum of uniform distributions converges to the normal distribution) or different distributions (e.g., the division of two different chi-square distributions approaches the F-distribution). Therefore, newer and more complex distributions can be developed using these basic building blocks. However, it is mathematically complex to create or model new distributions analytically, but, by using Monte Carlo risk simulation methods, new and unique distributions can be readily and easily created by simply adding, subtracting, multiplying, dividing, and applying any other combinations of mathematical operators among multiple simulation assumptions to generate your own unique probability distribution, without the need for complex mathematics.

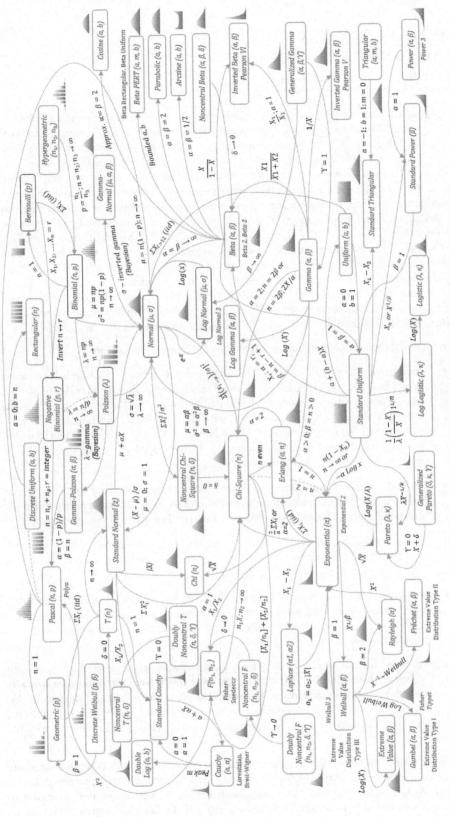

Figure 4A.3: Relationships Among Probability Distributions

APPENDIX—ROV COMPILER: PROTECT AND CONVERT EXCEL FILES INTO EXECUTABLE EXE

For the sake of completeness, this appendix illustrates the ROV Compiler software, which is extremely handy for Excel modelers. This software is meant to be used to convert Microsoft Excel 2007, 2010, and 2013 files to *extract an existing model into pure mathematical relationships and code such that the same model can be used as usual but the intellectual property of the model is protected*. You can now use Excel as a software development tool instead of as only a modeling tool. That is, suppose you are an expert in a certain industry such as pharmaceuticals, biotechnology, manufacturing, banking, insurance, aeronautics, and so forth, and further suppose that you have developed Excel models and worksheets that are appropriate for use by others in the same field. You can now use ROV Compiler to create executable EXE files from your existing Excel models, lock up the mathematical and computational logic into binary code and create extremely secure hardware-locked license protection of your file, and distribute the file like a software program. When run, the compiled file will have the exact look and feel of Excel, minus the ability of accessing critical calculation logic, plus the ability to be secured and licensed like a regular software program. There exists public domain software that will crack Excel passwords quickly and effortlessly, but such software will not work on compiled files.

By running the extracted model, several items are accomplished, namely:

- Any existing Excel 2007, 2010, 2013 files and beyond can be compiled–extracted from Excel XLS or XLSX files and turned into binary mathematical code and the file will become a self-executable EXE file that, when run, will open in Excel. The file will function exactly like an Excel file, with all of the Excel functionalities, but the end user will not have access to the calculations, functions, or logic. It will look and feel like Excel but the computations are all embedded in binary format that is encrypted and not accessible to the end user.

- All of the business intelligence and relationships are maintained but will no longer be visible to the end user, allowing the model creator to safely and securely distribute the model without losing control of any intellectual property or company secrets.

- The compiled model can be locked using an AES encryption (military-strength protection) and can only be accessible using the correct password or license key codes (with computer hardware locking algorithms).

- The compiled model cannot be changed by the end user. This feature maintains a strict quality control and prevents malicious tampering or accidental breakage of the model (e.g., equations and functions with broken links, wrong functions, and calculations, etc.).

The compiled file can also be used by third-party software applications in a Component Based Modeling environment. For instance, the end user might have his or her own software or database with predefined calculations. The compiled file is linked into and is a part of this existing proprietary system. This proprietary system simply obtains the inputs to link into the compiled file and the compiled model will perform the computations and return the required outputs.

Figure 4A.4 shows a sample screen shot of the security settings for the compiled file where you can convert your Excel file (Figure 4A.5) and enable advanced license protection that is hardware locked to the end user's computer, with some advanced encryption templates to which only you would have access. The license generated (Figure 4A.6) can only be used by the computer with the unique Hardware ID. The top of Figure 4A.7 shows the protected and compiled file, while the bottom picture shows the original file. Notice that the protected file looks and feels exactly the same as the original file, but all of the calculations, equations, computations, VBA codes, and so forth are completely protected and embedded inside compiled binary codes that cannot be cracked. Finally, if required, the executable file can be embedded into other proprietary software products and can be run in code (Figure 4A.8), without the need of ever opening up the Excel file. For more detailed information, you can watch the getting started videos on the ROV website:

www.realoptionsvaluation.com/rovcompiler.html.

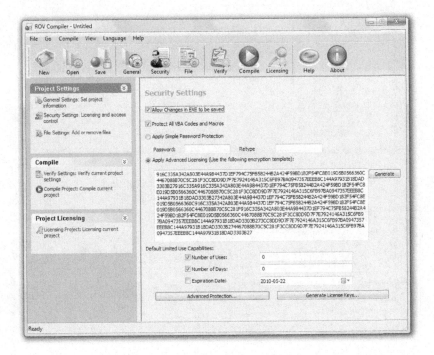

Figure 4A.4: ROV Compiler Protection

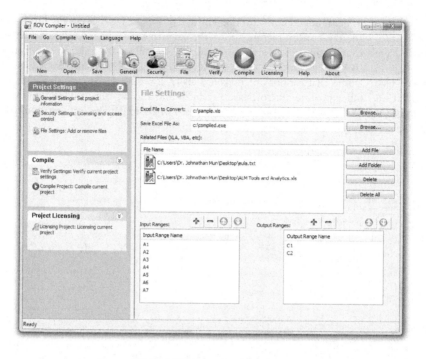

Figure 4A.5: ROV Compiler File Conversion

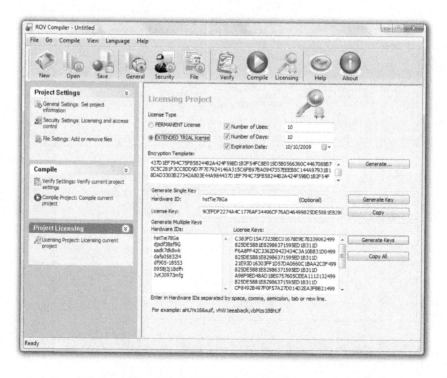

Figure 4A.6: ROV Compiler Licensing

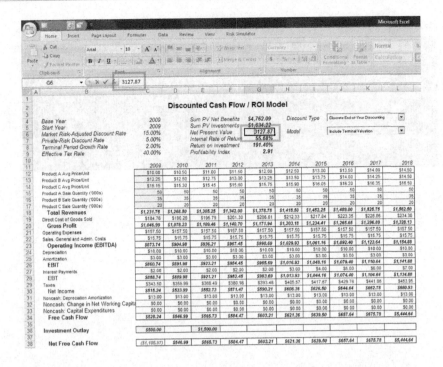

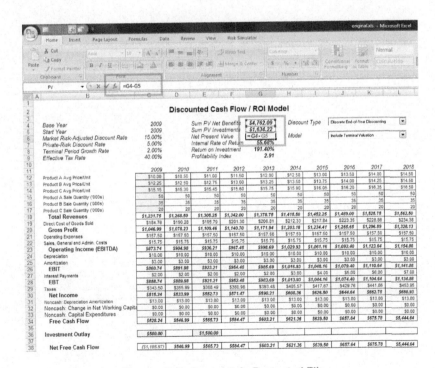

Figure 4A.7: Completely Protected File

```
C:\WINDOWS\system32\cmd.exe

D:\Johnathan\test\debug>ROVTargetEXE.exe /i "0.1,0.2,0.3,0.4" /p abcd1234
1:      0.25
2:      3.48602

D:\Johnathan\test\debug>ROVTargetEXE.exe /i "0.4,0.5,0.6,0.7" /p abcd1234
1:      0.55
2:      7.66924

D:\Johnathan\test\debug>_
```

Figure 4A.8: Console Model

APPENDIX—ROV EXTRACTOR AND EVALUATOR: RUNS EXTREME SUPER SPEED SIMULATIONS AND CONVERTS EXCEL MODELS INTO A CALCULATOR ENVIRONMENT

Yet another powerful tool is the ROV Risk Extractor and Evaluator software, which is meant to be used inside of Microsoft Excel 2010 and 2013 to extract an existing model into pure mathematical relationships and code such that the same model can be run completely outside and independent of Excel. By running the extracted model, several items are accomplished:

- All of the business intelligence and relationships are maintained but will no longer be visible to the end user, allowing the model creator to safely and securely distribute the model without losing control of any intellectual property or company secrets.

- A large model that can take a long time to run in Excel can now be run at extremely fast speeds in the lifted model. You can open ROV Extractor directly in Excel and select the specific cells to set as inputs and outputs before lifting the model (Figure 4A.9).

- The large Excel model can now be turned into a calculator-like environment (Figure 4A.10), where all the end user has to do is enter the inputs and obtain the outputs. Imagine it as akin to creating a very large Visual Basic function in Excel, but instead of a simple function with several lines of computations, this function is an entire Excel workbook with many interconnected worksheets.

- Large-scale Monte Carlo risk simulations with a large number of trials can be performed at very high speeds. Figure 4A.11 illustrates a model that was subjected to a 100,000-trial simulation and it took less than a few quick seconds to complete! If you are a large entity such as a bank or investment firm, or some large manufacturer requiring large-scale simulations to be run, this is the best platform to do so. You can develop the model in Excel, then lift the model using ROV Extractor, and run the simulations in ROV Evaluator.

- The extracted model can be locked using an AES encryption (military-strength protection) and can only be accessible using the correct password.

- Large models with many irrelevant parts are identified and, additionally, you can identify the main key inputs and outputs you wish to have modeled. For instance, in a model such as $A+B+C=D$, $B+E=F$, and if F is chosen as the key output, only B and E are relevant. Computational time for the model is decreased by identifying critical inputs, and the model can then be optimized to run even faster once the model thread is identified.

- The extracted model cannot be changed by the end user. Thus a strict quality control is maintained and malicious tampering or accidental breakage of the model (e.g., equations and functions with broken links, wrong functions and calculations, etc.) are prevented.

- The extracted file can also be used by third-party software applications in a Component Based Modeling environment. For instance, the end user might have his or her own software or database with predefined calculations. The extracted file is linked into and is a part of this existing proprietary system. This proprietary system simply obtains the inputs to link into the extracted file and the extracted model will perform the computations at high speed and return the required outputs.

For more detailed information, you can watch the getting started videos on the ROV website: www.realoptionsvaluation.com/rovextractor.html.

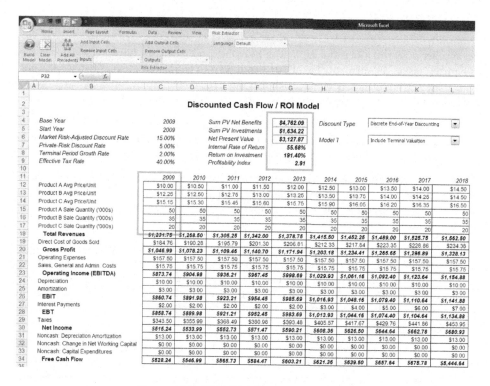

Figure 4A.9: ROV Risk Extractor in Excel

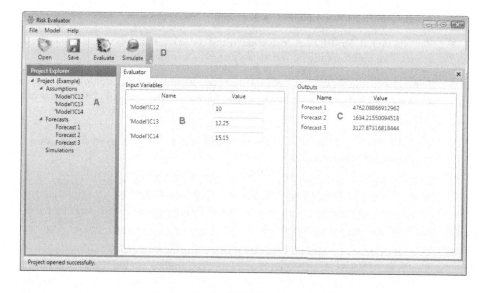

Figure 4A.10: ROV Risk Evaluator

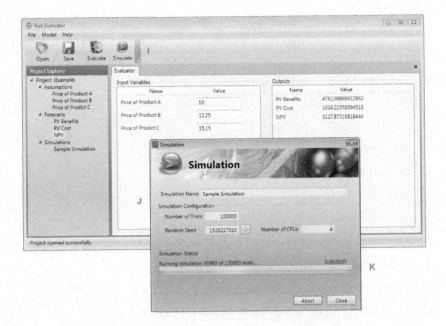

Figure 4A.11: Extreme Super Speed Simulation

EXERCISE 1: BASIC SIMULATION MODEL

This sample model illustrates how to use Risk Simulator for:

1. Running a Monte Carlo Risk Simulation

2. Using Forecast Charts

3. Interpreting the Risk Statistics

4. Setting Seed Values

5. Running Super Speed Simulation

6. Setting Run Preferences (Simulation Properties)

7. Extracting Simulation Data

8. Creating a Simulation Report and Forecast Statistics Table

9. Creating Forecast Statistics Using the RS Functions

10. Saving a Simulation Run's Forecast Charts

11. Creating New and Switching Among Simulation Profiles

12. Distributional Truncation and Multidimensional Simulation

Model Background

File Name: Basic Simulation Model.xls

Access: *Risk Simulator | Example Models | 02 Basic Simulation Model*

Prerequisites: Risk Simulator 2014 or later, Chapters 1 and 2 of *Modeling Risk*

The *Static and Dynamic Model* worksheet illustrates a very simple model with two input assumptions (revenue and cost) and an output forecast (income) as seen in Figure 4E1.A. The model on the left is a static model with single-point estimates while the model on the right is a dynamic model on which we will set Monte Carlo input assumptions and output forecasts. After running the simulation, the results can be extracted and further analyzed. In this model we can also learn to set different simulation preferences, to run a simulation, how to set seed values, and much more. To perform these exercises, you will need to have Risk Simulator version 2014 or later installed and working.

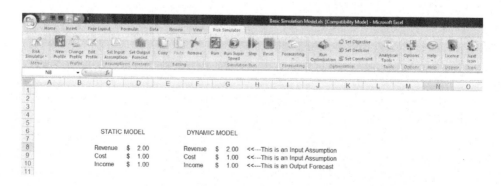

Figure 4E1.A: Basic Simulation Model

1. Running a Monte Carlo Risk Simulation

To set up and run a simulation model using Risk Simulator is as simple as 1-2-3, that is, create a new profile, set inputs and outputs, and then run. To follow along, open the example (click on *Risk Simulator | Example Models | 02 Basic Simulation Model*) and do the following:

1. Select *Risk Simulator | New Simulation Profile* (or click on the *New Profile* icon), provide it with a name (e.g., "Practice Simulation") and leave everything else as is (we later revisit some of these settings).

2. Select cell *G8* and click on *Risk Simulator | Set Input Assumption* (or click on the *Set Input Assumption* icon), then select *Triangular* distribution and set the *Min = 1.50, Most Likely = 2.00, Max = 2.25* and then hit *OK* (Figure 4E1.B).

3. Select cell *G9* and set another input assumption. This time use *Uniform* distribution with *Min = 0.85* and *Max = 1.25*.

4. Select cell *G10* and set that cell as the output forecast by clicking on *Risk Simulator | Set Output Forecast*. You can use the default name "Income" that it picked up from the model.

5. Select *Risk Simulator | Run Simulation* (or click on the *Run* icon) to start the simulation.

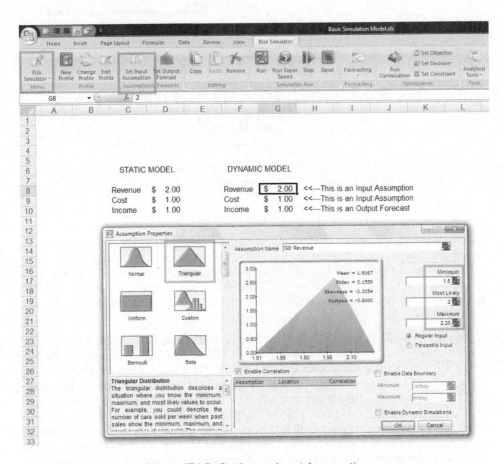

Figure 4E1.B: Setting an Input Assumption

Figure 4E1.C shows the simulation run. At the end of the simulation, click *OK*. There are a few things to notice here. The first is that the resulting model at the end of the simulation run returns the same results as the static model. That is, two dollars minus one dollar is equal to one dollar. However, what simulation does is create thousands of possible outcomes of "around two dollars" in revenue minus thousands of possible outcomes of "around one dollar" cost, resulting in the income of "around one dollar." The results are shown as a histogram, complete with the risk statistics, which we will review later in this exercise.

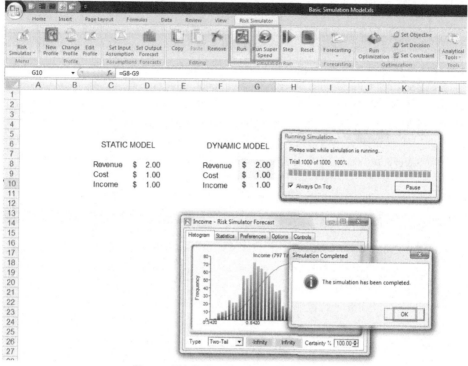

Figure 4E1.C: Running the Simulation

2. Using Forecast Charts

The forecast chart (Figure 4E1.D) is shown when the simulation is running. Once simulation is completed, the forecast chart can be used. The forecast chart has several tabs: *Histogram, Statistics, Preferences, Options,* and *Controls*. Of particular interest are the first two, the histogram and statistics tabs. For instance, the first tab shows the output forecast's probability distribution in the form of a histogram, where the specific values can be determined using the certainty boxes.

In the *Histogram* tab, select *Two-Tail*, enter *90* in the *Certainty* box, and hit *TAB* on your keyboard. The 90% confidence interval is shown (0.5269 and 1.1712). This result means that there is a 5% chance that the income will fall below $0.5269, and another 5% chance that it will be above $1.1712. Alternatively, you can select *Left-Tail* ≤ and enter *1.0* on the input box, hit *TAB*, and see that the left-tail certainty is 76.30%, indicating that there is a 76.30% chance that the income will fall at or below $1.0 (or that there is a 23.70% chance that income will exceed $1.0). Note that your results will *not* be exactly the same as what we illustrate here due to the theoretical fact that we are running a simulation of random numbers. Please do not be concerned at this point, and continue on to the next exercises for more details on how to get the same simulation results going forward.

3. Interpreting the Risk Statistics

The *Statistics* tab illustrates the statistical results of the forecast variable. Refer to Chapter 2 for more details on how to interpret and use these risk profile statistics in risk analysis and risk management. Note that your results will not be exactly the same as those illustrated here because a simulation (random number generation) was run, and by definition, the results will not be exactly the same every time. However, if a seed value is set (see next section), the results will be identical in every single run.

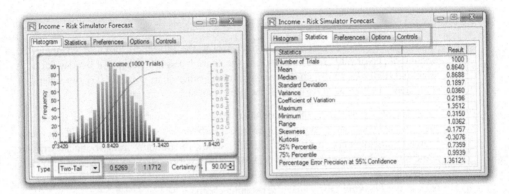

Figure 4E1.D: Simulation Results and Forecast Charts

Optional Exercises

For additional exercise, view the *Preferences, Options* and *Controls* tabs and play with some of the settings. Specifically, try the following:

Preferences:

1. Try selecting and deselecting the *Always Show Windows on Top* option. Navigate around different applications that might be open and notice the behavior of the forecast chart.

2. Run a simulation with at least three forecasts and select *Semitransparent When Inactive* on all three forecast charts (e.g., use your own model or in cell *G11*, set it to be *=G10*, in *G12*, set it also to be *=G10*, set these two cells *G11* and *G12* as output forecasts, and then run a simulation). Then, minimize all other software applications, leaving these three forecast charts visible, overlay one chart on top of another, then click anywhere on the desktop to deactivate the forecast charts. Notice how you can now compare different forecast charts.

3. Change the *Histogram Resolution* to different levels and view the *Histogram* tab to see how the shape changes.

4. Also, if you have multiple forecast charts up and running and you forget to reset the previous simulation (resetting the simulation will clear all the forecast charts and simulated data from temporary memory, allowing you to rerun another simulation), you can *Minimize All Charts, Close All Charts,* or *Copy* a specific chart (you can set up the chart any way you like and then copy the chart to clipboard and paste it into another software such as Microsoft Word or Microsoft PowerPoint) from this tab. Click on the *Excel* button to generate live editable probability histogram charts in Excel.

Options:

1. Play with the *Data Filter* by showing only limited data such as only 2 standard deviations from the mean, or a specific range of values. Go back to the *Histogram* tab and notice the change in the chart; go back to the *Statistics* tab and notice that the computed risk statistics are now based on the truncated data and not the entire dataset.

2. You can also select the *Statistic* to show, or the number of *Decimals* to show in the *Histogram* chart and *Statistics* tabs. This option may come in handy if you wish to obtain higher precision of the results (more decimals) or show fewer decimals for large value results.

Controls:

1. From this tab, you can control and change how the histogram looks by changing the orientation, color, 2D and 3D aspects of the chart, background, type of overlay curve to show (CDF versus PDF), chart types, and many other chart controls. Try out several of these items and see what happens to the histogram chart each time.

2. You can also perform a distributional fitting of the forecast results and obtain the theoretical versus empirical moments of the distribution (see the *Distributional Data Fitting* exercise in the next chapter for more details on how distribution fitting routines work), or show the fitted distribution's theoretical curve on top of the empirical histogram (first click on *Fit*, then select either *Continuous or Discrete* from the *Chart Overlay* droplist, and then go back to the *Histogram* tab to view the resulting charts).

3. Finally, you can change the *Chart Type* (Bar, Cylinder, Pyramid, and so forth), *Chart Title*, *Min* and *Max* values of the chart axes, and the *Decimals* to show on the chart. Try out several of these items and see what happens to the histogram chart each time.

If you are using Risk Simulator 2014 or later, you can click on the *Global View* link on the top right corner of the forecast chart to view all the aforementioned tabs and functionalities in a single view, or click on the *Normal View* link to return to the tabbed view described above.

4. Setting Seed Values

1. Reset the simulation by selecting *Risk Simulator | Reset Simulation*.

2. Select *Risk Simulator | Edit Simulation Profile* (Figure 4E1.E).

3. Select the *check box* for *Specify Random Number Sequence (Seed)* and enter in a seed value (e.g., *999*) and click *OK* (Figure 4E1.E).

4. Run the simulation and verify that the results are the same as the results obtained in Figure 4E1.E. In fact, run the simulation a few more times, and each time verify that the simulated statistical results are identical each time.

Note that the random number sequence or seed number has to be a positive integer value. Running the same model with the same assumptions and forecasts with an identical seed value and same number of trials will always yield the same results. The number of simulation trials to run can be set in the same run properties box (Figure 4E1.E). Setting a seed value is important especially when you wish to obtain the same values in each simulation run. Say, for example, that you need the live model to return the same results as a printed report during a live presentation. If the results in your live demonstration are slightly off compared to the printed results, questions may arise as to their validity. By having a seed value, the results are guaranteed to always be the same.

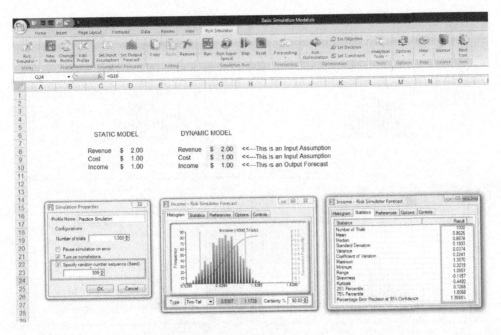

Figure 4E1.E: Using a Seed Value

Let us now revisit the confidence interval analysis after you have run another simulation with the seed value. Figure 4E1.F illustrates the results of these manipulations:

1. Select *Two-Tail,* enter a *Certainty* of *90,* and hit *TAB* on the keyboard. You will obtain the two-tailed 90% confidence interval of 0.5307 and 1.1739, which means that 90% of the time, the income level will be between these two values, with a 5% chance it will be below 0.5307 and 5% it will be above 1.1739.

2. To verify the 5% result above, select *Left-Tail <,* enter a *Certainty* of *5,* and hit *TAB.* You will obtain the value of 0.5307, indicating that there is a 5% chance you will receive an income less than 0.5307.

3. Next, select *Left-Tail ≤,* enter in the value *1,* and hit *TAB.* This time, instead of providing a probability to receive a value, you provide a value to receive the probability. In this case, it states that you have a 74.30% chance that your income will be less than or equal to the 1.000 value that your static single-point model had predicted. In fact, in Figure 4E1.E, you see that the mean or average income value is 0.8626. In other words, the *expected value* (mean) is not the same as the *value expected* (in your original single-point estimate static model).

4. Select *Right-Tail >,* enter in *1,* and hit *TAB.* Here you can see the complement of the Left-Tail ≤ value. In other words, the value you receive, 25.70%, indicates the probability you will make more than your target of 1.000, and if you take 100% minus 25.70%, you obtain 74.30%, the Left-Tail ≤ value. When doing this exercise, make sure you select the correct inequality signs (less than, less than or equal to, greater than, greater than or equal to).

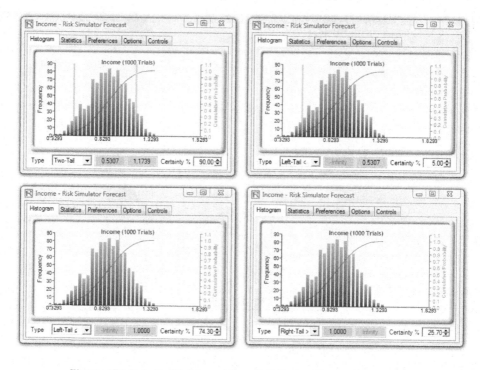

Figure 4E1.F: Left-, Right- and Two-Tail Probabilities (Simulation Results with Seed Values)

5. Running Super Speed Simulation

1. Reset the simulation by selecting *Risk Simulator | Reset Simulation*.

2. Select *Risk Simulator | Run Super Speed Simulation* (Figure 4E1.C).

Notice how much faster the super speed simulation runs. In fact, for practice, *Reset the Simulation, Edit Simulation Profile* and change the *Number of Trials* to *100,000*, and *Run Super Speed*. It should only take a few seconds to run. However, be aware that super speed simulation will not run if the model has errors, VBA (visual basic for applications), or links to external data sources or applications. In such situations, you will be notified and the regular speed simulation will be run instead. Regular speed simulations are always able to run even with errors, VBA, or external links.

6. Setting Run Preferences (Simulation Properties)

The run preferences or *Simulation Properties* dialog box that came up when you first created a new profile or edited the current profile (Figure 4E1.E), allows you to specify the *Number of Trials* to run in a particular simulation (by default it will be 1,000 trials). In theory, the higher the number of trials, the more precise the results (try rerunning the simulation again and this time, keep an eye on the *Percentage Error Precision at 95% Confidence* value in the *Statistics* tab, which should decrease as you increase the number of trials). Refer to Chapter 2 for more details on interpreting these risk statistics, and on error precision confidence, and for how to use them in making decisions. In addition, *Pause Simulation on Error* can be set up so that the simulation will stop running if a computational error in Excel is encountered (e.g., #NUM or #ERROR), which is a good tool for ascertaining if your model is set up correctly. If this option is not checked, any errors will be ignored and only the valid results will be used in the forecast charts. Correlations can also be specified between pairs of input assumptions, and if *Turn on Correlations* is selected, these specified correlations will be imputed in the simulation. See the *Correlation Risk Effects* exercise later in this chapter for how to set up correlations and to understand how correlations affect the outcome of your results, the theory of risk diversification, portfolio effects on distributional moments, etc.

7. Extracting Simulation Data

The simulation's assumptions and forecast data are stored in memory until the simulation is reset or when Excel is closed. If required, these raw data can be extracted into a separate Excel sheet. To extract the data, simply:

1. *Edit Simulation Profile*, reset the *Number of Trials* to 1,000 and then *Run* the simulation.

2. After the simulation is completed, select *Risk Simulator | Analytical Tools | Extract Data* (you can also access this function by clicking on the *Next* icon repeatedly until you get to the tools icon ribbon, and then click on the *Data Extraction* icon as shown in Figure 4E1.G).

3. Choose the relevant assumptions or forecasts to extract, select *New Excel Worksheet* as the extraction format and click *OK.*

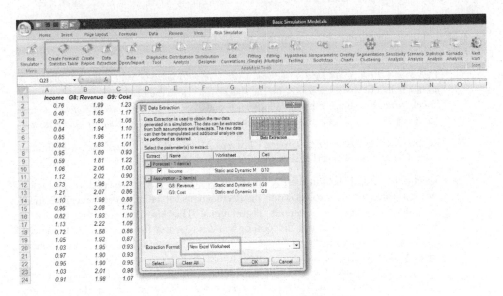

Figure 4E1.G: Extracting Simulation Data

Optional Exercise

1. The 1,000 simulated revenue and cost values will be extracted, as well as the computed forecast income variable (Figure 4E1.G). Note that if you had not first run a simulation, the extracted data report would be empty, as there are no values to extract. Try clicking on the *Select...* button a few times to see what happens.

2. Using the extracted data, apply Excel's functions to compute all of the risk statistics, for example, the mean, median, standard deviation, and so forth, and compare to make sure the results are identical to those obtained in Risk Simulator's forecast statistics tab. Hint: Use the following Excel functions for this exercise: AVERAGE(), STDEV(), VAR(), SKEW(), KURT(), MIN(), MAX().

8. Creating a Simulation Report and Forecast Statistics Table

The simulation's input assumptions and output forecasts, as well as the detailed risk statistics, can also be extracted after a simulation has been run. Assuming the simulation has already been run, simply:

1. Select *Risk Simulator | Analytical Tools | Create Report* (you can also access this function by clicking on the *Next* icon repeatedly until you get to the tools icon ribbon, and then click on the *Create Report* icon as shown in Figure 4E1.G). Spend some time reviewing the report that is generated.

2. Select *Risk Simulator | Analytical Tools | Create Forecast Statistics Table* (you can also access this function by clicking on the *Next* icon repeatedly until you get to the tools icon ribbon, and then click on the *Create Forecast Statistics Table* icon as shown in Figure 4E1.G). Here you can select the forecasts you wish to show. In this simple example, we only have one forecast, but in larger models, you can select multiple forecasts at once. We suggest you try creating this statistics table with the other exercises.

9. Creating Forecast Statistics Using the RS Functions

You can also obtain the forecast statistics not in a report format, but in a specific cell by using the Risk Simulator function call. For example, do the following:

1. Save the example file and then exit Excel and click on *Start | Programs | Real Options Valuation | Risk Simulator | Analytical Tools | Install Functions*. When the installation is complete in a few short seconds, hit the spacebar to close the black console pad and start Excel. Note: If you are running Windows 8 or 10, click on the *Windows button + C* and *Search* for the *Install Functions* app, right-click on the app and choose *Run As Administrator*.

2. Reopen the example at *Risk Simulator | Example Models | 02 Basic Simulation Model* and run a simulation in super speed *Risk Simulator | Run Super Speed Simulation*.

3. Select cell *G12* and click on the *FX* (insert function) icon in Excel or click on and select the *ALL* category and scroll down to the RS functions list. Here you see several set input assumption functions for various distributions. The last item on the RS list is RSForecastStatistic. Select this function or you can type this function directly in the cell. For instance, type in *=RSForecastStatistic(G10, "Average")* where G10 is the forecast output cell and "Average" is the statistic you wish to obtain. Remember to keep the quotes ("") and you can replace the Average parameter with any of the following: *Average, CoefficientofVariation, Median, Maximum, StandardDeviation, Minimum, Variance, Range, Skewness, Percentile75, Kurtosis, Certainty1.0, Percentile99.9*. In fact, you can use "PercentileXX.XX" and "CertaintyXX.XX" and just replace the X with your own number for a left-tail < value. The Percentile parameter means you enter the percentage and receive the value X, whereas for the Certainty parameter, you enter the value X and get the left-tail percentage.

4. Just for practice, reset the simulation, run a regular speed simulation, and notice that the statistics will keep changing as you run the simulation, and that it stops at the final result when the simulation completes. You can now use this function call as part of your model. One quick note: If you run a super speed simulation, the function call will not be updated automatically. You will have to select the cell with the function after the simulation is run, hit F2 on the keyboard, and then hit *Enter* to update the function calculation.

10. Saving a Simulation Run's Forecast Charts

Suppose you run a large model and want to save the forecast charts. You can do so in Risk Simulator by saving the results as a *Risk Sim* file format. Saving the forecast charts allows you to open the results without having to rerun the simulation, thereby saving you some time.

1. *Run* a simulation as usual.

2. Select *Risk Simulator | Analytical Tools | Data Extraction/Export* (you can also access this function by clicking on the *Next* icon repeatedly until you get to the tools icon ribbon, and then click on the *Data Extraction* icon). Here you select the Extraction Format as *Risk Simulator Data (Risk Sim)* file (Figure 4E1.H). Save the file to the desired location. You can now save and exit Excel.

3. Open Excel and select *Risk Simulator | Analytical Tools | Data Open/Import* (you can also access this function by clicking on the *Next* icon repeatedly until you get to the tools icon ribbon, and click on the *Data Open/Import* icon). Select the Risk Sim file you saved previously and the forecast charts will now reappear.

11. Creating New and Switching Among Simulation Profiles

The same model can have multiple Risk Simulator profiles. That is, different users of the same model can, in fact, create their own simulation input assumptions, forecasts, run preferences, and so forth. All these preferences are stored in separate simulation profiles and each profile can be run independently. This is a powerful feature that allows multiple users to run the same model their own way, or for the same user to run the model under different simulation conditions, thereby allowing for scenario analysis on Monte Carlo simulation. To create different profiles and switch among different profiles, simply:

1. Create several new profiles by clicking on *Risk Simulator | New Simulation Profile* and provide each new profile with a unique name.

2. Add the relevant assumptions and forecasts, or change the run preferences as desired in each simulation profile.

3. Switch among different profiles by clicking on *Risk Simulator | Change Active Simulation*.

Note that you can create as many profiles as you wish but each profile needs to have its own unique name. Also, you can select an existing profile and click on *Duplicate* (Figure 4E1.I) to duplicate all the input assumptions and output forecasts that are in this profile, which means you do not have to replicate all these manually. You can then change to this new profile and make any modifications as required. From this user interface, you can also *Delete* any unwanted profiles (but note that you need to have at least one profile active in the model, which means that you can delete any profile you choose but you cannot delete all of them as one profile must be left in the model). You can also click on a profile, click again on the name of the profile, and *rename* the profile as required.

Finally, as you save the Excel file, you will also save these profiles in the same Excel file. Profiles are stored in a special hidden segment of the Excel file and will be available to you as you open the Excel file in the future. For further practice, try saving the Excel file and then reopening the file again; notice that all your profiles and settings are still available. Just bear in mind that if you have multiple profiles, the last profile used will be the profile that is activated by default when the Excel file is opened the next time. Depending on what you are trying to do, you may need to remember to *Change the Profile* to the one you wish to use before you start running any simulations.

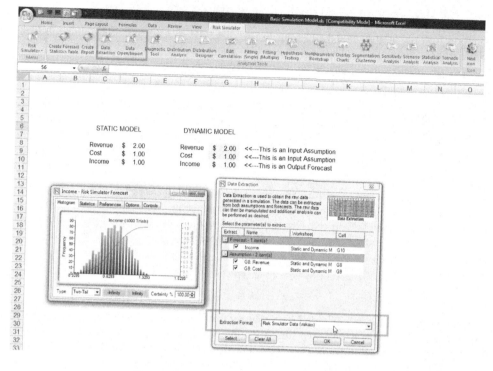

Figure 4E1.H: Extracting to a Risk Sim file

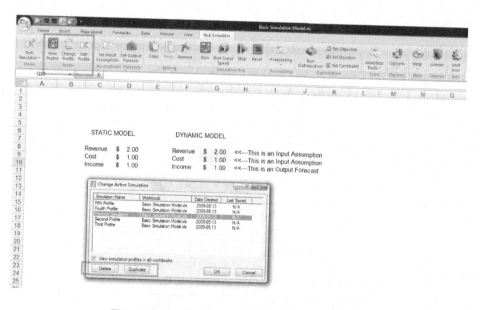

Figure 4E1.I: Multiple Profiles in Risk Simulator

12. Distributional Truncation, Alternate Parameters, and Multidimensional Simulation

Distributional truncation or *data boundaries* are typically not used by the average analyst but exist for truncating the distributional assumptions. For instance, if a normal distribution is selected, the theoretical boundaries are between negative infinity and positive infinity. However, in practice, the simulated variable exists only within some smaller range, and this range can then be entered to truncate the distribution appropriately. Not considering truncation is a major error users commit, especially when using the triangular distribution. The triangular distribution is very simple and intuitive. As a matter of fact, it is probably the most widely used distribution in Risk Simulator, apart from the normal and uniform distributions. Simplistically, the triangular distribution looks at the minimum value, the most probable value, and the maximum value. These three inputs are often confused with the worst-case, nominal-case, and best-case scenarios. This assumption is indeed incorrect.

In fact, a worst-case scenario can be translated as a highly unlikely condition that will still occur given a percentage of the time. For instance, one can model the economy as high, average, and low, analogous to the worst-case, nominal-case, and best-case scenarios. Thus, logic would dictate that the worst-case scenario might have, say, a 15 percent chance of occurrence, the nominal-case a 50 percent chance of occurrence, and a 35 percent chance that a best-case scenario will occur. This approach is what is meant by using a best-, nominal-, and worst-case scenario analysis. However, compare that to the triangular distribution, where the minimum and maximum cases will almost never occur, with a probability of occurrence set at zero!

For instance, see Figure 4E1.J, where the worst-, nominal-, and best-case scenarios are set as 5, 10, and 15, respectively. Note that at the extreme values, the probability of 5 or 15 occurring is virtually zero, as the areas under the curve (the measure of probability) of these extreme points are zero. In other words, 5 and 15 will almost never occur. Compare that to the economic scenario where these extreme values have either a 15 percent or 35 percent chance of occurrence. Instead, distributional truncation should be considered here. The same applies to any other distribution. Figure 4E1.K illustrates a truncated normal distribution where the extreme values do not extend to both positive and negative infinities, but are truncated at 7 and 13.

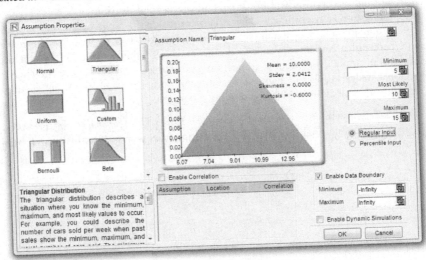

Figure 4E1.J: Sample Triangular Distribution

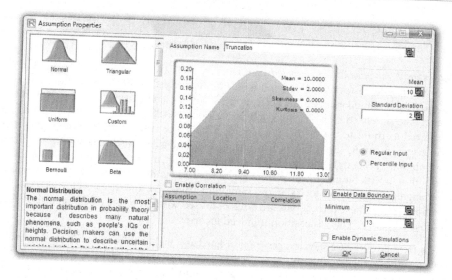

Figure 4E1.K: Truncating a Distribution

Another critical activity is looking at *Alternate Parameters*, that is, to look at the same distribution but through a different set of parameters. For instance, if a *normal distribution* is used in simulating market share, and the mean is set at *55* percent with a standard deviation of *45* percent, one should be extremely worried. Using Risk Simulator's *Percentile Input* selection in the *Set Input Assumption* user interface, the 10th and 90th percentiles indicate values of –2.67 percent and 112.67 percent (Figure 4E1.L). Clearly these values cannot exist under actual conditions. How can a product have –2.67 or 112.67 percent of the market share? The alternate-parameters function is a very powerful tool to use in conditions such as these. Almost always, the first thing that should be done is to use alternate parameters to ascertain the logical upper and lower values of an input parameter. So, even if you obtained the 55% and 45% through distributional fitting (which by the way, is correct, because the fit was probably very strong in the center of the normal distribution), but by virtue of a theoretical fitting routine, the entire normal distribution will be fitted, and the normal distribution's tails extend from negative infinity to positive infinity, which is clearly outside the range of the norm for market share. So, using the alternate parameters will quickly allow you to visualize the tenth and ninetieth percentiles, and then you can decide to change the distribution or still use the distribution but apply distributional truncation as discussed previously. See the exercise on distributional analysis tools in Chapter 5 for obtaining other percentiles for any distribution, other than the default 10% and 90% as described here.

Alternatively, use the *Risk Simulator | Analytical Tools | Distributional Fitting (Percentiles)* tool to obtain the distributional parameters by entering the worst-, nominal-, and best-case scenarios.

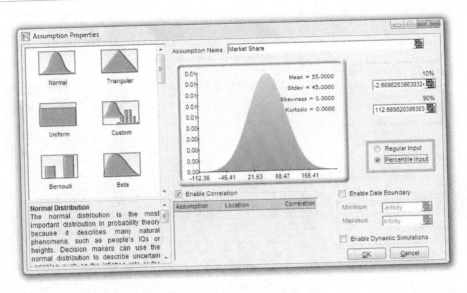

Figure 4E1.L: Alternate Parameters

Finally, Figures 4E1.M and 4E1.N illustrate how *multidimensional simulation* or *dynamic simulation* works. Suppose you have a model like the one shown, and further suppose that you have an input Triangular distribution assumption in cell G5, and you used the link icon to link its input parameters to other cells (H5, I5 and J5 for the minimum, most likely, and maximum values) as shown in Figure 4E1.M. Typically, this is a basic assumption and you are all done. However, what if the minimum, most likely, and maximum inputs are themselves uncertain? If that is the case then you can set an input assumption for these inputs (cells H5, I5, J5). In other words, if you have an assumption that is linked to other cells, and these other cells themselves are assumptions, you have just created a 2-layer simulation (of course you can add additional layers where these input cells are again linked to other cells that are simulated and so forth, creating a multidimensional simulation model). If you do this, remember to select the *Enable Dynamic Simulation* checkbox (Figure 4E1.M) on the assumption that links to other assumptions. So, if you ran a 1,000-trial simulation, instead of having a single Triangular distribution and picking random numbers from this single distribution, there are actually 1,000 triangular distributions, where at each trial, there will be new parameters for this Triangular distribution, and a random number is selected from this distribution, and then on the next trial, you repeat the entire process. This multidimensional simulation approach allows you to additionally simulate uncertain input parameters into the overall simulation model.

There is one little word of caution: Do not overdo the multidimensional layers, because suppose you are using a Triangular distribution with Min = A, Most Likely = B, and Max = C. And suppose A is a uniform distribution with Min = D and Max = E. If C is also another uniform distribution with Min − F and Max − G, all is well as long as E and F do not cross each other. Put another way, if you accidentally set E > F, then there will be times in a random simulation where the random value E is higher than F. This result means that A > C in the original distribution, which violates the input requirements, causing the simulation stop and creating an error (i.e., the maximum value is less than the minimum value in the Triangular distribution; this cannot work and the simulation stops). So, if you are confused by distributional truncation, it might be best to avoid using it.

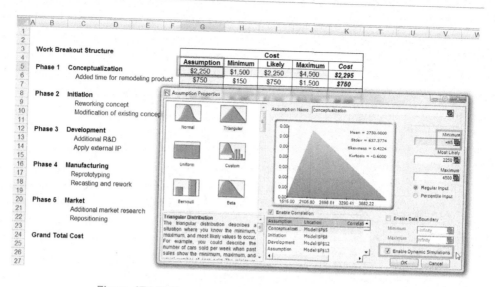

Figure 4E1.M: Dynamic or Multidimensional Simulation

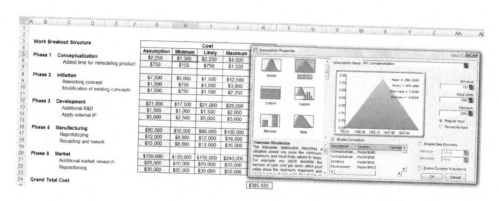

Figure 4E1.N: Input Parameter as an Assumption

EXERCISE 2: CORRELATION EFFECTS MODEL

This sample model illustrates how to use Risk Simulator for:

1. Setting Up a Simulation's Input Assumptions and Output Forecasts

2. Copying, Pasting, and Deleting Simulation Assumptions and Forecasts

3. Running Correlated Simulations, Comparing Results between Correlated and Uncorrelated Models

4. Extracting and Manually Computing and Verifying the Assumptions' Correlations

5. Pearson's Product Moment Linear Correlation and Spearman's Nonlinear Rank Correlation

Model Background

File Name: Correlation Risk Effects Model.xls

Access: *Risk Simulator | Example Models | 04 Correlation Risk Effects Model*

Prerequisites: Risk Simulator 2014 or later, Completed Basic Simulation Model Exercise, Chapter 4 of *Modeling Risk* (Section: Correlations and Precision Control)

   This model illustrates the effects of correlated simulation versus uncorrelated simulation. That is, whether a pair of simulated assumptions is not correlated, positively correlated, or negatively correlated, the results can sometimes be very different. In addition, the simulated assumptions' raw data are extracted after the simulation and manual computations of their pairwise correlations are performed. The results indicate that the input correlations hold after the simulation.

1. Setting Up a Simulation's Input Assumptions and Output Forecasts

Open the model *Risk Simulator | Example Models | 04 Correlation Risk Effects Model*. Go to the *Correlation Model* worksheet (Figure 4E2.A). Follow the instructions shown on the following pages to set up and run this model.

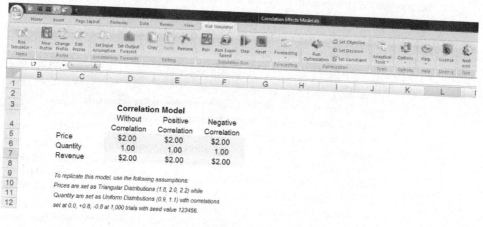

Figure 4E2.A: Correlation Model

2. Copying, Pasting, and Deleting Simulation Assumptions and Forecasts

We will replicate the assumptions and forecasts per the instructions on the worksheet by setting the input assumptions for price and quantity, and forecast outputs for revenue. When setting up the input assumptions, you can practice by setting up one assumption at a time, or set up a single assumption and then use the Risk Simulator *Copy* and *Paste* technique to replicate the assumptions across multiple cells at once. Follow these steps:

Procedures:

1. Create a new profile: *Risk Simulator | New Profile* (or use the New Profile icon) and give it a name.

2. Select cell *D5* for the price without correlation. Click on *Risk Simulator | Set Input Assumption* (or use the Set Input Assumption icon), select the *Triangular* distribution, and set the parameters as 1.8, 2.0, and 2.2 as instructed on the worksheet (Figure 4E2.B). Click *OK* when done.

3. Select cell *D5* again, after the assumption has been set, and click on *Risk Simulator | Copy Parameter* (or use the *Copy* icon in the Risk Simulator toolbar). Make sure you <u>do not</u> use Excel's copy or *Ctrl+C* or right-click *Copy*, because using Excel copy will only copy the cell contents, color, equations, and font. Only by using Risk Simulator's *Copy* can you copy the input assumption and its parameters.

4. Select cells *E5* and *F5* and click on *Risk Simulator | Paste Parameter* (or use the Paste icon in the Risk Simulator toolbar). Again, make sure you do not hit Enter and do not use Excel's paste function or *Ctrl+V*, as this will only paste the Excel cell contents and not the input assumptions (Figure 4E2.C).

5. Select cell *D6* and repeat the process above, this time using a *Uniform* distribution with 0.9 and 1.1 as the input parameters. *Copy/Paste* the parameters for cells *E6* and *F6*.

6. Select cell *D7* and set it as an output forecast by clicking on *Risk Simulator | Set Output Forecast* (or use the Set Output Forecast icon), and link the forecast name to cell *D4*. Then, select cell *D7* again, copy the parameter, and select cells *E7* and *F7* to paste the parameters using Risk Simulator *Copy* and *Paste*. Later, remember to review the tip presented in the next section for an important reminder on copying and pasting.

7. Next, set the correlations among the variables. There are two ways to set correlations: You can set correlations one pair of assumptions at a time or set them in a correlation matrix all at once. We will explore both approaches as follows:

   a. As cell E5 is supposed to be correlated to cell E6, select cell E5 and click on *Risk Simulator | Set Input Assumption* (or use the Set Input Assumption icon) once again. This time, look at the *pairwise correlation section* (Figure 4E2.D). You may click and drag to enlarge the user interface form as well as to increase the width of the three columns for assumptions, location, and correlation. Find the input assumption for E6, enter the correlation of *0.8* and hit *Enter* on the keyboard (Figure 4E2.D). Remember to hit *Enter* on the keyboard when you are done entering the correlation, otherwise the software will think that you are still typing in the input box. Click *OK* when done. For the sake of completeness, select cell E6 and again set an input assumption, and notice that by setting the assumption in cell E5 previously and correlating it to E6, cell E6 automatically correlates back to E5. Repeat the correlation process for cells F5 and F6.

b. Click on *Risk Simulator | Analytical Tools | Edit Correlations* and you will be provided with a correlation tool (Figure 4E2.E). Select the *Show Cell Name* checkbox and you can select the variables you wish to correlate or click on *Select All* to show all of them. In the correlation matrix section, enter the correlation value (correlations have to be between –1 and 1, and zeroes are allowed, of course). Notice that the correlation matrix shown is a full square matrix and the upper triangle mirrors the lower triangle. So, all you need to do is enter the correlation on either the upper or lower triangle and hit *Enter* on the keyboard. The value will be updated in both the upper and lower triangles. Click *OK* when done. Also, note that the user interface allows you to *Paste* in a correlation matrix. This tool comes in handy if you wish the correlation matrix to be visible in Excel. When you have an existing matrix in Excel, you can copy the matrix and then paste it here (making sure the matrix you copied is square and the upper and lower triangles have identical pairwise correlation values). You are now done with setting correlations. For the sake of completeness, you can select any one of the input assumptions and set assumption again to make sure that the correlations are set up correctly (Figure 4E2.D).

8. Run the simulation by clicking on *Risk Simulator | Run Simulation* (or use the Run Simulation icon) and interpret the results. Proceed to the next section for an interpretation of the results. You can also try running *Super Speed Simulation* for faster results.

TIP: For the copy and paste in Risk Simulator, this quick tip will come in handy when you are setting inputs and outputs on larger models. When you select a cell and use the Risk Simulator *Copy* function, it copies everything into Windows clipboard, including the cell's value, equation, function, color, font, and size, as well as Risk Simulator assumptions, forecasts, or decision variables. Then, as you apply the Risk Simulator *Paste* function, you have two options. The first option is to apply the Risk Simulator *Paste* directly, and *without* the cell's values, color, equation, function, font, and so forth. The second option is to apply the Risk Simulator *Paste* as well as including all cell values, color, font, equation, functions, and parameters will be pasted, akin to the example above.

TIP: You can also click on the *View Correlation Charts* tool to view sample representations of how different correlation levels look when variables are plotted on a scatter chart, and you can also use this tool to compute correlations of your raw data.

TIP: You can select multiple cells with assumptions and forecasts, and use Risk Simulator *Copy* and *Paste* functionalities.

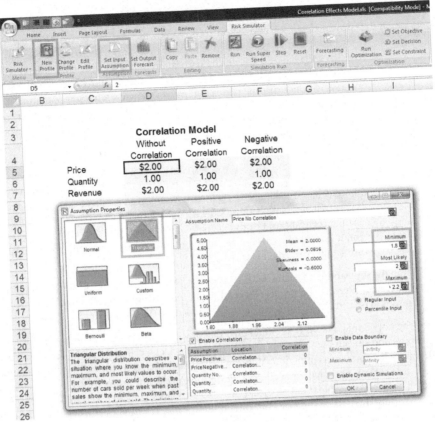

Figure 4E2.B: Setting an Input Assumption

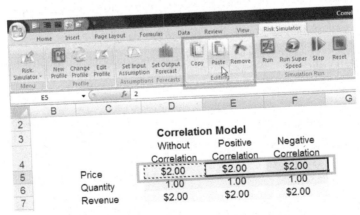

Figure 4E2.C: Simulation Parameter Copy and Paste

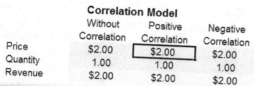

	Correlation Model		
	Without Correlation	Positive Correlation	Negative Correlation
Price	$2.00	$2.00	$2.00
Quantity	1.00	1.00	1.00
Revenue	$2.00	$2.00	$2.00

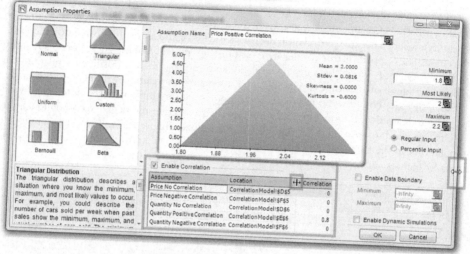

Figure 4E2.D: Pairwise Correlations (Manual)

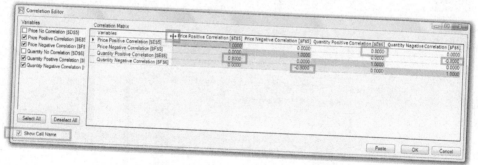

Figure 4E2.E: Pairwise Correlations (Matrix)

3. Running Correlated Simulations, Comparing Results of Correlated and Uncorrelated Models

The resulting simulation statistics indicate that the negatively correlated variables provide a tighter or smaller standard deviation or overall risk level on the model. This relationship exists because negative correlations provide a diversification effect on the variables and, hence, tend to make the standard deviation slightly smaller. Thus, we need to make sure to input correlations when there indeed are correlations between variables. Otherwise this interacting effect will not be accounted for in the simulation.

The positive correlation model has a larger standard deviation because a positive correlation tends to make both variables travel in the same direction, making the extreme ends wider and, hence, increases the overall risk. Therefore, the model without any correlations will have a standard deviation between the positive and negative correlation models.

Notice that the expected value or mean does not change much. In fact, if sufficient simulation trials are run, the theoretical and empirical values of the mean remain the same. The first moment (central tendency or expected value) does not change with correlations. Only the second moment (spread or risk and uncertainty) will change with correlations (Figure 4E2.F).

Note that this characteristic exists only in simple models with a positive relationship. That is, a Price × Quantity model is considered a "positive" relationship model (as is Price + Quantity), where a negative correlation decreases the range and a positive correlation increases the range. The opposite is true for negative relationship models. For instance, Price / Quantity or Price − Quantity would be a negative relationship model, where a positive correlation will reduce the range of the forecast variable, and a negative correlation will increase the range. Finally, for more complex models (e.g., larger models with multiple variables interacting with positive and negative relationships and sometimes with positive and negative correlations), the results are hard to predict and cannot be determined theoretically. Only by running a simulation can the true results of the range and outcomes be determined. In such a scenario, tornado analysis and sensitivity analysis would be more appropriate.

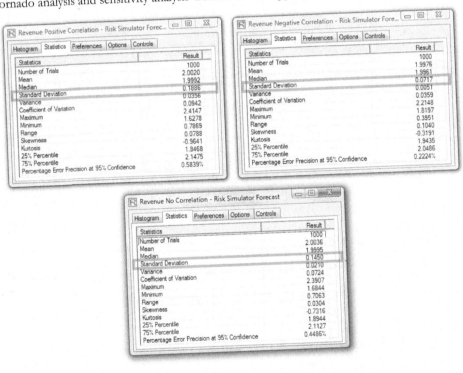

Figure 4E2.F: Risk Effects on Distributional Moments

4. Extracting and Manually Computing and Verifying the Assumptions' Correlations

For additional exercise, run the simulation and then extract the simulated data. Then run a correlation computation and see if the correlations are similar to what you have entered into Risk Simulator.

Procedures:

1. Run the simulation: *Risk Simulator | Run Simulation* (or use the Run Simulation icon). Click *OK* when simulation is done.

2. Extract the data: *Risk Simulator | Analytical Tools | Data Extraction and Export* (or use the Data Extraction icon under the Analytical Tools ribbon). Select *New Excel Worksheet* and you can click the *Select All…* button repeatedly to select only the forecasts, only the assumptions, or all forecasts and assumptions at once (Figure 4E2.G). Let's just select the checkboxes for *All* forecasts and assumptions and click *OK* to extract the data.

3. Go to the extracted data worksheet and use Excel's CORREL function to compute the pairwise correlations of the simulated data. For example, Figure 4E2.H illustrates that the computed correlations are +0.8 and –0.8 for the positive and negative correlation pairs, plus the uncorrelated pair is close to zero (the correlation is never exactly equal to zero because of the randomness effect, and 0.03 is statistically significantly identical to zero in this case). In other words, the correlations we inputted originally are maintained in the simulation model.

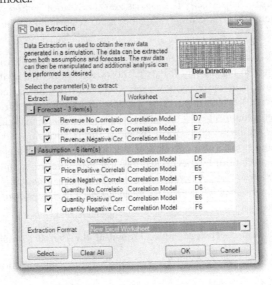

Figure 4E2.G: Data Extraction

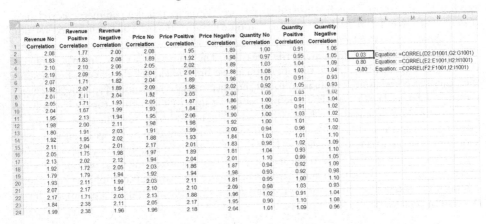

Revenue No Correlation	Revenue Positive Correlation	Revenue Negative Correlation	Price No Correlation	Price Positive Correlation	Price Negative Correlation	Quantity No Correlation	Quantity Positive Correlation	Quantity Negative Correlation		
2.08	1.77	2.00	2.08	1.95	1.89	1.00	0.91	1.06	0.03	Equation: =CORREL(D2:D1001,G2:G1001)
1.83	1.83	2.08	1.89	1.92	1.98	0.97	0.95	1.05	0.80	Equation: =CORREL(E2:E1001,H2:H1001)
2.10	2.10	2.06	2.05	2.02	1.89	1.03	1.04	1.09	-0.80	Equation: =CORREL(F2:F1001,I2:I1001)
2.19	2.09	1.95	2.04	2.04	1.88	1.08	1.03	1.04		
2.07	1.71	1.82	2.04	1.89	1.96	1.01	0.91	0.93		
1.92	2.07	1.89	2.09	1.98	2.02	0.92	1.05	0.93		
2.01	2.11	2.04	1.82	2.06	2.00	1.05	1.03	1.02		
2.05	1.71	1.93	2.05	1.87	1.86	1.00	0.91	1.04		
2.04	1.67	1.99	1.93	1.84	1.96	1.06	0.91	1.02		
1.95	2.13	1.94	1.95	2.06	1.90	1.00	1.03	1.02		
1.98	2.00	2.11	1.98	1.98	1.92	1.00	1.01	1.10		
1.80	1.91	2.03	1.91	1.99	2.00	0.94	0.96	1.02		
1.92	1.95	2.02	1.88	1.93	1.84	1.03	1.01	1.10		
2.11	2.04	2.01	2.17	2.01	1.83	0.98	1.02	1.09		
2.05	1.75	1.98	1.97	1.89	1.81	1.04	0.93	1.10		
2.13	2.02	2.12	1.94	2.04	2.01	1.10	0.99	1.05		
1.92	1.72	1.94	2.03	1.86	1.87	0.94	0.92	1.09		
1.79	1.79	1.94	1.92	1.94	1.98	0.93	0.92	0.98		
1.93	2.11	1.99	2.03	2.11	1.81	0.95	1.00	1.10		
2.07	2.17	1.94	2.10	2.10	2.09	0.98	1.03	0.93		
2.17	1.71	2.03	2.13	1.88	1.96	1.02	0.91	1.04		
1.84	2.38	2.11	2.05	2.17	1.95	0.90	1.10	1.08		
1.99	2.38	1.96	1.96	2.18	2.04	1.01	1.09	0.96		

Figure 4E2.H: Correlation of Simulated Values

5. Pearson's Product Moment Linear Correlation and Spearman's Nonlinear Rank Correlation

Typically, when we use the term *correlation*, we usually mean a linear correlation. And, of course, correlations can take on any value between −1 and +1, inclusive, which means that the correlation coefficient has a sign (direction) and magnitude (strength). The problem arises when there is nonlinearity and we use linear correlations. Figure 4E2.I illustrates a few scatter charts with a pairwise X and Y variables (e.g., hours of study and school grades). If we draw an imaginary best-fitting line in the scatter diagram, we can see the approximate correlation (we will show a computation of correlation in a moment, but for now, let's just visualize). Part A shows a relatively high positive correlation coefficient (R) of about 0.7 as an increase in X means an increase in Y, so there is a positive slope and therefore a positive correlation. Part B shows an even stronger negative correlation (negatively sloped, an increase of X means a decrease of Y and vice versa). It has slightly higher magnitude because the dots are closer to the line. In fact, when the dots are exactly on the line, as in Part D, the correlation is +1 (if positively sloped) or −1 (if negatively sloped), indicating a perfect correlation. Part C shows a situation where the curve is perfectly flat, or has zero correlation, where, regardless of the X value, Y remains unchanged, indicating that there is no relationship. These are all very basic and good.

The problem arises when there are nonlinear relationships (typically the case in many real-life situations) as shown in Figure 4E2.J. Part E shows an exponential relationship between X and Y. If we use a nonlinear correlation, we get +0.9, but if we use a linear correlation, it is much lower at 0.6 (Part F), which means that there is information that is not picked up by the linear correlation. The situation gets a lot worse when we have a sinusoidal relationship, as in Parts G and H. The nonlinear correlation picks up the relationship very nicely with a 0.9 correlation coefficient; using a linear correlation, the best-fitting line is literally a flat horizontal line, indicating zero correlation. However, just looking at the picture would tell you that there is a relationship. *So, we must therefore distinguish between linear and nonlinear correlations, because as we have seen in this exercise, correlation affects risk, and we are dealing with risk analysis!*

The linear correlation coefficient is also known as the *Pearson's product moment correlation coefficient*. It is computed by

$$R = \frac{\sum_{i=1}^{n}(X_i - \bar{X})(Y_i - \bar{Y})}{\sqrt{\sum_{i=1}^{n}(X_i - \bar{X})^2 (Y_i - \bar{Y})^2}}$$

and assumes that the underlying distribution is normal or near-normal such as the t-distribution. Therefore this is a parametric correlation. You can use Excel's *CORREL* function to compute this effortlessly. The nonlinear correlation is the *Spearman's nonparametric rank-based correlation*, which does not assume any underlying distribution, making it a nonparametric measure. The approach to Spearman's nonlinear correlation is very simple. Using the original data we first "linearize" the data and then apply the Pearson's correlation computation to get the Spearman's correlation. Typically, whenever there is nonlinear data, we can linearize it by either using a *LOG* function (or equivalently, an *LN* or natural log function) or a *RANK* function. The table shown next illustrates this effect. The original value is clearly nonlinear (it is 10^X where x is from 0 to 5). However, if you apply a log function, the data becomes linear (1, 2, 3, 4, 5) or when you apply ranks, the rank (either high to low or low to high) is also linear. Once we have linearized the data, we can apply the linear Pearson's correlation. To summarize, Spearman's nonparametric nonlinear correlation coefficient is obtained by first ranking the data and then applying Pearson's parametric linear correlation coefficient.

Value	LOG (VALUE)	RANK (VALUE)
1	0	1
10	1	2
100	2	3
1000	3	4
10000	4	5
100000	5	6

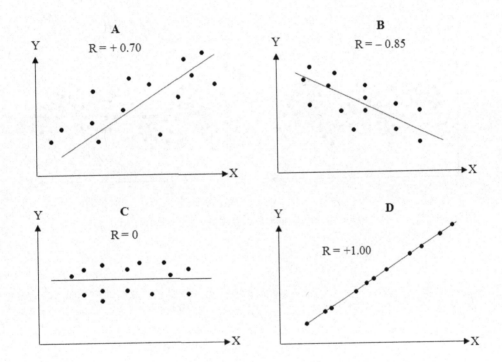

Figure 4E2.I: Linear Correlation of Simulated Values

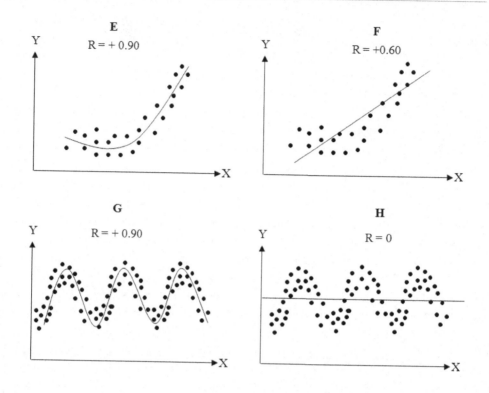

Figure 4E2.J: Nonlinear Correlation of Simulated Values

CHAPTER 5 –
PANDORA'S TOOLBOX

This chapter deals with the Risk Simulator software's analytical tools. These analytical tools are discussed through example applications of the Risk Simulator software, complete with step-by-step illustrations. These tools are very valuable to analysts working in the realm of risk analysis. The applicability of each tool is discussed in detail in this chapter. All of the example files used in this chapter are found by starting Excel, going to the *Risk Simulator | Example Models* menu. There are also multiple highly recommended step-by-step exercises at the end of this chapter that will provide detailed hands-on practice of the tools and techniques presented in this chapter, with more detailed interpretation of the results, as well as special tips and tricks.

TORNADO AND SENSITIVITY TOOLS IN SIMULATION

Theory

Tornado analysis is a powerful analytical tool that captures the static impacts of each variable on the outcome of the model; that is, the tool automatically perturbs each variable in the model a preset amount, captures the fluctuation on the model's forecast or final result, and lists the resulting perturbations ranked from the most significant to the least. Figures 5.1 through 5.6 illustrate the application of a tornado analysis. For instance, Figure 5.1 is a sample discounted cash flow model where the input assumptions in the model are shown. The question is, what are the critical success drivers that affect the model's output the most? That is, what really drives the net present value of $96.63 or which input variable impacts this value the most?

To follow along click on *Risk Simulator | Example Models | 22 Tornado and Sensitivity Charts (Linear)* to access the example model. Figure 5.2 shows this sample model where cell *G6*, containing the net present value, is chosen as the target result to be analyzed. The target cell's precedents in the model are used in creating the tornado chart. Precedents are all the input and intermediate variables that affect the outcome of the model. For instance, if the model consists of $A = B + C$, and where $C = D + E$, then B, D, and E are the precedents for A (C is not a precedent as it is only an intermediate calculated value). Figure 5.2 also shows the testing range of each precedent variable used to estimate the target result. If the precedent variables are simple inputs, then the testing range will be a simple perturbation based on the range chosen (e.g., the default is ±10%). Each precedent variable can be perturbed at different percentages if required. A wider range is important as it is better able to test extreme values rather than smaller perturbations around the expected values. In certain circumstances, extreme values may have a larger, smaller, or unbalanced impact (e.g., nonlinearities may occur where increasing or decreasing economies of scale and scope creep in for larger or smaller values of a variable) and only a wider range will capture this nonlinear impact.

Discounted Cash Flow Model

Base Year	2015	Sum PV Net Benefits		**$1,896.63**
Market Risk-Adjusted Discount Rate	15.00%	Sum PV Investments		**$1,800.00**
Private-Risk Discount Rate	5.00%	Net Present Value		**$96.63**
Annualized Sales Growth Rate	2.00%	Internal Rate of Return		18.80%
Price Erosion Rate	5.00%	Return on Investment		5.37%
Effective Tax Rate	40.00%			

	2015	2016	2017	2018	2019
Prod A Avg Price	$10.00	$9.50	$9.03	$8.57	$8.15
Prod B Avg Price	$12.25	$11.64	$11.06	$10.50	$9.98
Prod C Avg Price	$15.15	$14.39	$13.67	$12.99	$12.34
Prod A Quantity	50.00	51.00	52.02	53.06	54.12
Prod B Quantity	35.00	35.70	36.41	37.14	37.89
Prod C Quantity	20.00	20.40	20.81	21.22	21.65
Total Revenues	**$1,231.75**	**$1,193.57**	**$1,156.57**	**$1,120.71**	**$1,085.97**
Cost of Goods Sold	$184.76	$179.03	$173.48	$168.11	$162.90
Gross Profit	**$1,046.99**	**$1,014.53**	**$983.08**	**$952.60**	**$923.07**
Operating Expenses	$157.50	$160.65	$163.86	$167.14	$170.48
SG&A Costs	$15.75	$16.07	$16.39	$16.71	$17.05
Operating Income (EBITDA)	**$873.74**	**$837.82**	**$802.83**	**$768.75**	**$735.54**
Depreciation	$10.00	$10.00	$10.00	$10.00	$10.00
Amortization	$3.00	$3.00	$3.00	$3.00	$3.00
EBIT	**$860.74**	**$824.82**	**$789.83**	**$755.75**	**$722.54**
Interest Payments	$2.00	$2.00	$2.00	$2.00	$2.00
EBT	**$858.74**	**$822.82**	**$787.83**	**$753.75**	**$720.54**
Taxes	$343.50	$329.13	$315.13	$301.50	$288.22
Net Income	**$515.24**	**$493.69**	**$472.70**	**$452.25**	**$432.33**
Depreciation	$13.00	$13.00	$13.00	$13.00	$13.00
Change in Net Working Capital	$0.00	$0.00	$0.00	$0.00	$0.00
Capital Expenditures	$0.00	$0.00	$0.00	$0.00	$0.00
Free Cash Flow	**$528.24**	**$506.69**	**$485.70**	**$465.25**	**$445.33**
Investments	$1,800.00				

Financial Analysis

Present Value of Free Cash Flow	$528.24	$440.60	$367.26	$305.91	$254.62
Present Value of Investment Outlay	$1,800.00	$0.00	$0.00	$0.00	$0.00
Net Cash Flows	($1,271.76)	$506.69	$485.70	$465.25	$445.33

Figure 5.1: A Typical Discounted Cash Flow Analysis

Procedure

Use the following steps to create a tornado analysis:

- Select the single output cell (i.e., a cell with a function or equation) in an Excel model (e.g., cell *G6* is selected in our example).

- Select *Risk Simulator | Analytical Tools | Tornado Analysis.*

- Review the precedents and rename them as appropriate (renaming the precedents to shorter names allows a more visually pleasing tornado and spider chart) and click *OK*. Alternatively, click on *Use Cell Address* to apply cell locations as the variable names.

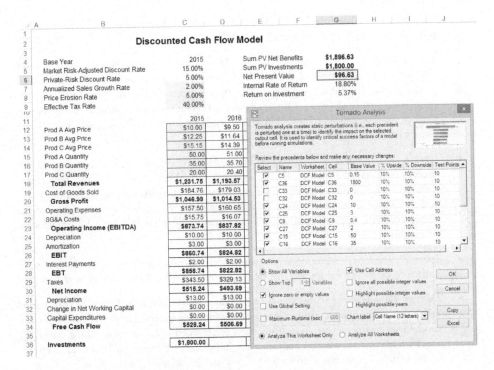

Figure 5.2: Running Tornado Analysis

Tips and Additional Notes on Running a Tornado Analysis

Here are some tips on running tornado analysis and further details on the options available in the tornado analysis user interface (Figure 5.2):

- Tornado analysis should never be run just once. It is meant as a model diagnostic tool, which means that it should ideally be run several times on the same model. For instance, in a large model, tornado can be run the first time using all of the default settings and all precedents should be shown (select *Show All Variables*). The result may be a large report and long (and potentially unsightly) tornado charts. Nonetheless, this analysis provides a great starting point to determine how many of the precedents are considered critical success factors. For example, the tornado chart may show that the first 5 variables have high impact on the output, while the remaining 200 variables have little to no impact, in which case, a second tornado analysis is run showing fewer variables (e.g., select the *Show Top 10 Variables* if the first 5 are critical, thereby creating a satisfactory report and tornado chart that shows a contrast between the key factors and less critical factors. You should never show a tornado chart with only the key variables without showing some less critical variables as a contrast to their effects on the output. Finally, the default testing points can be increased from ±10% of the parameter to some larger value to test for nonlinearities (the spider chart will show nonlinear lines and tornado charts will be skewed to one side if the precedent effects are nonlinear).

- *Use Cell Address* is always a good idea if your model is large, allowing you to identify the location (worksheet name and cell address) of a precedent cell. If this option is not selected, the software will apply its own fuzzy logic in an attempt to determine the name of each precedent variable (sometimes the names might end up being confusing in a large model with repeated variables or the names might be too long, possibly making the tornado chart unsightly).

- The *Analyze This Worksheet* and *Analyze All Worksheets* options allow you to control whether the precedents should only be part of the current worksheet or include all worksheets in the same workbook. This option comes in handy when you are only attempting to analyze an output based on values in the current sheet versus performing a global search of all linked precedents across multiple worksheets in the same workbook.

- *Use Global Setting* is useful when you have a large model and you wish to test all the precedents at say, ±50% instead of the default 10%. Instead of having to change each precedent's test values one at a time, you can select this option, change one setting, and *click somewhere else* in the user interface to change the entire list of the precedents. Deselecting this option will allow you control the changing of test points one precedent at a time.

- *Ignore Zero or Empty Values* is an option turned on by default where precedent cells with zero or empty values will not be run in the tornado. This is the typical setting.

- *Highlight Possible Integer Values* is an option that quickly identifies all possible precedent cells that currently have integer inputs. This function is sometimes important if your model uses switches (e.g., functions such as IF a cell is 1, then something happens, and IF a cell has a 0 value, something else happens, or integers such as 1, 2, 3, and so forth, which you do not wish to test). For instance, ±10% of a flag switch value of 1 will return a test value of 0.9 and 1.1, both of which are irrelevant and incorrect input values in the model, and Excel may interpret the function as an error. This option, when selected, will quickly highlight potential problem areas for tornado analysis. You can determine which precedents to turn on or off manually, or you can use the *Ignore Possible Integer Values* to turn all of them off simultaneously.

- The *Excel* button creates a live and editable chart in an Excel worksheet.

Results Interpretation

Figure 5.3 shows the resulting tornado analysis report, which indicates that capital investment has the largest impact on net present value (NPV), followed by tax rate, average sale price and quantity demanded of the product lines, and so forth. The report contains four distinct elements:

- In Figure 5.4, we see that by changing one of the inputs, e.g., Investment, by −10%, originally from $1,800 (*Base Case Value*) now to $1,620 (i.e., the *Input Downside*), the NPV base case of $96.63 increases to $276.63 (this is called the *Output Downside* as NPV is the output, and this result is when the input is changed to its lower value or −10% downside). Conversely, when Investment goes up +10% from $1,800 (*Base Case Value*) to $1,980 (i.e., the *Input Upside*), the NPV goes down to −$83.37 (this is called the *Output Upside* as NPV is the output, and this result occurs when the input is changed to its upper value or +10% upside). Clearly, this is a negative relationship (higher investment means lower NPV, and vice versa). The total net swing from − $83.37 to $276.63 is $360.00, which is termed the *Effective Range*. Then, the investment amount is changed back to its original value of $1,800 prior to proceeding onto the next input variable. In Figure 5.4, the next input tested was Tax Rate. In other words, one variable is tested at a time by perturbing a preset amount. Finally, the results in Figure 5.4 is generated by sorting the precedent variables using the *Effective Range* from highest to lowest. Finally, you can see that Investment and Tax Rate are negatively related to NPV, whereas Prices and Quantities of products A, B, C are positively related to NPV (i.e., the higher the price or quantity sold, the higher the project's NPV).

- The spider chart (Figure 5.5) illustrates these effects graphically. The y-axis is the NPV target value while the x-axis depicts the percentage change on each of the precedent value (the central point is the base case value at $96.63 at 0% change from the base value of each precedent). Positively sloped lines indicate a positive relationship or effect while negatively sloped lines indicate a negative relationship (e.g., investment is negatively sloped, which means that the higher the investment level, the lower the NPV). The absolute value of the slope indicates the magnitude of the effect computed as the percentage change in the result given a percentage change in the precedent (a steep line indicates a higher impact on the NPV y-axis given a change in the precedent x-axis).

- Figure 5.6's tornado chart plots the results in Figure 5.4's sensitivity table. As previously explained, Investment has the largest impact on NPV and has an inverse relationship with NPV. Therefore, in the tornado chart, the first horizontal bar is Investment (each bar represents a precedent variable—see the precedent variable names on the y-axis), and the values $1,980 and $1,620 at the end of the bars represent the input's upside and downside values. The x-axis is the output variable (NPV). Therefore, we can see that Investment is negatively related to NPV (the bar's right side has a lower input value whereas the x-axis on the right side represents a higher NPV). In Risk Simulator, the chart is in color and we can see that the right side of this Investment bar is red (lower end of the input) and green on the left side of the bar (upper end of the input). As additional explanation, the opposite is true for Price of Product A (third bar in the chart), where $11 (input upside) is on the right (the Risk Simulator report's chart will show the right part of the bar in green), indicating a higher NPV, and hence, a positive relationship between Price of Product A (input) and NPV (output). The left side of this bar would be red (input downside at $9), and on the left where NPV is a lower value. To recap, green bars on the right indicate that the precedent variable is positively related to the output, and red bars on the right indicate a negative relationship between the precedent input and resulting output variables.

Notes

Remember that tornado analysis is a *static* sensitivity analysis applied on each input variable in the model—that is, each variable is perturbed individually and the resulting effects are tabulated. This makes tornado analysis a key component to execute before running a simulation. One of the very first steps in risk analysis is where the most important impact drivers in the model are captured and identified. The next step is to identify which of these important impact drivers are uncertain. These uncertain impact drivers are the critical success drivers of a project, where the results of the model depend on these critical success drivers. These variables are the ones that should be simulated. Do not waste time simulating variables that are neither uncertain nor have little impact on the results. Tornado charts assist in identifying these critical success drivers quickly and easily. Following this example, it might be that price and quantity should be simulated, assuming that the required investment and effective tax rate are both known in advance and unchanging.

Tornado and Spider Charts

| Precedent Cell | Base Value: 96.626 | | | Input Changes | | |
	Output Downside	Output Upside	Effective Range	Input Downside	Input Upside	Base Case Value
Investment	$276.63	($83.37)	360.00	$1,620.00	$1,980.00	$1,800.00
Tax Rate	$219.73	($26.47)	246.20	36.00%	44.00%	40.00%
A Price	$3.43	$189.83	186.40	$9.00	$11.00	$10.00
B Price	$16.71	$176.55	159.84	$11.03	$13.48	$12.25
A Quantity	$23.18	$170.07	146.90	45.00	55.00	50.00
B Quantity	$30.53	$162.72	132.19	31.50	38.50	35.00
C Price	$40.15	$153.11	112.96	$13.64	$16.67	$15.15
C Quantity	$48.05	$145.20	97.16	18.00	22.00	20.00
Discount Rate	$138.24	$57.03	81.21	13.50%	16.50%	15.00%
Price Erosion	$116.80	$76.64	40.16	4.50%	5.50%	5.00%
Sales Growth	$90.59	$102.69	12.10	1.80%	2.20%	2.00%
Depreciation	$95.08	$98.17	3.08	$9.00	$11.00	$10.00
Interest	$97.09	$96.16	0.93	$1.80	$2.20	$2.00
Amortization	$96.16	$97.09	0.93	$2.70	$3.30	$3.00
CapEx	$96.63	$96.63	0.00	$0.00	$0.00	$0.00
Working Capital	$96.63	$96.63	0.00	$0.00	$0.00	$0.00

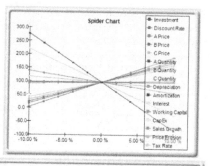

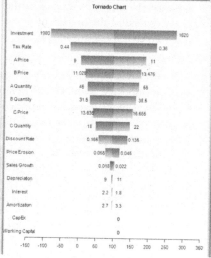

Figure 5.3: Tornado Analysis Report

| Precedent Cell | Base Value: 96.626 | | | Input Changes | | |
	Output Downside	Output Upside	Effective Range	Input Downside	Input Upside	Base Case Value
Investment	$276.63	($83.37)	360.00	$1,620.00	$1,980.00	$1,800.00
Tax Rate	$219.73	($26.47)	246.20	36.00%	44.00%	40.00%
A Price	$3.43	$189.83	186.40	$9.00	$11.00	$10.00
B Price	$16.71	$176.55	159.84	$11.03	$13.48	$12.25
A Quantity	$23.18	$170.07	146.90	45.00	55.00	50.00
B Quantity	$30.53	$162.72	132.19	31.50	38.50	35.00
C Price	$40.15	$153.11	112.96	$13.64	$16.67	$15.15
C Quantity	$48.05	$145.20	97.16	18.00	22.00	20.00
Discount Rate	$138.24	$57.03	81.21	13.50%	16.50%	15.00%
Price Erosion	$116.80	$76.64	40.16	4.50%	5.50%	5.00%
Sales Growth	$90.59	$102.69	12.10	1.80%	2.20%	2.00%
Depreciation	$95.08	$98.17	3.08	$9.00	$11.00	$10.00
Interest	$97.09	$96.16	0.93	$1.80	$2.20	$2.00
Amortization	$96.16	$97.09	0.93	$2.70	$3.30	$3.00
CapEx	$96.63	$96.63	0.00	$0.00	$0.00	$0.00
Working Capital	$96.63	$96.63	0.00	$0.00	$0.00	$0.00

Figure 5.4: Sensitivity Table

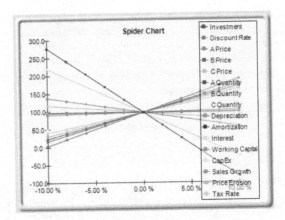

Figure 5.5: Spider Chart

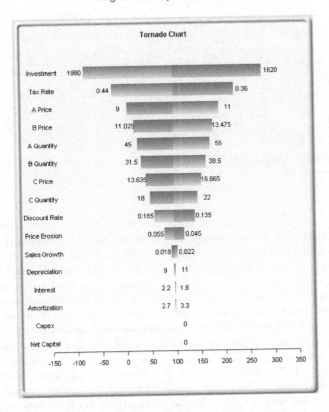

Figure 5.6: Tornado Chart

Although the tornado chart is easier to read, the spider chart is important to determine if there are any nonlinearities in the model. For instance, Figure 5.7 shows another spider chart where nonlinearities are fairly evident (the lines on the graph are not straight but curved). The example model used is *Risk Simulator | Example Models | 22 Tornado and Sensitivity Charts (Nonlinear)*, which applies the Black–Scholes option pricing model. Such nonlinearities cannot be ascertained from a tornado chart as readily, and may be important information in the model or provide decision makers important insight into the model's dynamics. For instance, in this Black–Scholes model, the fact that stock price and strike price are nonlinearly related to the option value is important to know. This characteristic implies that option value will not increase or decrease proportionally to the changes in stock or strike price, and that there might be some interactions between these two prices as well as other variables. As another example, an engineering model depicting nonlinearities might indicate that a particular part or component, when subjected to a high enough force or tension, will break. Clearly, it is important to understand such nonlinearities.

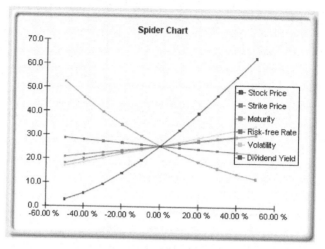

Figure 5.7: Nonlinear Spider Chart

SENSITIVITY ANALYSIS

Theory

A related feature is sensitivity analysis. While tornado analysis (tornado charts and spider charts) applies static perturbations *before* a simulation run, sensitivity analysis applies dynamic perturbations created *after* the simulation run. Tornado and spider charts are the results of static perturbations, meaning that each precedent or assumption variable is perturbed a preset amount one at a time, and the fluctuations in the results are tabulated. In contrast, sensitivity charts are the results of dynamic perturbations in the sense that multiple assumptions are perturbed simultaneously and their interactions in the model and correlations among variables are captured in the fluctuations of the results. Tornado charts therefore identify which variables drive the results the most and hence are suitable for simulation, whereas sensitivity charts identify the impact on the results when multiple interacting variables are simulated together in the model. This effect is clearly illustrated in Figure 5.8. Notice that the ranking of critical success drivers are similar to the tornado chart in the previous examples. However, if correlations are added between the assumptions, Figure 5.9 shows a very different picture. Notice for instance, price erosion had little impact on NPV but when some of the input assumptions are correlated, the interaction that exists between these correlated variables makes price erosion have more impact. Note that tornado analysis cannot capture these correlated dynamic relationships. Only after a simulation is run will such relationships become evident in a sensitivity analysis. A tornado chart's pre-simulation critical success factors will therefore sometimes be different from a sensitivity chart's post-simulation critical success factor. The post-simulation critical success factors should be the ones that are of interest as these more readily capture the model precedents' interactions.

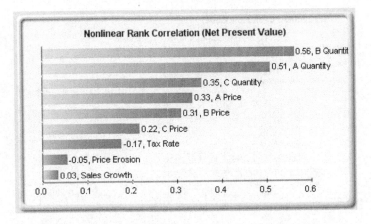

Figure 5.8: Sensitivity Chart Without Correlations

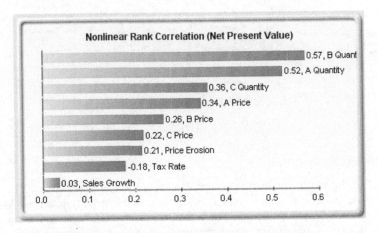

Figure 5.9: Sensitivity Chart With Correlations

Procedure

Use the following steps to create a sensitivity analysis:

- Open or create a model, define assumptions and forecasts, and run the simulation––the example here uses the *Risk Simulator | Example Models | 22 Tornado and Sensitivity Charts (Linear)* file.

- Select *Risk Simulator | Analytical Tools | Sensitivity Analysis*.

- Select the forecast of choice to analyze and click *OK* (Figure 5.10).

Note that sensitivity analysis cannot be run unless assumptions and forecasts have been defined and a simulation has been run.

Discounted Cash Flow Model

	2015				
Base Year	2015		Sum PV Net Benefits	$1,896.63	
Market Risk-Adjusted Discount Rate	15.00%		Sum PV Investments	$1,800.00	
Private-Risk Discount Rate	5.00%		Net Present Value	$96.63	
Annualized Sales Growth Rate	2.00%		Internal Rate of Return	18.80%	
Price Erosion Rate	5.00%		Return on Investment	5.37%	
Effective Tax Rate	40.00%				

	2015	2016	2017	2018	
Prod A Avg Price	$10.00	$9.50	$9.03	$8.57	
Prod B Avg Price	$12.25	$11.64	$11.06	$10.50	
Prod C Avg Price	$15.15	$14.39	$13.67	$12.99	
Prod A Quantity	50.00	51.00	52.02	53.06	
Prod B Quantity	35.00	35.70	36.41	37.14	
Prod C Quantity	20.00	20.40	20.81	21.22	
Total Revenues	**$1,231.75**	**$1,193.57**	**$1,156.57**	**$1,120.71**	
Cost of Goods Sold				$168.11	
Gross Profit				$952.60	
Operating Expenses				$167.14	
SG&A Costs				$16.71	
Operating Income (EBITD				$768.75	
Depreciation				$10.00	
Amortization				$3.00	
EBIT				$755.75	
Interest Payments				$2.00	
EBT				$753.75	
Taxes				$301.50	
Net Income				$452.25	
Depreciation				$13.00	
Change in Net Working Capita				$0.00	$0.00
Capital Expenditures	$0.00	$0.00	$0.00	$0.00	$0.00
Free Cash Flow	**$528.24**	**$506.69**	**$485.70**	**$465.25**	**$445.33**

Investments	$1,800.00	

Figure 5.10: Running Sensitivity Analysis

Results Interpretation

The results of the sensitivity analysis comprise a report and two key charts. The first is a nonlinear rank correlation chart (Figure 5.11) that ranks from highest to lowest the assumption-forecast correlation pairs. These correlations are nonlinear and nonparametric, making them free of any distributional requirements (i.e., an assumption with a Weibull distribution can be compared to another with a beta distribution). The results from this chart are fairly similar to that of the tornado analysis seen previously (of course, without the capital investment value, which we decided was a known value and hence was not simulated), with one special exception. Tax rate was relegated to a much lower position in the sensitivity analysis chart (Figure 5.11) as compared to the tornado chart (Figure 5.6). This is because by itself, tax rate will have a significant impact but once the other variables are interacting in the model, it appears that tax rate has less of a dominant effect (this is because tax rate has a smaller distribution as historical tax rates tend not to fluctuate too much, and also because tax rate is a straight percentage value of the income before taxes, where other precedent variables have a larger effect on NPV). This example proves that performing sensitivity analysis after a simulation run is important to ascertain if there are any interactions in the model and if the effects of certain variables still hold. The second chart (Figure 5.12) illustrates the percent variation explained; that is, of the fluctuations in the forecast, how much of the variation can be explained by each of the assumptions after accounting for all the interactions among variables? Notice that the sum of all variations explained is usually close to 100% (sometimes other elements impact the model but they cannot be captured here directly), and if correlations exist, the sum may sometimes exceed 100% (due to the interaction effects that are cumulative). Briefly, think of Figure 5.11 as nonlinear rank correlations (R) of each simulation input assumption to the output forecast, where each bar is a simulation input assumption. And Figure 5.12 as the R-square or coefficient of determination (0%–100%) showing the percent variation explained by each input simulation assumption on the output forecast variable.

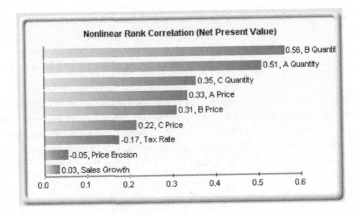

Figure 5.11: Rank Correlation Chart

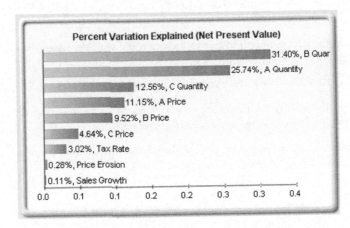

Figure 5.12: Contribution to Variance Chart

Notes

Tornado analysis is performed before a simulation run while sensitivity analysis is performed after a simulation run. Spider charts in tornado analysis can consider nonlinearities while rank correlation charts in sensitivity analysis can account for nonlinear and distributional-free conditions.

DISTRIBUTIONAL FITTING: SINGLE VARIABLE AND MULTIPLE VARIABLES

Theory

Another powerful simulation tool is distributional fitting; that is, how does an analyst or engineer determine which distribution to use for a particular input variable? What are the relevant distributional parameters? If no historical data exist, then the analyst must make assumptions about the variables in question. One approach is to use the Delphi method, where a group of experts are tasked with estimating the behavior of each variable. For instance, a group of mechanical engineers can be tasked with evaluating the extreme possibilities of a spring coil's diameter through rigorous experimentation or guesstimates. These values can be used as the variable's input parameters (e.g., uniform distribution with extreme values between 0.5 and 1.2). When testing is not possible (e.g., market share and revenue growth rate), management can still make estimates of potential outcomes and provide the best-case, most-likely case, and worst-case scenarios, whereupon a triangular or custom distribution can be created.

However, if reliable historical data are available, distributional fitting can be accomplished. Assuming that historical patterns hold and that history tends to repeat itself, then historical data can be used to find the best-fitting distribution with their relevant parameters to better define the variables to be simulated. Figures 5.13 through 5.15 illustrate a distributional-fitting example. The following illustration uses the *Data Fitting* file in the examples folder.

Procedure

Use the following steps to perform a distributional fitting model:

- Open a spreadsheet with existing data for fitting (e.g., use the *Risk Simulator | Example Models | 06 Data Fitting*).

- Select the data you wish to fit not including the variable name (data should be in a single column with multiple rows).

- Select *Risk Simulator | Analytical Tools | Distributional Fitting (Single-Variable)*.

- Select the specific distributions you wish to fit to or keep the default where all distributions are selected and click *OK* (Figure 5.13).

- Review the results of the fit, choose the relevant distribution you want and click *OK* (Figure 5.14).

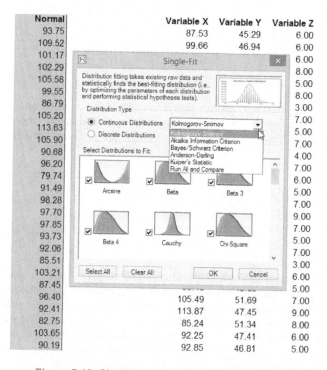

Figure 5.13: Single Variable Distributional Fitting

Results Interpretation

The null hypothesis (H$_o$) being tested is such that the fitted distribution is the same distribution as the population from which the sample data to be fitted come. Thus, if the computed p-value is lower than a critical alpha level (typically 0.10 or 0.05), then the distribution is the wrong distribution. Conversely, the *higher the p-value, the better the distribution fits the data*. Roughly, you can think of p-value as a *percentage explained*, that is, if the p-value is 0.9996 (Figure 5.14), then setting a normal distribution with a mean of 100.67 and a standard deviation of 10.40 explains about 99.96% of the variation in the data, indicating an especially good fit. The data was from a 1,000-trial simulation in Risk Simulator based on a normal distribution with a mean of 100 and a standard deviation of 10. Because only 1,000 trials were simulated, the resulting distribution is fairly close to the specified distributional parameters, and in this case, about a 99.96% precision.

Both the results (Figure 5.14) and the report (Figure 5.15) show the test statistic, p-value, theoretical statistics (based on the selected distribution), empirical statistics (based on the raw data), the original data (to maintain a record of the data used), and the assumption complete with the relevant distributional parameters (i.e., if you selected the option to automatically generate assumption and if a simulation profile already exists). The results also rank all the selected distributions and how well they fit the data.

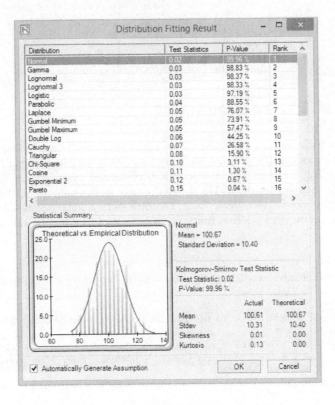

Figure 5.14: Distributional Fitting Result

Single Variable Distributional Fitting

Statistical Summary

Fitted Assumption	100.61	

Fitted Distribution **Normal**

Mean	100.67
Standard Deviation	10.40
Kolmogorov-Smirnov Statistic	0.02
P-Value for Test Statistic	0.9996

	Actual	Theoretical
Mean	100.61	100.67
Standard Deviation	10.31	10.40
Skewness	0.01	0.00
Excess Kurtosis	-0.13	0.00

Theoretical vs. Empirical Distribution

Original Fitted Data

73.53	78.21	78.52	79.50	79.72	79.74	81.56	82.08	82.68	82.75	83.34	83.64	84.09
84.66	85.00	85.35	85.51	86.04	86.79	86.82	86.91	87.02	87.03	87.45	87.53	87.66
88.05	88.45	88.51	89.95	90.19	90.54	90.68	90.96	91.25	91.49	91.56	91.94	92.06
92.36	92.41	92.45	92.70	92.80	92.84	93.21	93.26	93.48	93.73	93.75	93.77	93.82
94.00	94.15	94.51	94.57	94.64	94.69	94.95	95.57	95.62	95.71	95.78	95.83	95.97
96.20	96.24	96.40	96.43	96.47	96.61	96.88	97.00	97.07	97.21	97.23	97.48	97.70
97.77	97.85	98.15	98.17	98.24	98.28	98.32	98.33	98.35	98.65	99.03	99.27	99.46
99.47	99.55	99.73	99.96	100.08	100.24	100.36	100.42	100.44	100.48	100.49	100.83	101.17
101.28	101.34	101.45	101.46	101.55	101.73	101.74	101.81	102.29	102.55	102.58	102.60	102.70
103.17	103.21	103.22	103.32	103.34	103.45	103.65	103.66	103.72	103.81	103.90	103.99	104.46
104.57	104.76	105.20	105.44	105.50	105.52	105.58	105.66	105.87	105.90	105.90	106.29	106.35
106.59	107.01	107.68	107.70	107.93	108.17	108.20	108.34	108.42	108.43	108.49	108.70	109.15
109.22	109.35	109.52	109.75	110.04	110.16	110.25	110.54	111.05	111.06	111.44	111.76	111.90
111.95	112.07	112.19	112.29	112.32	112.42	112.48	112.85	112.92	113.50	113.59	113.63	113.70
114.13	114.14	114.21	114.91	114.95	115.40	115.58	115.66	116.58	116.98	117.60	118.67	119.24
119.52	124.14	124.16	124.39	132.30								

Figure 5.15: Distributional Fitting Report

FITTING MULTIPLE VARIABLES

For fitting multiple variables, the process is fairly similar to fitting individual variables. However, the data should be arranged in columns (i.e., each variable is arranged as a column) and all the variables are fitted. The same analysis is performed when fitting multiple variables as when single variables are fitted. The difference here is that only the final report will be generated and you do not get to review each variable's distributional rankings. If the rankings are important, run the single variable fitting procedure instead, on one variable at a time.

Procedure

- Open a spreadsheet with existing data for fitting (e.g., use the *Risk Simulator | Example Models | 06 Data Fitting*).

- Select the data you wish to fit (data should be in multiple columns with multiple rows).

- Select *Risk Simulator | Analytical Tools | Distributional Fitting (Multi-Variable)*.

- Review the data, choose the types of distributions you want to fit to, and click *OK*.

Notes

Notice that the statistical ranking methods used in the distributional fitting routines in the examples above are the Chi-Square test and Kolmogorov–Smirnov test (other distributional fitting methods are discussed in the next section). The former is used to test discrete distributions and the latter, continuous distributions. Briefly, a hypothesis test coupled with the maximum likelihood procedure with an internal optimization routine is used to find the best-fitting parameters on each distribution tested and the results are ranked from the best fit to the worst fit. There are other distributional fitting tests such as the Shapiro-Wilks, etc. However, these tests are very sensitive parametric tests and are highly inappropriate in Monte Carlo risk simulation distribution-fitting routines when different distributions are being tested. Due to their parametric requirements, these tests are most suited for testing normal distributions and distributions with normal-like behaviors (e.g., binomial distribution with a high number of trials and symmetrical probabilities) and will provide less accurate results when performed on nonnormal distributions. Take great care when using such parametric tests. The Kolmogorov–Smirnov and Chi-Square tests employed in Risk Simulator are nonparametric and semiparametric in nature and are better suited for fitting normal and nonnormal distributions. Additional distributional fitting methods are discussed next.

DISTRIBUTIONAL FITTING ALGORITHMS

Generally speaking, distributional fitting answers the questions: Which distribution does an analyst or engineer use for a particular input variable in a model? What are the relevant distributional parameters? Following are additional methods of distributional fitting available in Risk Simulator:

- Akaike Information Criterion (AIC). Rewards goodness-of-fit but also includes a penalty that is an increasing function of the number of estimated parameters (although AIC penalizes the number of parameters less strongly than other methods).

- Anderson–Darling (AD). When applied to testing if a normal distribution adequately describes a set of data, it is one of the most powerful statistical tools for detecting departures from normality and is powerful for testing normal tails. However, in non-normal distributions, this test lacks power compared to others.

- Kolmogorov–Smirnov (KS). A nonparametric test for the equality of continuous probability distributions that can be used to compare a sample with a reference probability distribution, making it useful for testing abnormally shaped distributions and non-normal distributions.

- Kuiper's Statistic (K). Related to the KS test making it as sensitive in the tails as at the median and also making it invariant under cyclic transformations of the independent variable, rendering it invaluable when testing for cyclic variations over time. In comparison, the AD test provides equal sensitivity at the tails as the median, but it does not provide the cyclic invariance.

- Schwarz/Bayes Information Criterion (SC/BIC). The SC/BIC test introduces a penalty term for the number of parameters in the model with a larger penalty than AIC.

The null hypothesis being tested is such that the fitted distribution is the same distribution as the population from which the sample data to be fitted comes. Thus, if the computed p-value is lower than a critical alpha level (typically 0.10 or 0.05), then the distribution is the wrong distribution (reject the null hypothesis). Conversely, the higher the p-value, the better the distribution fits the data (do not reject the null hypothesis, which means the fitted distribution is the correct distribution, or null hypothesis of H_0: $Error = 0$, where error is defined as the difference between the empirical data and the theoretical distribution). Roughly, you can think of p-value as a percentage explained; that is, for example, if the computed p-value of a fitted normal distribution is 0.9996, then setting a normal distribution with the fitted mean and standard deviation explains about 99.96% of the variation in the data, indicating an especially good fit. Both the results and the report show the test statistic, p-value, theoretical statistics (based on the selected distribution), empirical statistics (based on the raw data), the original data (to maintain a record of the data used), and the assumptions complete with the relevant distributional parameters (i.e., if you selected the option to automatically generate assumptions and if a simulation profile already exists). The results also rank all the selected distributions and how well they fit the data.

PERCENTILE DISTRIBUTIONAL FITTING TOOL

The Percentile Distributional Fitting tool in Risk Simulator is an alternate way of fitting probability distributions. There are several related tools and each has its own uses and advantages:

- Distributional Fitting (Percentiles). Uses an alternate method of entry (percentiles and first/second moment combinations) to find the best-fitting parameters of a specified distribution without the need for having raw data. This method is suitable for use when there are insufficient data or only when percentiles and moments are available, or as a means to recover the entire distribution with only two or three data points but the distribution type needs to be assumed or known.

- Distributional Fitting (Single Variable). Uses statistical methods to fit your raw data to all 50 distributions to find the best-fitting distribution and its input parameters. Multiple data points are required for a good fit, and the distribution type may or may not be known ahead of time.

- Distributional Fitting (Multiple Variables). Uses statistical methods to fit your raw data on multiple variables at the same time. This method uses the same algorithms as the single-variable fitting, but incorporates a pairwise correlation matrix between the variables. Multiple data points are required for a good fit, and the distribution type may or may not be known ahead of time.

- Custom Distribution (Set Assumption). Uses nonparametric resampling techniques to generate a custom distribution with the existing raw data and to simulate the distribution based on this empirical distribution. Fewer data points are required, and the distribution type is not known ahead of time. This tool is also suitable for subject matter expert (SME) estimates, the Delphi method, and management assumptions.

Quick Procedure

Click on *Risk Simulator | Analytical Tools | Distributional Fitting (Percentiles)*, choose the probability distribution and types of inputs you wish to use, enter the parameters, and click *Run* to obtain the results. Review the fitted R-square results and compare the empirical versus theoretical fitting results to determine if your distribution is a good fit.

BOOTSTRAP SIMULATION

Theory

Bootstrap simulation is a simple technique that estimates the reliability or accuracy of forecast statistics or other sample raw data. Bootstrap simulation can be used to answer a lot of confidence- and precision-based questions in simulation. For instance, suppose an identical model (with identical assumptions and forecasts but without any random seeds) is run by 100 different people, the results will clearly be slightly different. The question is, if we collected all the statistics from these 100 people, how will the mean be distributed, or the median, or the skewness, or excess kurtosis? Suppose one person has a mean value of say, 1.50 while another 1.52. Are these two values statistically significantly different from one another or are they statistically similar and the slight difference is due entirely to random chance? What about 1.53? So, how far is far enough to say that the values are statistically different? In addition, if a model's resulting skewness is −0.19 is this forecast distribution negatively skewed or is it statistically close enough to zero to state that this distribution is symmetrical and not skewed? Thus, if we bootstrapped this forecast 100 times, i.e., run a 1,000-trial simulation for 100 times and collect the 100 skewness coefficients, the skewness distribution would indicate how far zero is away from −0.19. If the 90% confidence on the bootstrapped skewness distribution contains the value zero, then we can state that on a 90% confidence level, this distribution is symmetrical and not skewed, and the value −0.19 is statistically close enough to zero. Otherwise, if zero falls outside of this 90% confidence area, then this distribution is negatively skewed. The same analysis can be applied to excess kurtosis and other statistics.

Essentially, bootstrap simulation is a hypothesis testing tool. Classical methods used in the past relied on mathematical formulas to describe the accuracy of sample statistics. These methods assume that the distribution of a sample statistic approaches a normal distribution, making the calculation of the statistic's standard error or confidence interval relatively easy. However, when a statistic's sampling distribution is not normally distributed or easily found, these classical methods are difficult to use. In contrast, bootstrapping analyzes sample statistics empirically by repeatedly sampling the data and creating distributions of the different statistics from each sampling. The classical methods of hypothesis testing are available in Risk Simulator and are explained in the next section. Classical methods provide higher power in their tests but rely on normality assumptions and can only be used to test the mean and variance of a distribution, as compared to bootstrap simulation, which provides lower power but is nonparametric and distribution-free, and can be used to test any distributional statistic.

Procedure

- *Run simulation* with assumptions and forecasts (e.g., use the *Risk Simulator | Example Models | 08 Hypothesis Testing and Bootstrap Simulation*).

- Select *Risk Simulator | Analytical Tools | Nonparametric Bootstrap.*

- Select only *one* forecast to bootstrap, select the statistic(s) to bootstrap, and enter the number of bootstrap trials and click *OK* (Figure 5.16).

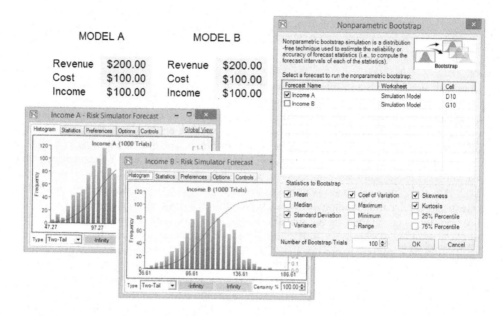

Figure 5.16: Nonparametric Bootstrap Simulation

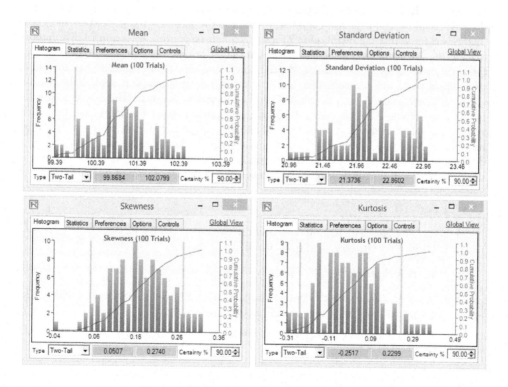

Figure 5.17: Bootstrap Simulation Results

Results Interpretation

Figure 5.17 illustrates some sample bootstrap results. The example file used was *Hypothesis Testing and Bootstrap Simulation*. For instance, the 90 percent confidence for the kurtosis statistic is between –0.2517 and 0.2299, such that the value 0 falls within this confidence, indicating that on a 90 percent confidence, the kurtosis of this forecast is not statistically significantly different from zero, or that this distribution can be considered as normal-tailed. Conversely, if the value 0 falls outside of this confidence, then the opposite is true, the distribution has excess kurtosis skewed (positive kurtosis if indicating fat tails if the forecast statistic is positive, and negative kurtosis with flat -tailed if the forecast statistic is negative). Similarly, in Figure 5.17, we can state that the distribution is positively skewed (the 90 percent confidence interval is from 0.0507 to 0.2740, and 0 falls outside of this interval).

Notes

The term *bootstrap* comes from the saying, "to pull oneself up by one's own bootstraps," and is applicable because this method uses the distribution of statistics themselves to analyze the statistics' accuracy. Nonparametric simulation is simply randomly picking golf balls from a large basket with replacement where each golf ball is based on a historical data point. Suppose there are 365 golf balls in the basket (representing 365 historical data points). Imagine if you will that the value of each golf ball picked at random is written on a large whiteboard. The results of the 365 balls picked with replacement are written in the first column of the board with 365 rows of numbers. Relevant statistics (e.g., mean, median, mode, standard deviation, and so forth) are calculated on these 365 rows. The process is then repeated, say, five thousand times. The whiteboard will now be filled with 365 rows and 5,000 columns. Hence, 5,000 sets of statistics (that is, there will be 5,000 means, 5,000 medians, 5,000 modes, 5,000 standard deviations, and so forth) are tabulated and their distributions shown. The relevant *statistics of the statistics* are then tabulated, where from these results one can ascertain how confident the simulated statistics are. Finally, bootstrap results are important because according to the *Law of Large Numbers* and *Central Limit Theorem* in statistics, the mean of the sample means is an unbiased estimator and approaches the true population mean when the sample size increases.

HYPOTHESIS TESTING

Theory

A hypothesis test is performed when testing the means and variances of two distributions to determine if they are statistically identical or statistically different from one another; that is, to see if the differences between the means and variances of two different forecasts that occur are based on random chance or if they are, in fact, statistically significantly different from one another.

This analysis is related to bootstrap simulation but with several differences. Classical hypothesis testing uses mathematical models and is based on theoretical distributions. This means that the precision and power of the test is higher than bootstrap simulation's empirically based method of simulating a simulation and letting the data tell the story. However, classical hypothesis tests are only applicable for testing two distributions' means and variances (and by extension, standard deviations) to see if they are statistically identical or different. In contrast, nonparametric bootstrap simulation can be used to test for any distributional statistics, making it more useful, but the drawback is its lower testing power. Risk Simulator provides both techniques from which to choose.

Procedure

- *Run Simulation* (e.g., use the *Risk Simulator | Example Models | 08 Hypothesis Testing and Bootstrap Simulation*).

- Select *Risk Simulator | Analytical Tools | Hypothesis Testing*.

- Select the *two forecasts* to test, select the type of hypothesis test you wish to run, and click *OK* (Figure 5.18).

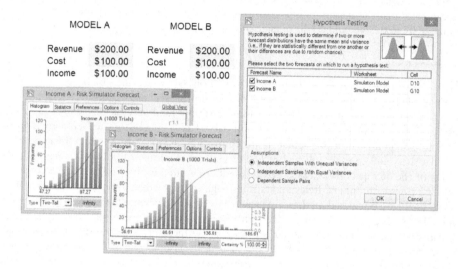

Figure 5.18: Hypothesis Testing

Results Interpretation

A two-tailed hypothesis test is performed on the null hypothesis (H_o) such that the two variables' population means are statistically identical to one another. The alternative hypothesis (H_a) is such that the population means are statistically different from one another. If the calculated p-values are less than or equal to 0.01, 0.05, or 0.10 alpha test levels, it means that the null hypothesis is rejected, which implies that the forecast means are statistically significantly different at the 1%, 5% and 10% significance levels. If the null hypothesis is not rejected when the p-values are high, the means of the two forecast distributions are statistically similar to one another. The same analysis is performed on variances of two forecasts at a time using the pairwise F-test. If the p-values are small, then the variances (and standard deviations) are statistically different from one another, otherwise, for large p-values, the variances are statistically identical to one another. The example file used was *Hypothesis Testing and Bootstrap Simulation* (Figure 5.19).

Hypothesis Test on the Means and Variances of Two Forecasts

Statistical Summary

A hypothesis test is performed when testing the means and variances of two distributions to determine if they are statistically identical or statistically different from one another. That is, to see if the differences between two means and two variances that occur are based on random chance or they are in fact different from one another. The two-variable t-test with unequal variances (the population variance of forecast 1 is expected to be different from the population variance of forecast 2) is appropriate when the forecast distributions are from different populations (e.g., data collected from two different geographical locations, two different operating business units, and so forth). The two-variable t-test with equal variances (the population variance of forecast 1 is expected to be equal to the population variance of forecast 2) is appropriate when the forecast distributions are from similar populations (e.g., data collected from two different engine designs with similar specifications, and so forth). The paired dependent two-variable t-test is appropriate when the forecast distributions are from similar populations (e.g., data collected from the same group of customers but on different occasions, and so forth).

A two-tailed hypothesis test is performed on the null hypothesis Ho such that the two variables' population means are statistically identical to one another. The alternative hypothesis is that the population means are statistically different from one another. If the calculated p-values are less than or equal to 0.01, 0.05, or 0.10, this means that the hypothesis is rejected, which implies that the forecast means are statistically significantly different at the 1%, 5% and 10% significance levels. If the null hypothesis is not rejected when the p-values are high, the means of the two forecast distributions are statistically similar to one another. The same analysis is performed on variances of two forecasts at a time using the pairwise F-test. If the p-values are small, then the variances (and standard deviations) are statistically different from one another, otherwise, for large p-values, the variances are statistically identical to one another.

Result

Hypothesis Test Assumption:	Unequal Variances
Computed t-statistic:	1.015722
P-value for t-statistic:	0.309885
Computed F-statistic:	1.063476
P-value for F-statistic:	0.330914

Figure 5.19: Hypothesis Testing Results

Notes

The two-variable t-test with unequal variances (the population variance of forecast 1 is expected to be different from the population variance of forecast 2) is appropriate when the forecast distributions are from different populations (e.g., data collected from two different geographical locations, or two different operating business units, and so forth). The two-variable t-test with equal variances (the population variance of forecast 1 is expected to be equal to the population variance of forecast 2) is appropriate when the forecast distributions are from similar populations (e.g., data collected from two different engine designs with similar specifications, and so forth). The paired dependent two-variable t-test is appropriate when the forecast distributions are from exactly the same population and subjects (e.g., data collected from the same group of patients before an experimental drug was used and after the drug was applied, and so forth).

DATA EXTRACTION, SAVING SIMULATION RESULTS, AND GENERATING REPORTS

A simulation's raw data can be very easily extracted using Risk Simulator's *Data Extraction* routine. Both assumptions and forecasts can be extracted but a simulation must first be run. The extracted data can then be used for a variety of other analyses and the data can be extracted to different formats—for use in spreadsheets, databases, and other software products.

Procedure

- Open or create a model, define assumptions and forecasts, and run the simulation.

- Select *Risk Simulator | Analytical Tools | Data Extraction*.

- Select the *Assumptions* and/or *Forecasts* from which you wish to extract the data and click *OK*.

The simulated data can be extracted to an Excel worksheet, a flat text file (for easy import into other software applications), or as *.risksim files (which can be reopened as Risk Simulator forecast charts at a later date). Finally, you can create a simulation report of all the assumptions and forecasts in the model by going to *Risk Simulator | Analytical Tools | Create Report*. This is an efficient way to gather all the simulation inputs and outputs in one concise report.

CUSTOM MACROS

Simulation can also be run while harnessing the power of Visual Basic for Applications (VBA) in Excel. For instance, the examples in Chapter 3 of *Modeling Risk* on running models with VBA codes can be used in tandem with Risk Simulator. For an illustration of how to set the macros or customized functions to run with simulation, see the VBA Macro hands-on exercise (Retirement Funding with Inflation) at the end of *Modeling Risk's* Chapter 3.

Currently, the existing Risk Simulator software does not allow direct access to its functionalities via Excel VBA. Instead, you can write VBA codes to execute certain functions between simulation trials. For example, a search algorithm or function in VBA can be written to compute your own proprietary model, insert these functions or models in your Excel model, then set assumptions and forecasts using Risk Simulator to run simulations. In other words, a single trial of your assumptions will be generated and populates the Excel worksheet, then the VBA code will trigger, and the forecast cells will collect the results in memory, then the next trial is triggered, until the total number of simulation trials is complete.

DISTRIBUTIONAL ANALYSIS TOOL

The distributional analysis tool is a statistical probability tool in Risk Simulator that is rather useful in a variety of settings. It can be used to compute the probability density function (PDF), which is also called the probability mass function (PMF) for discrete distributions (these terms are used interchangeably), where given some distribution and its parameters, we can determine the probability of occurrence given some outcome x. In addition, the cumulative distribution function (CDF) can be computed, which is the sum of the PDF values up to this x value. Finally, the inverse cumulative distribution function (ICDF) is used to compute the value x given the cumulative probability of occurrence. The following pages provide example uses of PDF, CDF, and ICDF. Also remember to try some of the exercises at the end of this chapter for more hands-on applications of probability distribution analysis using this tool.

This tool is accessible via *Risk Simulator | Analytical Tools | Distributional Analysis*. As an example of its use, Figure 5.20 shows the computation of a binomial distribution (i.e., a distribution with two outcomes, such as the tossing of a coin, where the outcome is either Heads or Tails, with some prescribed probability of heads and tails). Suppose we toss a coin two times and set the outcome Heads as a success. We use the binomial distribution with Trials = 2 (tossing the coin twice) and Probability = 0.50 (the probability of success, of getting Heads). Selecting the PDF and setting the range of values x as from 0 to 2 with a step size of 1 (this means we are requesting the values 0, 1, 2 for x), the resulting probabilities are provided in the table and in a graphic format, as well as the theoretical four moments of the distribution. As the outcomes of the coin toss is Heads-Heads, Tails-Tails, Heads-Tails, and Tails-Heads, the probability of getting exactly no Heads is 25 percent, of getting one Heads is 50%, and of getting two Heads is 25%. Similarly, we can obtain the exact probabilities of tossing the coin, say 20 times, as seen in Figure 5.21. The results are again presented both in tabular and graphic formats.

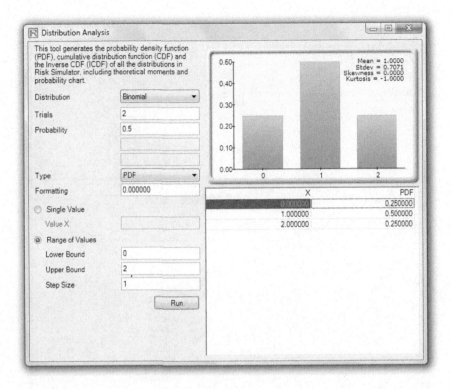

Figure 5.20: Distributional Analysis Tool (Binomial Distribution with 2 Trials)

As a side note, the binomial distribution describes the number of times a particular event occurs in a fixed number of trials, such as the number of heads in 10 flips of a coin or the number of defective items out of 50 items chosen. The three conditions underlying the binomial distribution are:

- For each trial, only two outcomes are possible that are mutually exclusive.

- The trials are independent—what happens in the first trial does not affect the next trial.

- The probability of an event occurring remains the same from trial to trial.

The probability of success (p) and the integer number of total trials (n) are the distributional parameters. The number of successful trials is denoted x. It is important to note that probability of success (p) of 0 or 1 are trivial conditions and do not require any simulations, and hence, are not allowed in the software.

Input requirements:

Probability of success > 0 and < 1 (that is, $0.0001 \leq p \leq 0.9999$)

Number of trials ≥ 1 or positive integers and ≤ 1000 (for larger trials, use the normal distribution with the relevant computed binomial mean and standard deviation as the normal distribution's parameters).

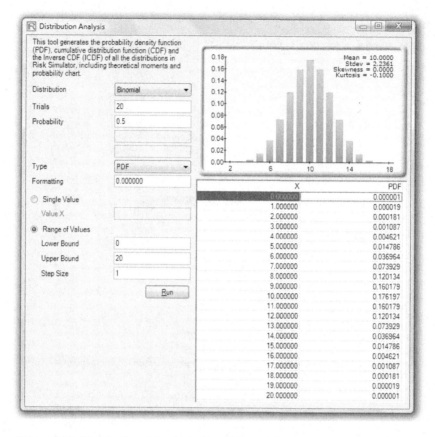

Figure 5.21: Distributional Analysis Tool (Binomial Distribution with 20 Trials)

Figure 5.22 shows the same binomial distribution but now the CDF is computed. The CDF is simply the sum of the PDF values up to the point x. For instance, in Figure 5.21, we see that the probabilities of 0, 1, and 2 are 0.000001, 0.000019, and 0.000181, whose sum is 0.000201, which is the value of the CDF at $x = 2$ in Figure 5.22. Whereas the PDF computes the probabilities of getting exactly 2 Heads, the CDF computes the probability of getting no more than 2 Heads or up to 2 Heads (or probabilities of 0, 1, and 2 Heads). Taking the complement (i.e., $1 - 0.00021$) obtains 0.999799, or 99.9799 percent, which is the probability of getting at least 3 Heads or more.

As another example, out of 20 projects where there is a 50% independent chance of success of each project, the probability of getting at least 8 successful projects is 86.84% (i.e., the sum of the probabilities of exactly 8, 9, 10, ..., 20 successful projects or 100% − the cumulative probability of 0 to 7 from Figure 5.22, or 100% − 13.16% = 86.84%). Alternatively, out of 20 independent projects, the probability of having no more than 12 successful project is 86.84% (CDF of 12 is 86.84% in Figure 5.22). The probability in this example is the same due to the 50% success probability in a binomial distribution which creates a symmetrical distribution (8 failures is the same as 12 successes out of 20 projects).

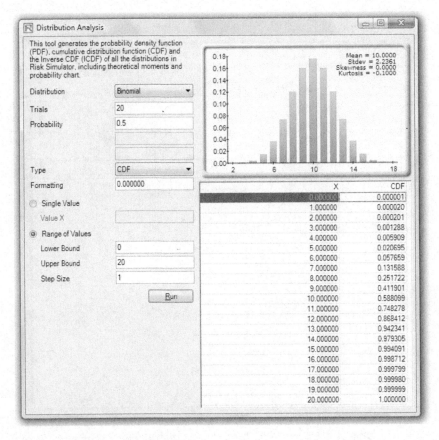

Figure 5.22: Distributional Analysis Tool (Binomial Distribution's CDF with 20 Trials)

Using this distributional analysis tool, distributions even more advanced can be analyzed, such as the gamma, beta, negative binomial, and many others in Risk Simulator. As further example of the tool's use in a continuous distribution and the ICDF functionality, Figure 5.23 shows the standard-normal distribution (normal distribution with a mean or *mu* of zero and standard deviation or *sigma* of one), where we apply the ICDF to find the value of x that corresponds to the cumulative probability of 97.50 percent (CDF). That is, a one-tail CDF of 97.50 percent is equivalent to a two-tail 95 percent confidence interval (there is a 2.50 percent probability in the right tail and 2.50 percent in the left tail, leaving 95 percent in the center or confidence interval area, which is equivalent to a 97.50 percent area for one tail). The result is the familiar Z-Score of 1.96. Therefore, using this distributional analysis tool, the standardized scores for other distributions and the exact and cumulative probabilities of other distributions can all be obtained quickly and easily. See the exercises at the end of this chapter for more hands-on applications using the binomial, negative binomial, and other distributions.

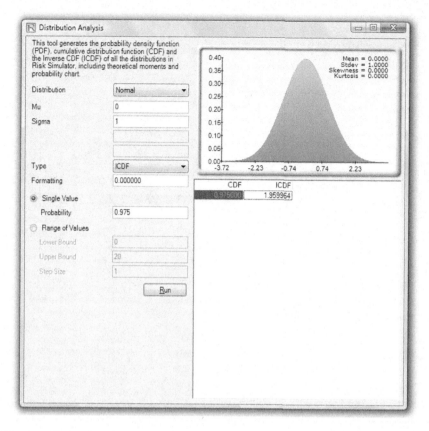

Figure 5.23: Distributional Analysis Tool (Normal Distribution's ICDF and Z-score)

SCENARIO ANALYSIS TOOL

The scenario analysis tool in Risk Simulator allows you to run multiple scenarios quickly and effortlessly by changing one or two input parameters to determine the output of a variable. Figure 5.24 illustrates how this tool works on the discounted cash flow sample model (*Risk Simulator | Example Models | 07 DCF, ROI, and Volatility*). In this example, cell *G6* (net present value) is selected as the output of interest, whereas cells *C9* (effective tax rate) and *C12* (product price) are selected as inputs to perturb. You can set the starting and ending values to test as well as the step size or the number of steps to run between these starting and ending values. The result is a scenario analysis table (Figure 5.25), where the row and column headers are the two input variables and the body of the table shows the net present values. This scenario analysis tool is available via *Risk Simulator | Analytical Tools | Scenario Analysis*.

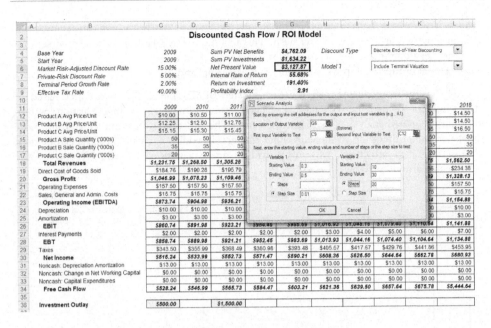

Figure 5.24: Scenario Analysis Tool

SCENARIO ANALYSIS TABLE

Output Variable:	$G$6	Initial Base Case Value:		$3,127.87				
Column Variable:	$C$12	Min: 10	Max: 30	Steps: 20	Stepsize:		Initial Base Case Value:	$10.00
Row Variable:	$C$9	Min: 0.3	Max: 0.5	Steps: ---	Stepsize:	0.01	Initial Base Case Value:	40.00%

	$10.00	$11.00	$12.00	$13.00	$14.00	$15.00	$16.00	$17.00	$18.00	$19.00	$20.00	$21.00	$22.00	$23.00	$24.00	...	$30.00
30.0%	$3,905	$4,134	$4,364	$4,594	$4,823	$5,053	$5,282	$5,512	$5,742	$5,971	$6,201	$6,430	$6,660	$6,890	$7,119	...	$8,497
31.0%	$3,827	$4,053	$4,280	$4,506	$4,732	$4,959	$5,185	$5,411	$5,638	$5,864	$6,090	$6,317	$6,543	$6,769	$6,996	...	$8,354
32.0%	$3,749	$3,972	$4,196	$4,419	$4,642	$4,865	$5,088	$5,311	$5,534	$5,757	$5,980	$6,203	$6,426	$6,649	$6,872	...	$8,210
33.0%	$3,672	$3,892	$4,111	$4,331	$4,551	$4,771	$4,990	$5,210	$5,430	$5,650	$5,869	$6,089	$6,309	$6,529	$6,748	...	$8,067
34.0%	$3,594	$3,811	$4,027	$4,243	$4,460	$4,676	$4,893	$5,109	$5,326	$5,542	$5,759	$5,975	$6,192	$6,408	$6,625	...	$7,924
35.0%	$3,516	$3,730	$3,943	$4,156	$4,369	$4,582	$4,796	$5,009	$5,222	$5,435	$5,648	$5,862	$6,075	$6,288	$6,501	...	$7,780
36.0%	$3,439	$3,649	$3,858	$4,068	$4,278	$4,488	$4,698	$4,908	$5,118	$5,328	$5,538	$5,748	$5,958	$6,168	$6,378	...	$7,637
37.0%	$3,361	$3,568	$3,774	$3,981	$4,188	$4,394	$4,601	$4,807	$5,014	$5,221	$5,427	$5,634	$5,841	$6,047	$6,254	...	$7,494
38.0%	$3,283	$3,487	$3,690	$3,893	$4,097	$4,300	$4,503	$4,707	$4,910	$5,114	$5,317	$5,520	$5,724	$5,927	$6,130	...	$7,350
39.0%	$3,206	$3,406	$3,606	$3,806	$4,006	$4,206	$4,406	$4,606	$4,806	$5,006	$5,206	$5,406	$5,607	$5,807	$6,007	...	$7,207
40.0%	$3,128	$3,325	$3,521	$3,718	$3,915	$4,112	$4,309	$4,505	$4,702	$4,899	$5,096	$5,293	$5,489	$5,686	$5,883	...	$7,064
41.0%	$3,050	$3,244	$3,437	$3,631	$3,824	$4,018	$4,211	$4,405	$4,598	$4,792	$4,985	$5,179	$5,372	$5,566	$5,759	...	$6,921
42.0%	$2,972	$3,163	$3,353	$3,543	$3,733	$3,924	$4,114	$4,304	$4,494	$4,685	$4,875	$5,065	$5,255	$5,446	$5,636	...	$6,777
43.0%	$2,895	$3,082	$3,269	$3,456	$3,643	$3,830	$4,017	$4,204	$4,390	$4,577	$4,764	$4,951	$5,138	$5,325	$5,512	...	$6,634
44.0%	$2,817	$3,001	$3,184	$3,368	$3,552	$3,735	$3,919	$4,103	$4,287	$4,470	$4,654	$4,838	$5,021	$5,205	$5,389	...	$6,491
45.0%	$2,739	$2,920	$3,100	$3,281	$3,461	$3,641	$3,822	$4,002	$4,183	$4,363	$4,543	$4,724	$4,904	$5,085	$5,265	...	$6,347
46.0%	$2,662	$2,839	$3,016	$3,193	$3,370	$3,547	$3,724	$3,902	$4,079	$4,256	$4,433	$4,610	$4,787	$4,964	$5,141	...	$6,204
47.0%	$2,584	$2,758	$2,932	$3,106	$3,279	$3,453	$3,627	$3,801	$3,975	$4,149	$4,322	$4,496	$4,670	$4,844	$5,018	...	$6,061
48.0%	$2,506	$2,677	$2,847	$3,018	$3,189	$3,359	$3,530	$3,700	$3,871	$4,041	$4,212	$4,382	$4,553	$4,724	$4,894	...	$5,918
49.0%	$2,429	$2,596	$2,763	$2,930	$3,098	$3,265	$3,432	$3,600	$3,767	$3,934	$4,101	$4,269	$4,436	$4,603	$4,771	...	$5,774
50.0%	$2,351	$2,515	$2,679	$2,843	$3,007	$3,171	$3,335	$3,499	$3,663	$3,827	$3,991	$4,155	$4,319	$4,483	$4,647	...	$5,631

Figure 5.25: Scenario Analysis Table

SEGMENTATION CLUSTERING TOOL

A final analytical technique of interest is that of segmentation clustering. Figure 5.26 illustrates a sample dataset. You can select the data and run the tool through *Risk Simulator | Analytical Tools | Segmentation Clustering*. Figure 5.26 shows a sample segmentation of two groups. That is, taking the original dataset, we run some internal algorithms (a combination or k-means hierarchical clustering and other method of moments in order to find the best-fitting groups or natural statistical clusters) to statistically divide or segment the original dataset into two groups. You can see the two-group memberships in Figure 5.26. Clearly, you can segment this dataset into as many groups as you wish. This technique is valuable in a variety of settings including marketing (market segmentation of customers into various customer relationship management groups etc.), physical sciences, engineering, and others.

The results from cluster analysis creates clusters of multiple groups, partitioned based on data similarity for exploratory data analysis and data mining (e.g., machine learning, pattern recognition, image analysis, bioinformatics, etc.). The objects in the same cluster are more similar to each other than to those in other clusters. In addition, cluster analysis can be used to discover data structures without providing an explanation or interpretation of the relationship among variables.

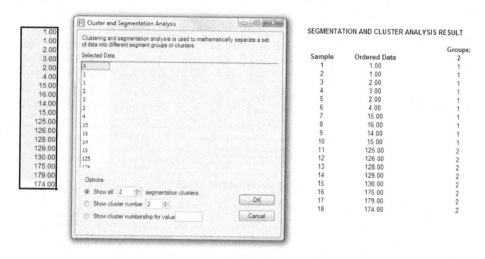

Figure 5.26: Segmentation Clustering Tool and Results

STRUCTURAL BREAK ANALYSIS

A structural break tests whether the coefficients in different datasets are equal, and this test is most commonly used in time-series analysis to test for the presence of a structural break. A time-series dataset can be divided into two subsets and each subset is tested on each other and on the entire dataset to statistically determine if indeed there is a break starting at a particular time period. The structural break test is often used to determine whether the independent variables have different impacts on different subgroups of the population, such as to test if a new marketing campaign, activity, major event, acquisition, divestiture, and so forth, have an impact on the time-series data. Suppose the dataset has 100 time-series data points, you can set various breakpoints to test, for instance, data points 10, 30 and 51 (this means that three structural break tests will be performed on the following dataset: data points 1-9 compared with 10-100; data points 1-29 compared with 30-100; and 1-50 compared with 51-100, to see if indeed at the start of data point 10, 30 and 51, whether there is a break in the underlying structure). A one-tailed hypothesis test is performed on the null hypothesis (H_o) such that the two data subsets are statistically similar to one another, that is, there is no statistically significant structural break. The alternative hypothesis (H_a) is that the two data subsets are statistically different from one another, indicating a possible structural break. If the calculated p-values are less than or equal to 0.01, 0.05, or 0.10, this means that the hypothesis is rejected, which implies that the two data subsets are statistically significantly different at the 1%, 5% and 10% significance levels. High p-values indicate there is no statistically significant structural break.

DETRENDING AND DESEASONALIZING

This tool in Risk Simulator deseasonalizes and detrends your original data to take out any seasonal and trending components. In forecasting models, the process of removing the effects of accumulating datasets from seasonality and trend to show only the absolute changes in values and to allow potential cyclical patterns to be identified after removing the general drift, tendency, twists, bends and effects of seasonal cycles of a set of time-series data. For example, a detrended dataset may be necessary to see a more accurate account of a company's sales in a given year more clearly by shifting the entire dataset from a slope to a flat surface to better see the underlying cycles and fluctuations.

Many time-series data exhibit seasonality where certain events repeat themselves after some time period or seasonality period (e.g., ski resorts' revenues are higher in winter than in summer, and this predictable cycle will repeat itself every winter). Seasonality periods represent how many periods would have to pass before the cycle repeats itself (e.g., 24 hours in a day, 12 months in a year, 4 quarters in a year, 60 minutes in an hour, and so forth). This tool deseasonalizes and detrends your original data to take out any seasonal components. A seasonal index greater than 1 indicates a high period or peak within the seasonal cycle and a value below 1 indicate a dip in the cycle.

PRINCIPAL COMPONENT ANALYSIS

Principal Component Analysis (PCA) is a way of identifying patterns in data, and recasting the data in such a way as to highlight their similarities and differences. Patterns of data are very difficult to find in high dimensions when multiple variables exist, and higher dimensional graphs are very difficult to represent and interpret. Once the patterns in the data are found, they can be compressed and the number of dimensions is now reduced. This reduction of data dimensions does not mean much reduction in loss of information. Instead, similar levels of information can now be obtained by less number of variables.

PCA is a statistical method that is used to reduce data dimensionality using covariance analysis among independent variables by applying an orthogonal transformation to convert a set of correlated variables data into a new set of values of linearly uncorrelated variables named principal components. The number of computed principal components will be less than or equal to the number of original variables. This statistical transformation is setup such that the first principal component has the largest possible variance accounting for as much of the variability in the data as possible, and each subsequent component has the highest variance possible under the constraint that it is orthogonal to or uncorrelated with the preceding components. Thus, PCA reveals the internal structure of the data in a way that best explains the variance in the data. Such dimensionality reduction is useful to process high-dimensional datasets while still retaining as much of the variance in the dataset as possible. PCA essentially rotates the set of points around their mean in order to align with the principal components. Therefore, PCA creates variables that are linear combinations of the original variables. The new variables have the property that the variables are all orthogonal. Factor analysis is similar to PCA, in that factor analysis also involves linear combinations of variables using correlations whereas PCA uses covariance to determine eigenvectors and eigenvalues relevant to the data using a covariance matrix. Eigenvectors can be thought of as preferential directions of a dataset or main patterns in the data. Eigenvalues can be thought of as quantitative assessment of how much a component represents the data. The higher the eigenvalues of a component, the more representative it is of the data.

As an example, PCA is useful when running multiple regression or basic econometrics when the number of independent variables are large or when there are significant multicollinearity in the independent variables. PCA can be run on the independent variables to reduce the number of variables and to eliminate any linear correlations among the independent variables. The extracted revised data obtained after running PCA can be used to rerun the linear multiple regression or linear basic econometric analysis. The resulting model will usually have slightly lower R-squared values but potentially higher statistical significance (lower p-value). Users can decide to use as many principal components as required based on the cumulative variance.

Questions

1. Name the key similarities and differences between a tornado chart and a spider chart. Then, compare tornado and spider charts with sensitivity analysis.

2. In distributional fitting, sometimes you may not get the distribution you thought is the right fit as the best choice. Why is this so? Also, why does the beta distribution usually come up as one of the top few candidates as the best-fitting distribution?

3. Briefly explain what a hypothesis test is.

4. How is bootstrap simulation related to precision and error control in simulation?

5. In sensitivity analysis, how is percent variation explained linked to rank correlation?

Additional hands-on exercises are presented after the appendix. These exercises require Risk Simulator to be installed, and apply the techniques presented in this chapter.

APPENDIX—GOODNESS-OF-FIT TESTS

Several statistical tests exist for deciding if a sample set of data comes from a specific distribution. The most commonly used are the Kolmogorov–Smirnov test and the Chi-Square test. Each test has its advantages and disadvantages. The following sections detail the specifics of these tests as applied in distributional fitting in Monte Carlo simulation analysis. Other less powerful tests such as the Jacque-Bera and Wilkes-Shapiro are not used in Risk Simulator as these are parametric tests and their accuracy depends on the dataset being normal or near-normal. Therefore, the results of these tests are oftentimes suspect or yield inconsistent results.

Kolmogorov–Smirnov Test

The Kolmogorov–Smirnov (KS) test is based on the empirical distribution function of a sample dataset and belongs to a class of *nonparametric* tests. This nonparametric characteristic is the key to understanding the KS test, which simply means that the distribution of the KS test statistic does not depend on the underlying cumulative distribution function being tested. Nonparametric simply means no predefined distributional parameters are required. In other words, the KS test is applicable across a multitude of underlying distributions. Another advantage is that it is an exact test as compared to the Chi-Square test, which depends on an adequate sample size for the approximations to be valid. Despite these advantages, the KS test has several important limitations. It only applies to continuous distributions, and it tends to be more sensitive near the center of the distribution than at the distribution's tails. Also, the distribution must be fully specified.

Given N ordered data points Y_1, Y_2, ... Y_N, the empirical distribution function is defined as $E_n = n_i / N$ where n_i is the number of points less than Y_i where Y_i are ordered from the smallest to the largest value. This is a step function that increases by $1/N$ at the value of each ordered data point.

The null hypothesis is such that the dataset follows a specified distribution while the alternate hypothesis is that the dataset does not follow the specified distribution. The hypothesis is tested using the KS statistic defined as $KS = \max_{1 \le i \le N} \left| F(Y_i) - \frac{i}{N} \right|$ where F is the theoretical cumulative distribution of the continuous distribution being tested that must be fully specified (i.e., the location, scale, and shape parameters cannot be estimated from the data).

The hypothesis regarding the distributional form is rejected if the test statistic, KS, is greater than the critical value obtained from the table below. *Notice that 0.03 to 0.05 are the most common levels of critical values (at the 1 percent, 5 percent, and 10 percent significance levels). Thus, any calculated KS statistic less than these critical values implies that the null hypothesis is not rejected and that the distribution is a good fit.* There are several variations of these tables that use somewhat different scaling for the KS test statistic and critical regions. These alternative formulations should be equivalent, but it is necessary to ensure that the test statistic is calculated in a way that is consistent with how the critical values were tabulated. However, the rule of thumb is that a KS test statistic less than 0.03 or 0.05 indicates a good fit.

TWO-TAILED ALPHA LEVEL	KS CRITICAL
10%	0.03858
5%	0.04301
1%	0.05155

Chi-Square Test

The Chi-Square (CS) goodness-of-fit test is applied to binned data (i.e., data put into classes) and an attractive feature of the CS test is that it can be applied to any univariate distribution for which you can calculate the cumulative distribution function. However, the values of the CS test statistic are dependent on how the data is binned, and the test requires a sufficient sample size in order for the CS approximation to be valid. This test is sensitive to the choice of bins. The test can be applied to discrete distributions such as the binomial and the Poisson, while the KS test is restricted to continuous distributions.

The null hypothesis is such that the dataset follows a specified distribution while the alternate hypothesis is that the dataset does not follow the specified distribution. The hypothesis is tested using the CS statistic defined as $\chi^2 = \sum_{i=1}^{k}(O_i - E_i)^2 / E_i$ where O_i is the observed frequency for bin i and E_i is the expected frequency for bin i. The expected frequency is calculated by $E_i = N(F(Y_U) - F(Y_L))$, where F is the cumulative distribution function for the distribution being tested, Y_U is the upper limit for class i, Y_L is the lower limit for class i, and N is the sample size.

The test statistic follows a CS distribution with $(k - c)$ degrees of freedom where k is the number of nonempty cells and c is the number of estimated parameters (including location and scale parameters and shape parameters) for the distribution + 1. For example, for a three-parameter Weibull distribution, $c = 4$. Therefore, the hypothesis that the data are from a population with the specified distribution is rejected if $\chi^2 > \chi^2(\alpha, k - c)$ where $\chi^2(\alpha, k - c)$ is the CS percent point function with $k - c$ degrees of freedom and a significance level of α.

Again, as the null hypothesis is such that the data follow some specified distribution, when applied to distributional fitting in Risk Simulator, a low p-value (e.g., less than 0.10, 0.05, or 0.01) indicates a bad fit (the null hypothesis is rejected) while a high p-value indicates a statistically good fit.

CHI-SQUARED GOODNESS-OF-FIT TEST SAMPLE CRITICAL VALUES
DEGREES OF FREEDOM 23

ALPHA LEVEL	CUTOFF
10%	32.00690
5%	35.17246
1%	41.63840

Akaike Information Criterion, Anderson–Darling, Kuiper's Statistic, and Schwarz/Bayes Criterion

Following are additional methods of distributional fitting available in Risk Simulator:

- Akaike Information Criterion (AIC). Rewards goodness-of-fit but also includes a penalty that is an increasing function of the number of estimated parameters (although AIC penalizes the number of parameters less strongly than other methods).

- Anderson–Darling (AD). When applied to testing if a normal distribution adequately describes a set of data, it is one of the most powerful statistical tools for detecting departures from normality and is powerful for testing normal tails. However, in non-normal distributions, this test lacks power compared to others.

- Kolmogorov–Smirnov (KS). A nonparametric test for the equality of continuous probability distributions that can be used to compare a sample with a reference probability distribution, making it useful for testing abnormally shaped distributions and non-normal distributions.

- Kuiper's Statistic (K). Related to the KS test making it as sensitive in the tails as at the median and also making it invariant under cyclic transformations of the independent variable, rendering it invaluable when testing for cyclic variations over time. In comparison, the AD test provides equal sensitivity at the tails as the median, but it does not provide the cyclic invariance.

- Schwarz/Bayes Information Criterion (SC/BIC). The SC/BIC test introduces a penalty term for the number of parameters in the model with a larger penalty than AIC.

The null hypothesis being tested is such that the fitted distribution is the same distribution as the population from which the sample data to be fitted comes. Thus, if the computed p-value is lower than a critical alpha level (typically 0.10 or 0.05), then the distribution is the wrong distribution (reject the null hypothesis). Conversely, the higher the p-value, the better the distribution fits the data (do not reject the null hypothesis, which means the fitted distribution is the correct distribution, or null hypothesis of H_0: *Error = 0*, where error is defined as the difference between the empirical data and the theoretical distribution). Roughly, you can think of p-value as a percentage explained; that is, for example, if the computed p-value of a fitted normal distribution is 0.9727, then setting a normal distribution with the fitted mean and standard deviation explains about 97.27% of the variation in the data, indicating an especially good fit. Both the results and the report show the test statistic, p-value, theoretical statistics (based on the selected distribution), empirical statistics (based on the raw data), the original data (to maintain a record of the data used), and the assumptions complete with the relevant distributional parameters (i.e., if you selected the option to automatically generate assumptions and if a simulation profile already exists). The results also rank all the selected distributions and how well they fit the data.

EXERCISE 1: TORNADO, SPIDER, SENSITIVITY, AND SCENARIO ANALYSES

This exercise illustrates how to use Risk Simulator for running:

1. Static Sensitivity, Dynamic Sensitivity, and Scenario Analysis

2. Tornado and Spider Analysis: Pre-simulation Sensitivity Analysis (Linear)

3. Tornado and Spider Analysis: Pre-simulation Sensitivity Analysis (Nonlinear)

4. Sensitivity Analysis: Post-simulation Sensitivity Analysis

5. Scenario Analysis

6. Optimization Basics

Model Background

File Name: Tornado and Sensitivity Charts (Linear).xls and Tornado and Sensitivity Charts (Nonlinear).xls

Access: *Risk Simulator | Example Models | 22 Tornado and Sensitivity Charts (Linear)*

Access: *Risk Simulator | Example Models | 23 Tornado and Sensitivity Charts (Nonlinear)*

Prerequisites: Risk Simulator 2014 or later, Chapter 4 of *Modeling Risk* (Section: Tornado and Sensitivity)

The example model we will use illustrates a simple discounted cash flow model and shows how sensitivity analysis can be performed both prior to running a simulation and after a simulation is run (Figure 5E1.A). Tornado and Spider charts are static sensitivity analysis tools useful for determining which variables impact the key results the most. That is, each precedent variable is perturbed a set amount and the key result is analyzed to determine which input variables are the critical success factors with the most impact. In contrast, sensitivity charts are dynamic, in that all precedent variables are perturbed together in a simultaneous fashion (the effects of autocorrelations, cross-correlations, and interactions are all captured in the resulting sensitivity chart). Therefore, a tornado static analysis is run *before* a simulation while a sensitivity analysis is run *after* a simulation.

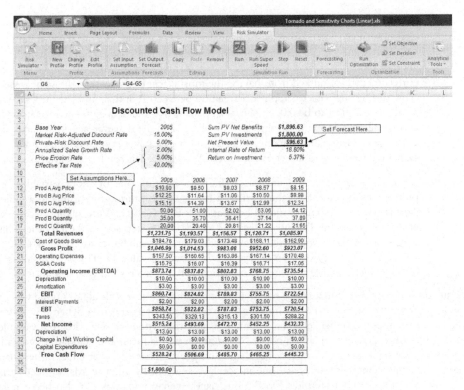

Figure 5E1.A: Sample Model

1. Static Sensitivity, Dynamic Sensitivity, and Scenario Analysis

Before we get started, there are a few terminology issues we need to get out of the way. There are similarities and differences among these terms and it is best to cover them up front as these terms are used throughout this exercise and the reports.

- *Static Sensitivity.* Just as the name indicates, this analysis is static, which means that if you have a model A + B = C and C is selected as the output to analyze, it will identify A and B as the inputs that precede C, or as its *precedents*. Then, because of the static nature of this analysis, we start off with A and B at their original values, and then we tweak A to see the effects on C, while holding B constant. Then, we revert A to its original value and tweak B to see the effects on C. Therefore, each precedent is tweaked one at a time, creating a static sensitivity table and chart. In Risk Simulator, we call this the tornado analysis, where we show the precedent with the largest effect first, followed by the second largest effect and so forth, creating a tornado funnel shape chart. Alternatively, if you take the tornado chart and put it on its side and let all the bars fall onto the x-axis as a baseline, we have a Pareto chart.

- *Dynamic Sensitivity.* In dynamic sensitivity, suppose we have another model, A + B + C = D. In this case, A, B, and C are, of course, the precedents to D. However, if only A and C are set as simulation assumptions, only A and C are considered inputs to be tested in a dynamic sensitivity model. This is because, to run a dynamic analysis, we need to dynamically change things, and the only way to do so is through the use of simulation. Therefore, *dynamic sensitivity can only be run after a simulation is run*. And because B is not an assumption, B is only a single-point estimate and cannot be tested.

Only A and C can be tested in a dynamic sensitivity (B can only be tested if we run a static sensitivity such as a tornado analysis). In addition, if you set correlations between A and C, the resulting sensitivity analysis will change. Suppose you have another model, A + B + C +...+ X + Y + Z, and suppose that the values are not correlated and are ranked from having the most effect to the least in the same order. Now further suppose we apply a correlation between A and Z, and let's just say we set the correlation to be +0.95. What happens is that the data generated for both A and Z will move together in the same direction, and the dynamic sensitivity analysis will pick up this relationship and will relegate A to a lower rank and increase Z to a higher rank in terms of effect on the model. We will see this result later in the exercise.

- *Scenario Analysis.* Scenario analysis is literally selecting one or more variables on purpose, changing these values within a range, and capturing the results in a table. Again, assume we have a model such as A + B + C = D. We can run a scenario analysis by changing B from the value 2 to 100 with a step size of 2 each time. This means that A and C will be left unchanged, whereas B will be set to 2, then 4, 6, 8..., 100 and each time, we keep an eye on the resulting value D. The final result is a scenario analysis table showing 50 scenarios of B and the resulting 50 scenarios of D.

Simulation and optimization analysis requires and implements these techniques in one way or another. For instance, simulation is nothing but scenario analysis run in a dynamic way for thousands of times in a statistical and mathematical algorithm with each scenario input variable having its own characteristics, like a normal distribution with a mean and standard deviation, and thus creating a specific distributional shape and probabilities of occurrence, rather than testing a straight range of values as done in scenario analysis. In other words, simulation is scenario analysis on super steroids! On the one hand, scenario analysis can also be seen as tornado static sensitivity analysis but performed on specific variables. On the other hand, static sensitivity runs scenario analysis with a specified range such as ±10% on all precedent variables, not just selected ones. Finally, dynamic sensitivity runs a simulation and then tests its sensitivity to the output, and this process combines both sensitivity analysis and simulation.

2. Tornado and Spider Charts: Pre-simulation Sensitivity Analysis (Linear)

To run this model, simply:

1. Start Excel and open the example model *Risk Simulator | Example Models | 22 Tornado and Sensitivity Charts (Linear).*

2. Go to the DCF Model worksheet and select the NPV result cell *G6.*

3. Go to *Risk Simulator | Analytical Tools | Tornado Analysis* (or click on the tornado icon) and click *OK* (Figure 5E1.B).

4. Go to the generated tornado analysis report worksheet and review the report (Figure 5E1.C). The report generated illustrates the sensitivity table (starting base value of the key variable as well as the perturbed values and the precedents). The precedent with the highest impact (range of output) is listed first. The tornado chart illustrates this analysis graphically. The Spider chart performs the same analysis but also accounts for nonlinear effects. That is, if the input variables have a nonlinear effect on the output variable, the lines on the Spider chart will be curved.

5. Go back to the DCF Model and rerun the tornado analysis. This time, spend a little more time on the user interface. You can test out various settings such as the ones listed below. In each setting, see the effects on the report.

o   *Show All Variables* versus *Show Top N Variables* allows you to decide how long the tornado chart and table should be. Sometimes in a large model there might be a significant number of precedents, and, in most cases, you do not need to see all of them, just the top few that have the largest impact on the model.

o   *Use Cell Address* is always a good idea if your model is large, allowing you to identify the location (worksheet name and cell address) of a precedent cell. If this option is not selected, the software will apply its own fuzzy logic in an attempt to determine the name of each precedent variable (sometimes the names might end up being confusing in a large model with repeated variables or the names might be too long, possibly making the tornado chart unsightly).

o   *Analyze This Worksheet* and *Analyze All Worksheets* options allow you to control if the precedents should only be part of the current worksheet or include all worksheets in the same workbook. This option comes in handy when you are only attempting to analyze an output based on values in the current sheet versus performing a global search of all linked precedents across multiple worksheets in the same workbook.

o   *Use Global Setting* is useful when you have a large model and you wish to test all the precedents at say, ±50% instead of the default 10%. Instead of having to change each precedent's test values one at a time, you can select this option, change one setting, and click somewhere else in the user interface and the entire list of the precedents will change. Deselecting this option will allow you control of changing test points one precedent at a time.

o   *Ignore Zero or Empty Values* is an option turned on by default where precedent cells with zero or empty values will not be run in the tornado. This is the typical setting.

o   *Highlight Possible Integer Values* is an option that quickly identifies all possible precedent cells that currently have integer inputs. This is sometimes important if your model uses switches (e.g., functions such as IF a cell is 1, then something happens, and IF a cell has a 0 value, something else happens, or integers such as 1, 2, 3, and so forth, which you do not wish to test). For instance, ±10% of a flag switch value of 1 will return a test value of 0.9 and 1.1, both of which are irrelevant and incorrect input values in the model, and Excel may interpret the function as an error. This option, when selected, will quickly highlight potential problem areas for tornado analysis and you can determine which precedents to turn on or off manually, or you can use the *Ignore Possible Integer Values* to turn all of them off simultaneously.

o   *Chart Label* is also very handy in that sometimes certain cell names are too long and they cut into the chart and table. If that is the case, select *Use Cell Address* for shorter and more precise chart labels.

Note: Tornado analysis should never be run just once. It is meant as a model diagnostic tool, which means that it should ideally be run several times on the same model. For instance, in a large model, tornado can be run the first time using all of the default settings and all precedents should be shown (select *Show All Variables*). This single analysis may result in a large report and long (and potentially unsightly) tornado charts. Nonetheless, it provides a great starting point to determine how many of the precedents are considered critical success factors (e.g., the tornado chart may show that the first 5 variables have high impact on the output, while the remaining 200 variables have little to no impact), in which case, a second tornado analysis is run showing fewer variables (e.g., select the *Show Top 10 Variables* if the first 5 are critical, thereby creating a nice report and a tornado chart that shows a contrast between the key factors and less critical factors; that is, you should never show a tornado chart with only the key variables without showing some less critical variables as a contrast to their effects on the output). Finally, the default testing points can be increased from the ±10% to some larger value to test for nonlinearities (the Spider chart will show nonlinear lines and tornado charts will be skewed to one side if the precedent effects are nonlinear).

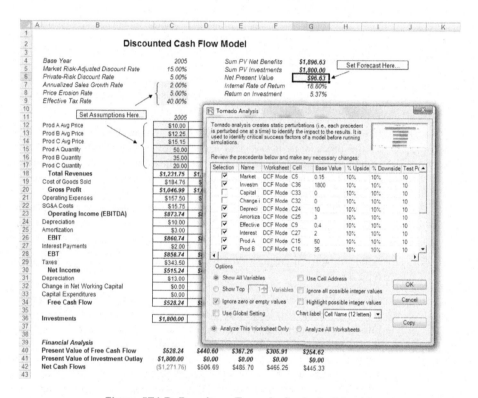

Figure 5E1.B: Running a Tornado Analysis (Linear)

Tornado and Spider Charts

Statistical Summary

One of the powerful simulation tools is the tornado chart—it captures the static impacts of each variable on the outcome of the model. That is, the tool automatically perturbs each precedent variable in the model a user-specified preset amount, captures the fluctuation on the model's forecast or final result, and lists the resulting perturbations ranked from the most significant to the least. Precedents are all the input and intermediate variables that affect the outcome of the model. For instance, if the model consists of A = B + C, where C = D + E, then B, D, and E are the precedents for A (C is not a precedent as it is only an intermediate calculated value). The range and number of values perturbed is user-specified and can be set to test extreme values rather than smaller perturbations around the expected values. In certain circumstances, extreme values may have a larger, smaller, or unbalanced impact (e.g., nonlinearities may occur where increasing or decreasing economies of scale and scope creep occurs for larger or smaller values of a variable) and only a wider range will capture this nonlinear impact.

A tornado chart lists all the inputs that drive the model, starting from the input variable that has the most effect on the results. The chart is obtained by perturbing each precedent input at some consistent range (e.g., ±10% from the base case) one at a time, and comparing their results to the base case. A spider chart looks like a spider with a central body and its many legs protruding. The positively sloped line indicates a positive relationship, while a negatively sloped line indicates a negative relationship. Further, spider charts can be used to visualize linear and nonlinear relationships. The tornado and spider charts help identify the critical success factors of an output cell in order to identify the inputs to simulate. The identified critical variables that are uncertain are the ones that should be simulated. Do not waste time simulating variables that are neither uncertain nor have little impact on the results.

Result

| | Base Value: 96.6261638553219 | | | Input Changes | | |
Precedent Cell	Output Downside	Output Upside	Effective Range	Input Downside	Input Upside	Base Case Value
C36: Investments	276.52616	-83.373836	360.00	$1,620.00	$1,980.00	$1,800.00
C9: Effective Tax Rate	219.72693	-26.474599	246.20	36.00%	44.00%	40.00%
C12: Prod A Avg Price	3.4255424	189.82679	186.40	$9.00	$11.00	$10.00
C13: Prod B Avg Price	16.706631	176.5457	159.84	$11.03	$13.48	$12.25
C15: Prod A Quantity	23.177498	170.07483	146.90	45.00	55.00	50.00
C16: Prod B Quantity	30.533	162.71933	132.19	31.50	38.50	35.00
C14: Prod C Avg Price	40.146587	153.10574	112.96	$13.64	$16.67	$15.15
C17: Prod C Quantity	48.047369	145.20496	97.16	18.00	22.00	20.00
C5: Market Risk-Adjusted Discount Rate	138.23913	57.029841	81.21	13.50%	16.50%	15.00%
C8: Price Erosion Rate	116.80381	76.640952	40.16	4.50%	5.50%	5.00%
C7: Annualized Sales Growth Rate	90.588354	102.68541	12.10	1.80%	2.20%	2.00%
C24: Depreciation	95.084173	98.168155	3.08	$9.00	$11.00	$10.00
C25: Amortization	96.163566	97.088761	0.93	$2.70	$3.30	$3.00
C27: Interest Payments	97.088761	96.163566	0.93	$1.80	$2.20	$2.00

Figure 5E1.C: Linear Tornado Analysis Report

3. Tornado and Spider Charts: Pre-simulation Sensitivity Analysis (Nonlinear)

1. Open the example model *Risk Simulator | Example Models | 23 Tornado and Sensitivity Charts (Nonlinear)*.

2. Go to the Black–Scholes Model worksheet and select the Black–Scholes result cell *E13*.

3. Go to *Risk Simulator | Analytical Tools | Tornado Analysis* (or click on the tornado icon) and this time, select *Use Global Settings* and change the percentage *upside* to *80%*. Then click somewhere else on the grid and the entire column of upside percentages will change to match your new input. Repeat to set the percentage *downside* to *80%*. Click *OK* when done (Figure 5E1.D).

4. Go to the generated report worksheet and examine the results. Notice the nonlinear effects in this model (Figure 5E1.E).

   a. Exercise Question: What do the green and red colors mean on the tornado chart?

   b. Exercise Question: What do the linear versus nonlinear spider chart lines mean and the symmetrical versus asymmetrical bars in the tornado chart mean?

   c. Exercise Question: What do the values beside the tornado chart's horizontal bars mean and what does the x-axis of the tornado chart represent?

   d. Exercise Question: What do the x-axis and y-axis values represent in the spider chart?

e. Exercise Question: What significance does the slope of the spider chart's lines have? For instance, what is the difference between a variable with a positive slope versus a negative slope, and how about comparing two lines where one is steeper and another is less steep? What about if you have a strictly vertical line or a strictly horizontal line?

f. Exercise Question: How do you compute the effective range on the tornado analysis report table?

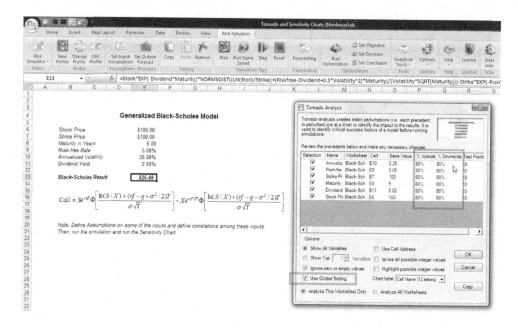

Figure 5E1.D: Running a Tornado Analysis (Nonlinear)

Tornado and Spider Charts

Statistical Summary

One of the powerful simulation tools is the tornado chart—it captures the static impacts of each variable on the outcome of the model. That is, the tool automatically perturbs each precedent variable in the model a user-specified preset amount, captures the fluctuation on the model's forecast or final result, and lists the resulting perturbations ranked from the most significant to the least. Precedents are all the input and intermediate variables that affect the outcome of the model. For instance, if the model consists of A = B + C, where C = D + E, then B, D, and E are the precedents for A (C is not a precedent as it is only an intermediate calculated value). The range and number of values perturbed is user-specified and can be set to test extreme values rather than smaller perturbations around the expected values. In certain circumstances, extreme values may have a larger, smaller, or unbalanced impact (e.g., nonlinearities may occur where increasing or decreasing economies of scale and scope creep occurs for larger or smaller values of a variable) and only a wider range will capture this nonlinear impact.

A tornado chart lists all the inputs that drive the model, starting from the input variable that has the most effect on the results. The chart is obtained by perturbing each precedent input at some consistent range (e.g., ±10% from the base case) one at a time, and comparing their results to the base case. A spider chart looks like a spider with a central body and its many legs protruding. The positively sloped line indicates a positive relationship, while a negatively sloped line indicates a negative relationship. Further, spider charts can be used to visualize linear and nonlinear relationships. The tornado and spider charts help identify the critical success factors of an output cell in order to identify the inputs to simulate. The identified critical variables that are uncertain are the ones that should be simulated. Do not waste time simulating variables that are neither uncertain nor have little impact on the results.

Result

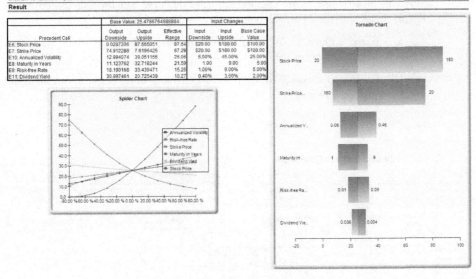

Figure 5E1.E: Nonlinear Tornado Analysis Report

4. Sensitivity Analysis: Post-simulation Sensitivity Analysis

To run this exercise, simply:

1. Go back to the linear model or reopen it from *Risk Simulator | Example Models | 22 Tornado and Sensitivity Charts (Linear)*.

2. Some sample input assumptions and forecasts have already been set for this model, so just run the simulation using *Risk Simulator | Run Simulation* (or click on the Run icon).

3. After the simulation is complete, click *OK* and then select *Risk Simulator | Analytical Tools | Sensitivity Analysis* (Figure 5E1.F). Select *Cell Name* for the Chart Label and click *OK* to run the analysis.

4. Go to the newly generated sensitivity report and review the results (Figure 5E1.G).

   a. Exercise Question: Is this sensitivity analysis a static or dynamic sensitivity?

   b. Exercise Question: What do the red and green bars mean in the sensitivity charts?

   c. Exercise Question: What is the nonlinear rank correlation (Spearman nonparametric rank correlation) and what does it measure? Why do we use it rather than a regular linear correlation (Pearson's product moment correlation coefficient)?

d. Exercise Question: What is the percent variation explained and what does it measure? How does it compare with the coefficient of determination (R-square) obtained from a regression analysis?

5. Reset the simulation (*Risk Simulator | Reset Simulation* (or click on the Reset icon) and go back to the model worksheet. Select cell *C7* annualized growth rate and set a correlation of *0.85* with the effective tax rate cell *C9* (Figure 5E1.H). Run the simulation and run the sensitivity analysis one more time and compare this new correlated simulation report (Figure 5E1.I) with the report without correlations (Figure 5E1.G).

a. Exercise Question: What happens to the sensitivity results when you have a correlated simulation?

b. Exercise Question: What happens to the ranking of C7 before a correlation and after a correlation?

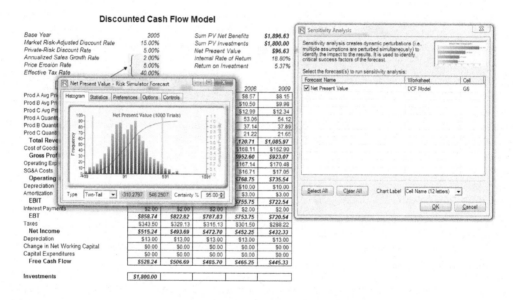

Figure 5E1.F: Dynamic Sensitivity Analysis

Sensitivity Analysis

Statistical Summary

Sensitivity charts are dynamic perturbations created after the simulation run. Sensitivity charts are dynamic perturbations in the sense that multiple assumptions are perturbed simultaneously and their interactions are captured in the fluctuations of the results. In contrast, Tornado charts are static perturbations, meaning that each precedent or assumption variable is perturbed a preset amount and the fluctuations in the results are tabulated. Tornado charts therefore identify which variables drive the results the most and hence are suitable for determining which variables to simulate (that is, they are used before a simulation), whereas Sensitivity charts identify the impact to the results when multiple interacting variables are simulated together in the model (that is, they are used after a simulation).

The Nonlinear Rank Correlation charts indicate the rank correlations between each assumption and the target forecast, and are depicted from the highest absolute value to the lowest absolute value. Positive correlations are shown in green while negative correlations are shown in red. Rank correlation is used instead of a regular correlation coefficient as it captures nonlinear effects between variables. In contrast, the Percent Variation Explained computes how much of the variation in the forecast variable can be explained by the variations in each of the assumptions by itself in a dynamic simulated environment. These charts show the sensitivity of the target forecast to the simulated assumptions.

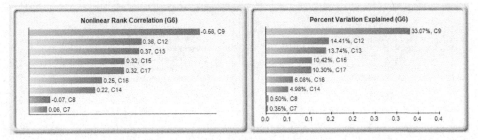

Figure 5E1.G: Dynamic Sensitivity Analysis Report

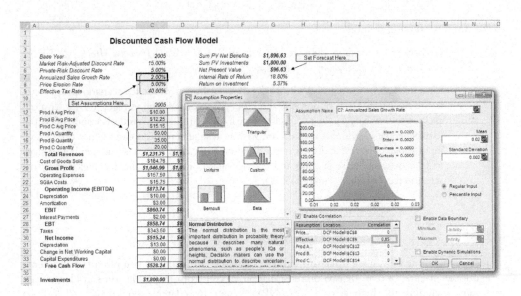

Figure 5E1.H: Correlated Simulation

Sensitivity Analysis

Statistical Summary

Sensitivity charts are dynamic perturbations created after the simulation run. Sensitivity charts are dynamic perturbations in the sense that multiple assumptions are perturbed simultaneously and their interactions are captured in the fluctuations of the results. In contrast, Tornado charts are static perturbations, meaning that each precedent or assumption variable is perturbed a preset amount and the fluctuations in the results are tabulated. Tornado charts therefore identify which variables drive the results the most and hence are suitable for determining which variables to simulate (that is, they are used before a simulation), whereas Sensitivity charts identify the impact to the results when multiple interacting variables are simulated together in the model (that is, they are used after a simulation).

The Nonlinear Rank Correlation charts indicate the rank correlations between each assumption and the target forecast, and are depicted from the highest absolute value to the lowest absolute value. Positive correlations are shown in green while negative correlations are shown in red. Rank correlation is used instead of a regular correlation coefficient as it captures nonlinear effects between variables. In contrast, the Percent Variation Explained computes how much of the variation in the forecast variable can be explained by the variations in each of the assumptions by itself in a dynamic simulated environment. These charts show the sensitivity of the target forecast to the simulated assumptions.

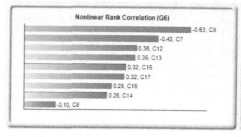 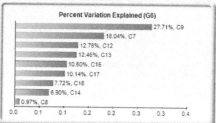

Figure 5E1.I: Dynamic Sensitivity Report of Correlated Simulation

5. Scenario Analysis

To run this exercise, simply:

1. Go back to the linear model or reopen it from *Risk Simulator | Example Models | 22 Tornado and Sensitivity Charts (Linear)*.

2. Click on *Risk Simulator | Analytical Tools | Scenario Analysis* (or use the scenario analysis icon in the Analytical Tools ribbon set) and input the values as seen in Figure 5E1.J. You can click on the link icons to link to a cell or type in the cell address directly. Location of output variable is the location of the cell you wish to test, and you can enter either one or two input variables to test and their starting and ending values as well as the number of steps to take between these starting and ending values or the step size to take. Review the scenario report results (Figure 5E1.K).

6. Optimization Basics

Just a quick note before we leave this exercise. The scenario analysis you ran a few moments ago looks at either a one- or two-dimensional table, and from this table you can identify the results, including the highest or lowest NPV values. In a later exercise, we will look at optimization, where you can have multidimensional scenario analysis that can take on billions and trillions of sets of combinations quickly and automatically, to find the optimal results.

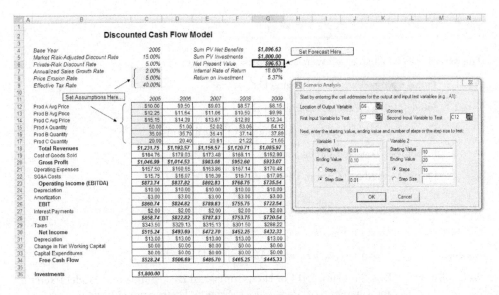

Figure 5E1.J: Scenario Analysis

SCENARIO ANALYSIS TABLE

Output Variable:	$G$6	Initial Base Case Value:		$96.63						Initial Base Case Value:		$10.00
Column Variable:	$C$12	Min:	10.00 Max:	20.00 Steps:	10.00 Stepsize:	---						
Row Variable:	$C$7	Min:	0.01 Max:	0.10 Steps:	---	Stepsize:	0.01 Initial Base Case Value:					2.00%

	$10.00	$11.00	$12.00	$13.00	$14.00	$15.00	$16.00	$17.00	$18.00	$19.00	$20.00
1.00%	$66.65	$158.35	$250.04	$341.74	$433.43	$525.13	$616.82	$708.52	$800.22	$891.91	$983.61
2.00%	$96.63	$189.83	$283.03	$376.23	$469.43	$562.63	$655.83	$749.03	$842.23	$935.43	$1,028.63
3.00%	$127.14	$221.87	$316.60	$411.34	$506.07	$600.80	$695.53	$790.27	$885.00	$979.73	$1,074.46
4.00%	$158.19	$254.49	$350.78	$447.07	$543.36	$639.65	$735.95	$832.24	$928.53	$1,024.82	$1,121.11
5.00%	$189.80	$287.68	$385.56	$483.44	$581.32	$679.20	$777.08	$874.96	$972.84	$1,070.72	$1,168.59
6.00%	$221.96	$321.46	$420.95	$520.45	$619.94	$719.44	$818.93	$918.43	$1,017.93	$1,117.42	$1,216.92
7.00%	$254.69	$355.83	$456.97	$558.11	$659.25	$760.39	$861.53	$962.67	$1,063.81	$1,164.95	$1,266.09
8.00%	$288.00	$390.81	$493.62	$596.44	$699.25	$802.06	$904.88	$1,007.69	$1,110.50	$1,213.31	$1,316.13
9.00%	$321.89	$426.40	$530.92	$635.43	$739.95	$844.46	$948.98	$1,053.49	$1,158.01	$1,262.52	$1,367.04
10.00%	$356.36	$462.61	$568.86	$675.10	$781.35	$887.60	$993.85	$1,100.10	$1,206.34	$1,312.59	$1,418.84

Figure 5E1.K: Scenario Analysis Report

EXERCISE 2: DATA FITTING

This sample model illustrates how to use Risk Simulator for:

1. Fitting a Single Variable to Existing Data

2. Fitting Multiple Variables to Existing Data

3. Simulating, Extracting Data, and Refitting to Distributions

4. Hypothesis Tests and Fitting Statistics

5. Delphi Method and Custom Distributions

Model Background

File Name: Data Fitting.xls

Access: *Risk Simulator | Example Models | 06 Data Fitting*

Prerequisites: Risk Simulator 2014 or later, Completed Basic Simulation Model Exercise, and Chapter 5 of *Modeling Risk* (Section: Distributional Fitting)

This example illustrates how existing sample data can be used to find the statistically best-fitting distribution. By doing so, we also confirm the simulation results through the distributional fitting routine, that is, we simulate a particular distribution, extract its raw data, and refit it back to all distributions.

1. Fitting a Single Variable to Existing Data

To run this model, simply:

1. Start Excel and open the example model at *Risk Simulator | Example Models | 06 Data Fitting*. Go to the *Raw Data* worksheet and select cells *C2:C201* (Figure 5E2.A).

2. Start a new profile by clicking *Risk Simulator | New Profile* (or click the New Profile icon).

3. Click on *Risk Simulator | Analytical Tools | Distributional Fitting (Single Variable)*.

4. Make sure *Fit Continuous Distributions* is selected and all distributions are checked then click *OK*. The resulting fit of all distributions is shown. Select the best fit that is ranked first, view the statistics, and click *OK*.

5. A report will be generated (Figure 5E2.B) indicating all the relevant statistics as well as the data used for fitting (for future reference). Note that if a simulation profile exists and if the *Automatically Generate Assumption* choice is selected, then the report will contain an assumption that is the best fit. Otherwise, only the type of distribution and its relevant input assumptions are provided. You can repeat this exercise on the remaining data points provided.

6. Go the report and select the cell with the assumption and then go to *Risk Simulator | Set Input Assumption* and you will be able to see the assumption and the parameters automatically set up for you (Figure 5E2.C). Compare the input parameters and distribution with those listed in the report.

7. Go back to the *Raw Data* worksheet and rerun the distributional fitting. This time make sure *Fit Discrete Distributions* is selected and all distributions are checked then click *OK*.

a. Exercise Question: What are the two tests used in distributional fitting?

b. Exercise Question: Do you want a low p-value or a high p-value when doing a distributional fitting, that is, are distributions with high p-values ranked better or worse than low p-values?

c. Exercise Question: What is a p-value anyway?

d. Exercise Question: What is the null hypothesis that is being tested?

e. Exercise Question: Are higher or lower values of the test statistics better?

Note: There are several key points to remember. First, more data implies a better statistical fit. Do not fit to very few data points and expect a good fit. Second, only positive discrete data (integers) can be fitted to discrete distributions. When negative values or continuous data exist, you should always fit to continuous distributions. Third, certain distributions are related to other distributions through their statistical properties. For example, a t-distribution becomes a normal distribution when degrees of freedom is high, a Poisson distribution can be used to approximate a binomial, or a normal can be used to approximate a Poisson, hypergeometric, and binomial. There are many other such relationships, and just because the fit is not exactly to the distribution expected does not mean the data are bad or the routine is incorrect. It simply means that another distribution is better suited for the data. Finally, distributions like beta and gamma are extremely flexible and can take on many shapes (we have another exercise that illustrates this), and so do not be surprised if these distributions sometimes show up as a high ranking fit.

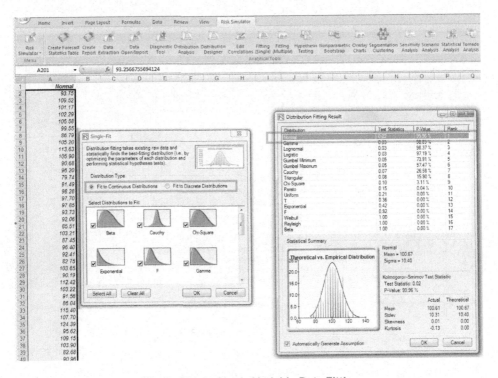

Figure 5E2.A: Single Variable Data Fitting

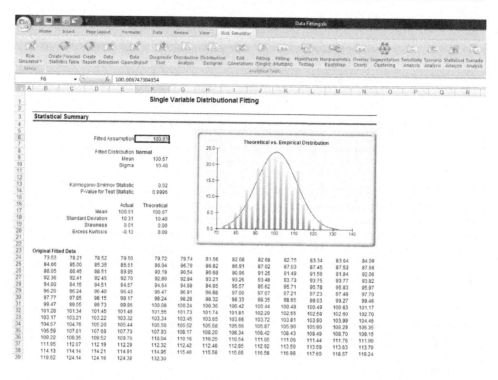

Figure 5E2.B: Single Variable Fitting Report

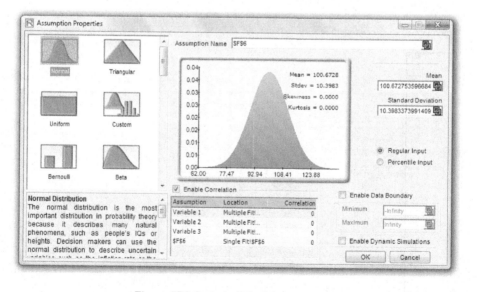

Figure 5E2.C: Auto Fitted Assumption

2. Fitting Multiple Variables to Existing Data

To run this model, simply:

1. Go to the *Raw Data* worksheet, create a new profile (*Risk Simulator | New Profile*) and select the area *C1:E201* and run the multiple variable fitting routine by selecting *Risk Simulator | Analytical Tools | Distributional Fitting (Multi-Variable)* (Figure 5E2.D).

2. Click on the *Distribution Type* list box on the top of the user interface. Then click on the *Distribution Type* droplist for the Binomial variable row and change it to *Discrete* distribution. Keep the other two variables as fitting to *Continuous* distribution. Keep the *Include Correlations Above Absolute Value* at its automatically computed value and the selection checked, and click *OK* to run the fitting routines.

3. Go to the newly generated report (Figure 5E2.E) and spend a minute reviewing the results. Then review the correlation matrix by going to *Risk Simulator | Analytical Tools | Edit Correlations* and clicking on *Select All* (Figure 5E2.F) to review the pairwise cross-correlations.

    a. Exercise Question: Why are all the correlations zero?

    b. Exercise Question: In layman's terms, what does statistically significant correlation mean?

    c. Exercise Question: What does the section that compares actual empirical versus theoretical distribution moments mean?

4. Rerun the multiple fitting routine by repeating steps 1 and 2 above, making sure you create a new profile with a new unique name so you can differentiate which fitted values are in which profile. When you repeat these steps, keep the *Include Correlations Above Absolute Value* and change the value to *0*. That is, all correlations, whether positive or negative, as long as it is not zero, will be used. Run the report and view the correlation matrix just like in Step 3 above to review the correlations.

Note: You can replicate the fitting routine on multiple variables simultaneously (variables must be arranged in columns) instead of one at a time. When performing a Multiple Variable Fitting, make sure to select the right distribution types for the variables. For example, select *continuous* for the first two and *discrete* for the third distribution in our model. Further, you can either select the data with the names or without the names, and if you do not select the variable name when fitting, you can enter the variable names in the fitting dialog box. Also, if you have an existing profile, you can select the *Automatically Generate Assumptions* option such that the report will have assumptions set up for you. Further, these assumptions will also include correlations. The question is then what correlation coefficient is significant for this dataset (i.e., is a correlation of 0.0151 significant or merely a residual effect of randomness and should not be incorporated? What about 0.016 or 0.15, and so forth)? Risk Simulator will automatically compute the statistical significance cutoff level (in this case, any correlation above the absolute value of 0.0907 is statistically significant) and if you select this option, the software will ignore all correlations below the absolute value of this significance level (we use absolute values because correlations can be either positive or negative).

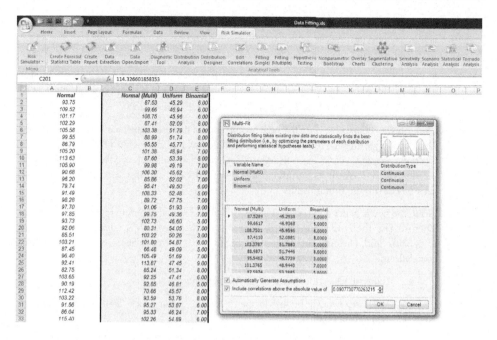

Figure 5E2.D: Multiple Variables Fitting

Multiple Variable Distributional Fitting

Statistical Summary

Variable Name	ormal (Multi)		Variable Name	Uniform		Variable Name	Binomial
Best-Fit Assumption	99.18		Best-Fit Assumption	49.83		Best-Fit Assumption	6.73

Fitted Distribution	Normal		Fitted Distribution	Uniform		Fitted Distribution	Gumbel (Maximum)
Mu	99.34		Minimum	44.84		Alpha	6.38
Sigma	10.48		Maximum	54.89		Beta	1.26

Kolmogorov-Smirnov Statistic	0.03		Kolmogorov-Smirnov Statistic	0.04		Kolmogorov-Smirnov Statistic	0.14
P-Value for Test Statistic	0.9845		P-Value for Test Statistic	0.8110		P-Value for Test Statistic	0.0005

	Actual	Theoretical		Actual	Theoretical		Actual	Theoretical
Mean	99.18	99.34	Mean	49.83	49.87	Mean	6.73	7.11
Standard Deviation	10.33	10.48	Standard Deviation	2.96	2.90	Standard Deviation	1.49	1.61
Skewness	-0.12	0.00	Skewness	0.02	0.00	Skewness	-0.51	1.14
Excess Kurtosis	0.19	0.00	Excess Kurtosis	-1.32	-1.20	Excess Kurtosis	-0.06	2.40

Correlation Matrix

	Normal	Uniform	Binomial
Normal	1		
Uniform	0.0007	1	
Binomial	-0.0693	-0.0044	1

Figure 5E2.E: Multiple Variables Fitting Report with Correlations

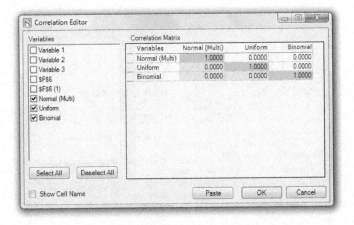

Figure 5E2.F: Not Statistically Significant Correlations

3. Simulating, Extracting Data, and Refitting to Distributions

For additional practice you can run a simulation on an assumption and run a fitting back to find the best distribution.

To run this example, simply:

1. Start a new workbook in Excel. Create a new profile by clicking *Risk Simulator | New Profile*. Then select cell *A1* and create an assumption *Risk Simulator | Set Input Assumption* (or use the Set Input Assumption icon). Select something simple such as *Normal* distribution and make the *Mean 100* and *Standard Deviation 10*.

2. Go to cell *A2*, set the equation *=A1*, and set this cell as a forecast *Risk Simulator | Set Output Forecast* (or use the Set Output Forecast icon).

3. Click on *Risk Simulator | Run Simulation*. At the end of simulation, you can refit the simulated data two ways, first using the forecast chart and, second, by extracting the data and refitting the distribution. We will work on both methods in this exercise.

    a. In the forecast chart, go to the *Controls* tab. Click on the *Fit* button and you can see that the 1,000 raw data captured in the forecast chart are all fitted to the best distribution, which in this case is normal, as expected. Here you can see the theoretical and empirical moments of the distribution (Figure 5E2.G) as well as the p-value of the fit.

    b. Extract the data *Risk Simulator | Analytical Tools | Data Extract and Export* to obtain the raw simulated data. Then, select the data, perform the single distributional fitting, and compare the results in the generated report with the forecast chart's controls tab fitting routine.

    c. Exercise Question: What are the differences between raw data fitting and using the forecast chart's controls tab fitting?

4. For practice, reset the simulation, edit the active profile to run 10,000 simulation trials, run the simulation at super speed, and perform a fitting using the forecast chart's controls section.

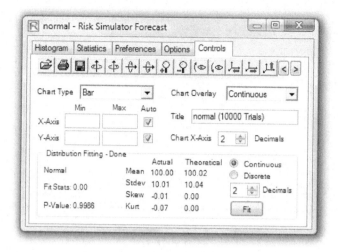

Figure 5E2.G: Forecast Chart Distributional Fit

4. Hypothesis Tests and Fitting Statistics

There is another exercise on Bootstrapping and Hypothesis Testing that will provide additional information and practice in running a hypothesis test. Nonetheless, briefly, the *null hypothesis* that is being tested in distribution fitting is that "The distribution being tested is the correct distribution." In other words, the algorithm or procedure in distribution fitting is fairly straightforward:

1. Using the data, go through each distribution one at a time.

2. For each distribution, perform an inverted optimization approach to find the best-fitting input parameters to the distribution that minimizes the fitting errors.

3. Perform the Kolmogorov–Smirnov or Chi-Square test to determine the fit.

4. Obtain the p-values of the fit.

5. Rank the distributions from best fit to the worst fit.

5. Delphi Method and Custom Distributions

In a distributional fitting environment, higher p-values are better. The question is how high a p-value do you need to be comfortable with the fit? Clearly a fit of 0.95 is great versus 0.10, which is not that good at all. But what about values in between these two? In most cases, it is really up to the user to make this determination. Nonetheless, in situations where you do not have data, or not enough data points exist or the p-value fit is really low, there is an alternative: the use of the Custom Distribution to make your own distribution. This customized distribution is powerful and applicable because it has multiple advantageous characteristics, including the fact that you will always get a 100% fit or a p-value of 1 because it is nonparametric in nature and the approach uses the data to tell the story. That is, every data point will be used in the distribution. This custom distribution is perfect for use in the Delphi subject matter expert approach as well as for historical simulation, where all historical data are used and simulated.

To run this example, simply:

1. Start a new workbook in Excel. Create a new profile by clicking *Risk Simulator | New Profile* and then enter some data like those shown in Figure 5E2.H. *Select the data* and click *Edit | Copy* in Excel or use *Ctrl+C* or right-click and copy the cells into the Windows clipboard.

2. Select any empty cell and set an assumption *Risk Simulator | Set Input Assumption.* Select the *Custom* distribution and click on *Create Distribution.* Then, in the custom distribution designer interface, just follow the numbers for the four steps: *1 Paste, 2 Update Chart, 3 Apply,* and *4 Close.* Then back in the set assumptions properties, click *OK* to set the assumption.

3. Click on the *Step Simulation* icon a few times to see the value in the cell changing. You will see that it is randomly selecting the numbers from the original dataset, where numbers that have the highest probability of occurrence or are repeated more often in the original dataset are selected more often, of course.

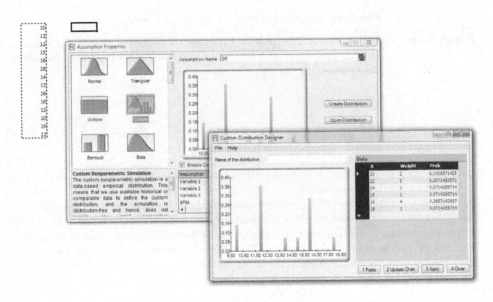

Figure 5E2.H: Custom Distribution

EXERCISE 3: DISTRIBUTIONAL ANALYSIS AND OVERLAY CHARTS

This sample model illustrates how to use Risk Simulator for:

1. Basics of PDF, CDF, ICDF, and Types of Probability Distributions

2. Distributional Analysis (Empirical Simulation and Theoretical PDF)

3. Simple Getting Started Applications of PDF and CDF

4. Computing Theoretical Probabilities of Events for Six Sigma Quality Control

5. Overlay Charts and Distributional Comparisons

Model Background

File Name: Overlay Charts.xls

Access: *Risk Simulator | Example Models | 14 Overlay Charts*

Prerequisites: Risk Simulator 2014 or later, Completed Basic Simulation Model Exercise, and Chapter 4 of *Modeling Risk* (Appendix: Understanding Probability Distributions)

1. Basics of PDF, CDF, ICDF, and Types of Probability Distributions

In this exercise, you will learn how to use the statistical probability *Distributional Analysis* tool in Risk Simulator that is very useful in a variety of settings. This tool can be used to compute the *probability density function* (PDF), which is also called the *probability mass function* (PMF) for discrete distributions (we will use these terms interchangeably), where given some distribution and its parameters, we can determine the probability of occurrence given some outcome x. In addition, the *cumulative distribution function* (CDF) can also be computed, which is the sum of the PDF values up to this x value. Finally, the *inverse cumulative distribution function* (ICDF) is used to compute the value x given the cumulative probability of occurrence.

2. Distributional Analysis (Empirical Simulation and Theoretical PDF)

Before we begin, let's briefly discuss the difference between using a simulation's resulting probabilities and using the statistical probability *Distributional Analysis* tool (Figure 5E3.A). If both the probability of an event happening and its probability distribution type are known for certain and the scenario is a basic situation (e.g., tossing a coin 10 times where no complex modeling is required), then the statistical probability analysis is sufficient, and the result will be a single probability value or a table of probability of outcomes. Conversely, in more complex situations where there are multiple variables and they are interacting with one another, and where a model needs to be built (e.g., cash flow return on investment model), we have no choice but to revert to risk simulation by setting multiple input assumptions and correlations, and running the simulation thousands of times to obtain the resulting probabilities.

3. Simple Getting Started Applications of PDF and CDF

This distributional analysis tool is accessible via *Risk Simulator | Analytical Tools | Distributional Analysis*. As an example, Figure 5E3.A shows the computation of a binomial distribution (i.e., a distribution with two outcomes, such as the tossing of a coin, where the outcome is either Heads or Tails, with some prescribed probability of heads and tails). Suppose we toss a coin two times, and set the outcome Heads as a success. We use the binomial distribution with Trials = 2 (tossing the coin twice) and Probability = *0.50* (the probability of success, of getting Heads). Selecting the PDF and setting the range of values *x* as from *0* to *2* with a step size of *1* (i.e., we are requesting the values 0, 1, 2 for *x*), the resulting probabilities are provided in the table and in a graphical format, as well as the theoretical four moments of the distribution. As the outcomes of the coin toss is Heads-Heads, Tails-Tails, Heads-Tails, and Tails-Heads, the probability of getting exactly no Heads is 25%, one Heads is 50%, and two Heads is 25%.

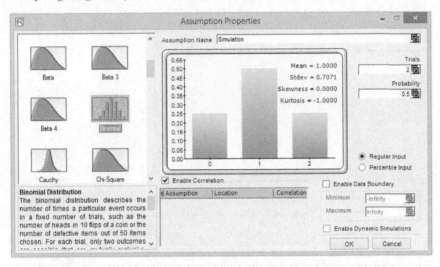

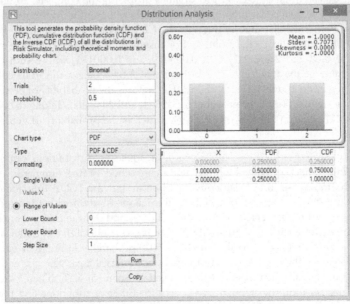

Figure 5E3.A: Distributional Analysis Tool

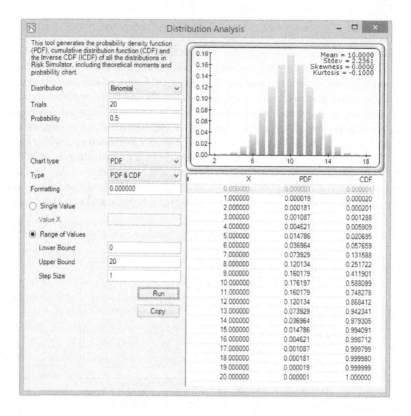

Figure 5E3.B: Binomial PDF and CDF

Similarly, we can obtain the exact probabilities of tossing the coin, say, 20 times, as seen in Figure 5E3.B. The results are presented both in table and graphical formats. Figure 5E3.B shows the same binomial distribution but now the CDF is computed. The CDF is simply the sum of the PDF values up to the point x. For instance, in Figure 5E3.B, we see that the probabilities of 0, 1, and 2 are 0.000001, 0.000019, and 0.000181, whose sum is 0.000201, which is the value of the CDF at $x = 2$ in Figure 5E3.B. Whereas the PDF computes the probabilities of getting exactly 2 Heads, the CDF computes the probability of getting no more than 2 Heads or up to 2 Heads (or probabilities of 0, 1, and 2 Heads). Taking the complement (i.e., $1 - 0.00021$) obtains 0.999799 or 99.9799% which is the probability of getting at least 3 Heads or more.

Using this *Distributional Analysis* tool, even more advanced distributions can be analyzed, such as the gamma, beta, negative binomial, and many others in Risk Simulator. As a further example of the tool's use in a continuous distribution and the ICDF functionality, Figure 5E3.C shows the standard-normal distribution (normal distribution with a mean of zero and standard deviation of one), where we apply the ICDF to find the value of x that corresponds to the cumulative probability of 97.50% (CDF). That is, a one-tail CDF of 97.50% is equivalent to a two-tail 95% confidence interval (there is a 2.50% probability in the right-tail and 2.50% in the left-tail, leaving 95% in the center or confidence interval area, which is equivalent to a 97.50% area for one-tail). The result is the familiar Z-Score of 1.96. Therefore, using this *Distributional Analysis* tool, the standardized scores for other distributions and the exact cumulative probabilities of other distributions can all be obtained quickly and easily.

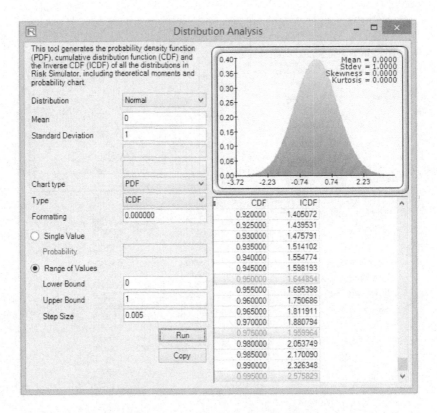

Figure 5E3.C: Standard-Normal CDF and ICDF

Figure 5E3.D illustrates another discrete distribution example by applying the Poisson distribution, a distribution that is used when trying to measure events occurring in a specific area and time (for instance, the average number of people standing in line at a McDonald's or waiting in line for a teller at a bank branch, the number of customers showing up at a restaurant, people missing their flights in a specific hour). Let us assume that the average number of people calling up a customer service center per hour is 2.5 individuals (we set Lambda or average value to *2.5* in Figure 5E3.D). We can determine that the probability of having 0 phone calls per hour is 8.20%, the probability of exactly 1 call per hour is 20.52%, 2 calls per hour is 25.65%, and so forth, by using the PDF function. Conversely, using the CDF function, we know that there is a 54.38% chance that you will get 0 or 1 or 2 calls per hour, or less than or equal to 2 calls per hour, or no more than 2 calls per hour. Of course, the probability of getting more than 2 calls is 100% – 54.38%, or 45.62% (the total probabilities for all numbers of calls will add to 100%). If you wish to be 99% sure that you will have enough customer sales representatives available to handle these incoming calls, you will need to have sufficient staff to handle up to 7 calls per hour.

- Exercise Question: How do you know what to set in terms of the upper bound and lower bound for the range of values to show in the table?

- Exercise Question: What is the probability of no more than 5 calls per hour?

- Exercise Question: What is the probability of at least 3 calls per hour?

- Exercise Question: What is the probability of exactly either 2 or 3 calls per hour?

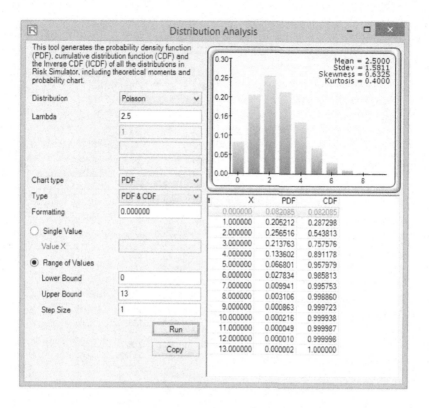

Figure 5E3.D: Poisson PDF and CDF

The negative binomial distribution is useful for modeling the distribution of the number of additional trials required on top of the number of successful occurrences required (R). For instance, in order to close a total of 10 sales opportunities, how many extra sales calls would you need to make above 10 calls given some probability of success in each call? The x-axis shows the number of additional calls required or the number of failed calls. The number of trials is not fixed, the trials continue until the Rth success, and the probability of success is the same from trial to trial. Probability of success (P) and number of successes required (R) are the distributional parameters. Such a model can be applied in a multitude of situations, such as the cost of sales cold calls, the budget required to train military recruits, and so forth. The simple example shown below illustrates how a negative binomial distribution works. Suppose that a salesperson is tasked with making cold calls and a resulting sale is considered a success while no sale means a failure. Suppose that, historically, the proportion of sales to all calls is 30%. We can model this scenario using the negative binomial distribution by setting the *Successes Required* (R) to equal 2 and the *Probability of Success* (P) as 0.3. For instance, say the salesperson makes 2 calls and the success rate is 30% per call and they are statistically independent of one another. There can be 4 possible outcomes (SS, SF, FS, FF, where S stands for success, and F for failure). The probability of SS is 0.3×0.3, or 9%; SF and FS are 0.3×0.7, or 21%; and FF is 0.7×0.7, or 49%. Therefore, there is a 9% chance that 2 calls are sufficient and no additional calls are needed to get the 2 successes required. In other words, $X = 0$ has a probability of 9% if we define X as the additional calls required beyond the 2 calls.

Extending to 3 calls, we have many possible outcomes, but the key outcomes we care about are 2 successful calls, which we can define as the following combinations: SSS, SSF, SFS, and FSS. Their respective probabilities are computed below (e.g., FSS is computed by $0.7 \times 0.3 \times 0.3 = 6.30\%$). Now, the combinatorial sequences SSS and SSF do not require a third call because the first two calls have already been successful. Further, SFF, FSF, FFS, and FFF all fail the required 2 call success as they only have either zero or one successful call. So, the sum total probability of the situations requiring a third call to make exactly 2 calls successful out of 3 is 12.60%. All other values are listed in the tool.

2 Call Example		
	Success	Failure
Call 1	30%	70%
Call 2	30%	70%

Success + Success	9%
Success + Failure	21%
Failure + Success	21%
Failure + Failure	49%
Sum	*100%*
Both Successful (R = 2)	9%

3 Call Example		
	Success	Failure
Call 1	30%	70%
Call 2	30%	70%
Call 3	30%	70%

Success + Success + Success	2.70%	*Not require 3rd call*
Success + Success + Failure	6.30%	*Not require 3rd call*
Success + Failure + Success	**6.30%**	***Requires 3rd call***
Failure + Success + Success	**6.30%**	***Requires 3rd call***
Success + Failure + Failure	14.70%	*Fails 2-call required*
Failure + Success + Failure	14.70%	*Fails 2-call required*
Failure + Failure + Success	14.70%	*Fails 2-call required*
Failure + Failure + Failure	34.30%	*Fails 2-call required*
Sum	*100.00%*	
Sum (Requires 3rd call)	**12.60%**	

Clearly, doing the above exercise for a large combinatorial problem with many required successes would be difficult and intractable. However, we can obtain the same results using Risk Simulator's *Distributional Analysis* tool running a negative binomial distribution with $R = 2$ and $P = 0.3$ (Figure 5E3.E). Notice that the probability of $X = 0$ is exactly what we had computed, 9%, and $X = 1$ yields 12.60%.

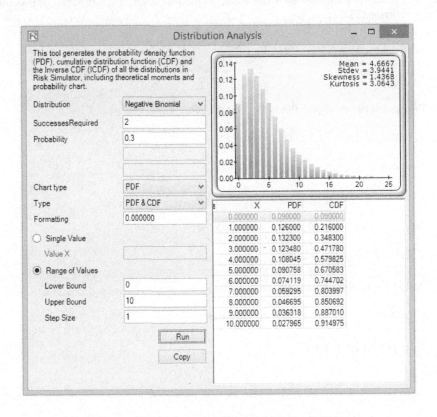

Figure 5E3.E: Negative Binomial PDF and CDF

4. Computing Theoretical Probabilities of Events for Six Sigma Quality Control

In this section, we continue using the *Distributional Analysis* tool and illustrate the manual computations used to obtain the exact probabilities of the occurrence of events for quality control purposes. These will be illustrated through some simple discrete distributions. The section continues with some continuous distributions for the purposes of theoretical hypotheses tests. Then hypothesis testing on empirically simulated data is presented, where we use theoretical distributions to simulate empirical data and run hypotheses tests.

Binomial Distribution

The binomial distribution describes the number of times a particular event occurs in a fixed number of trials, such as the number of heads in 10 flips of a coin or the number of defective items out of 50 items chosen. For each trial, only two outcomes are possible that are mutually exclusive. The trials are independent, where what happens in the first trial does not affect the next trial. The probability of an event occurring remains the same from trial to trial. Probability of success (p) and the number of total trials (n) are the distributional parameters. The number of successful trials is denoted x (the x-axis of the probability distribution graph). The input requirements in the distribution include *Probability of Success* > 0 and < 1 (e.g., $p \geq 0.0001$ and $p \leq 0.9999$), *Number of Trials* ≥ 1, and integers ≤ 1000.

Example: If the probability of obtaining a part that is defective is 50%, what is the probability that in selecting 4 parts at random, there will be no defective part, or 1 defective part, or 2 defective parts, and so forth? Recreate the probability mass function or probability density function (PDF):

Probability of no defects P($x = 0$): 6.25%:

$$C_0^4(.5)^0(.5)^{4-0} = \frac{4!}{0!(4-0)!}(.5)^0(.5)^{4-0} = \frac{1}{16} = 6.25\%$$

Probability of one defect P($x = 1$): 25.00%:

$$C_1^4(.5)^1(.5)^{4-1} = \frac{4!}{1!(4-1)!}(.5)^1(.5)^3 = \frac{4}{16} = 25\%$$

Probability of two defects P($x = 2$): 37.50%:

$$C_2^4(.5)^2(.5)^{4-2} = \frac{4!}{2!(4-2)!}(.5)^2(.5)^2 = \frac{6}{16} = 37.50\%$$

Probability of three defects P($x = 3$): 25.00%:

$$C_3^4(.5)^3(.5)^{4-3} = \frac{4!}{3!(4-3)!}(.5)^3(.5)^1 = \frac{4}{16} = 25\%$$

Probability of four defects P($x = 4$): 6.25%:

$$C_4^4(.5)^4(.5)^{4-4} = \frac{4!}{4!(4-4)!}(.5)^4(.5)^0 = \frac{1}{16} = 6.25\%$$

Total probabilities: 100.00%

where we define $P(x=0)$ as the probability (P) of the number of successes of an event (x), and the mathematical combination (C). In addition, you can sum up the probabilities to obtain the cumulative distribution function (CDF):

Probability of no defects $P(x = 0)$:

      6.25% computed as $P(x = 0)$

Probability of up to 1 defect $P(x \leq 1)$:

      31.25% computed as $P(x = 0) + P(x = 1)$

Probability of up to 2 defects $P(x \leq 2)$:

      68.75% computed as $P(x = 0) + P(x = 1) + P(x = 2)$

Probability of up to 3 defects $P(x \leq 3)$:

      93.75% computed as $P(x = 0) + P(x = 1) + P(x = 2) + P(x = 3)$

Probability of up to 4 defects $P(x \leq 4)$:

      100% computed as $P(x = 0) + P(x = 1) + P(x = 2) + P(x = 3) + P(x = 4)$

The same analysis can be performed using the Distribution Analysis tool in Risk Simulator. For instance, you can start the tool by clicking on *Risk Simulator | Analytical Tools | Distributional Analysis*, selecting *Binomial*, entering *4* for Trials and *0.5* for *Probability*, then selecting PDF as the type of analysis, and a range of between *0* and *4* with a step of *1*. The resulting table and PDF distribution is exactly as computed as seen in Figure 5E3.F. For practice, confirm the computed CDF values above using the *Distributional Analysis* tool. In addition, the four distributional moments can be determined using the tool.

Mean or Average	2.00
Standard Deviation	1.00
Skewness Coefficient	0.00
Kurtosis (Excess)	−0.50

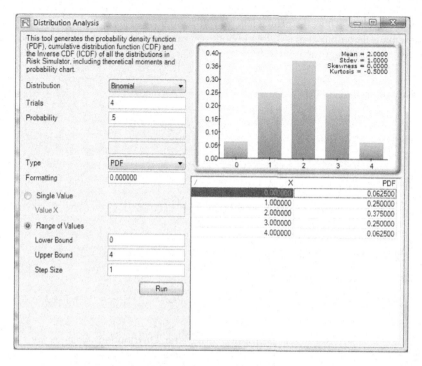

Figure 5E3.F: Distributional Analysis for a Binomial PDF

Poisson Distribution

The Poisson distribution describes the number of times an event occurs in a given space or time interval, such as the number of telephone calls per minute or the number of errors per page in a document (Figure 5E3.G). The number of possible occurrences in any interval is unlimited; the occurrences are independent. The number of occurrences in one interval does not affect the number of occurrences in other intervals, and the average number of occurrences must remain the same from interval to interval. Rate or Lambda is the only distributional parameter. The input requirement for the distribution is Rate > 0 and ≤ 1000.

Exercise Question: A tire service center has the capacity of servicing 6 customers in an hour. From prior experience, on average 3 show up an hour. The owner is afraid that there might insufficient manpower to handle an overcrowding of over 6 customers. What is the probability that there will be exactly 6 customers? What about 6 or more customers? Use Figures 5E3.G and 5E3.H to help you answer these questions.

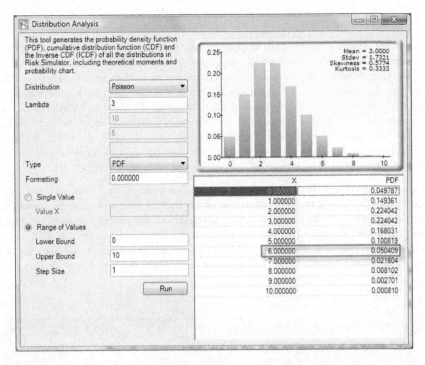

Figure 5E3.G: PDF of a Poisson

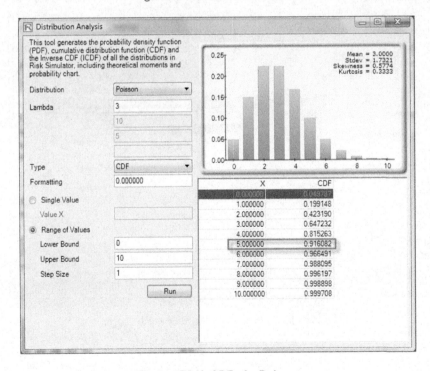

Figure 5E3.H: CDF of a Poisson

Normal Distribution

The normal distribution is the most important distribution in probability theory because it describes many natural phenomena, such as people's IQs or heights. Decision makers can use the normal distribution to describe uncertain variables such as the inflation rate or the future price of gasoline. Some value of the uncertain variable is the most likely (the mean of the distribution), the uncertain variable could as likely be above the mean as it could be below the mean (symmetrical about the mean), and the uncertain variable is more likely to be in the vicinity of the mean than farther away. Mean (μ) and standard deviation (σ) are the distributional parameters. The input requirements include Mean (which can take on any value) and Standard Deviation (which must be > 0 and can be any positive value).

Exercise Question: You observe that in the past, on average, your manufactured batteries last for 15 months with a standard deviation of 1.5 months. Assume that the battery life is normally distributed. If a battery is randomly selected, find the probability that it has a life of less than 16.5 months or over 16.5 months. Using the tool, we obtain CDF of X = 16.5 months as 84.13%, which means that there is 84.13% chance that the manufactured batteries last up to 16.5 months, and 1 − 0.8413 or 15.87% chance the batteries will last over 16.5 months (Figure 5E3.I).

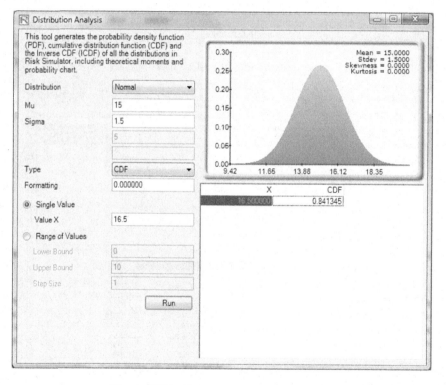

Figure 5E3.I: CDF of a Normal Distribution

Exercise Question: Alternatively, suppose you wish to provide a 12-month warranty on your batteries, that is, if the battery dies before 12 months, you will give a full refund. What are the chances that you may have to provide this refund?

Using the tool, we find that the CDF for X = 12 is a 2.28% chance that a refund will have to be issued (Figure 5E3.J).

So far, we have been computing the probabilities of events occurring using the PDF and CDF functions and tools. We can also reverse the analysis and obtain the X values given some probability, using the inverse cumulative distribution function (ICDF), as seen next.

Exercise Question: If the probability calculated in the above problem is too high and, hence, too costly for you and you wish to minimize the cost and probability of having to refund your customers down to a 1% probability, what would be a suitable warranty date (in months)?

The answer is that to provide anything less than an 11.51 month guarantee will most likely result in less than or equal to a 1% chance of a return. To obtain the results here, we use the ICDF analysis in the Distributional Analysis tool (Figure 5E3.K).

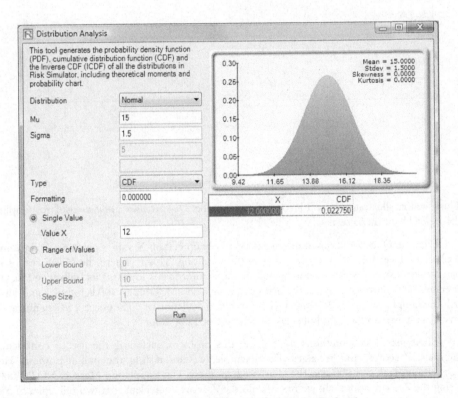

Figure 5E3.J: Probability of a Guarantee Refund

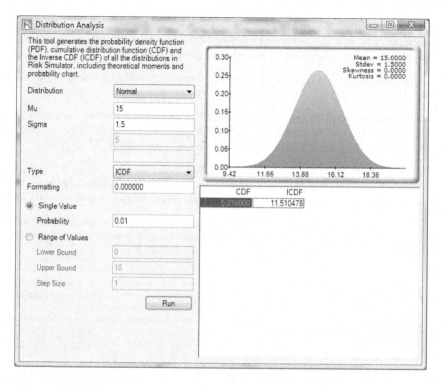

Figure 5E3.K: Obtaining the Inverse Cumulative Distribution Function (ICDF)

Hypothesis Tests in a Theoretical Situation

This section illustrates how to continue using the *Distributional Analysis* tool to simplify theoretical hypothesis tests.

Exercise Question: Sometimes, we need to obtain certain X values given a certainty and probability level for the purposes of hypothesis testing. This is where the ICDF comes in handy. For instance, suppose a light bulb manufacturer needs to test if its bulbs can last, on average, 1,000 burning hours. If the plant manager randomly samples 100 light bulbs and finds that the sample average is 980 hours with a standard deviation of 80 hours, at a 5% significance level (two-tails), do the light bulbs last an average of 1,000 hours?

There are several methods for solving this problem, including the use of confidence intervals, Z-scores, and p-values. For example, we are testing the null hypothesis Ho: Population Mean = 1,000 and the alternate hypothesis Ha: Population Mean is NOT 1,000. Using the Z-score approach, we first obtain the Z-score equivalent to a two-tail alpha of 5% (which means one-tail is 2.5%, and using the *Distributional Analysis* tool we get the Z = 1.96 at a CDF of 97.50%, equivalent to a one-tail p-value of 2.5%). Using the *Distributional Analysis* tool, set the distribution to Normal with a mean of zero and standard deviation of one (this is the standard-normal Z distribution). Then, compute the ICDF for 0.975 or 97.5% CDF, which provides an X value of 1.9599 or 1.96 (Figure 5E3.L).

Using the confidence interval formula, we get:

$$\mu \pm Z\left(\frac{s}{\sqrt{n}}\right)$$

$$1000 \pm 1.96\left(\frac{80}{\sqrt{100}}\right)$$

$$1000 \pm 15.68$$

This result means that the statistical confidence interval is between 984.32 and 1015.68. As the sample mean of 980 falls outside this confidence interval, we reject the null hypothesis and conclude that the true population mean is different from 1,000 hours.

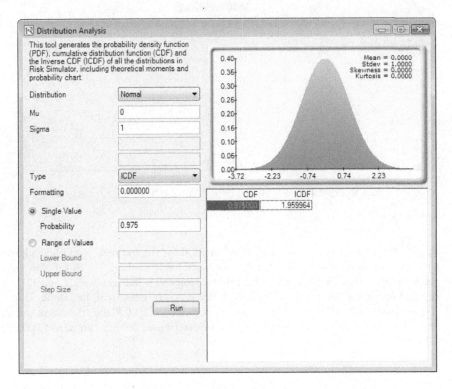

Figure 5E3.L: Standard-Normal Z-score

A much quicker and simpler approach is to use the *Distributional Analysis* tool directly. Seeing that we are performing a statistical sample, we first need to correct for small sampling size bias by correcting the standard deviation to get:

$$\frac{s}{\sqrt{n}} = \frac{80}{\sqrt{100}} = 8$$

Then we can find the CDF relating to the sample mean of 980. We see that the CDF p-value is 0.0062, less than the alpha of 0.025 one-tail (or 0.50 two-tail), which means we reject the null hypothesis and conclude that the population mean is statistically significantly different from the 1,000 hours tested (Figure 5E3.M).

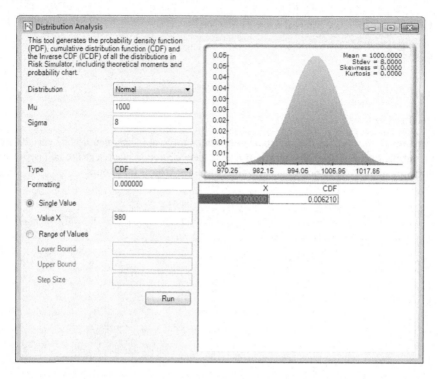

Figure 5E3.M: Obtaining P-Values Using the Distributional Analysis Tool

Yet another alternative is to use the ICDF method for the mean and sampling adjusted standard deviation and compute the X values corresponding to the 2.5% and 97.5% levels. The results indicate that the 95% two-tail confidence interval is between 984.32 and 1,015.68 as computed previously. Hence, 980 falls outside this range, meaning that the sample value of 980 is statistically far away from the hypothesized population of 1,000 (i.e., the unknown true population based on a statistical sampling test can be determined to be not equal to 1,000). See Figure 5E3.N.

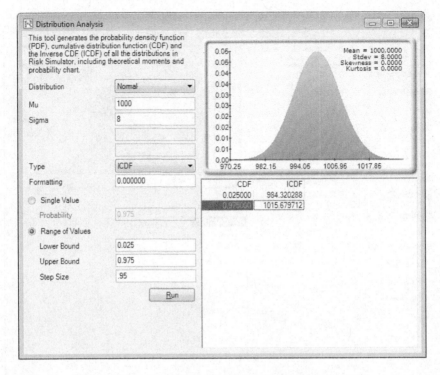

Figure 5E3.N: Computing Statistical Confidence Intervals

Note that we adjust the sampling standard deviation only because the population is large and we sample a small size. However, if the population standard deviation is known, we do not divide it by the square root of N (sample size).

Exercise Question: In another example, suppose it takes, on average, 20 minutes with a standard deviation of 12 minutes to complete a certain manufacturing task. Based on a sample of 36 workers, what is the probability that you will find someone completing the task taking between 18 and 24 minutes?

Again, we adjust the sampling standard deviation to be 12 divided by the square root of 36, or equivalent to 2. The CDFs for 18 and 24 are 15.86% and 97.72%, respectively, yielding the difference of 81.86%, which is the probability of finding someone taking between 18 and 24 minutes to complete the task. See Figure 5E3.O.

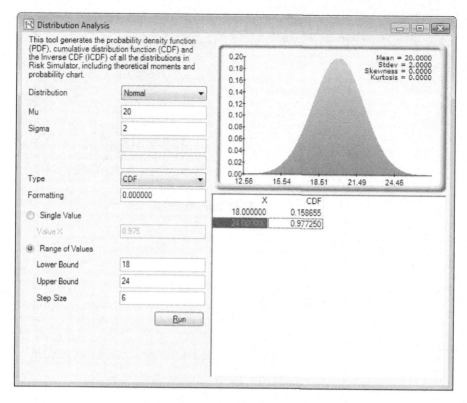

Figure 5E3.O: Sampling Confidence Interval

Exercise Question: Sometimes, when the sample size is small, we need to revert to using the Student's t-distribution. For instance, suppose a plant manager studies the life of a particular battery and samples 10 units. The sample mean is 5 hours with a sample standard deviation of 1 hour. What is the 95% confidence interval for the battery life?

Using the t-distribution, we set the degrees of freedom as $n-1$ or 9, with a mean location of 0 for a standard t-distribution. The ICDF for 0.975 or 97.5% (5% two-tail means 2.5% on one-tail, creating a complement of 97.5%) is equivalent to 2.262 (Figure 5E3.P). So, the 95% statistical confidence interval is:

$$\bar{x} \pm t \frac{s}{\sqrt{n}}$$

$$5 \pm 2.262 \frac{1}{\sqrt{10}}$$

$$5 \pm 0.71$$

Therefore, the confidence interval is between 4.29 and 5.71.

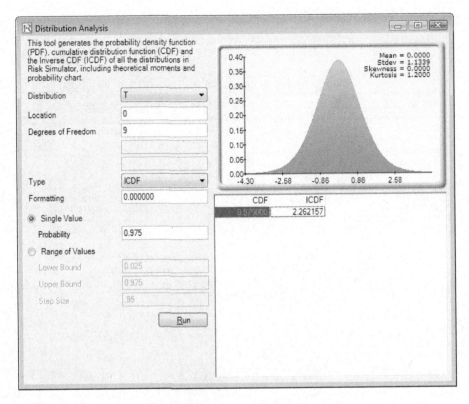

Figure 5E3.P: Standard T-Distribution

5. Overlay Charts and Distributional Comparisons

In this section, we will look at Overlay Charts in Risk Simulator. As you can already tell, sometimes it might be advantageous to overlay several probability distributions on top of one another to compare how they look, as well as to learn the characteristics of specific distributions. For instance, the binomial distribution we have been so fond of earlier in this exercise can take on a variety of shapes (Figure 5E3.Q) when different probabilities of success (*P*) and number of trials (*N*) are used. When *N* is a high value, the distribution becomes more symmetrical and approaches the normal distribution (due to the central limit theorem and the law of large numbers), and, in fact, the normal distribution is a good approximation when *N* is fairly large.

As another example, the beta distribution is a fairly flexible distribution where depending on the input parameters you use, you can get a variety of different shapes and sizes (Figure 5E3.R). Specifically, if *Alpha* = *Beta* = 1, the distribution is exactly that of a uniform distribution. When both *Alpha* = *Beta*, the distribution is fairly symmetrical. The larger the *Alpha* and *Beta* parameters, while at the same time being equal, makes the distribution more symmetrical and normal (notice that the skewness is zero and the excess kurtosis is close to zero, indicative of a normal distribution). Further, when *Alpha* < *Beta*, we have a positive skew, and if *Alpha* > *Beta*, we have a negative skew. Further, if either *Alpha* or *Beta* is 1 and the other is 2, we have a triangular distribution, when *Alpha* = *Beta* = 2, we have a mound distribution, and if *Alpha* = 2 and *Beta* > *Alpha*, we have a lognormal distribution.

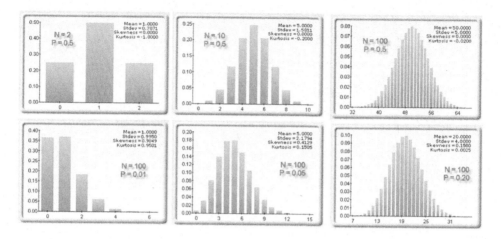

Figure 5E3.Q: The Faces of Binomial and Central Limit Theorem
Top Row: (N=2, P=0.5), (N=10, P=0.5), (N=100, P=0.5)
Bottom Row: (N=100, P=0.01), (N=100, P=0.05), (N=100, P=0.2)

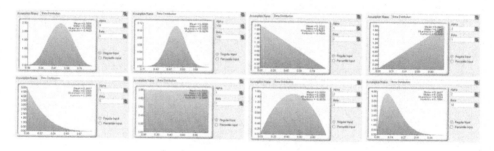

Figure 5E3.R: The Faces of Beta Distribution
Top Row: (α=5, β=5), (α=100, β=100), (α=1, β=2), (α=2, β=1)
Bottom Row: (α=1, β=5), (α=1, β=1), (α=2, β=2), (α=2, β=10)

We will now work on an exercise to run the *Overlay Chart* tool by comparing and overlaying input assumptions with forecast outputs (Figure 5E3.S), as well as looking at comparing input assumptions with various distributions or with the same distribution using different input parameters (Figure 5E3.T). To get started with this exercise, follow the instructions below:

1. Start Excel, open the example model *Risk Simulator | Example Models | 14 Overlay Charts*, and run a simulation by selecting *Risk Simulator | Run Simulation* (or clicking on the Run Simulation icon). You can also run super speed simulation if you wish. Click *OK* when the simulation is done.

2. Click on *Risk Simulator | Analytical Tools | Overlay Charts* and replicate some of the overlay charts in Figure 5E3.S, specifically:

   a. Overlay PDF Bar chart with Revenue A, Revenue E, Income A, Income E

   b. Overlay PDF Line chart with Revenue A, Revenue B, Income A, Income B

   c. Overlay PDF Bar chart with Revenue A, Revenue B, Revenue C (turn confidence on and off)

d. Overlay 3D Bar chart with Revenue A, Revenue C, Revenue E

e. Overlay Time Series Area chart with Revenue A, Revenue E, Income A, and Income E

f. Overlay Time Series Area chart with Revenues A to E

g. Overlay Time Series 3D Bar chart with Revenues A to E

h. Overlay Time Series 3D Bar Stack chart with Revenue A, Revenue E, Income A, and Income E

3. Open a new workbook in Excel and create a new profile. Go to an empty cell and set an input assumption. Use the Beta distribution, set the parameters to be Alpha = 2, Beta =3, and give it a name (e.g., "Beta 2,3"). Then, go down to the next cell and set another assumption with a Beta (2,4) distribution, and then another cell with Beta (2,5), while naming them appropriately each time. Run a simulation, and run the overlay chart. Select these three assumptions for the overlay chart and run the PDF line chart (Figure 5E3.T).

Note: With a similar approach, you can now keep trying and comparing other theoretical distributions using the input assumptions method. Remember, if only assumptions are used in the overlay chart, the theoretical distributions will be shown. If only output forecasts are chosen, the empirical distributions will be shown, and if both assumptions and forecasts are chosen, the theoretical distributions will be overlaid against the empirical distribution results. In all cases, the theoretical distributions look like nice smooth curves, whereas empirical distributions are shown as bars or irregular curves. Of course, you can change the colors of each variable by clicking on the color tags beside each selected distribution.

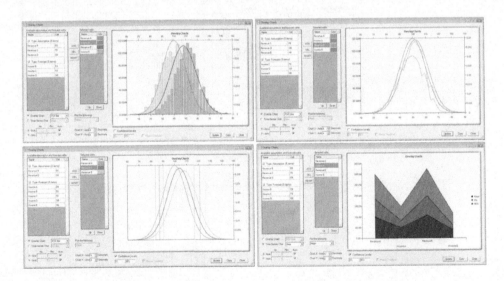

Figure 5E3.S: Various Types of Overlay Charts (continues)

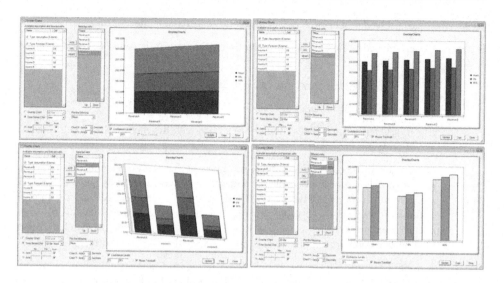

Figure 5E3.S Various Types of Overlay Charts (continued)

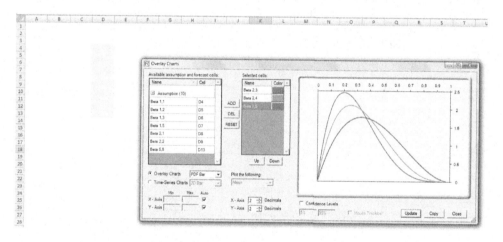

Figure 5E3.T: The Faces of Beta on Overlay Chart

EXERCISE 4: BOOTSTRAP SIMULATION, HYPOTHESIS TESTING, AND SEGMENTATION CLUSTERING

This sample model illustrates how to use Risk Simulator for:

1. Nonparametric Bootstrap Simulation

2. Theoretical Hypothesis Tests

3. Segmentation Clustering

Model Background

File Name: Hypothesis Testing and Bootstrap Simulation.xls

Access: *Risk Simulator | Example Models | 08 Hypothesis Testing and Bootstrap Simulation*

Prerequisites: Risk Simulator 2014 or later, Completed the Basic Simulation Exercise

1. Nonparametric Bootstrap Simulation

Bootstrap simulation is a simple technique that estimates the reliability or accuracy of forecast statistics or other sample raw data. Essentially, bootstrap simulation is used in hypothesis testing where we use the empirical resampling approach, that is, using the actual simulated data and resampling the simulation multiple times. In contrast, classical or traditional methods rely on mathematical formulas to describe the accuracy of sample statistics where these methods assume that the distribution of a sample statistic approaches a normal distribution, making the calculation of the statistic's standard error or confidence interval relatively easy. We used these methods in the previous exercise, "Distributional Analysis and Overlay Charts," and will use them in the next segment of this exercise, where additional theoretical hypothesis tests are run. However, when a statistic's sampling distribution is not normally distributed or easily found, these classical methods are difficult to use or are invalid. In contrast, bootstrapping analyzes sample statistics empirically by repeatedly sampling the data and creating distributions of the different statistics from each sampling.

In essence, nonparametric bootstrap simulation can be thought of as simulation based on a simulation. Thus, after running a simulation, the resulting statistics are displayed, but the accuracy of such statistics and their statistical significance are sometimes in question. For instance, if a simulation run's skewness statistic is –0.10, is this distribution truly negatively skewed or is the slight negative value attributable to random chance? What about –0.15, –0.20, and so forth? That is, how far is far enough such that this distribution is considered to be negatively skewed? The same question can be applied to all the other statistics. Is one distribution statistically identical to another distribution with regard to some computed statistics or are they significantly different? Figure 5E4.A to 6E4.C illustrate some sample bootstrap results. For instance, the 90% confidence for the skewness statistic is between 0.0500 and 0.2585, such that the value 0 falls outside of this confidence interval, indicating that on a 90% confidence, the skewness of this forecast is statistically significantly different from zero, or that this distribution can be considered as positively skewed and not symmetrical. Conversely, if the value 0 falls inside of this confidence, then the opposite is true, the distribution is symmetrical.

Think of it another way… If I have a simple or complicated model (Figure 5E4.A) and if there is no seed value set in the simulation, each time I run the simulation, I get slightly different values. So, suppose the resulting distribution's skew is 0.1650. How do I test to see if this is just random white noise such that this value is close enough to zero to say it is statistically significantly no different from zero? Or perhaps it is statistically significantly positive. Well, I call up 100 of my best buddies and send them each the same model and ask all of them to do me a big favor and run the simulation 1,000 trials (Figure 5E4.B). This means each person will have his or her own forecast chart and forecast statistics. So, there will be 100 averages, 100 standard deviations, 100 skew, 100 kurtosis, and so forth. I call each of them back up and gather all the data and plot the 100 skews in a histogram, and the result is the bootstrapped simulation as shown in Figure 5E4.C. So, if 90 out of 100 of my buddies (90% confidence interval in Figure 5E4.C), call me back and provide me a positive skew value, chances are that the real skew is positive! In fact, in Figure 5E4.C, we actually see that almost 100% of the values are positive, indicating a statistically significant positive skew. In contrast, if the 90% confidence interval straddles zero (the range is positive and negative), such as for the kurtosis measure in Figure 5E4.C, or in the analogy, 90 out of a 100 friends who call me up provide me both positive and negative values close to zero, I cannot tell if the kurtosis is statistically different than zero and I would correctly infer that there is zero kurtosis.

In other words, bootstrap simulation can be thought of as running a statistical analysis on the statistics, or getting the precision and confidence interval of the statistics, or determining if the simulated forecast statistic is statistically significant. It works well because according to the Law of Large Numbers and Central Limit Theorem in statistics, the mean of the sample means is an unbiased estimator and approaches the true population mean when the sample size increases.

To run the exercise, follow the steps below:

1. Start Excel and open the example model *Risk Simulator | Example Models | 08 Hypothesis Testing and Bootstrap Simulation*. Run a simulation as usual by going to *Risk Simulator | Run Simulation* (or click on the Run icon), and click *OK* when the simulation is done (Figure 5E4.A).

2. Click on *Risk Simulator | Analytical Tools | Nonparametric Bootstrap* (or click on the Next icon repeatedly until you see the Analytical Tools ribbon set, and from here you can click on the Nonparametric Bootstrap icon). In our example, select *Income A* and then check some of the statistics you wish to test, including *mean, skew,* and *kurtosis* (Figure 5E4.B) and click *OK.*

3. Review bootstrap simulation results and create two-tailed confidence intervals for 90%, 95% and 99%.

   a. Exercise Question: Why do we use these 90%, 95% and 99% confidence levels?

   b. Exercise Question: Why do we use two tails? When can and should we use one tail, and if so, should it be a left-tail or right-tail confidence?

MODEL A   MODEL B

Revenue $200.00   Revenue $200.00
Cost $100.00   Cost $100.00
Income $100.00   Income $100.00

To replicate this model, start by creating a Simulation
(Simulation I New Profile), then, set the random seed
revenue cells and provide them a Normal distribution
deviation of 20 (select one
select Normal and enter th
each of the cost cells. Fina
the simulation.

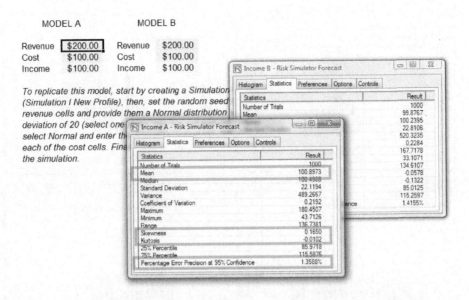

Figure 5E4.A: Simulation Modeling Results

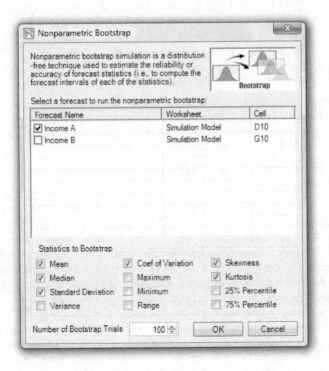

Figure 5E4.B: Running a Bootstrap Simulation

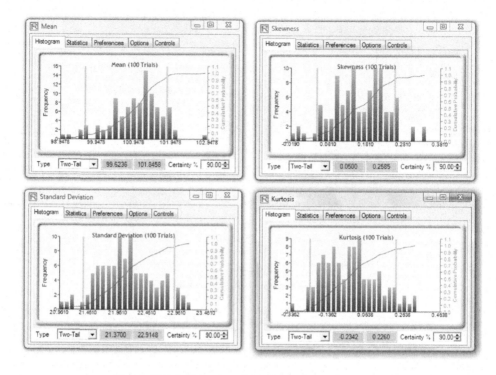

Figure 5E4.C: Bootstrap Results and Interpretation

2. Theoretical Hypothesis Tests

To run the hypothesis test, use the following procedures:

1. Rerun the same simulation and click on *Risk Simulator | Analytical Tools | Hypothesis Test*, and choose two forecasts at a time (in our example model, there are only two forecasts, so make sure both of them are chosen). Select the type of statistical tests you wish to run (for this example, keep the default selection) and click *OK*.

2. Review the created statistical analysis report and try to understand the results of the hypothesis test.

A hypothesis test is performed when testing the means and variances of two distributions to determine if they are statistically identical or statistically different from one another (Figures 5E4.D and 5E4.E). It is performed to see if the differences between two means and two variances that occur are based on random chance or are, in fact, different from one another. The two-variable t-test with unequal variances (the population variance of forecast 1 is expected to be different from the population variance of forecast 2) is appropriate when the forecast distributions are from different populations (e.g., data collected from two different geographical locations, two different operating business units, and so forth). The two-variable t-test with equal variances (the population variance of forecast 1 is expected to be equal to the population variance of forecast 2) is appropriate when the forecast distributions are from similar populations (e.g., data collected from two different engine designs with similar specifications and so forth). The paired dependent two-variable t-test is appropriate when the forecast distributions are from similar populations (e.g., data collected from the same group of customers but on different occasions, and so forth). A two-tailed hypothesis test is performed on the null hypothesis Ho such that the two variables' population means are statistically identical to one another.

The alternative hypothesis is that the population means are statistically different from one another. If the calculated p-values are less than or equal to 0.01, 0.05, or 0.10, this means that the hypothesis is rejected, which implies that the forecast means are statistically significantly different at the 1%, 5%, and 10% significance levels. If the null hypothesis is not rejected when the p-values are high, the means of the two forecast distributions are statistically similar to one another. The same analysis is performed on variances of two forecasts at a time using the pairwise F-test. If the p-values are small, then the variances (and standard deviations) are statistically different from one another; otherwise, for large p-values, the variances are statistically identical to one another.

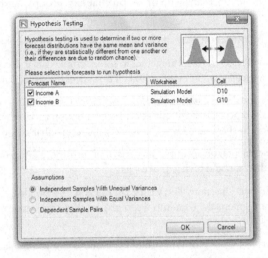

Figure 5E4.D: Hypothesis Test Types

Hypothesis Test on the Means and Variances of Two Forecasts

Statistical Summary

A hypothesis test is performed when testing the means and variances of two distributions to determine if they are statistically identical or statistically different from one another. That is, to see if the differences between two means and two variances that occur are based on random chance or they are in fact different from one another. The two-variable t-test with unequal variances (the population variance of forecast 1 is expected to be different from the population variance of forecast 2) is appropriate when the forecast distributions are from different populations (e.g., data collected from two different geographical locations, two different operating business units, and so forth). The two-variable t-test with equal variances (the population variance of forecast 1 is expected to be equal to the population variance of forecast 2) is appropriate when the forecast distributions are from similar populations (e.g., data collected from two different engine designs with similar specifications, and so forth). The paired dependent two-variable t-test is appropriate when the forecast distributions are from similar populations (e.g., data collected from the same group of customers but on different occasions, and so forth).

A two-tailed hypothesis test is performed on the null hypothesis Ho such that the two variables' population means are statistically identical to one another. The alternative hypothesis is that the population means are statistically different from one another. If the calculated p-values are less than or equal to 0.01, 0.05, or 0.10, this means that the hypothesis is rejected, which implies that the forecast means are statistically significantly different at the 1%, 5% and 10% significance levels. If the null hypothesis is not rejected when the p-values are high, the means of the two forecast distributions are statistically similar to one another. The same analysis is performed on variances of two forecasts at a time using the pairwise F-test. If the p-values are small, then the variances (and standard deviations) are statistically different from one another, otherwise, for large p-values, the variances are statistically identical to one another.

Result

Hypothesis Test Assumption:	Unequal Variances
Computed t-statistic:	1.015722
P-value for t-statistic:	0.309885
Computed F-statistic:	1.063476
P-value for F-statistic:	0.330914

Figure 5E4.E: Hypothesis Test Results

3. Segmentation Clustering

Segmentation clustering is the technique of taking a large dataset and running some algorithms that combine k-means hierarchical analysis, data clustering with centroids and Euclidean mean distance measures, and other methods of moments to find the best-fitting groups or natural statistical clusters to statistically divide or segment the original dataset into multiple naturally occurring groups. You can see the two-group memberships in Figure 5E4.F, which illustrates how this is done, and Figure 5E4.G shows the results of segmenting into two, three, and four groups. Clearly you can segment this dataset into as many groups as you wish. This technique is valuable in a variety of settings including marketing (market segmentation of customers into various customer relationship management or profitability groups, and so forth), physical sciences, engineering, and others.

To run the exercise on segmentation clustering, follow the steps below:

1. Start a new worksheet in Excel and enter in some sample data in a column. You can reuse the sample dataset shown in Figure 5E4.F. Then select the data (Figure 5E4.F).

2. Click on *Risk Simulator | Analytical Tools | Segmentation Clustering*, and choose any one of the three options. To get started, simply select the first option to *Show All Segmentation Clusters*, select *2* clusters to show, and click *OK*. Review the results that are generated.

3. Repeat the segmentation example but this time use more clusters; for example, set *4* clusters and then run and review the results.

    a. Exercise Question: The values 251123 and 284456 look similar but why, when you segment the data into 4 groups, are these two values assigned to different group memberships?

    b. Exercise Question: What other applications can you think of that might benefit from using segmentation clustering techniques?

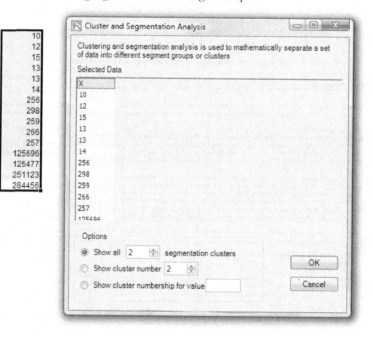

Figure 5E4.F: Segmentation Clustering

SEGMENTATION AND CLUSTER ANALYSIS RESULT

Sample	Ordered Data	Groups: 2	3	4
1	10	1	1	1
2	12	1	1	1
3	15	1	1	1
4	13	1	1	1
5	13	1	1	1
6	14	1	1	1
7	256	1	1	1
8	298	1	1	1
9	259	1	1	1
10	266	1	1	1
11	257	1	1	1
12	125696	1	2	2
13	125477	1	2	2
14	251123	2	3	3
15	284456	2	3	4

Figure 5E4.G: Clustering Results

EXERCISE 5: DATA DIAGNOSTICS AND STATISTICAL ANALYSIS

This sample model illustrates how to use Risk Simulator for:

1. Running Data Diagnostics

2. Running Statistical Analysis

Model Background

File Name: Regression Diagnostics.xls

Access: *Risk Simulator | Example Models | 16 Regression Diagnostics*

Prerequisites: Risk Simulator 2014 or later, Chapter 7 (Pitfalls of Forecasting)

Sometimes when you have a lot of data, what do you do with it? In this exercise, we will look at two powerful tools in Risk Simulator for running data diagnostics and statistical analysis.

1. Running Data Diagnostics

To run this exercise, use the following procedures:

1. Start Excel and open the example model *Risk Simulator | Example Models | 16 Regression Diagnostics*.

2. Go to the *Time Series Data* worksheet and select the data you want to analyze, including the data headers (Figure 5E5.A).

3. Click on *Risk Simulator | Analytical Tools | Diagnostic Tool*, select the dependent variable, and click *OK*.

    a. Exercise Question: What are some of the basic requirements and assumptions in a multiple regression analysis? In other words, if these assumptions are violated, your regression analysis and other related forecast methods will be biased and sometimes invalid.

4. Review the generated report and try to understand what each test is for and how to interpret the results. You can review the Pitfalls of Forecasting section for more high-level explanations of these tests and what they do:

    o   Heteroskedasticity

    o   Micronumerosity

    o   Outliers

    o   Nonlinearity

    o   Autocorrelation of the Dependent Variable

        ▪   Autocorrelation

        ▪   Partial Autocorrelation

    o   Distributive Lags of the Independent Variables

    o   Test for Normality and Sphericity of Errors

- o   Nonstationarity Analysis of Dependent Variable

    - ▪   Brownian motion stochastic process parameter estimation

    - ▪   Mean-reversion stochastic process parameter estimation

    - ▪   Jump-diffusion stochastic process parameter estimation

- o   Multicollinearity Analysis of Independent Variables

    - ▪   Correlation Matrix

    - ▪   Variance Inflation Factor

- o   Correlation Analysis of All Variables

    - ▪   Linear Correlation

    - ▪   Nonlinear Correlation

    - ▪   Statistical Significance Tests of Correlations

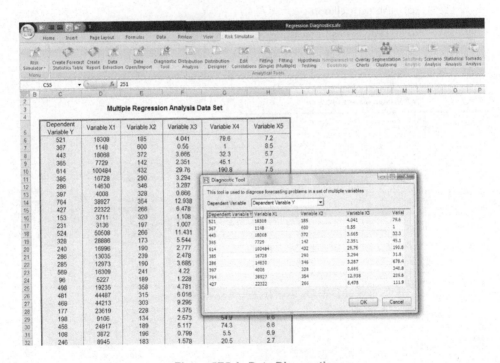

Figure 5E5.A: Data Diagnostics

2. Running Statistical Analysis

To run this exercise, use the following procedures:

1. Select the data you wish to analyze (Figure 5E5.B). You can use the same model (Regression Diagnostics) or you can open another example in *Risk Simulator | Example Models | 18 Statistical Analysis*. Then go to the *Data* worksheet, making sure the data to analyze are selected.

2. Click on *Risk Simulator | Analytical Tools | Statistical Analysis*, and choose whether the dataset selected is a single variable or multiple variables arranged in columns, and click *OK*.

3. You can now select the tests to run or keep and run all tests by default, and click *OK*.

   a. Exercise Question: When you are done reviewing the forecast charts, how do you close them all at once without having to exit each one individually?

4. Review the generated report and try to understand what each test is for and how to interpret the results. This tool runs and tests the following items:

- o Descriptive Statistics

- o Single Variable Distributional Fitting

- o Hypothesis Test (t-Test on the Population Mean of One Variable)

- o Nonlinear Extrapolation

- o Test for Normality

- o Stochastic Process Parameter Estimations

- o Autocorrelation

- o Time-Series Forecasting

- o Linear Trend Line Projection

Multiple Regression Analysis Data Set

Dependent Variable Y	Variable X1	Variable X2	Variable X3	Variable X4	Variable X5
521	18308	185	4.041	79.6	7.2
367	1148	600	0.55	1	8.5
443	18068	372			
365	7729	142			
614	100484	432			
385	16728	290			
286	14630	346			
397	4008	328			
784	38927	354			
427	22322	266			
153	3711	320			
231	3136	197			
524	50508	266			
328	28886	173			
240	16998	190			
286	13035	239			
285	12973	190			
569	16309	241			
96	5227	189			
498	19235	358			
481	44487	315			
468	44213	303			
177	23619	228		4.375	55	5.1
198	9106	134	2.573	54.9	8.6
458	24917	189	5.117	74.3	6.6
108	3872	196	0.799	5.5	6.9
246	8945	183	1.578	20.5	2.7
291	2373	417	1.202	10.9	5.5
68	7128	233	1.109	123.7	7.2
311	23624	349	7.73	1042	6.6
606	5242	284	1.515	12.5	6.9
512	92629	499	17.99	381	7.2
426	28795	231	6.629	136.1	5.8
47	4487	143	0.639	9.3	4.1
265	48799	249	10.847	264.9	6.4

Figure 5E5.B: Statistical Analysis

SECTION FOUR –
RISK PREDICTION

CHAPTER 6 –
TOMORROW'S FORECAST
TODAY

Forecasting is the act of predicting the future, whether it is based on historical data or speculation about the future when no history exists. When historical data exist, a quantitative or statistical approach is best, but if no historical data exist, then a qualitative or judgmental approach is usually the only recourse. Figure 6.1 lists the most common methodologies for forecasting.

DIFFERENT TYPES OF
FORECASTING TECHNIQUES

Generally, forecasting can be divided into quantitative and qualitative approaches. Qualitative forecasting is used when little to no reliable historical, contemporaneous, or comparable data exist. Several qualitative methods exist such as the Delphi or expert opinion approach (a consensus-building forecast by field experts, marketing experts, or internal staff members), management assumptions (target growth rates set by senior management), as well as market research or external data or polling and surveys (data obtained through third-party sources, industry and sector indexes, or active market research). These estimates can be either single-point estimates (an average consensus) or a set of prediction values (a distribution of predictions). The latter can be entered into Risk Simulator as a custom distribution and the resulting predictions can be simulated; that is, running a nonparametric simulation using the prediction data points as the custom distribution.

For quantitative forecasting, the available data or data that need to be forecasted can be divided into time-series (values that have a time element to them, such as revenues at different years, inflation rates, interest rates, market share, failure rates, and so forth), cross-sectional (values that are time-independent, such as the grade point average of sophomore students across the nation in a particular year, given each student's levels of SAT scores, IQ, and number of alcoholic beverages consumed per week), or mixed panel (mixture between time-series and panel data, e.g., predicting sales over the next 10 years given budgeted marketing expenses and market share projections, which means that the sales data are time-series but exogenous variables such as marketing expenses and market share exist to help to model the forecast predictions).

Here is a quick review of each methodology and several quick getting started examples in using the software. More detailed descriptions and example models of each of these techniques are found throughout this and the next chapter.

- *ARIMA.* Autoregressive integrated moving average (ARIMA, also known as Box–Jenkins ARIMA) is an advanced econometric modeling technique. ARIMA looks at historical time-series data and performs back-fitting optimization routines to account for historical autocorrelation (the relationship of a variable's values over time, that is, how a variable's data is related to itself over time), accounts for the stability of the data to correct for the nonstationary characteristics of the data, and learns over time by correcting its forecasting errors. Think of ARIMA as an advanced multiple regression model on steroids, where time-series variables are modeled and predicted using its historical data as well as other time-series explanatory variables. Advanced knowledge in econometrics is typically required to build good predictive models using this approach. Suitable for time-series and mixed-panel data (not applicable for cross-sectional data).

- *Auto ARIMA.* The Auto-ARIMA module automates some of the traditional ARIMA modeling by automatically testing multiple permutations of model specifications and returns the best-fitting model. Running the Auto-ARIMA module is similar to running regular ARIMA forecasts. The differences being that the required P, D, Q inputs in ARIMA are no longer required and that different combinations of these inputs are automatically run and compared. Suitable for time-series and mixed-panel data (not applicable for cross-sectional data).

- *Basic Econometrics.* *Econometrics* refers to a branch of business analytics, modeling, and forecasting techniques for modeling the behavior or forecasting certain business, economic, finance, physics, manufacturing, operations, and any other variables. Running the Basic Econometrics models is similar to regular regression analysis except that the dependent and independent variables are allowed to be modified before a regression is run. Suitable for all types of data.

- *Basic Auto Econometrics.* This methodology is similar to basic econometrics, but thousands of linear, nonlinear, interacting, lagged, and mixed variables are automatically run on your data to determine the best-fitting econometric model that describes the behavior of the dependent variable. It is useful for modeling the effects of the variables and for forecasting future outcomes, while not requiring the analyst to be an expert econometrician. Suitable for all types of data.

- *Combinatorial Fuzzy Logic.* Fuzzy sets deal with approximate rather than accurate binary logic. Fuzzy values are between 0 and 1. This weighting schema is used in a combinatorial method to generate the optimized time-series forecasts. Suitable for time-series only.

- *Custom Distributions.* Using Risk Simulator, expert opinions can be collected and a customized distribution can be generated. This forecasting technique comes in handy when the dataset is small, when the Delphi method is used, or the goodness-of-fit is bad when applied to a distributional fitting routine. Suitable for all types of data.

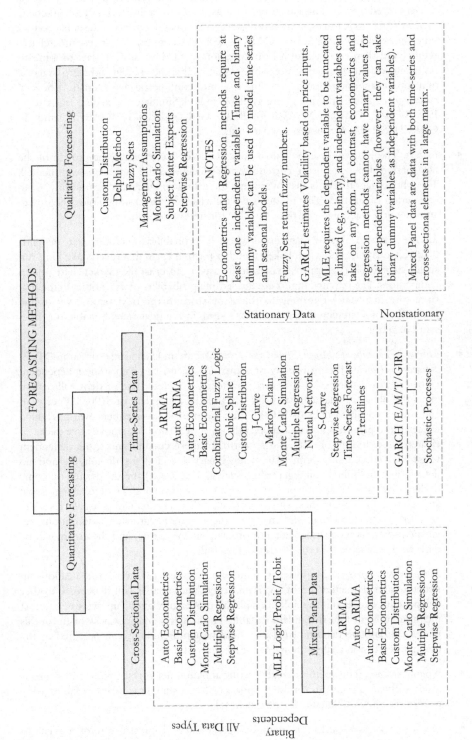

Figure 6.1: Forecasting Methods

- *GARCH.* The generalized autoregressive conditional heteroskedasticity (GARCH) model is used to model historical and forecast future volatility levels of a marketable security (e.g., stock prices, commodity prices, oil prices, etc.). The dataset has to be a time series of raw price levels. GARCH will first convert the prices into relative returns and then run an internal optimization to fit the historical data to a mean-reverting volatility term structure, while assuming that the volatility is heteroskedastic in nature (changes over time according to some econometric characteristics). Several variations of this methodology are available in Risk Simulator, including EGARCH, EGARCH-T, GARCH-M, GJR-GARCH, GJR-GARCH-T, IGARCH, and T-GARCH. Suitable for time-series data only.

- *J-Curve.* The J-curve, or exponential growth curve, is one where the growth of the next period depends on the current period's level and the increase is exponential. This phenomenon means that over time, the values will increase significantly, from one period to another. This model is typically used in forecasting biological growth and chemical reactions over time. Suitable for time-series data only.

- *Markov Chains.* A Markov chain exists when the probability of a future state depends on a previous state and when linked together forms a chain that reverts to a long-run steady state level. This approach is typically used to forecast the market share of two competitors. The required inputs are the starting probability of a customer in the first store (the first state) returning to the same store in the next period, versus the probability of switching to a competitor's store in the next state. Suitable for time-series data only.

- *Maximum Likelihood on Logit, Probit, and Tobit.* Maximum likelihood estimation (MLE) is used to forecast the probability of something occurring given some independent variables. For instance, MLE is used to predict if a credit line or debt will default given the obligor's characteristics (30 years old, single, salary of $100,000 per year, and total credit card debt of $10,000), or the probability a patient will have lung cancer if the person is a male between the ages of 50 and 60, smokes five packs of cigarettes per month or year, and so forth. In these circumstances, the dependent variable is limited (i.e., limited to being binary 1 and 0 for default/die and no default/live, or limited to integer values such as 1, 2, 3, etc.) and the desired outcome of the model is to predict the probability of an event occurring. Traditional regression analysis will not work in these situations (the predicted probability is usually less than zero or greater than one, and many of the required regression assumptions are violated, such as independence and normality of the errors, and the errors will be fairly large). Suitable for cross-sectional data only.

- *Multivariate Regression.* Multivariate regression is used to model the relationship structure and characteristics of a certain dependent variable as it depends on other independent exogenous variables. Using the modeled relationship, we can forecast the future values of the dependent variable. The accuracy and goodness-of-fit for this model can also be determined. Linear and nonlinear models can be fitted in the multiple regression analysis. Suitable for all types of data.

- *Neural Network.* This method creates artificial neural networks, nodes, and neurons inside software algorithms for the purposes of forecasting time-series variables using pattern recognition. Suitable for time-series data only.

- *Nonlinear Extrapolation.* In this methodology, the underlying structure of the data to be forecasted is assumed to be nonlinear over time. For instance, a dataset such as 1, 4, 9, 16, 25 is considered to be nonlinear (these data points are from a squared function). Suitable for time-series data only.

- *S-Curves.* The S-curve, or logistic growth curve, starts off like a J-curve, with exponential growth rates. Over time, the environment becomes saturated (e.g., market saturation, competition, overcrowding), the growth slows, and the forecast value eventually ends up at a saturation or maximum level. The S-curve model is typically used in forecasting market share or sales growth of a new product from market introduction until maturity and decline, population dynamics, and other naturally occurring phenomenon. Suitable for time-series data only.

- *Spline Curves.* Sometimes there are missing values in a time-series dataset. For instance, interest rates for years 1 to 3 may exist, followed by years 5 to 8, and then year 10. Spline curves can be used to interpolate the missing years' interest rate values based on the data that exist. Spline curves can also be used to forecast or extrapolate values of future time periods beyond the time period of available data. The data can be linear or nonlinear. Suitable for time-series data only.

- *Stochastic Process Forecasting.* Sometimes variables are stochastic and cannot be readily predicted using traditional means. Nonetheless, most financial, economic, and naturally occurring phenomena (e.g., motion of molecules through the air) follow a known mathematical law or relationship. Although the resulting values are uncertain, the underlying mathematical structure is known and can be simulated using Monte Carlo risk simulation. The processes supported in Risk Simulator include Brownian motion random walk, mean-reversion, jump-diffusion, and mixed processes, useful for forecasting nonstationary time-series variables. Suitable for time-series data only.

- *Time-Series Analysis and Decomposition.* In well-behaved time-series data (typical examples include sales revenues and cost structures of large corporations), the values tend to have up to three elements: a base value, trend, and seasonality. Time-series analysis uses these historical data and decomposes them into these three elements, and recomposes them into future forecasts. In other words, this forecasting method, like some of the others described, first performs a back-fitting (backcast) of historical data before it provides estimates of future values (forecasts). Suitable for time-series data only.

- *Trendlines.* This method fits various curves such as linear, nonlinear, moving average, exponential, logarithmic, polynomial, and power functions on existing historical data. Suitable for time-series data only.

RUNNING THE FORECASTING TOOL IN RISK SIMULATOR

In general, to create forecasts, several quick steps are required:

- Start Excel and enter in or open existing historical data.

- Select the data and click on *Risk Simulator | Forecasting*.

- Select the relevant sections (Box–Jenkins ARIMA, Time-series Analysis, Multivariate Regression, Stochastic Forecasting, Nonlinear Extrapolation, etc.) and enter the relevant inputs.

Figure 6.2 illustrates the *Forecasting* tool and the various methodologies available in Risk Simulator.

Figure 6.2: Risk Simulator's Forecasting Methods

The following provides a quick review of each methodology and several quick getting started examples in using the software. The example data files used to create these examples are included in the Risk Simulator software and can be accessed through the following menu: *Risk Simulator | Example Models.*

TIME-SERIES ANALYSIS

Theory

Figure 6.3 lists the eight most common time-series models, segregated by seasonality and trend. For instance, if the data variable has no trend or seasonality, then a single moving average model or a single exponential-smoothing model would suffice. However, if seasonality exists but no discernable trend is present, either a seasonal additive or seasonal multiplicative model would be better, and so forth.

	NO SEASONALITY	WITH SEASONALITY
WITHOUT TREND	Single Moving Average	Seasonal Additive
WITHOUT TREND	Single Exponential Smoothing	Seasonal Multiplicative
WITH TREND	Double Moving Average	Holt–Winters Additive
WITH TREND	Double Exponential Smoothing	Holt–Winters Multiplicative

Figure 6.3: The Eight Most Common Time-Series Methods

Procedure

- Start Excel and type in or open an existing spreadsheet with the relevant historical data (the following example uses the *Risk Simulator | Example Models | Time-Series Forecasting* file).

- Make sure you start a new simulation profile or that there is an existing profile in the model if you want the forecast results to automatically generate Monte Carlo assumptions.

- Select the historical data not including the variable name (data should be listed in a single column).

- Select *Risk Simulator | Forecasting | Time-Series Analysis*.

- Choose the model to apply, enter the relevant assumptions, and click *OK*.

To follow along in this example, choose Auto Model Selection, enter 4 for seasonality periods per cycle, and forecast for 4 periods (Figure 6.4).

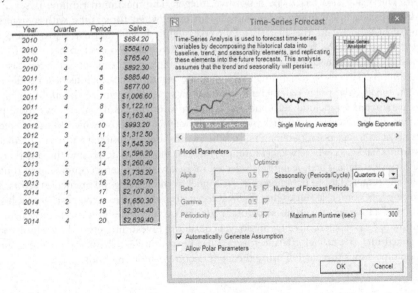

Figure 6.4: Time-Series Analysis

Results Interpretation

Figure 6.5 illustrates the sample results generated by using the *Forecasting* tool. The model used was a Holt–Winters multiplicative model. Notice that in Figure 6.5, the model-fitting and forecast chart indicate that the trend and seasonality are picked up nicely by the Holt–Winters multiplicative model. The time-series analysis report provides the relevant optimized alpha, beta, and gamma parameters, the error measurements, fitted data, forecast values, and forecast-fitted graph. The parameters are simply for reference. Alpha captures the memory effect of the base level changes over time, beta is the trend parameter that measures the strength of the trend, while gamma measures the seasonality strength of the historical data. The analysis decomposes the historical data into these three elements and then recomposes them to forecast the future. The fitted data illustrate the historical data as well as the fitted data using the recomposed model and show how close the forecasts are in the past (a technique called backcasting). The forecast values are either single-point estimates or assumptions (if the automatically generated assumptions option is chosen and if a simulation profile exists). The graph illustrates the historical, fitted, as well as forecast values. The chart is a powerful communication and visual tool to see how good the forecast model is.

Notes

This time-series analysis module contains the eight time-series models seen in Figure 6.3. You can choose the specific model to run based on the trend and seasonality criteria or choose the Auto Model Selection, which will automatically iterate through all eight methods, optimize the parameters, and find the best-fitting model for your data. Alternatively, if you choose one of the eight models, you can also deselect the *optimize* checkboxes and enter your own alpha, beta, and gamma parameters. In addition, you would need to enter the relevant seasonality periods if you choose the automatic model selection or any of the seasonal models. The seasonality input must be a positive integer (e.g., if the data is quarterly, enter 4 as the number of seasons or cycles a year, or enter 12 if monthly data, or any other positive integer representing the data periods of a full cycle—a droplist preset with these inputs is available or apply the *Custom* selection to enter in your own positive integer value). Next, enter the number of periods to forecast. This value also has to be a positive integer. The maximum runtime is set at 300 seconds. Typically, no changes are required. However, when forecasting with a significant amount of historical data, the analysis might take slightly longer and if the processing time exceeds this runtime, the process will be terminated. You can also elect to have the forecast automatically generate assumptions; that is, instead of single-point estimates, the forecasts will be assumptions. However, to automatically generate assumptions, a simulation profile must first exist. Finally, the polar parameters option allows you to optimize the alpha, beta, and gamma parameters to include zero and one. Certain forecasting software allows these polar parameters while others do not. Risk Simulator allows you to choose which to use. Typically, there is no need to use polar parameters. In other words, before running a forecast prediction, we first run a backcast, where we test multiple forecast models to determine the one that best fits the historical data. Then, using this selected model, we run internal optimization routines to obtain the required input parameters in the model by minimizing the prediction errors. This methodology, of course, assumes that the best forecast of the future is the past, or that history repeats itself. However, if certain structural shifts and changes are predicted to occur in the near future (e.g., new disruptive technology, acquisition, divestiture, etc.), these shifts can be incorporated into the model *after* the forecast has been run. See Chapter 7 for the technical details on time-series forecasting using the eight decomposition methods.

Holt-Winter's Multiplicative

The analysis was run with alpha = 0.2429, beta = 1.0000, gamma = 0.7797, and seasonality = 4

Time-Series Analysis Summary

When both seasonality and trend exist, more advanced models are required to decompose the data into their base elements: a base-case level (L) weighted by the alpha parameter; a trend component (b) weighted by the beta parameter; and a seasonality component (S) weighted by the gamma parameter. Several methods exist but the two most common are the Holt-Winters' additive seasonality and Holt-Winters' multiplicative seasonality methods. In the Holt-Winter's additive model, the base case level, seasonality, and trend are added together to obtain the forecast fit.

The best-fitting test for the moving average forecast uses the root mean squared errors (RMSE). The RMSE calculates the square root of the average squared deviations of the fitted values versus the actual data points.

Mean Squared Error (MSE) is an absolute error measure that squares the errors (the difference between the actual historical data and the forecast-fitted data predicted by the model) to keep the positive and negative errors from canceling each other out. This measure also tends to exaggerate large errors by weighting the large errors more heavily than smaller errors by squaring them, which can help when comparing different time-series models. Root Mean Square Error (RMSE) is the square root of MSE and is the most popular error measure, also known as the quadratic loss function. RMSE can be defined as the average of the absolute values of the forecast errors and is highly appropriate when the cost of the forecast errors is proportional to the absolute size of the forecast error. The RMSE is used as the selection criteria for the best-fitting time-series model.

Mean Absolute Percentage Error (MAPE) is a relative error statistic measured as an average percent error of the historical data points and is most appropriate when the cost of the forecast error is more closely related to the percentage error than the numerical size of the error. Finally, an associated measure is the Theil's U statistic, which measures the naivety of the model's forecast. That is, if the Theil's U statistic is less than 1.0, then the forecast method used provides an estimate that is statistically better than guessing.

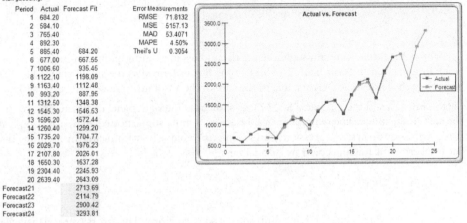

Period	Actual	Forecast Fit	Error Measurements	
1	684.20		RMSE	71.8132
2	584.10		MSE	5157.13
3	765.40		MAD	53.4071
4	892.30		MAPE	4.50%
5	885.40	684.20	Theil's U	0.3054
6	677.00	667.55		
7	1006.60	935.45		
8	1122.10	1198.09		
9	1163.40	1112.48		
10	993.20	887.95		
11	1312.50	1348.38		
12	1545.30	1546.53		
13	1596.20	1572.44		
14	1260.40	1299.20		
15	1735.20	1704.77		
16	2029.70	1976.23		
17	2107.80	2026.01		
18	1650.30	1637.28		
19	2304.40	2245.93		
20	2639.40	2643.09		
Forecast21		2713.69		
Forecast22		2114.79		
Forecast23		2900.42		
Forecast24		3293.81		

Figure 6.5: Example Holt–Winters Forecast Report

MULTIVARIATE REGRESSION

Theory

It is assumed that the user is sufficiently knowledgeable about the fundamentals of regression analysis. The general bivariate linear regression equation takes the form of $Y = \beta_0 + \beta_1 X + \varepsilon$, where β_0 is the intercept, β_1 is the slope, and ε is the error term. It is bivariate as there are only two variables, a Y or dependent variable, and an X or independent variable, where X is also known as the regressor (sometimes a bivariate regression is also known as a univariate regression as there is only a single independent variable X). The dependent variable is named as such as it *depends* on the independent variable, for example, sales revenue depends on the amount of marketing costs expended on a product's advertising and promotion, making the dependent variable sales and the independent variable marketing costs. An example of a bivariate regression is seen as simply inserting the best-fitting line through a set of data points in a two-dimensional plane, as seen on the left panel in Figure 6.6. In other cases, a multivariate regression can be performed, where there are multiple or k number of independent X variables or regressors, where the general regression equation will now take the form of $Y = \beta_0 + \beta_1 X_1 + \beta_2 X_2 + \beta_3 X_3 ... + \beta_k X_k + \varepsilon$. In this case, the best-fitting line will be within a $k + 1$ dimensional plane.

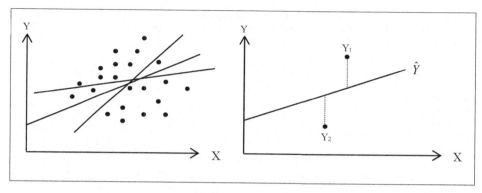

Figure 6.6: Bivariate Regression

However, fitting a line through a set of data points in a scatter plot as in Figure 6.6 may result in numerous possible lines. The best-fitting line is defined as the single unique line that minimizes the total vertical errors, that is, the sum of the absolute distances between the actual data points (Y_i) and the estimated line $(\hat{Y})$, as shown on the right panel of Figure 6.6. To find the best-fitting unique line that minimizes the errors, a more sophisticated approach is applied, using regression analysis. Regression analysis finds the unique best-fitting line by requiring that the total errors be minimized, or by calculating

$$Min \sum_{i=1}^{n} (Y_i - \hat{Y}_i)^2$$

where only one unique line minimizes this sum of squared errors. The errors (vertical distances between the actual data and the predicted line) are squared to avoid the negative errors from canceling out the positive errors. Solving this minimization problem with respect to the slope and intercept requires calculating first derivatives and setting them equal to zero:

$$\frac{d}{d\beta_0} \sum_{i=1}^{n} (Y_i - \hat{Y}_i)^2 = 0 \ \ and \ \ \frac{d}{d\beta_1} \sum_{i=1}^{n} (Y_i - \hat{Y}_i)^2 = 0$$

which yields the bivariate regression's least squares equations:

$$\beta_1 = \frac{\sum_{i=1}^{n} (X_i - \bar{X})(Y_i - \bar{Y})}{\sum_{i=1}^{n} (X_i - \bar{X})^2} = \frac{\sum_{i=1}^{n} X_i Y_i - \dfrac{\sum_{i=1}^{n} X_i \sum_{i=1}^{n} Y_i}{n}}{\sum_{i=1}^{n} X_i^2 - \dfrac{\left(\sum_{i=1}^{n} X_i\right)^2}{n}}$$

$$\beta_0 = \bar{Y} - \beta_1 \bar{X}$$

For multivariate regression, the analogy is expanded to account for multiple independent variables, where $Y_i = \beta_1 + \beta_2 X_{2,i} + \beta_3 X_{3,i} + \varepsilon_i$ and the estimated slopes can be calculated by:

$$\hat{\beta}_2 = \frac{\sum Y_i X_{2,i} \sum X_{3,i}^2 - \sum Y_i X_{3,i} \sum X_{2,i} X_{3,i}}{\sum X_{2,i}^2 \sum X_{3,i}^2 - \left(\sum X_{2,i} X_{3,i}\right)^2}$$

$$\hat{\beta}_3 = \frac{\sum Y_i X_{3,i} \sum X_{2,i}^2 - \sum Y_i X_{2,i} \sum X_{2,i} X_{3,i}}{\sum X_{2,i}^2 \sum X_{3,i}^2 - \left(\sum X_{2,i} X_{3,i}\right)^2}$$

In running multivariate regressions, great care must be taken to set up and interpret the results. For instance, a good understanding of econometric modeling is required (e.g., identifying regression pitfalls such as structural breaks, multicollinearity, heteroskedasticity, autocorrelation, specification tests, nonlinearities, and so forth) before a proper model can be constructed.

Procedure

- Start Excel and type in or open your existing dataset (the illustration below uses *Risk Simulator | Example Models | 09 Multiple Regression* in the examples folder).

- Check to make sure that the data are arranged in columns and select the data including the variable headings, and click on *Risk Simulator | Forecasting | Multiple Regression*.

- *Select the dependent variable* and check the relevant options (lags, stepwise regression, nonlinear regression, and so forth) and click *OK* (Figure 6.7).

Results Interpretation

Figure 6.8 illustrates a sample multivariate regression result report generated. The report comes complete with all the regression results, analysis of variance results, fitted chart, and hypothesis test results. See Chapter 7 for the technical details on interpreting the results from a regression analysis.

STEPWISE REGRESSION

One powerful automated approach to regression analysis is "stepwise regression" and based on its namesake, the regression process proceeds in multiple steps. There are several ways to set up these stepwise algorithms including the correlation approach, forward method, backward method, and the forward and backward method (these methods are all available in Risk Simulator).

In the correlation method, the dependent variable (Y) is correlated to all the independent variables (X), and starting with the X variable with the highest absolute correlation value, a regression is run, then subsequent X variables are added until the p-values indicate that the new X variable is no longer statistically significant. This approach is quick and simple but does not account for interactions among variables, and an X variable, when added, will statistically overshadow other variables.

In the forward method, we first correlate Y with all X variables, run a regression for Y on the highest absolute value correlation of X, and obtain the fitting errors. Then, correlate these errors with the remaining X variables and choose the highest absolute value correlation among this remaining set and run another regression. Repeat the process until the p-value for the latest X variable coefficient is no longer statistically significant then stop the process.

In the backward method, run a regression with Y on all X variables and reviewing each variable's p-value, systematically eliminate the variable with the largest p-value, then run a regression again, repeating each time until all p-values are statistically significant.

In the forward and backward method, apply the forward method to obtain three X variables then apply the backward approach to see if one of them needs to be eliminated because it is statistically insignificant. Then repeat the forward method, and then the backward method until all remaining X variables are considered.

Multiple Regression Analysis Data Set

Aggravated Assault	Bachelor's Degree	Police Expenditure Per Capita	Population in Millions	Population Density (Persons/Sq Mile)	Unemployment Rate
521	18308	185	4.041	79.6	7.2
367	1148	600	0.55	1	8.5
443	18068	372	3.665	32.3	5.7
365	7729	142	2.351	45.1	7.3
614	100484				
385	16728				
286	14630				
397	4008				
764	38927				
427	22322				
153	3711				
231	3136				
524	50508				
328	28886				
240	16996				
286	13035				
285	12973				
569	16309				
96	5227				
498	19235				
481	44487				
468	44213				
177	23619				
198	9106				
458	24917				
108	3872				
246	8945				
291	2373				
68	7128				
311	23624	349	7.73	1042	6.6

Figure 6.7: Running a Multivariate Regression

Regression Analysis Report

Regression Statistics

R-Squared (Coefficient of Determination)	0.3272
Adjusted R-Squared	0.2508
Multiple R (Multiple Correlation Coefficient)	0.5720
Standard Error of the Estimates (SEy)	149.6720
Number of Observations	50

The R-Squared or Coefficient of Determination indicates that 0.33 of the variation in the dependent variable can be explained and accounted for by the independent variables in this regression analysis. However, in a multiple regression, the Adjusted R-Squared takes into account the existence of additional independent variables or regressors and adjusts this R-Squared value to a more accurate view of the regression's explanatory power. Hence, only 0.25 of the variation in the dependent variable can be explained by the regressors.

The Multiple Correlation Coefficient (Multiple R) measures the correlation between the actual dependent variable (Y) and the estimated or fitted (Y) based on the regression equation. This is also the square root of the Coefficient of Determination (R-Squared).

The Standard Error of the Estimates (SEy) describes the dispersion of data points above and below the regression line or plane. This value is used as part of the calculation to obtain the confidence interval of the estimates later.

Regression Results

	Intercept	Bachelor's Degree	Police Expenditure Per Capita	Population in Millions	Population Density (Persons/Sq Mile)	Unemployment Rate
Coefficients	57.9555	-0.0035	0.4644	25.2377	-0.0086	16.5579
Standard Error	108.7901	0.0035	0.2535	14.1172	0.1016	14.7996
t-Statistic	0.5327	-1.0066	1.8316	1.7877	-0.0843	1.1188
p-Value	0.5969	0.3197	0.0738	0.0807	0.9332	0.2693
Lower 5%	-161.2966	-0.0106	-0.0466	-3.2137	-0.2132	-13.2687
Upper 95%	277.2076	0.0036	0.9753	53.6891	0.1961	46.3845

Degrees of Freedom		Hypothesis Test	
Degrees of Freedom for Regression	5	Critical t-Statistic (99% confidence with df of 44)	2.6923
Degrees of Freedom for Residual	44	Critical t-Statistic (95% confidence with df of 44)	2.0154
Total Degrees of Freedom	49	Critical t-Statistic (90% confidence with df of 44)	1.6802

The Coefficients provide the estimated regression intercept and slopes. For instance, the coefficients are estimates of the true; population b values in the following regression equation Y = b0 + b1X1 + b2X2 + ... + bnXn. The Standard Error measures how accurate the predicted Coefficients are, and the t-Statistics are the ratios of each predicted Coefficient to its Standard Error.

The t-Statistic is used in hypothesis testing, where we set the null hypothesis (Ho) such that the real mean of the Coefficient = 0, and the alternate hypothesis (Ha) such that the real mean of the Coefficient is not equal to 0. A t-test is is performed and the calculated t-Statistic is compared to the critical values at the relevant Degrees of Freedom for Residual. The t-test is very important as it calculates if each of the coefficients is statistically significant in the presence of the other regressors. This means that the t-test statistically verifies whether a regressor or independent variable should remain in the regression or it should be dropped.

The Coefficient is statistically significant if its calculated t-Statistic exceeds the Critical t-Statistic at the relevant degrees of freedom (df). The three main confidence levels used to test for significance are 90%, 95% and 99%. If a Coefficient's t-Statistic exceeds the Critical level, it is considered statistically significant. Alternatively, the p-Value calculates each t-Statistic's probability of occurrence, which means that the smaller the p-Value, the more significant the Coefficient. The usual significant levels for the p-Value are 0.01, 0.05, and 0.10, corresponding to the 99%, 95%, and 90% confidence levels.

The Coefficients with their p-Values highlighted in blue indicate that they are statistically significant at the 90% confidence or 0.10 alpha level, while those highlighted in red indicate that they are not statistically significant at any other alpha levels.

Analysis of Variance

	Sums of Squares	Mean of Squares	F-Statistic	p-Value	Hypothesis Test	
Regression	479388.49	95877.70	4.28	0.0029	Critical F-statistic (99% confidence with df of 5 and 44)	3.4651
Residual	985675.19	22401.71			Critical F-statistic (95% confidence with df of 5 and 44)	2.4270
Total	1465063.68				Critical F-statistic (90% confidence with df of 5 and 44)	1.9828

The Analysis of Variance (ANOVA) table provides an F-test of the regression model's overall statistical significance. Instead of looking at individual regressors as in the t-test, the F-test looks at all the estimated Coefficients' statistical properties. The F-Statistic is calculated as the ratio of the Regression's Mean of Squares to the Residual's Mean of Squares. The numerator measures how much of the regression is explained, while the denominator measures how much is unexplained. Hence, the larger the F-Statistic, the more significant the model. The corresponding p-Value is calculated to test the null hypothesis (Ho) where all the Coefficients are simultaneously equal to zero, versus the alternate hypothesis (Ha) that they are all simultaneously different from zero, indicating a significant overall regression model. If the p-Value is smaller than the 0.01, 0.05, or 0.10 alpha significance, then the regression is significant. The same approach can be applied to the F-Statistic by comparing the calculated F-Statistic with the critical F values at various significance levels.

Forecasting

Period	Actual (Y)	Forecast (F)	Error (E)
1	521.0000	299.5124	221.4876
2	367.0000	487.1243	(120.1243)
3	443.0000	353.2789	89.7211
4	365.0000	276.3296	88.6704
5	614.0000	776.1336	(162.1336)
6	385.0000	298.9993	86.0007
7	286.0000	354.8718	(68.8718)
8	397.0000	312.6155	84.3845
9	764.0000	529.7550	234.2450
10	427.0000	347.7034	79.2966
11	153.0000	266.2526	(113.2526)
12	231.0000	264.6375	(33.6375)
13	524.0000	408.8009	117.1991
14	328.0000	272.2226	55.7774
15	240.0000	231.7882	8.2118
16	286.0000	257.8862	28.1138
17	285.0000	314.9521	(29.9521)
18	569.0000	335.3140	233.6860
19	96.0000	282.0356	(186.0356)
20	498.0000	370.2062	127.7938
21	481.0000	340.8742	140.1258
22	468.0000	427.5118	40.4882
23	177.0000	274.5298	(97.5298)
24	198.0000	294.7795	(96.7795)
25	458.0000	295.2180	162.7820

RMSE: 140.4048

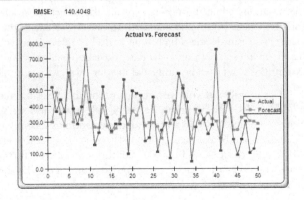

Figure 6.8: Multivariate Regression Results

STOCHASTIC FORECASTING

Theory

A stochastic process is a mathematically defined equation that can create a series of outcomes over time, outcomes that are not deterministic in nature; that is, an equation or process that does not follow any simple discernible rule such as price will increase X percent every year or revenues will increase by this factor of X plus Y percent. A stochastic process is by definition nondeterministic, and one can plug numbers into a stochastic process equation and obtain different results every time. For instance, the path of a stock price is stochastic in nature, and one cannot reliably predict the exact stock price path with any certainty. However, the price evolution over time is enveloped in a process that generates these prices. *The process is fixed and predetermined, but the outcomes are not.* Hence, by stochastic simulation, we create multiple pathways of prices, obtain a statistical sampling of these simulations, and make inferences on the potential pathways that the actual price may undertake given the nature and parameters of the stochastic process used to generate the time series. Four stochastic processes are included in Risk Simulator's Forecasting tool, including Geometric Brownian motion or random walk, which is the most common and prevalently used process due to its simplicity and wide-ranging applications. The other three stochastic processes are the mean-reversion process, jump-diffusion process, and a mixed process.

The interesting thing about stochastic process simulation is that historical data is not necessarily required; that is, the model does not have to fit any sets of historical data. Simply compute the expected returns and the volatility of the historical data or estimate them using comparable external data or make assumptions about these values.

Procedure

- Start the module by selecting *Risk Simulator | Forecasting | Stochastic Processes.*

- Select the desired stochastic process, enter the required inputs, click on update chart a few times to make sure the process is behaving the way you expect it to, and click *OK* (Figure 6.9).

Results Interpretation

Figure 6.10 shows the results of a sample stochastic process. The chart shows a sample set of the iterations while the report explains the basics of stochastic processes. In addition, the forecast values (mean and standard deviation) for each time period is provided. Using these values, you can decide which time period is relevant to your analysis, and set assumptions based on these mean and standard deviation values using the normal distribution. These assumptions can then be simulated in your own custom model.

For example, if you wish to determine the Year 1 forecast using the stochastic process model results, find an empty cell (e.g., cell A100) and set a simulation input assumption as Normal (mean of 101.38 and standard deviation of 23.05) based on the results in Figure 6.10. Then, in a nearby cell (e.g., cell A101), set it to equal the assumption cell's value (i.e., in cell A101, set it to be =A100), and make this a simulation forecast cell. Run the simulation, and using the forecast chart, you can determine Year 1's predicted mean simulated value, percentiles, and confidence intervals.

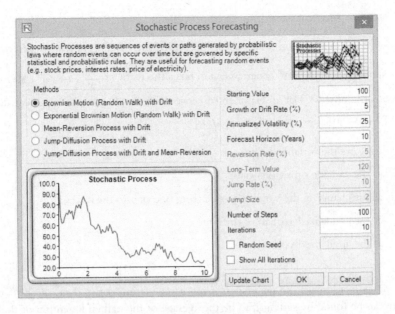

Figure 6.9: Stochastic Process Forecasting

Stochastic Process Forecasting

Statistical Summary

A stochastic process is a sequence of events or paths generated by probabilistic laws. That is, random events can occur over time but are governed by specific statistical and probabilistic rules. The main stochastic processes include Random Walk or Brownian Motion, Mean-Reversion, and Jump-Diffusion. These processes can be used to forecast a multitude of variables that seemingly follow random trends but yet are restricted by probabilistic laws.

The Random Walk Brownian Motion process can be used to forecast stock prices, prices of commodities, and other stochastic time-series data given a drift or growth rate and a volatility around the drift path. The Mean-Reversion process can be used to reduce the fluctuations of the Random Walk process by allowing the path to target a long-term value, making it useful for forecasting time-series variables that have a long-term rate such as interest rates and inflation rates (these are long-term target rates by regulatory authorities or the market). The Jump-Diffusion process is useful for forecasting time-series data when the variable can occasionally exhibit random jumps, such as oil prices or price of electricity (discrete exogenous event shocks can make prices jump up or down). Finally, these three stochastic processes can be mixed and matched as required.

The results on the right indicate the mean and standard deviation of all the iterations generated at each time step. If the Show All Iterations option is selected, each iteration pathway will be shown in a separate worksheet. The graph generated below shows a sample set of the iteration pathways.

Stochastic Process: Brownian Motion (Random Walk) with Drift

Start Value	100	Steps	100.00	Jump Rate	N/A
Drift Rate	5.00%	Iterations	10.00	Jump Size	N/A
Volatility	25.00%	Reversion Rate	N/A	Random Seed	55854670
Horizon	10	Long-Term Value	N/A		

Time	Mean	Stdev
0.0000	100.00	0.00
0.1000	98.06	6.89
0.2000	101.50	6.48
0.3000	105.49	12.28
0.4000	101.57	13.37
0.5000	100.30	15.67
0.6000	100.13	16.14
0.7000	98.76	11.87
0.8000	101.04	16.68
0.9000	100.64	19.47
1.0000	101.38	23.05
1.1000	102.63	17.22
1.2000	109.72	21.37
1.3000	107.89	21.87
1.4000	107.56	21.69
1.5000	105.21	18.97
1.6000	109.58	22.32
1.7000	110.51	27.93
1.8000	113.67	27.43
1.9000	115.78	32.78
2.0000	118.85	37.28
2.1000	117.83	35.05
2.2000	118.48	40.23
2.3000	126.34	42.98
2.4000	124.39	34.83
2.5000	122.94	35.30
2.6000	122.31	37.64
2.7000	127.76	42.62
2.8000	130.45	52.67
2.9000	128.91	52.78
3.0000	136.85	57.63
3.1000	137.70	67.81
3.2000	130.76	71.52
3.3000	132.69	76.17
3.4000	138.17	89.47
3.5000	138.36	91.45
3.6000	135.20	88.22
3.7000	132.61	77.40
3.8000	134.30	73.48
3.9000	132.51	67.49
4.0000	130.63	68.48

Figure 6.10: Stochastic Forecast Result

Brownian Motion Random Walk Process

The Brownian motion random walk process takes the form of $\dfrac{\delta S}{S} = \mu(\delta t) + \sigma \varepsilon \sqrt{\delta t}$ for regular options simulation, or a more generic version takes the form of $\dfrac{\delta S}{S} = (\mu - \sigma^2 / 2)\delta t + \sigma \varepsilon \sqrt{\delta t}$ for a geometric process. For an exponential version, we simply take the exponentials, and as an example, we have $\dfrac{\delta S}{S} = \exp\left[\mu(\delta t) + \sigma \varepsilon \sqrt{\delta t}\right]$.

The following are the variable definitions:

S as the variable's previous value

δS as the change in the variable's value from one step to the next

μ as the annualized growth or drift rate

σ as the annualized volatility

In order to estimate the parameters from a set of time-series data, the drift rate and volatility can be found by setting μ to be the average of the natural logarithm of the relative returns $\ln\dfrac{S_t}{S_{t-1}}$, while σ is the standard deviation of all $\ln\dfrac{S_t}{S_{t-1}}$ values.

Mean-Reversion Process

The following describes the mathematical structure of a mean-reverting process with drift: $\dfrac{\delta S}{S} = \eta(\bar{S}e^{\mu(\delta t)} - S)\delta t + \mu(\delta t) + \sigma \varepsilon \sqrt{\delta t}$. In order to obtain the rate of reversion and long term rate, using the historical data points, run a regression such that $Y_t - Y_{t-1} = \beta_0 + \beta_1 Y_{t-1} + \varepsilon$ and we find $\eta = -\ln[1+\beta_1]$ and $\bar{S} = -\beta_0 / \beta_1$.

The following are the variable definitions:

η as the rate of reversion to the mean

$\bar{S}$ as the long-term value the process reverts to

Y as the historical data series

β_0 as the intercept coefficient in a regression analysis

β_1 as the slope coefficient in a regression analysis

Jump Diffusion Process

A jump diffusion process is similar to a random walk process but there is a probability of a jump at any point in time. The occurrences of such jumps are completely random but its probability and magnitude are governed by the process itself. The model is defined as: $\dfrac{\delta S}{S} = \eta(\bar{S}e^{\mu(\delta t)} - S)\delta t + \mu(\delta t) + \sigma \varepsilon \sqrt{\delta t} + \theta F(\lambda)(\delta t)$ for a jump diffusion process.

The following are the variable definitions:

θ as the jump size of S

$F(\lambda)$ as the inverse of the Poisson cumulative probability distribution

λ as the jump rate of S

The jump size can be found by computing the ratio of the post-jump to the pre-jump levels, and the jump rate can be imputed from past historical data. The other parameters are found the same way as above.

NONLINEAR EXTRAPOLATION

Theory

Extrapolation involves making statistical forecasts by using historical trends that are projected for a specified period of time into the future. It is only used for time-series forecasts. For cross-sectional or mixed panel data (time-series with cross-sectional data), multivariate regression is more appropriate. This methodology is useful when major changes are not expected, that is, causal factors are expected to remain constant or when the causal factors of a situation are not clearly understood. It also helps discourage the introduction of personal biases into the process. Extrapolation is fairly reliable, relatively simple, and inexpensive. However, extrapolation, which assumes that recent and historical trends will continue, produces large forecast errors if discontinuities occur within the projected time period; that is, pure extrapolation of time series assumes that all we need to know is contained in the historical values of the series being forecasted. If we assume that past behavior is a good predictor of future behavior, extrapolation is appealing. This makes it a useful approach when all that is needed are many short-term forecasts.

This methodology estimates the $f(x)$ function for any arbitrary x value, by interpolating a smooth nonlinear curve through all the x values, and using this smooth curve, extrapolates future x values beyond the historical dataset. The methodology employs either the polynomial functional form or the rational functional form (a ratio of two polynomials). Typically, a polynomial functional form is sufficient for well-behaved data, however, rational functional forms are sometimes more accurate (especially with polar functions, i.e., functions with denominators approaching zero).

Procedure

- Start Excel and enter your data or open an existing worksheet with historical data to forecast (the illustration shown next uses *Risk Simulator | Example Models | 10 Nonlinear Extrapolation* from the examples folder).

- *Select the time-series data* and select *Risk Simulator | Forecasting | Nonlinear Extrapolation.*

- *Select the extrapolation type* (automatic selection, polynomial function, or rational function are available but in this example, use automatic selection) and enter the number of forecast period desired (Figure 6.11) and click *OK.*

Results Interpretation

The report (Figure 6.12) shows the extrapolated forecast values, the error measurements, and the graphical representation of the extrapolation results. The error measurements should be used to check the validity of the forecast and are especially important when used to compare the forecast quality and accuracy of extrapolation versus time-series analysis.

Notes

When the historical data is smooth and follows some nonlinear patterns and curves, extrapolation is better than time-series analysis. However, when the data patterns follow seasonal cycles and a trend, time-series analysis will provide better results. It is always advisable to run both time-series analysis and extrapolation and compare the results to see which has a lower error measure and a better fit.

Historical Sales Revenues
Polynomial Growth Rates

Year	Month	Period	Sales
2014	1	1	$1.00
2014	2	2	$6.73
2014	3	3	$20.52
2014	4	4	$45.25
2014	5	5	$83.59
2014	6	6	$138.01
2014	7	7	$210.87
2014	8	8	$304.44
2014	9	9	$420.89
2014	10	10	$562.34
2014	11	11	$730.85
2014	12	12	$928.43

Historical Net Income
Sinusoidal Growth Rates

Year	Month	Period	Income
2014	1	1	$84.15
2014	2	2	$90.93
2014	3	3	$14.11
2014	4	4	($75.68)
2014	5	5	($95.89)
2014	6	6	($27.94)
2014	7	7	$65.70
2014	8	8	$98.94
2014	9	9	$41.21
2014	10	10	($54.40)
2014	11	11	($100.00)
2014	12	12	($53.66)
2015	1	13	$42.02
2015	2	14	$99.06
2015	3	15	$65.03
2015	4	16	($28.79)
2015	5	17	($96.14)
2015	6	18	($75.10)

Extrapolation

Nonlinear Extrapolation is used to make statistical time-series forecast projections by applying historical trends. It is useful when the historical trends are nonlinear and well behaved. The extrapolation is best used for short-term forecasts.

Function Type

⦿ Automatic Selection ◯ Polynomial Function ◯ Rational Function

Number of Extrapolation Periods [6]

OK   Cancel

Figure 6.11: Running a Nonlinear Extrapolation

Nonlinear Extrapolation

Statistical Summary

Extrapolation involves making statistical projections by using historical trends that are projected for a specified period of time into the future. It is only used for time-series forecasts. For cross-sectional or mixed panel data (time-series with cross-sectional data), multivariate regression is more appropriate. This methodology is useful when major changes are not expected, that is, causal factors are expected to remain constant or when the causal factors of a situation are not clearly understood. It also helps discourage the introduction of personal biases into the process. Extrapolation is fairly reliable, relatively simple, and inexpensive. However, extrapolation, which assumes that recent and historical trends will continue, produces large forecast errors if discontinuities occur within the projected time period. That is, pure extrapolation of time series assumes that all we need to know is contained in the historical values of the series that is being forecasted. If we assume that past behavior is a good predictor of future behavior, extrapolation is appealing. This makes it a useful approach when all that is needed are many short-term forecasts.

This methodology estimates the f(x) function for any arbitrary x value, by interpolating a smooth nonlinear curve through all the x values, and using this smooth curve, extrapolates future x values beyond the historical data set. The methodology employs either the polynomial functional form or the rational functional form (a ratio of two polynomials). Typically, a polynomial functional form is sufficient for well-behaved data, however, rational functional forms are sometimes more accurate (especially with polar functions, i.e., functions with denominators approaching zero).

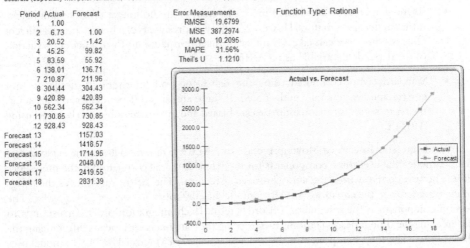

Period	Actual	Forecast		Error Measurements			Function Type: Rational
1	1.00			RMSE	19.6799		
2	6.73	1.00		MSE	387.2974		
3	20.52	-1.42		MAD	10.2095		
4	45.25	99.82		MAPE	31.56%		
5	83.59	55.92		Theil's U	1.1210		
6	138.01	136.71					
7	210.87	211.96					
8	304.44	304.43					
9	420.89	420.89					
10	562.34	562.34					
11	730.85	730.85					
12	928.43	928.43					
Forecast 13		1157.03					
Forecast 14		1418.57					
Forecast 15		1714.95					
Forecast 16		2048.00					
Forecast 17		2419.55					
Forecast 18		2831.39					

Figure 6.12: Nonlinear Extrapolation Results

BOX–JENKINS ARIMA ADVANCED TIME-SERIES FORECASTS

Theory

One very powerful advanced times-series forecasting tool is the ARIMA or *Auto Regressive Integrated Moving Average* approach, which assembles three separate tools into a comprehensive model. The first tool segment is the autoregressive or "AR" term, which corresponds to the number of lagged value of the residual in the unconditional forecast model. In essence, the model captures the historical variation of actual data to a forecasting model and uses this variation or residual to create a better predicting model. The second tool segment is the integration order or the "I" term. This integration term corresponds to the number of differencing the time-series data to be forecasted goes through to make the data stationary. This element accounts for any nonlinear growth rates existing in the data. The third tool segment is the moving average or "MA" term, which is essentially the moving average of lagged forecast errors. By incorporating this lagged forecast errors, the model in essence learns from its forecast errors or mistakes and corrects for them through a moving average calculation. The ARIMA model follows the Box–Jenkins methodology with each term representing steps taken in the model construction until only random noise remains. Also, ARIMA modeling uses correlation techniques in generating forecasts. ARIMA can be used to model patterns that may not be visible in plotted data. In addition, ARIMA models can be mixed with exogenous variables, but make sure that the exogenous variables have enough data points to cover the additional number of periods to forecast. Finally, be aware that ARIMA cannot and should not be used to forecast stochastic processes or time-series data that are stochastic in nature—use the Stochastic Process module to forecast instead.

There are many reasons why an ARIMA model is superior to usual time-series analysis and multivariate regressions. The common finding in time series analysis and multivariate regression is that the error residuals are correlated with their own lagged values. This autocorrelation violates the standard assumption of regression theory that disturbances are not correlated with other disturbances. The primary problems associated with serial correlation are:

- Regression analysis and basic time-series analysis are no longer efficient among the different linear estimators. However, as the error residuals can help to predict current error residuals, we can take advantage of this information to form a better prediction of the dependent variable using ARIMA.

- Standard errors computed using the regression and time-series formula are not correct and are generally understated. If there are lagged dependent variables set as the regressors, regression estimates are biased and inconsistent but can be fixed using ARIMA.

Autoregressive Integrated Moving Average or ARIMA(p,d,q) models are the extension of the AR model that uses three components for modeling the serial correlation in the time series data. The first component is the autoregressive (AR) term. The AR(p) model uses the p lags of the time series in the equation. An AR(p) model has the form: $y_t = a_1 y_{t-1} + ... + a_p y_{t-p} + e_t$. The second component is the integration (d) order term. Each integration order corresponds to differencing the time series. I(1) means differencing the data once. I(d) means differencing the data d times. The third component is the moving average (MA) term. The MA(q) model uses the q lags of the forecast errors to improve the forecast. An MA(q) model has the form: $y_t = e_t + b_1 e_{t-1} + ... + b_q e_{t-q}$. Finally, an ARMA(p,q) model has the combined form: $y_t = a_1 y_{t-1} + ... + a_p y_{t-p} + e_t + b_1 e_{t-1} + ... + b_q e_{t-q}$.

Procedure

- Start Excel and enter your data or open an existing worksheet with historical data to forecast (the illustration shown next uses the example file in *Risk Simulator | Example Models | 21 Time-Series Forecasting*).

- Click on *Risk Simulator | Forecasting | ARIMA* and select the time-series data.

- Enter the relevant *P, D,* and *Q* parameters (positive integers only, example: 1, 0, 1) and enter the number of forecast periods desired, and click *OK*.

Results Interpretation

In interpreting the results of an ARIMA model, most of the specifications are identical to the multivariate regression analysis (see Chapter 7, Using the Past to Predict the Future, for more technical details about interpreting the multivariate regression analysis and ARIMA models). However, there are several additional sets of results specific to the ARIMA analysis as seen in Figure 6.13. The first is the addition of Akaike Information Criterion (AIC) and Schwarz Criterion (SC), which are often used in ARIMA model selection and identification. That is, AIC and SC are used to determine if a particular model with a specific set of p, d, and q parameters is a good statistical fit. The SC imposes a greater penalty for additional coefficients than the AIC but, generally, the model with the lowest AIC and SC values should be chosen. Finally, an additional set of results called the autocorrelation (AC) and partial autocorrelation (PAC) statistics are provided in the ARIMA report.

For instance, if autocorrelation AC(1) is nonzero, it means that the series is first-order autocorrelated. If AC dies off more or less geometrically with increasing lags, it implies that the series follows a low-order autoregressive process. If AC drops to zero after a small number of lags, it implies that the series follows a low-order moving average process. In contrast, PAC measures the correlation of values that are k periods apart after removing the correlation from the intervening lags. If the pattern of autocorrelation can be captured by an autoregression of order less than k, then the partial autocorrelation at lag k will be close to zero. The Ljung–Box Q-statistics and their p-values at lag k are also provided, where the null hypothesis being tested is such that there is no autocorrelation up to order k. The dotted lines in the plots of the autocorrelations are the approximate two standard error bounds. If the autocorrelation is within these bounds, it is not significantly different from zero at approximately the 5% significance level. Finding the right ARIMA model takes practice and experience. These AC, PAC, SC, and AIC are highly useful diagnostic tools to help identify the correct model specification. Finally, the ARIMA parameter results are obtained using sophisticated optimization and iterative algorithms, which means that although the functional forms look like those of a multivariate regression, they are not the same. ARIMA is a much more computationally intensive and advanced econometric approach.

ARIMA (Autoregressive Integrated Moving Average)

Regression Statistics

R-Squared (Coefficient of Determination)	0.9999	Akaike Information Criterion (AIC)	4.6213
Adjusted R-Squared	0.9999	Schwarz Criterion (SC)	4.6632
Multiple R (Multiple Correlation Coefficient)	1.0000	Log Likelihood	-1005.13
Standard Error of the Estimates (SEy)	297.52	Durbin-Watson (DW) Statistic	1.8588
Number of Observations	435	Number of Iterations	5

Autoregressive Integrated Moving Average or ARIMA(p,d,q) models are the extension of the AR model that use three components for modeling the serial correlation in the time-series data. The first component is the autoregressive (AR) term. The AR(p) model uses the p lags of the time series in the equation. An AR(p) model has the form: y(t)=a(1)*y(t-1)+...+a(p)*y(t-p)+e(t). The second component is the integration (d) order term. Each integration order corresponds to differencing the time series. I(1) means differencing the data once. I(d) means differencing the data d times. The third component is the moving average (MA) term. The MA(q) model uses the q lags of the forecast errors to improve the forecast. An MA(q) model has the form: y(t)=e(t)+b(1)*e(t-1)+...+b(q)*e(t-q). Finally, an ARMA(p,q) model has the combined form: y(t)=a(1)*y(t-1)+...+a(p)*y(t-p)+e(t)+b(1)*e(t-1)+...+b(q)*e(t-q).

The R-Squared, or Coefficient of Determination, indicates the percent variation in the dependent variable that can be explained and accounted for by the independent variables in this regression analysis. However, in a multiple regression, the Adjusted R-Squared takes into account the existence of additional independent variables or regressors and adjusts this R-Squared value to a more accurate view the regression's explanatory power. However, under some ARIMA modeling circumstances (e.g., with nonconvergence models), the R-Squared tends to be unreliable.

The Multiple Correlation Coefficient (Multiple R) measures the correlation between the actual dependent variable (Y) and the estimated or fitted (Y) based on the regression equation. This correlation is also the square root of the Coefficient of Determination (R-Squared).

The Standard Error of the Estimates (SEy) describes the dispersion of data points above and below the regression line or plane. This value is used as part of the calculation to obtain the confidence interval of the estimates later.

The AIC and SC are often used in model selection. SC imposes a greater penalty for additional coefficients. Generally, the user should select a model with the lowest value of the AIC and SC.

The Durbin-Watson statistic measures the serial correlation in the residuals. Generally, DW less than 2 implies positive serial correlation.

Regression Results

	Intercept	AR(1)	MA(1)
Coefficients	-0.0626	1.0055	0.4936
Standard Error	0.3108	0.0006	0.0420
t-Statistic	-0.2013	1691.1373	11.7633
p-Value	0.8406	0.0000	0.0000
Lower 5%	0.4498	1.0065	0.5628
Upper 95%	-0.5749	1.0046	0.4244

Degrees of Freedom		Hypothesis Test	
Degrees of Freedom for Regression	2	Critical t-Statistic (99% confidence with df of 432)	2.5873
Degrees of Freedom for Residual	432	Critical t-Statistic (95% confidence with df of 432)	1.9655
Total Degrees of Freedom	434	Critical t-Statistic (90% confidence with df of 432)	1.6484

The Coefficients provide the estimated regression intercept and slopes. For instance, the coefficients are estimates of the true, population b values in the following regression equation Y = b0 + b1X1 + b2X2 + ... + bnXn. The Standard Error measures how accurate the predicted Coefficients are, and the t-Statistics are the ratios of each predicted Coefficient to its Standard Error.

The t-Statistic is used in hypothesis testing, where we set the null hypothesis (Ho) such that the real mean of the Coefficient = 0, and the alternate hypothesis (Ha) such that the real mean of the Coefficient is not equal to 0. A t-test is is performed and the calculated t-Statistic is compared to the critical values at the relevant Degrees of Freedom for Residual. The t-test is very important as it calculates if each of the coefficients is statistically significant in the presence of the other regressors. This means that the t-test statistically verifies whether a regressor or independent variable should remain in the regression or it should be dropped.

The Coefficient is statistically significant if its calculated t-Statistic exceeds the Critical t-Statistic at the relevant degrees of freedom (df). The three main confidence levels used to test for significance are 90%, 95% and 99%. If a Coefficient's t-Statistic exceeds the Critical level, it is considered statistically significant. Alternatively, the p-Value calculates each t-Statistic's probability of occurrence, which means that the smaller the p-Value, the more significant the Coefficient. The usual significant levels for the p-value are 0.01, 0.05, and 0.10, corresponding to the 99%, 95%, and 90% confidence levels.

The Coefficients with their p-Values highlighted in blue indicate that they are statistically significant at the 90% confidence or 0.10 alpha level, while those highlighted in red indicate that they are not statistically significant at any other alpha levels.

Figure 6.13: Box–Jenkins ARIMA Forecast Report (continues)

Analysis of Variance

	Sums of Squares	Mean of Squares	F-Statistic	p-Value	Hypothesis Test	
Regression	38415447.53	19207723.76	3171851.1	0.0000	Critical F-statistic (99% confidence with df of 2 and 432)	4.6546
Residual	2616.05	6.06			Critical F-statistic (95% confidence with df of 2 and 432)	3.0166
Total	38418063.58				Critical F-statistic (90% confidence with df of 2 and 432)	2.3149

The Analysis of Variance (ANOVA) table provides an F-test of the regression model's overall statistical significance. Instead of looking at individual regressors as in the t-test, the F-test looks at all the estimated Coefficients' statistical properties. The F-Statistic is calculated as the ratio of the Regression's Mean of Squares to the Residual's Mean of Squares. The numerator measures how much of the regression is explained, while the denominator measures how much is unexplained. Hence, the larger the F-Statistic, the more significant the model. The corresponding p-Value is calculated to test the null hypothesis (Ho) where all the Coefficients are simultaneously equal to zero, versus the alternate hypothesis (Ha) that they are all simultaneously different from zero, indicating a significant overall regression model. If the p-Value is smaller than the 0.01, 0.05, or 0.10 alpha significance, then the regression is significant. The same approach can be applied to the F-Statistic by comparing the calculated F-Statistic with the critical F values at various significance levels.

Autocorrelation

Time Lag	AC	PAC	Lower Bound	Upper Bound	Q-Stat	Prob
1	0.9921	0.9921	(0.0958)	0.0958	431.1216	-
2	0.9841	(0.0105)	(0.0958)	0.0958	858.3037	-
3	0.9760	(0.0109)	(0.0958)	0.0958	1,275.4818	-
4	0.9678	(0.0142)	(0.0958)	0.0958	1,688.5499	-
5	0.9594	(0.0098)	(0.0958)	0.0958	2,095.4825	-
6	0.9509	(0.0113)	(0.0958)	0.0958	2,496.1572	-
7	0.9423	(0.0124)	(0.0958)	0.0958	2,890.5594	-
8	0.9336	(0.0147)	(0.0958)	0.0958	3,278.5669	-
9	0.9247	(0.0121)	(0.0958)	0.0958	3,660.1152	-
10	0.9156	(0.0139)	(0.0958)	0.0958	4,035.1192	-

If autocorrelation AC(1) is nonzero, it means that the series is first order serially correlated. If AC(k) dies off more or less geometrically with increasing lag , it implies that the series follows a low-order autoregressive process. If AC(k) drops to zero after a small number of lags, it implies that the series follows a low-order moving-average process. Partial correlation PAC(k) measures the correlation of values that are k periods apart after removing the correlation from the intervening lags. If the pattern of autocorrelation can be captured by an autoregression of order less than k, then the partial autocorrelation at lag k will be close to zero. Ljung-Box Q-statistics and their p-values at lag k has the null hypothesis that there is no autocorrelation up to order k. The dotted lines in the plots of the autocorrelations are the approximate two standard error bounds. If the autocorrelation is within these bounds, it is not significantly different from zero at (approximately) the 5% significance level.

Forecasting

Period	Actual (Y)	Forecast (F)	Error (E)	RMSE:
2	139.4000	139.6056	(0.2056)	2.4523
3	139.7000	140.0069	(0.3069)	
4	139.7000	140.2586	(0.5586)	
5	140.7000	140.1343	0.5657	
6	141.2000	141.6948	(0.4948)	
7	141.7000	141.6741	0.0259	
8	141.9000	142.4339	(0.5339)	
9	141.0000	142.3587	(1.3587)	
10	140.5000	141.0466	(0.5466)	
11	140.4000	140.9447	(0.5447)	
12	140.0000	140.8451	(0.8451)	
13	140.0000	140.2948	(0.2948)	
14	139.9000	140.5663	(0.6663)	
15	139.8000	140.2823	(0.4823)	
16	139.6000	140.2726	(0.6726)	
17	139.6000	139.9775	(0.3775)	
18	139.6000	140.1232	(0.5231)	

Figure 6.13: Box–Jenkins ARIMA Forecast Report (continued)

AUTO ARIMA (BOX–JENKINS ARIMA TIME-SERIES) FORECASTS

Theory

This tool provides analyses identical to the ARIMA module except that the Auto-ARIMA module automates some of the traditional ARIMA modeling by automatically testing multiple permutations of model specifications and returns the best-fitting model. Running the Auto-ARIMA module is similar to running regular ARIMA forecasts. The differences being that the P, D, Q inputs are no longer required and that different combinations of these inputs are automatically run and compared.

Procedure

- Start Excel and enter your data or open an existing worksheet with historical data to forecast (the illustration shown in Figure 6.14 uses the example file located at *Risk Simulator | Example Models | 01 Advanced Forecasting Models*).

- In the *Auto ARIMA* worksheet, select *Risk Simulator | Forecasting | Auto-ARIMA*. You can also access the method through the Forecasting icons ribbon or right-clicking anywhere in the model and selecting the forecasting shortcut menu.

- Click on the link icon and link to the existing time-series data, enter the number of forecast periods desired, and click *OK*.

ARIMA and AUTO ARIMA Note

For ARIMA and Auto ARIMA, you can model and forecast future periods either by using only the dependent variable (*Y*), that is, the *Time Series Variable* by itself, or you can insert additional exogenous variables ($X_1, X_2,..., X_n$) just as in a regression analysis where you have multiple independent variables. You can run as many forecast periods as you wish if you only use the time-series variable (*Y*). However, if you add exogenous variables (*X*), be sure to note that your forecast periods are limited to the number of exogenous variables' data periods minus the time-series variable's data periods. For example, you can only forecast up to 5 periods if you have time-series historical data of 100 periods and only if you have exogenous variables of 105 periods (100 historical periods to match the time-series variable and 5 additional future periods of independent exogenous variables to forecast the time-series dependent variable).

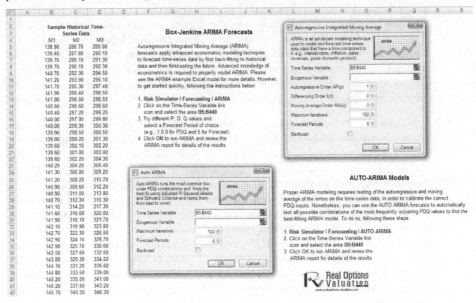

Figure 6.14: AUTO-ARIMA Module

BASIC ECONOMETRICS

Theory

Econometrics refers to a branch of business analytics, modeling, and forecasting techniques for modeling the behavior or forecasting certain business, financial, economic, physical science, and other variables. Running the Basic Econometrics models is similar to regular regression analysis except that the dependent and independent variables are allowed to be modified before a regression is run. The report generated is the same as shown previously in the Multiple or Multivariate Regression section and the interpretations are identical to those described previously.

Procedure

- Start Excel and enter your data or open an existing worksheet with historical data to forecast (the illustration shown in Figure 6.15 uses the file example located at *Risk Simulator | Example Models | 01 Advanced Forecasting Models*).

- *Select the data* in the *Basic Econometrics* worksheet and select *Risk Simulator | Forecasting | Basic Econometrics*.

- Enter the desired dependent and independent variables (see Figure 6.15 for examples) and click *OK* to run the model and report, or click on *Show Results* to view the results before generating the report in case you need to make any changes to the model.

Notes

- See Chapter 7 for details on interpreting the regression outputs and, by extension, the outputs from a basic econometrics analysis.

- To run an econometric model, simply select the data (B5:G55) including headers and click on *Risk Simulator | Forecasting | Basic Econometrics*. You can then type in the variables and their modifications for the dependent and independent variables (Figure 6.15). Note that only one variable is allowed as the Dependent Variable (Y), whereas multiple variables are allowed in the Independent Variables (X) section, separated by a semicolon (;) and that basic mathematical functions can be used (e.g., LN, LOG, LAG, +, -, /, *, TIME, RESIDUAL, DIFF). Click on *Show Results* to preview the computed model and click *OK* to generate the econometric model report.

- You can also automatically generate Multiple Models by entering a sample model and using the predefined *INTEGER(N)* variable as well as *Shifting Data* up or down specific rows repeatedly. For instance, if you use the variable *LAG(VAR1, INTEGER1)* and you set *INTEGER1* to be between *MIN* = 1 and *MAX* = 3, then the following three models will be run: first *LAG(VAR1,1)*, then *LAG(VAR1,2)*, and, finally, *LAG(VAR1,3)*. Also, sometimes you might want to test if the time-series data has structural shifts or if the behavior of the model is consistent over time by shifting the data and then running the same model. For example, if you have 100 months of data listed chronologically, you can shift down 3 months at a time for 10 times (i.e., the model will be run on months 1–100, 4–100, 7–100, etc.). Using this *Multiple Models* section in Basic Econometrics, you can run hundreds of models by simply entering a single model equation if you use these predefined integer variables and shifting methods.

Basic Econometrics Data Set

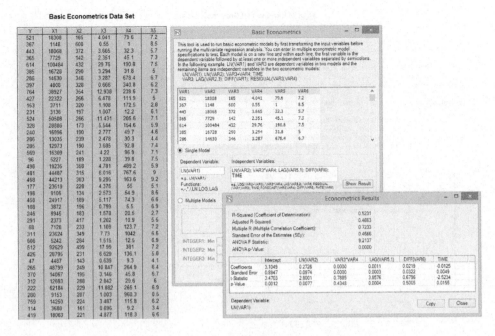

Figure 6.15: Basic Econometrics Module

J-CURVE AND S-CURVE FORECASTS

Theory

The J-curve, or exponential growth curve, is one where the growth of the next period depends on the current period's level and the increase is exponential. This phenomenon means that over time, the values will increase significantly, from one period to another. This model is typically used in forecasting biological growth and chemical reactions over time.

Procedure

- Start Excel and select *Risk Simulator | Forecasting | JS Curves*.

- Select the J- or S-curve type, enter the required input assumptions (see Figures 6.16 and 6.17 for examples), and click *OK* to run the model and report.

J-Curve Exponential Growth Curves

In mathematics, a quantity that grows exponentially is one whose growth rate is always proportional to its current size. Such growth is said to follow an exponential law. This implies that for any exponentially growing quantity, the larger the quantity gets, the faster it grows. But it also implies that the relationship between the size of the dependent variable and its rate of growth is governed by a strict law, of the simplest kind: direct proportion. The general principle behind exponential growth is that the larger a number gets, the faster it grows. Any exponentially growing number will eventually grow larger than any other number which grows at only a constant rate for the same amount of time. This forecast method is also called a J curve due to its shape resembling the letter J. There is no maximum level of this growth curve. Other growth curves include S-curves and Markov Chains.

To generate a J curve forecast, follow the instructions below:

1. Click on **Risk Simulator I Forecasting I JS Curves**
2. Select Exponential J Curve and enter in the desired inputs
   (e.g., Starting Value of 100, Growth Rate of 5 percent, End Period of 100)
3. Click OK to run the forecast and spend some time reviewing the forecast report

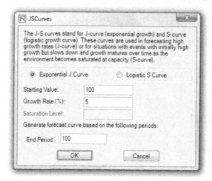

Figure 6.16: J-curve Forecast

The S-curve, or logistic growth curve, starts off like a J-curve, with exponential growth rates. Over time, the environment becomes saturated (e.g., market saturation, competition, overcrowding), the growth slows, and the forecast value eventually ends up at a saturation or maximum level. The S-curve model is typically used in forecasting market share or sales growth of a new product from market introduction until maturity and decline, population dynamics, growth of bacterial cultures, and other naturally occurring variables. Figure 6.17 illustrates a sample S-curve.

Logistic S Curve

A logistic function or logistic curve models the S-curve of growth of some variable X. The initial stage of growth is approximately exponential; then, as competition arises, the growth slows, and at maturity, growth stops. These functions find applications in a range of fields, from biology to economics. For example, in the development of an embryo, a fertilized ovum splits, and the cell count grows: 1, 2, 4, 8, 16, 32, 64, etc. This is exponential growth. But the fetus can grow only as large as the uterus can hold; thus other factors start slowing down the increase in the cell count; and the rate of growth slows (but the baby is still growing, of course). After a suitable time, the child is born and keeps growing. Ultimately, the cell count is stable; the person's height is constant; the growth has stopped, at maturity. The same principles can be applied to population growth of animals or humans, and the market penetration and revenues of a product, with an initial growth spurt in market penetration, but over time, the growth slows due to competition and eventually the market declines and matures.

1. Click on **Risk Simulator | Forecasting | JS Curves**
2. Enter in the required inputs (see below for an example)
3. Click **OK** and review the forecast report

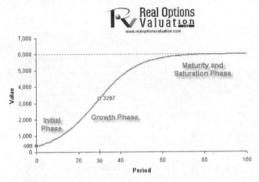

Figure 6.17: S-curve Forecast

GARCH VOLATILITY FORECASTS

Theory

The generalized autoregressive conditional heteroskedasticity (GARCH) model is used to model historical and forecast future volatility levels of a marketable security (e.g., stock prices, commodity prices, oil prices, etc.). The dataset has to be a time series of raw price levels. GARCH will first convert the prices into relative returns and then run an internal optimization to fit the historical data to a mean-reverting volatility term structure, while assuming that the volatility is heteroskedastic in nature (changes over time according to some econometric characteristics). The theoretical specifics of a GARCH model are outside the purview of this book.

Procedure

- Start Excel, open the example file *Advanced Forecasting Model*, go to the *GARCH* worksheet, and select *Risk Simulator | Forecasting | GARCH*.

- Click on the link icon, select the *Data Location* and enter the required input assumptions (see Figure 6.18), and click *OK* to run the model and report.

Notes

The typical volatility forecast situation requires P = 1, Q = 1; Periodicity = number of periods per year (12 for monthly data, 52 for weekly data, 252 or 365 for daily data); Base = minimum of 1 and up to the periodicity value; and Forecast Periods = number of annualized volatility forecasts you wish to obtain. There are several GARCH models available in Risk Simulator, including EGARCH, EGARCH-T, GARCH-M, GJR-GARCH, GJR-GARCH-T, IGARCH, and T-GARCH.

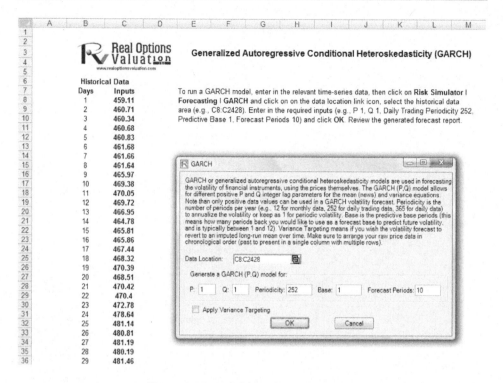

	A	B	C	D	E	F	G	H	I	J	K	L	M
1													
2													
3													
4													
5													
6		Historical Data											
7		Days	Inputs										
8		1	459.11										
9		2	460.71										
10		3	460.34										
11		4	460.68										
12		5	460.83										
13		6	461.68										
14		7	461.66										
15		8	461.64										
16		9	465.97										
17		10	469.38										
18		11	470.05										
19		12	469.72										
20		13	466.95										
21		14	464.78										
22		15	465.81										
23		16	465.86										
24		17	467.44										
25		18	468.32										
26		19	470.39										
27		20	468.51										
28		21	470.42										
29		22	470.4										
30		23	472.78										
31		24	478.64										
32		25	481.14										
33		26	480.81										
34		27	481.19										
35		28	480.19										
36		29	481.46										

Generalized Autoregressive Conditional Heteroskedasticity (GARCH)

To run a GARCH model, enter in the relevant time-series data, then click on **Risk Simulator I Forecasting I GARCH** and click on on the data location link icon, select the historical data area (e.g., C8:C2428). Enter in the required inputs (e.g., P 1, Q 1, Daily Trading Periodicity 252, Predictive Base 1, Forecast Periods 10) and click OK. Review the generated forecast report.

Figure 6.18: GARCH Volatility Forecast

GARCH models are used mainly in analyzing financial time-series data to ascertain their conditional variances and volatilities. These volatilities are then used to value the options as usual, but the amount of historical data necessary for a good volatility estimate remains significant. Usually, several dozen—and even up to hundreds—of data points are required to obtain good GARCH estimates. GARCH is a term that incorporates a family of models that can take on a variety of forms, known as GARCH(p,q), where p and q are positive integers that define the resulting GARCH model and its forecasts. In most cases for financial instruments, a GARCH(1,1) is sufficient and is most generally used. For instance, a GARCH (1,1) model takes the form of:

$$y_t = x_t \gamma + \varepsilon_t$$
$$\sigma_t^2 = \omega + \alpha \varepsilon_{t-1}^2 + \beta \sigma_{t-1}^2$$

The first equation's dependent variable (y_t) is a function of exogenous variables (x_t) with an error term (ε_t). The second equation estimates the variance (squared volatility σ_t^2) at time t, which depends on a historical mean (ω), news about volatility from the previous period, measured as a lag of the squared residual from the mean equation (ε_{t-1}^2), and volatility from the previous period (σ_{t-1}^2). The exact modeling specification of a GARCH model is beyond the scope of this book. Suffice it to say that detailed knowledge of econometric modeling (model specification tests, structural breaks, and error estimation) is required to run a GARCH model, making it less accessible to the general analyst. Another problem with GARCH models is that the model usually does not provide a good statistical fit. That is, it is impossible to predict the stock market and, of course, equally if not harder to predict a stock's volatility over time.

Note that the GARCH function has several inputs as follow:

- *Time-Series Data.* The time series of data in chronological order (e.g., stock prices). Typically, dozens of data points are required for a decent volatility forecast.

- *Periodicity,* A positive integer indicating the number of periods per year (e.g., 12 for monthly data, 252 for daily trading data, etc.), assuming you wish to annualize the volatility. To obtain periodic volatility, enter 1.

- *Predictive Base.* The number of periods back (of the time-series data) to use as a base to forecast volatility. The higher this number, the longer the historical base is used to forecast future volatility.

- *Forecast Period.* A positive integer indicating how many future periods beyond the historical stock prices you wish to forecast.

- *Variance Targeting.* This variable is set as False by default (even if you do not enter anything here) but can be set as True. False means the omega variable is automatically optimized and computed. The suggestion is to leave this variable empty. If you wish to create mean-reverting volatility with variance targeting, set this variable as True.

- *P.* The number of previous lags on the mean equation.

- *Q.* The number of previous lags on the variance equation.

The following lists some of the GARCH specifications used in Risk Simulator with two underlying distributional assumptions: one for normal distribution and the other for the t-distribution.

For the GARCH-M models, the conditional variance equations are the same in the six variations but the mean questions are different and assumption on Z_t can be either normal distribution or t-distribution. The estimated parameters for GARCH-M with normal distribution are those five parameters in the mean and conditional variance equations. The estimated parameters for GARCH-M with the t-distribution are those five parameters in the mean and conditional variance equations plus another parameter, the degrees of freedom for the t-distribution. In contrast, for the GJR models, the mean equations are the same in the six variations and the differences are that the conditional variance equations and the assumption on Z_t can be either a normal distribution or t-distribution. The estimated parameters for EGARCH and GJR-GARCH with normal distribution are those four parameters in the conditional variance equation. The estimated parameters for GARCH, EARCH, and GJR-GARCH with t-distribution are those parameters in the conditional variance equation plus the degrees of freedom for the t-distribution. More technical details of GARCH methodologies fall outside of the scope of this book.

	$Z_t \sim$ Normal Distribution	$Z_t \sim$ T-Distribution
GARCH-M Variance in Mean Equation	$y_t = c + \lambda \sigma_t^2 + \varepsilon_t$ $\varepsilon_t = \sigma_t z_t$ $\sigma_t^2 = \omega + \alpha \varepsilon_{t-1}^2 + \beta \sigma_{t-1}^2$	$y_t = c + \lambda \sigma_t^2 + \varepsilon_t$ $\varepsilon_t = \sigma_t z_t$ $\sigma_t^2 = \omega + \alpha \varepsilon_{t-1}^2 + \beta \sigma_{t-1}^2$
GARCH-M Standard Deviation in Mean Equation	$y_t = c + \lambda \sigma_t + \varepsilon_t$ $\varepsilon_t = \sigma_t z_t$ $\sigma_t^2 = \omega + \alpha \varepsilon_{t-1}^2 + \beta \sigma_{t-1}^2$	$y_t = c + \lambda \sigma_t + \varepsilon_t$ $\varepsilon_t = \sigma_t z_t$ $\sigma_t^2 = \omega + \alpha \varepsilon_{t-1}^2 + \beta \sigma_{t-1}^2$
GARCH-M Log Variance in Mean Equation	$y_t = c + \lambda \ln(\sigma_t^2) + \varepsilon_t$ $\varepsilon_t = \sigma_t z_t$ $\sigma_t^2 = \omega + \alpha \varepsilon_{t-1}^2 + \beta \sigma_{t-1}^2$	$y_t = c + \lambda \ln(\sigma_t^2) + \varepsilon_t$ $\varepsilon_t = \sigma_t z_t$ $\sigma_t^2 = \omega + \alpha \varepsilon_{t-1}^2 + \beta \sigma_{t-1}^2$
GARCH	$y_t = x_t \gamma + \varepsilon_t$ $\sigma_t^2 = \omega + \alpha \varepsilon_{t-1}^2 + \beta \sigma_{t-1}^2$	$y_t = \varepsilon_t$ $\varepsilon_t = \sigma_t z_t$ $\sigma_t^2 = \omega + \alpha \varepsilon_{t-1}^2 + \beta \sigma_{t-1}^2$
EGARCH	$y_t = \varepsilon_t$ $\varepsilon_t = \sigma_t z_t$ $\ln(\sigma_t^2) = \omega + \beta \cdot \ln(\sigma_{t-1}^2) +$ $\alpha \left[\left\lvert \dfrac{\varepsilon_{t-1}}{\sigma_{t-1}} \right\rvert - E(\lvert \varepsilon_t \rvert) \right] + r \dfrac{\varepsilon_{t-1}}{\sigma_{t-1}}$ $E(\lvert \varepsilon_t \rvert) = \sqrt{\dfrac{2}{\pi}}$	$y_t = \varepsilon_t$ $\varepsilon_t = \sigma_t z_t$ $\ln(\sigma_t^2) = \omega + \beta \cdot \ln(\sigma_{t-1}^2) +$ $\alpha \left[\left\lvert \dfrac{\varepsilon_{t-1}}{\sigma_{t-1}} \right\rvert - E(\lvert \varepsilon_t \rvert) \right] + r \dfrac{\varepsilon_{t-1}}{\sigma_{t-1}}$ $E(\lvert \varepsilon_t \rvert) = \dfrac{2\sqrt{v-2}\,\Gamma((v+1)/2)}{(v-1)\Gamma(v/2)\sqrt{\pi}}$
GJR-GARCH	$y_t = \varepsilon_t$ $\varepsilon_t = \sigma_t z_t$ $\sigma_t^2 = \omega + \alpha \varepsilon_{t-1}^2 +$ $r\varepsilon_{t-1}^2 d_{t-1} + \beta \sigma_{t-1}^2$ $d_{t-1} = \begin{cases} 1 & \text{if } \varepsilon_{t-1} < 0 \\ 0 & \text{otherwise} \end{cases}$	$y_t = \varepsilon_t$ $\varepsilon_t = \sigma_t z_t$ $\sigma_t^2 = \omega + \alpha \varepsilon_{t-1}^2 +$ $r\varepsilon_{t-1}^2 d_{t-1} + \beta \sigma_{t-1}^2$ $d_{t-1} = \begin{cases} 1 & \text{if } \varepsilon_{t-1} < 0 \\ 0 & \text{otherwise} \end{cases}$

MARKOV CHAINS

Theory

A Markov chain exists when the probability of a future state depends on a previous state and when linked together forms a chain that reverts to a long-run steady state level. This Markov approach is typically used to forecast the market share of two competitors. The required inputs are the starting probability of a customer in the first store (first state) returning to the same store in the next period versus the probability of switching to a competitor's store in the next state.

Procedure

- Start Excel and select *Risk Simulator | Forecasting | Markov Chain*.

- Enter the required input assumptions (see Figure 6.19 for an example) and click *OK* to run the model and report.

Note

Set both probabilities to 10 percent and rerun the Markov chain, and you will see the effects of switching behaviors very clearly in the resulting chart shown in Figure 6.19.

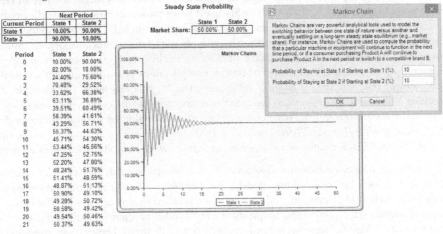

Figure 6.19: Markov Chains (Switching Regimes)

MAXIMUM LIKELIHOOD MODELS ON LOGIT, PROBIT, AND TOBIT

Theory

Limited Dependent Variables describe the situation where the dependent variable contains data that are limited in scope and range, such as binary responses (*0* or *1*), truncated, ordered, or censored data. For instance, given a set of independent variables (e.g., age, income, education level of credit card or mortgage loan holders), we can model the probability of defaulting on mortgage payments, using maximum likelihood estimation (MLE). The response or dependent variable Y is binary, that is, it can have only two possible outcomes that we denote as *1* and *0* (e.g., Y may represent presence/absence of a certain condition, defaulted/not defaulted on previous loans, success/failure of some device, answer yes/no on a survey, etc.) and we also have a vector of independent variable regressors X, which are assumed to influence the outcome Y. A typical ordinary least squares regression approach is invalid because the regression errors are heteroskedastic and non-normal, and the resulting estimated probability estimates will return nonsensical values of above *1* or below *0*. MLE analysis handles these problems using an iterative optimization routine to maximize a log likelihood function when the dependent variables are limited.

A Logit or Logistic regression is used for predicting the probability of occurrence of an event by fitting data to a logistic curve. It is a generalized linear model used for binomial regression, and like many forms of regression analysis, it makes use of several predictor variables that may be either numerical or categorical. MLE applied in a binary multivariate logistic analysis is used to model dependent variables to determine the expected probability of success of belonging to a certain group. The estimated coefficients for the Logit model are the logarithmic odds ratios and they cannot be interpreted directly as probabilities. A quick computation is first required and the approach is simple.

Specifically, the Logit model is specified as *Estimated Y = LN[P_i/(1–P_i)]* or, conversely, *P_i = EXP(Estimated Y)/(1+EXP(Estimated Y))*, and the coefficients β_i are the log odds ratios. So, taking the antilog or *EXP(β_i)* we obtain the odds ratio of *P_i/(1–P_i)*. This means that with an increase in a unit of *βi* the log odds ratio increases by this amount. Finally, the rate of change in the probability *dP/dX = $\beta_i P_i$(1–P_i)*. The Standard Error measures how accurate the predicted Coefficients are, and the t-Statistics are the ratios of each predicted Coefficient to its Standard Error and are used in the typical regression hypothesis test of the significance of each estimated parameter. To estimate the probability of success of belonging to a certain group (e.g., predicting if a smoker will develop respiratory complications given the amount smoked per year), simply compute the *Estimated Y* value using the MLE coefficients. For example, if the model is *Y = 1.1 + 0.005 (Cigarettes)* then someone smoking 100 packs per year has an *Estimated Y of 1.1 + 0.005(100) = 1.6*. Next, compute the inverse antilog of the odds ratio by doing: *EXP(Estimated Y)/[1 + EXP(Estimated Y)] = EXP(1.6)/(1+ EXP(1.6)) = 0.8320.* So, such a person has an *83.20%* chance of developing some respiratory complications in his lifetime.

A Probit model (sometimes also known as a Normit model) is a popular alternative specification for a binary response model, which employs a Probit function estimated using maximum likelihood estimation, and the approach is called Probit regression. The Probit and Logistic regression models tend to produce very similar predictions where the parameter estimates in a logistic regression tend to be 1.6 to 1.8 times higher than they are in a corresponding Probit model. The choice of using a Probit or Logit is entirely up to convenience, and the main distinction is that the logistic distribution has a higher kurtosis (fatter tails) to account for extreme values. For example, suppose that house ownership is the decision to be modeled, and this response variable is binary (home purchase or no home purchase) and depends on a series of independent variables X_i such as income, age, and so forth, such that *I_i = β_0 + $\beta_1 X_1$ +...+ $\beta_n X_n$*, where the larger the value of I_i, the higher the probability of home ownership. For each family, a critical *I** threshold exists, where if exceeded, the house is purchased, otherwise, no home is purchased, and the outcome probability (*P*) is assumed to be normally distributed, such that *P_i = CDF(I)* using a standard-normal cumulative distribution function (*CDF*). Therefore, use the estimated coefficients exactly like those of a regression model and using the *Estimated Y* value, apply a standard-normal distribution (you can use Excel's *NORMSDIST* function or Risk Simulator's *Distributional Analysis* tool by selecting Normal distribution and setting the mean to be *0* and standard deviation to be *1*). Finally, to obtain a Probit or probability unit measure, set *I_i + 5* (this is because whenever the probability *P_i < 0.5*, the estimated *I_i* is negative, due to the fact that the normal distribution is symmetrical around a mean of zero).

The Tobit model (Censored Tobit) is an econometric and biometric modeling method used to describe the relationship between a non-negative dependent variable Y_i and one or more independent variables X_i. A Tobit model is an econometric model in which the dependent variable is censored; that is, the dependent variable is censored because values below zero are not observed. The Tobit model assumes that there is a latent unobservable variable Y^*. This variable is linearly dependent on the X_i variables via a vector of β_i coefficients that determine their inter-relationships. In addition, there is a normally distributed error term U_i to capture random influences on this relationship. The observable variable Y_i is defined to be equal to the latent variables whenever the latent variables are above zero and Y_i is assumed to be zero otherwise. That is, $Y_i = Y^*$ if $Y^* > 0$ and $Y_i = 0$ if $Y^* = 0$. If the relationship parameter β_i is estimated by using ordinary least squares regression of the observed Y_i on X_i, the resulting regression estimators are inconsistent and yield downward-biased slope coefficients and an upward-biased intercept. Only MLE would be consistent for a Tobit model. In the Tobit model, there is an ancillary statistic called sigma, which is equivalent to the standard error of estimate in a standard ordinary least squares regression, and the estimated coefficients are used the same way as in a regression analysis.

Procedure

- Start Excel and open the example file *Advanced Forecasting Model*, go to the *MLE* worksheet, select the dataset including the headers, and click on *Risk Simulator | Forecasting | Maximum Likelihood.*

- Select the dependent variable from the drop-down list (see Figure 6.20) and click *OK* to run the model and report.

Binary Logistic Maximum Likelihood Forecast: Logit, Probit, Tobit

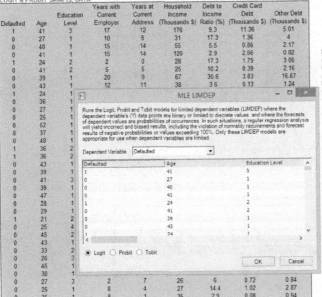

Maximum Likelihood Estimates or MLE on a binary multivariate logistic analysis, which is used to model dependent variables to determine the expected probability of success of belonging to a certain group. For instance, given a set of independent variables (e.g., age, income, and education level of credit card or mortgage loan holders), we can model the probability of credit loan default using MLE, or finding the probability a person will contract a specific illness or survive this disease given the person's age, social status, blood pressure, medications taken, and so forth. A typical regression model is invalid because the errors are heteroskedastic and non-normal, and the resulting probability estimates will sometimes be above 1 or below 0. MLE analysis handles these problems using an iterative optimization routine.

The data here represents a sample of several hundred previous loans, credit, or debt issues. The data show whether each loan had defaulted or not, as well as the specifics of each loan applicant's age, education level (1-3 indicating high school, university, or graduate professional education), years with current employer and so forth. The idea is to model these empirical data to see which variables affect the default behavior of individuals, using Risk Simulator's Maximum Likelihood Models. The resulting model will help the bank or credit issuer compute the expected probability of default of an individual credit holder of having specific characteristics.

Figure 6.20: Maximum Likelihood Models

SPLINE (CUBIC SPLINE INTERPOLATION AND EXTRAPOLATION)

Theory

Sometimes there are missing values in a time-series dataset. For instance, interest rates for years 1 to 3 may exist, followed by years 5 to 8, and then year 10. Spline curves can be used to interpolate the missing years' interest rate values based on the data that exist. Spline curves can also be used to forecast or extrapolate values of future time periods beyond the time period of available data. The data can be linear or nonlinear. Figure 6.21 illustrates how a cubic spline is run and Figure 6.22 shows the resulting forecast report from this module. The *Known X* values represent the values on the x-axis of a chart (in our example, this is Years of the known interest rates, and, usually, the x-axis values are those that are known in advance such as time or years) and the *Known Y* values represent the values on the y-axis of a time-series chart (in our case, the known Interest Rates). The y-axis variable is typically the variable you wish to interpolate missing values from or extrapolate the values into the future.

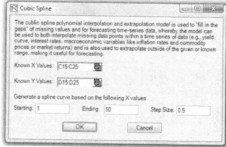

Cubic Spline Interpolation and Extrapolation

The cubic spline polynomial interpolation and extrapolation model is used to "fill in the gaps" of missing spot yields and term structure of interest rates whereby the model can be used to both interpolate missing data points within a time series of interest rates (as well as other macroeconomic variables such as inflation rates and commodity prices or market returns) and also used to extrapolate outside of the given or known range, useful for forecasting purposes.

Years	Spot Yields	
0.0833	4.55%	These are the yields
0.2500	4.47%	that are known and
0.5000	4.52%	are used as inputs in
1.0000	4.39%	the Cubic Spline
2.0000	4.13%	Interpolation and
3.0000	4.16%	Extrapolation model
5.0000	4.26%	
7.0000	4.38%	
10.0000	4.56%	
20.0000	4.88%	
30.0000	4.84%	

To run the Cubic Spline forecast, click on **Risk Simulator | Forecasting | Cubic Spline** and then click on the link icon and select C15:C25 as the Known X values (values on the x-axis of a time-series chart) and D15:D25 as the Known Y values (make sure the length of Known X and Y values are the same). Enter the desired forecast periods (e.g., Starting 1, Ending 50, Step Size 0.5). Click OK and review the generated forecasts and chart.

Figure 6.21: Cubic Spline Module

Procedure

- Start Excel and open the example file *Advanced Forecasting Model*, go to the *Cubic Spline* worksheet, select the dataset excluding the headers, and click on *Risk Simulator | Forecasting | Cubic Spline*.

- The data location is automatically inserted into the user interface if you first select the data, or you can also manually click on the link icon and link the *Known X* values and *Known Y* values (see Figure 6.21 for an example), then enter the required *Starting* and *Ending* values to extrapolate and interpolate, as well as the required *Step Size* between these starting and ending values. Click *OK* to run the model and report (see Figure 6.22).

Cubic Spline Forecasts

The cubic spline polynomial interpolation and extrapolation model is used to "fill in the gaps" of missing values and for forecasting time-series data, whereby the model can be used to both interpolate missing data points within a time series of data (e.g., yield curve, interest rates, macroeconomic variables like inflation rates and commodity prices or market returns) and also used to extrapolate outside of the given or known range, making it useful for forecasting.

Spline Interpolation and Extrapolation Results

X	Fitted Y	Notes
1.0	4.39%	Interpolate
1.5	4.21%	Interpolate
2.0	4.13%	Interpolate
2.5	4.13%	Interpolate
3.0	4.16%	Interpolate
3.5	4.19%	Interpolate
4.0	4.22%	Interpolate
4.5	4.24%	Interpolate
5.0	4.26%	Interpolate
5.5	4.29%	Interpolate
6.0	4.32%	Interpolate
6.5	4.35%	Interpolate
7.0	4.38%	Interpolate
7.5	4.41%	Interpolate
8.0	4.44%	Interpolate
8.5	4.47%	Interpolate
9.0	4.50%	Interpolate
9.5	4.53%	Interpolate
10.0	4.56%	Interpolate
10.5	4.59%	Interpolate

These are the known value inputs in the Cubic Spline Interpolation and Extrapolation model:

Observation	Known X	Known Y
1	0.0833	4.55%
2	0.2500	4.47%
3	0.5000	4.52%
4	1.0000	4.39%
5	2.0000	4.13%
6	3.0000	4.16%
7	5.0000	4.26%
8	7.0000	4.38%
9	10.0000	4.56%
10	20.0000	4.88%
11	30.0000	4.84%

Figure 6.22: Spline Forecast Results

NEURAL NETWORK AND COMBINATORIAL FUZZY LOGIC FORECASTING METHODOLOGIES

Theory: Neural Network

The term Neural Network is often used to refer to a network or circuit of biological neurons, while modern usage of the term often also refers to artificial neural networks comprising artificial neurons, or nodes, recreated in a software environment. Such networks attempt to mimic the neurons in the human brain in ways of thinking and identifying patterns and, in our situation, identifying patterns for the purposes of forecasting time-series data. In Risk Simulator, the methodology is found inside the ROV BizStats module located at *Risk Simulator | ROV BizStats | Neural Network* as well as in *Risk Simulator | Forecasting | Neural Network*. Figure 6.23 shows the Neural Network forecast methodology results and Figure 6.24 charts the historical data and forecast data.

Procedure

- Click on *Risk Simulator | Forecasting | Neural Network*.

- Start by either manually entering data or pasting some data from the clipboard (e.g., select and copy some data from Excel, start this tool, and paste the data by clicking on the Paste button).

- Select if you wish to run a *Linear* or *Nonlinear* (*Cosine, Hyperbolic*, or *Logistic*) Neural Network model, enter in the desired number of Forecast Periods (e.g., 5), the number of hidden *Layers* in the Neural Network (e.g., 3), and number of *Testing Periods* (e.g., 5).

- Click *Run* to execute the analysis and review the computed results and charts. You can also *Copy* the results and chart to the clipboard and paste them in another software application.

Notes

Note that the number of hidden layers in the network is an input parameter and will need to be calibrated with your data. Typically, the more complicated the data pattern, the higher the number of hidden layers you would need and the longer it would take to compute. It is recommended that you start at 3 layers. The testing period is simply the number of data points used in the final calibration of the Neural Network model, and we recommend using at least the same number of periods you wish to forecast as the testing period.

Theory: Combinatorial Fuzzy Logic

In contrast, the term fuzzy logic is derived from fuzzy set theory to deal with reasoning that is approximate rather than accurate—as opposed to crisp logic, where binary sets have binary logic, fuzzy logic variables may have a truth value that ranges between 0 and 1 and is not constrained to the two truth values of classic propositional logic. This fuzzy weighting schema is used together with a combinatorial method to yield time-series forecast results in Risk Simulator as illustrated in Figure 6.25, and is most applicable when applied to time-series data that has seasonality and trend. This methodology is found inside the ROV BizStats module in Risk Simulator, at *Risk Simulator | ROV BizStats | Combinatorial Fuzzy Logic* as well as in *Risk Simulator | Forecasting | Combinatorial Fuzzy Logic*.

Procedure

1. Click on *Risk Simulator | Forecasting | Combinatorial Fuzzy Logic*.

2. Start by either manually entering data or pasting some data from the clipboard (e.g., select and copy some data from Excel, start this tool, and paste the data by clicking on the Paste button).

3. Select the variable you wish to run the analysis on from the drop-down list, and enter in the seasonality period (e.g., 4 for quarterly data, 12 for monthly data, etc.) and the desired number of Forecast Periods (e.g., 5).

4. Click *Run* to execute the analysis and review the computed results and charts. You can also *Copy* the results and chart to the clipboard and paste them in another software application.

Notes

Note that neither neural networks nor fuzzy logic techniques have yet been established as valid and reliable methods in the business forecasting domain, on either a strategic, tactical, or operational level. Much research is still required in these advanced forecasting fields. Nonetheless, Risk Simulator provides the fundamentals of these two techniques for the purposes of running time-series forecasts. To build more robust models, we recommend that you do not use any of these techniques in isolation, but, rather, in combination with the other Risk Simulator forecasting methodologies. Finally, you need sufficient data points to run these analyses with any level of confidence.

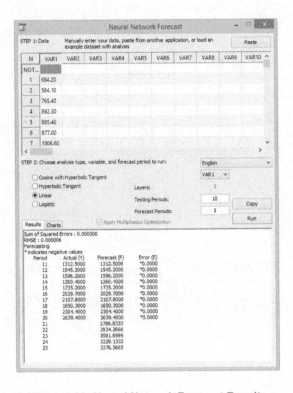

Figure 6.23: Neural Network Forecast Results

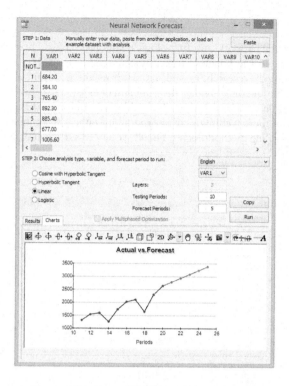

Figure 6.24: Neural Network Forecast Chart

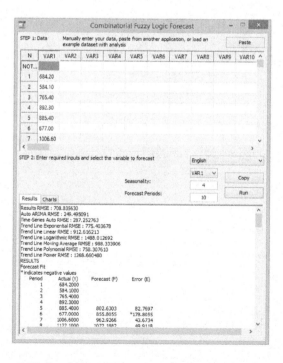

Figure 6.25: Combinatorial Fuzzy Logic Time-series Forecast

TRENDLINE FORECASTS

Theory

Trendlines can be used to determine if a set of time-series data follows any appreciable time-series trend. Trends can be linear or nonlinear (such as exponential, logarithmic, moving average, power, or polynomial curves).

Procedure

1. Select the data you wish to analyze, click on *Risk Simulator | Forecasting | Trendline*. Select the relevant trendlines you wish to apply on the data (e.g., select all methods by default), enter in the number of periods to forecast (e.g., 6 periods), and click *OK* (Figure 6.26).

2. Review the report to determine which of these test trendlines provide the best fit and best forecast for your data.

Notes

Figure 6.27 shows example shapes of the various trendlines, and the technical details of each trendline is noted below. Trendlines can also be used to forecast future periods (Figure 6.28).

*   Exponential trendline is useful when data values rise or fall at constantly increasing rates. Exponential trendlines cannot be computed if the dataset contains zero or negative values. The equation for the exponential trendline is $y = be^{xc}$, where b and c are constants and e is the natural exponential or base of the natural log (2.718).

*   Linear trendline is best for fitting straight lines for simple linear datasets. The dataset is linear if the pattern in its data points looks like a straight line. A linear trendline usually shows that something is increasing or decreasing at a steady rate. The equation for the line is $y = a + b_1 x$, where a and b are constants.

*   Logarithmic trendline is useful when the rate of change in the data increases or decreases quickly and then levels out. A logarithmic trendline requires positive values. Examples include population growth of animals or bacteria in a fixed-space area, where the population hits a maximum sustainable level as space and resources decrease and competition increases with the increase in population. The equation for the line is $y = a + b_1 ln(x)$, where a and b are constants.

*   Moving Average trendline evens out fluctuations in the dataset to show a pattern or trend. A moving average uses a set number of data points and averages them, then uses the average as a point in the line. For example, if Period is set to 2, the average of the first two data points is used as the first point in the moving average trendline. The average of the second and third data points is used as the second point in the trendline, and so on. The points move and the averaging number of period remains the same, hence the term moving average.

*   Polynomial or curvilinear trendline is useful when your data fluctuates such as when analyzing gains and losses over a large dataset over time. The power or order of the polynomial can be determined by the number of fluctuations in the data or by how many bends (hills and valleys) appear in the curve. For example, an Order 2 polynomial has only one hill or valley, an Order 3 has one or two hills or valleys, and an Order 4 has up to three hills or valleys. The equation for the n-order polynomial line is $y = a + b_1 x + b_2 x^2 + \cdots + + b_n x^n$, where a and b are constants.

- Power trendline is useful for datasets that compare measurements that increase at a specific rate, for example, the acceleration of a race car at some fixed time intervals. Power trendlines cannot be computed if the data contain zero or negative values. The equation for the power trendline is $y = bx^c$, where b and c are constants.

Historical Sales Revenues

Year	Quarter	Period	Sales
2010	1	1	$684.20
2010	2	2	$584.10
2010	3	3	$765.40
2010	4	4	$892.30
2011	1	5	$885.40
2011	2	6	$677.00
2011	3	7	$1,006.60
2011	4	8	$1,122.10
2012	1	9	$1,163.40
2012	2	10	$993.20
2012	3	11	$1,312.50
2012	4	12	$1,545.30
2013	1	13	$1,596.20
2013	2	14	$1,260.40
2013	3	15	$1,735.20
2013	4	16	$2,029.70
2014	1	17	$2,107.80
2014	2	18	$1,650.30
2014	3	19	$2,304.40
2014	4	20	$2,639.40

Figure 6.26: Trendline Methods

Trendlines

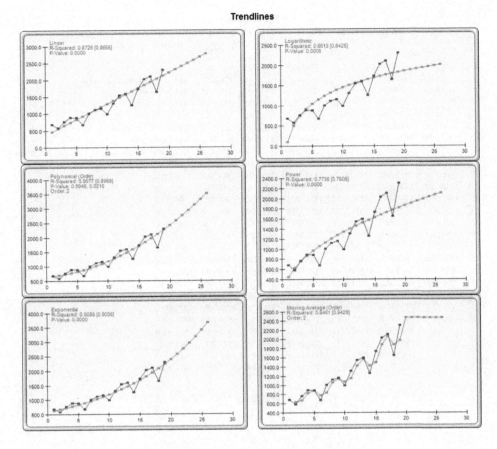

Figure 6.27: Trendline Charts and Results

Forecasts

Fitted and Forecast Data

Period	Actual Data	Linear	Logarithmic	Polynomial	Power	Exponential	Moving Average
1	684.2000	467.8014	105.2121	673.9569	452.2725	630.6812	
2	584.1000	560.4271	512.0838	701.4808	627.9345	676.7394	634.1500
3	765.4000	653.0527	750.0885	736.2383	760.8163	726.1612	674.7500
4	892.3000	745.6783	918.9555	778.2292	871.8234	779.1922	828.8500
5	885.4000	838.3040	1049.9389	827.4537	968.9645	836.0960	888.8500
6	677.0000	930.9296	1156.9601	883.9117	1056.3163	897.1555	781.2000
7	1006.6000	1023.5553	1247.4453	947.6032	1136.2870	962.6742	841.8000
8	1122.1000	1116.1809	1325.8272	1018.5283	1210.4384	1032.9776	1064.3500
9	1163.4000	1208.8065	1394.9648	1096.6869	1279.8511	1108.4152	1142.7500
10	993.2000	1301.4322	1456.8106	1182.0790	1345.3089	1189.3620	1078.3000
11	1312.5000	1394.0578	1512.7569	1274.7046	1407.4022	1276.2202	1152.8500
12	1545.3000	1486.6835	1563.8318	1374.5638	1466.5881	1369.4217	1428.9000
13	1596.2000	1579.3091	1610.8162	1481.6565	1523.2293	1469.4296	1570.7500
14	1260.4000	1671.9347	1654.3170	1595.9827	1577.6194	1576.7410	1428.3000
15	1735.2000	1764.5604	1694.8152	1717.5425	1629.9995	1691.8892	1497.8000
16	2029.7000	1857.1860	1732.6988	1846.3357	1680.5711	1815.4467	1882.4500
17	2107.8000	1949.8117	1768.2850	1982.3625	1729.5040	1948.0275	2068.7500
18	1650.3000	2042.4373	1801.8365	2125.6229	1776.9435	2090.2905	1879.0500
19	2304.4000	2135.0629	1833.5735	2276.1167	1823.0143	2242.9429	1977.3500
20	2639.4000	2227.6886	1863.6822	2433.8441	1867.8251	2406.7435	2471.9000
		2320.3142	1892.3217	2598.8050	1911.4709	2582.5062	2471.9000
		2412.9398	1919.6285	2770.9994	1954.0353	2771.1048	2471.9000
		2505.5655	1945.7213	2950.4274	1995.5926	2973.4766	2471.9000
		2598.1911	1970.7035	3137.0889	2036.2089	3190.6275	2471.9000
		2690.8168	1994.6657	3330.9839	2075.9435	3423.6367	2471.9000
		2783.4424	2017.6879	3532.1125	2114.8495	3673.6625	2471.9000

Error Estimates

Method	RMSE
Linear	204.0672
Logarithmic	332.7298
Polynomial	173.6690
Power	283.6811
Exponential	173.3855
Moving Average	138.8412

Figure 6.28: Trendline Backfit and Forecast Fit

Questions and Exercises

1. What are the differences between time-series forecasting techniques and nonlinear extrapolation?

2. Which forecasting method requires existing data and which method does not?

3. How do you use the software to perform qualitative forecasts?

4. Replicate all the examples in this chapter.

5. Time-series data that exhibit seasonality are easier to forecast than data that exhibit cyclicality. Is this statement true and why or why not?

The following pages present additional hands-on exercises on forecasting, and review all the techniques covered in this chapter.

EXERCISE: FORECASTING

This sample exercise illustrates how to use Risk Simulator for running:

1. Autoregressive Integrated Moving Average (ARIMA)
2. AUTO ARIMA
3. Basic Econometrics & Auto Econometrics
4. Cubic Spline
5. Custom Distribution
6. GARCH
7. J-Curve (Exponential Curve)
8. Markov Chain Process
9. Maximum Likelihood (Logit, Probit, Tobit)
10. Nonlinear Extrapolation
11. Multiple Regression
12. S-Curve (Logistic Curve)
13. Stochastic Processes (Random Walk, Brownian Motion, Mean-Reversion, Jump-Diffusion)
14. Time Series Decomposition
15. Trendlines

It is assumed that you have reviewed Chapter 6 for all the technical and usability details of these forecasting methods and are somewhat familiar with the purpose of each.

1. ARIMA

Autoregressive Integrated Moving Average (ARIMA) forecasts apply advanced econometric modeling techniques to forecast time-series data by first *back-fitting* to historical data and then *forecasting* the future. Advanced knowledge of econometrics is required to properly model ARIMA. Please see the ARIMA example Excel model for more details. However, to get started quickly, follow the instructions below:

1. Start Excel and open the example model *Risk Simulator | Example Models | 01 Advanced Forecast Models.*

2. Go to the *ARIMA and AUTO ARIMA* worksheet.

3. Select the data area *B5:B440* and click on *Risk Simulator | Forecasting | ARIMA* and click *OK* (you can keep the default settings for now). Spend some time reviewing the generated ARIMA report.

4. Next, go back to the worksheet and rerun ARIMA. This time you can try different P, D, Q values and enter a different Forecast Period of choice (e.g., *1,0,0* for P, D, Q, and *5* for Forecast… remember that these inputs have to be 0 or positive integers).

5. Run ARIMA again, but this time, click on the link icon to select the dataset *B5:B440* on the worksheet for the time-series variable and *C5:D445* for the exogenous variables.

   a. Exercise Question: What does exogenous variable mean?

b. Exercise Question: What types of variables might be well-suited for ARIMA forecasting?

c. Exercise Question: What types of data are appropriate for ARIMA? Time-series, cross-sectional, or mixed-panel data?

d. Exercise Question: What are the P, D, Q values used for?

e. Exercise Question: How does ARIMA compare with multiple regression analysis?

Note: For ARIMA and AUTO ARIMA, you can run as many forecast periods as you wish if you only use the time-series variable (*Y*). If you add exogenous variables (*X*), note that your forecast period is limited to the number of exogenous variables' data periods minus the time-series variable's data periods. For example, you can only forecast up to 5 periods if you have time-series historical data of 100 periods and only if you have exogenous variables of 105 periods (100 historical periods to match the time-series variable and 5 additional future periods of independent exogenous variables to forecast the time-series dependent variable).

2. AUTO ARIMA

Proper ARIMA modeling requires testing of the autoregressive and moving average of the errors on the time-series data in order to calibrate the correct *P, D, Q* inputs. Nonetheless, you can use the AUTO ARIMA forecasts to automatically test all possible combinations of the most frequently occurring *P, D, Q* values to find the best-fitting ARIMA model. To do so, follow these steps:

1. Start Excel and open the example model *Risk Simulator | Example Models | 01 Advanced Forecast Models*.

2. Go to the *ARIMA and AUTO ARIMA* worksheet.

3. Select the data area *B5:B440* and click on *Risk Simulator | Forecasting | Auto ARIMA* and click *OK*. Review the ARIMA report for details of the results.

4. Run ARIMA again, but this time, click on the link icon to select the dataset *B5:B440* on the worksheet for the time-series variable and *C5:D445* for the exogenous variables.

    a. Exercise Question: What is the difference between ARIMA and AUTO ARIMA?

    b. Exercise Question: What additional information is provided in the report and what input parameters are no longer required?

3. BASIC ECONOMETRICS & AUTO ECONOMETRICS

To run an econometric model, follow the instructions below:

1. Start Excel and open the example model *Risk Simulator | Example Models | 01 Advanced Forecast Models*.

2. Go to the *Basic Econometrics* worksheet.

3. Select the data area *B5:G55* and click on *Risk Simulator | Forecasting | Basic Econometrics* and then type in the variables and their modifications for the dependent and independent variables.

      a.   Dependent Variable: VAR1

      b.   Independent Variables: VAR2; VAR3; VAR4; VAR5; VAR6

4.   Click on *Show Results* to preview the computed model and click *OK* to generate the econometric model report.

5.   Go back to the data and rerun *Basic Econometrics.* This time, set up the model:

      a.   Dependent Variable: LN(VAR1)

      b.   Independent Variable: LN(VAR2); VAR3*VAR4; LAG(VAR5,1); DIFF(VAR6); TIME

6.   Go back to the data one more time and rerun *Basic Econometrics.* This time, select the *Multiple Models* option. Run the initial model with *VAR1* as the dependent variable and *LAG(VAR5,INTEGER1); VAR3*VAR4* as the independent variable, set *INTEGER1* to be between *1* and *3*, Sort by Adjusted R-Square, and *Shift Data 1 Row Down 5 Times* and click *OK.*

      a.   Exercise Question: What happens when you perform a shift to multiple econometric models?

      b.   Exercise Question: How do you model linear, nonlinear, interacting, lag, lead, log, natural log, time-series, difference, and ratios?

7.   Go back to the data, select *Risk Simulator | Forecasting | Auto Econometrics* and this time select *Linear and Nonlinear Interacting,* and then click *OK.* Review the generated report.

Note: Only one variable is allowed as the Dependent Variable (*Y*), whereas multiple variables are allowed in the Independent Variables (*X*) section, separated by a semicolon (;) and basic mathematical functions can be used (e.g., *LN, LOG, LAG, +, -, /, *, TIME, RESIDUAL, DIFF*). You can also automatically generate *Multiple Models* by entering a sample model and using the predefined '*INTEGER(N)*' variable as well as *Shifting Data* up or down specific rows repeatedly. For instance, if you use the variable *LAG(VAR1, INTEGER1)* and you set *INTEGER1* to be between *MIN* = 1 and *MAX* = 3, then the following three models will be run: *LAG(VAR1,1),* then *LAG(VAR1,2),* and, finally, *LAG(VAR1,3).* Using this *Multiple Models* section in *Basic Econometrics,* you can run hundreds of models by simply entering a single model equation if you use these predefined integer variables and shifting methods.

4. CUBIC SPLINE

The cubic spline polynomial interpolation and extrapolation model is used to "fill in the gaps" of missing values in that it can be used to both interpolate missing data points within a time series (e.g., interest rates as well as other macroeconomic variables such as inflation rates and commodity prices or market returns) and to extrapolate outside of the given or known range, useful for forecasting purposes.

To run the Cubic Spline forecast, follow the instructions below:

1.   Start Excel and open the example model *Risk Simulator | Example Models | 01 Advanced Forecast Models.*

2.   Go to the *Cubic Spline* worksheet.

3.   Select the data area *C15:D25* and click on *Risk Simulator | Forecasting | Cubic Spline* (check to make sure *C15:C25* is set as the *Known X* values and *D15:D25* is set as the *Known Y*

values). Enter the desired forecast periods *Starting = 1, Ending = 50, Step Size = 0.5* and click *OK.* Review the generated forecasts and chart.

    a.   Exercise Question: How do you know which variable should be set as the known *Y* versus the known *X*?

    b.   Exercise Question: What is a spline curve supposed to do?

    c.   Exercise Question: Is this methodology more appropriate for time-series data and can it be used for cross-sectional datasets with missing intermediate values?

5. CUSTOM DISTRIBUTION

To create a custom distribution assumption, follow the instructions below:

1.   Start Excel and open the example model *Risk Simulator | Example Models | 01 Advanced Forecast Models.*

2.   Go to the *Custom Distribution and Delphi* worksheet.

3.   Create a new profile by clicking on *Risk Simulator | New Simulation Profile.*

4.   Select the data area *B14:C24* and click on *Edit | Copy* in Excel or use *CTRL+C* to copy the data into temporary clipboard memory and then select any empty cell in the worksheet.

5.   Click on *Risk Simulator | Set Input Assumption* and select *Custom* distribution, then click on *Create Distribution.* Then, in the custom distribution designer interface, just click on and follow each of the four steps: *1 Paste, 2 Update Chart, 3 Apply,* and *4 Close.* Finally, back in the set assumptions properties, click *OK* to set the assumption.

6.   Click on the *Step Simulation* icon a few times to see the value in the cell changing and you will see that it is randomly selecting the numbers from the original dataset, where numbers that have the highest probability of occurrence or that are repeated more often in the original dataset are selected more often, of course.

    a.   Exercise Question: Why is the custom distribution considered a nonparametric simulation?

    b.   Exercise Question: Is it better to use data fitting to find the best-fitting distribution to run a simulation or to use a custom distribution?

    c.   Exercise Question: What is the p-value for the distributional fitting if we were to apply a hypothesis test to see what the goodness-of-fit is for a custom distribution?

6. GARCH

To run a GARCH model, follow the instructions below:

1.   Start Excel and open the example model *Risk Simulator | Example Models | 01 Advanced Forecast Models.*

2.   Go to the *GARCH* worksheet.

3.   Select the data area *C8:C2428* and click on *Risk Simulator | Forecasting | GARCH* (you can also click on the data location link icon to select the historical data area or preselect the data area before starting the GARCH routine). Enter in the required inputs: $P = 1, Q = 1, Daily$

Trading Periodicity = 252, Predictive Base = 1, Forecast Periods = 10 and click *OK*. Review the generated forecast report and chart.

    a.   Exercise Question: What variables are most appropriate for running a GARCH model?

    b.   Exercise Question: Can cross-sectional data be used to run GARCH or is it only restricted to time-series data?

    c.   Exercise Question: What does GARCH forecast?

    d.   Exercise Question: Briefly describe what GARCH is used for.

    e.   Exercise Question: Why is number of days set to 252? Why is it not 365?

7. J-CURVE (EXPONENTIAL CURVE)

In mathematics, a quantity that grows exponentially is one whose growth rate is always proportional to its current size. Such growth is said to follow an exponential law. This law implies that for any exponentially growing quantity, the larger the quantity gets, the faster it grows. But it also implies that the relationship between the size of the dependent variable and its rate of growth is governed by a strict law: direct proportion. This forecast method is also called a J-curve due to its shape resembling the letter J. There is no maximum level of this growth curve.

To generate a J-curve forecast, follow the instructions below:

1.   Start Excel and open the example model *Risk Simulator | Example Models | 01 Advanced Forecast Models*.

2.   Go to the *J-Curve* worksheet.

3.   Click on *Risk Simulator | Forecasting | JS Curves* and click on *J-Curve*, and use *Starting Value = 100, Growth Rate = 5 percent, End Period = 100* and click *OK* to run the forecast and spend some time reviewing the forecast report.

    a.   Exercise Question: Can J-Curves be used to forecast cross-sectional data or are they only appropriate for time-series data?

8. MARKOV CHAIN PROCESS

The Markov process is useful for studying the evolution of systems over multiple and repeated trials in successive time periods. The system's state at a particular time is unknown, and we are interested in knowing the probability that a particular state exists. For instance, Markov chains are used to compute the probability that a particular machine or equipment will continue to function in the next time period, or whether a consumer purchasing Product A will continue to purchase Product A in the next period or switch to a competitive Product B.

To generate a Markov process, follow the instructions below:

1.   Start Excel and open the example model *Risk Simulator | Example Models | 01 Advanced Forecast Models*.

2.   Go to the *Markov* worksheet.

3.   Click on *Risk Simulator | Forecasting | Markov Chain* and enter in the value *10* (representing 10%) for both state probabilities and click *OK* to create the report and chart. Review the chart and see what happens when the probability is low.

4. Rerun the Markov Chain and this time, set the probabilities to both be at 90%.

    a. Exercise Question: What is the difference between a stochastic process forecast and a Markov chain forecast?

    b. Exercise Question: What happens when the state probabilities are small? Why are there such high levels of switching back and forth on the chart as compared to a much lower fluctuation level with high probabilities?

9. MAXIMUM LIKELIHOOD (LOGIT, PROBIT AND TOBIT)

Maximum Likelihood Estimates, or MLE, is a binary multivariate logistic analysis used to model dependent variables to determine the expected probability of success of belonging to a certain group. For instance, given a set of independent variables (e.g., age, income, and education level of credit card or mortgage loan holders), we can model the probability of credit loan default using MLE, or we can determine the probability a person will contract a specific illness or survive this disease given the person's age, social status, blood pressure, medications taken, and so forth. A typical regression model is invalid because the errors are heteroskedastic and non-normal, and the resulting estimated probability estimates will sometimes be above 1 or below 0. MLE analysis handles these problems using an iterative optimization routine. The data here represent a sample of several hundred previous loans, credit, or debt issues. The data show whether each loan had defaulted or not, as well as the specifics of each loan applicant's age, education level (1-3 indicating high school, university, or graduate professional education), years with current employer, and so forth. The idea is to model these empirical data to see which variables affect the default behavior of individuals, using Risk Simulator's Maximum Likelihood Models. The resulting model will help the bank or credit issuer compute the expected probability of default of an individual credit holder having specific characteristics.

To run the analysis, follow the instructions below:

1. Start Excel and open the example model *Risk Simulator | Example Models | 01 Advanced Forecast Models*.

2. Go to the *MLE* worksheet.

3. Select the data area including the headers or cells *B4:J504* and click on *Risk Simulator | Forecasting | Maximum Likelihood*. Select the *Dependent Variable* as *Defaulted* and click *OK*.

    a. Exercise Question: What does limited dependent variable mean?

    b. Exercise Question: What types of dependent variable data can be used in this Logit, Probit, and Tobit model?

    c. Exercise Question: Follow the instructions above to compute the expected probability of default of an individual with the following information:

Age	35
Education Level	2
Years with Current Employer	10
Years at Current Address	10
Household Income (Thousands $)	50
Debt to Income Ratio (%)	0
Credit Card Debt (Thousands $)	0
Other Debt (Thousands $)	0

10. NONLINEAR EXTRAPOLATION

Nonlinear Extrapolation involves making statistical projections by using historical trends that are projected for a specified period of time into the future. It is only used for time-series forecasts. Extrapolation is fairly reliable, relatively simple, and inexpensive. However, extrapolation, which assumes that recent and historical trends will continue, produces large forecast errors if discontinuities occur within the projected time period.

To run the nonlinear extrapolation model, follow these steps:

1. Start Excel and open the example model *Risk Simulator | Example Models | 01 Advanced Forecast Models.*

2. Go to the *Nonlinear Extrapolation* worksheet.

3. Select the data area excluding the headers or cells *E13:E24* and click on *Risk Simulator | Forecasting | Nonlinear Extrapolation.* Input the number of periods to forecast as *3*, use the *Automatic Selection* option, and click *OK.* Review the report and chart that are created.

    a. Exercise Question: What is a polynomial function versus a rational function?

    b. Exercise Question: How many periods into the future may be considered a reasonable forecast assuming that there are 12 periods of historical data?

    c. Exercise Question: Would this model be appropriate for cross-sectional data?

11. MULTIPLE REGRESSION

To run the multiple regression analysis, follow these steps:

1. Start Excel and open the example model *Risk Simulator | Example Models | 01 Advanced Forecast Models.*

2. Go to the *Regression* worksheet.

3. Select the data area including the headers or cells *B5:G55* and click on *Risk Simulator | Forecasting | Regression Analysis.* Select the *Dependent Variable* as the variable Y, leave everything else alone, and click *OK.* Review the generated report.

    a. Exercise Question: Which of the independent variables are statistically insignificant and how can you tell? That is, which statistic did you use?

    b. Exercise Question: How good is the initial model's fit?

    c. Exercise Question: Delete the entire variable columns of data that are insignificant and rerun the regression (i.e., select the column headers in Excel's grid, right-click and delete). Compare the R-Square and Adjusted R-Square values for both regressions. What can you determine?

    d. Exercise Question: Will R-Square always increase when you have more independent variables, regardless of their being statistically significant? How about Adjusted R-Square? Which is a more conservative and appropriate goodness-of-fit measure?

    e. Exercise Question: What can you do to increase the Adjusted R-Square of this model? Hint: Consider nonlinearity and some other econometric modeling techniques.

    f. Exercise Question: Run an Auto Econometric model on this dataset and select the nonlinear and interacting option and see what happens. Does the generated model better fit the data?

12. LOGISTIC S-CURVE

A logistic function or logistic curve models the S-curve of growth of some variable X. The initial stage of growth is approximately exponential; then, as competition arises, the growth slows, and at maturity, growth stops. These functions find applications in a range of fields, from biology to economics. For example, in the development of an embryo, a fertilized ovum splits, and the cell count grows: 1, 2, 4, 8, 16, 32, 64, etc. This is exponential growth. But the fetus can grow only as large as the uterus can hold; thus other factors start slowing down the increase in the cell count, and the rate of growth slows (but the baby is still growing, of course). After a suitable time, the child is born and keeps growing. Ultimately, the cell count is stable; the person's height is constant; the growth has stopped, at maturity. The same principles can be applied to population growth of animals or humans, and the market penetration and revenues of a product, with an initial growth spurt in market penetration, but over time, the growth slows due to competition and eventually the market declines and matures.

To generate an S-curve forecast, follow the instructions below:

1. Start Excel and open the example model *Risk Simulator | Example Models | 01 Advanced Forecast Models*.

2. Go to the *S-Curve* worksheet.

3. Click on *Risk Simulator | Forecasting | JS Curves* and click on *S-Curve*. Use *Starting Value = 200, Growth Rate = 10 percent, Saturation Level = 6000, End Period = 100* and click *OK* to run the forecast. Spend some time reviewing the forecast report.

   a. Exercise Question: Can S-Curves be used to forecast cross-sectional data or are they only appropriate for time-series data?

   b. Exercise Question: How would one obtain the value of the saturation level? What does saturation level mean?

13. STOCHASTIC PROCESSES (RANDOM WALK, BROWNIAN MOTION, MEAN-REVERSION, JUMP-DIFFUSION)

A stochastic process is a sequence of events or paths generated by probabilistic laws. That is, random events can occur over time but are governed by specific statistical and probabilistic rules. The main stochastic processes include Random Walk or Brownian motion, Mean-Reversion and Jump-Diffusion. These processes can be used to forecast a multitude of variables that seemingly follow random trends but yet are restricted by probabilistic laws. We can use Risk Simulator's Stochastic Process module to simulate and create such processes. These processes can be used to forecast a multitude of time-series data including stock prices, interest rates, inflation rates, oil prices, electricity prices, commodity prices, and so forth.

To run this forecast method, follow the instructions below:

1. Start Excel and open the example model *Risk Simulator | Example Models | 01 Advanced Forecast Models*.

2. Click on *Risk Simulator | Forecasting | Stochastic Processes*.

3. Enter a set of relevant inputs or use the existing inputs as a test case. Then, you can select the relevant process to simulate. Click *Update Chart* several times to view the updated computation of a single path each time. When ready, click *OK* to generate the process.

4. Rerun the stochastic process module and try out other processes. Using the default sample inputs, modify some of them and see what happens to the sample generated path as you click *Update Chart* repeatedly. For instance, select the mean-reversion process and change

the reversion rate from 5% to 1%, and then to 10% to see what happens to the chart when you click on *Update Chart* a few times. Be very careful with your choice of inputs because sometimes large values will invalidate the process and it will not run.

    a.   Exercise Question: How does a mean-reversion process compare to a Brownian motion random walk process?

    b.   Exercise Question: What types of variables might be best suited for a random walk process versus a mean-reversion process versus a jump-diffusion process?

14. TIME SERIES DECOMPOSITION

Time-series forecasting decomposes the historical data into the baseline, trend, and seasonality, if any. The models then apply an optimization procedure to find the alpha, beta, and gamma parameters for the baseline, trend, and seasonality coefficients and then recompose them into a forecast. In other words, this methodology first applies a "backcast" to find the best-fitting model and best-fitting parameters of the model that minimizes forecast errors, and then proceeds to "forecast" the future based on the historical data that exist. This process, of course, assumes that the same baseline growth, trend, and seasonality hold going forward. Even if they do not, say, when there exists a structural shift (e.g., company goes global, has a merger, spin-off, and so forth), the baseline forecasts can be computed and then the required adjustments can be made to the forecasts.

To run these forecast models, follow the steps below:

1.   Start Excel and open the example model *Risk Simulator | Example Models | 01 Advanced Forecast Models.*

2.   Go to the *Time Series Decomposition* worksheet.

3.   Create a new profile at *Risk Simulator | New Simulation Profile* if you wish the software to automatically generate assumptions for the forecast. Otherwise, if you do not need the assumption, a new profile is not required.

4.   Select the data excluding the headers or cells *E25:E44.*

5.   Click on *Risk Simulator | Forecasting | Time Series Analysis* and choose *Auto Model Selection,* set *Forecast = 4, Periods and Seasonality = 4.* Note that you can only select *Create Simulation Assumptions* if an existing Simulation Profile exists. Click *OK* to run the analysis. Review the generated report and chart.

    a.   Exercise Question: What do the alpha, beta, and gamma mean or represent?

    b.   Exercise Question: What are the three elements that a time-series analysis decomposes into?

    c.   Exercise Question: Can time series analysis be used to forecast cross-sectional data? How about for panel data?

    d.   Exercise Question: How accurate are the forecast results? How can you tell? What does each of the error measures represent in the report?

    e.   Exercise Question: How is heteroskedasticity modeled in this forecast method? Hint: Look at each of the input assumptions automatically set up in the report.

15. TRENDLINES

To run trendlines analysis, follow the steps below:

1. Start Excel and open the example model *Risk Simulator | Example Models | 01 Advanced Forecast Models*.

2. Go to the *Time Series Decomposition* worksheet.

3. Select the data excluding the headers or cells *E25:E44*.

4. Click on *Risk Simulator | Forecasting | Trendlines*, select the trendlines you wish to run or leave everything checked by default, and click *OK* to run. Review the generated report.

   a. Exercise Question: Is a low p-value or a high p-value a better fit?

   b. Exercise Question: Would you rather have a low or high R-Squared value, and what does R-Square here represent?

CHAPTER 7 – USING THE PAST TO PREDICT THE FUTURE

One of the more difficult tasks in risk analysis is forecasting, which includes the forecasting of any variable's future outcomes, for example, sales, revenues, machine failure rates, demand, costs, market share, competitive threats, and so forth. Recall from Chapter 6, Tomorrow's Forecast Today, that the most common quantitative or statistical approaches to forecasting include econometric modeling, multivariate regression, time-series analysis, nonlinear extrapolation, stochastic processes, autoregressive integrated moving average (ARIMA), generalized autoregressive conditional heteroskedasticity (GARCH), and others. Data can be time-dependent, cross-sectional, or panel-based (a mixture of time-dependent and cross-sectional data), and specific methods are applicable for specific types of data. Chapter 6 explores the basics of these methods, how to use Risk Simulator to forecast using these approaches, as well as some fundamental theories to these approaches. This chapter explores in more depth the time-series and regression analysis through example computations. We start with time-series analysis by exploring the eight most common time-series methods or models as seen in Figure 7.1. Regression analysis is discussed, including the many pitfalls and dangers of applying regression analysis as a novice.

TIME-SERIES FORECASTING METHODOLOGY

Figure 7.1 lists the eight most common time-series models, segregated by seasonality and trend. For instance, if the data variable has no trend or seasonality, then a single moving average model or a single exponential-smoothing model would suffice. However, if seasonality exists but no discernable trend is present, either a seasonal additive or seasonal multiplicative model would be better, and so forth. The following sections explore these models in more detail. These computational examples use monthly data with a seasonality of 4. However, in practice, any periodicity can be used (e.g., minutes, hours, days, months, quarters, years, untimed, etc.) and any seasonality period can be applied (e.g., 1 for annual data, 12 for monthly data, 4 for quarterly data, 24 for hourly data, etc.).

	NO SEASONALITY	WITH SEASONALITY
NO TREND Single Moving Average	Single Moving Average	Seasonal Additive
	Single Exponential Smoothing	Seasonal Multiplicative
WITH TREND	Double Moving Average	Holt–Winters Additive
	Double Exponential Smoothing	Holt–Winters Multiplicative

Figure 7.1: The Eight Most Common Time-Series Methods

NO TREND AND NO SEASONALITY

Single Moving Average

The single moving average is applicable when time-series data with no trend and no seasonality exist. The approach simply uses an average of the actual historical data to project future outcomes. This average is applied consistently moving forward, hence the term moving average.

The value of the moving average (MA) for a specific length (n) is simply the summation of actual historical data (Y) arranged and indexed in time sequence (i):

$$MA_n = \frac{\sum_{i=1}^{n} Y_i}{n}$$

An example computation of a 3-month single moving average is seen in Figure 7.2. Here we see that there are 39 months of actual historical data and a 3-month moving average is computed.[33] Additional columns of calculations also exist in the example, calculations that are required to estimate the error of measurements in using this moving-average approach. These errors are important as they can be compared across multiple moving averages (i.e., 3-month, 4-month, 5-month, and so forth), as well as other time-series models (e.g., single moving average, seasonal additive model, and so forth) to find the best fit that minimizes these errors. Figures 7.3 to 7.5 show the calculations used in the moving average model. Notice that the forecast-fit value in period 4 of 198.12 is a 3-month average of the prior three periods (months 1 through 3). The forecast-fit value for period 5 would then be the 3-month average of months 2 through 4. This process is repeated moving forward until month 40 (Figure 7.4) where every month after that, the forecast is fixed at 664.97. Clearly, this approach is not suitable if there is a trend (upward or downward over time) or if there is seasonality. Thus, error estimation is important when choosing the optimal time-series forecast model. Figure 7.3 illustrates a few additional columns of calculations required for estimating the forecast errors. The values from these columns are used in Figure 7.5's error estimation.

Single Moving Average (3 Months)

Month	Actual	Forecast Fit	$\|Error\|$	$Error^2$	$\dfrac{\|Y_t - \hat{Y}_t\|}{Y_t}$	$\left[\dfrac{\hat{Y}_t - Y_t}{Y_{t-1}}\right]^2$	$\left[\dfrac{Y_t - Y_{t-1}}{Y_{t-1}}\right]^2$	$Error$	$[E_t - E_{t-1}]^2$
1	265.22	-	-	-	-	-	-	-	-
2	146.64	-	-	-	-	-	-	-	-
3	182.50	-	-	-	-	-	-	-	-
4	118.54	198.12	79.57	6332.12	67.13%	0.19	0.12	79.57	-
5	180.04	149.23	30.81	949.43	17.11%	0.07	0.27	-30.81	12185.39
6	167.45	160.36	7.09	50.20	4.23%	0.00	0.00	-7.09	562.99
7	231.75	155.34	76.41	5838.18	32.97%	0.21	0.15	-76.41	4805.61
8	223.71	193.08	30.63	938.22	13.69%	0.02	0.00	-30.63	2095.60
9	192.98	207.64	14.66	214.91	7.60%	0.00	0.02	14.66	2051.18
10	122.29	216.15	93.86	8808.84	76.75%	0.24	0.13	93.86	6271.97
11	336.65	179.66	157.00	24647.46	46.63%	1.65	3.07	-157.00	62925.98
12	186.50	217.31	30.81	949.17	16.52%	0.01	0.20	30.81	35270.22
13	194.27	215.15	20.88	435.92	10.75%	0.01	0.00	20.88	98.60
14	149.19	239.14	89.95	8091.27	60.29%	0.21	0.05	89.95	4771.05
15	210.06	176.65	33.41	1115.94	15.90%	0.05	0.17	-33.41	15216.99
16	272.91	184.50	88.40	7815.04	32.39%	0.18	0.09	-88.40	3024.67
17	191.93	210.72	18.79	352.98	9.79%	0.00	0.09	18.79	11489.77
18	286.94	224.96	61.97	3840.48	21.60%	0.10	0.25	-61.97	6522.06
19	226.76	250.59	23.83	567.99	10.51%	0.01	0.04	23.83	7362.34
20	303.38	235.21	68.17	4647.58	22.47%	0.09	0.11	-68.17	8465.03
21	289.72	272.36	17.36	301.32	5.99%	0.00	0.00	-17.36	2582.12
22	421.59	273.29	148.30	21993.55	35.18%	0.26	0.21	-148.30	17146.25
23	264.47	338.23	73.76	5440.32	27.89%	0.03	0.14	73.76	49310.98
24	342.30	325.26	17.04	290.41	4.98%	0.00	0.09	-17.04	8244.63
25	339.86	342.79	2.93	8.56	0.86%	0.00	0.00	2.93	398.71
26	439.90	315.54	124.35	15463.53	28.27%	0.13	0.09	-124.35	16199.87
27	315.54	374.02	58.48	3420.05	18.53%	0.02	0.08	58.48	33428.15
28	438.62	365.10	73.52	5404.80	16.76%	0.05	0.15	-73.52	17423.61
29	400.94	398.02	2.92	8.54	0.73%	0.00	0.01	-2.92	4983.77
30	437.37	385.03	52.34	2739.41	11.97%	0.02	0.01	-52.34	2442.13
31	575.77	425.64	150.13	22539.03	26.07%	0.12	0.10	-150.13	9563.01
32	407.33	471.36	64.03	4099.56	15.72%	0.01	0.09	64.03	45863.59
33	681.92	473.49	208.43	43442.59	30.57%	0.26	0.45	-208.43	74232.65
34	475.78	555.01	79.23	6277.13	16.65%	0.01	0.09	79.23	82746.68
35	581.17	521.68	59.49	3539.49	10.24%	0.02	0.05	-59.49	19243.79
36	647.82	579.62	68.20	4651.17	10.53%	0.01	0.01	-68.20	75.79
37	650.81	568.26	82.55	6814.39	12.68%	0.02	0.00	-82.55	205.92
38	677.54	626.60	50.94	2594.71	7.52%	0.01	0.00	-50.94	999.26
39	666.56	658.72	7.84	61.47	1.18%	0.00	0.00	-7.84	1857.46
Forecast 40	-	664.97	-	-	-	-	-	-	-
Forecast 41	-	664.97	-	-	-	-	-	-	-
Forecast 42	-	664.97	-	-	-	-	-	-	-

RMSE	79.00
MSE	6241.27
MAD	63.00
MAPE	20.80%
Thiel's U	0.80

$$MA_n = \frac{\sum_{i=1}^{n} Y_i}{n} \quad \forall\, i = 1, \ldots, N$$

Figure 7.2: Single Moving Average (3 Months)

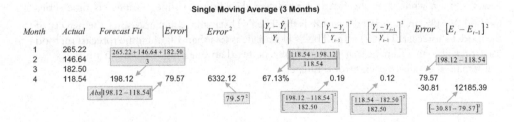

Figure 7.3: Calculating Single Moving Average

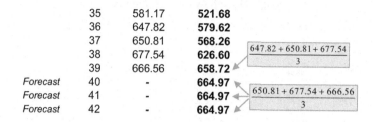

Figure 7.4: Forecasting with a Single Moving Average

Error Estimation (RMSE, MSE, MAD, MAPE, Theil's U)

Several different types of errors can be calculated for time-series forecast methods, including the mean-squared error (*MSE*), root mean-squared error (*RMSE*), mean absolute deviation (*MAD)*, and mean absolute percent error (*MAPE*).

The *MSE* is an absolute error measure that squares the errors (the difference between the actual historical data and the forecast-fitted data predicted by the model) to keep the positive and negative errors from canceling each other out. This measure also tends to exaggerate large errors by weighting the large errors more heavily than smaller errors by squaring them, which can help when comparing different time-series models. The *MSE* is calculated by simply taking the average of the *Error²* column in Figure 7.1. RMSE is the square root of *MSE* and is the most popular error measure, also known as the *quadratic loss function*. RMSE can be defined as the average of the absolute values of the forecast errors and is highly appropriate when the cost of the forecast errors is proportional to the absolute size of the forecast error.

The *MAD* is an error statistic that averages the distance (absolute value of the difference between the actual historical data and the forecast-fitted data predicted by the model) between each pair of actual and fitted forecast data points. *MAD* is calculated by taking the average of the |*Error*| column in Figure 7.1, and is most appropriate when the cost of forecast errors is proportional to the absolute size of the forecast errors.

The *MAPE* is a relative error statistic measured as an average percent error of the historical data points and is most appropriate when the cost of the forecast error is more closely related to the percentage error than the numerical size of the error. This error estimate is calculated by taking the average of the $\left|\dfrac{Y_t - \hat{Y}_t}{Y_t}\right|$ column in Figure 7.1, where Y_t is the historical data at time *t*, while $\hat{Y}_t$ is the fitted or predicted data point at time *t* using this time-series method. Finally, an associated measure is the Theil's U statistic, which measures the naivety of the model's forecast. That is, if the Theil's U statistic is less than 1.0, then the forecast method used provides an estimate that is statistically better than guessing. Figure 7.5 provides the mathematical details of each error estimate.

RMSE	79.00
MSE	6241.27
MAD	63.00
MAPE	20.80%
Thiel's U	0.80

$$RMSE = \sqrt{\sum_{i=1}^{n} \frac{(Error^2)_i}{n}} = \sqrt{MSE}$$

$$MSE = \sum_{i=1}^{n} \frac{(Error^2)_i}{n} = RMSE^2$$

$$MAD = \sum_{i=1}^{n} \frac{|Error|_i}{n}$$

$$MAPE = \sum_{i=1}^{n} \frac{\left|\frac{Y_t - \hat{Y}_t}{Y_t}\right|_i}{n}$$

$$Theil's\,U = \sqrt{\frac{\sum_{i=1}^{n}\left[\frac{\hat{Y}_t - Y_t}{Y_{t-1}}\right]^2_i}{\sum_{i=1}^{n}\left[\frac{Y_t - Y_{t-1}}{Y_{t-1}}\right]^2_i}}$$

Figure 7.5: Error Estimation

Single Exponential Smoothing

The second approach to use when no discernable trend or seasonality exists is the single exponential-smoothing method. This method weights past data with exponentially decreasing weights going into the past; that is, the more recent the data value, the greater its weight. This weighting largely overcomes the limitations of moving averages or percentage-change models. The weight used is termed the *alpha* measure. The method is illustrated in Figures 7.6 and 7.7 and uses the following model:

$$ESF_t = \alpha Y_{t-1} + (1 - \alpha)ESF_{t-1}$$

where the exponential smoothing forecast (ESF_t) at time t is a weighted average between the actual value one period in the past (Y_{t-1}) and last period's forecast (ESF_{t-1}), weighted by the alpha parameter (α).

Figure 7.7 shows an example of the computation. Notice that the first forecast-fitted value for month 2 or $\hat{Y}_2$ is always the previous month's actual value (Y_1). The mathematical equation gets used only at month 3 or starting from the second forecast-fitted period.

The following are some sample calculations:

Forecast Fit for period 2 = Actual value in period 1 or 265.22

Forecast Fit for period 3 = 0.1 × 146.64 + (1 – 0.1) × 265.22 = 253.36

Forecast Fit for period 4 = 0.1 × 182.50 + (1 – 0.1) × 253.36 = 246.28

Single Exponential Smoothing

Alpha		RMSE
0.10		126.26

Month	Actual	Forecast Fit
1	265.22	
2	146.64	265.22
3	182.50	253.36
4	118.54	246.28
5	180.04	233.50
6	167.45	228.16
7	231.75	222.09
8	223.71	223.05
9	192.98	223.12
10	122.29	220.10
11	336.65	210.32
12	186.50	222.96
13	194.27	219.31
14	149.19	216.81
15	210.06	210.04
16	272.91	210.05
17	191.93	216.33
18	286.94	213.89
19	226.76	221.20
20	303.38	221.75
21	289.72	229.92
22	421.59	235.90
23	264.47	254.46
24	342.30	255.47
25	339.86	264.15
26	439.90	271.72
27	315.54	288.54
28	438.62	291.24
29	400.94	305.98
30	437.37	315.47
31	575.77	327.66
32	407.33	352.47
33	681.92	357.96
34	475.78	390.35
35	581.17	398.90
36	647.82	417.12
37	650.81	440.19
38	677.54	461.26
39	666.56	482.88
Forecast 40	-	501.25

$$ESF_t = \alpha \, Y_{t-1} + (1 - \alpha) \, ESF_{t-1}$$

Figure 7.6: Single Exponential Smoothing

Single Exponential Smoothing

Alpha
0.10

Month	Actual	Forecast Fit
1	265.22	
2	146.64	265.22
3	182.50	253.36
4	118.54	246.28
5	180.04	233.50
6	167.45	228.16
7	231.75	222.09
8	223.71	223.05

$$\hat{Y}_2 = Y_1 = 265.22$$

$$0.1(146.64) + (1 - 0.1)265.22$$

$$\text{ESF}_t = \alpha \, Y_{t-1} + (1 - \alpha) \, \text{ESF}_{t-1}$$

Figure 7.7: Calculating Single Exponential Smoothing

Optimizing Forecasting Parameters

Clearly, in the single exponential-smoothing method, the alpha parameter was arbitrarily chosen as 0.10. In fact, the optimal alpha has to be obtained for the model to provide a good forecast. Using the model in Figure 7.6, Excel's Solver add-in package is applied to find the optimal alpha parameter that minimizes the forecast errors. Figure 7.8 illustrates Excel's Solver add-in dialog box, where the target cell is set to the *RMSE* as the objective to be minimized by methodically changing the alpha parameter. As alpha should only be allowed to vary between 0.00 and 1.00 (because alpha is a weight given to the historical data and past period forecasts, and weights can never be less than zero or greater than one), additional constraints are also set up. The resulting optimal alpha value that minimizes forecast errors calculated by Solver is 0.4476. Therefore, entering this alpha value into the model will yield the best forecast values that minimize the errors. Risk Simulator's time-series forecast module takes care of finding the optimal alpha level automatically as well as allows the integration of risk simulation parameters (see Chapter 6 for details), but we show the manual approach here using Solver as an illustrative example.

Throughout this chapter, the alpha (α), beta (β), and gamma (γ) are the decision variables to be optimized, where each of these variables represents the weight of the time-series data's *Level* (α), *Trend* (β), and *Seasonality* (γ), and each variable can take on any value between 0% and 100% (i.e., between 0 and 1, inclusive). The objective in the optimization is to minimize the forecast errors, which typically means minimizing *RMSE*. In other words, the minimum *RMSE* model implies the least amount of forecast errors or the highest level of accuracy achievable in the forecast model, or the best-fitting model given the historical data.

Figure 7.8: Optimizing Parameters in Single Exponential Smoothing

WITH TREND BUT NO SEASONALITY

For data that exhibit a trend but no seasonality, the double moving average and double exponential-smoothing methods work rather well.

Double Moving Average

The double moving average method will smooth out past data by performing a moving average on a subset of data that represents a moving average of an original set of data. That is, a second moving average is performed on the first moving average. The second moving average application captures the trending effect of the data. Figures 7.9 and 7.10 illustrate the computation involved. The example shown is a 3-month double moving average and the forecast value obtained in period 40 is calculated using the following:

$$Forecast_{t+1} = 2MA_{1,t} - MA_{2,t} + \frac{2}{m-1}\left[MA_{1,t} - MA_{2,t}\right]$$

where the forecast value is twice the amount of the first moving average (MA_1) at time t, less the second moving average estimate (MA_2) plus the difference between the two moving averages multiplied by a correction factor (two divided into the number of months in the moving average, m, less one).

Period	Actual	3-month MA_1	3-month MA_2	Forecast Fit
1	265.22	-	-	-
2	146.64	-	-	-
3	182.50	-	-	-
4	118.54	198.12	-	-
5	180.04	149.23	-	-
6	167.45	160.36	169.24	-
7	231.75	155.34	154.98	142.61
8	223.71	193.08	169.59	156.08
9	192.98	207.64	185.35	240.05
10	122.29	216.15	205.62	252.20
11	336.65	179.66	201.15	237.20
12	186.50	217.31	204.37	136.68
13	194.27	215.15	204.04	243.18
14	149.19	239.14	223.86	237.37
15	210.06	176.65	210.31	269.69
16	272.91	184.50	200.10	109.33
17	191.93	210.72	190.62	153.32
18	286.94	224.96	206.73	250.90
19	226.76	250.59	228.76	261.44
20	303.38	235.21	236.92	294.26
21	289.72	272.36	252.72	231.78
22	421.59	273.29	260.28	311.64
23	264.47	338.23	294.62	299.29
24	342.30	325.26	312.26	425.44
25	339.86	342.79	335.42	351.26
26	439.90	315.54	327.86	357.51
27	315.54	374.02	344.12	290.91
28	438.62	365.10	351.55	433.82
29	400.94	398.02	379.04	392.19
30	437.37	385.03	382.71	435.96
31	575.77	425.64	402.90	389.66
32	407.33	471.36	427.34	471.13
33	681.92	473.49	456.83	559.39
34	475.78	555.01	499.95	506.81
35	581.17	521.68	516.72	665.12
36	647.82	579.62	552.10	531.58
37	650.81	568.26	556.52	634.66
38	677.54	626.60	591.49	591.73
39	666.56	658.72	617.86	696.81
Forecast 40	-	664.97	650.10	740.45

$$Forecast_{t+1} = 2MA_{1,t} - MA_{2,t} + \frac{2}{m-1}\left[MA_{1,t} - MA_{2,t}\right]$$

Figure 7.9: Double Moving Average (3 Months)

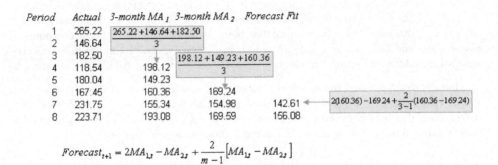

$$Forecast_{t+1} = 2MA_{1,t} - MA_{2,t} + \frac{2}{m-1}\left[MA_{1,t} - MA_{2,t}\right]$$

Figure 7.10: Calculating Double Moving Average

Double Exponential Smoothing

The second approach to use when the data exhibit a trend but no seasonality is the double exponential-smoothing method. Double exponential smoothing involves applying single exponential smoothing twice, once to the original data and then a second time to the resulting single exponential-smoothing data. An alpha (α) weighting parameter is used on the first or single exponential smoothing (*SES*) while a beta (β) weighting parameter is used on the second or double exponential smoothing (*DES*). This approach is useful when the historical data series is not stationary. Figure 7.11 illustrates the double exponential-smoothing model, while Figure 7.12 shows Excel's Solver add-in dialog box used to find the optimal alpha and beta parameters that minimizes the forecast errors. Risk Simulator's time-series forecast module takes care of finding the optimal alpha level automatically as well as allow the integration of risk simulation parameters (see Chapter 6 for details), but we show the manual approach here using Solver as an illustrative example. Figure 7.13 shows the computational details. The forecast is calculated using the following:

$$DES_t = \beta\,(SES_t - SES_{t-1}) + (1 - \beta)\,DES_{t-1}$$
$$SES_t = \alpha\,Y_t + (1 - \alpha)(SES_{t-1} + DES_{t-1})$$

The double exponential smoothing algorithm starts with a time series of historical data (denoted as the *Actual* column in Figure 7.11) in chronological order. The example historical data shows 39 periods and we need to forecast 4 periods into the future (periods 40–43). The first step is to create the *SES* and *DES* columns using the two equations shown above. To get started and as placeholders, set $\alpha = 0.1593$ and $\beta = 0.3913$ so that these two columns can be computed. See Figure 7.13 for more detailed calculations of these two columns.

Then, create the last column called *Forecast Fit* (Figure 7.11). This last column is computed using the equation:

$$F_t = SES_{t-1} + N \times DES_{t-1}$$

Note that in the equation above, $N = 1$ for all in-sample forecasts (i.e., for periods 3–39). It is typically standard to leave out the first two periods' forecast fit values in a double exponential smoothing method to avoid any zero outlier issues for the beginning periods. For instance, period 3's forecast fit is $246.33 + 1 \times (-7.40) = 238.93$, and period 4's forecast fit is $229.94 + 1 \times (-10.93) = 219.01$, and so forth. Notice the multiplier is always set to 1. Conversely, when we perform out-of-sample forecasts, the multiplier $N \geq 1$. For instance, the first forecast (period 40) value is computed as $690.24 + 1 \times 27.91 = 718.14$ (rounded) and second forecast (period 41) value is $690.24 + 2 \times 27.91 = 746.05$ (rounded), and so forth, with each successive future forecast increasing the index N by 1.

The reason for the index N to increment by 1 in each out-of-sample forecast is because the *SES* and *DES* columns can only be computed until the last period of the *Actual* data. In other words, there are 39 actual historical data points, which means we can only compute 39 rows of *SES* and *DES*. In turn, only 39 periods of *Forecast Fit* can be computed as well. To extrapolate and forecast beyond this set of historical data, the incremental index N is required.

Finally, to get the best-fitting α and β parameters, optimization is used to minimize the *RMSE* errors (Figure 7.12) and the optimized values are found to be $\alpha = 0.1593$ and $\beta = 0.3919$. Note that both parameters must be between 0 and 1, inclusive. Figure 7.11 shows the calculations and results of the entire double exponential-smoothing algorithm.

		Alpha 0.1593	Beta 0.3919	RMSE 70.81
Period	Actual	SES	DES	Forecast Fit
1	265.22	265.22	0.00	-
2	146.64	246.33	-7.40	-
3	182.50	229.94	-10.93	238.93
4	118.54	203.01	-17.20	219.01
5	180.04	184.89	-17.56	185.81
6	167.45	167.35	-17.55	167.33
7	231.75	162.85	-12.44	149.80
8	223.71	162.09	-7.86	150.42
9	192.98	160.41	-5.44	154.23
10	122.29	149.76	-7.48	154.96
11	336.65	173.24	4.65	142.28
12	186.50	179.27	5.19	177.90
13	194.27	186.02	5.80	184.46
14	149.19	185.03	3.14	191.82
15	210.06	191.66	4.51	188.17
16	272.91	208.39	9.30	196.17
17	191.93	213.59	7.69	217.69
18	286.94	231.74	11.79	221.28
19	226.76	240.86	10.74	243.53
20	303.38	259.85	13.98	251.60
21	289.72	276.35	14.97	273.82
22	421.59	312.07	23.10	291.32
23	264.47	323.91	18.69	335.17
24	342.30	342.55	18.67	342.60
25	339.86	357.82	17.33	361.22
26	439.90	385.46	21.38	375.15
27	315.54	392.30	15.68	406.84
28	438.62	412.85	17.59	407.97
29	400.94	425.74	15.75	430.44
30	437.37	440.83	15.49	441.49
31	575.77	475.35	22.95	456.32
32	407.33	483.81	17.27	498.30
33	681.92	529.88	28.56	501.08
34	475.78	545.27	23.40	558.44
35	581.17	570.66	24.18	568.67
36	647.82	603.28	27.49	594.84
37	650.81	633.96	28.74	630.77
38	677.54	665.06	29.66	662.69
39	666.56	690.24	27.91	694.72
Forecast 40	-	-	-	718.14
Forecast 41	-	-	-	746.05
Forecast 42	-	-	-	773.95
Forecast 43	-	-	-	801.86

$$DES_t = \beta\left(SES_t - SES_{t-1}\right) + (1-\beta)DES_{t-1}$$

$$SES_t = \alpha Y_t + (1-\alpha)\left(SES_{t-1} + DES_{t-1}\right)$$

$$Forecast\ F_t = SES_{t-1} + N \times DES_{t-1}$$

(where N is the future forecast period)

Figure 7.11: Double Exponential Smoothing

Figure 7.12: Optimizing Parameters in Double Exponential Smoothing

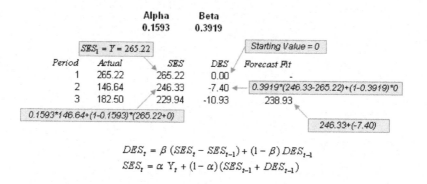

$$DES_t = \beta\,(SES_t - SES_{t-1}) + (1 - \beta)\,DES_{t-1}$$
$$SES_t = \alpha\,Y_t + (1 - \alpha)\,(SES_{t-1} + DES_{t-1})$$

Figure 7.13: Calculating Double Exponential Smoothing

NO TREND BUT WITH SEASONALITY

Additive Seasonality

If the time-series data have no appreciable trend but exhibit seasonality, then the additive seasonality and multiplicative seasonality methods apply. The additive seasonality method is illustrated in Figures 7.14 and 7.15.

The additive seasonality model breaks the historical data into a level (L) or base-case component as measured by the alpha parameter (α), and a seasonality (S) component measured by the gamma parameter (γ). The resulting forecast value is simply the addition of this base case level to the seasonality value. (Please be aware that all calculations are rounded). Quarterly seasonality is assumed in the example.

Additive Seasonality With No Trend

	Level Alpha 0.33	Seasonal Gamma 0.40		RMSE 93.54

Period	Actual	Level	Seasonality	Forecast Fit
1	265.22	-	87.00	-
2	146.64	-	-31.59	-
3	182.50	-	4.27	-
4	118.54	178.23	-59.68	-
5	180.04	150.44	63.85	265.22
6	167.45	166.29	-18.38	118.86
7	231.75	186.25	20.90	170.56
8	223.71	217.93	-33.28	126.57
9	192.98	188.97	39.72	281.78
10	122.29	173.22	-31.51	170.58
11	336.65	219.70	59.63	194.12
12	186.50	219.73	-33.26	186.42
13	194.27	198.47	22.01	259.45
14	149.19	192.67	-36.34	166.96
15	210.06	178.90	48.15	252.31
16	272.91	220.40	1.32	145.63
17	191.93	203.94	8.29	242.41
18	286.94	242.86	-3.91	167.60
19	226.76	221.90	30.69	291.01
20	303.38	248.05	23.10	223.23
21	289.72	258.93	17.36	256.34
22	421.59	313.26	41.35	255.02
23	264.47	287.34	9.09	343.95
24	342.30	297.73	31.76	310.44
25	339.86	305.81	24.09	315.09
26	439.90	336.05	66.55	347.16
27	315.54	326.40	1.05	345.15
28	438.62	352.64	53.62	358.16
29	400.94	360.53	30.67	376.73
30	437.37	363.89	69.35	427.08
31	575.77	432.65	58.34	364.94
32	407.33	406.90	32.17	486.27
33	681.92	486.59	97.07	437.57
34	475.78	460.45	47.56	555.94
35	581.17	480.80	75.29	518.79
36	647.82	524.78	68.82	512.97
37	650.81	534.22	104.94	621.84
38	677.54	565.45	73.58	581.79
39	666.56	573.87	82.31	640.74

$Level \, L_t = \alpha(Y_t - S_{t-s}) + (1-\alpha)(L_{t-1})$

$Seasonality \, S_t = \gamma(Y_t - L_t) + (1-\gamma)(S_{t-s})$

$Forecast \, F_{t+m} = L_t + S_{t+m-s}$

Figure 7.14: Seasonal Additive (Seasonality = 4)

As explained, when there is seasonality in the data but a trend does not exist, the seasonal additive (Figure 7.14) or seasonal multiplicative (Figure 7.15) models may be appropriate. The main difference between these two approaches is that the additive model uses addition and subtraction versus multiplication and division, and, of course, the optimized α and γ parameters would also be different to compensate for these differences in mathematical operations.

Figure 7.14 shows the model setup for a seasonal additive model and Figure 7.15 explores in more detail the actual computations. Typically, to get started, the *Actual* column lists the historical time-series data in chronological order. The data in this example has a seasonality of 4 periods (i.e., quarterly data where there are 4 quarters in a year, representing one full cycle) the *Level* column starts on period 4 (the seasonality) and the forecast fit which is one period forecast out, starts at period 5.

For the *Level* calculations, the first value is simply the average of the previous *Actual* values for the entire season. As the seasonality in this example is 4, the first *Level* value is computed as the average of *265.22, 146.64, 182.5, and 118.54* or *178.23*. Starting from L_{s+1} onwards, the *Level* is computed using the equation in Figure 7.14, where we compute $\alpha(Y_t - S_{t-s}) +$ $(1-\alpha)(L_{t-1})$ or *0.3261 × (180.04 − 87.00) + (1 − 0.3261) × 178.23 = 150.45* (rounded). Note that in this case the optimized α is 0.3261, the Y_t represents the actual historical data point for the same period t, S_{t-s} represents the *Seasonality* value s periods back from period t ($s = 4$ in this example), and L_{t-1} represents the previous period's calculated *Level* (i.e., 178.23 in this example). All subsequent values in the *Level* column are calculated the same way.

For the *Seasonality* calculations, as there are 4 periods in this season, the first 4 figures are computed using the Y_t−*Value of the First Level* or *265.22 − 178.23 = 87.00* (rounded) for the first seasonality value, *146.64 − 178.23 = −31.59* for the second period, and so forth, until the fourth period (or whatever period, depending on the seasonality of the data). All *Seasonality* calculations after the first s periods are computed using the equation seen in Figure 7.15. For instance, period 5's *Seasonality* factor is computed as $\gamma(Y_t - L_t) + (1 - \gamma)S_{t-s}$ or *0.4033 × (180.04 − 150.44) + (1 − 0.4033) × 87.00 = 63.85*.

Finally, the *Forecast Fit* model is calculated one period out at a time. As an example, the period 5 *Forecast Fit* value is computed as $L_t + S_{t+m-s}$ or *178.23 + 87.00 = 265.23* (rounded). All subsequent periods are calculated in the same fashion going forward. For future forecast periods beyond the seasonality periodicity (i.e., seasonality in this example is 4, which means we can use the last 4 periods' seasonality factors in forecasting periods 40–43, but for periods 44 onward, we call this beyond the historical seasonality period), we replicate the last seasonality factors. This means that the confidence in future forecasts beyond the seasonality periodicity will be less accurate in general, due to insufficient seasonal data, and we therefore assume that the seasonality will repeat itself going forward. This is clearly one of the shortcomings of the current methodology.

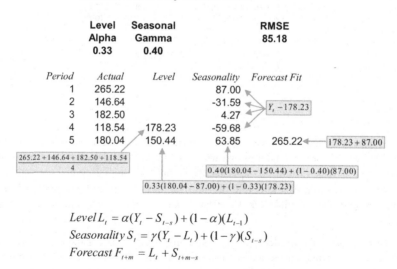

Additive Seasonality With No Trend

	Level Alpha 0.33	Seasonal Gamma 0.40	RMSE 85.18

Period	Actual	Level	Seasonality	Forecast Fit
1	265.22		87.00	
2	146.64		-31.59	$Y_t - 178.23$
3	182.50		4.27	
4	118.54	178.23	-59.68	
5	180.04	150.44	63.85	265.22 ← $178.23 + 87.00$

$\dfrac{265.22 + 146.64 + 182.50 + 118.54}{4}$

$0.40(180.04 - 150.44) + (1 - 0.40)(87.00)$

$0.33(180.04 - 87.00) + (1 - 0.33)(178.23)$

$Level\ L_t = \alpha(Y_t - S_{t-s}) + (1 - \alpha)(L_{t-1})$
$Seasonality\ S_t = \gamma(Y_t - L_t) + (1 - \gamma)(S_{t-s})$
$Forecast\ F_{t+m} = L_t + S_{t+m-s}$

Figure 7.15: Calculating Seasonal Additive

Multiplicative Seasonality

Similarly, the multiplicative seasonality model requires the alpha and gamma parameters. The difference being that the model is multiplicative, for example, the forecast value is the multiplication between the base case level and seasonality factor. Figures 7.16 and 7.17 illustrate the computations required. Quarterly seasonality is assumed in the example. (Please be aware that all calculations are rounded).

Multiplicative Seasonality With No Trend

		Level Alpha 0.22	Seasonal Gamma 0.64	RMSE 95.65
Period	Actual	Level	Seasonality	Forecast Fit
1	265.22	-	1.49	-
2	146.64	-	0.82	-
3	182.50	-	1.02	-
4	118.54	178.23	0.67	-
5	180.04	165.35	1.23	265.22
6	167.45	173.93	0.91	136.04
7	231.75	185.72	1.17	178.11
8	223.71	219.61	0.89	123.53
9	192.98	205.42	1.04	270.67
10	122.29	189.36	0.74	187.42
11	336.65	211.65	1.44	221.04
12	186.50	211.10	0.89	188.67
13	194.27	205.43	0.98	220.57
14	149.19	204.47	0.73	152.37
15	210.06	191.32	1.22	294.08
16	272.91	217.55	1.12	169.58
17	191.93	212.61	0.93	213.50
18	286.94	252.73	0.99	156.05
19	226.76	237.67	1.05	308.43
20	303.38	245.03	1.20	266.66
21	289.72	259.92	1.05	228.13
22	421.59	297.16	1.26	257.56
23	264.47	286.97	0.97	311.99
24	342.30	286.78	1.19	343.32
25	339.86	295.18	1.11	300.72
26	439.90	307.02	1.37	373.34
27	315.54	311.30	1.00	297.12
28	438.62	323.87	1.30	371.87
29	400.94	331.95	1.17	360.91
30	437.37	328.97	1.34	455.55
31	575.77	384.87	1.32	328.02
32	407.33	368.95	1.17	499.11
33	681.92	416.60	1.47	433.22
34	475.78	402.47	1.24	560.30
35	581.17	411.24	1.38	529.84
36	647.82	442.93	1.36	482.55
37	650.81	442.86	1.47	651.26
38	677.54	466.08	1.38	549.47
39	666.56	470.02	1.40	642.45

$$Level\ L_t = \alpha(Y_t / S_{t-s}) + (1-\alpha)(L_{t-1})$$
$$Seasonality\ S_t = \gamma(Y_t / L_t) + (1-\gamma)(S_{t-s})$$
$$Forecast\ F_{t+m} = L_t S_{t+m-s}$$

Figure 7.16: Seasonal Multiplicative

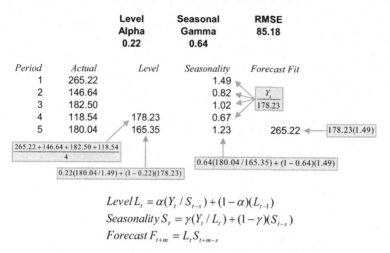

$$Level\ L_t = \alpha(Y_t / S_{t-s}) + (1-\alpha)(L_{t-1})$$
$$Seasonality\ S_t = \gamma(Y_t / L_t) + (1-\gamma)(S_{t-s})$$
$$Forecast\ F_{t+m} = L_t S_{t+m-s}$$

Figure 7.17: Calculating Seasonal Multiplicative (Seasonality = 4)

WITH SEASONALITY AND WITH TREND

When both seasonality and trend exist, more advanced models are required to decompose the data into their base elements: a base case level (L) weighted by the alpha parameter (α); a trend component (b) weighted by the beta parameter (β); and a seasonality component (S) weighted by the gamma parameter (γ). Several methods exist but the two most common are the Holt–Winters additive seasonality and Holt–Winters multiplicative seasonality methods.

Holt–Winters Additive Seasonality

Figures 7.18 and 7.19 illustrate the required computations for determining a Holt–Winters additive forecast model. The Holt–Winters additive seasonality model is a combination of the seasonal additive and double exponential-smoothing models described previously. Similar to seasonal additive and seasonal multiplicative models, the difference between the two Holt–Winters models is that the additive model uses addition and subtraction versus multiplication and division, and, of course, the optimized α, β, and γ parameters would also be different to compensate for these differences in mathematical operations. Figure 7.18 shows the setup of the algorithm, starting from the historical time-series data or *Actual* column, followed by the *Level*, *Trend*, and *Seasonality* columns. The Holt–Winters algorithm assumes that any time-series data can be decomposed into these three components, each with its own weighting schema, set between 0 and 1 inclusive, namely, α for the strength of the *Level*, β for the strength of the *Trend*, and γ for the strength of the *Seasonality* effects. In other words, each of the weights can take on any value between 0% and 100%. The calculations proceed as usual, and can be seen in more detail in Figure 7.19.

Holt-Winters Additive Seasonality With Trend

	Level Alpha 0.05	Trend Beta 1.00	Seasonal Gamma 0.24		RMSE 77.03
Period	Actual	Level	Trend	Seasonality	Forecast Fit
1	265.22	-	-	87.00	-
2	146.64	-	-	-31.59	-
3	182.50	-	-	4.27	-
4	118.54	178.23	0.00	-59.68	-
5	180.04	174.03	-4.20	67.96	265.22
6	167.45	171.27	-2.76	-25.06	138.25
7	231.75	171.42	0.15	17.45	172.79
8	223.71	177.07	5.65	-34.69	111.89
9	192.98	179.89	2.81	55.06	250.69
10	122.29	180.96	1.07	-32.96	157.64
11	336.65	188.78	7.83	48.11	199.48
12	186.50	197.82	9.04	-29.20	161.92
13	194.27	203.53	5.71	39.94	261.92
14	149.19	207.90	4.37	-39.01	176.27
15	210.06	209.79	1.89	36.86	260.38
16	272.91	216.14	6.35	-8.99	182.49
17	191.93	219.01	2.87	24.19	262.43
18	286.94	227.01	8.00	-15.76	182.87
19	226.76	232.79	5.78	26.78	271.87
20	303.38	242.20	9.41	7.50	229.58
21	289.72	252.30	10.10	27.30	275.80
22	421.59	271.02	18.71	23.34	246.64
23	264.47	287.17	16.15	15.15	316.51
24	342.30	304.87	17.70	14.54	310.82
25	339.86	322.08	17.21	25.06	349.87
26	439.90	343.09	21.01	40.61	362.63
27	315.54	360.97	17.88	0.91	379.26
28	438.62	381.07	20.10	24.65	393.38
29	400.94	399.93	18.86	19.41	426.24
30	437.37	417.70	17.77	35.69	459.40
31	575.77	442.34	24.64	32.06	436.38
32	407.33	462.83	20.49	5.81	491.63
33	681.92	492.14	29.31	59.45	502.72
34	475.78	517.45	25.31	17.50	557.14
35	581.17	543.06	25.62	33.48	574.81
36	647.82	572.29	29.23	22.20	574.49
37	650.81	601.02	28.73	57.18	660.98
38	677.54	631.24	30.22	24.27	647.26
39	666.56	660.07	28.82	27.14	694.95

$$Level\ L_t = \alpha(Y_t - S_{t-s}) + (1-\alpha)(L_{t-1} + b_{t-1})$$
$$Trend\ b_t = \beta(L_t - L_{t-1}) + (1-\beta)(b_{t-1})$$
$$Seasonality\ S_t = \gamma(Y_t - L_t) + (1-\gamma)(S_{t-s})$$
$$Forecast\ F_{t+m} = L_t + mb_t + S_{t+m-s}$$

Figure 7.18: Holt–Winters Additive

Figures 7.18 and 7.19 show the Holt–Winters additive model. The first period value of *Level (L)* is computed as the average of *265.22, 146.64, 182.50, and 118.54* or *178.23*. All subsequent *Levels* are calculated as $\alpha(Y_t - S_{t-s}) + (1 - \alpha)(L_{t-1} + b_{t-1})$ or *0.0493 × (180.04 – 87) + (1 – 0.0493) × (178.23 + 0) = 174.03* (as an example for period 5). The optimized α = 0.0493, β = 1.0000, and γ = 0.2351.

The *Trend (b)* calculation starts at period *s+1* or in this case, starting in period 5, we use the equation $\beta(L_t - L_{t-1}) + (1 - \beta)b_{t-1}$ or *1.00 × (174.03 – 178.23) + (1 – 1.00) × 0.00 = –4.20*. All subsequent calculations proceed the same way. For instance, the *Trend* for period 6 is such that we have *1.00 × (171.27 – 174.03) + (1 – 1.00) × (–4.2) = –2.76*, and so forth.

The *Seasonality (S)* factor for all periods within *s* (in this case, *s* is 4), the *Seasonality* is computed as $Y_t - L_s$ or *Actual(t)–Level(s)* computed to be *265.22 – 178.23 = 87.00* (rounded) for period 1, *146.64 – 178.23 = –31.59* for period 2, and so forth. Starting from period *s + 1*, the *Seasonality* factor becomes $\gamma(Y_t - L_t) + (1 - \gamma)S_{t-s}$ or computed as *0.2351 × (180.04 – 174.03) + (1 – 0.2351) × 87.00 = 67.96*. All subsequent periods use the same calculation approach.

Finally, for the *Forecast Fit* column, compute $L_t + mb_t + S_{t+m-s}$ for future forecast period *m* or *178.23 + (1 × 0) + 87 = 265.22* (rounded) starting from the *s + 1* period. All subsequent periods proceed the same way. Note that *m = 1* always when in-sample forecast fit is calculated, and use $m \geq 1$ when calculating out-of-sample forecasts.

Just like the seasonal models discussed previously, this means that the confidence in future forecasts beyond the seasonality periodicity will be less accurate in general, due to insufficient seasonal data, and we therefore assume that the seasonality will repeat itself going forward. This is clearly one of the shortcomings of this methodology.

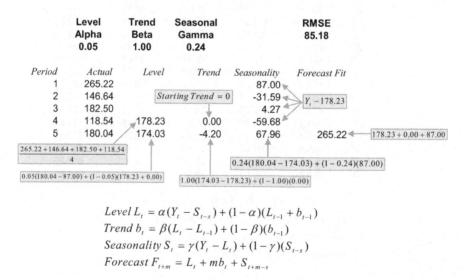

Holt-Winters Additive Seasonality With Trend

	Level Alpha 0.05	Trend Beta 1.00	Seasonal Gamma 0.24		RMSE 85.18

Period	Actual	Level	Trend	Seasonality	Forecast Fit
1	265.22			87.00	
2	146.64	*Starting Trend = 0*		-31.59	$Y_t - 178.23$
3	182.50			4.27	
4	118.54	178.23	0.00	-59.68	
5	180.04	174.03	-4.20	67.96	265.22

265.22 + 146.64 + 182.50 + 118.54 / 4

0.05(180.04 – 87.00) + (1 – 0.05)(178.23 + 0.00)

1.00(174.03 – 178.23) + (1 – 1.00)(0.00)

0.24(180.04 – 174.03) + (1 – 0.24)(87.00)

178.23 + 0.00 + 87.00

$Level\ L_t = \alpha(Y_t - S_{t-s}) + (1 - \alpha)(L_{t-1} + b_{t-1})$

$Trend\ b_t = \beta(L_t - L_{t-1}) + (1 - \beta)(b_{t-1})$

$Seasonality\ S_t = \gamma(Y_t - L_t) + (1 - \gamma)(S_{t-s})$

$Forecast\ F_{t+m} = L_t + mb_t + S_{t+m-s}$

Figure 7.19: Calculating Holt–Winters Additive (Seasonality = 4)

Holt–Winters Multiplicative Seasonality

Figures 7.20 and 7.21 show the required computation for determining a Holt–Winters multiplicative forecast model when both trend and seasonality exist.

Holt-Winters Multiplicative Seasonality With Trend

	Level Alpha 0.04	Trend Beta 1.00	Seasonal Gamma 0.27		RMSE 79.15
Period	Actual	Level	Trend	Seasonality	Forecast Fit
1	265.22	-	-	1.49	-
2	146.64	-	-	0.82	-
3	182.50	-	-	1.02	-
4	118.54	178.23	0.00	0.67	-
5	180.04	176.12	-2.10	1.36	265.22
6	167.45	175.11	-1.02	0.86	143.18
7	231.75	176.01	0.90	1.10	178.26
8	223.71	182.75	6.75	0.82	117.67
9	192.98	187.75	5.00	1.27	257.93
10	122.29	190.90	3.15	0.80	165.60
11	336.65	198.12	7.22	1.27	214.19
12	186.50	206.17	8.06	0.84	167.87
13	194.27	211.98	5.81	1.17	272.12
14	149.19	216.64	4.66	0.77	174.13
15	210.06	219.27	2.63	1.18	280.20
16	272.91	225.66	6.39	0.94	186.67
17	191.93	229.53	3.88	1.08	272.38
18	286.94	238.53	9.00	0.89	179.57
19	226.76	245.48	6.95	1.11	292.61
20	303.38	254.99	9.51	1.01	237.70
21	289.72	264.63	9.63	1.09	286.13
22	421.59	281.63	17.00	1.05	243.42
23	264.47	296.40	14.77	1.05	331.98
24	342.30	312.20	15.80	1.03	314.05
25	339.86	327.45	15.25	1.07	355.98
26	439.90	345.45	18.00	1.11	361.10
27	315.54	361.12	15.67	1.00	382.29
28	438.62	378.54	17.42	1.07	389.23
29	400.94	395.15	16.61	1.06	424.62
30	437.37	411.07	15.91	1.10	458.54
31	575.77	432.37	21.30	1.09	428.40
32	407.33	451.03	18.66	1.02	484.20
33	681.92	476.14	25.11	1.16	496.30
34	475.78	498.73	22.59	1.06	551.41
35	581.17	521.70	22.97	1.10	569.70
36	647.82	547.93	26.23	1.07	556.94
37	650.81	573.70	25.77	1.15	665.46
38	677.54	600.92	27.22	1.08	635.58
39	666.56	627.35	26.43	1.09	690.07

$$Level\ L_t = \alpha(Y_t / S_{t-s}) + (1-\alpha)(L_{t-1} + b_{t-1})$$
$$Trend\ b_t = \beta(L_t - L_{t-1}) + (1-\beta)(b_{t-1})$$
$$Seasonality\ S_t = \gamma(Y_t / L_t) + (1-\gamma)(S_{t-s})$$
$$Forecast\ F_{t+m} = (L_t + mb_t)S_{t+m-s}$$

Figure 7.20: Holt–Winters Multiplicative

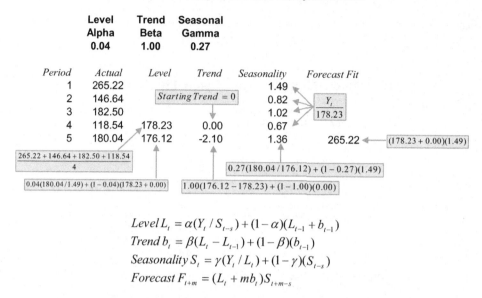

Holt-Winters Multiplicative Seasonality With Trend

	Level	Trend	Seasonal
	Alpha	Beta	Gamma
	0.04	1.00	0.27

Period	Actual	Level	Trend	Seasonality	Forecast Fit
1	265.22			1.49	
2	146.64	Starting Trend = 0		0.82	Y_t
3	182.50			1.02	178.23
4	118.54	178.23	0.00	0.67	
5	180.04	176.12	-2.10	1.36	265.22 ← (178.23 + 0.00)(1.49)

$$\frac{265.22 + 146.64 + 182.50 + 118.54}{4}$$

$$0.27(180.04/176.12) + (1 - 0.27)(1.49)$$

$$0.04(180.04/1.49) + (1 - 0.04)(178.23 + 0.00)$$

$$1.00(176.12 - 178.23) + (1 - 1.00)(0.00)$$

$$\text{Level } L_t = \alpha(Y_t / S_{t-s}) + (1 - \alpha)(L_{t-1} + b_{t-1})$$
$$\text{Trend } b_t = \beta(L_t - L_{t-1}) + (1 - \beta)(b_{t-1})$$
$$\text{Seasonality } S_t = \gamma(Y_t / L_t) + (1 - \gamma)(S_{t-s})$$
$$\text{Forecast } F_{t+m} = (L_t + mb_t)S_{t+m-s}$$

Figure 7.21: Calculating Holt–Winters Multiplicative (Seasonality = 4)

REGRESSION ANALYSIS

This section deals with using regression analysis for forecasting purposes. It is assumed that the reader is sufficiently knowledgeable about the fundamentals of regression analysis. Instead of focusing on the detailed theoretical mechanics of the regression equation, we instead look at the basics of applying regression analysis and work through the various relationships that a regression analysis can capture, as well as the common pitfalls in regression, including the problems of outliers, nonlinearities, heteroskedasticity, autocorrelation, and structural breaks.

The general bivariate linear regression equation takes the form of $Y = \beta_0 + \beta_1 X + \varepsilon$ where β_0 is the intercept, β_1 is the slope, and ε is the error term. It is bivariate as there are only two variables, a Y or dependent variable and an X or independent variable, where X is also known as the regressor (sometimes a bivariate regression is also known as a univariate regression as there is only a single independent variable X). The dependent variable is named as such as it *depends* on the independent variable; for example, sales revenue depends on the amount of marketing costs expended on a product's advertising and promotion, making the dependent variable sales and the independent variable marketing costs. An example of a bivariate regression is seen as simply inserting the best-fitting line through a set of data points in a two-dimensional plane as seen on the left panel in Figure 7.22. In other cases, a multivariate regression can be performed, where there are multiple or n number of independent X variables, where the general regression equation will now take the form of $Y = \beta_0 + \beta_1 X_1 + \beta_2 X_2 + \beta_3 X_3 + ... + \beta_n X_n + \varepsilon$. In this case, the best-fitting line will be within an $n + 1$ dimensional plane.

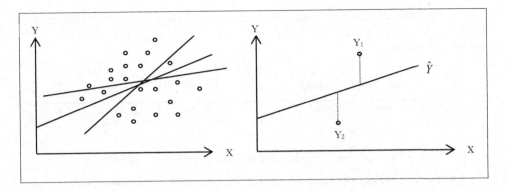

Figure 7.22: Bivariate Regression

However, fitting a line through a set of data points in a scatter plot as in Figure 7.22 may result in numerous possible lines. The best-fitting line is defined as the single unique line that minimizes the total vertical errors, that is, the sum of the absolute distances between the actual data points (Y_i) and the estimated line $(\hat{Y})$ as shown on the right panel of Figure 7.22. In order to find the best fitting line that minimizes the errors, a more sophisticated approach is required, that is, regression analysis. Regression analysis therefore finds the unique best-fitting line by requiring that the total errors be minimized, or by calculating

$$Min \sum_{i=1}^{n} (Y_i - \hat{Y}_i)^2$$

where only one unique line minimizes this sum of squared errors. The errors (vertical distance between the actual data and the predicted line) are squared to avoid the negative errors from canceling out the positive errors. Solving this minimization problem with respect to the slope and intercept requires calculating a first derivative and setting them equal to zero:

$$\frac{d}{d\beta_0} \sum_{i=1}^{n} (Y_i - \hat{Y}_i)^2 = 0 \quad \text{and} \quad \frac{d}{d\beta_1} \sum_{i=1}^{n} (Y_i - \hat{Y}_i)^2 = 0$$

which yields the *Least Squares Regression Equations* seen in Figure 7.23.

$$\beta_1 = \frac{\sum_{i=1}^{n}(X_i - \bar{X})(Y_i - \bar{Y})}{\sum_{i=1}^{n}(X_i - \bar{X})^2} = \frac{\sum_{i=1}^{n} X_i Y_i - \frac{\sum_{i=1}^{n} X_i \sum_{i=1}^{n} Y_i}{n}}{\sum_{i=1}^{n} X_i^2 - \frac{\sum_{i=1}^{n}(X_i)^2}{n}}$$

$$\text{and} \quad \beta_0 = \bar{Y} - \beta_1 \bar{X}$$

Figure 7.23: Least Squares Regression Equations

Example: Given the following sales amounts ($ millions) and advertising sizes (measured as linear inches by summing up all the sides of an ad) for a local newspaper, answer the following questions.

Advertising size (inch)	12	18	24	30	36	42	48
Sales ($ millions)	5.9	5.6	5.5	7.2	8.0	7.7	8.4

(a) Which is the dependent variable and which is the independent variable?

   The independent variable is advertising size, whereas the dependent variable is sales.

(b) Manually calculate the slope (β_1) and the intercept (β_0) terms.

X	Y	XY	X^2	Y^2
12	5.9	70.8	144	34.81
18	5.6	100.8	324	31.36
24	5.5	132.0	576	30.25
30	7.2	216.0	900	51.84
36	8.0	288.0	1296	64.00
42	7.7	323.4	1764	59.29
48	8.4	403.2	2304	70.56
$\Sigma(X)=210$	$\Sigma(Y)=48.3$	$\Sigma(XY)=1534.2$	$\Sigma(X^2)=7308$	$\Sigma(Y^2)=342.11$

$$\beta_1 = \frac{1534.2 - \frac{210(48.3)}{7}}{7308 - \frac{210^2}{7}} = 0.0845 \quad and \quad \beta_0 = \frac{48.3}{7} - 0.0845\left[\frac{210}{7}\right] = 4.3643$$

(c) What is the estimated regression equation?

   $Y = 4.3643 + 0.0845X$ or Sales $= 4.3643 + 0.0845$(Size)

(d) What would the level of sales be if we purchase a 28-inch ad?

   $Y = 4.3643 + 0.0845\ (28) = \$6.73$ million dollars in sales.

Note that we only predict or forecast and cannot say for certain. This is only an expected value or on average.

Regression Output

Using the data in the previous example, a regression analysis can be performed using either Excel's Data Analysis add-in or Risk Simulator software.[34] Figure 7.24 shows Excel's regression analysis output. Notice that the coefficients on the intercept and X variable confirm the results we obtained in the manual calculation.

Regression Statistics	
Multiple R	0.9026
R Square	0.8146
Adjusted R Square	0.7776
Standard Error	0.5725
Observations	7

ANOVA

	df	SS	MS	F	Significance F
Regression	1	7.2014	7.2014	21.9747	0.0054
Residual	5	1.6386	0.3277		
Total	6	8.8400			

	Coefficients	Standard Error	t Stat	P-value	Lower 95%	Upper 95%
Intercept	4.3643	0.5826	7.4911	0.0007	2.8667	5.8619
X Variable 1	0.0845	0.0180	4.6877	0.0054	0.0382	0.1309

Figure 7.24: Regression Output from Excel's Data Analysis Add-In

The same regression analysis can be performed using Risk Simulator.[35] The results obtained through Risk Simulator are seen in Figure 7.25. Notice again the identical answers to the slope and intercept calculations. Clearly, there are significant amounts of additional information obtained through the Excel and Risk Simulator analyses. Most of these additional statistical outputs pertain to goodness-of-fit measures, that is, a measure of how accurate and statistically reliable the model is.

Regression Analysis Report

Regression Statistics

R-Squared (Coefficient of Determination)	0.3272
Adjusted R-Squared	0.2508
Multiple R (Multiple Correlation Coefficient)	0.5720
Standard Error of the Estimates (SEy)	149.6720
Number of Observations	50

The R-Squared or Coefficient of Determination indicates that 0.33 of the variation in the dependent variable can be explained and accounted for by the independent variables in this regression analysis. However, in a multiple regression, the Adjusted R-Squared takes into account the existence of additional independent variables or regressors and adjusts this R-Squared value to a more accurate view of the regression's explanatory power. Hence, only 0.25 of the variation in the dependent variable can be explained by the regressors.

The Multiple Correlation Coefficient (Multiple R) measures the correlation between the actual dependent variable (Y) and the estimated or fitted (Y) based on the regression equation. This is also the square root of the Coefficient of Determination (R-Squared).

The Standard Error of the Estimates (SEy) describes the dispersion of data points above and below the regression line or plane. This value is used as part of the calculation to obtain the confidence interval of the estimates later.

Regression Results

	Intercept	X1	X2	X3	X4	X5
Coefficients	57.9555	-0.0035	0.4644	25.2377	-0.0086	16.5579
Standard Error	108.7901	0.0035	0.2535	14.1172	0.1016	14.7996
t-Statistic	0.5327	-1.0066	1.8316	1.7877	-0.0843	1.1188
p-Value	0.5969	0.3197	0.0738	0.0807	0.9332	0.2693
Lower 5%	-161.2966	-0.0106	-0.0466	-3.2137	-0.2132	-13.2687
Upper 95%	277.2076	0.0036	0.9753	53.6891	0.1961	46.3845

Degrees of Freedom		Hypothesis Test	
Degrees of Freedom for Regression	5	Critical t-Statistic (99% confidence with df of 44)	2.6923
Degrees of Freedom for Residual	44	Critical t-Statistic (95% confidence with df of 44)	2.0154
Total Degrees of Freedom	49	Critical t-Statistic (90% confidence with df of 44)	1.6802

The Coefficients provide the estimated regression intercept and slopes. For instance, the coefficients are estimates of the true; population b values in the following regression equation Y = b0 + b1X1 + b2X2 + ... + bnXn. The Standard Error measures how accurate the predicted Coefficients are, and the t-Statistics are the ratios of each predicted Coefficient to its Standard Error.

The t-Statistic is used in hypothesis testing, where we set the null hypothesis (Ho) such that the real mean of the Coefficient = 0, and the alternate hypothesis (Ha) such that the real mean of the Coefficient is not equal to 0. A t-test is is performed and the calculated t-Statistic is compared to the critical values at the relevant Degrees of Freedom for Residual. The t-test is very important as it calculates if each of the coefficients is statistically significant in the presence of the other regressors. This means that the t-test statistically verifies whether a regressor or independent variable should remain in the regression or it should be dropped.

The Coefficient is statistically significant if its calculated t-Statistic exceeds the Critical t-Statistic at the relevant degrees of freedom (df). The three main confidence levels used to test for significance are 90%, 95% and 99%. If a Coefficient's t-Statistic exceeds the Critical level, it is considered statistically significant. Alternatively, the p-Value calculates each t-Statistic's probability of occurrence, which means that the smaller the p-Value, the more significant the Coefficient. The usual significant levels for the p-Value are 0.01, 0.05, and 0.10, corresponding to the 99%, 95%, and 90% confidence levels.

The Coefficients with their p-Values highlighted in blue indicate that they are statistically significant at the 90% confidence or 0.10 alpha level, while those highlighted in red indicate that they are not statistically significant at any other alpha levels.

Analysis of Variance

	Sums of Squares	Mean of Squares	F-Statistic	p-Value	Hypothesis Test	
Regression	479388.49	95877.70	4.28	0.0029	Critical F-statistic (99% confidence with df of 5 and 44)	3.4651
Residual	985675.19	22401.71			Critical F-statistic (95% confidence with df of 5 and 44)	2.4270
Total	1465063.68				Critical F-statistic (90% confidence with df of 5 and 44)	1.9828

The Analysis of Variance (ANOVA) table provides an F-test of the regression model's overall statistical significance. Instead of looking at individual regressors as in the t-test, the F-test looks at all the estimated Coefficients' statistical properties. The F-Statistic is calculated as the ratio of the Regression's Mean of Squares to the Residual's Mean of Squares. The numerator measures how much of the regression is explained, while the denominator measures how much is unexplained. Hence, the larger the F-Statistic, the more significant the model. The corresponding p-Value is calculated to test the null hypothesis (Ho) where all the Coefficients are simultaneously equal to zero, versus the alternate hypothesis (Ha) that they are all simultaneously different from zero, indicating a significant overall regression model. If the p-Value is smaller than the 0.01, 0.05, or 0.10 alpha significance, then the regression is significant. The same approach can be applied to the F-Statistic by comparing the calculated F-Statistic with the critical F values at various significance levels.

Forecasting

Period	Actual (Y)	Forecast (F)	Error (E)
1	521.0000	299.5124	221.4876
2	367.0000	487.1243	(120.1243)
3	443.0000	353.2789	89.7211
4	365.0000	276.3296	88.6704
5	614.0000	776.1336	(162.1336)
6	385.0000	298.9993	86.0007
7	286.0000	354.8718	(68.8718)
8	397.0000	312.6155	84.3845
9	764.0000	529.7550	234.2450
10	427.0000	347.7034	79.2966
11	153.0000	266.2526	(113.2526)
12	231.0000	264.6375	(33.6375)
13	524.0000	406.8009	117.1991
14	328.0000	272.2226	55.7774
15	240.0000	231.7882	8.2118
16	286.0000	257.8862	28.1138
17	285.0000	314.9521	(29.9521)
18	569.0000	335.3140	233.6860
19	96.0000	282.0356	(186.0356)
20	498.0000	370.2062	127.7938
21	481.0000	340.8742	140.1258
22	468.0000	427.5118	40.4882
23	177.0000	274.5298	(97.5298)
24	198.0000	294.7795	(96.7795)
25	458.0000	295.2180	162.7820
26	108.0000	269.6195	(161.6195)

RMSE: 140.4048

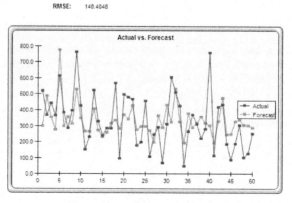

Figure 7.25: Regression Output from Risk Simulator Software

Goodness-of-Fit

Goodness-of-fit statistics provide a glimpse into the accuracy and reliability of the estimated regression model. They usually take the form of a t-statistic, F-statistic, R-squared statistic, adjusted R-squared statistic, Durbin–Watson statistic, and their respective probabilities. (See the t-statistic, F-statistic, and critical Durbin–Watson tables at the end of this book for the corresponding critical values used later in this chapter). The following sections discuss some of the more common regression statistics and their interpretation.

The R-squared (R^2), or coefficient of determination, is an error measurement that looks at the percent variation of the dependent variable that can be explained by the variation in the independent variable for a regression analysis. The coefficient of determination can be calculated by:

$$R^2 = 1 - \frac{\sum_{i=1}^{n}(Y_i - \hat{Y}_i)^2}{\sum_{i=1}^{n}(Y_i - \overline{Y})^2} = 1 - \frac{SSE}{TSS}$$

where the coefficient of determination is one less the ratio of the sums of squares of the errors (*SSE*) to the total sums of squares (*TSS*). In other words, the ratio of *SSE* to *TSS* is the unexplained portion of the analysis, thus, one less the ratio of *SSE* to *TSS* is the explained portion of the regression analysis.

Figure 7.26 provides a graphical explanation of the coefficient of determination. The estimated regression line is characterized by a series of predicted values ($\hat{Y}$); the average value of the dependent variable's data points is denoted $\overline{Y}$; and the individual data points are characterized by Y_i. Therefore, the total sum of squares, that is, the total variation in the data or the total variation about the average dependent value, is the total of the difference between the individual dependent values and its average (seen as the total squared distance of $Y_i - \overline{Y}$ in Figure 7.26). The explained sum of squares, the portion that is captured by the regression analysis, is the total of the difference between the regression's predicted value and the average dependent variable's dataset (seen as the total squared distance of $\hat{Y} - \overline{Y}$ in Figure 7.26). The difference between the total variation (*TSS*) and the explained variation (*ESS*) is the unexplained sums of squares, also known as the sums of squares of the errors (*SSE*).

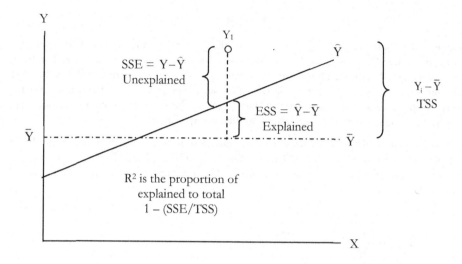

Figure 7.26: Explaining the Coefficient of Determination

Another related statistic, the adjusted coefficient of determination, or the adjusted R-squared ($\bar{R}^2$), corrects for the number of independent variables (k) in a multivariate regression through a degrees of freedom correction to provide a more conservative estimate:

$$\bar{R}^2 = 1 - \frac{\sum_{i=1}^{n}(Y_i - \hat{Y}_i)^2 / (k-2)}{\sum_{i=1}^{n}(Y_i - \bar{Y})^2 / (k-1)} = 1 - \frac{SSE / (k-2)}{TSS / (k-1)}$$

The adjusted R-squared should be used instead of the regular R-squared in multivariate regressions because every time an independent variable is added into the regression analysis, the R-squared will increase; indicating that the percent variation explained has increased. This increase occurs even when nonsensical regressors are added. The adjusted R-squared takes the added regressors into account and penalizes the regression accordingly, providing a much better estimate of a regression model's goodness-of-fit.

Other goodness-of-fit statistics include the t-statistic and the F-statistic. The former is used to test if *each* of the estimated slope and intercept(s) is statistically significant, that is, if it is statistically significantly different from zero (therefore making sure that the intercept and slope estimates are statistically valid). The latter applies the same concepts but simultaneously for the entire regression equation including the intercept and slope(s). Using the previous example, the following illustrates how the t-statistic and F-statistic can be used in a regression analysis. (See the t-statistic and F-statistic tables at the end of the book for their corresponding critical values). It is assumed that the reader is somewhat familiar with hypothesis testing and tests of significance in basic statistics.

Example: Given the information from the regression analysis output in Figure 7.27, interpret the following:

ANOVA

	df	SS	MS	F	Significance F
Regression	1	7.2014	7.2014	21.9747	0.0054
Residual	5	1.6386	0.3277		
Total	6	8.8400			

	Coefficients	Standard Error	t Stat	P-value	Lower 95%	Upper 95%
Intercept	4.3643	0.5826	7.4911	0.0007	2.8667	5.8619
X Variable 1	0.0845	0.0180	4.6877	0.0054	0.0382	0.1309

Figure 7.27: ANOVA and Goodness-of-Fit Table

(a) Perform a hypothesis test on the slope and intercept to see if they are *each* significant at a two-tailed alpha (α) of 0.05.

The null hypothesis H_o is such that the slope $\beta_1 = 0$ and the alternate hypothesis H_a is such that $\beta_1 \neq 0$. The t-statistic calculated is 4.6877, which exceeds the t-critical (2.9687 obtained from the t-statistic table at the end of this book) for a two-tailed alpha of 0.05 and degrees of freedom $n - k = 7 - 1 = 6$.[36] Therefore, the null hypothesis is rejected and one can state that the slope is statistically significantly different from 0, indicating that the regression's estimate of the slope is statistically significant. This hypothesis test can also be performed by looking at the t-statistic's corresponding p-value (0.0054), which is less than the alpha of 0.05, which means the null hypothesis is rejected.[37] The hypothesis test is then applied to the intercept, where the null hypothesis H_o is such that the intercept $\beta_0 = 0$ and the alternate hypothesis H_a is such that $\beta_0 \neq 0$. The t-statistic calculated is 7.4911, which exceeds the critical *t* value of 2.9687 for $n - k$ ($7 - 1 = 6$) degrees of freedom, so, the null hypothesis is rejected indicating that the intercept is statistically significantly different from 0, meaning that the regression's estimate of the intercept if statistically significant. The calculated p-value (0.0007) is also less than the alpha level, which means the null hypothesis is also rejected.

(b) Perform a hypothesis test to see if both the slope and intercept are significant as a whole. In other words, if the estimated model is statistically significant at an alpha (α) of 0.05.

The simultaneous null hypothesis H_o is such that $\beta_0 = \beta_1 = 0$ and the alternate hypothesis H_a is $\beta_0 \neq \beta_1 \neq 0$. The calculated F-value is 21.9747, which exceeds the critical F-value (5.99 obtained from the table at the end of this book) for k (1) degrees of freedom in the numerator and $n - k$ ($7 - 1 = 6$) degrees of freedom for the denominator, so the null hypothesis is rejected indicating that both the slope and intercept are simultaneously significantly different from 0 and that the model as a whole is statistically significant. This result is confirmed by the p-value of 0.0054 (significance of F), which is less than the alpha value, thereby rejecting the null hypothesis and confirming that the regression as a whole is statistically significant.

(c) Using Risk Simulator's regression output in Figure 7.28, interpret the R^2 value. How is it related to the correlation coefficient?

The calculated R^2 is 0.8146, meaning that 81.46 percent of the variation in the dependent variable can be explained by the variation in the independent variable. The R^2 is simply the square of the correlation coefficient, that is, the correlation coefficient between the independent and dependent variable is 0.9026.

Regression Statistics

R-Squared (Coefficient of Determination)	0.8146
Adjusted R-Squared	0.7776
Multiple R (Multiple Correlation Coefficient)	0.9026
Standard Error of the Estimates (SEy)	0.5725
Number of Observations	7

Regression Results

	Intercept	Ad Size
Coefficients	4.3643	0.0845
Standard Error	0.5826	0.0180
t-Statistic	7.4911	4.6877
p-Value	0.0007	0.0054
Lower 5%	2.8667	0.0382
Upper 95%	5.8619	0.1309

Figure 7.28: Additional Regression Output from Risk Simulator

Regression Assumptions

The following six assumptions are the requirements for a regression analysis to work:

1. The relationship between the dependent and independent variables is linear.

2. The expected value of the errors or residuals is zero.

3. The errors are independently and normally distributed.

4. The variance of the errors is constant or homoskedastic and not varying over time.

5. The errors are independent and uncorrelated with the explanatory variables.

6. The independent variables are uncorrelated to each other meaning that no multicollinearity exists.

One very simple method to verify some of these assumptions is to use a scatter plot. This approach is simple to use in a bivariate regression scenario. If the assumption of the linear model is valid, the plot of the observed dependent variable values against the independent variable values should suggest a linear band across the graph with no obvious departures from linearity. Outliers may appear as anomalous points in the graph, often in the upper right-hand or lower left-hand corner of the graph. However, a point may be an outlier in either an independent or dependent variable without necessarily being far from the general trend of the data.

If the linear model is not correct, the shape of the general trend of the X-Y plot may suggest the appropriate function to fit (e.g., a polynomial, exponential, or logistic function). Alternatively, the plot may suggest a reasonable transformation to apply. For example, if the X-Y plot arcs from lower left to upper right so that data points either very low or very high in the independent variable lie below the straight line suggested by the data, while the middle data points of the independent variable lie on or above that straight line, taking square roots or logarithms of the independent variable values may promote linearity.

If the assumption of equal variances or homoskedasticity for the dependent variable is correct, the plot of the observed dependent variable values against the independent variable should suggest a band across the graph with roughly equal vertical width for all values of the independent variable. That is, the shape of the graph should suggest a tilted cigar and not a wedge or a megaphone.

A fan pattern like the profile of a megaphone, with a noticeable flare either to the right or to the left in the scatter plot, suggests that the variance in the values increases in the direction where the fan pattern widens (usually as the sample mean increases), and this in turn suggests that a transformation of the dependent variable values may be needed.

As an example, Figure 7.29 shows a scatter plot of two variables: sales revenue (dependent variable) and marketing costs (independent variable). Clearly, there is a positive relationship between the two variables, as is evident from the regression results in Figure 7.30, where the slope of the regression equation is a positive value (0.7447). The relationship is also statistically significant at 0.05 alpha and the coefficient of determination is 0.43, indicating a somewhat weak but statistically significant relationship.

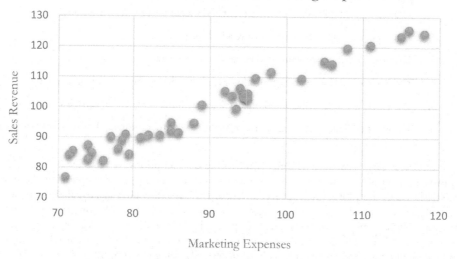

Figure 7.29: Scatter Plot Showing a Positive Relationship

Regression Statistics

R-Squared (Coefficient of Determination)	0.4300
Adjusted R-Squared	0.4185
Multiple R (Multiple Correlation Coefficient)	0.6557
Standard Error of the Estimates (SEy)	2732.90
Number of Observations	50

Regression Results

	Intercept	Marketing
Coefficients	26.8970	0.7447
Standard Error	12.1431	0.1237
t-Statistic	2.2150	6.0219
p-Value	0.0315	0.0000

Figure 7.30: Bivariate Regression Results for Positive Relationship

Compare that to a multiple linear regression in Figure 7.31, where another independent variable, pricing structure of the product, is added. The regression's adjusted coefficient of determination (adjusted R-squared) is now 0.62, indicating a much stronger regression model.[38] The pricing variable shows a negative relationship to the sales revenue, a very much expected result, as according to the law of demand in economics, a higher price point necessitates a lower quantity demanded, hence lower sales revenues. The t-statistics and corresponding probabilities (p-values) also indicate a statistically significant relationship.

Regression Statistics

R-Squared (Coefficient of Determination)	0.6360	
Adjusted R-Squared	0.6206	ADJ. R-SQUARED
Multiple R (Multiple Correlation Coefficient)	0.7975	IS HIGHER
Standard Error of the Estimates (SEy)	1745.80	
Number of Observations	50	

Regression Results

	Intercept	Marketing	Price	
Coefficients	877.9700	0.6507	-8.1382	HIGHLY
Standard Error	165.3895	0.1015	1.5787	SIGNIFICANT
t-Statistic	5.3085	6.4090	-5.1550	RELATIONSHIPS
p-Value	0.0000	0.0000	0.0000	

Figure 7.31: Multiple Linear Regression Results for Positive and Negative Relationships

In contrast, Figure 7.32 shows a scatter plot of two variables with little to no relationship, which is confirmed by the regression result in Figure 7.33, where the coefficient of determination is 0.066, close to being negligible. In addition, the calculated t-statistic and corresponding probability indicate that the marketing-expenses variable is statistically insignificant at the 0.05 alpha level meaning that the regression equation is not significant (a fact that is also confirmed by the low F-statistic).

Figure 7.32: Scatter Plot Showing No Relationship

Regression Statistics

R-Squared (Coefficient of Determination)	0.0660	LOW R-SQUARED
Adjusted R-Squared	0.0462	INDICATING LITTLE
Multiple R (Multiple Correlation Coefficient)	0.2569	RELATIONSHIP
Standard Error of the Estimates (SEy)	13661.00	
Number of Observations	50	

Regression Results

	Intercept	Marketing
Coefficients	82.9660	0.2265
Standard Error	13.7445	0.1233
t-Statistic	6.0363	1.8369
p-Value	0.0000	0.0724

Figure 7.33: Multiple Regression Results Showing No Relationship

THE PITFALLS OF FORECASTING: OUTLIERS, NONLINEARITY, MULTICOLLINEARITY, HETEROSKEDASTICITY, AUTOCORRELATION, AND STRUCTURAL BREAKS

Forecasting is a balance between art and science. Using Risk Simulator can take care of the science, but it is almost impossible to take the art out of forecasting. In forecasting, experience and subject-matter expertise counts. One effective way to support this point is to look at some of the more common problems and violations of the required underlying assumptions of the data and forecast interpretation. Clearly there are many other technical issues, but the following list is sufficient to illustrate the pitfalls of forecasting and why sometimes the art (i.e., experience and expertise) is important:

- Out-of-Range Forecasts
- Nonlinearities
- Interactions
- Self-Selection Bias
- Survivorship Bias
- Control Variables
- Omitted Variables
- Redundant Variables
- Multicollinearity
- Bad-Fitting Model or Bad Goodness-of-Fit
- Error Measurements
- Structural Breaks
- Structural Shifts
- Model Errors (Granger Causality and Causality Loops)
- Autocorrelation
- Serial Correlation
- Leads and Lags
- Seasonality
- Cyclicality
- Specification Errors and Incorrect Econometric Methods
- Micronumerosity
- Bad Data and Data Collection Errors
- Nonstationary Data, Random Walks, Non-Predictability, and Stochastic Processes (Brownian Motion, Mean-Reversion, Jump-Diffusion, Mixed Processes)
- Nonspherical and Dependent Errors
- Heteroskedasticity and Homoskedasticity
- Many other technical issues!

These errors predominantly apply to time-series data, cross-sectional data, and mixed-panel data. However, the following potential errors apply only to time-series data: Autocorrelation, Heteroskedasticity, and Nonstationarity.

Analysts sometimes use historical data to make *out-of-range forecasts* that, depending on the forecast variable, could be disastrous. Take a simple yet extreme case of a cricket. Did you know that if you caught some crickets, put them in a controlled lab environment, raised the ambient temperature, and counted the average number of chirps per minute, these chirps are relatively predictable? You might get a pretty good fit and a high R-squared value. So, the next time you go out on a date with your spouse or significant other and hear some crickets chirping on the side of the road, stop and count the number of chirps per minute. Then, using your regression forecast equation, you can approximate the temperature, and the chances are that you would be fairly close to the actual temperature. But here are some problems: Suppose you take the poor cricket and toss it into an oven at 450 degrees Fahrenheit, what happens? Well, you are going to hear a large "pop" instead of the predicted 150 chirps per minute! Conversely, toss it into the freezer at -32 degrees Fahrenheit and you will not hear the negative chirps that were predicted in your model. That is the problem of out-of-sample or out-of-range forecasts.

Suppose that in the past, your company spent different amounts in marketing each year and saw improvements in sales and profits as a result of these marketing campaigns. Further assume that, historically, the firm spends between $10M and $20M in marketing each year, and for every dollar spent in marketing, you get five dollars back in net profits. Does that mean the CEO should come up with a plan to spend $500M in marketing the next year? After all, the prediction model says there is a 5× return, meaning the firm will get $2.5B in net profit increase. Clearly this is not going to be the case. If it were, why not keep spending infinitely? The issue here is, again, an out-of-range forecast as well as *nonlinearity*. Revenues will not increase linearly at a multiple of five for each dollar spent in marketing expense, going on infinitely. Perhaps there might be some initial linear relationship, but this will most probably become nonlinear, perhaps taking the shape of a logistic S-curve, with a high-growth early phase followed by some diminishing marginal returns and eventual saturation and decline. After all, how many iPhones can a person own? At some point you have reached your total market potential and any additional marketing you spend will further flood the media airwaves and eventually cut into and reduce your profits. This is the issue of *interactions* among variables.

Think of this another way. Suppose you are a psychologist and are interested in student aptitude in writing essays under pressure. So you round up 100 volunteers, give them a pretest to determine their IQ levels, and divide the students into two groups: the brilliant Group A and the not-so-brilliant Group B, without telling the students, of course. Then you administer a written essay test twice to both groups; the first test has a 30-minute deadline and the second test, with a different but comparably difficult question, a 60-minute window. You then determine if time and intelligence has an effect on exam scores. A well thought out experiment, or so you think. The results might differ depending on whether you gave the students the 30-minute test first and then the 60-minute test or vice versa. As the not-so-brilliant students will tend to be anxious during an exam, taking the 30-minute test first may increase their stress level, possibly causing them to give up easily. Conversely, taking the longer 60-minute test first might make them ambivalent and not really care about doing it well. Of course, we can come up with many other issues with this experiment. The point is, there might be some interaction among the sequence of exams taken, intelligence, and how students fare under pressure, and so forth.

The student volunteers are just that, volunteers, and so there might be a *self-selection bias*. Another example of self-selection is a clinical research program on sports-enhancement techniques that might only attract die-hard sports enthusiasts, whereas the couch potatoes among us will not even bother participating, let alone be in the mediagraphics readership of the sports magazines in which the advertisements were placed. Therefore, the sample might be biased even before the experiment ever started. Getting back to the student test-taking volunteers, there is also an issue of *survivorship bias*, where the really not-so-brilliant students just never show up for the essay test, possibly because of their negative affinity towards exams. This fickle-mindedness and many other variables that are not *controlled* for in the experiment may actually be reflected in the exam grade. What about the students' facility with English or whatever language the exam was administered in? How about the number of beers they had the night before (being hung over while taking an exam does not help your grades at all)? These are all *omitted variables*, which means that the predictability of the model is reduced should these variables not be accounted for. It is like trying to predict the company's revenues the next few years without accounting for the price increase you expect, the recession the country is heading into, or the introduction of a new, revolutionary product line.

However, sometimes too much data can actually be bad. Now, let us go back to the students again. Suppose you undertake another research project and sample another 100 students, obtain their grade point average at the university, and ask them how many parties they go to on average per week, the number of hours they study on average per week, the number of beers they have per week (the drink of choice for college students), and the number of dates they go on per week. The idea is to see which variable, if any, affects a student's grade on average. A reasonable experiment, or so you think… The issue in this case is *redundant variables* and, perhaps worse, severe *multicollinearity*. In other words, chances are, the more parties they attend, the more people they meet, the more dates they go on per week, and the more drinks they would have on the dates and at the parties, and being drunk half the time, the less time they have to study! All variables in this case are highly correlated to each other. In fact, you probably only need one variable, such as hours of study per week, to determine the average student's grade point. Adding in all these exogenous variables confounds the forecast equation, making the forecast less reliable.

In fact, as you see later in this chapter, when you have severe multicollinearity, which just means there are multiple variables ("multi") that are changing together ("co-") in a linear fashion ("linearity"), the regression equation cannot be run. In less severe multicollinearity such as with redundant variables, the adjusted R-square might be high but the p-values will be high as well, indicating that you have a *bad-fitting* model. The prediction errors will be large. While it might be counterintuitive, the problem of multicollinearity, of having too much data, is worse than having less data or having omitted variables. And speaking of bad-fitting models, what is a good R-square *goodness-of-fit* value? This, too, is subjective. How good is your prediction model, and how accurate is it? Unless you measure accuracy using some statistical procedures for your *error measurements* such as those provided by Risk Simulator (e.g., mean absolute deviation, root mean square, p-values, Akaike and Schwartz criterion, and many others) and perhaps input a distributional assumption around these errors to run a simulation on the model, your forecasts may be highly inaccurate.

Another issue is *structural breaks*. For example, remember the poor cricket? What happens when you take a hammer and smash it? Well, there goes your prediction model! You just had a structural break. A company filing for bankruptcy will see its stock price plummet and delisted on the stock exchange, a major natural catastrophe or terrorist attack on a city can cause such a break, and so forth. *Structural shifts* are less severe changes, such as a recessionary period, or a company going into new international markets, engaged in a merger and acquisition, and so forth, where the fundamentals are still there but values might be shifted upward or downward.

Sometimes you run into a *causality loop* problem. We know that correlation does not imply causation. Nonetheless, sometimes there is a *Granger causation*, which means that one event causes another but in a specified direction, or sometimes there is a *causality loop*, where you have different variables that loop around and perhaps back into themselves. Examples of loops include systems engineering where changing an event in the system causes some ramifications across other events, which feeds back into itself causing a feedback loop. Here is an example of a causality loop going the wrong way: Suppose you collect information on crime rate statistics for the 50 states in the United States for a specific year, and you run a regression model to predict the crime rate using police expenditures per capita, gross state product, unemployment rate, number of university graduates per year, and so forth. And further suppose you see that police expenditures per capita is highly predictive of crime rate, which, of course, makes sense, and say the relationship is positive, and if you use these criteria as your prediction model (i.e., the dependent variable is crime rate and independent variable is police expenditure), you have just run into a causality loop issue. That is, you are saying that the higher the police expenditure per capita, the higher the crime rate! Well, then, either the cops are corrupt or they are not really good at their jobs! A better approach might be to use the previous year's police expenditure to predict this year's crime rate; that is, using a *lead* or *lag* on the data. So, more crime necessitates a larger police force, which will, in turn, reduce the crime rate, but going from one step to the next takes time and the lags and leads take the time element into account. Back to the marketing problem, if you spend more on marketing now, you may not see a rise in net income for a few months or even years. Effects are not immediate and the time lag is required to better predict the outcomes.

Many time-series data, especially financial and economic data, are *autocorrelated;* that is, the data are correlated to itself in the past. For instance, January's sales revenue for the company is probably related to the previous month's performance, which itself may be related to the month before. If there is *seasonality* in the variable, then perhaps last January's sales are related to the last 12 months, or January of the year before, and so forth. These seasonal cycles are repeatable and somewhat predictable. You sell more ski tickets in winter than in summer, and, guess what, next winter you will again sell more tickets than next summer, and so forth. In contrast, *cyclicality* such as the business cycle, the economic cycle, the housing cycle, and so forth, is a lot less predictable. You can use autocorrelations (relationship to your own past) and lags (one variable correlated to another variable lagged a certain number of periods) for predictions involving seasonality, but, at the same time, you would require additional data. Usually, you will need historical data of at least two seasonal cycles in length to even start running a seasonal model with any level of confidence, otherwise you run into a problem of *micronumerosity,* or lack of data. Regardless of the predictive approach used, the issue of *bad data* is always a concern. Either badly coded data or just data from a bad source, incomplete data points, and *data collection errors* are always a problem in any forecast model.

Next, there is the potential for a *specification error* or using the *incorrect econometric model* error. You can run a seasonal model where there are no seasonalities, thus creating a specification problem, or use an ARIMA when you should be using a GARCH model, creating an econometric model error. Sometimes there are variables that are considered *nonstationary;* that is, the data are not well behaved. These types of variables are really not predictable. An example is stock prices. Try predicting stock prices and you quickly find out that you cannot do a reasonable job at all. Stock prices usually follow something called a random walk, where values are randomly changing all over the place. The mathematical relationship of this random walk is known and is called a *stochastic process,* but the exact outcome is not known for certain. Typically, simulations are required to run random walks, and these stochastic processes come in a variety of forms, including the Brownian motion (e.g., ideal for stock prices), mean-reversion (e.g., ideal for interest rates and inflation), jump-diffusion (e.g., ideal for price of oil and price of electricity), and mixed processes of several forms combined into one. In this case, picking the wrong process is also a specification error.

In most forecasting methods, we assume that the forecast errors are *spherical* or *normally distributed.* That is, the forecast model is the best-fitting model one can develop that minimizes all the forecast errors, which means whatever errors that are left over are random white noise that is normally distributed (a normal distribution is symmetrical, which means you are equally likely to be underestimating as you are overestimating the forecast). If the errors are not normal and skewed, you are either overestimating or underestimating things, and adjustments need to be made. Further, these errors, because they are random, should be random over time, which means that they should be *identically and independently distributed as normal,* or *i.i.d. normal.* If they are not, then you have some autocorrelations in the data and should be building an autocorrelation model instead.

Finally, if the errors are i.i.d. normal, then the data are *homoskedastic*; that is, the forecast errors are identical over time. Think of it as a tube that contains all your data, and you put a skinny stick in that tube. The amount of wiggle room for that stick is the error of your forecast (and, by extension, if your data is spread out, the tube's diameter is large and the wiggle room is large, which means that the error is large; conversely, if the diameter of the tube is small, the error is small, such that if the diameter of the tube is exactly the size of the stick, the prediction error is zero and your R-squared goodness-of-fit is 100 percent). The amount of wiggle room is constant going into the future. This condition is ideal and what you want. The problem is, especially in nonstationary data or data with some *outliers*, that there is *heteroskedasticity*, which means that instead of a constant diameter tube, you now have a cone, with a small diameter initially that increases over time. This fanning out (see Figure 7.41) means that there is an increase in wiggle room or errors the further out you go in time. An example of this fanning out is stock prices, where if the stock price today is $50, you can forecast and say that there is a 90 percent probability the stock price will be between $48 and $52 tomorrow, or between $45 and $55 in a week, and perhaps between $20 and $100 in six months, holding everything else constant. In other words, the prediction errors increase over time.

So you see, there are many potential issues in forecasting. Knowing your variables and the theory behind the behavior of these variables is an art that depends a lot on experience, comparables with other similar variables, historical data, and expertise in modeling. There is no such thing as a single model that will solve all these issues automatically. See the sections on Data Diagnostics and Statistical Analysis in Chapter 5's exercises for the two tools in Risk Simulator that help in identifying some of these problems.

Other than being good modeling practice to create scatter plots prior to performing regression analysis, the scatter plot can also sometimes, on a fundamental basis, provide significant amounts of information regarding the behavior of the data series. Blatant violations of the regression assumptions can be spotted easily and effortlessly, without the need for more detailed and fancy econometric specification tests. For instance, Figure 7.34 shows the existence of outliers. Figure 7.35's regression results, which include the outliers, indicate that the coefficient of determination is only 0.252 as compared to 0.447 in Figure 7.36 when the outliers are removed.

Values may not be identically distributed because of the presence of outliers. Outliers are anomalous values in the data. Outliers may have a strong influence over the fitted slope and intercept, giving a poor fit to the bulk of the data points. Outliers tend to increase the estimate of residual variance, lowering the chance of rejecting the null hypothesis. They may be due to recording errors, which may be correctable, or they may be due to the dependent-variable values not all being sampled from the same population. Apparent outliers may also be due to the dependent-variable values being from the same, but nonnormal, population. Outliers may show up clearly in an X-Y scatter plot of the data, as points that do not lie near the general linear trend of the data. A point may be an unusual value in either an independent or dependent variable without necessarily being an outlier in the scatter plot.

The method of least squares involves minimizing the sum of the squared vertical distances between each data point and the fitted line. Because of this, the fitted line can be highly sensitive to outliers. In other words, least squares regression is not resistant to outliers, thus, neither is the fitted-slope estimate. A point vertically removed from the other points can cause the fitted line to pass close to it, instead of following the general linear trend of the rest of the data, especially if the point is relatively far horizontally from the center of the data (the point represented by the mean of the independent variable and the mean of the dependent variable). Such points are said to have high leverage: the center acts as a fulcrum, and the fitted line pivots toward high-leverage points, perhaps fitting the main body of the data poorly. A data point that is extreme in dependent variables but lies near the center of the data horizontally will not have much effect on the fitted slope, but by changing the estimate of the mean of the dependent variable, it may affect the fitted estimate of the intercept.

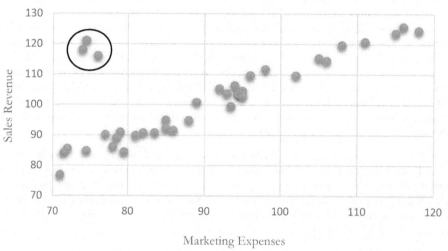

Figure 7.34: Scatter Plot Showing Outliers

Regression Statistics

R-Squared (Coefficient of Determination)	0.2520
Adjusted R-Squared	0.2367
Multiple R (Multiple Correlation Coefficient)	0.5020
Standard Error of the Estimates (SEy)	3417.60

Regression Results

	Intercept	Marketing
Coefficients	53.2690	0.4857
Standard Error	11.6769	0.1207
t-Statistic	4.5619	4.0247
p-Value	0.0000	0.0002

Figure 7.35: Regression Results with Outliers

Regression Statistics

R-Squared (Coefficient of Determination)	0.4470	HIGHER R-SQUARED
Adjusted R-Squared	0.4343	WHEN OUTLIERS
Multiple R (Multiple Correlation Coefficient)	0.6686	ARE REMOVED
Standard Error of the Estimates (SEy)	2524.90	

Regression Results

	Intercept	Marketing
Coefficients	19.4470	0.8229
Standard Error	13.4006	0.1365
t-Statistic	1.4512	6.0267
p-Value	0.1532	0.0000

Figure 7.36: Regression Results with Outliers Deleted

However, great care should be taken when deciding if the outliers should be removed. Although in most cases when outliers are removed, the regression results look better, *a priori* justification must first exist. For instance, if one is regressing the performance of a particular firm's stock returns, outliers caused by downturns in the stock market should be included; these are not truly outliers as they are inevitabilities in the business cycle. Forgoing these outliers and using the regression equation to forecast one's retirement fund based on the firm's stocks will yield incorrect results at best. In contrast, suppose the outliers are caused by a single nonrecurring business condition (e.g., merger and acquisition) and such business structural changes are not forecast to recur; then these outliers should be removed and the data cleansed prior to running a regression analysis.

Figure 7.37 shows a scatter plot with a nonlinear relationship between the dependent and independent variables. In a situation such as this one, a linear regression will not be optimal. A nonlinear transformation should first be applied to the data before running a regression. One simple approach is to take the natural logarithm of the independent variable (other approaches include taking the square root or raising the independent variable to the second or third power) and regress the sales revenue on this transformed marketing-cost data series. Figure 7.38 shows the regression results with a coefficient of determination at 0.938, as compared to 0.707 in Figure 7.39 when a simple linear regression is applied to the original data series without the nonlinear transformation.

If the linear model is not the correct one for the data, then the slope and intercept estimates and the fitted values from the linear regression will be biased, and the fitted slope and intercept estimates will not be meaningful. Over a restricted range of independent or dependent variables, nonlinear models may be well approximated by linear models (this is, in fact, the basis of linear interpolation), but for accurate prediction, a model appropriate to the data should be selected. An examination of the X-Y scatter plot may reveal whether the linear model is appropriate. If there is a great deal of variation in the dependent variable, it may be difficult to decide what the appropriate model is; in this case, the linear model may do as well as any other, and has the virtue of simplicity. Refer to the appendix on detecting and fixing heteroskedasticity for specification tests of nonlinearity and heteroskedasticity as well as ways to fix them.

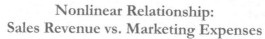

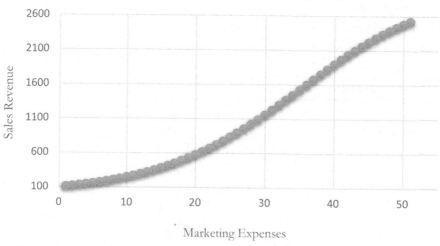

Figure 7.37: Scatter Plot Showing a Nonlinear Relationship

Regression Statistics		
R-Squared (Coefficient of Determination)	0.9380	MUCH HIGHER
Adjusted R-Squared	0.9364	SIGNIFICANCE
Multiple R (Multiple Correlation Coefficient)	0.9685	WITH NONLINEAR
Standard Error of the Estimates (SEy)	101.74	TRANSFORMATION

Regression Results		
	Intercept	LN(Marketing)
Coefficients	10.2080	5.3783
Standard Error	1.0618	0.2001
t-Statistic	9.6141	26.8750
p-Value	0.0000	0.0000

Figure 7.38: Regression Results Using a Nonlinear Transformation

However, great care should be taken here as the original linear data series of marketing costs should not be added with the nonlinearly transformed marketing costs in the regression analysis. Otherwise, multicollinearity occurs; that is, marketing costs are highly correlated to the natural logarithm of marketing costs, and if both are used as independent variables in a multivariate regression analysis, the assumption of no multicollinearity is violated and the regression analysis breaks down. Figure 7.40 illustrates what happens when multicollinearity strikes. Notice that the coefficient of determination (0.938) is the same as the nonlinear transformed regression (Figure 7.38). However, the adjusted coefficient of determination went down from 0.9364 (Figure 7.38) to 0.9358 (Figure 7.40). In addition, the previously statistically significant marketing-costs variable in Figure 7.39 now becomes insignificant (Figure 7.40) with a probability or p-value increasing from close to zero to 0.4661. A basic symptom of multicollinearity is low t-statistics coupled with a high R-squared (Figure 7.40). See *Appendix 9–Detecting and Fixing Multicollinearity* for further details on detecting multicollinearity in a regression.

Regression Statistics

R-Squared (Coefficient of Determination)	0.7070	LINEAR REGRESSION
Adjusted R-Squared	0.7013	RETURNS LOWER
Multiple R (Multiple Correlation Coefficient)	0.8408	R-SQUARED THAN
Standard Error of the Estimates (SEy)	477.72	NONLINEAR MODEL

Regression Results

	Intercept	Marketing
Coefficients	33.3580	0.0164
Standard Error	0.6335	0.0015
t-Statistic	52.6580	10.7720
p-Value	0.0000	0.0000

Figure 7.39: Regression Results Using Linear Data

Regression Statistics

R-Squared (Coefficient of Determination)	0.9380	WATCH OUT FOR
Adjusted R-Squared	0.9358	MULTICOLLINEARITY
Multiple R (Multiple Correlation Coefficient)	0.9685	
Standard Error of the Estimates (SEy)	100.59	

Regression Results

	Intercept	Marketing	LN(Marketing)
Coefficients	9.0966	-0.0011	5.6542
Standard Error	1.8510	0.0015	0.4606
t-Statistic	4.9143	-0.7349	12.2750
p-Value	0.0000	0.4660	0.0000

NOTE THAT NONLINEAR OVERTAKES LINEAR MODEL... A SYMPTOM THAT MULTICOLLINEARITY MAY EXIST: LOW P-VALUE AND HIGH R-SQUARED

Figure 7.40: Regression Results Using both Linear and Nonlinear Transformations

Another common violation is heteroskedasticity, that is, the variance of the errors increases over time. Figure 7.41 illustrates this case, where the width of the vertical data fluctuations increases or fans out over time. In this example, the data points have been changed to exaggerate the effect. However, in most time-series analysis, checking for heteroskedasticity is a much more difficult task. See *Appendix 9–Detecting and Fixing Heteroskedasticity* for further details. And correcting for heteroskedasticity is an even greater challenge.[39] Notice in Figure 7.42 that the coefficient of determination dropped significantly when heteroskedasticity exists. As is, the current regression model is insufficient and incomplete.

If the variance of the dependent variable is not constant, then the error's variance will not be constant. The most common form of such heteroskedasticity in the dependent variable is that the variance of the dependent variable may increase as the mean of the dependent variable increases for data with positive independent and dependent variables.

Unless the heteroskedasticity of the dependent variable is pronounced, its effect will not be severe: the least-squares estimates will still be unbiased, and the estimates of the slope and intercept will either be normally distributed if the errors are normally distributed, or at least normally distributed asymptotically (as the number of data points becomes large) if the errors are not normally distributed. The estimate for the variance of the slope and overall variance will be inaccurate, but the inaccuracy is not likely to be substantial if the independent-variable values are symmetric about their mean.

Heteroskedasticity of the dependent variable is usually detected informally by examining the X-Y scatter plot of the data before performing the regression. If both nonlinearity and unequal variances are present, employing a transformation of the dependent variable may have the effect of simultaneously improving the linearity and promoting equality of the variances. Otherwise, a weighted least-squares linear regression may be the preferred method of dealing with nonconstant variance of the dependent variable.

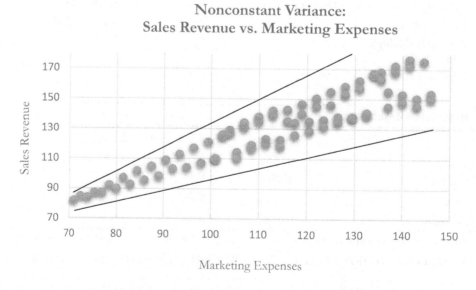

Figure 7.41: Scatter Plot Showing Heteroskedasticity with Nonconstant Variance

Regression Statistics

R-Squared (Coefficient of Determination)	0.3980	WATCH OUT FOR
Adjusted R-Squared	0.3858	HETEROSKEDASTICITY!
Multiple R (Multiple Correlation Coefficient)	0.6309	

Regression Results

	Intercept	Marketing
Coefficients	1.5742	0.9586
Standard Error	16.7113	0.1701
t-Statistic	0.0942	5.6371
p-Value	0.9253	0.0000

Figure 7.42: Regression Results with Heteroskedasticity

OTHER TECHNICAL ISSUES IN REGRESSION ANALYSIS

If the data to be analyzed by linear regression violate one or more of the linear regression assumptions, the results of the analysis may be incorrect or misleading. For example, if the assumption of independence is violated, then linear regression is not appropriate. If the assumption of normality is violated or outliers are present, then the linear regression goodness-of-fit test may not be the most powerful or informative test available, and this could mean the difference between detecting a linear fit or not. A nonparametric, robust, or resistant regression method, a transformation, a weighted least-squares linear regression, or a nonlinear model may result in a better fit. If the population variance for the dependent variable is not constant, a weighted least-squares linear regression or a transformation of the dependent variable may provide a means of fitting a regression adjusted for the inequality of the variances. Often, the impact of an assumption violation on the linear regression result depends on the extent of the violation (such as how nonconstant the variance of the dependent variable is, or how skewed the dependent variable population distribution is). Some small violations may have little practical effect on the analysis, while other violations may render the linear regression result useless and incorrect.

Other potential assumption violations include:

- Lack of independence in the dependent variable.

- Independent variable is random, not fixed.

- Special problems with few data points.

- Special problems with regression through the origin.

Lack of Independence in the Dependent Variable

Whether the independent-variable values are independent of each other is generally determined by the structure of the experiment from which they arise. The dependent-variable values collected over time may be autocorrelated. For serially correlated dependent-variable values, the estimates of the slope and intercept will be unbiased, but the estimates of their variances will not be reliable and, hence, the validity of certain statistical goodness-of-fit tests will be flawed. An ARIMA model may be better in such circumstances.

The Independent Variable is Random, Not Fixed

The usual linear regression model assumes that the observed independent variables are fixed, not random. If the independent values are not under the control of the experimenter (i.e., are observed but not set), and if there is in fact underlying variance in the independent variable, but the variance is the same, the linear model is called an errors-in-variables model or a structural model. The least-squares fit will still give the best linear predictor of the dependent variable, but the estimates of the slope and intercept will be biased (will not have expected values equal to the true slope and variance). A stochastic forecast model may be a better alternative here.

Special Problems with Few Data Points or Micronumerosity

If the number of data points is small (also termed *micronumerosity*), it may be difficult to detect assumption violations. With small samples, assumption violations such as nonnormality or heteroskedasticity of variances are difficult to detect even when they are present. With a small number of data points, linear regression offers less protection against violation of assumptions. With few data points, it may be hard to determine how well the fitted line matches the data, or whether a nonlinear function would be more appropriate.

Even if none of the test assumptions are violated, a linear regression on a small number of data points may not have sufficient power to detect a significant difference between the slope and zero, even if the slope is nonzero. The power depends on the residual error, the observed variation in the independent variable, the selected significance alpha level of the test, and the number of data points. Power decreases as the residual variance increases, decreases as the significance level is decreased (i.e., as the test is made more stringent), increases as the variation in observed independent variable increases, and increases as the number of data points increases. If a statistical significance test with a small number of data points produces a surprisingly nonsignificant probability value, then lack of power may be the reason. The best time to avoid such problems is in the design stage of an experiment, when appropriate minimum sample sizes can be determined, perhaps in consultation with an econometrician, before data collection begins.

Special Problems with Regression Through the Origin

The effects of nonconstant variance of the dependent variable can be particularly severe for a linear regression when the line is forced through the origin: the estimate of variance for the fitted slope may be much smaller than the actual variance, making the test for the slope nonconservative (more likely to reject the null hypothesis that the slope is zero than what the stated significance level indicates). In general, unless there is a structural or theoretical reason to assume that the intercept is zero, it is preferable to fit both the slope and intercept.

REGRESSION AND FORECASTING DIAGNOSTIC TOOL

The regression and forecasting diagnostic tool is the advanced analytical tool in Risk Simulator used to determine the econometric properties of your data. The diagnostics include checking the data for heteroskedasticity, nonlinearity, outliers, specification errors, micronumerosity, stationarity and stochastic properties, normality and sphericity of the errors, and multicollinearity. Each test is described in more detail in their respective reports in the model.

Procedure

- Open the example model (*Risk Simulator | Example Models | Regression Diagnostics*), and go to the *Time-Series Data* worksheet, and *select the data* including the variable names (cells *C5:H55*).

- Click on *Risk Simulator | Analytical Tools | Diagnostic Tool.*

- Check the data and select the *Dependent Variable Y* from the drop-down menu. Click *OK* when finished (Figure 7.43).

A common violation in forecasting and regression analysis is heteroskedasticity; that is, the variance of the errors increases over time (see Figure 7.44 for test results using the diagnostic tool). Visually, the width of the vertical data fluctuations increases or fans out over time, and, typically, the coefficient of determination (R-squared coefficient) drops significantly when heteroskedasticity exists. If the variance of the dependent variable is not constant, then the error's variance will not be constant. Unless the heteroskedasticity of the dependent variable is pronounced, its effect will not be severe: The least-squares estimates will still be unbiased, and the estimates of the slope and intercept will either be normally distributed if the errors are normally distributed or at least normally distributed asymptotically (as the number of data points becomes large) if the errors are not normally distributed. The estimate for the variance of the slope and overall variance will be inaccurate, but the inaccuracy is not likely to be substantial if the independent-variable values are symmetric about their mean.

If the number of data points is small (micronumerosity), it may be difficult to detect assumption violations. With small sample sizes, assumption violations such as nonnormality or heteroskedasticity of variances are difficult to detect even when they are present. With a small number of data points, linear regression offers less protection against violation of assumptions. With few data points, it may be hard to determine how well the fitted line matches the data, or whether a nonlinear function would be more appropriate. Even if none of the test assumptions are violated, a linear regression on a small number of data points may not have sufficient power to detect a significant difference between the slope and zero, even if the slope is nonzero. The power depends on the residual error, the observed variation in the independent variable, the selected significance alpha level of the test, and the number of data points. Power decreases as the residual variance increases, decreases as the significance level is decreased (i.e., as the test is made more stringent), increases as the variation in observed independent variable increases, and increases as the number of data points increases.

Values may not be identically distributed because of the presence of outliers. Outliers are anomalous values in the data. Outliers may have a strong influence over the fitted slope and intercept, giving a poor fit to the bulk of the data points. Outliers tend to increase the estimate of residual variance, lowering the chance of rejecting the null hypothesis; that is, creating higher prediction errors. They may be due to recording errors, which may be correctable, or they may be due to the dependent-variable values not all being sampled from the same population. Apparent outliers may also be due to the dependent-variable values being from the same, but nonnormal, population. However, a point may be an unusual value in either an independent or dependent variable without necessarily being an outlier in the scatter plot. In regression analysis, the fitted line can be highly sensitive to outliers. In other words, least squares regression is not resistant to outliers, thus, neither is the fitted-slope estimate. A point vertically removed from the other points can cause the fitted line to pass close to it, instead of following the general linear trend of the rest of the data, especially if the point is relatively far horizontally from the center of the data.

Multiple Regression Analysis Data Set

Dependent Variable Y	Variable X1	Variable X2	Variable X3	Variable X4	Variable X5
521	18308	185	4.041	79.6	7.2
367	1148	600	0.55	1	8.5
443	18068	372	3.665	32.3	5.7
365	7729				
614	100484				
385	16728				
286	14630				
397	4008				
764	38927				
427	22322				
153	3711				
231	3136				
524	50508				
328	28886				
240	16996				
286	13035				
285	12973				
569	16309				
96	5227				
498	19235				
481	44487				
468	44213				
177	23619				
198	9106		134	2.573	54.9	8.6
458	24917	189	5.117	74.3	6.6
108	3872	196	0.799	5.5	6.9
246	8945	183	1.578	20.5	2.7
291	2373	417	1.202	10.9	5.5
68	7128	233	1.109	123.7	7.2

Diagnostic Tool

This tool is used to diagnose forecasting problems in a set of multiple variables.

Dependent Variable: Dependent Variable Y

Dependent Variable Y	Variable X1	Variable X2	Variable X3	Variab
521	18308	185	4.041	79.6
367	1148	600	0.55	1
443	18068	372	3.665	32.3
365	7729	142	2.351	45.1
614	100484	432	29.76	190.8
385	16728	290	3.294	31.8
286	14630	346	3.287	678.4
397	4008	328	0.666	340.8
764	38927	354	12.938	239.6
427	22322	266	6.478	111.9

OK   Cancel

Figure 7.43: Running the Data Diagnostic Tool

However, great care should be taken when deciding if the outliers should be removed. Although in most cases when outliers are removed, the regression results look better, *a priori* justification must first exist. For instance, if one is regressing the performance of a particular firm's stock returns, outliers caused by downturns in the stock market should be included; these are not truly outliers as they are inevitabilities in the business cycle. Forgoing these outliers and using the regression equation to forecast one's retirement fund based on the firm's stocks will yield incorrect results at best. In contrast, suppose the outliers are caused by a single nonrecurring business condition (e.g., merger and acquisition) and such business structural changes are not forecast to recur; then these outliers should be removed and the data cleansed prior to running a regression analysis. The analysis here only identifies outliers and it is up to the user to determine if they should remain or be excluded.

Sometimes, a nonlinear relationship between the dependent and independent variables is more appropriate than a linear relationship. In such cases, running a linear regression will not be optimal. If the linear model is not the correct form, then the slope and intercept estimates and the fitted values from the linear regression will be biased, and the fitted slope and intercept estimates will not be meaningful. Over a restricted range of independent or dependent variables, nonlinear models may be well approximated by linear models (this is, in fact, the basis of linear interpolation), but for accurate prediction, a model appropriate to the data should be selected. A nonlinear transformation should first be applied to the data before running a regression. One simple approach is to take the natural logarithm of the independent variable (other approaches include taking the square root or raising the independent variable to the second or third power) and run a regression or forecast using the nonlinearly transformed data.

Diagnostic Results

Variable	Heteroskedasticity		Micronumerosity	Outliers			Nonlinearity	
	W-Test p-value	Hypothesis Test result	Approximation result	Natural Lower Bound	Natural Upper Bound	Number of Potential Outliers	Nonlinear Test p-value	Hypothesis Test result
Y			no problems	-7.86	671.70	2		
Variable X1	0.2543	Homoskedastic	no problems	-21377.95	64713.03	3	0.2458	linear
Variable X2	0.3371	Homoskedastic	no problems	77.47	445.93	2	0.0335	nonlinear
Variable X3	0.3649	Homoskedastic	no problems	-5.77	15.69	3	0.0305	nonlinear
Variable X4	0.3066	Homoskedastic	no problems	-295.96	628.21	4	0.9298	linear
Variable X5	0.2495	Homoskedastic	no problems	3.35	9.38	3	0.2727	linear

Figure 7.44: Results from Tests of Outliers, Heteroskedasticity, Micronumerosity, and Nonlinearity

Another typical issue when forecasting time-series data is whether the independent-variable values are truly independent of each other or are actually dependent. Dependent variable values collected over a time series may be autocorrelated. For serially correlated dependent-variable values, the estimates of the slope and intercept will be unbiased, but the estimates of their forecast and variances will not be reliable and, hence, the validity of certain statistical goodness-of-fit tests will be flawed. For instance, interest rates, inflation rates, sales, revenues, and many other time-series data are typically autocorrelated, where the value in the current period is related to the value in a previous period, and so forth (clearly, the inflation rate in March is related to February's level, which, in turn, is related to January's level, etc.). Ignoring such blatant relationships will yield biased and less accurate forecasts. In such events, an autocorrelated regression model or an ARIMA model may be better suited (*Risk Simulator | Forecasting | ARIMA*). Finally, the autocorrelation functions of a series that is nonstationary tend to decay slowly (see nonstationary report in the model).

If autocorrelation AC(*1*) is nonzero, it means that the series is first-order serially correlated. If AC(*k*) dies off more or less geometrically with increasing lag, it implies that the series follows a low-order autoregressive process. If AC(*k*) drops to zero after a small number of lags, it implies that the series follows a low-order moving average process. Partial correlation PAC(*k*) measures the correlation of values that are *k* periods apart after removing the correlation from the intervening lags. If the pattern of autocorrelation can be captured by an autoregression of order less than *k*, then the partial autocorrelation at lag *k* will be close to zero. Ljung–Box Q-statistics and their p-values at lag *k* have the null hypothesis that there is no autocorrelation up to order *k*. The dotted lines in the plots of the autocorrelations are the approximate two standard error bounds. If the autocorrelation is within these bounds, it is not significantly different from zero at the 5 percent significance level.

Autocorrelation measures the relationship to the past of the dependent *Y* variable to itself. Distributive lags, in contrast, are time-lag relationships between the dependent *Y* variable and different independent *X* variables. For instance, the movement and direction of mortgage rates tend to follow the Federal Funds Rate but at a time lag (typically 1 to 3 months). Sometimes, time lags follow cycles and seasonality (e.g., ice-cream sales tend to peak during the summer months and are therefore related to last summer's sales, 12 months in the past). The distributive lag analysis (Figure 7.45) shows how the dependent variable is related to each of the independent variables at various time lags, when all lags are considered simultaneously, to determine which time lags are statistically significant and should be considered.

Autocorrelation

Time Lag	AC	PAC	Lower Bound	Upper Bound	Q-Stat	Prob
1	0.0580	0.0580	-0.2828	0.2828	0.1786	0.6726
2	-0.1213	-0.1251	-0.2828	0.2828	0.9754	0.6140
3	0.0590	0.0756	-0.2828	0.2828	1.1879	0.7607
4	0.2423	0.2232	-0.2828	0.2828	4.4865	0.3442
5	0.0067	-0.0078	-0.2828	0.2828	4.4890	0.4814
6	-0.2654	-0.2345	-0.2828	0.2828	8.6516	0.1941
7	0.0814	0.0939	-0.2828	0.2828	9.0524	0.2489
8	0.0634	-0.0442	-0.2828	0.2828	9.3012	0.3175
9	0.0204	0.0673	-0.2828	0.2828	9.3276	0.4076
10	-0.0190	0.0865	-0.2828	0.2828	9.3512	0.4991
11	0.1035	0.0790	-0.2828	0.2828	10.0648	0.5246
12	0.1658	0.0978	-0.2828	0.2828	11.9466	0.4500
13	-0.0524	-0.0430	-0.2828	0.2828	12.1394	0.5162
14	-0.2050	-0.2523	-0.2828	0.2828	15.1738	0.3684
15	0.1782	0.2089	-0.2828	0.2828	17.5315	0.2881
16	-0.1022	-0.2591	-0.2828	0.2828	18.3296	0.3050
17	-0.0861	0.0808	-0.2828	0.2828	18.9141	0.3335
18	0.0418	0.1987	-0.2828	0.2828	19.0559	0.3884
19	0.0869	-0.0821	-0.2828	0.2828	19.6894	0.4135
20	-0.0091	-0.0269	-0.2828	0.2828	19.6966	0.4770

Distributive Lags

P-Values of Distributive Lag Periods of Each Independent Variable

Variable	1	2	3	4	5	6	7	8	9	10	11	12
X1	0.8467	0.2045	0.3336	0.9105	0.9757	0.1020	0.9205	0.1267	0.5431	0.9110	0.7495	0.4016
X2	0.6077	0.9900	0.8422	0.2851	0.0638	0.0032	0.8007	0.1551	0.4823	0.1126	0.0519	0.4383
X3	0.7394	0.2396	0.2741	0.8372	0.9808	0.0464	0.8355	0.0545	0.6828	0.7354	0.5093	0.3500
X4	0.0061	0.6739	0.7932	0.7719	0.6748	0.8627	0.5586	0.9046	0.5726	0.6304	0.4812	0.5707
X5	0.1591	0.2032	0.4123	0.5599	0.6416	0.3447	0.9190	0.9740	0.5185	0.2856	0.1489	0.7794

Figure 7.45: Autocorrelation and Distributive Lag Results

Another requirement in running a regression model is the assumption of normality and sphericity of the error term. If the assumption of normality is violated or outliers are present, then the linear regression goodness-of-fit test may not be the most powerful or informative test available. Choosing the most appropriate test could mean the difference between detecting a linear fit or not. If the errors are not independent and not normally distributed, it may indicate that the data might be autocorrelated or suffer from nonlinearities or other more destructive errors. Independence of the errors can also be detected in the heteroskedasticity tests (Figure 7.46).

The normality test on the errors performed is a nonparametric test, which makes no assumptions about the specific shape of the population from where the sample is drawn, allowing for smaller sample datasets to be analyzed. This test evaluates the null hypothesis of whether the sample errors were drawn from a normally distributed population versus an alternate hypothesis that the data sample is not normally distributed. If the calculated D-statistic is greater than or equal to the D-critical values at various significance values, then reject the null hypothesis and accept the alternate hypothesis (the errors are not normally distributed). Otherwise, if the D-statistic is less than the D-critical value, do not reject the null hypothesis (the errors are normally distributed). This test relies on two cumulative frequencies: one derived from the sample dataset and the second from a theoretical distribution based on the mean and standard deviation of the sample data.

Sometimes, certain types of time-series data cannot be modeled using any other methods except for a stochastic process, because the underlying events are stochastic in nature. For instance, you cannot adequately model and forecast stock prices, interest rates, price of oil, and other commodity prices using a simple regression model because these variables are highly uncertain and volatile, and do not follow a predefined static rule of behavior; in other words, the process is not stationary. Stationarity is checked here using the Runs Test, while another visual clue is found in the Autocorrelation report (the ACF tends to decay slowly). A stochastic process is a sequence of events or paths generated by probabilistic laws. That is, random events can occur over time but are governed by specific statistical and probabilistic rules. The main stochastic processes include random walk or Brownian motion, mean reversion, and jump diffusion. These processes can be used to forecast a multitude of variables that seemingly follow random trends but are restricted by probabilistic laws. The process-generating equation is known in advance, but the actual results generated are unknown (Figure 7.47).

Test Result

		Errors	Relative Frequency	Observed	Expected	O-E
Regression Error Average	0.00					
Standard Deviation of Errors	141.83	-219.04	0.02	0.02	0.0612	-0.0412
D Statistic	0.1036	-202.53	0.02	0.04	0.0766	-0.0366
D Critical at 1%	0.1138	-186.04	0.02	0.06	0.0948	-0.0348
D Critical at 5%	0.1225	-174.17	0.02	0.08	0.1097	-0.0297
D Critical at 10%	0.1458	-162.13	0.02	0.10	0.1265	-0.0265
Null Hypothesis: The errors are normally distributed.		-161.62	0.02	0.12	0.1272	-0.0072
		-160.39	0.02	0.14	0.1291	0.0109
Conclusion: The errors are normally distributed at the		-145.40	0.02	0.16	0.1526	0.0074
1% alpha level.		-138.92	0.02	0.18	0.1637	0.0163
		-133.81	0.02	0.20	0.1727	0.0273
		-120.76	0.02	0.22	0.1973	0.0227
		-120.12	0.02	0.24	0.1985	0.0415

Figure 7.46: Test for Normality of Errors

The random walk Brownian motion process can be used to forecast stock prices, prices of commodities, and other stochastic time-series data given a drift or growth rate and volatility around the drift path. The mean-reversion process can be used to reduce the fluctuations of the random walk process by allowing the path to target a long-term value, making it useful for forecasting time-series variables that have a long-term rate such as interest rates and inflation rates (these are long-term target rates by regulatory authorities or the market). The jump-diffusion process is useful for forecasting time-series data when the variable can occasionally exhibit random jumps, such as oil prices or price of electricity (discrete exogenous event shocks can make prices jump up or down). These processes can also be mixed and matched as required.

A note of caution is required here. The stochastic parameters calibration shows all the parameters for all processes and does not distinguish which process is better and which is worse or which process is more appropriate to use. It is up to the user to make this determination. For instance, if we see a 283 percent reversion rate, chances are a mean-reversion process is inappropriate, or a very high jump rate of, say, 100 percent most probably means that a jump-diffusion process is probably not appropriate, and so forth. Further, the analysis cannot determine what the variable is and what the data source is. For instance, is the raw data from historical stock prices or is it the historical prices of electricity or inflation rates or the molecular motion of subatomic particles, and so forth. Only the user would know such information, and, hence, using *a priori* knowledge and theory, be able to pick the correct process to use (e.g., stock prices tend to follow a Brownian motion random walk whereas inflation rates follow a mean-reversion process, or a jump-diffusion process is more appropriate should you be forecasting the price of electricity).

Multicollinearity exists when there is a linear relationship between the independent variables. When this occurs, the regression equation cannot be estimated at all. In near collinearity situations, the estimated regression equation will be biased and provide inaccurate results. This situation is especially true when a step-wise regression approach is used, where the statistically significant independent variables will be thrown out of the regression mix earlier than expected, resulting in a regression equation that is neither efficient nor accurate. One quick test of the presence of multicollinearity in a multiple regression equation is that the R-squared value is relatively high while the t-statistics are relatively low.

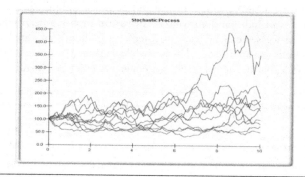

Statistical Summary

The following are the estimated parameters for a stochastic process given the data provided. It is up to you to determine if the probability of fit (similar to a goodness-of-fit computation) is sufficient to warrant the use of a stochastic process forecast, and if so, whether it is a random walk, mean-reversion, or a jump-diffusion model, or combinations thereof. In choosing the right stochastic process model, you will have to rely on past experiences and *a priori* economic and financial expectations of what the underlying data set is best represented by. These parameters can be entered into a stochastic process forecast (**Simulation | Forecasting | Stochastic Processes**).

Periodic

Drift Rate	-1.48%	Reversion Rate	283.89%	Jump Rate	20.41%
Volatility	88.84%	Long-Term Value	327.72	Jump Size	237.89

Probability of stochastic model fit: 46.48%

A high fit means a stochastic model is better than conventional models.

Runs	20	Standard Normal	-1.7321
Positive	25	P-Value (1-tail)	0.0416
Negative	25	P-Value (2-tail)	0.0833
Expected Run	26		

A low p-value (below 0.10, 0.05, 0.01) means that the sequence is not random and hence suffers from stationarity problems, and an ARIMA model might be more appropriate. Conversely, higher p-values indicate randomness and stochastic process models might be appropriate.

Figure 7.47: Stochastic Process Parameter Estimation

Another quick test is to create a correlation matrix between the independent variables. A high cross-correlation indicates a potential for autocorrelation. The rule of thumb is that a correlation with an absolute value greater than 0.75 is indicative of severe multicollinearity. Another test for multicollinearity is the use of the Variance Inflation Factor (VIF), obtained by regressing each independent variable to all the other independent variables, obtaining the R-squared value, and calculating the VIF. A VIF exceeding 2.0 can be considered as severe multicollinearity. A VIF exceeding 10.0 indicates destructive multicollinearity (Figure 7.48).

Correlation Matrix

CORRELATION	X2	X3	X4	X5
X1	0.333	0.959	0.242	0.237
X2	1.000	0.349	0.319	0.120
X3		1.000	0.196	0.227
X4			1.000	0.290

Variance Inflation Factor

VIF	X2	X3	X4	X5
X1	1.12	12.46	1.06	1.06
X2	N/A	1.14	1.11	1.01
X3		N/A	1.04	1.05
X4			N/A	1.09

Figure 7.48: Multicollinearity Errors

The correlation matrix lists the Pearson's product moment correlations (commonly referred to as the Pearson's R) between variable pairs. The correlation coefficient ranges between –1.0 and + 1.0, inclusive. The sign indicates the direction of association between the variables, while the coefficient indicates the magnitude or strength of association. The Pearson's R only measures a linear relationship and is less effective in measuring nonlinear relationships.

To test whether the correlations are significant, a two-tailed hypothesis test is performed and the resulting p-values are computed. P-values less than 0.10, 0.05, and 0.01 are highlighted in blue to indicate statistical significance. In other words, a p-value for a correlation pair that is less than a given significance value is statistically significantly different from zero, indicating that there is a significant linear relationship between the two variables.

The Pearson's product moment correlation coefficient (R) between two variables (x and y) is related to the covariance (*cov*) measure where

$$R_{x,y} = \frac{COV_{x,y}}{s_x s_y}$$

The benefit of dividing the covariance by the product of the two variables' standard deviations (s) is that the resulting correlation coefficient is bounded between –1.0 and +1.0, inclusive. This parameter makes the correlation a good relative measure to compare among different variables (particularly with different units and magnitude). The Spearman rank-based nonparametric correlation is also included in the analysis. The Spearman's R is related to the Pearson's R in that the data is first ranked and then correlated. The rank correlations provide a better estimate of the relationship between two variables when one or both of them is nonlinear.

It must be stressed that a significant correlation does not imply causation. Associations between variables in no way imply that the change of one variable causes another variable to change. Two variables that are moving independently of each other but in a related path may be correlated but their relationship might be spurious (e.g., a correlation between sunspots and the stock market might be strong, but one can surmise that there is no causality and that this relationship is purely spurious).

STATISTICAL ANALYSIS TOOL

Another very powerful tool in Risk Simulator is the *Statistical Analysis* tool, which determines the statistical properties of the data. The diagnostics run include checking the data for various statistical properties, from basic descriptive statistics to testing for and calibrating the stochastic properties of the data.

Procedure

- Open the example model (*Risk Simulator | Example Models | Statistical Analysis*), go to the *Data* worksheet, and *select the data* including the variable names (cells *C5:E55*).

- Click on *Risk Simulator | Analytical Tools | Statistical Analysis* (Figure 7.49).

- Check the data type; that is, whether the data selected are from a single variable or multiple variables arranged in rows. In our example, we assume that the data areas selected are from multiple variables. Click *OK* when finished.

- Choose the statistical tests you wish to perform. The suggestion (and by default) is to choose all the tests. Click *OK* when finished (Figure 7.50).

Spend some time going through the reports generated to get a better understanding of the statistical tests performed (sample reports are shown in Figures 7.51 through 7.54).

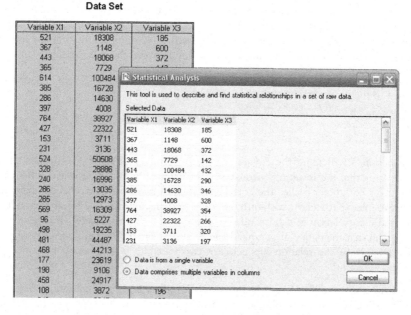

Figure 7.49: Running the Statistical Analysis Tool

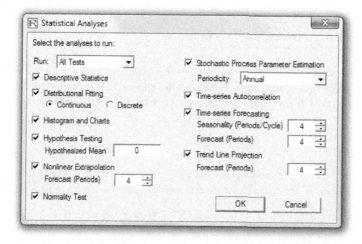

Figure 7.50: Statistical Tests

Descriptive Statistics

Analysis of Statistics

Almost all distributions can be described within 4 moments (some distributions require one moment, while others require two moments, and so forth). Descriptive statistics quantitatively capture these moments. The first moment describes the location of a distribution (i.e., mean, median, and mode) and is interpreted as the expected value, expected returns, or the average value of occurrences.

The Arithmetic Mean calculates the average of all occurrences by summing up all of the data points and dividing them by the number of points. The Geometric Mean is calculated by taking the power root of the products of all the data points and requires them to all be positive. The Geometric Mean is more accurate for percentages or rates that fluctuate significantly. For example, you can use Geometric Mean to calculate average growth rate given compound interest with variable rates. The Trimmed Mean calculates the arithmetic average of the data set after the extreme outliers have been trimmed. As averages are prone to significant bias when outliers exist, the Trimmed Mean reduces such bias in skewed distributions.

The Standard Error of the Mean calculates the error surrounding the sample mean. The larger the sample size, the smaller the error such that for an infinitely large sample size, the error approaches zero, indicating that the population parameter has been estimated. Due to sampling errors, the 95% Confidence Interval for the Mean is provided. Based on an analysis of the sample data points, the actual population mean should fall between these Lower and Upper Intervals for the Mean.

Median is the data point where 50% of all data points fall above this value and 50% below this value. Among the three first moment statistics, the median is least susceptible to outliers. A symmetrical distribution has the Median equal to the Arithmetic Mean. A skewed distribution exists when the Median is far away from the Mean. The Mode measures the most frequently occurring data point.

Minimum is the smallest value in the data set while Maximum is the largest value. Range is the difference between the Maximum and Minimum values.

The second moment measures a distribution's spread or width, and is frequently described using measures such as Standard Deviations, Variances, Quartiles, and Inter-Quartile Ranges. Standard Deviation indicates the average deviation of all data points from their mean. It is a popular measure as is associated with risk (higher standard deviations mean a wider distribution, higher risk, or wider dispersion of data points around the mean) and its units are identical to original data set's. The Sample Standard Deviation differs from the Population Standard Deviation in that the former uses a degree of freedom correction to account for small sample sizes. Also, Lower and Upper Confidence Intervals are provided for the Standard Deviation and the true population standard deviation falls within this interval. If your data set covers every element of the population, use the Population Standard Deviation instead. The two Variance measures are simply the squared values of the standard deviations.

The Coefficient of Variability is the standard deviation of the sample divided by the sample mean, proving a unit-free measure of dispersion that can be compared across different distributions (you can now compare distributions of values denominated in millions of dollars with one in billions of dollars, or meters and kilograms, etc.). The First Quartile measures the 25th percentile of the data points when arranged from its smallest to largest value. The Third Quartile is the value of the 75th percentile data point. Sometimes quartiles are used as the upper and lower ranges of a distribution as it truncates the data set to ignore outliers. The Inter-Quartile Range is the difference between the third and first quartiles, and is often used to measure the width of the center of a distribution.

Skewness is the third moment in a distribution. Skewness characterizes the degree of asymmetry of a distribution around its mean. Positive skewness indicates a distribution with an asymmetric tail extending toward more positive values. Negative skewness indicates a distribution with an asymmetric tail extending toward more negative values.

Kurtosis characterizes the relative peakedness or flatness of a distribution compared to the normal distribution. It is the fourth moment in a distribution. A positive Kurtosis value indicates a relatively peaked distribution. A negative kurtosis indicates a relatively flat distribution. The Kurtosis measured here has been centered to zero (certain other kurtosis measures are centered around 3.0). While both are equally valid, centering across zero makes the interpretation simpler. A high positive Kurtosis indicates a peaked distribution around its center and leptokurtic or fat tails. This indicates a higher probability of extreme events (e.g., catastrophic events, terrorist attacks, stock market crashes) than is predicted in a normal distribution.

Summary Statistics

Statistics	Variable X1		
Observations	50.0000	Standard Deviation (Sample)	172.9140
Arithmetic Mean	331.9200	Standard Deviation (Population)	171.1761
Geometric Mean	281.3247	Lower Confidence Interval for Standard Deviation	148.6090
Trimmed Mean	325.1739	Upper Confidence Interval for Standard Deviation	207.7947
Standard Error of Arithmetic Mean	24.4537	Variance (Sample)	29899.2588
Lower Confidence Interval for Mean	283.0125	Variance (Population)	29301.2736
Upper Confidence Interval for Mean	380.8275	Coefficient of Variability	0.5210
Median	307.0000	First Quartile (Q1)	204.0000
Mode	47.0000	Third Quartile (Q3)	441.0000
Minimum	764.0000	Inter-Quartile Range	237.0000
Maximum	717.0000	Skewness	0.4838
Range		Kurtosis	-0.0952

Figure 7.51: Sample Statistical Analysis Tool Report

Hypothesis Test (t-Test on the Population Mean of One Variable)

Statistical Summary

Statistics from Dataset:		Calculated Statistics:	
Observations	50	t-Statistic	13.5734
Sample Mean	331.92	P-Value (right-tail)	0.0000
Sample Standard Deviation	172.91	P-Value (left-tailed)	1.0000
		P-Value (two-tailed)	0.0000
User Provided Statistics:			
		Null Hypothesis (Ho):	μ = Hypothesized Mean
Hypothesized Mean	0.00	Alternate Hypothesis (Ha):	μ < > Hypothesized Mean

Notes: "<>" denotes "greater than" for right-tail, "less than" for left-tail, or "not equal to" for two-tail hypothesis tests.

Hypothesis Testing Summary

The one-variable t-test is appropriate when the population standard deviation is not known but the sampling distribution is assumed to be approximately normal (the t-test is used when the sample size is less than 30 but is also appropriate and in fact, provides more conservative results with larger data sets). This t-test can be applied to three types of hypothesis tests: a two-tailed test, a right-tailed test, and a left-tailed test. All three tests and their respective results are listed below for your reference.

Two-Tailed Hypothesis Test

A two-tailed hypothesis tests the null hypothesis Ho such that the population mean is statistically identical to the hypothesized mean. The alternative hypothesis is that the real population mean is statistically different from the hypothesized mean when tested using the sample dataset. Using a t-test, if the computed p-value is less than a specified significance amount (typically 0.10, 0.05, or 0.01), this means that the population mean is statistically significantly different than the hypothesized mean at 10%, 5% and 1% significance value (or at the 90%, 95%, and 99% statistical confidence). Conversely, if the p-value is higher than 0.10, 0.05, or 0.01, the population mean is statistically identical to the hypothesized mean and any differences are due to random chance.

Right-Tailed Hypothesis Test

A right-tailed hypothesis tests the null hypothesis Ho such that the population mean is statistically less than or equal to the hypothesized mean. The alternative hypothesis is that the real population mean is statistically greater than the hypothesized mean when tested using the sample dataset. Using a t-test, if the p-value is less than a specified significance amount (typically 0.10, 0.05, or 0.01), this means that the population mean is statistically significantly greater than the hypothesized mean at 10%, 5% and 1% significance value (or 90%, 95%, and 99% statistical confidence). Conversely, if the p-value is higher than 0.10, 0.05, or 0.01, the population mean is statistically similar or less than the hypothesized mean.

Left-Tailed Hypothesis Test

A left-tailed hypothesis tests the null hypothesis Ho such that the population mean is statistically greater than or equal to the hypothesized mean. The alternative hypothesis is that the real population mean is statistically less than the hypothesized mean when tested using the sample dataset. Using a t-test, if the p-value is less than a specified significance amount (typically 0.10, 0.05, or 0.01), this means that the population mean is statistically significantly less than the hypothesized mean at 10%, 5%, and 1% significance value (or 90%, 95%, and 99% statistical confidence). Conversely, if the p-value is higher than 0.10, 0.05, or 0.01, the population mean is statistically similar or greater than the hypothesized mean and any differences are due ti random chance.

Because the t-test is more conservative and does not require a known population standard deviation as in the Z-test, we only use this t-test.

Figure 7.52: Sample Statistical Analysis Tool Report
(Hypothesis Testing of One Variable)

Test for Normality

The Normality test is a form of nonparametric test, which makes no assumptions about the specific shape of the population from which the sample is drawn, allowing for smaller sample data sets to be analyzed. This test evaluates the null hypothesis of whether the data sample was drawn from a normally distributed population, versus an alternate hypothesis that the data sample is not normally distributed. If the calculated p-value is less than or equal to the alpha significance value then reject the null hypothesis and accept the alternate hypothesis. Otherwise, if the p-value is higher than the alpha significance value, do not reject the null hypothesis. This test relies on two cumulative frequencies: one derived from the sample data set, the second from a theoretical distribution based on the mean and standard deviation of the sample data. An alternative to this test is the Chi-Square test for normality. The Chi-Square test requires more data points to run compared to the Normality test used here.

Test Result

		Data	Relative Frequency	Observed	Expected	O-E
Data Average	331.92	47.00	0.02	0.02	0.0497	-0.0297
Standard Deviation	172.91	68.00	0.02	0.04	0.0635	-0.0235
D Statistic	0.0859	87.00	0.02	0.06	0.0783	-0.0183
D Critical at 1%	0.1150	96.00	0.02	0.08	0.0862	-0.0062
D Critical at 5%	0.1237	102.00	0.02	0.10	0.0918	0.0082
D Critical at 10%	0.1473	108.00	0.02	0.12	0.0977	0.0223
Null Hypothesis: The data is normally distributed.		114.00	0.02	0.14	0.1038	0.0362
		127.00	0.02	0.16	0.1180	0.0420
Conclusion: The sample data is normally distributed at		153.00	0.02	0.18	0.1504	0.0296
the 1% alpha level.		177.00	0.02	0.20	0.1851	0.0149
		186.00	0.02	0.22	0.1994	0.0206
		188.00	0.02	0.24	0.2026	0.0374
		198.00	0.02	0.26	0.2193	0.0407
		222.00	0.02	0.28	0.2625	0.0175
		231.00	0.02	0.30	0.2797	0.0203
		240.00	0.02	0.32	0.2975	0.0225
		246.00	0.02	0.34	0.3096	0.0304
		251.00	0.02	0.36	0.3199	0.0401
		265.00	0.02	0.38	0.3494	0.0306
		280.00	0.02	0.40	0.3820	0.0180
		285.00	0.02	0.42	0.3931	0.0269
		286.00	0.04	0.46	0.3953	0.0647
		291.00	0.02	0.48	0.4065	0.0735
		303.00	0.02	0.50	0.4336	0.0664
		311.00	0.02	0.52	0.4519	0.0681

Figure 7.53: Sample Statistical Analysis Tool Report (Normality Test)

Stochastic Process - Parameter Estimations

Statistical Summary

A stochastic process is a sequence of events or paths generated by probabilistic laws. That is, random events can occur over time but are governed by specific statistical and probabilistic rules. The main stochastic processes include Random Walk or Brownian Motion, Mean-Reversion, and Jump-Diffusion. These processes can be used to forecast a multitude of variables that seemingly follow random trends but yet are restricted by probabilistic laws. The process-generating equation is known in advance but the actual results generated is unknown.

The Random Walk Brownian Motion process can be used to forecast stock prices, prices of commodities, and other stochastic time-series data given a drift or growth rate and a volatility around the drift path. The Mean-Reversion process can be used to reduce the fluctuations of the Random Walk process by allowing the path to target a long-term value, making it useful for forecasting time-series variables that have a long-term rate such as interest rates and inflation rates (these are long-term target rates by regulatory authorities or the market). The Jump-Diffusion process is useful for forecasting time-series data when the variable can occasionally exhibit random jumps, such as oil prices or price of electricity (discrete exogenous event shocks can make prices jump up or down). Finally, these three stochastic processes can be mixed and matched as required.

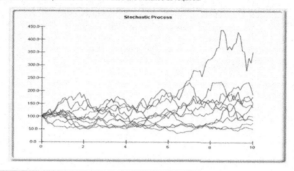

Statistical Summary

The following are the estimated parameters for a stochastic process given the data provided. It is up to you to determine if the probability of fit (similar to a goodness-of-fit computation) is sufficient to warrant the use of a stochastic process forecast, and if so, whether it is a random walk, mean-reversion, or a jump-diffusion model, or combinations thereof. In choosing the right stochastic process model, you will have to rely on past experiences and a priori economic and financial expectations of what the underlying data set is best represented by. These parameters can be entered into a stochastic process forecast (**Simulation I Forecasting I Stochastic Processes**).
(Annualized)

Drift Rate	5.86%	Reversion Rate	N/A	Jump Rate	16.33%
Volatility	7.04%	Long-Term Value	N/A	Jump Size	21.33

Probability of stochastic model fit: 4.63%

Figure 7.54: Sample Statistical Analysis Tool Report (Forecasting)

Questions

1. Explain what each of the following terms means:

    a. Time-series analysis

    b. Ordinary least squares

    c. Regression analysis

    d. Heteroskedasticity

    e. Autocorrelation

    f. Multicollinearity

    g. ARIMA

2. What is the difference between the R-squared versus the adjusted R-squared measure in a regression analysis? When is each applicable and why?

3. Explain why if each of the following is not detected properly or corrected for in the model, the estimated regression model will be flawed:

    a. Heteroskedasticity

    b. Autocorrelation

    c. Multicollinearity

4. Based on the data in the chapter examples, recreate the following using Excel:

    a. Double moving average model

    b. Single exponential-smoothing model

    c. Additive seasonality model

    d. Holt–Winters multiplicative model

5. Explain briefly how to fix the problem of nonlinearity in the dataset.

APPENDIX—FORECAST INTERVALS

The forecast interval estimated in a forecast (an approach also used by Risk Simulator) is illustrated in Figure 7A.1. The confidence interval (*CI*) is estimated by $\hat{Y}_i \pm Z\left[\dfrac{RMSE}{N-T}\right]N$ where $\hat{Y}_i$ is the *i*th forecast estimate; Z is the standard-normal statistic (see the standard-normal tables at the end of this book); *RMSE* is the root mean squared error previously calculated; N is the number of historical data points; and T is the forecast period. When N is a relatively small number (usually less than 30), then the same analysis can be performed using the *t*-statistic in place of the *Z*-value (see the t-statistic table at the end of this book).

Clearly, this approach is a modification of the more common confidence interval estimate of $\hat{Y}_i \pm Z\dfrac{\sigma}{\sqrt{n}}$ applicable within a dataset. Here, it is assumed that $\left[\dfrac{RMSE}{N-T}\right]N \approx \dfrac{\sigma}{\sqrt{n}}$ and the inclusion of the T variable is simply to adjust for the added degrees of freedom when forecasting outside of the original dataset.

Confidence Interval Estimation for Forecast

Period	Raw Data
1	265.22
2	146.64
3	182.50
4	118.54
5	180.04
6	167.45
7	231.75
8	223.71
9	192.98
10	122.29
11	336.65
12	186.50
13	194.27
14	149.19
15	210.06
36	647.82
37	650.81
38	677.54
39	666.56

Forecast Values

	Forecast	5%	95%
	710.07	586.91	833.23
	701.52	575.03	828.01
	756.04	626.04	886.04
	818.99	685.27	952.71
	794.37	656.71	932.02
Estimated RMSE	72.951		

$$CI = \hat{Y} \pm Z\left[\frac{RMSE}{(N-T)}\right]N$$

Period	Forecast (T)	Stdev	Z-statistic	Lower	Upper
40	1	74.87	1.645	586.91	833.23
41	2	76.89	1.645	575.03	828.01
42	3	79.03	1.645	626.03	886.04
43	4	81.29	1.645	685.27	952.71
44	5	83.68	1.645	656.71	932.02

RMSE	72.951
Data Points (N)	39

Figure 7A.1: Forecast Interval Estimation

APPENDIX—ORDINARY LEAST SQUARES

The following illustrates the concept of the ordinary least-squares regression line. Figure 7A.2 shows the data on the dependent variable (Y) and independent variable (X) as well as the results estimated using Excel's solver add-in. Arbitrary starting points of the slope and intercept values are fitted back into the data points and the squared residuals are calculated. Then, the optimal slope and intercept values are calculated through minimizing the sum of the squared residuals.

	A	B	C	D	E	F	G	H
1	Y	X	Slope	Intercept	Predicted	Residual	Squared Resid	
2	1000	3	91.98	2489.16	2765.09	1765.09	3115530.48	
3	3333	3	91.98	2489.16	2765.09	-567.91	322525.70	
4	2222	3	91.98	2489.16	2765.09	543.09	294942.99	
5	1111	2	91.98	2489.16	2673.11	1562.11	2440188.73	
6	5555	3	91.98	2489.16	2765.09	-2789.91	7783617.14	
7	2222	2	91.98	2489.16	2673.11	451.11	203500.54	
8	2222	3	91.98	2489.16	2765.09	543.09	294942.99	
9	5555	3	91.98	2489.16	2765.09	-2789.91	7783617.14	
10	4444	7	91.98	2489.16	3132.99	-1311.01	1718743.79	
11	3333	6	91.98	2489.16	3041.02	-291.98	85255.17	
12	2222	7	91.98	2489.16	3132.99	910.99	829905.16	
13	1111	8	91.98	2489.16	3224.97	2113.97	4468858.59	
14	5555	7	91.98	2489.16	3132.99	-2422.01	5866126.11	
15	2222	6	91.98	2489.16	3041.02	819.02	670785.76	
16	2222	7	91.98	2489.16	3132.99	910.99	829905.16	
17	5555	6	91.98	2489.16	3041.02	-2513.98	6320120.01	
18	4444	5	91.98	2489.16	2949.04	-1494.96	2234908.63	
19	1111	6	91.98	2489.16	3041.02	1930.02	3724958.34	
20	2222	4	91.98	2489.16	2857.06	635.06	403304.67	
21	3333	5	91.98	2489.16	2949.04	-383.96	147426.11	
22	2222	4	91.98	2489.16	2857.06	635.06	403304.67	
23	1111	4	91.98	2489.16	2857.06	1746.06	3048735.05	
24								
25		┌ Optimization Parameter					┌ Excel Estimated Parameter	
26		Intercept			2489.16		Intercept	2489.16
27		Slope			91.98		Slope	91.98
28		Sum of Squared Residuals			52991202.91			
29								

Figure 7A.2: Using Optimization to Estimate Regression Intercept and Slope

To get started, make sure Excel's Solver is added in by clicking on *File | Excel Options | Add-Ins | Excel Add-Ins | Go | Solver Add-In*. Verify that the check-box beside *Solver Add-In* is selected (Figure 7A.3).

Then, back in the Excel model, click on *Data (tab) | Solver* and make sure the *sum of squared residuals* (cell E28) is set as the target cell to minimize through systematically changing the intercept and slope values (cells E26 and E27) as seen in Figure 7A.4.

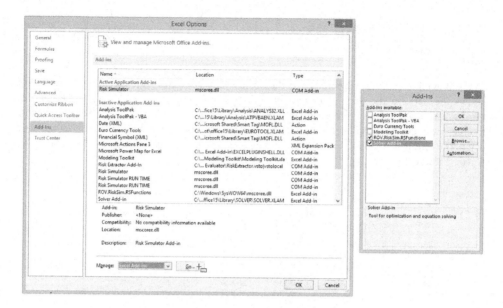

Figure 7A.3: Excel Solver Add-In

Figure 7A.4: Excel Solver Parameters

Solving yields an intercept value of 2489.16 and a slope of 91.98. These results can be verified using Excel's built-in *slope* and *intercept* functions (Figure 7A.5). In other words, the ordinary least-squares regression equation approach is the unique line (as described by an intercept and slope) that minimizes all possible vertical errors (total sum of squared residuals), making it the best-fitting line through a dataset.

Optimization Parameter	
Intercept	2489.16
Slope	91.98
Sum of Squared Residuals	52991202.91

Excel Estimated Parameter	
Intercept	2489.16
Slope	91.98

Figure 7A.5: Optimized Ordinary Least Squares Results

APPENDIX—DETECTING AND FIXING HETEROSKEDASTICITY

Several tests exist to test for the presence of heteroskedasticity. These tests also are applicable for testing misspecifications and nonlinearities. The simplest approach is to graphically represent each independent variable against the dependent variable as illustrated earlier in the chapter. Another approach is to apply one of the most widely used model, the White's test, where the test is based on the null hypothesis of no heteroskedasticity against an alternate hypothesis of heteroskedasticity of some unknown general form. The test statistic is computed by an auxiliary or secondary regression, where the squared residuals or errors from the first regression are regressed on all possible (and nonredundant) cross products of the regressors.

For example, suppose the following regression is estimated:

$$Y = \beta_0 + \beta_1 X + \beta_2 Z + \varepsilon_t$$

The test statistic is then based on the auxiliary regression of the errors (ε):

$$\varepsilon_t^2 = \alpha_0 + \alpha_1 X + \alpha_2 Z + \alpha_3 X^2 + \alpha_4 Z^2 + \alpha_5 XZ + v_t$$

The nR^2 statistic is the White's test statistic, computed as the number of observations (n) times the centered R-squared from the test regression. White's test statistic is asymptotically distributed as a χ^2 with degrees of freedom equal to the number of independent variables (excluding the constant) in the test regression. The White's test is also a general test for model misspecification, because the null hypothesis underlying the test assumes that the errors are both homoskedastic and independent of the regressors, and that the linear specification of the model is correct. Failure of any one of these conditions could lead to a significant test statistic. Conversely, a nonsignificant test statistic implies that none of the three conditions is violated. For instance, the resulting F-statistic is an omitted variable test for the joint significance of all cross products, excluding the constant.

One method to fix heteroskedasticity is to make it homoskedastic by using a weighted least squares (WLS) approach. For instance, suppose the following is the original regression equation:

$$Y = \beta_0 + \beta_1 X_1 + \beta_2 X_2 + \beta_3 X_3 + \varepsilon$$

Further suppose that X_2 is heteroskedastic. Then transform the data used in the regression into:

$$Y = \frac{\beta_0}{X_2} + \beta_1 \frac{X_1}{X_2} + \beta_2 + \beta_3 \frac{X_3}{X_2} + \frac{\varepsilon}{X_2}$$

The model can be redefined as the following WLS regression:

$$Y_{WLS} = \beta_0^{WLS} + \beta_1^{WLS} X_1 + \beta_2^{WLS} X_2 + \beta_3^{WLS} X_3 + v$$

Alternatively, the Park's test can be applied to test for heteroskedasticity and to fix it. The Park's test model is based on the original regression equation, uses its errors, and creates an auxiliary regression that takes the form of:

$$\ln e_i^2 = \beta_1 + \beta_2 \ln X_{k,i}$$

Suppose β_2 is found to be statistically significant based on a t-test, then heteroskedasticity is found to be present in the variable $X_{k,i}$. The remedy, therefore, is to use the following regression specification:

$$\frac{Y}{\sqrt{X_k^{\beta_2}}} = \frac{\beta_1}{\sqrt{X_k^{\beta_2}}} + \frac{\beta_2 X_2}{\sqrt{X_k^{\beta_2}}} + \frac{\beta_3 X_3}{\sqrt{X_k^{\beta_2}}} + \varepsilon$$

APPENDIX—DETECTING AND FIXING MULTICOLLINEARITY

Multicollinearity exists when there is a linear relationship between the independent variables. When this occurs, the regression equation cannot be estimated at all. In near collinearity situations, the estimated regression equation will be biased and provide inaccurate results. This situation is especially true when a step-wise regression approach is used, where the statistically significant independent variables will be thrown out of the regression mix earlier than expected, resulting in a regression equation that is neither efficient nor accurate. As an example, suppose the following multiple regression analysis exists, where $Y_i = \beta_1 + \beta_2 X_{2,i} + \beta_3 X_{3,i} + \varepsilon_i$

Then the estimated slopes can be calculated through

$$\hat{\beta}_2 = \frac{\sum Y_i X_{2,i} \sum X_{3,i}^2 - \sum Y_i X_{3,i} \sum X_{2,i} X_{3,i}}{\sum X_{2,i}^2 \sum X_{3,i}^2 - \left(\sum X_{2,i} X_{3,i}\right)^2}$$

$$\hat{\beta}_3 = \frac{\sum Y_i X_{3,i} \sum X_{2,i}^2 - \sum Y_i X_{2,i} \sum X_{2,i} X_{3,i}}{\sum X_{2,i}^2 \sum X_{3,i}^2 - \left(\sum X_{2,i} X_{3,i}\right)^2}$$

Now suppose that there is perfect multicollinearity, that is, there exists a perfect linear relationship between X_2 and X_3, such that $X_{3,i} = \lambda X_{2,i}$ for all positive values of λ. Substituting this linear relationship into the slope calculations for β_2, the result is indeterminate. In other words, we have

$$\hat{\beta}_2 = \frac{\sum Y_i X_{2,i} \sum \lambda^2 X_{2,i}^2 - \sum Y_i \lambda X_{2,i} \sum \lambda X_{2,i}^2}{\sum X_{2,i}^2 \sum \lambda^2 X_{2,i}^2 - \left(\sum \lambda X_{2,i}^2\right)^2} = \frac{0}{0}$$

The same calculation and results apply to β_3, which means that the multiple regression analysis breaks down and cannot be estimated given a perfect collinearity condition.

One quick test of the presence of multicollinearity in a multiple regression equation is that the R-squared value is relatively high while the t-statistics are relatively low. (See Figure 7.40 for an illustration of this effect). Another quick test is to create a correlation matrix between the independent variables. A high cross-correlation indicates a potential for multicollinearity. The rule of thumb is that a correlation with an absolute value greater than 0.75 is indicative of severe multicollinearity. Another test for multicollinearity is the use of the variance inflation factor (VIF), obtained by regressing each independent variable to all the other independent variables, obtaining the R-squared value and calculating the VIF of that variable by estimating:

$$VIF_i = \frac{1}{(1 - R_i^2)}$$

A high VIF value indicates a high R-squared near unity. As a rule of thumb, a VIF value greater than 10 is usually indicative of destructive multicollinearity.

APPENDIX—DETECTING AND FIXING AUTOCORRELATION

One very simple approach to test for autocorrelation is to graph the time series of a regression equation's residuals. If these residuals exhibit some cyclicality, then autocorrelation exists. Another more robust approach to detect autocorrelation is the use of the Durbin–Watson statistic, which estimates the potential for a first-order autocorrelation. The Durbin–Watson test also identifies model misspecification. That is, if a particular time-series variable is correlated to itself one period prior. Many time-series data tend to be autocorrelated to their historical occurrences. This relationship can be due to multiple reasons, including the variables' spatial relationships (similar time and space), prolonged economic shocks and events, psychological inertia, smoothing, seasonal adjustments of the data, and so forth.

The Durbin–Watson statistic is estimated by the sum of the squares of the regression errors for one period prior, to the sum of the current period's errors:

$$DW = \frac{\sum (\varepsilon_t - \varepsilon_{t-1})^2}{\sum \varepsilon_t^2}$$

There is a Durbin–Watson critical statistic table at the end of the book that provides a guide as to whether a statistic implies any autocorrelation.

Another test for autocorrelation is the Breusch–Godfrey test, where for a regression function in the form of:

$$Y = f(X_1, X_2, ..., X_k)$$

Estimate this regression equation and obtain its errors ε_t. Then, run the secondary regression function in the form of:

$$Y = f(X_1, X_2, ..., X_k, \varepsilon_{t-1}, \varepsilon_{t-2}, \varepsilon_{t-p})$$

Obtain the R-squared value and test it against a null hypothesis of no autocorrelation versus an alternate hypothesis of autocorrelation, where the test statistic follows a Chi-Square distribution of p degrees of freedom:

$$R^2(n-p) \sim \chi^2_{df=p}$$

Fixing autocorrelation requires more advanced econometric models including the applications of ARIMA (Auto Regressive Integrated Moving Average) or ECM (Error Correction Models). However, one simple fix is to take the lags of the dependent variable for the appropriate periods, add them into the regression function, and test for their significance, for instance:

$$Y_t = f\left(Y_{t-1}, Y_{t-2}, \ldots, Y_{t-p}, X_1, X_2, \ldots, X_k\right)$$

SECTION FIVE – RISK DIVERSIFICATION

CHAPTER 8 – THE SEARCH FOR THE OPTIMAL DECISION

In most simulation models, there are variables over which you have control, such as how much to charge for a product or how much to invest in a project. These controlled variables are called decision variables. Finding the optimal values for decision variables can make the difference between reaching an important goal and missing that goal. This chapter details the optimization process at a high-level, while Chapter 9, Optimization Under Uncertainty provides several step-by-step examples of resource optimization and portfolio optimization solved using Risk Simulator software.

WHAT IS AN OPTIMIZATION MODEL?

In today's competitive global economy, companies are faced with many difficult decisions. These decisions include allocating financial resources, building or expanding facilities, managing inventories, and determining product-mix strategies (Figure 8.1). Such decisions might involve thousands or millions of potential alternatives. Considering and evaluating each of them would be impractical or even impossible. A model can provide valuable assistance in incorporating relevant variables when analyzing decisions, and finding the best solutions for making decisions. Models capture the most important features of a problem and present them in a form that is easy to interpret. Models often provide insights that intuition alone cannot. An optimization model has three major elements: decision variables, constraints, and an objective. In short, the optimization methodology finds the best combination or permutation of decision variables (e.g., which products to sell and which projects to execute) in every conceivable way such that the objective is maximized (e.g., revenues and net income) or minimized (e.g., risk and costs) while still satisfying the constraints (e.g., budget and resources).

Obtaining optimal values generally requires that you search in an iterative or ad hoc fashion. This search involves running one iteration for an initial set of values, analyzing the results, changing one or more values, rerunning the model, and repeating the process until you find a satisfactory solution. This process can be very tedious and time consuming even for small models, and often it is not clear how to adjust the values from one iteration to the next.

A more rigorous method systematically enumerates all possible alternatives. This approach guarantees optimal solutions if the model is correctly specified. Suppose that an optimization model depends on only two decision variables. If each variable has 10 possible values, trying each combination requires 100 iterations (10^2 alternatives). If each iteration is very short (e.g., 2 seconds), then the entire process could be done in approximately three minutes of computer time.

However, instead of two decision variables, consider six, then consider that trying all combinations requires 1,000,000 iterations (10^6 alternatives). It is easily possible for complete enumeration to take weeks, months, or even years to carry out.

What is Optimization?

An approach used to find the combination of inputs to achieve the best possible output subject to satisfying certain prespecified constraints and conditions

- What stocks to pick in a portfolio, as well as the weights of each stock as a percent of total budget
- Optimal staffing needs for a production line
- Project strategy selection and prioritization
- Inventory optimization
- Optimal pricing and royalty rates
- Utilization of employees for workforce planning
- Configuration of machines for production scheduling
- Location of facilities for distribution
- Tolerances in manufacturing design
- Treatment policies in waste management

Figure 8.1: What Is Optimization?

THE TRAVELING FINANCIAL PLANNER

A very simple example is in order. Figure 8.2 illustrates the traveling financial planner problem. Suppose the traveling financial planner has to make three sales trips to New York, Chicago, and Seattle. Further suppose that the order of arrival at each city is irrelevant. All that is important in this simple example is to find the lowest total cost possible to cover all three cities. Figure 8.2 also lists the flight costs from these different cities.

The problem here is cost minimization, suitable for optimization. One basic approach to solving this problem is through an ad hoc or brute force method. That is, manually list all six possible permutations as seen in Figure 8.3. Clearly the cheapest itinerary is going from the east coast to the west coast, going from New York to Chicago and finally on to Seattle.[40] Here, the problem is simple and can be calculated manually, as there were three cities and, hence, six possible itineraries.[41] However, add two more cities and the total number of possible itineraries jumps to 120.[42] Performing an ad hoc calculation will be fairly intimidating and time consuming. On a larger scale, suppose there are 100 cities on the salesman's list; the possible itineraries will be as many as 9.3×10^{157}. The problem will take many years to calculate manually, which is where optimization software steps in, automating the search for the optimal itinerary.

The example illustrated up to now is a deterministic optimization problem, that is, the airline ticket prices are known ahead of time and are assumed to be constant. Now suppose the ticket prices are not constant but are uncertain, following some distribution (e.g., a ticket from Chicago to Seattle averages $325, but is never cheaper than $300 and usually never exceeds $500).[43] The same uncertainty applies to tickets for the other cities. The problem now becomes an *optimization under uncertainty*. Ad hoc and brute force approaches simply do not work. Software such as Risk Simulator can take over this optimization problem and automate the entire process seamlessly. The next section discusses the terms required in an optimization under uncertainty. Chapter 9 illustrates several additional business cases and models with step-by-step instructions.

> Optimization problems can be solved using different approaches including the use of simplex or graphical methods, brute force, mathematically taking calculus derivatives, or using software that apply smart algorithms and search heuristics to efficiently identify the optimal solutions.

Traveling Financial Planning Problem

- You have to travel and visit clients in New York, Chicago, and Seattle... You may start from any city and you will stay at your final city, i.e., you will need to purchase three airline tickets.
- Your goal is to travel as cheaply as possible given these rates:
    - Seattle to Chicago: $325
    - Chicago to Seattle: $225
    - New York to Seattle: $350
    - Seattle to New York: $375
    - Chicago to New York: $325
    - New York to Chicago: $325
- How do you solve the problem?
    - Ad-hoc approach: start trying different combinations
    - Enumeration: look at all possible alternatives

Figure 8.2: Traveling Financial Planner Problem

Multiple Combinations

- Seattle–Chicago–New York: $325 + $325 = $650
- Seattle–New York–Chicago: $375 + $325 = $700
- Chicago–Seattle–New York: $225 + $375 = $600
- Chicago–New York–Seattle: $325 + $350 = $675
- New York–Seattle–Chicago: $350 + $325 = $675
- New York–Chicago–Seattle: $325 + $225 = $550

Additionally, say you want to include San Antonio and Denver... For the 5 cities, you now have $5! = 5 \times 4 \times 3 \times 2 \times 1 = 120$ combinations

What about 100 different cities? We would have $100! = 100 \times 99 \times 98 \times ... \times 1 = 93,326,215,443,944,200,000,000,000,...,000 = 9.3 \times 10^{157}$ combinations!

Figure 8.3: Multiple Combinations of the Traveling Financial Planner Problem

THE LINGO OF OPTIMIZATION

Before embarking on solving an optimization problem, it is vital to understand the terminology of optimization—the terms used to describe certain attributes of the optimization process. These words include: decision variables, constraints, and objectives.

Decision variables are quantities over which you have control; for example, the amount of a product to make, the number of dollars to allocate among different investments, or which projects to select from among a limited set. As an example, portfolio optimization analysis includes a go or no-go decision on particular projects. In addition, the dollar or percentage budget allocation across multiple projects also can be structured as decision variables.

Constraints describe relationships among decision variables that restrict the values of the decision variables. For example, a constraint might ensure that the total amount of money allocated among various investments cannot exceed a specified amount or, at most, one project from a certain group can be selected, budget constraints, timing restrictions, minimum returns, or risk tolerance levels.

Objectives give a mathematical representation of the model's desired outcome, such as maximizing profit or minimizing cost, in terms of the decision variables. In financial analysis, for example, the objective may be to maximize returns while minimizing risks (maximizing the Sharpe's ratio or returns-to-risk ratio).

Conceptually, an optimization model might look like Figure 8.4.

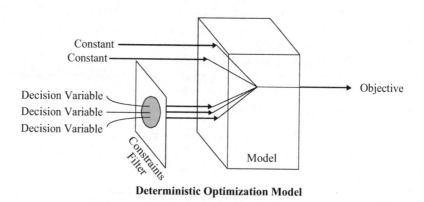

Deterministic Optimization Model

Figure 8.4: Visualizing Optimization I

The solution to an optimization model provides a set of values for the decision variables that optimizes (maximizes or minimizes) the associated objective. If the real business conditions were simple and if the future were predictable, all data in an optimization model would be constant, making the model deterministic.

In many cases, however, a deterministic optimization model cannot capture all the relevant intricacies of a practical decision-making environment. When a model's data are uncertain and can only be described probabilistically, the objective will have some probability distribution for any chosen set of decision variables. You can find this probability distribution by simulating the model using Risk Simulator. An optimization model under uncertainty has several additional elements, including assumptions and forecasts.

Assumptions capture the uncertainty of model data using probability distributions, whereas forecasts are the frequency distributions of possible results for the model. Forecast statistics are summary values of a forecast distribution, such as the mean, standard deviation, and variance. The optimization process (Figure 8.5) controls the optimization by maximizing or minimizing the objective.

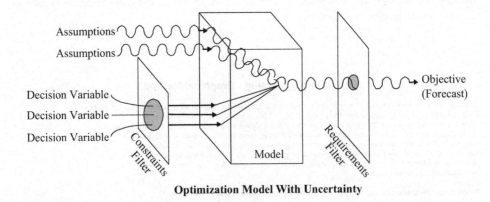

Optimization Model With Uncertainty

Figure 8.5: Visualizing Optimization II

Each optimization model has one objective, a variable that mathematically represents the model's objective in terms of the assumption and decision variables. Optimization's job is to find the optimal (minimum or maximum) value of the objective by selecting and improving different values for the decision variables. When model data are uncertain and can only be described using probability distributions, the objective itself will have some probability distribution for any set of decision variables.

Before embarking on solving an optimization problem, the analyst first has to understand the lingo of optimization: objectives, constraints, decision variables, assumption, and forecasts.

SOLVING OPTIMIZATION GRAPHICALLY AND USING EXCEL'S SOLVER

Figure 8.6 illustrates a simple multiple constraint optimization problem solved using the graphical method. In this simple example of deterministic linear optimization with linear constraints, the graphical approach is easy to implement. However, great care should be taken when nonlinear constraints exist.[44] Sometimes, optimization models are specified incorrectly. For instance, Figure 8.7 shows problems arising with unbounded solutions (with a solution set at infinity), no feasible solution (where the constraints are too restrictive and impossible to satisfy), and multiple solutions (this is good news for management as they can choose from among several equally optimal solutions).

Figure 8.8 illustrates the same problem but solved using Excel's Solver add-in.[45] Solver is clearly a more powerful approach than the manual graphical method. This situation is especially true when multiple decision variables exist as a multidimensional graph would be required.[46] Figures 8.9 and 8.10 show the use of Excel's Solver to optimize a portfolio of projects—the former assumes an integer optimization, where projects are either a go or no-go decision, whereas the latter assumes a continuous optimization, where projects can be funded anywhere from 0 percent to 100 percent.[47]

There is one major limitation of Excel's Solver. Specifically, it assumes static and deterministic optimization models and cannot account for risk and uncertainty. In the next chapter, we will see how Risk Simulator can be used to run static optimization as well as dynamic optimization and stochastic optimization to account for risks and uncertainty, as well as run investment efficient frontiers.

Linear Programming - Graphical Method

Say there are two products X and Y being manufactured. Product X provides a $20 profit and product Y a $15 profit. Product X takes 3 hours to manufacture and product Y takes 2 hours to produce. In any given week, the manufacturing equipment can make both products but has a maximum capacity of 300 hours. In addition, based on market demand, management has determined that they cannot sell more than 80 units of X and 100 units of Y in a given week and prefers not to have any inventory on hand. Therefore, management has set these demand levels as the maximum output for products X and Y respectively. The issue now becomes what is the optimal production levels of both X and Y such that profits would be maximized in any given week?

Based on the situation above, we can formulate a linear optimization routine where we have:

The Objective Function:	Max 20X + 15Y
subject to Constraints:	3X + 2Y = 300
	X = 80
	Y = 100

We can more easily visualize the constraints by plotting them out one at a time as follows:

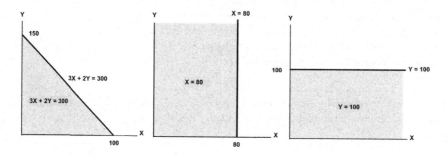

Figure 8.6: Solving Optimization using Linear Programming (continues)

The graph below shows the combination of all three constraints. The shaded region shows the feasible area, where all constraints are simultaneously satisfied. Hence, the optimal should fall within this shaded region.

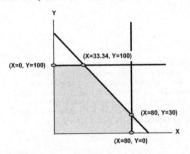

We can easily calculate the intersection points of the constraints. For example, the intersection between Y = 100 and 3X + 2Y = 300 is obtained by solving the equations simultaneously. Substituting, we get 3X + 2(100) = 300. Solving yields X = 33.34 and Y = 100.

Similarly, the intersection between X = 80 and 3X + 2Y = 300 can be obtained by solving the equations simultaneously. Substituting yields 3(80) + 2Y = 300. Solving yields Y = 30 and X = 80.

The other two edges are simply intersections between the axes. Hence, when X = 80, Y = 0 for the X = 80 line and Y = 100 and X = 0 for the Y = 100 line.

From linear programming theory, one of these four intersection edges or extreme values is the optimal solution. One method is simply to substitute each of the end points into the objective function and see which solution set provides the highest profit level.

Using the objective function where Profit = 20X + 15Y and substituting each of the extreme value sets:

When X = 0 and Y = 100:   Profit = \$20 (0) + \$15 (100) = \$1,500
When X = 33.34 and Y = 100:   Profit = \$20 (33.34) + \$15 (100) = \$2,167
When X = 80 and Y = 30:   Profit = \$20 (80) + \$15 (30) = \$2,050
When X = 80 and Y = 0:   Profit = \$20 (80) + \$15 (0) = \$1,600

Here, we see that when X = 33.34 and Y = 100, the profit function is maximized. We can also further verify this by using any combinations of X and Y within the feasible (shaded) area above. For instance, X =10 and Y =10 is a combination which is feasible but their profit outcome is only \$20 (10) + \$15 (10) = \$350. We can calculate an infinite combinations of X and Y sets but the optimal combination is always going to be at extreme value edges.

We can easily verify which extreme value will be the optimal solution set by drawing the objective function line. If we set the objective function to be:

20X + 15Y = 0   we get X = 20, Y = 15
20X + 15Y = 1000   we get X = 60, Y = 80

If we keep shifting the profit function upwards to the right, we will keep intersecting with the extreme value edges. The edge which provides the highest profit function is the optimal solution set.

In our example, point B is the optimal solution, which was verified by our calculations above, where X = 33.34 and Y = 100.

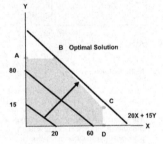

Figure 8.6: Solving Optimization using Linear Programming (continued)

Linear Programming - Potential Problems

There could be potential problems when dealing with linear programming. The three most frequently occurring problems include: Unbounded Solutions, No Feasible Solutions and Multiple Optimal Solutions.

Unbounded Solutions

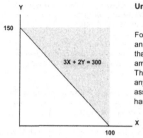

For instance, if the only constraint was such that 3X + 2Y = 300, we have an unbounded problem. This means the machine can keep working greater than 300 hours without stop. Hence, optimally, in order to generate the most amount of profit, we would keep making products X and Y up to an infinite level. This is essentially management heaven, to produce as much as possible without any budgetary or resource constraints. Obviously, if this is the case, we should assume that the problem has not been defined correctly and perhaps an error has occurred in our mathematical models.

No Feasible Solution

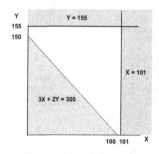

Now suppose we have the following constraints:

$$3X + 2Y = 300$$
$$X = 101$$
$$Y = 155$$

There exists no area where all constraints are binding simultaneously. In essence, any solution generated will by definition not be feasible since there will always be a constraint that is violated. Given a situation like this, it may be that the problem has been framed incorrectly or that we may have to request that management loosens some of its tight constraints since based on their expectations, the project is just not do-able. Additional resources are required (greater than 300 hours by purchasing additional machines or hiring more workers) or that the minimum required production levels (155 and 101) be reduced.

Multiple Solutions

Here, we have two extreme values (B and C) that intersect the profit objective function. Both these solution sets are optimal. This is good news for management since they have the option of choosing either combination of X and Y production levels. Other qualitative factors may be utilized on top of quantitative analytical results.

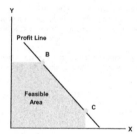

Figure 8.7: Potential Problems of Linear Programming

Linear Programming - Excel Solver Method

Using the same previous problem, where we have the following:

The Objective Function: Max 20X + 15Y

subject to Constraints: 3X + 2Y = 300
                                 X = 80
                                 Y = 100

We can utilize Excel's Solver add-in to provide a quick analytical solution.

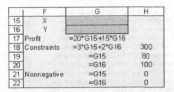

First, we need to set up the spreadsheet model. We have an X and Y variable which is to be solved. Next, we have the profit objective function in cell G17 and the constraints in cells G18 through H22. In order for Solver to perform the calculation, we needed to include two additional requirements, the nonnegative constraints, where we are setting both X and Y to be positive values only. Negative values of production are impossible. Cells H18 to H22 are the target values for the constraints. We then start Solver by clicking on Tools and Solver. (If Solver is not available, you may have to first add it in by clicking on Tools/Add-Ins and selecting Solver. Then, go back to Tools/Solver to run the program).

Set the profit calculation as the target cell ($G$17) and select maximization. Set the X and Y unknowns as the cells to change ($G$15:$G$16). Next, click on Add to add the constraints. The constraints could be added one at a time or in a batch group. Add $G$18:$G$20 to be less than or equal to $H$18:$H$20. Then, add in the nonnegative constraints where $G$21:$G$22 is greater than or equal to zero ($H$21:$H$22).

If we let Solver calculate the results, we would obtain the following, where the optimal solution set is when:

X	33.33	
Y	100	
Profit	$2,167	
Constraints	300	300
	33.33	80
	100	100
Nonnegative	33.33	0
	100	0

Figure 8.8: Using Excel's Solver in Linear Programming

Integer Portfolio Optimization and Integer Linear Programming

	Cost	Return	Risk	Return-Risk Ratio	Allocation	Weighted Cost	Risk Return	Weighted Risk
Project A	$500,000	19%	32%	0.594	0%	$0	0.000	0%
Project B	$625,000	23%	39%	0.590	0%	$0	0.000	0%
Project C	$345,000	15%	22%	0.682	100%	$345,000	0.682	22%
Project D	$290,000	16%	29%	0.552	0%	$0	0.000	0%
Project E	$450,000	17%	25%	0.680	100%	$450,000	0.680	25%
					Sum	$795,000	1.362	47%

Budget Constraint $1,000,000
Each project must be between 10% and 50% allocated in funds

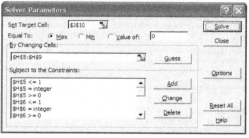

Suppose you have 5 projects you wish to allocate a fixed budget of $500,000 (this is your constraint) among, such that you will maximize the return to risk ratio (this is the objective function) subject to the requirements that each of these projects can be allocated anywhere between 10% and 50% of its total cost. You cannot allocate more than 50% of the cost of a project since you are only in the beginning stages of development while at least 10% of the project should be funded since all five projects have been previously found to be financially feasible. Using Excel's Solver add-in (use Tools/Add-Ins/Solver and then Tools/Solver) we calculate the optimal weights that will maximize the return to risk ratio.

Target cell is the objective function, which in this case is the total return to risk ratio weighted by each project, which is to be maximized. Next, add additional constraints including the budget constraint where the total cost allocated in the portfolio is = the budget constraint. In addition, for each project weight, set them to be = 0 and = 1 as well as weight as integers. This is essentially the difference between the prior linear programming and optimization routine which allows fractional projects to be executed while in integer linear programming, projects are either chosen (1.0) or not (0.0) and nothing in between is allowed (integer constraint).

Figure 8.9: Excel Solver on Integer Linear Programming

Portfolio Optimization and Linear Programming

	Cost	Return	Risk	Return-Risk Ratio	Allocation	Weighted Cost	Total Risk-Return	Weighted Risk
Project A	$500,000	19%	32%	0.594	10%	$50,000	0.059	3%
Project B	$625,000	23%	39%	0.590	10%	$62,500	0.059	4%
Project C	$345,000	15%	22%	0.682	50%	$172,500	0.341	11%
Project D	$290,000	16%	29%	0.552	50%	$145,000	0.276	15%
Project E	$450,000	17%	25%	0.680	16%	$70,000	0.106	4%
					Sum	$500,000	0.841	36%

Budget Constraint $500,000
Each project must be between 10% and 50% allocated in funds

Suppose you have 5 projects you wish to allocate a fixed budget of $500,000 (this is your constraint) among, such that you will maximize the return to risk ratio (this is the objective function) subject to the requirements that each of these projects can be allocated anywhere between 10% and 50% of its total cost. You cannot allocate more than 50% of the cost of a project since you are only in the beginning stages of development while at least 10% of the project should be funded since all five projects have been previously found to be financially feasible. Using Excel's Solver add-in (use Tools/Add-Ins/Solver and then Tools/Solver) we calculate the optimal weights that will maximize the return to risk ratio.

Target cell is the objective function, which in this case is the total return to risk ratio weighted by each project, which is to be maximized. Next, add additional constraints including the budget constraint where the total cost allocated in the portfolio is = the budget constraint. In addition, for each project weight, set them to be = 0.1 and = 0.5.

Figure 8.10: Excel Solver on Continuous Linear Programming

Questions

1. What is the difference between deterministic optimization and optimization under uncertainty?

2. Define then compare and contrast each of the following:

    a. Objective

    b. Constraint

    c. Decision variable

3. Explain what some of the problems are in a graphical linear programming approach and if they can be easily solved.

4. What are some of the approaches to solve an optimization problem? List each approach as well as their corresponding pros and cons.

CHAPTER 9 –
OPTIMIZATION UNDER
UNCERTAINTY

This chapter looks at the optimization process and methodologies in more detail as they pertain to using Risk Simulator. These methodologies include the use of continuous versus discrete integer optimization, as well as static versus dynamic and stochastic optimizations. The chapter then proceeds with several example optimization models to illustrate how the optimization process works. The first is the application of *continuous* optimization under uncertainty for a simple project selection model, where the idea is to allocate 100% of an individual's investment among several different asset classes (e.g., different types of mutual funds or investment styles: growth, value, aggressive growth, income, global, index, contrarian, momentum, and so forth). The second project deals with *discrete integer* optimization, where the idea is to look at several competing and nonmutually exclusive project choices, each with a different return, risk, and cost profile. The job of the analyst here is to find the best combination of projects that will satisfy the firm's budget constraints while maximizing the portfolio's total value. The chapter continues by running a portfolio investment efficient frontier by applying some of the advanced settings in Risk Simulator, continued by a stochastic optimization model where simulation is iteratively combined with optimization methods. Next, small case applications in the military on using portfolio optimization and efficient frontier are shown, together with a case on applying the optimal pricing structure on various goods and services by examining the price elasticity of demand. The chapter concludes with several appendices on running optimization outside of Excel (using ROV Optimizer for linking to large databases and for running large portfolios at super speed) and computing portfolio risk and return levels, as well as a detailed step-by-step set of hands-on exercises on setting up and running your own optimization routines.

OPTIMIZATION ALGORITHMS

Many algorithms exist to run optimization and many different procedures exist when optimization is coupled with Monte Carlo simulation. In Risk Simulator, there are three distinct optimization procedures and optimization types as well as different decision variable types. For instance, Risk Simulator can handle *Continuous Decision Variables* (1.2535, 0.2215, and so forth), *Integer Decision Variables* (e.g., 1, 2, 3, 4 or 1.5, 2.5, 3.5, and so forth), *Binary Decision Variables* (1 and 0 for go and no-go decisions), and *Mixed Decision Variables* (both integers and continuous variables). On top of that, Risk Simulator can handle *Linear Optimization* (i.e., when both the objective and constraints are all linear equations and functions) and *Nonlinear*

Optimizations (i.e., when the objective and constraints are a mixture of linear and nonlinear functions and equations).

As far as the optimization process is concerned, Risk Simulator can be used to run a *Discrete Optimization*, that is, an optimization that is run on a discrete or static model, where no simulations are run. In other words, all the inputs in the model are static and unchanging. This optimization type is applicable when the model is assumed to be known and no uncertainties exist. Also, a discrete optimization can first be run to determine the optimal portfolio and its corresponding optimal allocation of decision variables before more advanced optimization procedures are applied. For instance, before running a stochastic optimization problem, a discrete optimization is first run to determine if solutions to the optimization problem exist before a more protracted analysis is performed.

Next, *Dynamic Optimization* is applied when Monte Carlo simulation is used together with optimization. Another name for such a procedure is *Simulation-Optimization*. That is, a simulation is first run, then the results of the simulation are applied in the Excel model, and then an optimization is applied to the simulated values. In other words, a simulation is run for N trials, and then an optimization process is run for M iterations until the optimal results are obtained or an infeasible set is found. Using Risk Simulator's optimization module, you can choose which forecast and assumption statistics to use and replace in the model after the simulation is run. Then, these forecast statistics can be applied in the optimization process. This approach is useful when you have a large model with many interacting assumptions and forecasts, and when some of the forecast statistics are required in the optimization. For example, if the standard deviation of an assumption or forecast is required in the optimization model (e.g., computing the Sharpe Ratio in asset allocation and optimization problems where we have mean divided by standard deviation of the portfolio), then this approach should be used.

The *Stochastic Optimization* process, in contrast, is similar to the dynamic optimization procedure with the exception that the entire dynamic optimization process is repeated T times. That is, a simulation with N trials is run, and then an optimization is run with M iterations to obtain the optimal results. Then the process is replicated T times. The results will be a forecast chart of each decision variable with T values. In other words, a simulation is run and the forecast or assumption statistics are used in the optimization model to find the optimal allocation of decision variables. Then, another simulation is run, generating different forecast statistics, and these new updated values are then optimized, and so forth. Hence, the final decision variables will each have their own forecast chart, indicating the range of the optimal decision variables. For instance, instead of obtaining single-point estimates in the dynamic optimization procedure, you can now obtain a distribution of the decision variables, hence, a range of optimal values for each decision variable, also known as a stochastic optimization.

Finally, an Efficient Frontier optimization procedure applies the concepts of marginal increments and shadow pricing in optimization. That is, what would happen to the results of the optimization if one of the constraints were relaxed slightly? Say for instance, if the budget constraint is set at $1 million. What would happen to the portfolio's outcome and optimal decisions if the constraint were now $1.5 million, or $2 million, and so forth. This is the concept of the Markowitz efficient frontier in investment finance, where if the portfolio standard deviation is allowed to increase slightly, what additional returns will the portfolio generate? This process is similar to the dynamic optimization process with the exception that *one* of the constraints is allowed to change, and with each change, the simulation and optimization process is run. This process is best applied manually using Risk Simulator. This process can be run either manually (rerunning the optimization several times) or automatically (using Risk Simulator's changing constraint and efficient frontier functionality). As example, the manual process is: Run a dynamic or stochastic optimization, then rerun another optimization with a new constraint, and repeat that procedure several times. This manual process is important, as by changing the constraint, the analyst can determine if the results are similar or different, and, hence, whether it is worthy of any additional analysis, or to determine how far a marginal increase in the constraint should be to obtain a significant change in the objective and decision variables. This is done by comparing the forecast distribution of each decision variable after running a stochastic optimization. Alternatively, the automated efficient frontier approach will be shown later in the chapter.

One item is worthy of consideration. Other software products exist that supposedly perform stochastic optimization, but, in fact, they do not. For instance, after a simulation is run, then *one* iteration of the optimization process is generated, and then another simulation is run, then the *second* optimization iteration is generated and so forth. This process is simply a waste of time and resources; that is, in optimization, the model is put through a rigorous set of algorithms, where multiple iterations (ranging from several to thousands of iterations) are required to obtain the optimal results. Hence, generating *one* iteration at a time is a waste of time and resources. The same portfolio can be solved using Risk Simulator in under a minute as compared to multiple hours using such a backward approach. Also, such a simulation-optimization approach will typically yield bad results and is not a stochastic optimization approach. Be extremely careful of such methodologies when applying optimization to your models.

The following are two example optimization problems. One uses continuous decision variables while the other uses discrete integer decision variables. In either model, you can apply discrete optimization, dynamic optimization, or stochastic optimization, or even manually generate efficient frontiers with shadow pricing. Any of these approaches can be used for these two examples. Therefore, for simplicity, only the model setup is illustrated and it is up to the user to decide which optimization process to run. Also, the continuous decision variable example uses the nonlinear optimization approach (because the portfolio risk computed is a nonlinear function, and the objective is a nonlinear function of portfolio returns divided by portfolio risks) while the second example of an integer optimization is an example of a linear optimization model (its objective and all of its constraints are linear). Therefore, these two examples encapsulate all of the procedures aforementioned.

CONTINUOUS OPTIMIZATION

Figure 9.1 illustrates the sample continuous optimization model. The example here uses the example file located at *Risk Simulator | Example Models | 11 Continuous Optimization*. In this example, there are 10 distinct asset classes (e.g., different types of mutual funds, stocks, or assets) where the idea is to most efficiently and effectively allocate the portfolio holdings such that the best *bang for the buck* is obtained; that is, to generate the best portfolio returns possible given the risks inherent in each asset class. In order to truly understand the concept of optimization, we must delve more deeply into this sample model to see how the optimization process can best be applied.

The model shows the 10 asset classes and each asset class has its own set of annualized returns and annualized volatilities. These return and risk measures are annualized values such that they can be consistently compared across different asset classes. Returns are computed using the geometric average of the relative returns while the risks are computed using the logarithmic relative stock returns approach. See the first appendix to this chapter for details on computing the annualized volatility and annualized returns on a stock or asset class.

	Asset Class Description	Annualized Returns	Volatility Risk	Allocation Weights	Required Minimum Allocation	Required Maximum Allocation	Return to Risk Ratio	Returns Ranking (Hi-Lo)	Risk Ranking (Lo-Hi)	Return to Risk Ranking (Hi-Lo)	Allocation Ranking (Hi-Lo)
						ASSET ALLOCATION OPTIMIZATION MODEL					
	Asset Class 1	10.54%	12.36%	10.00%	5.00%	35.00%	0.8524	9	2	7	1
	Asset Class 2	11.25%	16.23%	10.00%	5.00%	35.00%	0.6929	7	8	10	1
	Asset Class 3	11.84%	15.64%	10.00%	5.00%	35.00%	0.7570	6	7	9	1
	Asset Class 4	10.64%	12.35%	10.00%	5.00%	35.00%	0.8615	8	1	5	1
	Asset Class 5	13.25%	13.28%	10.00%	5.00%	35.00%	0.9977	5	4	2	1
	Asset Class 6	14.21%	14.39%	10.00%	5.00%	35.00%	0.9875	3	6	3	1
	Asset Class 7	15.53%	14.25%	10.00%	5.00%	35.00%	1.0898	1	5	1	1
	Asset Class 8	14.95%	16.44%	10.00%	5.00%	35.00%	0.9094	2	9	4	1
	Asset Class 9	14.16%	16.50%	10.00%	5.00%	35.00%	0.8584	4	10	6	1
	Asset Class 10	10.06%	12.50%	10.00%	5.00%	35.00%	0.8045	10	3	8	1
	Portfolio Total	*12.6419%*	*4.58%*	*100.00%*							
	Return to Risk Ratio	*2.7596*									

Specifications of the optimization model:

Objective: *Maximize Return to Risk Ratio (C18)*
Decision Variables: *Allocation Weights (E6:E15)*
Restrictions on Decision Variables: *Minimum and Maximum Required (F6:G15)*
Constraints: *Portfolio Total Allocation Weights 100% (E17 is set to 100%)*

Additional specifications:

1. One can always maximize portfolio total returns or minimize the portfolio total risk.
2. Incorporate Monte Carlo simulation in the model by simulating the returns and volatility of each asset class and apply Simulation-Optimization techniques.
3. The portfolio can be optimized as is without simulation using Static Optimization techniques.

Figure 9.1: Continuous Optimization Model

The Allocation Weights in column E hold the decision variables, which are the variables that need to be tweaked and tested such that the total weight is constrained at 100% (cell E17). Typically, to start the optimization, we will set these cells to a uniform value, where in this case, cells E6 to E15 are set at 10% each. In addition, each decision variable may have specific restrictions in its allowed range. In this example, the lower and upper allocations allowed are 5% and 35%, as seen in columns F and G. This means that each asset class may have its own allocation boundaries. Next, column H shows the return to risk ratio, which is simply the return percentage divided by the risk percentage, where the higher this value, the higher the *bang for the buck*. The remaining model shows the individual asset class rankings by returns, risk, return to risk ratio, and allocation. In other words, these rankings show at a glance which asset class has the lowest risk, or the highest return, and so forth.

The portfolio's total returns in cell C17 is *SUMPRODUCT(C6:C15, E6:E15)*, that is, the sum of the allocation weights multiplied by the annualized returns for each asset class. In other words, we have $R_P = \omega_A R_A + \omega_B R_B + \omega_C R_C + \omega_D R_D$, where R_P is the return on the portfolio, $R_{A,B,C,D}$ are the individual returns on the projects, and $\omega_{A,B,C,D}$ are the respective weights or capital allocation across each project.

In addition, the portfolio's diversified risk in cell D17 is computed by taking

$$\sigma_P = \sqrt{\sum_{i=1}^{n} \omega_i^2 \sigma_i^2 + \sum_{i=1}^{n} \sum_{j=1}^{m} 2\omega_i \omega_j \rho_{i,j} \sigma_i \sigma_j}$$. Here, $\rho_{i,j}$ are the respective cross-correlations between

the asset classes. Hence, if the cross-correlations are negative, there are risk diversification effects, and the portfolio risk decreases. However, to simplify the computations here, we assume zero correlations among the asset classes through this portfolio risk computation, but assume the correlations when applying simulation on the returns as will be seen later. Therefore, instead of applying static correlations among these different asset returns, we apply the correlations in the simulation assumptions themselves, creating a more dynamic relationship among the simulated return values.

Finally, the return to risk ratio or Sharpe Ratio is computed for the portfolio. This value is seen in cell C18 and represents the objective to be maximized in this optimization exercise. To summarize, we have the following specifications in this example model:

Objective:	Maximize Return to Risk Ratio (C18)
Decision Variables:	Allocation Weights (E6:E15)
Restrictions on Decision Variables:	Minimum and Maximum Required (F6:G15)
Constraints:	Total Allocation Weights Sum to 100% (E17)

Procedure

- Open the example file at *Risk Simulator | Example Models | 11 Continuous Optimization* and start a new profile by clicking on *Risk Simulator | New Profile* and provide it a name.

- The first step in optimization is to set the decision variables. Select cell E6 and set the first decision variable (*Risk Simulator | Optimization | Set Decision*) and click on the link icon to select the name cell (B6), as well as the lower bound and upper bound values at cells F6 and G6. Then, using Risk Simulator *Copy*, copy this cell E6 decision variable and paste the decision variable to the remaining cells in E7 to E15.

- The second step in optimization is to set the constraint. There is only one constraint here, that is, the total allocation in the portfolio must sum to 100%. So, click on *Risk Simulator | Optimization | Constraints...* and select *ADD* to add a new constraint. Then, select the cell E17 and make it equal (=) to 100%. Click *OK* when done.

- The final step in optimization is to set the objective function and start the optimization by selecting the objective cell C18 and *Risk Simulator | Optimization | Set Objective* and then run the optimization by selecting *Risk Simulator | Optimization | Run Optimization* and selecting the optimization of choice (Static Optimization, Dynamic Optimization, or Stochastic Optimization). To get started, select *Static Optimization*. Check to make sure the objective cell is set for C18 and select *Maximize*. You can now review the decision variables and constraints if required, or click *OK* to run the static optimization.

- Once the optimization is complete, you may select *Revert* to revert back to the original values of the decision variables as well as the objective, or select *Replace* to apply the optimized decision variables. Typically, Replace is chosen after the optimization is done.

Figure 9.2 shows the screen shots of the preceding procedural steps. You can add simulation assumptions on the model's returns and risk (columns C and D) and apply the dynamic optimization and stochastic optimization for additional practice.

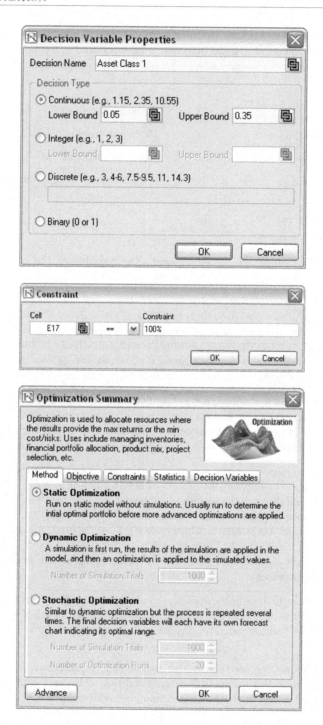

Figure 9.2: Running Continuous Optimization in Risk Simulator

Results Interpretation

The optimization's final results are shown in Figure 9.3, where the optimal allocation of assets for the portfolio is seen in cells E6:E15. Given the restrictions of each asset fluctuating between 5% and 35%, and where the sum of the allocation must equal 100%, the allocation which maximizes the return to risk ratio is seen in Figure 9.3.

A few important things must be noted when reviewing the results and optimization procedures performed thus far:

- The correct way to run the optimization is to maximize the *bang for the buck* or returns to risk Sharpe Ratio as we have done.

- If instead we maximized the total portfolio returns, the optimal allocation result is trivial and does not require optimization to obtain. That is, simply allocate 5% (the minimum allowed) to the lowest 8 assets, 35% (the maximum allowed) to the highest returning asset, and the remaining (25%) to the second-best returns asset. Optimization is not required. However, when allocating the portfolio this way, the risk is a lot higher as compared to when maximizing the returns to risk ratio, although the portfolio returns by themselves are higher.

- In contrast, one can minimize the total portfolio risk, but the returns will now be less.

The following table illustrates the results from the three different objectives being optimized.

Objective:	Portfolio Returns	Portfolio Risk	Portfolio Returns to Risk Ratio
Maximize Returns to Risk Ratio	12.69%	4.52%	2.8091
Maximize Returns	13.97%	6.77%	2.0636
Minimize Risk	12.38%	4.46%	2.7754

From the table, the best approach is to maximize the returns to risk ratio, that is, for the same amount of risk, this allocation provides the highest amount of return. Conversely, for the same amount of return, this allocation provides the lowest amount of risk possible. This approach of *bang for the buck* or returns to risk ratio is the cornerstone of the Markowitz efficient frontier in modern portfolio theory. That is, if we constrained the total portfolio risk levels and successively increased it over time we would obtain several efficient portfolio allocations for different risk characteristics. Thus, different efficient portfolio allocations can be obtained for different individuals with different risk preferences.

ASSET ALLOCATION OPTIMIZATION MODEL

Asset Class Description	Annualized Returns	Volatility Risk	Allocation Weights	Required Minimum Allocation	Required Maximum Allocation	Return to Risk Ratio	Returns Ranking (Hi-Lo)	Risk Ranking (Lo-Hi)	Return to Risk Ranking (Hi-Lo)	Allocation Ranking (Hi-Lo)
Asset Class 1	10.54%	12.36%	11.09%	5.00%	35.00%	0.8524	9	2	7	4
Asset Class 2	11.25%	16.23%	6.87%	5.00%	35.00%	0.6929	7	8	10	10
Asset Class 3	11.84%	15.64%	7.78%	5.00%	35.00%	0.7570	6	7	9	9
Asset Class 4	10.64%	12.35%	11.22%	5.00%	35.00%	0.8615	8	1	5	3
Asset Class 5	13.25%	13.28%	12.08%	5.00%	35.00%	0.9977	5	4	2	2
Asset Class 6	14.21%	14.39%	11.04%	5.00%	35.00%	0.9875	3	6	3	5
Asset Class 7	15.53%	14.25%	12.30%	5.00%	35.00%	1.0898	1	5	1	1
Asset Class 8	14.95%	16.44%	8.90%	5.00%	35.00%	0.9094	2	9	4	7
Asset Class 9	14.16%	16.50%	8.37%	5.00%	35.00%	0.8584	4	10	6	8
Asset Class 10	10.06%	12.50%	10.35%	5.00%	35.00%	0.8045	10	3	8	6
Portfolio Total	*12.6920%*	*4.52%*	*100.00%*							
Return to Risk Ratio	*2.8091*									

Specifications of the optimization model:

Objective:	*Maximize Return to Risk Ratio (C18)*
Decision Variables:	*Allocation Weights (E6:E15)*
Restrictions on Decision Variables:	*Minimum and Maximum Required (F6:G15)*
Constraints:	*Portfolio Total Allocation Weights 100% (E17 is set to 100%)*

Additional specifications:

1. One can always maximize portfolio total returns or minimize the portfolio total risk.
2. Incorporate Monte Carlo simulation in the model by simulating the returns and volatility of each asset class and apply Simulation-Optimization techniques.
3. The portfolio can be optimized as is without simulation using Static Optimization techniques.

Figure 9.3: Continuous Optimization Results

DISCRETE INTEGER OPTIMIZATION

Sometimes, the decision variables are not continuous but discrete integers (e.g., 1, 2, 3) or binary (e.g., 0 and 1). We can use such binary decision variables as on-off switches or go/no-go decisions. Figure 9.4 illustrates a project selection model where there are 12 projects listed. The example here uses the file found in *Risk Simulator | Example Models | 12 Optimization Discrete*. Each project like before, has its own returns (ENPV and NPV for expanded net present value and net present value—the ENPV is simply the NPV plus any strategic real options values), costs of implementation, risks, and so forth. If required, this model can be modified to include required full-time equivalences (FTE) and other resources of various functions, and additional constraints can be set on these additional resources. The inputs into this model are typically linked from other spreadsheet models. For instance, each project will have its own discounted cash flow or returns on investment model. The application here is to maximize the portfolio's Sharpe Ratio subject to some budget allocation. Many other versions of this model can be created, for instance, maximizing the portfolio returns, or minimizing the risks, or add additional constraints where the total number of projects chosen cannot exceed 6, and so forth and so on. All of these items can be run using this existing model.

Projects	ENPV	Cost	Risk $	Risk %	Return to Risk Ratio	Profitability Index	Selection
Project 1	$458.00	$1,732.44	$54.96	12.00%	8.33	1.26	1.0000
Project 2	$1,954.00	$859.00	$1,914.92	98.00%	1.02	3.27	1.0000
Project 3	$1,599.00	$1,845.00	$1,551.03	97.00%	1.03	1.87	1.0000
Project 4	$2,251.00	$1,645.00	$1,012.95	45.00%	2.22	2.37	1.0000
Project 5	$849.00	$458.00	$925.41	109.00%	0.92	2.85	1.0000
Project 6	$758.00	$52.00	$560.92	74.00%	1.35	15.58	1.0000
Project 7	$2,845.00	$758.00	$5,633.10	198.00%	0.51	4.75	1.0000
Project 8	$1,235.00	$115.00	$926.25	75.00%	1.33	11.74	1.0000
Project 9	$1,945.00	$125.00	$2,100.60	108.00%	0.93	16.56	1.0000
Project 10	$2,250.00	$458.00	$1,912.50	85.00%	1.18	5.91	1.0000
Project 11	$549.00	$45.00	$263.52	48.00%	2.08	13.20	1.0000
Project 12	$525.00	$105.00	$309.75	59.00%	1.69	6.00	1.0000
Total	$17,218.00	$8,197.44	$7,007	40.70%			12.00
Goal:	MAX	< =$5000					<=6
Sharpe Ratio	2.4573						

ENPV is the expected NPV of each investment or project, while Cost can be the total cost of investment, and Risk is the Coefficient of Variation of the project's ENPV.

Figure 9.4: Discrete Integer Optimization Model

Procedure

- Open the example file at *Risk Simulator | Example Models | 12 Discrete Optimization* and start a new profile by clicking on *Risk Simulator | New Profile* and provide it a name.

- The first step in optimization is to set up the decision variables. Set the first decision variable by selecting cell J4, and select *Risk Simulator | Optimization | Set Decision*, click on the link icon to select the name cell (B4), and select the *Binary* variable. Then, using Risk Simulator *Copy*, copy this J4 decision variable cell and paste the decision variable to the remaining cells in J5 to J15.

- The second step in optimization is to set the constraint. There are two constraints here, that is, the total budget allocation in the portfolio must be less than $5,000 and the total number of projects must not exceed 6. So, click on *Risk Simulator | Optimization | Constraints...* and select *ADD* to add a new constraint. Then, select the cell D17 and make it less than or equal (<=) to 5000. Repeat the step by setting cell J17 <= 6.

- The final step in optimization is to set the objective function and start the optimization by selecting cell C19 and selecting *Risk Simulator | Optimization | Set Objective* and then run the optimization (*Risk Simulator | Optimization | Run Optimization*) and selecting the optimization of choice (Static Optimization, Dynamic Optimization, or Stochastic Optimization). To get started, select *Static Optimization*. Check to make sure that the objective cell is C19 and select *Maximize*. You can now review the decision variables and constraints if required, or click *OK* to run the static optimization.

Figure 9.5 shows the screenshots of the foregoing procedural steps. You can add simulation assumptions on the model's ENPV and Risk (columns C and F) and apply the dynamic optimization and stochastic optimization for additional practice.

Results Interpretation

Figure 9.6 shows a sample optimal selection of projects that maximizes the Sharpe Ratio. In contrast, one can always maximize total revenues, but as before, this process is trivial and simply involves choosing the highest returning project and going down the list until you run out of money or exceed the budget constraint. Doing so will yield theoretically undesirable projects as the highest yielding projects typically hold higher risks. Now, if desired, you can replicate the optimization using a stochastic or dynamic optimization by adding in assumptions in the ENPV and Risk values.

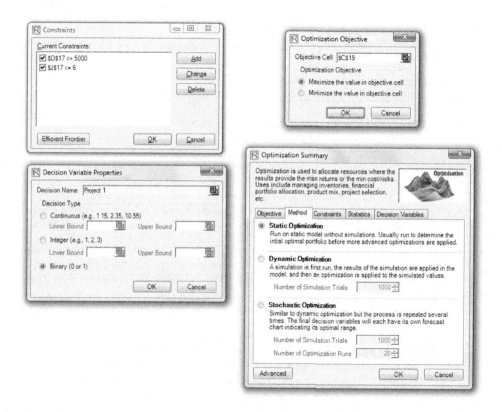

Figure 9.5: Running Discrete Integer Optimization in Risk Simulator

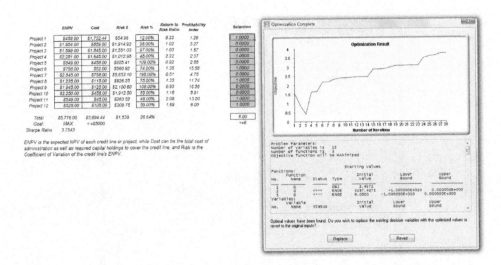

	ENPV	Cost	Risk $	Risk %	Return to Risk Ratio	Profitability Index		Selection
Project 1	$458.00	$1,732.44	$54.96	12.00%	8.33	1.26		1.0000
Project 2	$1,954.00	$859.00	$1,914.92	98.00%	1.02	3.27		0.0000
Project 3	$1,599.00	$1,545.00	$1,551.03	97.00%	1.03	1.87		0.0000
Project 4	$2,251.00	$1,645.00	$1,012.95	45.00%	2.22	2.37		1.0000
Project 5	$849.00	$458.00	$925.41	109.00%	0.92	2.85		0.0000
Project 6	$758.00	$52.00	$560.92	74.00%	1.35	15.58		1.0000
Project 7	$2,845.00	$758.00	$5,653.10	198.00%	0.51	4.75		0.0000
Project 8	$1,235.00	$115.00	$926.25	75.00%	1.33	11.74		0.0000
Project 9	$1,945.00	$125.00	$2,100.60	108.00%	0.93	16.56		0.0000
Project 10	$2,250.00	$458.00	$1,912.50	85.00%	1.18	5.91		0.0000
Project 11	$549.00	$45.00	$263.52	48.00%	2.08	13.20		1.0000
Project 12	$529.00	$105.00	$209.75	39.00%	1.69	6.00		1.0000
Total	$5,776.00	$3,694.44	$1,539	26.64%				6.00
Goal:	MAX	<=5000						<=6
Sharpe Ratio	3.7543							

ENPV is the expected NPV of each credit line or project, while Cost can be the total cost of administration as well as required capital holdings to cover the credit line, and Risk is the Coefficient of Variation of the credit line's ENPV.

Figure 9.6: Optimal Selection of Projects That Maximizes the Sharpe Ratio

EFFICIENT FRONTIER AND ADVANCED OPTIMIZATION SETTINGS

Figure 9.7 shows the efficient frontier constraints for optimization. You can get to this interface by clicking on the *Efficient Frontier* button *after* you have set some constraints. You can now make these constraints changing. That is, each of the constraints can be created to step through between some minimum and maximum value. As an example, the constraint in cell J17 <= 6 can be set to run between 4 and 8 (Figure 9.7). That is, five optimizations will be run, each with the following constraints: J17 <= 4, J17 <= 5, J17 <= 6, J17 <= 7, and J17 <= 8. The optimal results will then be plotted as an efficient frontier and the report will be generated (Figure 9.8).

Specifically, following are the steps required to create a changing constraint:

- In an optimization model (i.e., a model with Objective, Decision Variables, and Constraints already set up), click on *Risk Simulator | Optimization | Constraints* and then click on *Efficient Frontier*.

- Select the constraint you want to change or step (e.g., J17), enter the parameters for Min, Max, and Step Size (Figure 9.7), and click *ADD,* then *OK,* and *OK* again. You should *deselect* the D17 <= 5000 constraint before running.

- Run Optimization as usual (*Risk Simulator | Optimization | Run Optimization*). You can choose static, dynamic, or stochastic. To get started, select the *Static Optimization* to run.

- The results will be shown as a user interface (Figure 9.8). Click on *Create Report* to generate a report worksheet with all the details of the optimization runs.

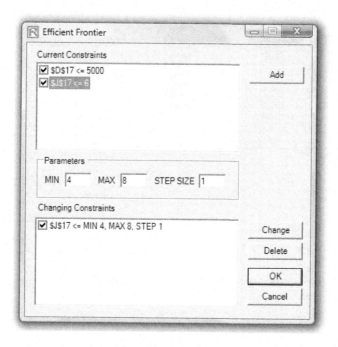

Figure 9.7: Generating Changing Constraints in an Efficient Frontier

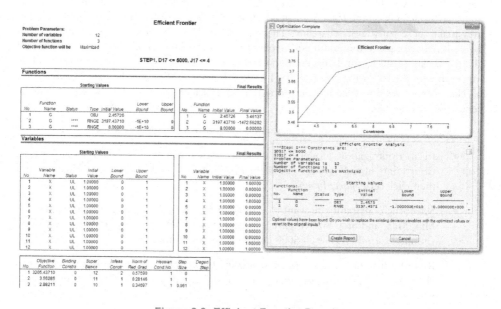

Figure 9.8: Efficient Frontier Results

STOCHASTIC OPTIMIZATION

This example illustrates the application of stochastic optimization using a sample model with four asset classes each with different risk and return characteristics. The idea here is to find the best portfolio allocation such that the portfolio's bang for the buck, or returns to risk ratio, is maximized. That is, the goal is to allocate 100 percent of an individual's investment among several different asset classes (e.g., different types of mutual funds or investment styles: growth, value, aggressive growth, income, global, index, contrarian, momentum, etc.). This model is different from others because there exist several simulation assumptions (risk and return values for each asset in columns C and D), as seen in Figure 9.9.

A simulation is run, then optimization is executed, and the entire process is repeated multiple times to obtain distributions of each decision variable. The entire analysis can be automated using Stochastic Optimization.

In order to run an optimization, several key specifications on the model have to be identified first:

Objective:	Maximize Return to Risk Ratio (C12)
Decision Variables:	Allocation Weights (E6:E9)
Restrictions on Decision Variables:	Minimum and Maximum Required (F6:G9)
Constraints:	Portfolio Total Weights 100% (E11=100%)
Simulation Assumptions:	Return and Risk Values (C6:D9)

The model shows the various asset classes. Each asset class has its own set of annualized returns and annualized volatilities. These return and risk measures are annualized values such that they can be consistently compared across different asset classes. Returns are computed using the geometric average of the relative returns, while the risks are computed using the logarithmic relative stock returns approach. See the second appendix in this chapter on volatility models for computational details.

Column E, the Allocation Weights, holds the decision variables, which are the variables that need to be tweaked and tested such that the total weight is constrained at 100% (cell E11). Typically, to start the optimization, we will set these cells to a uniform value. In this case, cells E6 to E9 are set at 25% each. In addition, each decision variable may have specific restrictions in its allowed range. In this example, the lower and upper allocations allowed are 10% and 40%, as seen in columns F and G. This setting means that each asset class may have its own allocation boundaries.

	A	B	C	D	E	F	G	H
1								
2								
3			ASSET ALLOCATION OPTIMIZATION MODEL					
4								
5		Asset Class Description	Annualized Returns	Volatility Risk	Allocation Weights	Required Minimum Allocation	Required Maximum Allocation	Return to Risk Ratio
6		Asset 1	10.60%	12.41%	25.00%	10.00%	40.00%	0.8544
7		Asset 2	11.21%	16.16%	25.00%	10.00%	40.00%	0.6937
8		Asset 3	10.61%	15.93%	25.00%	10.00%	40.00%	0.6660
9		Asset 4	10.52%	12.40%	25.00%	10.00%	40.00%	0.8480
10								
11		Portfolio Total	10.7356%	7.17%	100.00%			
12		Return to Risk Ratio	1.4970					

Figure 9.9: Asset Allocation Model Ready for Stochastic Optimization

Next, column H shows the return to risk ratio, which is simply the return percentage divided by the risk percentage for each asset, where the higher this value, the higher the bang for the buck. The remaining parts of the model show the individual asset class rankings by returns, risk, return to risk ratio, and allocation. In other words, these rankings show at a glance which asset class has the lowest risk, or the highest return, and so forth.

Running an Optimization

To run this model, simply click on *Risk Simulator | Optimization | Run Optimization*. Alternatively, and for practice, you can set up the model using the following steps:

1. Open the example model at *Risk Simulator | Example Models | 13 Stochastic Optimization*.

2. Start a new profile (*Risk Simulator | New Profile*).

3. For stochastic optimization, set distributional assumptions on the risk and returns for each asset class. That is, select cell *C6*, set an assumption (*Risk Simulator | Set Input Assumption*), and make your own assumption as required. Repeat for cells C7 to D9.

4. Select cell *E6*, define the decision variable (*Risk Simulator | Optimization | Set Decision* or click on the Set Decision D icon), and make it a *Continuous Variable*. Then link the decision variable's name and minimum/maximum required to the relevant cells (B6, F6, G6).

5. Then use the Risk Simulator *Copy* on cell *E6*, select cells *E7 to E9*, and use Risk Simulator Paste (*Risk Simulator | Copy Parameter* and *Risk Simulator | Paste Parameter*, or use the copy and paste icons). Remember not to use Excel's regular copy and paste functions.

6. Next, set up the optimization's constraints by selecting *Risk Simulator | Optimization | Constraints*, selecting *ADD*, and selecting the cell *E11* and making it equal 100% (total allocation, and do not forget the % sign).

7. Select cell *C12*, the objective to be maximized, and make it the objective: *Risk Simulator | Optimization | Set Objective* or click on the O icon.

8. Run the optimization by going to *Risk Simulator | Optimization | Run Optimization*. Review the different tabs to make sure that all the required inputs in steps 2 and 3 are correct. Select *Stochastic Optimization* and let it run for *500 trials* repeated *20 times* (Figure 9.10 illustrates these setup steps).

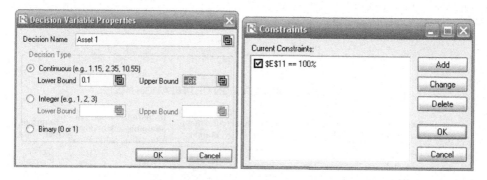

Figure 9.10: Setting Up the Stochastic Optimization Problem (continues)

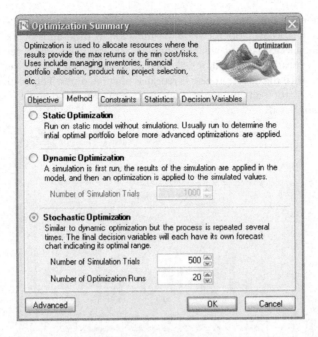

Figure 9.10: Setting Up the Stochastic Optimization Problem (continued)

Click *OK* when the simulation completes and a detailed stochastic optimization report will be generated along with forecast charts of the decision variables.

Viewing and Interpreting Forecast Results

Stochastic optimization is performed when a simulation is first run and then the optimization is run. Then the whole analysis is repeated multiple times. The result is a distribution of each decision variable rather than a single-point estimate (Figure 9.11). So instead of saying you should invest 30.53% in Asset 1, the optimal decision is to invest between 30.19% and 30.88% as long as the total portfolio sums to 100%. This way, the results provide management or decision makers a range of flexibility in the optimal decisions, and all the while accounting for the risks and uncertainties in the inputs.

Notes

- *Super Speed Simulation with Optimization.* You can also run stochastic optimization with super speed simulation. To do this, first reset the optimization by resetting all four decision variables back to 25%. Next select *Run Optimization,* click on the *Advanced* button (Figure 9.10), and select the checkbox for *Run Super Speed Simulation.* Then, in the run optimization user interface, select *Stochastic Optimization* on the *Method* tab and set it to run 500 trials and 20 optimization runs, and click *OK.* This approach will integrate the super speed simulation with optimization. Notice how much faster the stochastic optimization runs. You can now quickly rerun the optimization with a higher number of simulation trials.

- *Simulation Statistics for Stochastic and Dynamic Optimization.* Notice that if there are input simulation assumptions in the optimization model (i.e., these input assumptions are required to run the dynamic or stochastic optimization routines), the *Statistics* tab is now populated in the *Run Optimization* user interface. You can select from the droplist the statistics you want, such as average, standard deviation, coefficient of variation, conditional mean, conditional variance, a specific percentile, and so forth. Thus, if you run a stochastic optimization, a simulation of thousands of trials will first run; then the selected statistic will be computed and this value will be temporarily placed in the simulation assumption cell; then an optimization will be run based on this statistic; then the entire process is repeated multiple times. This method is important and useful for banking applications in computing Conditional Value at Risk or Conditional VaR.

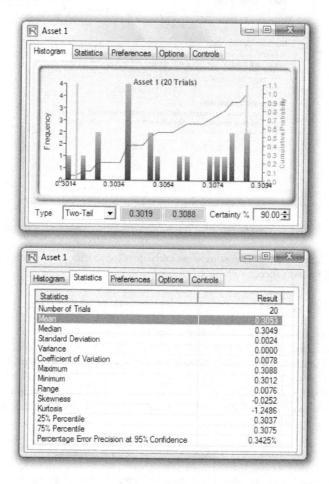

Figure 9.11: Simulated Results from the Stochastic Optimization Approach

OPTIMIZATION APPLICATION EXAMPLE: MILITARY PORTFOLIO AND EFFICIENT FRONTIER

This section illustrates a sample model from the ROV Modeling Toolkit—another software tool developed by Real Options Valuation, Inc., that contains more than 300 models and 800 functions. Figure 9.12 shows a model with 20 projects with different risk-return characteristics as well as several qualitative measures such as strategic score, military readiness score, tactical score, comprehensive score, and so forth. These scores are obtained through subject-matter experts, for instance, decision makers, leaders, and managers of organizations, where their expert opinions are gathered through the double-blind Delphi method. After being scrubbed (e.g., extreme values are eliminated, large data variations are analyzed, multiple iterations of the Delphi method are performed, etc.), their respective scores can be entered into a Distributional Fitting routine to find the best-fitting distribution, or used to develop a Custom Distribution for each project.

The central idea of this model is to find the best portfolio allocation such that the portfolio's total comprehensive strategic score and profits are maximized. That is, it is used to find the best project mix in the portfolio that maximizes the total *Profit*Score* measure, where *Profit* points to the portfolio level net returns after considering the risks and costs of each project and the *Score* measures the total comprehensive score of the portfolio, all the while being subject to the constraints on number of projects, budget constraint, full-time equivalent (FTE) resource restrictions, and strategic ranking constraints.

Objective:	Maximize total portfolio returns times the portfolio comprehensive score (C28)
Decision Variables:	Allocation or go/no-go decision (J5:J24)
Restrictions on Decision Variables:	Binary decision variables (0 or 1)
Constraints:	Total cost (E26) is less than or equal to $3800 (in thousands or millions of dollars), and less than or equal to 10 projects selected (J26) in the entire portfolio
	FTE resources have to be less than or equal to 80 (M26), total strategic ranking for the entire portfolio must be less than or equal to 100 (F26)

Military Portfolio Optimization

Project Name	ENPV	NPV	Cost	Strategy Ranking	Return to Rank Ratio	Profitability Index	Selection	Military Score	Tactical Score	FTE Resources	Comprehensive Score
Project 1	$458.00	$150.76	$1,732.44	1.20	381.67	1.09	1	8.10	2.31	1.20	1.98
Project 2	$1,954.00	$245.00	$859.00	9.80	199.39	1.29	1	1.27	4.83	2.50	1.76
Project 3	$1,599.00	$458.00	$1,845.00	9.70	164.85	1.25	1	9.88	4.75	3.60	2.77
Project 4	$2,251.00	$529.00	$1,645.00	4.50	500.22	1.32	1	8.83	1.61	4.50	2.07
Project 5	$849.00	$564.00	$458.00	10.90	77.89	2.23	1	5.02	6.25	5.50	2.94
Project 6	$758.00	$135.00	$52.00	7.40	102.43	3.60	1	3.64	5.79	9.20	3.26
Project 7	$2,845.00	$311.00	$758.00	19.80	143.69	1.41	1	5.27	6.47	12.50	4.04
Project 8	$1,235.00	$754.00	$115.00	7.50	164.67	7.56	1	9.80	7.16	5.30	3.63
Project 9	$1,945.00	$198.00	$125.00	10.80	180.09	2.58	1	5.68	2.39	6.30	2.16
Project 10	$2,250.00	$785.00	$458.00	8.50	264.71	2.71	1	8.29	4.41	4.50	2.67
Project 11	$549.00	$35.00	$45.00	4.80	114.38	1.78	1	7.52	4.65	4.90	2.75
Project 12	$525.00	$75.00	$105.00	5.90	88.98	1.71	1	5.54	5.09	5.20	2.69
Project 13	$816.00	$451.00	$48.00	2.80	184.29	10.40	1	2.51	2.17	4.60	1.66
Project 14	$499.00	$458.00	$351.00	9.40	53.09	2.30	1	9.41	9.49	9.90	4.85
Project 15	$859.00	$125.00	$421.00	6.50	132.15	1.30	1	6.91	9.62	7.20	4.25
Project 16	$684.00	$458.00	$124.00	3.90	226.67	4.69	1	7.06	9.98	7.50	4.46
Project 17	$956.00	$124.00	$521.00	15.40	62.06	1.24	1	1.25	2.50	8.60	2.07
Project 18	$854.00	$164.00	$512.00	21.00	40.67	1.32	1	3.09	2.90	4.30	1.70
Project 19	$195.00	$45.00	$5.00	1.20	162.50	10.00	1	5.25	1.22	4.10	1.86
Project 20	$210.00	$85.00	$21.00	1.00	210.00	5.05	1	2.01	4.06	5.20	2.50
Total	$22,191.00		$10,200.44	162.00			20	116.32	97.65	116.60	56.08
Profit/Rank	$136.98										
Profit*Score	$1,244,365.33	Maximize	<=$3800	<=100			x <=10			<=80	

Budget	Comprehensive Score	Tactical Score	Military Score	Allowed Projects	ROI-RANK Objective
$3,800.00	33.15	62.64	58.58	10	$470,235.60
$4,800.00	36.33	68.85	66.86	11	$521,645.92
$5,800.00	38.40	70.46	75.69	12	$623,557.79
$6,800.00	39.94	72.14	82.31	13	$659,947.99
$7,800.00	39.76	70.05	86.54	14	$676,279.81

Figure 9.12: The Project Selection Optimization Model

Running an Optimization

To run this preset model, simply open the profile (*Risk Simulator | Change Profile*) and select *Military Portfolio and Efficient Frontier*. Then run the optimization (*Risk Simulator | Optimization | Run Optimization*) or, for practice, set up the model yourself by following these steps:

1. Start a new profile (*Risk Simulator | New Profile*) and give it a name.

2. In this example, all the allocations are required to be binary (0 or 1) values, so, first select cell J5 and make this a decision variable in the Integer Optimization worksheet. Select cell J5 and define it as a decision variable (*Risk Simulator | Optimization | Set Decision*, or click on the Set Decision icon) and make it a Binary Variable. This setting automatically sets the minimum to 0 and maximum to 1 and can only take on a value of 0 or 1. Then use the Risk Simulator *Copy* on cell J5, select cells J6 to J24, and use Risk Simulator *Paste* (*Risk Simulator | Copy Parameter* and *Risk Simulator | Paste Parameter*, or use the Risk Simulator copy and paste icons, not the Excel copy/paste).

3. Next, set up the optimization's constraints by selecting *Risk Simulator | Optimization | Constraints* and selecting *ADD*. Then link to cell *E26*, and make it *<= 3800*, select *ADD* one more time, click on the link icon, and point to cell *J26* and set it to *<=10*. Continue with adding the other constraints (cell *M26 <= 80* and *F26 <= 100*).

4. Select cell *C28*, the objective to be maximized, select *Risk Simulator | Optimization | Set Objective*, choose *Maximize* and *OK*.

5. Then select *Risk Simulator | Optimization | Run Optimization*. Review the different tabs to make sure that all the required inputs in steps 2 and 3 are correct. You may now select the optimization method of choice (e.g., *Static Optimization*) and click *OK* to run the optimization. The model setup is illustrated in Figure 9.13.

Note: Remember that if you want to run either a dynamic or stochastic optimization routine, make sure that first you have assumptions defined in the model. That is, make sure that some of the cells in C5:C24 and E5:F24 are assumptions. The suggestion for this model is to run a *Static Optimization*.

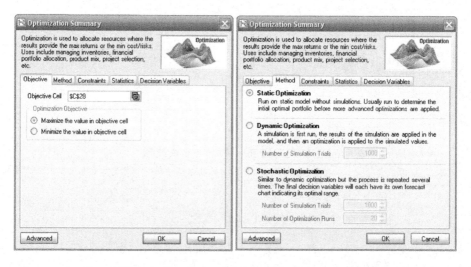

Figure 9.13: Setting Up an Optimization Model (continues)

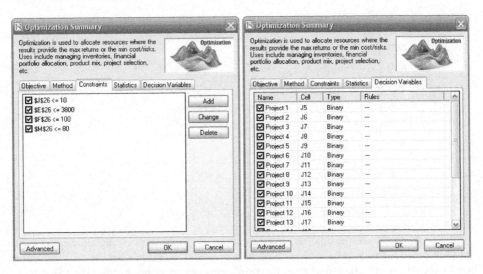

Figure 9.13: Setting Up an Optimization Model (continued)

Portfolio Efficient Frontier

Clearly, running the optimization procedure will yield an optimal portfolio of projects where the constraints are satisfied. This result represents a single optimal portfolio point on the efficient frontier, for example, Portfolio B on the chart in Figure 9.14. Then, by subsequently changing some of the constraints, for instance, by increasing the budget and allowed projects, we can rerun the optimization to produce another optimal portfolio given these new constraints. Therefore, a series of optimal portfolio allocations can be determined and graphed. This graphical representation of all optimal portfolios is called the *Portfolio Efficient Frontier*. At this juncture, each point represents a portfolio allocation, for instance, Portfolio B might represent projects 1, 2, 5, 6, 7, 8, 10, 15, and so forth, while Portfolio C might represent projects 2, 6, 7, 9, 12, 15, and so forth, each resulting in different tactical, military, or comprehensive scores, and portfolio returns. It is up to the decision maker to decide which portfolio represents the best decision and if sufficient resources exist to execute these projects. Typically, in an efficient frontier analysis, you would select projects where the marginal increase in benefits is positive and the slope is steep. In addition, you would select Portfolio D rather than Portfolio E because the marginal increase is negative on the y-axis (e.g., Tactical Score). That is, spending too much money may actually reduce the overall tactical score, and, hence, this portfolio should not be selected. Also, in comparing portfolios A and B, you would be more inclined to choose B as the slope is steep and the same increase in budget requirements (x-axis) would return a much higher percentage Tactical Score (y-axis). The decision to choose between portfolios C and D would depend on available resources and the decision maker deciding if the added benefits warrant and justify the added budget and costs.

Budget	Comprehensive Score	Tactical Score	Military Score	Allowed Projects	ROI-RANK Objective
$3,800	33.15	62.64	58.58	10	$470,236
$4,800	36.33	68.85	66.86	11	$521,646
$5,800	38.40	70.46	75.69	12	$623,558
$6,800	39.94	72.14	82.31	13	$659,948
$7,800	39.76	70.05	86.54	14	$676,280

Figure 9.14: Portfolio Efficient Frontier (continues)

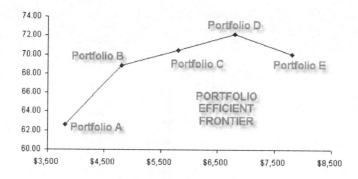

Figure 9.14: Portfolio Efficient Frontier (continued)

To further enhance the analysis, you can obtain the optimal portfolio allocations for C and D and then run a simulation on each optimal portfolio to decide what the probability that D will exceed C in value is, and whether this probability of occurrence justifies the added costs.

OPTIMIZATION APPLICATION EXAMPLE:
OPTIMAL PRICING WITH ELASTICITY

This section illustrates another sample model from the ROV Modeling Toolkit. This model is used to find the optimal pricing levels that will maximize revenues through the use of historical elasticity levels. The price elasticity of demand is a basic concept in microeconomics, which can be briefly described as the percentage change of quantity divided by the percentage change in prices. For example, if, in response to a 10% fall in the price of a good, the quantity demanded increases by 20%, the price elasticity of demand would be 20% / (−10 %) = −2. In general, a fall in the price of a good is expected to increase the quantity demanded, so the price elasticity of demand is negative but in some literature, the negative sign is omitted for simplicity (denoting only the absolute value of the elasticity). We can use this concept in several ways, including the point elasticity by taking the first derivative of the inverse of the demand function and multiplying it by the ratio of price to quantity at a particular point on the demand curve:

$$\varepsilon_d = \frac{\delta Q}{\delta P} \cdot \frac{P}{Q}$$

where ε is the price elasticity of demand, P is price, and Q is quantity demanded. Instead of using instantaneous point elasticities, this example uses the discrete version, where we define elasticity as:

$$\varepsilon_d = \frac{\%\Delta Q}{\%\Delta P} = \frac{\frac{Q_2 - Q_1}{\frac{Q_2 + Q_1}{2}}}{\frac{P_2 - P_1}{\frac{P_2 + P_1}{2}}} = \frac{Q_2 - Q_1}{Q_2 + Q_1} \cdot \frac{P_2 + P_1}{P_2 - P_1}$$

To further simplify things, we assume that in a category of hotel rooms, cruise ship tickets, airline tickets, or any other products with various categories (e.g., standard room, executive room, suite, etc.), there is an average price and average quantity of units sold per period. Therefore, we can further simplify the equation to:

$$\varepsilon_d = \frac{Q_2 - Q_1}{\overline{Q}} \div \frac{P_2 - P_1}{\overline{P}} = \frac{\overline{P}}{\overline{Q}} \cdot \frac{Q_2 - Q_1}{P_2 - P_1}$$

where we now use the average price and average quantity demanded values $\overline{P}, \overline{Q}$.

If we have in each category the average price and average quantity sold, as in the model, we can compute the expected quantity sold given a new price provided we have the historical elasticity of demand values. See Figure 9.15.

	Historical Analysis		
	Average	Average	Average
	Price	Quantity	Total
Type	Sold	Sold	Revenue
Single	$750	200	$150,000.00
Double	$812	180	$146,160.00
Deluxe	$865	150	$129,750.00
Executive	$1,085	100	$108,500.00
Premium Suite	$1,195	75	$89,625.00
Presidential	$1,458	50	$72,900.00

Figure 9.15: Sample Historical Pricing

In other words, if we take:

$$Q_1 - \varepsilon_d (P_2 - P_1) \frac{\overline{Q}}{\overline{P}} = Q_2$$

we would get:

$$Q_1 - \left[\frac{\overline{P}}{\overline{Q}} \cdot \frac{Q_2 - Q_1}{P_2 - P_1} \right] (P_2 - P_1) \frac{\overline{Q}}{\overline{P}} = Q_2$$

To illustrate, suppose the price elasticity of demand for a single room during high season at a specific hotel property is 3.15 (we use the absolute value), where the average price last season was $750 and the average quantity of rooms sold was 200 units. What would happen if prices were to change from $750 ($P_1$) to $800 ($P_2$)? That is, what would happen to the quantity sold from 200 units (Q_1)? See Figure 9.16. Note that ε is a negative value but we simplify as a positive value here to be consistent with economic literature.

	Historical Analysis			Price	Allocated	Projected
	Average	Average	Average	Elasticity	New	Quantity
	Price	Quantity	Total	of Demand	Price	Sold
Type	Sold	Sold	Revenue			
Single	$750	200	$150,000.00	3.15	$800.00	158
Double	$812	180	$146,160.00	2.85	$800.00	188
Deluxe	$865	150	$129,750.00	2.55	$1,000.00	90
Executive	$1,085	100	$108,500.00	2.35	$1,000.00	118
Premium Suite	$1,195	75	$89,625.00	1.65	$1,000.00	95
Presidential	$1,458	50	$72,900.00	1.45	$1,000.00	73

Figure 9.16: Elasticity Simulation

Using the preceding equation, we compute the newly predicted quantity demanded at $800 per night to be:

$$Q_2 = Q_1 - \varepsilon_d (P_2 - P_1) \frac{\overline{Q}}{\overline{P}} = 200 - 3.15 (800 - 750) \frac{200}{750} = 158$$

The higher the price, the lower the quantity demanded, and vice versa. Indeed, the entire demand curve can be reconstructed by applying different price levels. For instance, the demand curve for the single room is reconstructed in Figure 9.17.

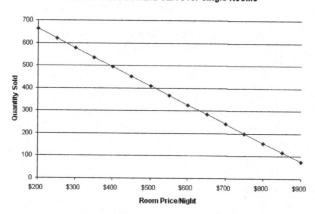

Reconstructed Demand Curve for Single Rooms

Figure 9.17: Reconstructed Demand Curve for Single Rooms

Optimization Procedures

Using the principles of price elasticity of demand, we can now figure out the optimal pricing structure of these hotel rooms by setting:

Objective:	Maximize total revenues
Constraints:	Number of rooms available per type
Decision Variables:	Price to charge for each type of room

This model already has the optimization set up. To run it directly, do the following:

1. Go to the Model worksheet and click on *Risk Simulator | Change Profile* and choose the *Optimal Pricing with Elasticity* profile.

2. Click on the Run Optimization icon or click on *Risk Simulator | Optimization | Run Optimization.*

3. Select the Method tab and select either Static Optimization if you wish to view the resulting optimal prices or Stochastic Optimization to run simulation with optimization multiple times, to obtain a range of optimal prices.

The results from a stochastic optimization routine are seen in the *Report* worksheet. In addition, several forecast charts will be visible once the stochastic optimization routine completes. For instance, looking at the Executive suites, select *Two-Tail*, type 90 in the Certainty box, and hit *TAB* on the keyboard to obtain the 90% confidence level (e.g., the optimal price to charge for the season is between $991 and $993 per night). See Figure 9.18.

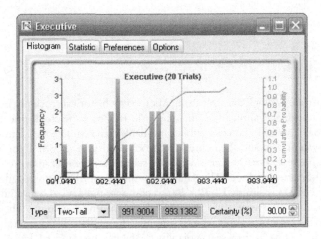

Figure 9.18: Distribution of Stochastic Optimization Decision Variable

To reset the model manually, do the following:

1. Go to the *Model* worksheet, click on *Risk Simulator | New Profile*, and give the new profile a name.

2. Reset the values on prices. That is, enter *800* for cells *H7, H8* and *1000* for cells *H9* to *H12*. We choose these values so that we determine the initial starting prices that are easy to remember, versus the optimized price levels later on.

3. Set the objective. Select cell *J15* and click on the *O* (set objective) icon or click *Risk Simulator | Optimization | Set Objective*.

4. Set the decision variables. Select cell *H7* and click on the *D* (set decision variable) icon or click *Risk Simulator | Optimization | Set Decision*. Select *Continuous* and give it the relevant lower and upper bounds (see columns M and N) or click on the link icons and link the lower and upper bounds (cells *M7* and *N7*).

5. Set the constraints. Click on the *C* icon or *Risk Simulator | Optimization | Constraints* and add the capacity constraints on the maximum number of available rooms (e.g., click *ADD* and link cell *I7* and make it "*<= 250*" and so forth.

6. Click on the *Run Optimization* icon or click on *Risk Simulator | Optimization | Run Optimization*.

7. Select the *Method* tab and select either *Static Optimization* if you wish to view the resulting optimal prices, or *Stochastic Optimization* to run simulation with optimization multiple times, to obtain a range of optimal prices. But remember that to run a stochastic optimization procedure, you need to have assumptions set up. Select cell *G7* and click on *Risk Simulator | Set Input Assumption* and set an assumption of your choice or choose Normal distribution and use the default values. Repeat for cells *G8* to *G12*, one at a time, and then you can run a stochastic optimization.

APPENDIX—COMPUTING ANNUALIZED RETURNS AND RISK FOR PORTFOLIO OPTIMIZATION

Figure 9A.1 illustrates a quick example using Microsoft's historical stock prices for computing the annualized return and annualized volatility risk. It shows the stock prices for Microsoft downloaded from Yahoo! Finance, a publicly available free resource (you can start by visiting http://finance.yahoo.com and then entering a stock symbol, e.g., MSFT for Microsoft, then click on *Quotes: Historical Prices*, select *Weekly*, and select the period of interest to download the data to a spreadsheet for analysis). The data in columns A and B are downloaded from Yahoo. The formula in cell D3 is simply *LN(B3/B4)* to compute the natural logarithmic value of the relative returns week after week, and is copied down the entire column. The formula in cell E3 is *STDEV(D3:D54)*SQRT(52)*, which computes the annualized (by multiplying the square root of the number of weeks in a year) volatility (by taking the standard deviation of the entire 52 weeks of the year 2004 data). The formula in cell E3 is then copied down the entire column to compute a moving window of annualized volatilities. The volatility used in this example is the average of a 52-week moving window, which covers 2 years of data; that is, cell M8's formula is *AVERAGE(E3:E54)*, where cell E54 has the following formula: *STDEV(D54:D105)*SQRT(52)*, and, of course, row 105 is January 2003. This means that the 52-week moving window captures the average volatility over a 2-year period and it will smooth the volatility such that infrequent but extreme spikes will not dominate the volatility computation. Of course, a median volatility should also be computed. If the median is far off from the average, the distribution of volatilities is skewed and the median should be used, otherwise, the average should be used. Finally, these 52 volatilities can be fed into Monte Carlo simulation, using the Risk Simulator software's custom distribution to run a nonparametric simulation or to perform data fitting procedure to find the best-fitting distribution to simulate.

In contrast, we can compute the annualized returns either using the arithmetic average method or the geometric average method. Cell G3 computes the absolute percentage return for the week where the formula for the cell is *(B3–B4)/B4*, and the formula is copied down the entire column. Then, the moving average window is computed in cell H3 as *AVERAGE(G3:G54)*52*, where the average weekly returns are obtained and annualized by multiplying it with 52, the number of weeks in a year. Note that averages are additive and can be multiplied directly by the number of weeks in a year versus volatility, which is not additive. Only volatility squared is additive, which means that the periodic volatility computed previously needs to be multiplied by the square root of 52. The arithmetic average return in cell M14 is, hence, the average of a 52-week period of the moving average computed as *AVERAGE(H3:H54)*. Similarly, the geometric average return is the average of the 52-week moving window of the geometric returns, that is, cell M15 is simply *AVERAGE(I3:I54)*, where in cell I3, we have *(POWER(B3/B54,1/52)-1)*52*, the geometric average computation. The arithmetic growth rate is typically higher that the geometric growth rate when the returns period to period are volatile. Typically, the geometric growth rate (with a moving average window) should be used.

	A	B	C D	E	F	G	H	I	J	K	L	M
1	**Historical Data**		**Volatility Computations**		**Returns Computations**							
2	Week	Closing Price	LN Relative Returns	Moving Average Volatilities	Relative Returns	Absolute Returns	Moving Average Absolute Returns	Moving Average Geometric Returns				
3	27-Dec-04	26.64	-0.0108	17.87%	0.9892	-1.08%	10.04%	7.69%				
4	20-Dec-04	26.93	0.0019	17.84%	1.0019	0.19%	11.98%	9.55%				
5	13-Dec-04	26.88	-0.0045	17.85%	0.9956	-0.44%	11.27%	10.22%				
6	6-Dec-04	27.00	-0.0055	18.00%	0.9945	-0.55%	14.36%	10.14%		*One-Year Annualized Volatility Analysis*		
7	29-Nov-04	27.15	0.0235	18.13%	1.0238	2.38%	17.50%	13.31%				
8	22-Nov-04	26.52	-0.0098	18.03%	0.9903	-0.97%	16.17%	13.52%		Average Annualized Volatility	21.89%	
9	15-Nov-04	26.78	-0.0011	18.10%	0.9989	-0.11%	19.56%	15.54%		Median Annualized Volatility	22.30%	
10	8-Nov-04	26.81	0.0223	18.20%	1.0225	2.25%	18.13%	18.05%				
11	1-Nov-04	26.22	0.0468	18.28%	1.0480	4.80%	13.56%	14.26%				
12	25-Oct-04	25.02	0.0084	17.71%	1.0085	0.85%	8.63%	7.21%		*One-Year Annualized Returns Analysis*		
13	18-Oct-04	24.81	-0.0092	17.80%	0.9908	-0.92%	6.02%	6.24%				
14	11-Oct-04	25.04	0.0000	19.68%	1.0000	0.00%	-1.09%	5.38%		Arithmetic Average Return	8.54%	
15	4-Oct-04	25.04	-0.0091	19.69%	0.9909	-0.91%	-0.46%	-2.99%		Geometric Average Return	6.16%	
16	27-Sep-04	25.27	0.0346	19.68%	1.0352	3.52%	-0.13%	-1.45%				
17	20-Sep-04	24.41	-0.0082	19.62%	0.9919	-0.81%	-0.50%	-5.50%				
18	13-Sep-04	24.61	0.0008	20.52%	1.0008	0.08%	-5.59%	-1.57%				
19	7-Sep-04	24.59	0.0139	21.30%	1.0140	1.40%	0.05%	-7.74%				
20	30-Aug-04	24.25	-0.0127	21.25%	0.9874	-1.26%	-1.51%	-3.56%				
21	23-Aug-04	24.56	0.0123	22.29%	1.0124	1.24%	6.77%	-2.45%				
22	16-Aug-04	24.26	0.0066	22.29%	1.0066	0.66%	6.70%	3.10%				
23	9-Aug-04	24.10	-0.0041	22.42%	0.9959	-0.41%	8.68%	3.59%				
24	2-Aug-04	24.20	-0.0488	22.42%	0.9524	-4.76%	8.92%	6.62%				

Figure 9A.1: Computing Annualized Return and Risk

APPENDIX—ROV MODELER SUITE: SERVER-BASED APPLICATIONS FOR RUNNING DATA-INTENSIVE MODELS AT EXTREMELY HIGH SPEEDS

Throughout the book, we look at individual Excel-based models to simplify the discussions and explanations. Nonetheless, these Excel models are limited in that they can only run on a limited set of data (e.g., Excel has a maximum number of rows and columns per worksheet) and might be much slower than, say, a bank would consider optimal (because of Excel's computational overhead of including graphics, equations, and cell-by-cell platform). Banks typically have thousands, if not millions, of transactions per day across all their branches, and some of these credit and market risk analyses have to be done frequently and quickly. In this appendix, we introduce the server-based applications, where millions of data points and computations can be run within seconds or minutes on a server. The same analytics and models in the two software programs (Risk Simulator and Real Options SLS) described throughout this book are now run in pure mathematical software codes, making the computations blazing fast and capable of handling large datasets.

This server-based software is called ROV Modeler Suite and it is divided into a few application modules:

- *ROV Risk Modeler.* Risk Modeler is a simulation and analytical module that focuses on general analytics and modeling, forecasting, and simulation, as well as credit risk and market risk for Basel II and Basel III based on a bank's existing data tables. It provides many models to simulate, fit, forecast, and value, and reports the results to the user. Existing data tables are based on the user's requirements such as linking to an existing database (e.g., Oracle OFDM, SQL, CSV, DSN, ODBC, Excel, flat text files, and other proprietary database systems), manually inputting data, or setting simulation assumptions, and so forth. This module can be used for computing, forecasting, and simulating risk analytics including historical back-fitting, time-series forecasts (ARIMA), volatility computations (GARCH), credit and market risk (PD, LGD, VAR, EAD), and other applications.

- *ROV Risk Optimizer.* Risk Optimizer is an advanced optimization module that can be used to optimize large portfolios and to find optimal decision variables. The decision variables can be discrete, continuous, integer, or binary, and the objective function can be linear or nonlinear. In addition, Risk Optimizer allows the user to link to existing data tables to run simulations, find the best-fitting models, and couple these techniques with optimization. It works exactly like Risk Simulator's optimization module described throughout this chapter, but it runs completely independently of Excel at super high speeds.

- *ROV Risk Valuator.* Risk Valuator is the application of more than 600 functions and models. Users can input the required data for the selected model and this application will return the computed results very quickly. This module is useful for valuing derivative instruments, debt instruments, exotic options, and options-embedded instruments, as well as multiple types of financial models.

The 600-plus advanced models are categorized into the following groups of applications:

- o Advanced Math Functions
- o Basic Finance Models
- o Basic Options Models
- o Bond Math, Options, Pricing, and Yields
- o Credit Risk Analysis
- o Delta Gamma Hedging
- o Exotic Options and Derivatives
- o Financial Ratios
- o Forecasting, Extrapolation, and Interpolation
- o Probability Distributions
- o Put-Call Parity and Option Sensitivities
- o Real Options Analysis
- o Value at Risk, Volatility, Portfolio Risk and Return

System Architecture

The entire system architecture of this server-based application can be divided into three parts: the first level is the product's main application, which is the user interface; the second level is the data map, which is used to input the data to compute from various methods such as linking to existing databases or manually inputting the data, and so forth; the last level is the lowest level, which links the database to a *query*, *insert*, and *get* value function to and from data tables. Figure 9A.2 illustrates the system architecture.

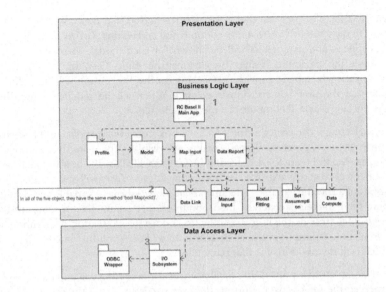

Figure 9A.2: System Architecture of Risk Modeler

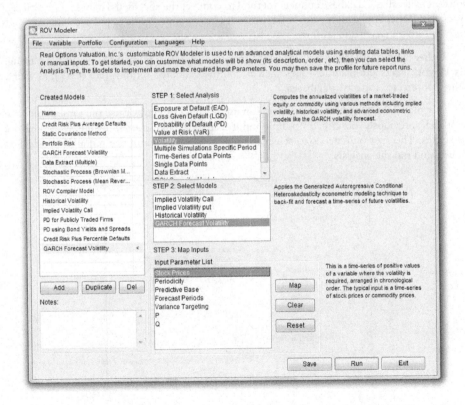

Figure 9A.3: Risk Modeler Main Application User Interface (Level 1)

Figure 9A.3 illustrates the first level of the system architecture, the user interface. A user can create new profiles for saving the data that will be used in the procedure (*File* I *New Profile*). In *Step 1*, the user selects the Analysis type, and, based on the type chosen, a list of models will be shown in *Step 2*. The user can then select models and *Add* as many as required, which will then appear in the *Created Models* list box for updating and editing. In *Step 3*, the list of required input assumptions and parameters will be shown for each model. The user can then map, clear, or reset the parameter values by clicking the *Map, Clear,* or *Reset* buttons (short descriptions for each step are provided). Clicking on the *Save* button will save all the data to the Profile that the user had previously created. When all the required inputs have been populated, clicking *Run* will compute the models selected.

When selecting a parameter in the *Step 3* list box in the main application and clicking the *MAP* button, the *Input Parameter Mapping* dialog will display. There are five methods afforded to the user, as seen in Figure 9A.4. Selecting *Data Link* will allow the user to link to an existing database or Excel to access existing data. Selecting *Manual Input* will show a dialog requiring manual input of a specific variable. Selecting *Data Compute* shows a variable and data calculator to compute the parameter's value by incorporating other parameters or constants. Selecting *Set Assumption* will provide the user the ability to choose the simulation distribution and input the risk simulation assumption values. Selecting *Model Fitting* will fit some existing data to 24 potential relevant distributions for that parameter.

There are seven types of ODBC data connect for accessing existing data (Figure 9A.5). For instance, in the Oracle data connect, the user needs to set up the required login inputs such as User and Password to access the database. When clicking on the *OK* button, the software will call the database connect method to connect the specified database. For different types of ODBC applications, the software codes are wrapped with popular calling methods such as *Connect, Query,* and so forth.

Other types of database and software connections are also possible, for example, through Excel worksheets and plain text files such as comma-delimited settings files (CSV), as well as other proprietary software databases.

For the *Risk Optimizer* module, users can input values directly or use the same three-level approach previously described to link input variables and output results with existing databases. The user only needs to select the required model, input the required parameters' values, and run the analysis.

Figure 9A.4: Input Parameter Mapping User Interface (Level 2)

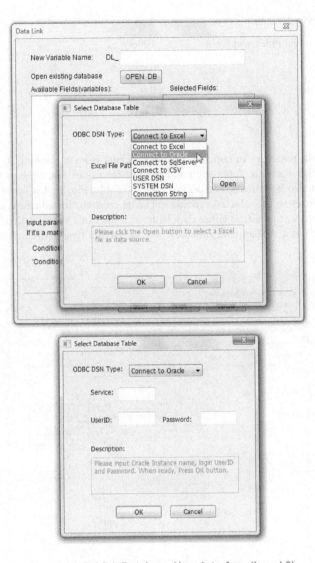

Figure 9A.5: Link Database User Interface (Level 3)

Risk Modeler

This section includes a simple example showcasing how to use Risk Modeler. After Risk Modeler has been successfully installed, start the application to show the main user dialog. Click on *File | New Profile* to create a new profile. Then select *Probability of Default (PD)* in the *Step 1* list box and *PD for Publicly Traded Firms* in *Step 2*. Next, click on *Market Value Equity* in *Step 3* (Figure 9A.6). Then, click on *MAP* and the program will open another dialog named *Input Parameter Mapping*. Click on the *Manual Input* radio button and hit *Next* (Figure 9A.7).

When the *Manual Input* dialog opens (Figure 9A.8), enter a variable name such as *Var1* and click the third radio button to manually input 3000. Then click on *Finish* to close this dialog. The program will return to the main application dialog. Using the same method, enter the following values for the required input parameters (enter any variable name as required):

Market Equity Volatility	0.45
Book Value Liabilities and Debt	10000
Risk-free	0.05
Growth Rate	0.07
Maturity	1.00

Alternatively, the user can copy multiple data points from an existing spreadsheet, a text file, or some other software application and paste these values directly into the data area. A flat text file can also be uploaded to populate this variable. Finally, for some special models, the input parameter to the selected variable might be constant for all cases, and the software allows the ability to populate an entire data table with the same value (e.g., risk-free rate for a specific time period is the same regardless of the transaction type or credit listing).

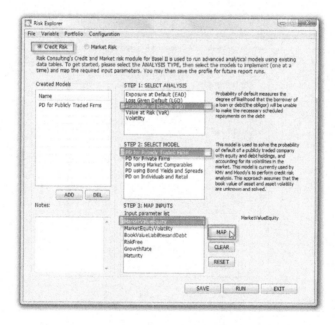

Figure 9A.6: Using Risk Modeler

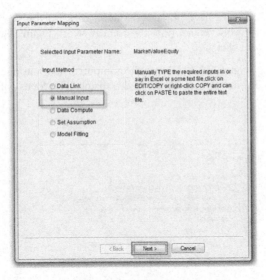

Figure 9A.7: Parameter Mapping

Figure 9A.8: Manual Inputs

When all the parameters have populated values, click on the *Run* button in the main application dialog. There are several options the user can select (Figure 9A.9). For this example, select the first choice and click *OK*.

The *Results* dialog (Figure 9A.10) shows the computed values using the input parameters specified. Click the *OK* button to close the *Results* dialog. The focus will return to the *Main* application dialog.

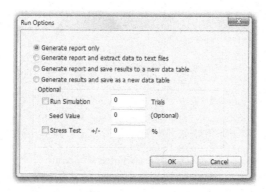

Figure 9A.9: Running the Report

Figure 9A.10: Results

Risk Optimizer

Here is another simple example showcasing how to use the *Risk Optimizer* module. After the Risk Modeler Suite has been successfully installed, start the Risk Optimizer application. The user interface has several tabs: *Method, Decision Variables, Constraints, Statistics,* and *Objective* (Figure 9A.11). To get started, select the *Method* tab and click on *Static Optimization*.

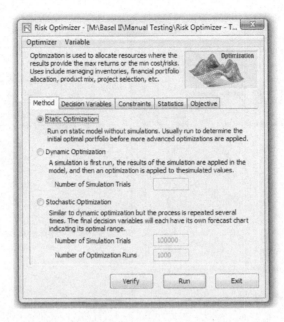

Figure 9A.11: Risk Optimizer

Next, click on the *Decision Variables* tab and *Add* to add some variables. For instance, we have 4 different variables (*Asset1* to *Asset4*), and each asset can be set to take continuous, integer, binary, or discrete values. For our simple illustration, set the variables to all be *Continuous* between 0.10 and 0.40 (i.e., only asset allocations between 10% and 40% are allowed). Keep adding 4 different asset classes as decision variables as shown in Figure 9A.12.

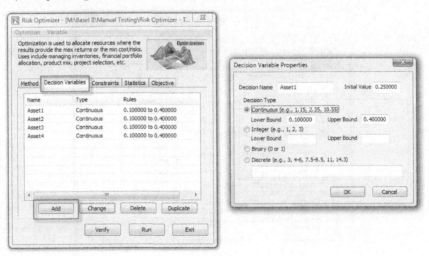

Figure 9A.12: Setting Decision Variables

Next, click on the *Constraints* tab and *Add* (Figure 9A.13). Then, in the *Expression* input box, enter the constraints (you can double-click on the list of variables and the variable string will be transferred up to the *Expression* box). In our simple example, the sum of the decision variables must equal 1.0 (i.e., the total allocation of asset classes must total 100% in an investment portfolio).

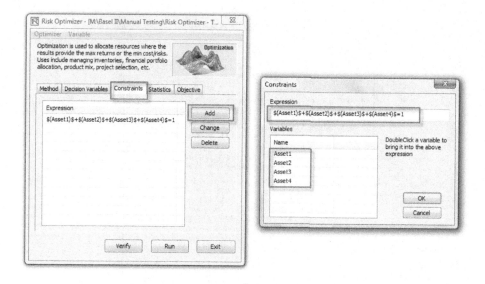

Figure 9A.13: Setting Constraints

Next, select the *Objective* tab and decide if you wish to run *Maximization* or *Minimization* on your objective. In addition, enter the relevant *Objective Function* expression as outlined in Figure 9A.14. You can double-click on the list of Variables to bring the variable name string to the *Objective Expression* input box. When completed, click on *Run* to obtain the results of your optimization (Figure 9A.15).

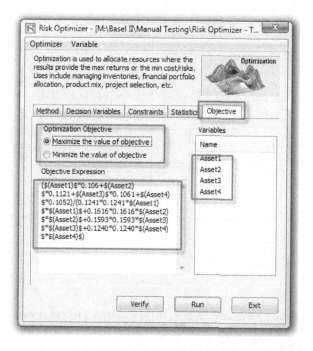

Figure 9A.14: Setting the Optimization Objective

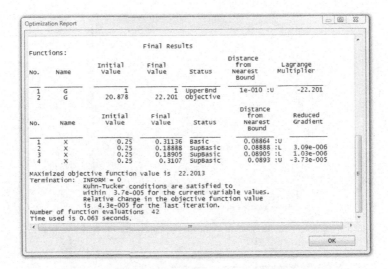

Figure 9A.15: Optimization Results

You may also use Risk Optimizer to link to an existing database such as Oracle or generate your own data tables to optimize (Figure 9A.16). For instance, clicking on the *Variable | Variable Management* menu accesses the *Variable Management* tool, which will, in turn, allow you to *Add, Edit,* or *Delete* variables. In addition, by clicking on *Add*, the familiar *Input Parameter Mapping* tool appears (Figure 9A.7), allowing you to link, compute, paste, simulate, or fit existing data for use in the optimization process.

Finally, if *Dynamic* or *Stochastic Optimization* is selected (Figure 9A.11), and if the variables have risk simulation assumptions associated with them, you can then access the *Statistics* tab, whereby you can make use of the simulated statistical properties to run stochastic optimization on. It is highly suggested that you try some of the example profiles such as the Markowitz efficient frontier and stochastic optimization.

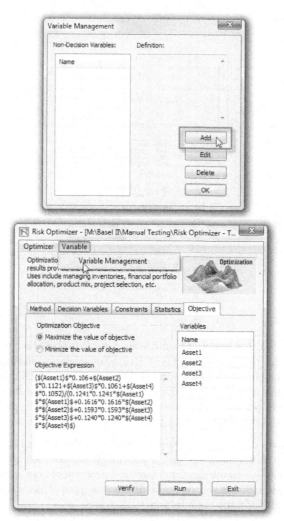

Figure 9A.16: Variable Management

Risk Valuator

Risk Valuator is used to perform quick computations from simple and basic models to advanced analytical models, and can handle single point values or a series of values. After installing the software, start Risk Valuator. Simply select the model type in the *Model Category* box and select the model of interest in the *Model Selection* box (Figure 9A.17). The required input parameters will then be listed. Single point inputs (e.g., 10 or 10.4532) will be in the *single input parameters* area, whereas multiple data requirements will be shown in the *multiple series input parameters* area. When entering a single series of multiple data points, use commas or spaces to separate the values (e.g., a time series of 6 months of interest rates can be entered either as 0.12, 0.124, 0.112, 0.1, 0.09, 0.16 or simply as 0.12 0.124 0.112 0.1 0.09 0.16).

Sometimes, certain models, such as the Value at Risk (VaR) model using the standard correlation method, require different columns of data and a correlation matrix. For instance, the goal is to compute the portfolio VaR using this model, where there are three asset classes, each with its own amounts, specific daily volatility for each asset class, and a square correlation matrix among these asset classes. In such a situation, the amounts and volatility inputs will have to be entered as a single column (hit *Enter* at the end of entering a value, to create a new line, designating a new asset class), and the correlation matrix will be separated by commas for the same row with different columns, and semicolons for different rows. This Risk Valuator module does not allow the user to link to various databases or simulate. To do so, use the Risk Modeler module instead. Many of the same models exist in both places. The Risk Valuator module is used to quickly obtain results without having to link to databases and so forth. Risk Valuator can also be used to compute more advanced models such as the Box–Jenkins ARIMA forecast (Figure 9A.18). In summary, Risk Modeler can be used to run highly data-intensive models, and it allows the user to link to existing databases and yet run forecasting, simulation, and optimization algorithms, coupled with the advanced analytical models for credit and market risks as specified by Basel II and Basel III.

This appendix only illustrates the basics of this tool, whereas the user manual and getting started videos available at *http://www.realoptionsvaluation.com/rovmodeler.html* provide much more detail on how to use the ROV Modeler Suite with Oracle and other databases, linking to and from other data sources, embedding ROV Compiler files, performing computations and data validation, executing SQL commands for data cleansing, running simulations, and many other approaches.

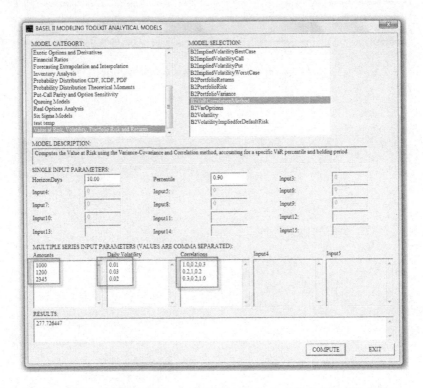

Figure 9A.17: Portfolio Value at Risk Model Solved Using Risk Valuator

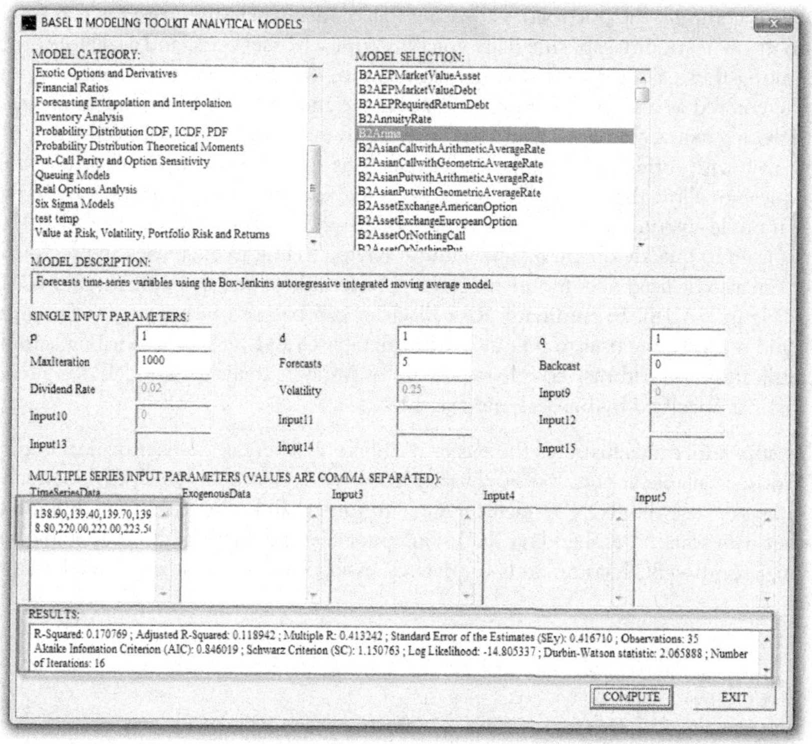

Figure 9A.18: Complex ARIMA Model Solution

EXERCISE: OPTIMIZATION

This sample model illustrates how to use Risk Simulator for:

1. Running Static, Dynamic, and Stochastic Optimization with Continuous Decision Variables

2. Optimization with Discrete Integer Decision Variables

3. Efficient Frontier and Advanced Optimization Settings

Model Background

File Name:	Basic Simulation Model.xls
Access:	*Risk Simulator	Example Models	11 Optimization Continuous*
Access:	*Risk Simulator	Example Models	12 Optimization Discrete*
Access:	*Risk Simulator	Example Models	13 Optimization Stochastic*
Prerequisites:	Risk Simulator 2014 or later, Chapters 8 and 9 of *Modeling Risk*

1. Running Static, Dynamic, and Stochastic Optimization with Continuous Decision Variables

Figure 9E.A illustrates the sample continuous optimization model. In this example, there are 10 distinct asset classes (e.g., different types of mutual funds, stocks, or assets) where the idea is to most efficiently and effectively allocate the portfolio holdings such that the best bang for the buck is obtained. In other words, we want to generate the best portfolio returns possible given the risks inherent in each asset class. In order to truly understand the concept of optimization, we will have to delve more deeply into this sample model to see how the optimization process can best be applied. The model shows the 10 asset classes and each asset class has its own set of annualized returns and annualized volatilities. These return and risk measures are annualized values such that they can be consistently compared across different asset classes. Returns are computed using the geometric average of the relative returns, while the risks are computed using the logarithmic relative stock returns approach.

ASSET ALLOCATION OPTIMIZATION MODEL

Asset Class Description	Annualized Returns	Volatility Risk	Allocation Weights	Required Minimum Allocation	Required Maximum Allocation	Return to Risk Ratio	Returns Ranking (Hi-Lo)	Risk Ranking (Lo-Hi)	Return to Risk Ranking (Hi-Lo)	Allocation Ranking (Hi-Lo)
Asset Class 1	10.54%	12.36%	10.00%	5.00%	35.00%	0.8524	9	2	7	1
Asset Class 2	11.25%	16.23%	10.00%	5.00%	35.00%	0.6929	7	8	10	1
Asset Class 3	11.84%	15.64%	10.00%	5.00%	35.00%	0.7570	6	7	9	1
Asset Class 4	10.64%	12.35%	10.00%	5.00%	35.00%	0.8615	8	1	5	1
Asset Class 5	13.25%	13.28%	10.00%	5.00%	35.00%	0.9977	5	4	2	1
Asset Class 6	14.21%	14.39%	10.00%	5.00%	35.00%	0.9875	3	6	3	1
Asset Class 7	15.53%	14.25%	10.00%	5.00%	35.00%	1.0898	1	5	1	1
Asset Class 8	14.95%	16.44%	10.00%	5.00%	35.00%	0.9094	2	9	4	1
Asset Class 9	14.16%	16.50%	10.00%	5.00%	35.00%	0.8584	4	10	6	1
Asset Class 10	10.06%	12.50%	10.00%	5.00%	35.00%	0.8045	10	3	8	1
Portfolio Total	*12.6419%*	*4.58%*	*100.00%*							
Return to Risk Ratio	*2.7596*									

Specifications of the optimization model:

Objective: Maximize Return to Risk Ratio (C18)
Decision Variables: Allocation Weights (E6:E15)
Restrictions on Decision Variables: Minimum and Maximum Required (F6:G15)
Constraints: Portfolio Total Allocation Weights 100% (E17 is set to 100%)

Additional specifications:

1. One can always maximize portfolio total returns or minimize the portfolio total risk.
2. Incorporate Monte Carlo simulation in the model by simulating the returns and volatility of each asset class and apply Simulation-Optimization techniques.
3. The portfolio can be optimized as is without simulation using Static Optimization techniques.

Figure 9E.A: Continuous Optimization Model

The Allocation Weights in column E holds the decision variables, which are the variables that need to be tweaked and tested such that the total weight is constrained at 100% (cell E17). Typically, to start the optimization, we will set these cells to a uniform value, where in this case, cells E6 to E15 are set at 10% each. In addition, each decision variable may have specific restrictions in its allowed range. In this example, the lower and upper allocations allowed are 5% and 35%, as seen in columns F and G. This means that each asset class may have its own allocation boundaries. Next, column H shows the return to risk ratio, which is simply the return percentage divided by the risk percentage; the higher this value, the higher the bang for the buck. The remaining columns show the individual asset class rankings by returns, risk, return to risk ratio, and allocation. In other words, these rankings show at a glance which asset class has the lowest risk, or the highest return, and so forth. The portfolio's total returns in cell C17 is $SUMPRODUCT(C6:C15, E6:E15)$, that is, the sum of the allocation weights multiplied by the annualized returns for each asset class. In other words, we have $R_P = \omega_A R_A + \omega_B R_B + \omega_C R_C + \omega_D R_D$, where R_P is the return on the portfolio, $R_{A,B,C,D}$ are the individual returns on the projects, and $\omega_{A,B,C,D}$ are the respective weights or capital allocation across each project. In addition, the portfolio's diversified risk in cell D17 is computed by

taking $\sigma_P = \sqrt{\sum_{i=1}^{i} \omega_i^2 \sigma_i^2 + \sum_{i=1}^{n} \sum_{j=1}^{m} 2\omega_i \omega_j \rho_{i,j} \sigma_i \sigma_j}$. Here, $\rho_{i,j}$ are the respective cross-correlations

between the asset classes—hence, if the cross-correlations are negative, there are risk diversification effects, and the portfolio risk decreases. However, to simplify the computations here, we assume zero correlations among the asset classes through this portfolio risk computation, but assume the correlations when applying simulation on the returns as will be seen later. Therefore, instead of applying static correlations among these different asset returns, we apply the correlations in the simulation assumptions themselves, creating a more dynamic relationship among the simulated return values. Finally, the return to risk ratio or Sharpe Ratio is computed for the portfolio. This value is seen in cell C18 and represents the objective to be maximized in this optimization exercise.

The following are the specifications in this example optimization model:

Objective:	Maximize Return to Risk Ratio (C18)
Decision Variables:	Allocation Weights (E6:E15)
Restrictions on Decision Variables:	Minimum and Maximum Required (F6:G15)
Constraints:	Total Allocation Weights Sum to 100% (E17)

Procedure

1. Start Excel and open the example file *Risk Simulator | Example Models | 11 Optimization Continuous.*

2. Start a new profile with *Risk Simulator | New Profile* (or click on the New Profile icon) and give it a name.

3. The first step in optimization is to set the decision variables. Select cell *E6* and set the first decision variable (*Risk Simulator | Optimization | Set Decision*) or click on the *D* icon. Then click on the link icon to select the name cell (*B6*), as well as the lower bound and upper bound values at cells *F6* and *G6*. Then, using Risk Simulator *Copy*, copy this cell *E6* decision variable and paste the decision variable to the remaining cells in *E7* to *E15.*

4. The second step in optimization is to set the constraint. There is only one constraint here, that is, the total allocation in the portfolio must sum to 100%. So, click on *Risk Simulator | Optimization | Constraints...* or click on the *C* icon, and select *ADD* to add a new constraint. Then, select the cell *E17* and make it equal (=) to *100%.* Click *OK* when done.

    a. Exercise Question: Would you get the same results if you set *E7* = 1 instead of 100%?

    b. Exercise Question: In the constraints user interface, what does the Efficient Frontier button mean and how does it work?

5. The final step in optimization is to set the objective function. Select cell *C18* and click on *Risk Simulator | Optimization | Set Objective* or click on the *O* icon. Check to make sure the objective cell is set for *C18* and select *Maximize.*

6. Start the optimization by going to *Risk Simulator | Optimization | Run Optimization* or click on the *Run* Optimization icon and select the optimization of choice (Static Optimization, Dynamic Optimization, or Stochastic Optimization). To get started, select *Static Optimization.* You can now review the objective, decision variables, and constraints in each tab if required, or click *OK* to run the static optimization.

    a. Exercise Question: In the Run Optimization user interface, click on the *Statistics* tab and you see that there is nothing there. Why?

7. Once the optimization is complete, you may select *Revert* to revert back to the original values of the decision variables as well as the objective, or select *Replace* to apply the optimized decision variables. Typically, Replace is chosen after the optimization is done. Then review the Results Interpretation section below before proceeding to the next step in the exercise.

8. Now reset the decision variables by typing *10%* back into all cells from *E6* to *E15.* Then, select cell *C6* and *Risk Simulator | Set Input Assumption* and use the default *Normal* distribution and the default parameters. This is only an example run and we really do not need to spend time to set proper distributions. Repeat setting the normal assumptions for cells *C7* to *C15.*

    a.   Exercise Question: Should you or should you not copy the first assumption in cell C6 and then copy and paste the parameters to cells C7:C15? And if we copy and paste the assumptions, what is the difference between using Risk Simulator *Copy* and *Paste* functions as opposed to using Excel's copy and paste function? What happens when you first hit Escape before applying Risk Simulator Paste?

    b.   Exercise Question: Why do we need to enter 10% back into the cells?

9.   Now run the optimization *Risk Simulator | Optimization | Run Optimization* and this time select *Dynamic Optimization* in the *Method* tab. When completed, click on *Revert* to go back to the original 10% decision variables.

    a.   Exercise Question: What was the difference between the static optimization run in Step 6 above and dynamic optimization?

10.   Now run the optimization *Risk Simulator | Optimization | Run Optimization* a third time, but this time, select *Stochastic Optimization* in the *Method* tab. Then notice several things.

    a.   First, click on the *Statistics* tab and see that this tab is now populated. Why is this the case and how do you use this statistics tab?

    b.   Second, click on the *Advanced* button and select the checkbox *Run Super Speed Simulation*. Then click *OK* to run the optimization. What do you see? How is super speed integrated into stochastic optimization?

11.   Access the advanced options by going to *Risk Simulator | Optimization | Run Optimization* and clicking the *Advanced* button. Spend some time trying to understand what each element means and how it is pertinent to optimization.

12.   After running the stochastic optimization, a report is created. Spend some time reviewing the report and try to understand what it means, as well as review the forecast charts generated for each decision variable.

Figure 9E.B shows the screen shots of the procedural steps given above. You can add simulation assumptions on the model's returns and risk (columns C and D) and apply the dynamic optimization and stochastic optimization for additional practice.

Results Interpretation

The optimization's final results are shown in Figure 9E.C, where the optimal allocation of assets for the portfolio is seen in cells E6:E15. That is, given the restrictions of each asset fluctuating between 5% and 35%, and where the sum of the allocation must equal 100%, the allocation that maximizes the return to risk ratio is seen in Figure 9E.C. A few important things have to be noted when reviewing the results and optimization procedures performed thus far:

- The correct way to run the optimization is to maximize the bang for the buck or returns to risk Sharpe Ratio as we have done.

- If instead we maximized the total portfolio returns, the optimal allocation result is trivial and does not require optimization to obtain. That is, simply allocate 5% (the minimum allowed) to the lowest 8 assets, 35% (the maximum allowed) to the highest returning asset, and the remaining (25%) to the second-best returns asset. Optimization is not required. However, when allocating the portfolio this way, the risk is a lot higher as compared to when maximizing the returns to risk ratio, although the portfolio returns by themselves are higher.

- Conversely, one can minimize the total portfolio risk, but the returns will be less.

The following table illustrates the results from the three different objectives being optimized:

Objective:	Portfolio Returns	Portfolio Risk	Portfolio Returns to Risk Ratio
Maximize Returns to Risk Ratio	12.69%	4.52%	2.8091
Maximize Returns	13.97%	6.77%	2.0636
Minimize Risk	12.38%	4.46%	2.7754

From the table it can be seen that the best approach is to maximize the returns to risk ratio. That is, for the same amount of risk, this allocation provides the highest amount of return. Conversely, for the same amount of return, this allocation provides the lowest amount of risk possible. This approach of bang for the buck or returns to risk ratio is the cornerstone of the Markowitz efficient frontier in modern portfolio theory. That is, if we constrained the total portfolio risk level and successively increased it over time, we will obtain several efficient portfolio allocations for different risk characteristics. Thus, different efficient portfolio allocations can be obtained for different individuals with different risk preferences.

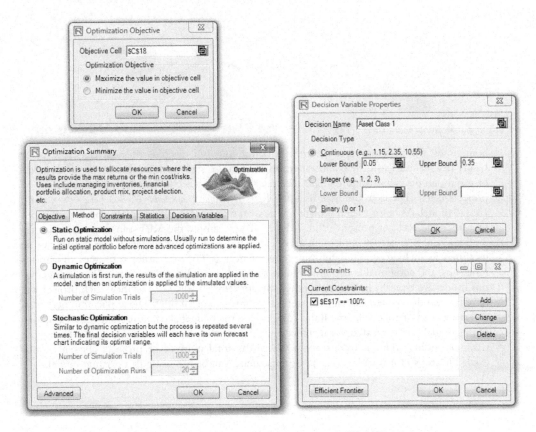

Figure 9E.B: Running Continuous Optimization in Risk Simulator

ASSET ALLOCATION OPTIMIZATION MODEL

Asset Class Description	Annualized Returns	Volatility Risk	Allocation Weights
Asset Class 1	10.54%	12.36%	11.09%
Asset Class 2	11.25%	16.23%	6.86%
Asset Class 3	11.84%	15.64%	7.78%
Asset Class 4	10.64%	12.35%	11.23%
Asset Class 5	13.25%	13.28%	12.09%
Asset Class 6	14.21%	14.39%	11.04%
Asset Class 7	15.53%	14.25%	12.30%
Asset Class 8	14.95%	16.44%	8.90%
Asset Class 9	14.16%	16.50%	8.37%
Asset Class 10	10.06%	12.50%	10.35%
Portfolio Total	12.6919%	4.52%	100.00%
Return to Risk Ratio	2.8091		

Figure 9E.C: Continuous Optimization Results

2. Optimization with Discrete Integer Decision Variables

Sometimes, the decision variables are not continuous but discrete integers (e.g., 1, 2, 3) or binary (e.g., 0 and 1). In the binary situation, we can use such optimization as on-off switches or go/no-go decisions. Figure 9E.D illustrates a project selection model where there are 12 projects listed. The example here uses the *Risk Simulator | Example Models | 12 Optimization Discrete* model. As before, each project has its own returns (ENPV and NPV for expanded net present value and net present value—the ENPV is simply the NPV plus any strategic real options values), costs of implementation, risks, and so forth. If required, this model can be modified to include required full-time equivalences (FTE) and other resources of various functions, and additional constraints can be set on these additional resources. The inputs into this model are typically linked from other spreadsheet models. For instance, each project will have its own discounted cash flow or returns on investment model. The application here is to maximize the portfolio's Sharpe Ratio subject to some budget allocation. Many other versions of this model can be created, for instance, maximizing the portfolio returns, or minimizing the risks, or adding additional constraints where the total number of projects chosen cannot exceed 6, and so forth and so on. All of these items can be run using this existing model.

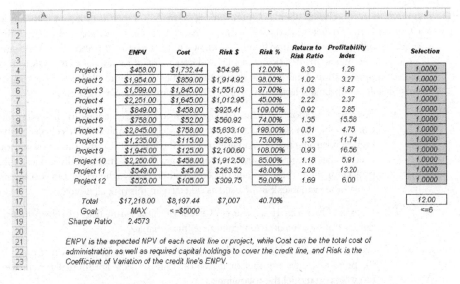

	ENPV	Cost	Risk $	Risk %	Return to Risk Ratio	Profitability Index	Selection
Project 1	$458.00	$1,732.44	$54.96	12.00%	8.33	1.26	1.0000
Project 2	$1,954.00	$859.00	$1,914.92	98.00%	1.02	3.27	1.0000
Project 3	$1,599.00	$1,845.00	$1,551.03	97.00%	1.03	1.87	1.0000
Project 4	$2,251.00	$1,645.00	$1,012.95	45.00%	2.22	2.37	1.0000
Project 5	$849.00	$458.00	$925.41	109.00%	0.92	2.85	1.0000
Project 6	$758.00	$52.00	$560.92	74.00%	1.35	15.58	1.0000
Project 7	$2,845.00	$758.00	$5,633.10	198.00%	0.51	4.75	1.0000
Project 8	$1,235.00	$115.00	$926.25	75.00%	1.33	11.74	1.0000
Project 9	$1,945.00	$125.00	$2,100.60	108.00%	0.93	16.56	1.0000
Project 10	$2,250.00	$458.00	$1,912.50	85.00%	1.18	5.91	1.0000
Project 11	$549.00	$45.00	$263.52	48.00%	2.08	13.20	1.0000
Project 12	$525.00	$105.00	$309.75	59.00%	1.69	6.00	1.0000
Total	$17,218.00	$8,197.44	$7,007	40.70%			12.00
Goal:	MAX	<=$5000					<=6
Sharpe Ratio	2.4573						

ENPV is the expected NPV of each credit line or project, while Cost can be the total cost of administration as well as required capital holdings to cover the credit line, and Risk is the Coefficient of Variation of the credit line's ENPV.

Figure 9E.D: Discrete Integer Optimization Model

Procedure

1. Open the example file and start a new profile by clicking on *Risk Simulator | New Profile* and give it a name.

2. The first step in optimization is to set up the decision variables. Set the first decision variable by selecting cell *J4*, and select *Risk Simulator | Optimization | Set Decision* or click on the *D* icon. Then, click on the link icon to select the name cell (*B4*), and select the *Binary* variable. Then, using Risk Simulator *Copy*, copy this cell *J4* decision variable and paste the decision variable to the remaining cells in *J5* to *J15*. This is the best method if you have only several decision variables and you can name each decision variable with a unique name for identification later.

    a. Exercise Question: What is the main purpose of linking the name to cell B4 before doing the copy and paste parameters?

3. The second step in optimization is to set the constraint. There are two constraints here: The total budget allocation in the portfolio must be less than $5,000 and the total number of projects must not exceed 6. So, click on *Risk Simulator | Optimization | Constraints...* or click on the *C* icon and select *ADD* to add a new constraint. Then, select the cell *D17* and make it *D17 <= 5000*. Repeat by setting cell *J17 <= 6*.

    a. Exercise Question: Why do we use <= instead of =?

    b. Exercise Question: Sometimes when there are no feasible results or the optimization does not run, changing the equal sign to the inequality helps. Why?

    c. Exercise Question: What would you do if you wanted D17 < 5000 instead of <= 5000?

    d. Exercise Question: Explain what would happen to the binding constraints if you set only one constraint and it is D17 <= 8200 or only J17 <= 12?

4. The final step in optimization is to set the objective function and start the optimization by selecting cell *C19* and selecting *Risk Simulator | Optimization | Set Objective* then, run the optimization using *Risk Simulator | Optimization | Run Optimization* and selecting the

optimization of choice (Static Optimization, Dynamic Optimization, or Stochastic Optimization). To get started, select *Static Optimization*. Check to make sure that the objective cell is either the Sharpe Ratio or portfolio returns to risk ratio and select *Maximize*. You can now review the decision variables and constraints if required, or click *OK* to run the static optimization. Figure 9E.E shows the settings and Figure 9E.F shows a sample set of results of optimal selection of projects that maximizes the Sharpe Ratio.

    a. Exercise Question: If instead you maximized total revenues by changing the existing objective, this becomes a trivial model and simply involves choosing the highest returning project and going down the list until you run out of money or exceed the budget constraint. Doing so will yield theoretically undesirable projects as the highest yielding projects typically hold higher risks. Do you agree? What other variables can be used as objective in this model, if any?

    b. Exercise Question: If we use coefficient of variation instead of return to risk ratio, would we maximize or minimize this variable?

    c. Exercise Question: How would you model a situation where, say, one project is the prerequisite for another or if two or more projects are mutually exclusive? How do you model the following?

        i. You cannot do Project 2 by itself without Project 1, but you can do Project 1 on its own without Project 2.

        ii. Either Project 3 or Project 4 can be chosen but not both.

        iii. Each project has some full time equivalence (FTE) employees required to be involved, and the company has a limited number of FTEs.

5. Now add simulation assumptions on the model's ENPV and cost variables (columns C and D) and apply dynamic optimization for additional practice.

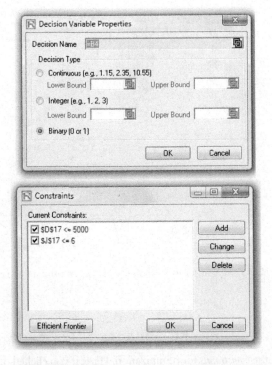

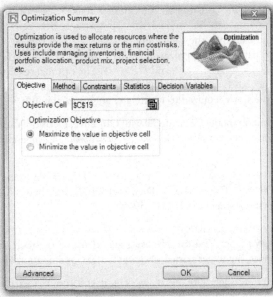

Figure 9E.E: Running Discrete Integer Optimization in Risk Simulator

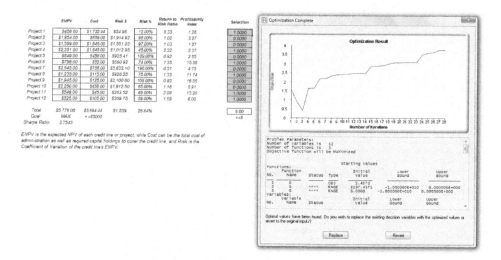

Figure 9E.F: Optimal Selection of Projects That Maximizes the Sharpe Ratio

3. Efficient Frontier and Advanced Optimization Settings

Figure 9E.G shows the *Constraints* for optimization. Here, if you clicked on the *Efficient Frontier* button *after* you have set some constraints, you can now make these constraints changing. That is, each of the constraints can be created to step through between some maximum and minimum value. As an example, the constraint in cell *J17 <= 6* can be set to run between *4* and *8* (Figure 9E.G). That is, five optimizations will be run, each with the following constraints: *J17 <= 4, J17 <= 5, J17 <= 6, J17 <= 7,* and *J17 <= 8*. The optimal results will then be plotted as an efficient frontier and the report will be generated (Figure 9E.H). Specifically, the following illustrates the steps required to create a changing constraint:

1. In an optimization model (i.e., a model with Objective, Decision Variables and Constraints already set up), click on *Risk Simulator | Optimization | Cons*traints and click on *Efficient Frontier.*

2. Select the constraint you want to change or step, *J17*, and enter the parameters for *Min, Max,* and *Step Size* (Figure 9E.G). Then click *ADD* and then *OK* and *OK* again. Also, *uncheck* the first constraint of *D17 <= 5000.*

3. Run Optimization as usual, *Risk Simulator | Optimization | Run Optimization* or click on the *Run Optimization* icon. You can choose static, dynamic or stochastic when running an efficient frontier, but to get started, choose the static optimization routine.

    a. Exercise Question: What happens if you run a stochastic optimization with efficient frontier? What is the step-by-step process that it goes through?

    b. Exercise Question: What happens if you do not uncheck the first constraint?

4. The results will be shown as a user interface (Figure 9E.H). Click on *Create Report* to generate a report worksheet with all the details of the optimization runs.

    a. Exercise Question: How do you interpret the efficient frontier? Is a steeper curve better or a flatter curve? Can the curve slope downwards and if so, what does that mean?

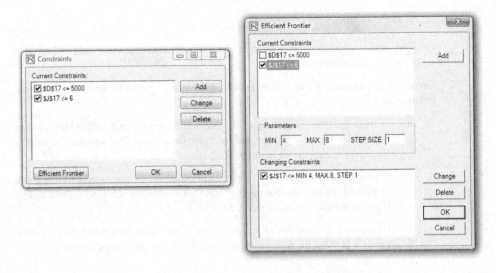

Figure 9E.G: Generating Changing Constraints in an Efficient Frontier

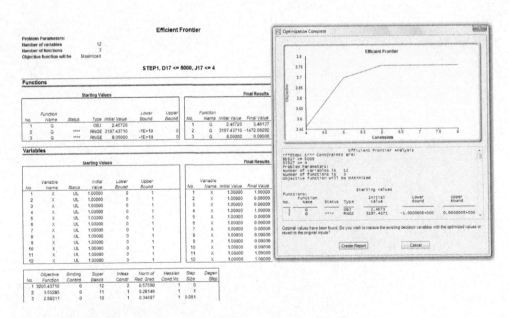

Figure 9E.H: Efficient Frontier Results

Questions

1. Compare and contrast between a discrete versus continuous decision variable when used in an optimization under uncertainty.

2. Create an Excel model for a continuous optimization problem with the following parameters:

    a. A stock portfolio consisting of four individual stocks, each with its own return and risk profile—each return and risk value has its own distributional assumption that is correlated to one another.

    b. The optimization problem is to efficiently allocate your resources to these that individual stocks such that the best bang for the buck is achieved—use a Sharpe Ratio (portfolio returns to risk ratio).

    c. Optimize this portfolio of stocks through the Sharpe Ratio and progressively create and show the Markowitz efficient frontier of stock allocations.

SECTION SIX – RISK MITIGATION

CHAPTER 10 – WHAT'S SO REAL ABOUT "REAL OPTIONS" AND WHY ARE THEY OPTIONAL?

This chapter provides the reader a cursory look at and quick introduction to real options analysis. It explains why only running simulations, forecasting, and optimization are not sufficient in a comprehensive risk management paradigm. That is, time-series forecasting and Monte Carlo simulation are used for *identifying, predicting,* and *quantifying* risks. The question that should be asked is, so what and what next? Quantifying and understanding risk is one thing, but turning this information into *actionable intelligence* is another. Real options analysis, when applied appropriately, allows you to *value* risk, create strategies to *mitigate* risk, and how to position yourself to *take advantage* of risk. It is highly recommended that you refer to *Real Options Analysis: Tools and Techniques,* Second Edition (Wiley Finance, 2005) also by the author, in order to learn more about the theoretical as well as pragmatic step-by-step computational details of real options analysis.

WHAT ARE REAL OPTIONS?

In the past, corporate investment decisions were cut and dried. Buy a new machine that is more efficient, make more products costing a certain amount, and if the benefits outweigh the costs, execute the investment. Hire a larger pool of sales associates, expand the current geographical area, and if the marginal increase in forecast sales revenues exceeds the additional salary and implementation costs, start hiring. Need a new manufacturing plant? Show that the construction costs can be recouped quickly and easily by the increase in revenues the plant will generate through new and improved products, and the initiative is approved.

However, real-life business conditions are a lot more complicated. Your firm decides to go with an e-commerce strategy, but multiple strategic paths exist. Which path do you choose? What are the options you have? If you choose the wrong path, how do you get back on the right track? How do you value and prioritize the paths that exist? You are a venture capitalist firm with multiple business plans to consider. How do you value a start-up firm with no proven track record? How do you structure a mutually beneficial investment deal? What is the optimal timing to a second or third round of financing?

Real options are useful not only in valuing a firm through its strategic business options, but also as a strategic business tool in capital investment decisions. For instance, should a firm invest millions in a new facility expansion initiative? How does a firm choose among several seemingly cashless, costly, and unprofitable information-technology infrastructure projects?

Should a firm indulge its billions in a risky research and development initiative? The consequences of a wrong decision can be disastrous or even terminal for certain firms. In a traditional discounted cash-flow model, these questions cannot be answered with any certainty. In fact, some of the answers generated through the use of the traditional discounted cash-flow model are flawed because the model assumes a static, one-time decision-making process whereas the real options approach takes into consideration the strategic managerial options that certain projects create under uncertainty and management's flexibility in exercising or abandoning these options at different points in time, when the level of uncertainty has decreased or has become known over time.

> Business conditions are fraught with uncertainty and risks. These uncertainties hold with them valuable information. When uncertainty becomes resolved through the passage of time, actions, and events, managers can make the appropriate midcourse corrections through a change in business decisions and strategies. Real options incorporate this learning model, akin to having a strategic road map, whereas traditional analyses that neglect this managerial flexibility will grossly undervalue certain projects and strategies.

The real options approach incorporates a learning model, such that management makes better and more informed strategic decisions when some levels of uncertainty are resolved through the passage of time, actions, and events. Traditional discounted cash-flow analysis assumes a static investment decision and assumes that strategic decisions are made initially with no recourse to choose other pathways or options in the future. To create a good analogy of real options, visualize it as a strategic road map of long and winding roads with multiple perilous turns and branches along the way. Imagine the intrinsic and extrinsic value of having such a road map or global positioning system when navigating through unfamiliar territory, as well as having road signs at every turn to guide you in making the best and most informed driving decisions. Such a strategic map is the essence of real options.

The answer to evaluating such projects lies in real options analysis, which can be used in a variety of settings, including pharmaceutical drug development, oil and gas exploration and production, manufacturing, start-up valuation, venture capital investment, information technology infrastructure, research and development, mergers and acquisitions, e-commerce and e-business, intellectual capital development, technology development, facility expansion, business project prioritization, enterprise risk management, business unit capital budgeting, licenses, contracts, intangible asset valuation, and the like. The following section illustrates some business cases and how real options can assist in identifying and capturing additional strategic value for a firm.

THE REAL OPTIONS SOLUTION IN A NUTSHELL

Simply defined, real options is a systematic approach and integrated solution using financial theory, economic analysis, management science, decision sciences, statistics, and econometric modeling in applying options theory in valuing real physical assets, as opposed to financial assets, in a dynamic and uncertain business environment where business decisions are flexible in the context of strategic capital investment decision making, valuing investment opportunities, and project capital expenditures. Real options are crucial in:

- Identifying different corporate investment decision pathways or projects that management can navigate given highly uncertain business conditions.

- Valuing each of the strategic decision pathways and what it represents in terms of financial viability and feasibility.

- Prioritizing these pathways or projects based on a series of qualitative and quantitative metrics.

- Optimizing the value of strategic investment decisions by evaluating different decision paths under certain conditions or using a different sequence of pathways that can lead to the optimal strategy.

- Timing the effective execution of investments and finding the optimal trigger values and cost or revenue drivers.

- Managing existing or developing new optionalities and strategic decision pathways for future opportunities.

ISSUES TO CONSIDER

Strategic options do have significant intrinsic value, but this value is only realized when management decides to execute the strategies. Real options theory assumes that management is logical and competent and that management acts in the best interests of the company and its shareholders through the maximization of wealth and minimization of risk of losses. For example, suppose a firm owns the rights to a piece of land that fluctuates dramatically in price. An analyst calculates the volatility of prices and recommends that management retain ownership for a specified time period, where within this period there is a good chance that the price of real estate will triple. Therefore, management owns an *option to wait* and defer sale for a particular time period. The value of the real estate is therefore higher than the value that is based on today's sale price. The difference is simply this option to wait. However, the value of the real estate will not command the higher value if prices do triple but management decides not to execute the option to sell. In that case, the price of real estate goes back to its original levels after the specified period, and then management finally relinquishes its rights.

Was the analyst right or wrong? What was the true value of the piece of land? Should it have been valued at its explicit value on a deterministic case where you know what the price of land is right now, and therefore this is its value; or should it include some types of optionality where there is a good probability that the price of land could triple in value, hence, the piece of land is truly worth more than it is now and should therefore be valued accordingly? The latter is the real options view. The additional strategic optionality value can only be obtained if the option is executed; otherwise, all the options in the world are worthless. This idea of *explicit* versus *implicit* value becomes highly significant when management's compensation is tied directly to the actual performance of particular projects or strategies.

To further illustrate this point, suppose the price of the land in the market is currently $10 million. Further, suppose that the market is highly liquid and volatile and that the firm can easily sell off the land at a moment's notice within the next 5 years, the same amount of time the firm owns the rights to the land. If there is a 50 percent chance the price will increase to $15 million and a 50 percent chance it will decrease to $5 million within this time period, is the property worth an expected value of $10 million? If the price rises to $15 million, management should be competent and rational enough to execute the option and sell that piece of land immediately to capture the additional $5 million premium. However, if management acts inappropriately or decides to hold off selling in the hopes that prices will rise even further, the property value may eventually drop back down to $5 million. Now, how much is this property really worth? What if there happens to be an *abandonment option*? Suppose there is a perfect counterparty to this transaction who decides to enter into a contractual agreement whereby, for a contractual fee, the counterparty agrees to purchase the property for $10 million within the next 5 years, regardless of the market price and executable at the whim of the firm that owns the property. Effectively, a safety net has been created whereby the minimum floor value of the property has been set at $10 million (less the fee paid). That is, there is a limited downside but an unlimited upside, as the firm can always sell the property at market price if it exceeds the floor value. Hence, this strategic *abandonment option* has increased the value of the property significantly. Logically, with this *abandonment option* in place, the value of the land with the option is definitely worth more than $10 million. The land price is stochastic and uncertain with some volatility (risk) and has some inherent probability distribution. The distribution's left tail is the downside risk and the right tail is upside value, and having an abandonment option (in this example, a price protection of $10 million) means that you take a really sharp knife and you slice off the distribution's left tail at $10 million because the firm will never have to deal with the situation of selling the land at anything lower than $10 million. What happens is that the distribution's left tail risk has been truncated and reduced, making the distribution now positively skewed; and the expected return or average value moves to the right. In other words, strategic real options in this case provided a *risk reduction and value enhancement strategy* to the firm. Therefore, this option has value (e.g., insurance policies require a premium or price to obtain, and you can think of this abandonment option as a price protection insurance against any downside movements), and the idea is to determine what is the fair market value, whether the option is indeed worth it, the optimal timing to execute the option, and so forth. The real options approach seeks to value this additional inherent flexibility. Real options analysis allows the firm to determine how much this safety downside insurance or abandonment option is worth (i.e., what is the fair market value of the contractual fee to obtain the option?), the optimal trigger price (i.e., at what price will make it optimal to sell the land?), and the optimal timing (i.e., what is the optimal amount of time to hold on to the land?).

IMPLEMENTING REAL OPTIONS ANALYSIS

First, it is vital to understand that real options analysis is *not* a simple set of equations or models. It is an *entire decision-making process* that enhances the traditional decision analysis approaches. It takes what has been tried-and-true financial analytics and evolves it to the next step by pushing the envelope of analytical techniques. In addition, it is vital to understand that 50 percent of the value in real options analysis is simply thinking about it. Another 25 percent of the value comes from the number crunching activities, while the final 25 percent comes from the results interpretation and explanation to management. Several issues should be considered when attempting to implement real options analysis:

- **Tools**—The correct tools are important. These tools must be more comprehensive than initially required because analysts will grow into them over time. Do not be restrictive in choosing the relevant tools. Always provide room for expansion. Advanced tools will relieve the analyst of detailed model building and let him or her focus instead on 75 percent of the value—thinking about the problem and interpreting the results. Chapter 11 illustrates the use of Real Options Super Lattice Solver (SLS) software and how even complex and customized real options problems can be solved with great ease.

- **Resources**—The best tools in the world are useless without the relevant human resources to back them up. Tools do not eliminate the analyst, but enhance the analyst's ability to effectively and efficiently execute the analysis. The right people with the right tools will go a long way. Because there are only a few true real options experts in the world who truly understand the theoretical underpinnings of the models as well the practical applications, care should be taken in choosing the correct team. A team of real options experts is vital in the success of the initiative. A company should consider building a team of in-house experts to implement real options analysis and to maintain the ability for continuity, training, and knowledge transfer over time. Knowledge and experience in the theories, implementation, training, and consulting are the core requirements of this team of individuals. This is why training is vital. For instance, the CRM/CQRM certification program provides analysts and managers the opportunity to immerse themselves into the theoretical and real-life applications of simulation, forecasting, optimization, and real options (for details please see *www.realoptionsvaluation.com*).

- **Senior Management Buy-in**—The analysis buy-in has to be top-down where senior management drives the real options analysis initiative. A bottom-up approach where a few inexperienced junior analysts try to impress the powers that be will fail miserably.

TYPES OF REAL OPTIONS STRATEGIES

Abandonment Option

An abandonment option provides the holder the right but not the obligation to sell off and abandon some project, asset, or property that it owns, at a prespecified price and term. This option helps hedge downside risks and losses by being able to salvage some value of a failed project or asset that is out-of-the-money (e.g., sell intellectual property and assets, abandon and walk away from a project, and execute buyback or sellback provisions). Additional examples include *Exit and Salvage* (sale of assets and intellectual property to reduce losses); *Divestitures; Spin-offs; Contractual Buyback Provisions; Stop and Abandon* (stop before executing the next phase); *Termination for Convenience; Early Exit;* and *Guaranteed Buyback or Salvage Value.*

Barrier Option

A barrier option means that the option becomes live and available for execution and, consequently, the value of the strategic option depends on either breaching or not breaching an artificial barrier. Examples include *Protective Barriers* (options become live only if a project's net profits are above a certain level); *Price Protection* (a vendor contract that becomes null if market prices go above or below a certain threshold); and any other *Options-Embedded Contracts* that get *knocked in-the-money* or *out-of-the-money* if a certain benchmark is surpassed.

Chooser Option

A chooser option implies that management has the flexibility to choose among several strategies. Examples of chooser options include contractual obligations allowing the holder to *Choose One or Multiple Options* (to expand, abandon, switch, or contract, and combinations of other exotic options).

Contraction Option

A contraction option provides management the right and ability to contract its existing operations under the right conditions, thereby saving on operating expenses. The option provides a reduction in downside risk but still allows the firm to participate in reduced benefits (e.g., a counterparty takes over or joins in some activities to share profits and share risks, which helps reduce your firm's risk of failure or reduce severe losses in a risky but potentially profitable venture). Additional examples include *Outsourcing, Alliances, Sub-Contractors, Leasing, Joint Venture, Foreign Partnerships, Co-Development,* and *Co-Marketing.*

Deferment Option (Optimal Timing, Option to Wait, Option to Execute)

A *deferment option* is also known as an *option to wait* or *option to execute*. This option allows decision makers to buy additional time to wait for new information by prenegotiating pricing and other contractual terms to obtain the option but not the obligation to purchase or execute something in the future should conditions warrant it (wait and see before executing). Examples of options to wait and defer include *Proof of Concept* (run a small-scale project first to better determine the costs, schedule, and market risks of a project versus jumping in right now and blindly taking the risk); *Build, Buy, or Lease* (develop internally or using commercially available technology or products); *Multiple Contracts* (contracts in place that may or not be executed); *Market Research* (to obtain valuable information before deciding); *Venture Capital* (small seed investment with a right of first refusal before executing large-scale financing); *Contract Negotiations* (negotiate with vendors for competitive sustainment and strategic capability and availability); *Research & Development* (parallel implementation of alternatives while waiting on technical success of the main project, and no need to delay the project because of one bad component in the project); *Prototyping; Advanced Concept Technology Demonstration* (test before full-scale implementation); *Right of First Refusal Contracts; Value of Information* (wait and see to obtain better demand or cost inputs, capability, schedule, and other metrics); *Hedging* (Call- and Put-like options to execute something in the future with agreed upon terms now); and other wait-and-see options.

Expansion Option

An expansion option provides management the right and ability to expand into different markets, products and strategies or to expand its current operations under the right conditions. This option allows companies to take advantage of upside opportunities by having existing platform, structure, or technology that can be readily expanded (e.g., utility peaking plants, larger oil platforms, early/leapfrog technology development, larger capacity or technology-in-place for future expansion). Spending a little more money upfront to have a prebuilt facility that is ready to be expanded is oftentimes cheaper in the long run than to restart any development in the future (e.g., a larger prebuilt deep-sea oil platform at the start of development in drydock is cheaper than re-initiating a secondary development in the future by building in the middle of the ocean). Some additional examples include *Platform Technologies, Mergers and Acquisitions, Pre-Built Expansion Capabilities, Geographical, Technological, and Market Expansion,* as well as *Reusability and Scalability Options* (pre-built into existing infrastructure).

Sequential Compound Option

A sequential compound option means that the execution and value of future strategic options depend on previous options in sequence of execution. Significant value exists if you can phase out investments over time, thereby reducing the risk of a one-time up-front investment (e.g., pharmaceutical and high technology development and manufacturing usually comes in phases or stages). Some examples include *Stage-Gate Implementation* (high-risk project development); *Prototyping; Low-Rate-Initial-Production; Technical Feasibility Tests; Market Research* (prior to launching a new product); *Technology Demonstration Competitions; Multiple Staged Contracts with Options to Abandon; Termination for Convenience; Built-in Flexibility* (ability to execute different courses of action at specific stages of development); *Milestones; Stage-Gate Research & Development; Phased Options;* and *Platform Technologies.*

Switching Option

A switching option provides the right and ability but not the obligation to switch among different sets of business operating conditions, including different technologies, markets, or products. This option provides the ability to choose among several options, thereby improving strategic flexibility to maneuver within the realm of uncertainty (maintain a foot in one door while exploring another to decide if it makes sense to switch or stay put). Examples include *Ability to Switch* (among various raw input materials to use when prices of each raw material fluctuate significantly); readiness and capability risk mitigation by switching vendors in an *Open Architecture* through *Multiple Vendors* and *Modular Design;* and *Switching Between Several Raw Materials* to cheaper inputs used in manufacturing.

EXECUTION TYPES

And for all of these options, you can have different allowed execution times, including American, European, Bermudan, and Asian options. American options allow you to execute at any time before and up to and including the expiration date. European options allow you to execute only on a specific date, typically the expiration date itself. Bermudan options are a mix between European and American in that there is a blackout or vesting period when you cannot execute the option, but you can do so at any time after this blackout period and up to and including expiration (e.g., an employee stock option usually has a 10-year maturity and a 4-year vesting period, where you cannot exercise the option within this first 4 years and you lose the option if you leave your job during this vesting period, but once this requisite service period has passed, the option is yours and you can exercise it at any time between year 4 and year 10). Finally, Asian options are look-back options, where specific conditions in the option are dependent on some factor in the future (e.g., United Airlines buys some Airbus A380 planes where they sign the purchase order today for delivery of the planes in two years, and the price of the plane is dependent on the average market price between now and two years, a period that is in the future when the purchase order was placed, but will be the past once the planes and final payment changes hands two years from now, and both parties can lookback to this pricing period to obtain the final sale price of the planes). So, you can have an American Abandonment option or a European Abandonment option, and so forth.

INDUSTRY LEADERS EMBRACING REAL OPTIONS

Industries using real options as a tool for strategic decision making started with oil and gas and mining companies and later expanded into utilities, biotechnology, and pharmaceuticals, and now into telecommunications, high-tech, and across all industries. The following examples relate how real options have been or should be used in different kinds of companies.

Automobile and Manufacturing Industry

In automobile and manufacturing, General Motors (GM) applies real options to create *switching options* in producing its new series of autos. This option is essentially to use a cheaper resource over a given period of time. GM holds excess raw materials and has multiple global vendors for similar materials with excess contractual obligations above what it projects as necessary. The excess contractual cost is outweighed by the significant savings of switching vendors when a certain raw material becomes too expensive in a particular region of the world. By spending the additional money in contracting with vendors and meeting their minimum purchase requirements, GM has essentially paid the premium on purchasing an *option to switch,* which is important especially when the price of raw materials fluctuates significantly in different regions around the world. Having an option here provides the holder a hedging vehicle against pricing risks.

Computer Industry

In the computer industry, HP–Compaq used to forecast sales in foreign countries months in advance. It then configured, assembled, and shipped the highly specific configuration printers to these countries. However, given that demand changes rapidly and forecast figures are seldom correct, the preconfigured printers usually suffer the higher inventory holding cost or the cost of technological obsolescence. HP–Compaq can create an *option to wait* and defer making any decisions too early through building assembly plants in these foreign countries. Parts can then be shipped and assembled in specific configurations when demand is known, possibly weeks in advance rather than months in advance. These parts can be shipped anywhere in the world and assembled in any configuration necessary, while excess parts are interchangeable across different countries. The premium paid on this option is building the assembly plants, and the upside potential is the savings in making wrong demand forecasts.

Airline Industry

In the airline industry, Boeing spends billions of dollars and takes several years to decide if a certain aircraft model should even be built. Should the wrong model be tested in this elaborate strategy, Boeing's competitors may gain a competitive advantage relatively quickly. Because so many technical, engineering, market, and financial uncertainties are involved in the decision-making process, Boeing can conceivably create an *option to choose* through parallel development of multiple plane designs simultaneously, knowing well the increasing cost of developing multiple designs simultaneously with the sole purpose of eliminating all but one in the near future. The added cost is the premium paid on the option. However, Boeing will be able to decide which model to abandon or continue when these uncertainties and risks become known over time. Eventually, all the models will be eliminated save one. This way, the company can hedge itself against making the wrong initial decision and benefit from the knowledge gained through parallel development initiatives.

Oil and Gas Industry

In the oil and gas industry, companies spend millions of dollars to refurbish their refineries and add new technology to create an *option to switch* their mix of outputs among heating oil, diesel, and other petrochemicals as a final product, using real options as a means of making capital and investment decisions. This option allows the refinery to switch its final output to one that is more profitable based on prevailing market prices, to capture the demand and price cyclicality in the market.

Telecommunications Industry

In the telecommunications industry, in the past, companies like Sprint and AT&T installed more fiber-optic cable and other telecommunications infrastructure than any other company in order to create a *growth option* in the future by providing a secure and extensive network and to create a high barrier to entry, providing a first-to-market advantage. Imagine having to justify to the board of directors the need to spend billions of dollars on infrastructure that will not be used for years to come. Without the use of real options, this decision would have been impossible to justify.

Real Estate Industry

In the real estate arena, leaving land undeveloped creates an option to develop at a later date at a more lucrative profit level. However, what is the *optimal wait time* or the *optimal trigger price* to maximize returns? In theory, one can wait for an infinite amount of time, and real options provide the solution for the optimal timing and optimal price trigger value.

Utilities Industry

In the utilities industry, firms have created an *option to execute* and an *option to expand* by installing cheap-to-build inefficient energy generator *peaker* plants to be used only when electricity prices are high and to shut down when prices are low. The price of electricity tends to remain constant until it hits a certain capacity utilization trigger level, when prices shoot up significantly. Although this occurs infrequently, the possibility still exists, and by having a cheap standby plant, the firm has created the option to turn on the expanded capacity generation whenever it becomes necessary, to capture this upside price fluctuation.

Pharmaceutical Research and Development Industry

In pharmaceutical or research and development initiatives, real options can be used to justify the large investments in what seems to be cashless and unprofitable under the discounted cash flow method but actually creates *sequential compound options* in the future. Under the myopic lenses of a traditional discounted cash flow analysis, the high initial investment of, say, a billion dollars in research and development may return a highly uncertain projected few million dollars over the next few years. Management will conclude under a net present value analysis that the project is not financially feasible. However, a cursory look at the industry indicates that research and development is performed everywhere. Hence, management must see an intrinsic strategic value in research and development. How is this intrinsic strategic value quantified? A real options approach would optimally time and spread the billion dollar initial investment into a multiple-stage investment structure. At each stage, management has an *option to wait* and see what happens as well as the *option to abandon* or the *option to expand* into the subsequent stages. The ability to defer cost and proceed only if situations are permissible creates value for the investment.

High-Tech and e-Business Industry

In e-business strategies, real options can be used to prioritize different e-commerce initiatives and to justify those large initial investments that have an uncertain future. Real options can be used in e-commerce to create incremental investment stages compared to a large one-time investment (invest a little now, wait and see before investing more) as well as create *options to abandon* and other future growth options.

Mergers and Acquisitions

In valuing a firm for acquisition, you should not only consider the revenues and cash flows generated from the firm's operations but also the strategic options that come with the firm. For instance, if the acquired firm does not operate up to expectations, an *abandonment option* can be executed where it can be sold for its intellectual property and other tangible assets. If the firm is highly successful, it can be spun off into other industries and verticals or new products and services can be eventually developed through the execution of an *expansion option*. In fact, in mergers and acquisition, several strategic options exist. For instance, a firm acquires other entities to enlarge its existing portfolio of products or geographic location or to obtain new technology (*expansion option*); or to divide the acquisition into many smaller pieces and sell them off as in the case of a corporate raider (*abandonment option*); or it merges to form a larger organization due to certain synergies and immediately lays off many of its employees (*contraction option*). If the seller does not value its real options, it may be leaving money on the negotiation table. If the buyer does not value these strategic options, it is undervaluing a potentially highly lucrative acquisition target.

All these cases where the high cost of implementation with no apparent payback in the near future seems foolish and incomprehensible in the traditional discounted cash flow sense are fully justified in the real options sense when taking into account the strategic options the practice creates for the future, the uncertainty of the future operating environment, and management's flexibility in making the right choices at the appropriate time.

EXPANSION AND COMPOUND OPTIONS: THE CASE OF THE OPERATING SYSTEM

You are the Chief Technology Officer of a large multinational corporation, and you know that your firm's systems are antiquated and require an upgrade (e.g., to some new cloud-based online collaboration tool, or to the new Windows 10, Server 2016, SAP HANA system, or some other hardware upgrade). You arrange a meeting with the CEO, letting him in on the situation. The CEO quips back immediately, saying that he will support your initiative if you can prove to him that the monetary benefits outweigh the costs of implementation—a simple and logical request. You immediately arrange for a demonstration of the new operating system, and the highly technical experts from the vendor (e.g., Microsoft, SAP, Oracle) provide you and your boss a marvelous presentation of the system's capabilities and value-added enhancements that took in excess of a few million dollars and several years to develop. The system even fixes itself in times of dire circumstances and is overall more reliable and stable than its predecessors. You get more excited by the minute and have made up your mind to get the much-needed product upgrade. There is still one hurdle, the financial hurdle, to prove not only that the new system provides a better operating environment, but also that the plan of action is financially sound. Granted, the more efficient and sophisticated system will make your boss's secretary a much happier person and, hence, more productive. Then again, so will an extra week's worth of vacation and a bigger bonus check, both of which are a lot cheaper and easier to implement. The new system will not help your sales force sell more products and generate higher revenues because the firm looks state-of-the-art only if a customer questions what version of Windows operating system you are using—hardly an issue that will arise during a sales call. Then again, when has using the latest software ever assisted in closing a deal, especially when you are a contract global-freight and logistics solutions provider?

You lose sleep over the next few days pondering the issue, and you finally decide to assemble a task force made up of some of your top IT personnel. The six of you sit in a room considering the same issues and trying to brainstorm a few really good arguments. You link up the value-added propositions provided in the Microsoft technician's presentation and come up with a series of potential cost reduction drivers. Principally, the self-preservation and self-fixing functionality will mean less technical assistance and help-desk calls, freeing up resources and perhaps leading to the need for fewer IT people on staff. Your mind races through some quick figures, you feel your heart pounding faster, and you see a light at the end of the tunnel. Finally you will have your long-awaited operating system, and all your headaches will go away. Wait, not only does it reduce the help-desk time, but also it increases efficiency because employees will no longer have to call or hold for technical assistance.

Your team spends the next few days scouring through mountains of data on help-desk calls and issues—thank goodness for good record-keeping and relational databases. Looking for issues that could potentially become obsolete with the new system, you find that at least 20 percent of your help-desk calls could be eliminated by having the new system in place because it is more stable, is capable of self-fixing these critical issues, can troubleshoot internal hardware conflicts, and so forth. Besides, doesn't employee morale count? Satisfied with your analysis, you approach the CEO and show him your findings.

Impressed with your charts and analytical rigor in such a short time frame, he asks several quick questions and points out several key issues. The cost reduction in technical assistance is irrelevant because you need these people to install and configure the new system. The start-up cost and learning curve might be steep, and employees may initially have a tough time adjusting to the new operating environment—help-desk calls may actually increase in the near future, albeit slowing down in time. But the firm's mission has always been to cultivate its employees and not to fire them needlessly. Besides, there are five people on staff at the help desk and a 20 percent reduction means one less full-time employee out of 5,000 in the entire firm—hardly a cost reduction strategy! As for the boss's secretary's productivity, you noticed two first-class air tickets to Maui on his desk, and you are pretty sure one of them is for her. Your mind races with alternate possibilities—including taking a trip to Hawaii with a high-powered digital-zoom camera but deciding against it on your way out. He notices your wandering eyes and tries to change the subject. You still have not sufficiently persuaded your boss on getting the new operating system, and you are up a tree and out on a limb. Thoughts of going shopping for a camera haunt you for the rest of the day.

Sound familiar? Firms wrestle with similar decisions daily, and vendors wrestling with how to make their products more marketable have to first address this financial and strategic issue. Imagine you are the sales director for Microsoft, or any software and hardware vendor for that matter. How do you close a sale like this?

Performing a series of simple traditional analyses using a discounted cash flow methodology or economic justification based on traditional analyses will fail miserably, as we have seen above. The quantifiable financial benefits do not exceed the high implementation costs. How do you justify and correctly value such seemingly cashless and cash-flow draining projects? The answer lies in real options. Instead of being myopic and focusing on current savings, the implementation of large-scale servers or operating systems will generate future strategic options for the firm. That is, having the servers and system in place provides you a springboard to a second-, third-, or fourth-phase IT implementation. That is, having a powerful connected system gives you the technical feasibility to pursue online collaboration, global data access, videoconferencing, digital signatures, encryption security, remote installations, document recovery, and the like, which would be impossible to do without it. Hence, the value of upgrading to a new system provides the firm an *expansion option,* which is the right and ability, but not the obligation, to invest and pursue some of these value-added technologies. Some of these technologies such as security enhancements and global data access can be highly valuable to your global freight company's supply chain management. You may further delineate certain features into groups of options to execute at the same time—that is, create a series of *sequential compound options* where the success of one group of initiatives depends on the success of another in sequence, similar to a stage-gate investment process. Notice that using an extrapolation of the traditional analytic approaches would be inappropriate here because all these implementation possibilities are simply options that a senior manager has, and not guaranteed execution by any means. When you view the whole strategic picture, value is created and identified where there was not any before, thereby making you able to clearly justify financially your plans for the upgrade. You would be well on your way to getting your new operating system installed.

EXPANSION OPTIONS: THE CASE OF THE E-BUSINESS INITIATIVE

Turn back the clock to the year 2000, when the e-business boom has just barely started, and the investment bank you worked for had decided to join the Internet age. You get a decree from the powers that be to come up with a solid e-commerce initiative. The CEO calls you into his office and spends an hour expounding on the wisdom of bringing the firm closer to the electronic Web. After hours of meetings, you are tasked with performing a feasibility analysis, choosing the right strategy, and valuing the wisdom of going e-commerce. Well, it sounds simple enough, or so you think… The next two weeks are spent with boardroom meetings, conference calls with e-commerce consulting firms, and bottles of Alka-Seltzer. Being a newly endowed expert on the e-business strategies after spending two weeks in Tahiti on a supposedly world-renowned e-commerce crash course, you realize you really still know nothing. One thing is for certain: the Internet has revolutionized the way businesses are run. The traditional *Sun Tzu* business environment of "know thy enemy and know thyself and in a hundred battles you will be victorious" had not met the Internet. The competitive playing field has been leveled, and your immediate competitors are no longer the biggest threat. The biggest threat is globalization, when new competitors halfway around the world crawl out of the woodwork and take half of your market share just because they have a fancy website capable of attracting, diverting, and retaining Web traffic, and capable of taking orders around the world, and you do not. Perhaps the CEO is right; it is a do-or-die scenario. When a 12-year-old girl can transform her parent's fledgling trinket store into an overnight success by going to the Internet, technology seems to be the biggest foe of all. You either ride the technological wave or are swept under.

Of course, back to the future in the year 2015, you can look back at companies like Google, Facebook, Twitter, and others, and only wished you had the power of hindsight. But back in 2000, you were convinced of the necessity of e-commerce and the strong desire to keep your job, you came up with a strategic game plan.

You look at the e-commerce options you have and try to ascertain the correct path to traverse, knowing very well that if you pick the wrong one, it can be ultimately disastrous, for you and your firm, in that particular order. In between updating your curriculum vitae, you decide to spend some time pondering the issues. You realize that there are a large number of options in going e-commerce, and you have decided on several potential pathways to consider as they are most appropriate to the firm's core business.

Do we simply create a static website with nice graphics, text explaining what we do, and perhaps a nice little map showing where we are located and the hours of availability, and get fired? Do we perhaps go a little further and provide traditional banking services on the Web? Perhaps a way for our customers to access their accounts, pay bills, trade stocks, apply for loans, and perhaps get some free stock advice or free giveaways and pop-up ads to divert traffic on the Web? Perhaps we can take it to the extreme and use state-of-the-art technology to enable items like digital television access, live continuous streaming technology, equity trading on smartphones and tablets, interaction with and direct access to floor specialists and traders on the New York Stock Exchange for the larger clients, and all the while using servers in Enron-like offshore tax havens (all the while assuming you don't get caught and implode like Enron did). The potentials are endless.

You suddenly feel queasy with the inkling of impending doom. What about competition? Ameritrade and a dozen other online trading firms currently exist. Most major banks are already on the Web, and they provide the same services. What makes us so special? Then again, if we do not follow the other players, we may be left out in the cold. Perhaps there are some ways to differentiate our services. Perhaps some sort of geographical expansion; after all, the Internet is global, so why shouldn't we be? What about market penetration effects and strategies, country risk analysis, legislative and regulatory risks? What if the strategy is unsuccessful? What will happen then? Competitive effects are unpredictable. The threats of new entrants and low barriers to entry may elicit even more competitors than you currently have. Is the firm ready to play in the big leagues and fight with the virtual offshore banking services? Globalization—what an ugly word it is right about now. What about new technology: Do we keep spending every time something new comes out? What about market share, market penetration, positioning, and being first to market with a new and exciting product? What about future growth opportunities, e-traffic management, and portal security? The lists go on and on. Perhaps you should take a middle ground, striking an alliance with established investment banking firms with the applicable IT infrastructure already in place. Why build when you can buy? You reach for your Alka-Seltzer and realize you need something much stronger.

How do you prioritize these potential strategies, perform a financial and strategic feasibility analysis, and make the right decision? Will the firm survive if we go down the wrong path? If we find out we are on the wrong path, can we navigate our way back to the right one? What options can we create to enable this? Which of these strategies is optimal? Upon identifying what these strategies are, including all their downstream *expansion options,* you can then value each of these strategic pathways. The identification, valuation, prioritization, and selection of strategic projects are where real options analysis can provide great insights and value. Each project initiative should not be viewed in its current state. Instead, all downstream opportunities should be viewed and considered as well. Otherwise, wrong decisions can be made because only projects with immediate value will be chosen, while projects that carry with them great future potential are abandoned simply because management is setting its sights on the short term.

EXPANSION AND SEQUENTIAL OPTIONS: THE CASE OF THE PHARMACEUTICAL R&D

Being the chief chemist of a small pharmaceutical firm that is thinking of developing a certain drug useful in gene therapy, you have the responsibility to determine the right biochemical compounds to create. Understanding very well that the future of the firm rests on pursuing and developing the right portfolio of drugs, you take your evaluation task rather seriously. Currently, the firm's management is uncertain whether to proceed with developing a group of compounds and is also uncertain regarding the drug development's financial feasibility. From historical data and personal experience, you understand that development "home runs" are few and far between. As a matter of fact, you realize that less than 5 percent of all compounds developed are superstars. However, if the right compounds are chosen, the firm will own several valuable patents and bolster its chances of receiving future rounds of funding. Armed with that future expectation, you evaluate each potential compound with care and patience.

For example, one of the compounds you are currently evaluating is called Creatosine. Management knows that Creatosine, when fully developed, can be taken orally, but has the potential to be directly injected into the bloodstream, which increases its effectiveness. Because there is great uncertainty in the development of Creatosine, management decides to develop the oral version for now and wait for a period of several years before deciding on investing additional funds to develop the injectable version. Thus, management has created an *expansion option*—that is, the option but not the obligation to expand Creatosine into an injectable version at any time between now and several years. By incorporating real options strategy, your firm has mitigated its risks in developing the drug into both an oral and injectable form at initiation. By waiting, scientific and market risks become resolved through the passage of time, and your firm can then decide whether to pursue the second injectable phase. This risk-hedging phenomenon is common in financial options and is applicable here for real options.

However, there are other drug compounds to analyze as well. You go through the list with a fine-tooth comb and realize that you must evaluate each drug by not only its biochemical efficacies, but also by its financial feasibility. Given the firm's current capital structure, you would need to not only value, prioritize, and select the right compounds, but also find the optimal portfolio mix of compounds, subject to budget, timing, and risk constraints. On top of that, you would have to value your firm as a whole in terms of a portfolio of strategic options. The firm's value lies not only in its forecast revenues less its costs subject to time valuation of money but also in all the current research and development initiatives under way, where a single home run will double or triple the firm's valuation. These so-called future *growth options,* which are essentially growth opportunities that the firm has, are highly valuable. These *growth options* are simply *expansion options* because your firm owns the right infrastructure, resources, and technology to pursue these future opportunities but not the obligation to do so unless both internal research and external market conditions are amenable.

Another approach you decide to use is to create a strategic development road map, knowing that every drug under development has to go through multiple phases. At each phase, depending on the research results, management can decide to continue its development to the next phase or abandon it assuming it does not meet certain prespecified criteria. That is, management has the *option to choose* whether a certain compound will continue to the next stage. Certain drugs in the initial phases go through a *sequential compound option,* where the success of the third phase, for example, depends on the success of the second phase, which in turn depends on the success of the first phase in the stage-gate drug development cycle. Valuing such sequences of options using a traditional approach of taking expected values with respect to the probabilities of success is highly dubious and incorrect. The valuation will be incorrect at best and highly misleading at worst, driving management to select the wrong mix of compounds at the wrong time.

EXPANSION AND SWITCHING OPTIONS: THE CASE OF THE OIL AND GAS EXPLORATION AND PRODUCTION

The oil and gas industry is fraught with strategic options problems because oil and gas exploration and production involves significant amounts of risk and uncertainty. For example, when drilling for oil, the reservoir properties, fluidic properties, trap size and geometry, porosity, seal containment, oil and gas in place, expulsion force, losses due to migration, development costs, and so forth are all unknowns. How then is a reservoir engineer going to recommend to management the value of a particular drill site? Let us explore some of the more frequent real options problems encountered in this industry.

Being a fresh M.B.A. graduate from a top finance program, you are hired by a second-tier independent oil and gas firm, and your first task is to value several primary and secondary reservoir recovery wells. You are called into your boss's office, and she requested that you do an independent financial analysis on a few production wells. You were given a stack of technical engineering documents to review. After spending a fortnight scouring through several books on the fundamentals of the oil and gas industry, you finally have some basic understanding of the intricacies of what a secondary recovery well is. Needing desperately to impress your superiors, you decide to investigate a little further into some new analytics for solving these types of recovery-well problems.

Based on your incomplete understanding of the problem, you begin to explore all the possibilities and come to the conclusion that the best analytics to use may be the application of a Monte Carlo simulation and real options analysis. Instead of simply coming up with the value of the project, you decide to also identify where value can be added to the projects by incorporating strategic real optionality. Suppose that the problem you are analyzing is a primary drilling site that has its own natural energy source, complete with its gas cap on one side and a water drive on the other. These energy sources maintain a high upward pressure on the oil reservoir to increase the ease of drilling and, therefore, the site's productivity. However, knowing that the level of energy may not be sustainable for a long time and its efficacy is unknown currently, you recognize that one of the strategies is to create an *expansion option* to drill a secondary recovery well near the primary site. Instead of drilling, you can use this well to inject water or gas into the ground, thereby increasing the upward pressure and keeping the reservoir productive. Building this secondary well is an option and not an obligation for the next few years. Another option that is on the table is hydraulic fracturing or fracking, where a high-pressure mixture of water, sand, and chemicals is directed at the rock strata to release the oil and gas trapped beneath. The secondary well can also be drilled vertically or horizontally to the rock layer to create new pathways to release the trapped gas or the pathways can be used to extend existing channels for the oil to flow.

The first recommendation seems to make sense given that the geological structure and reservoir size are difficult to estimate. Yet these are not the only important considerations, the price of oil in the market is also something that fluctuates dramatically and should be considered. Assuming that the price of oil is a major factor in management's decisions, your second recommendation includes separating the project into two stages. The first stage is to drill multiple wells in the primary reservoir, which will eventually maximize on its productivity. At that time a second phase can be implemented through smaller satellite reservoirs in the surrounding areas that are available for drilling but are separated from the primary reservoir by geological faults. This second stage is also an *expansion option* on the first: When the price of oil increases, the firm is then able to set up new rigs over the satellite reservoirs, drill, and complete these wells. Then, using the latest technology in subsurface robotics, the secondary wells can be tied back into the primary platform, thereby increasing and expanding the productivity of the primary well by some expansion factor. Obviously, although this is a strategic option that the firm has, the firm does not have the obligation to drill secondary wells unless the market price of oil is favorable enough. Using some basic intuition, you plug some numbers into your models and create the optimal oil price levels such that secondary drillings are profitable. However, given your brief conversation with your boss and your highly uncertain career future, you decide to dig into the strategy a little more.

Perhaps the company already has several producing wells at the reservoir. If that is so, the analysis should be tweaked such that instead of being an *expansion option* by drilling more wells, the firm can retrofit these existing wells in strategic locations from producers into injectors, creating a *switching option*. Instead of drilling more wells, the company can use the existing wells to inject gas, water, or chemical mixtures (i.e., perform fracking) into the surrounding geological areas in the hopes that this will increase the energy source, break through the rock strata, and forcing the trapped oil to surface at a higher rate. These secondary production wells should be switched into injectors when the recovery rate of the secondary wells is relatively low and the marginal benefits of the added productivity on primary wells far outstrip the retrofit costs. In addition, some of the deep-sea drilling platforms that are to be built in the near future can be made into *expansion options,* where slightly larger platforms are built at some additional cost (premium paid to create this option), such that if oil prices are optimally high, the flexible capacity inherent in this larger platform can be executed to boost production.

Finally, depending on the situation involved, you can also create a *sequential compound option* for the reservoir. That is, the firm can segregate its activities into different phases. Specifically, we can delineate the strategic option into four phases. Phases I to III are exploration wells, and Phase IV is a development well.

- Phase I: Start by performing seismic surveys to get information on the structures of subsurface reservoirs (the costs incurred include shooting the survey, processing data, mapping, and so forth).

- Phase II: If large structures are found, drill exploration wells; if not, then abandon the project now.

- Phase III: If the exploration well succeeds industrially or commercially (evaluated on factors such as cost, water depth, oil price, rock, reservoir, and fluid properties), drill more delineation or "step out" wells to define the reservoir.

- Phase IV: If the reservoir is productive enough, commit more money for full development (platform building, setting platform, drilling development wells).

ABANDONMENT OPTIONS: THE
CASE OF THE MANUFACTURER

You work for a midsize hardware manufacturing firm located in the heartland of America. Having recently attended a corporate finance seminar on real options, you set out to determine whether you can put some of your newfound knowledge to good use within the company. Currently, your firm purchases powerful laser-guided robotic fabrication equipment for state-of-the-art 3D Additive Printing Technology, Photopolymerization, Fused Deposition Modeling, and Selective Laser Sintering. Your main clients include companies like Airbus, Boeing, Lockheed Martin, Pratt & Whitney, Rolls-Royce, and Honeywell. Each of these equipment run in the tens of millions of dollars and have to be specially ordered more than a year in advance, due to their unique and advanced specifications. They break down easily, and if any one of the main machines that your firm owns breaks down, it can be disastrous because part of the manufacturing division may have to be shut down temporarily for a period exceeding a year. So, is it always desirable to have at least one fabrication tool under order at all times, just as a precaution? A major problem arises when the newly ordered tool arrives, but the remaining ones are fully functional and require no replacement. The firm has simply lost millions of dollars. In retrospect, certainly having a backup machine sitting idle that costs millions of dollars is not optimal. However, millions can also be lost if indeed a tool breaks down and a replacement is a year away. The question is what do you do, and how can real options be used in this case, both as a strategic decision-making tool and valuation model?

Using traditional analysis, you come up to a dead end, as the tool's breakdown has never been consistent and the ordered parts never arrive on schedule. Turning to real options, you decide to create a strategic option with the vendor. Instead of having to wait more than a year before a new machine arrives, while during that time not knowing when your existing machines will break down, you decide to create a mutually agreeable contract. Your firm decides to put up a certain amount of money and to enter into a contractual agreement whereby the vendor will put you on its preferred list. In addition, your firm spends some development funds to retrofit your manufacturing equipment to an open architecture and modular configuration, allowing quickly replaceable and interchangeable parts. This cuts down delivery time from one year to two months. If your firm does not require the equipment, you will have to pay a penalty exit fee equivalent to a certain percentage of the machine's dollar value amount, within a specified period, on a ratcheted scale, with different exit penalties at different exit periods. In essence, you have created an *abandonment option* where your firm has the right not to purchase the equipment should circumstances force your hand, but hedging yourself to obtain the machine at a moment's notice should there be a need. The price of the option's premium is the contractual price paid for such an arrangement. The savings come in the form of not having to close down part of your plant, losing potential revenues, incur higher costs, and having a bad reputation. By incorporating real options insights into the problem, the firm saves tens of millions of dollars, ends up with the optimal decision, reduces the amount of potential downtime, and upgrades its equipment with modular open architecture configuration suitable for future growth and inclusion of any new disruptive technology.

EXPANSION AND BARRIER OPTIONS: THE CASE OF THE LOST VENTURE CAPITALIST

You work in a venture capital firm and are in charge of the selection of strategic business plans and performing financial analysis on their respective financial feasibility and operational viability. The firm gets more than a thousand business plans a year, and your boss does not have the time to go through each of them in detail and relies on you to sniff out the ones with the maximum potential in the least amount of time. Besides, the winning plans do not wait for money. They often have money chasing after them. Having been in the field of venture capital funding for 20 years and having survived the bursting of the dot.com bubble, your judgment is highly valued in the firm. However, with the changing economic and competitive landscape, even seemingly bad ideas may turn into the next IPO success story. Given the opportunity of significant investment returns, the money lost on bad ideas is a necessary evil in not losing out on the next eBay, Google, PayPal, Facebook, Twitter, or Yahoo! just because the CEO is not a brilliant business plan author.

Your qualitative judgment may still be valid, but the question is what next? What do you do after you have selected your top 100 candidates? How do you efficiently allocate the firm's capital to minimize risk and maximize return? Picking the right firms the wrong way only gets you so far, especially when banking on start-ups hoping for new technological breakthroughs. A diversified portfolio of firms is always prudent, but a diversified portfolio of the right firms is much better. Prioritizing, ranking, and coming up with a solid financing structure for funding start-ups is tricky business, especially when traditional valuation methodologies do not work.

The new economy provides many challenges for the corporate decision maker. Market equity value of a firm now depends on expectations and anticipation of future opportunities in novel technologies rather than on a traditional bricks-and-mortar environment. This shift in underlying fundamentals from tangible goods to technological innovation has created an issue in valuing the firm. Even the face of the intangibles created by technological innovation has changed. In most cases, a significant portion of a firm's value or its strategic investment options is derived from the firm's intangibles. Intangibles generally refer to elements in a business that augment the revenue-generating process but do not themselves have a physical or monetary appearance while still holding significant value to the firm. Intangibles may range from more traditional items like intellectual property, property rights, patents, branding, and trademarks to a new generation of so-called e-intangibles created in the new economy.

Examples of this new generation of e-intangibles include items like marketing intangible, process and product technologies, trade dress, customer loyalty, branding, proprietary software, speed, search engine efficiency, online data catalogs, server efficiency, traffic control and diversion, streaming technology, content, experience, collaborative filtering, universal-resource-locator naming conventions, hubs, social networking, Web page hits, imprints, blogs, and community relationships. New entries in the e-commerce economy over the past decade include the financial sector (bank wires, online bill payments, online investing), healthcare sector (cross-border medical teaching), publication and retail auctions (e-books, e-magazines, open sourced papers and books, eBay) to the Amazon, Google, Facebook, and Twitters of the world. The new trend seems to continue, and new start-ups emerge in scores by the minute to include sophisticated and complex structures like online cross-border banking services, virtual offshore banks, cross-border medical diagnostic imaging, cloud-based applications, and online-server game playing. However, other less sophisticated e-business strategies on the cloud and Software as a Service (SaaS) strategy have also been booming of late, including service-based websites, which provide a supposedly value-added service at no charge to the consumers such as online greeting cards and online e-invitations. Lower barriers to entry and significant threat of new entrants and substitution effects characterize these strategies.

Even using fairly well-known models like the discounted cash flow analysis is insufficient to value these types of firms. For instance, as a potential venture capitalist, how do you go about identifying the intangibles and intellectual property created when traditional financial theory is insufficient to justify or warrant such outrageous price-to-earnings multiples? Trying to get on the bandwagon in initial public offerings with large capital gains is always a good investment strategy, but randomly investing in start-ups with little to no fundamental justification of potential future profitability is a whole other issue. Perhaps there is a fundamental shift in the way the economy works today or is expected to work in the future as compared to the last few decades. Whether there is indeed an irrational exuberance in the economy, or whether there is perhaps a shift in the fundamentals, we need a newer, more accurate, and sophisticated method of quantifying the value of such intangibles.

How do you identify, value, select, prioritize, justify, optimize, time, and manage large corporate investment decisions with high levels of uncertainty such that when a decision is made, the investment becomes irreversible? How do you value and select among several start-up firms to determine whether they are ideal venture candidates, and how do you create an optional financing structure? These types of cashless return investments provide no immediate increase in revenues, and the cost savings are only marginal compared to their costs. How do you justify such outrageous market equity prices?

There must be a better way to value these investment opportunities. Having read press releases by Motley Fool on Credit Suisse First Boston, and how the firm used real options to value stocks of different companies, you begin looking into the possibilities of applying real options yourself. The start-up firm has significant value even when its cash flow situation is hardly something to be desired because the firm has strategic *growth options*. That is, a particular start-up may have some technology that may seem untested today, but it has the *option to expand* into the marketplace quickly and effortlessly should the technology prove to be highly desirable in the near future. Obviously the firm has the right to also pursue other ancillary technologies but only if the market conditions are conducive enough. The venture firm can capitalize on this *option to expand* by hedging itself with multiple investments within a venture portfolio. The firm can also create strategic value through setting up contractual agreements with a *barrier option* and *option to defer* where for the promise of seed financing, the venture firm has the right of first refusal, but not the obligation, to invest in a second- or third-round (so-called Series B and Series C financing) should the start-up achieve certain management-set goals or barriers. The cost of this *barrier option* is seed financing, which is akin to the premium paid on a stock option. Should the option be in-the-money, the option will be executed through second- and third-round financing. By obtaining this strategic option, the venture firm has locked itself into a guaranteed favorable position should the start-up be highly successful, similar to the characteristics of a financial call option of unlimited upside potential. At the same time, the venture firm has hedged itself against missing the opportunity with limited downside proportional to the expenditure of a minimal amount of seed financing. In other words, for a smaller-sized seed investment, the venture firm can invest in more companies, while at the same time keep its foot at the door, ready to pounce and enter if the startup shows great promise, otherwise lose only a smaller amount should the firm fail, instead of simply jumping and investing all-in, all the time.

When venture capital firms value a group of companies, they should consider all the potential upsides available to these companies. These strategic options may very well prove valuable. A venture firm can also hedge itself through the use of barrier-type or deferment options. The venture firm should then go through a process of portfolio optimization analysis to decide what proportion of its funds should be disseminated to each of the chosen firms. This portfolio optimization analysis will maximize returns and minimize the risks borne by the venture firm on a portfolio level subject to budget or other constraints.

COMPOUND EXPANSION OPTIONS: THE CASE OF THE INTERNET START-UP

In contrast to the venture capitalist, one can look at the start-up entrepreneur. How do you obtain venture funding, and how do you position the firm such that it is more attractive to the potential investor? Your core competency is in developing desktop software and cloud-based apps, not financial valuation. How do you then structure the financing agreements such that they will be more attractive yet at the same time not detrimental to your operations, strategic plans, or worse, your personal equity stake? What are your projected revenues and costs? How do you project these values when you haven't even started your business yet? Are you undervaluing your firm, intellectual capital, and its potential such that an unscrupulous venture firm will capitalize on your lack of sophistication and take a larger piece of the pie for itself? What are your strategic alternatives when you are up and running, and how do you know it's optimal for you to proceed with the next phase of your business plan?

All these questions can be answered and valued through a real options framework. Knowing what strategic options your firm has is significant because this value-added insight not only provides the firm an overall strategic road map but also increases its value. The real option that may exist in this case is something akin to a *compound expansion option*. For example, the firm can expand its product and service offerings by branching out into ancillary technologies or different applications, or expanding into different vertical markets. However, these expansions will most certainly occur in stages, and the progression from one stage to another depends heavily on the success of the previous stages.

WHAT THE EXPERTS ARE SAYING

The trend in the market is quickly approaching the acceptance of real options, as can be seen from the following sample publication excerpts below.

According to an article by Credit Suisse (2009):

"Real options will become an increasingly important tool in security analysis. Real options provide the analytical flexibility that standard valuation frameworks lack."

According to an article in Forbes Business Finance (2007):

"An even more accurate method for evaluating risk in space projects is called real options analysis. It has changed valuation from the old static NPV model to a dynamic model based on specific risks."

IBM Institute for Business Value (2002) says that:

"Real options recognize that today's investments give investors the choice of pursuing further investments later, if conditions appear favorable, or abandoning the project if the environment has deteriorated. The capital investment made today provides future flexibility that can and must be valued, but is often missed by traditional DCF or ROI measures. Borrowing from both finance and strategy, real options can provide a way to analyze the value of investing in initiatives made under uncertainty."

According to an article by some MIT professors (2001):

"The integration of real options analysis will radically change the design of public and private systems. It will change the processes of system design, the way planners deal with uncertainly and risk. It will also change the outcomes, the kinds of elements designers build into the system as they develop it. Real options analysis explains this coming evolution, and presents cases documenting the changes in attitude and the results already occurring."

According to an article by the Center of Economics of Innovation and Technological Change (2007):

"Real options show that risk can be influenced through managerial flexibility, which becomes a central instrument for value creation."

According to an article in Bloomberg Wealth Manager (November 2001):

"Real options provide a powerful way of thinking and I can't think of any analytical framework that has been of more use to me in the past five years that I've been in this business."

According to a Wall Street Journal article (February 2000):

"Investors who, after its IPO in 1997, valued only Amazon.com's prospects as a book business would have concluded that the stock was significantly overpriced and missed the subsequent extraordinary price appreciation. Though assessing the value of real options is challenging, without doing it an investor has no basis for deciding whether the current stock price incorporates a reasonable premium for real options or whether the shares are simply overvalued."

CFO Europe (July/August 1999) cites the importance of real options in that:

"A lot of companies have been brainwashed into doing their valuations on a one-scenario discounted cash flow basis and sometimes our recommendations are not what intuition would suggest, and that's where the real surprises come from, and with real options, you can tell exactly where they came from."

According to a Business Week article (June 1999):

"The real options revolution in decision making is the next big thing to sell to clients and has the potential to be the next major business breakthrough. Doing this analysis has provided a lot of intuition you didn't have in the past and that as it takes hold, it's clear that a new generation of business analysts will be schooled in options thinking. Silicon Valley is fast embracing the concepts of real options analytics, in its tradition of fail fast so that other options may be sought after."

In Products Financiers (April 1999):

"Real options is a new and advanced technique that handles uncertainty much better than traditional evaluation methods. Because many managers feel that uncertainty is the most serious issue they have to face, there is no doubt that this method will have a bright future as any industry faces uncertainty in its investment strategies."

A Harvard Business Review article (September/October 1998) hits home:

"Unfortunately, the financial tool most widely relied on to estimate the value of a strategy is the discounted cash flow, which assumes that we will follow a predetermined plan regardless of how events unfold. A better approach to valuation would incorporate both the uncertainty inherent in business and the active decision making required for a strategy to succeed. It would help executives to think strategically on their feet by capturing the value of doing just that— of managing actively rather than passively and real options can deliver that extra insight."

This chapter provides a novel approach to applying real options to answering these issues and more. In particular, a real options framework is presented. It takes into account managerial flexibility in adapting to ever-changing strategic, corporate, economic, and financial environments over time as well as the fact that in the real business world, opportunities and uncertainty exist and are dynamic in nature. This book provides a real options process framework to identify, justify, time, prioritize, value, and manage corporate investment strategies under uncertainty in the context of applying real options. The recommendations, strategies, and methodologies outlined here are not meant to replace traditional discounted cash flow analysis but to complement it when the situation and the need arise. The entire analysis could be done, or parts of it could be adapted to a more traditional approach. In essence, the process methodology outlined starts with traditional analyses and continues with value- and insight-adding analytics, including Monte Carlo simulation, forecasting, real options analysis, and portfolio optimization. The real options approach outlined is not the only viable alternative nor will it provide a set of infallible results. However, if utilized correctly with the traditional approaches, it may lead to a set of more robust, accurate, insightful, and plausible results. The insights generated through real options analytics provide significant value in understanding a project's true strategic value.

CRITICISMS, CAVEATS, AND MISUNDERSTANDINGS IN REAL OPTIONS

Before embarking on a real options analysis, analysts should be aware of several caveats. The following five requirements need to be satisfied before a real options analysis can be run:

- *A financial model must exist.* Real options analysis requires the use of an existing discounted cash flow model, as real options build on the existing tried-and-true approaches of current financial modeling techniques. If a model does not exist, it means that strategic decisions have already been made and no financial justifications are required, and, hence, there is no need for financial modeling or real options analysis.

- *Uncertainties must exist.* Otherwise, the option value is worthless. If everything is known for certain in advance, then a discounted cash flow model is sufficient. In fact, when volatility (a measure of risk and uncertainty) is zero, everything is certain, the real options value is zero, and the total strategic value of the project or asset reverts to the net present value in a discounted cash flow model.

- *Uncertainties must affect decisions* when the firm is actively managing the project and these uncertainties must affect the results of the financial model. These uncertainties will then become risks, and real options can be used to hedge the downside risk and take advantage of the upside uncertainties.

- *Management must have strategic flexibility or options* to make midcourse corrections when actively managing the projects. Otherwise, do not apply real options analysis when there are no options or management flexibility to value.

- *Management must be smart enough and credible enough to execute the options when it becomes optimal to do so.* Otherwise, all the options in the world are useless unless they are executed appropriately, at the right time, and under the right conditions.

There are also several criticisms against real options analysis. It is vital that the analyst understands what they are and what the appropriate responses are.

- *Real options analysis is merely an academic exercise and is not practical in actual business applications.* Nothing is further from the truth. Although it was true in the past that real options analysis was merely academic, many corporations have begun to embrace and apply real options analysis. Also, its concepts are very pragmatic and with the use of the Real Options *Super Lattice Solver* software, even very difficult problems can be easily solved, as will become evident in the next chapter. This book and software have helped bring the theoretical a lot closer to practice. Firms are using it and universities are teaching it. It is only a matter of time before real options analysis becomes part of standard financial analysis.

- *Real options analysis is just another way to bump up and incorrectly increase the value of a project to get it justified.* Again, nothing is further from the truth. If a project has significant strategic options but the analyst does not value them appropriately, he or she is leaving money on the table. In fact, the analyst will be incorrectly undervaluing the project or asset. Also, one of the foregoing requirements states that one should never run real options analysis unless strategic options and flexibility exist. If they do not exist, then the option value is zero, but if they do exist, neglecting their valuation will grossly and significantly underestimate the project or asset's value.

- *Real options analysis ends up choosing the highest risk projects as the higher the volatility, the higher the option value.* This criticism is also incorrect. The option value is zero if no options exist. However, if a project is highly risky and has high volatility, then real options analysis becomes more important. That is, if a project is strategic but is risky, then you better incorporate, create, integrate, or obtain strategic real options to reduce and hedge the downside risk and take advantage of the upside uncertainties. Therefore, this argument is actually heading in the wrong direction. It is not that real options will overinflate a project's value, but for risky projects, you should create or obtain real options to reduce the risk and increase the upside, thereby increasing the total strategic value of the project. Also, although an option value is always greater than or equal to zero, sometimes the cost to obtain certain options may exceed its benefit, making the entire strategic value of the option negative, although the option value itself is always zero or positive.

So, it is incorrect to say that real options will always increase the value of a project or only risky projects are selected. People who make these criticisms do not truly understand how real options work. However, having said that, real options analysis is just another financial analysis tool, and the old axiom of *garbage in, garbage out* still holds. But if care and due diligence are exercised, the analytical process and results can provide highly valuable insights. In fact, this author believes that 50 percent (rounded, of course) of the challenge and value of real options analysis is simply *thinking about it*. Understanding that you have options, or obtaining options to hedge the risks and take advantage of the upside, and to think in terms of strategic options, is half the battle. Another 25 percent of the value comes from actually running the analysis and obtaining the results. The final 25 percent of the value comes from being able to explain it to management, to your clients, and to yourself, such that the results become actionable intelligence that can be capitalized and acted upon, and not merely another set of numbers.

Questions

1. Create your own definition of real options analysis.

2. What are some of the possible approaches used to solve a real options analysis problem?

3. In choosing the right methodology to be used in a real options analysis, what are some of the key requirements that should be considered?

4. What are the necessary conditions that must exist before real options analysis can be applied on a project?

5. What is the major limitation of only using Monte Carlo simulation to perform risk analysis?

CHAPTER 11 – THE BLACK BOX MADE TRANSPARENT: REAL OPTIONS SLS

The Real Options Super Lattice Software (SLS) comprises several modules, including the Single Super Lattice Solver (SLS), Multiple Super Lattice Solver (MSLS), Multinomial Lattice Solver (MNLS), Lattice Maker, SLS Excel Solution, Advanced Exotic Financial Options Valuator, and SLS Functions. These modules are highly powerful and customizable binomial and multinomial lattice solvers, as well as closed-form models (partial differential equations, variance reduction, path-dependent simulation, and other analytical models) that can be used to solve many types of options (including the three main families of options: *real options,* which deals with physical and intangible assets; *financial options,* which deals with financial assets and the investments of such assets; and *employee stock options,* which deals with financial assets provided to employees within a corporation). Note: See *Software Download and Install* at the end of this book for installation instructions and prerequisites for this software.

- The **Single Asset Model** is used primarily for solving options with a *single underlying asset* using binomial lattices. Even highly complex options with a single underlying asset can be solved using the SLS.

- The **Multiple Asset Model** is used for solving options with *multiple underlying assets* and sequential compound options with *multiple phases* using binomial lattices. Highly complex options with multiple underlying assets and phases can be solved using the MSLS.

- The **Multinomial Model** uses *multinomial lattices* (trinomial, quadranomial, pentanomial) to solve specific options that cannot be solved using binomial lattices.

- The **Lattice Maker** is used to create lattices in Excel with visible and live equations, useful for running Monte Carlo simulations with the Risk Simulator software (an Excel add-in, risk-based simulation, forecasting, and optimization software also developed by Real Options Valuation, Inc.) or for linking to and from other spreadsheet models. The lattices generated also include decision lattices where the strategic decisions to execute certain options and the optimal timing to execute these options are shown.

- The **Advanced Exotic Financial Options Valuator** is a comprehensive calculator of more than 250 functions and models, from basic options to exotic options (e.g., from Black–Scholes to multinomial lattices to closed-form differential equations and analytical methods for valuing exotic options, as well as other options-related models such as bond options, volatility computations, delta-gamma hedging, etc.). This valuator complements the ROV Risk Modeler and ROV Valuator software tools, with more than 800 functions and models between them, also developed by Real Options Valuation, Inc. (ROV), which are capable of running at extremely fast speeds, handling large datasets, and linking into existing ODBC-compliant databases (e.g., Oracle, SAP, Access, Excel, CSV, etc.).

- The **SLS Excel Solution** implements the SLS and MSLS computations within the Excel environment, allowing users to access the SLS and MSLS functions directly in Excel. This feature facilitates model building, formula and value linking and embedding, and running simulations, and provides the user sample templates to create such models.

- The **SLS Functions** are additional real options and financial options models accessible directly through Excel. This module facilitates model building, linking and embedding, and running simulations.

- The **Option Charts** are used to visually analyze the payoff structure of the options under analysis, the sensitivity and scenario tables of options to various inputs, convergence of the lattice results, and other valuable analyses.

The SLS software was created by the author. This software also accompanies the materials presented at different training courses on real options, simulation, and employee stock options valuation taught by Dr. Mun. While the software and its models are based on his books, the training courses cover the real options subject matter in more depth, including the solution of sample business cases and the framing of real options of actual cases. It is highly suggested that the user familiarizes him- or herself with the fundamental concepts of real options in *Real Options Analysis: Tools and Techniques,* Second Edition (Wiley 2005) prior to attempting an in-depth real options analysis using this software. This chapter does not cover some of the fundamental topics already discussed in that book.

Note: The first edition of *Real Options Analysis: Tools and Techniques* published in 2002 shows the *Real Options Analysis Toolkit* software, an older precursor to the *Super Lattice Solver,* also created by Dr. Johnathan Mun. The *Real Options Super Lattice Solver* supersedes the *Real Options Analysis Toolkit* by providing the following enhancements, and is introduced in *Real Options Analysis,* Second Edition (2005):

- Runs 100× faster and is completely customizable and flexible.

- All inconsistencies, computation errors, and bugs have been fixed and verified.

- Allows for changing input parameters over time (customized options).

- Allows for changing volatilities over time.

- Incorporates Bermudan (vesting and blackout periods) and Customized Options.

- Flexible modeling capabilities in creating or engineering your own customized options.

- Includes general enhancements to accuracy, precision, and analytical prowess.

- Includes more than 250 exotic options models (closed-form, exotic, multinomial lattice).

As the creator of both the Super Lattice Solver and Real Options Analysis Toolkit (ROAT) software, the author suggests that the reader focuses on using the Super Lattice Solver because it provides many powerful enhancements and analytical flexibility over its predecessor, ROAT.

The software will work on most foreign operating systems such as foreign language Windows or Excel, and the SLS software has been tested to work on most international Windows operating systems with just a quick change in settings going to *Control Panel | Region (Clock, Language, Regions) | Formats* and select *English* for language and location as *United States*. This change is required because the numbering convention is different in foreign countries (e.g., one thousand dollars and fifty cents is written as 1,000.50 in the United States versus 1.000,50 in certain European countries). You should also check in the *Additional Settings* button for decimal settings using periods (".").

SINGLE ASSET SUPER LATTICE SOLVER

Figure 11.1 illustrates the SLS software's main screen. After installing the software, the user can access the SLS main screen by *double clicking* on the *Real Options SLS* icon on the desktop or in Windows 8 or 10, you can also click on the *Windows button + C*, then select *Search* and enter *Real Options SLS* as the search term. From this main screen, you can run the Single Asset model, Multiple Asset model, Multinomial model, Lattice Maker, and Advanced Exotic Financial Options Valuator; open example models; or open an existing model. You can move your mouse over any one of the items to obtain a short description of what that module does. Finally, Real Options SLS supports 12 languages, including English, Arabic, Chinese (Simplified), Chinese (Traditional), French, German, Italian, Japanese, Korean, Portuguese, Russian, and Spanish, and you can change the language using the droplist on the main screen. You can also purchase or install a newly obtained permanent license from this main screen by clicking on each of the two license links. Refer to *Software Download and Install* at the end of this book to obtain and install the 30-day trial license. To access the SLS Functions, SLS Excel Solutions, or a sample volatility computation file, go to *Start | Programs | Real Options Valuation | Real Options SLS | Real Options SLS* and select the relevant module or in Windows 8 or 10, click on the *Windows button + C*, then select *Search* and enter *SLS Excel Solution* or *SLS Excel Function* as the search term, and click on the relevant searched result to open the files.

Single Asset SLS Examples

To help you get started, several simple examples are in order. A simple European call option is computed in this example using SLS. To follow along, in the main screen, click on New Single Asset Model and then click on *File | Examples | Plain Vanilla Call Option I*. This example file will be loaded into the SLS software as seen in Figure 11.2. The starting PV Underlying Asset or starting stock price is $100, and the Implementation Cost or strike price is $100 with a 5-year maturity. The annualized risk-free rate of return is 5 percent, and the historical, comparable, or future expected annualized volatility is 10 percent. Click on *RUN* (or Alt-R) and a 100-step binomial lattice is computed with the results indicating a value of $23.3975 for both the European and American call options. Benchmark values using Black–Scholes and partial differential Closed-Form American approximation models as well as standard plain-vanilla Binomial American and Binomial European Call and Put Options with 1,000-step binomial lattices are also computed. Notice that only the American and European options are selected and the computed results are for these simple plain-vanilla American and European call options.

Figure 11.1: Single Super Lattice Solver (SLS)

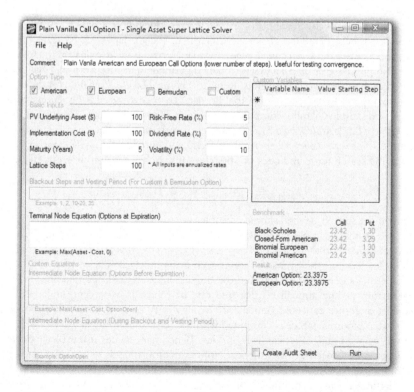

Figure 11.2: SLS Results of a Simple European and American Call Option

The benchmark results use both closed-form models (Black–Scholes and Closed-Form Approximation models) and 1,000-step binomial lattices on plain-vanilla options. You can change the steps to *1000* in the basic inputs section to verify that the answers computed are equivalent to the benchmarks as shown in Figure 11.3. Notice that, of course, the values computed for the American and European options are identical to each other and identical to the benchmark values of $23.4187, as it is never optimal to exercise a standard plain-vanilla call option early if there are no dividends. Be aware that the higher the lattice step, the longer it takes, of course, to compute the results. It is advisable to start with lower lattice steps to make sure the analysis is robust and then progressively increase lattice steps to check for results convergence.

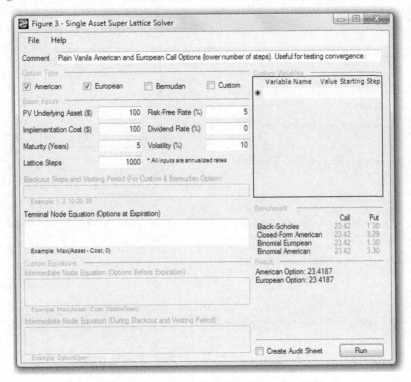

Figure 11.3: SLS Comparing Results with Benchmarks

Alternatively, you can enter Terminal and Intermediate Node Equations for a call option to obtain the same results. Notice that using 100 steps and creating your own Terminal Node Equation of *Max(Asset-Cost,0)* and Intermediate Node Equation of *Max(Asset-Cost,OptionOpen)* will yield the same answer. When entering your own equations, make sure that *Custom* option is first checked.

> When entering your own custom equations, make sure that Custom
> option is first checked.

Figure 11.4 illustrates how the analysis is done. Notice that the value $23.3975 in Figure 11.4 agrees with the value in Figure 11.2. The Terminal Node Equation is the computation that occurs at maturity, while the Intermediate Node Equation is the computation that occurs at all periods prior to maturity, and is computed using backward induction. The term *"OptionOpen"* represents "keeping the option open" and is often used in the Intermediate Node Equation when analytically representing the fact that the option is not executed but kept open for possible future execution. Therefore, in Figure 11.4, the Intermediate Node Equation *Max(Asset-Cost,OptionOpen)* represents the profit maximization decision of either executing the option or leaving it open for possible future execution. In contrast, the Terminal Node Equation of *Max(Asset-Cost,0)* represents the profit maximization decision at maturity of either executing the option if it is in-the-money or allowing it to expire worthless if it is at-the-money or out-of-the-money.

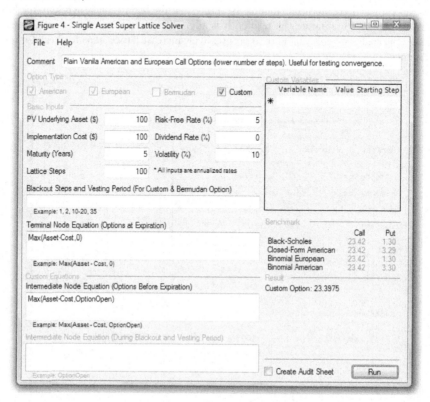

Figure 11.4: Custom Equation Inputs

In addition, you can create an Audit Worksheet in Excel to view a sample 10-step binomial lattice by checking the box *Generate Audit Worksheet*. For instance, loading the example file *Plain Vanilla Call Option I* and selecting the box creates a worksheet as seen in Figure 11.5. There are several items that should be noted about this audit worksheet:

- The audit worksheet generated will show the first 10 steps of the lattice, regardless of how many you enter. That is, if you enter 1,000 steps, the first 10 steps will be generated. If a complete lattice is required, simply enter 10 steps in the SLS and the full 10-step lattice will be generated instead. The Intermediate Computations and Results are for the Super Lattice, based on the number of lattice steps entered and not based on the 10-step lattice generated. To obtain the Intermediate Computations for 10-step lattices, simply rerun the analysis inputting *10* as the lattice steps. This way, the Audit Worksheet generated will be for a 10-step lattice, and the results from SLS will now be comparable (Figure 11.6).

- The worksheet only provides values as it is assumed that the user was the one who entered the terminal and intermediate equations, hence there is really no need to recreate these equations in Excel again. The user can always reload the SLS file and view the equations or print out the form if required (by clicking on *File | Print*).

The software also allows you to save or open analysis files. That is, all the inputs in the software will be saved and can be retrieved for future use. The results will not be saved because you may accidentally delete or change an input and the results will no longer be valid. In addition, rerunning the super lattice computations will only take a few seconds, and it is always advisable for you to rerun the model when opening an old analysis file.

You may also enter Blackout Steps. These are the steps on the super lattice that will have different behaviors than the terminal or intermediate steps. For instance, you can enter *1000* as the lattice steps, *0-400* as the blackout steps, and some Blackout Equation (e.g., *OptionOpen*). This means that for the first 400 steps, the option holder can only keep the option open. Other examples include entering *1, 3, 5, 10* if these are the lattice steps where blackout periods occur. You will have to calculate the relevant steps within the lattice where the blackout exists. For instance, if the blackout exists in years 1 and 3 on a 10-year, 10-step lattice, then steps 1, 3 will be the blackout dates. This blackout step feature comes in handy when analyzing options with holding periods, vesting periods, or periods where the option cannot be executed. Employee stock options have blackout and vesting periods, and certain contractual real options have periods during which the option cannot be executed (e.g., cooling-off periods, or proof of concept periods).

If equations are entered into the Terminal Node Equation box and American, European, or Bermudan Options are chosen, the terminal node equation you entered will be the one used in the super lattice for the terminal nodes. However, for the intermediate nodes, the American option will assume the same terminal node equation plus the ability to keep the option open; the European option will assume that the option can only be kept open and not executed; while the Bermudan option will assume that during the blackout lattice steps, the option will be kept open and cannot be executed. If you also wish to enter the Intermediate Node Equation, the *Custom* option should be first chosen (otherwise you cannot use the Intermediate Node Equation box). The *Custom* option result will use all the equations you have entered in the Terminal, Intermediate, and Intermediate with Blackout sections.

The Custom Variables list is where you can add, modify, or delete custom variables, the variables that are required beyond the basic inputs. For instance, when running an abandonment option, you will require the salvage value. You can add this in the Custom Variables list, provide it a name (a variable's name must be a single word without spaces), the appropriate value, and the starting step when this value becomes effective. For example, if you have multiple salvage values (i.e., if salvage values change over time), you can enter the same variable name (e.g., *salvage*) several times, but each time, its value changes and you can specify when the appropriate salvage value becomes effective. For instance, in a 10-year, 100-step super lattice problem where there are two salvage values—$100 occurring within the first 5 years and increases to $150 at the beginning of Year 6—you can enter two salvage variables with the same name: $100 with a starting step of 0 and $150 with a starting step of 51. Be careful here as Year 6 starts at step 51 and not 61. That is, for a 10-year option with a 100-step lattice, we have Steps 1–10 = Year 1; Steps 11–20 = Year 2; Steps 21–30 = Year 3; Steps 31–40 = Year 4; Steps 41–50 = Year 5; Steps 51–60 = Year 6; Steps 61–70 = Year 7; Steps 71–80 = Year 8; Steps 81–90 = Year 9; and Steps 91–100 = Year 10. Finally, incorporating 0 as a blackout step indicates that the option cannot be executed immediately.

> A Custom Variable's name must be a single continuous word.

Option Valuation Audit Sheet

Assumptions

PV Asset Value ($)	$100.00
Implementation Cost ($)	$100.00
Maturity (Years)	5.00
Risk-free Rate (%)	5.00%
Dividends (%)	0.00%
Volatility (%)	10.00%
Lattice Steps	100
Option Type	European

Terminal Equation
Intermediate Equation
Intermediate Equation (Blackouts)

Intermediate Computations

Stepping Time (dt)	0.0500
Up Step Size (up)	1.0226
Down Step Size (down)	0.9779
Risk-neutral Probability	0.5504

Results

Auditing Lattice Result (10 steps)	23.19
Super Lattice Results)	23.40

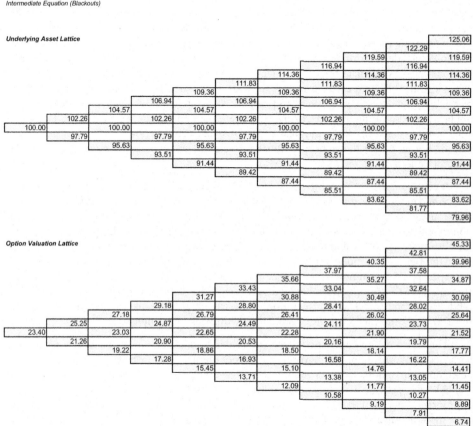

Figure 11.5: SLS-Generated Audit Worksheet

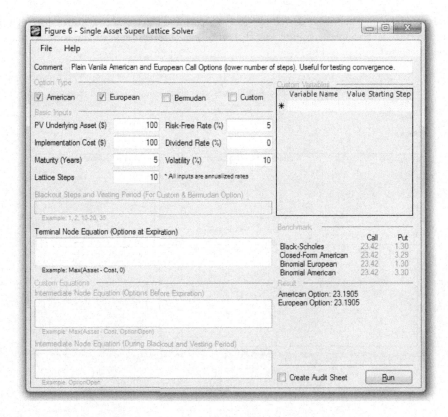

Figure 11.6: SLS Results with a 10-step Lattice

MULTIPLE ASSET SUPER LATTICE SOLVER

The MSLS is an extension of the SLS in that the MSLS can be used to solve options with multiple underlying assets and multiple phases. The MSLS allows the user to enter multiple underlying assets as well as multiple valuation lattices (Figure 11.7). These valuation lattices can call to user-defined custom variables. Some examples of the types of options that the MSLS can be used to solve include:

- Sequential Compound Options (two-, three-, four-, five-, and multiple-phased sequential options)

- Simultaneous Compound Options (multiple underlying assets with multiple simultaneous options)

- Chooser and Switching Options (choosing among several options and/or several underlying assets)

- Floating Options (choosing between calls and puts)

- Multiple Asset Options (3D binomial option models)

The MSLS software has several areas including a *Maturity* and *Comment* area. The *Maturity* value is a global value for the entire option, regardless of how many underlying or valuation lattices exist. The *Comment* field is for your personal notes describing the model you are building. There is also a *Blackout and Vesting Period Steps* section and a *Custom Variables* list similar to the SLS. The MSLS also allows you to create audit worksheets. Notice, too, that the user interface is resizable (e.g., you can click and drag the right side of the form to make it wider, as shown in Figure 11.8).

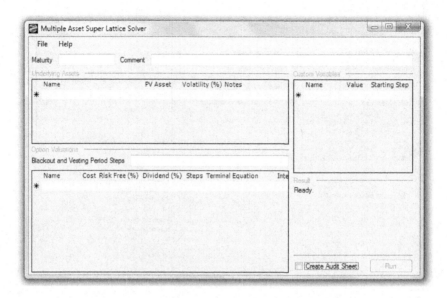

Figure 11.7: Multiple Super Lattice Solver

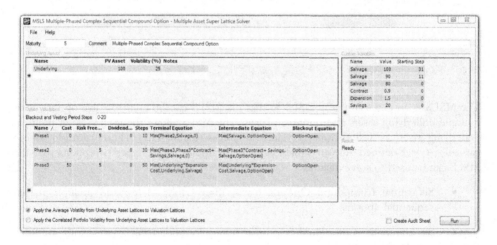

Figure 11.8: Resized Multiple Super Lattice Solver

To illustrate the power of the MSLS, a simple illustration is in order. Double click on the *Real Options SLS icon on the desktop* or in Windows 8 or 10, you can also click on the *Windows button + C*, then select *Search* and enter *Real Options SLS* as the search term. In the Main Screen, click on *New Multiple Asset Option Model*, and then select *File | Examples | Simple Two Phased Sequential Compound Option*. Figure 11.9 shows the MSLS example loaded. In this simple example, a single underlying asset is created with two valuation phases.

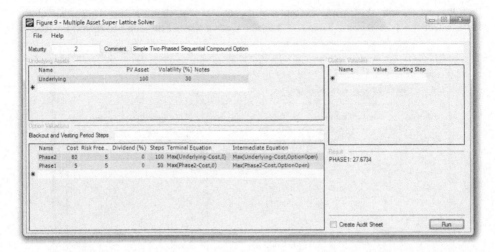

Figure 11.9: MSLS Solution to a Simple Two-phased Sequential Compound Option

The strategy tree for this option is seen in Figure 11.10. The project is executed in two phases—the first phase within the first year costs $5 million, while the second phase occurs within two years but only after the first phase is executed, and costs $80 million, both in present value dollars. The PV Asset of the project is $100 million (NPV is therefore $15 million) and faces 30 percent volatility in its cash flows. The computed strategic value using the MSLS is $27.67 million, indicating that there is a $12.67 million in option value. That is, spreading out and staging the investment into two phases has significant value (an expected value of $12.67 million to be exact). See the sections on compound options for more examples later in the chapter.

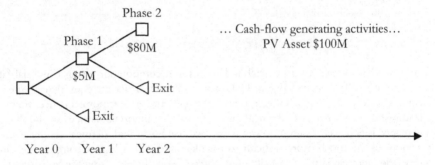

Figure 11.10: Strategy Tree for Two-phased Sequential Compound Option

MULTINOMIAL SUPER LATTICE SOLVER

The Multinomial Lattice Solver (MNLS) is another module of the Real Options Super Lattice Solver software. The MNLS applies multinomial lattices—where multiple branches stem from each node—such as trinomials (three branches), quadranomials (four branches), and pentanomials (five branches). Figure 11.11 illustrates the MNLS module. The module has a Basic Inputs section, where all of the common inputs for the multinomials are listed. Then, there are four sections with four different multinomial applications complete with the additional required inputs and results for both American and European call and put options.

To follow along with this simple example, in the *Main Screen*, click on *New Multinomial Option Model*, select *File | Examples | Trinomial American Call Option*, set dividend to 0, and hit *Run*.

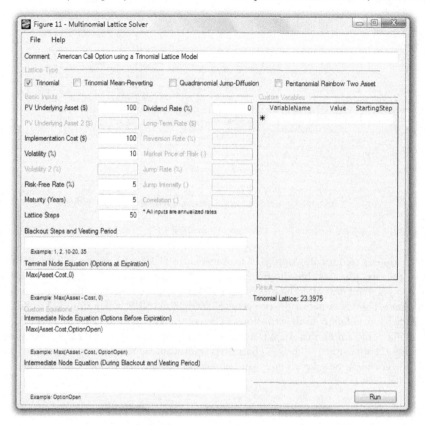

Figure 11.11: Multinomial Lattice Solver

Figure 11.11 shows a sample call and put option computation using trinomial lattices. Note that the results shown in Figure 11.11 using a 50-step lattice are equivalent to the results shown in Figure 11.2 using a 100-step binomial lattice. In fact, a trinomial lattice or any other multinomial lattice provides identical answers to the binomial lattice at the limit, but convergence is achieved faster at lower steps. Because both yield identical results at the limit but trinomials are much more difficult to calculate and take a longer computation time, in practice, the binomial lattice is usually used instead. Nonetheless, using the SLS software, the computation times are only seconds, making this traditionally difficult to run model computable almost instantly. However, a trinomial is required only under one special circumstance: when the underlying asset follows a mean-reverting process.

With the same logic, quadranomials and pentanomials yield identical results as the binomial lattice with the exception that these multinomial lattices can be used to solve the following different special limiting conditions:

- *Trinomials.* Results are identical to binomials and are most appropriate when used to solve mean-reverting underlying assets.

- *Quadranomials.* Results are identical to binomials and are most appropriate when used to solve options whose underlying assets follow jump-diffusion processes.

- *Pentanomials.* Results are identical to binomials and are most appropriate when used to solve two underlying assets that are combined, called rainbow options (e.g., price and quantity are multiplied to obtain total revenues, but price and quantity each follows a different underlying lattice with its own volatility, but both underlying parameters could be correlated to one another).

SLS LATTICE MAKER

The Lattice Maker module is capable of generating binomial lattices and decision lattices with visible formulas in an Excel spreadsheet (it is compatible with Excel 2007, 2010, and 2013). Figure 11.12 illustrates an example option generated using this module. The illustration shows the module inputs (you can obtain this module by clicking on *Create a Lattice* from the *Main Screen*) and the resulting output lattice. Notice that the visible equations are linked to the existing spreadsheet, which means this module will come in handy when running Monte Carlo simulations or when used to link to and from other spreadsheet models. The results can also be used as a presentation and learning tool to peep inside the analytical black box of binomial lattices. Last but not least, a decision lattice is also available with specific decision nodes indicating expected optimal times of execution of certain options in this module. The results generated from this module are identical to those generated using the SLS and Excel functions, but have the added advantage of a visible lattice (lattices of up to 200 steps can be generated using this module).

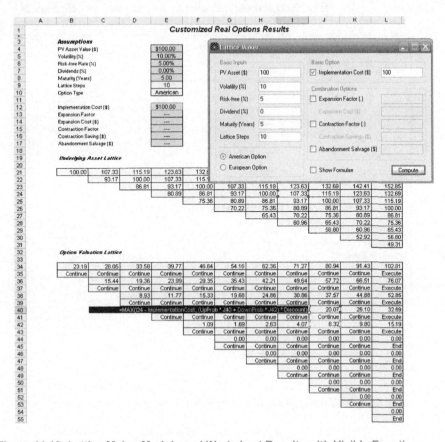

Figure 11.12: Lattice Maker Module and Worksheet Results with Visible Equations

SLS EXCEL SOLUTION (SLS, MSLS, AND CHANGING VOLATILITY MODELS IN EXCEL)

The SLS software also allows you to create your own models in Excel using customized functions. This is an important functionality because certain models may require linking from other spreadsheets or databases, run certain Excel macros and functions, or certain inputs need to be simulated, or inputs may change over the course of modeling your options. This Excel compatibility allows you the flexibility to innovate within the Excel spreadsheet environment. Specifically, the sample worksheet solves the SLS, MSLS, and Changing Volatility model.

To illustrate, Figure 11.13 shows a Customized Abandonment Option solved using SLS (from the *Single Asset Module*, click on *File | Examples | Abandonment Customized Option*). The same problem can be solved using the *SLS Excel Solution* by clicking on *Start | Programs | Real Options Valuation | Real Options SLS | Excel Solution* or in Windows 8 and 10, click on the *Windows button + C*, select *Search* and enter *SLS Excel Solution* to search, and click on the item found called *Excel Solution*. The sample solution is seen in Figure 11.14. Notice that the results are the same using the SLS versus the SLS Excel Solution file. The only difference is that in the Excel Solution, the function (Figure 11.14) has an added input, specifically, the *Option Type*. If the option type value is set to 0, you get an American option; 1 for European option; 2 for Bermudan option; and 3 for customized options. You can use the template provided by simply clicking on *File | Save As* in Excel and use the new file for your own modeling needs.

Figure 11.13: Customized Abandonment Option Using SLS

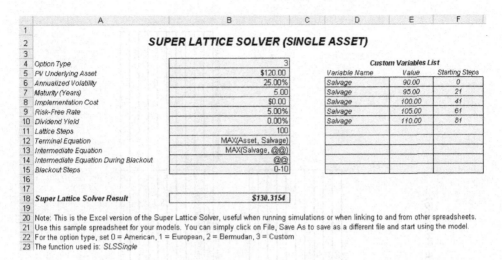

SUPER LATTICE SOLVER (SINGLE ASSET)

	A	B
4	Option Type	3
5	PV Underlying Asset	$120.00
6	Annualized Volatility	25.00%
7	Maturity (Years)	5.00
8	Implementation Cost	$0.00
9	Risk-Free Rate	5.00%
10	Dividend Yield	0.00%
11	Lattice Steps	100
12	Terminal Equation	MAX(Asset, Salvage)
13	Intermediate Equation	MAX(Salvage, @@)
14	Intermediate Equation During Blackout	@@
15	Blackout Steps	0-10
18	**Super Lattice Solver Result**	**$130.3154**

Custom Variables List

Variable Name	Value	Starting Steps
Salvage	90.00	0
Salvage	95.00	21
Salvage	100.00	41
Salvage	105.00	61
Salvage	110.00	81

20 Note: This is the Excel version of the Super Lattice Solver, useful when running simulations or when linking to and from other spreadsheets.
21 Use this sample spreadsheet for your models. You can simply click on File, Save As to save as a different file and start using the model.
22 For the option type, set 0 = American, 1 = European, 2 = Bermudan, 3 = Custom
23 The function used is: *SLSSingle*

Figure 11.14: Customized Abandonment Option Using SLS Excel Solution

Similarly, the MSLS can also be solved using the SLS Excel Solver. Figure 11.15 shows a complex multiple-phased sequential compound option solved using the SLS Excel Solver. The results shown are identical to the results generated from the MSLS module (example file: *Multiple Phased Complex Sequential Compound Option*). One small note of caution here is that if you add or reduce the number of option valuation lattices, make sure you change the function's link for the *MSLS Result* to incorporate the right number of rows; otherwise the analysis will not compute properly. For example, the default shows three option valuation lattices, and by selecting the *MSLS Results* cell in the spreadsheet and clicking on *Insert | Function*, you will see that the function links to cells A27:I29 for these three rows for the OVLattices input in the function. If you add another option valuation lattice, change the link to A27:I30, and so forth. You can also leave the list of custom variables as is. The results will not be affected if these variables are not used in the custom equations.

Finally, Figure 11.16 shows a Changing Volatility and Changing Risk-free Rate Option. In this model, the volatility and risk-free yields are allowed to change over time and a nonrecombining lattice is required to solve the option. In most cases, it is recommended that you create option models without the changing volatility term structure because getting a single volatility is difficult enough let alone a series of changing volatilities over time. If different volatilities that are uncertain need to be modeled, run a Monte Carlo simulation on volatilities instead. This model should only be used when the volatilities are modeled robustly, are rather certain, and change over time. The same advice applies to a changing risk-free rate term structure.

MULTIPLE SUPER LATTICE SOLVER (MULTIPLE ASSET & MULTIPLE PHASES)

Maturity (Years)	5.00
Blackout Steps	0-20
Correlation*	

MSLS Result $134.0802

Underlying Asset Lattices

Lattice Name	PV Asset	Volatility
Underlying	100.00	25.00

Custom Variables

Name	Value	Starting Steps
Salvage	100.00	31
Salvage	90.00	11
Salvage	80.00	0
Contract	0.90	0
Expansion	1.50	0
Savings	20.00	0

Option Valuation Lattices

Lattice Name	Cost	Riskfree	Dividend	Steps	Terminal Equation	Intermediate Equation	Intermediate Equation for Blackout
Phase3	50.00	5.00	0.00	50	Max(Underlying*Expansion-Cost Underlying,Salvage)	Max(Underlying*Expansion-Cost,Salvage,@@)	@@
Phase2	0.00	5.00	0.00	30	Max(Phase3,Phase3*Contract+Savings,Salvage,0)	Max(Phase3*Contract+Savings,Salvage,@@)	@@
Phase1	0.00	5.00	0.00	10	Max(Phase2,Salvage,0)	Max(Salvage,@@)	@@

Note: This is the Excel version of the Multiple Super Lattice Solver, useful when running simulations or when linking to and from other spreadsheets.
Use this sample spreadsheet for your models. You can simply click on File, Save As to save as a different file and start using the model.
*Because this is an Excel solution, the correlation function is not supported and is linked to an empty cell.

Figure 11.15: Complex Sequential Compound Option Using SLS Excel Solver

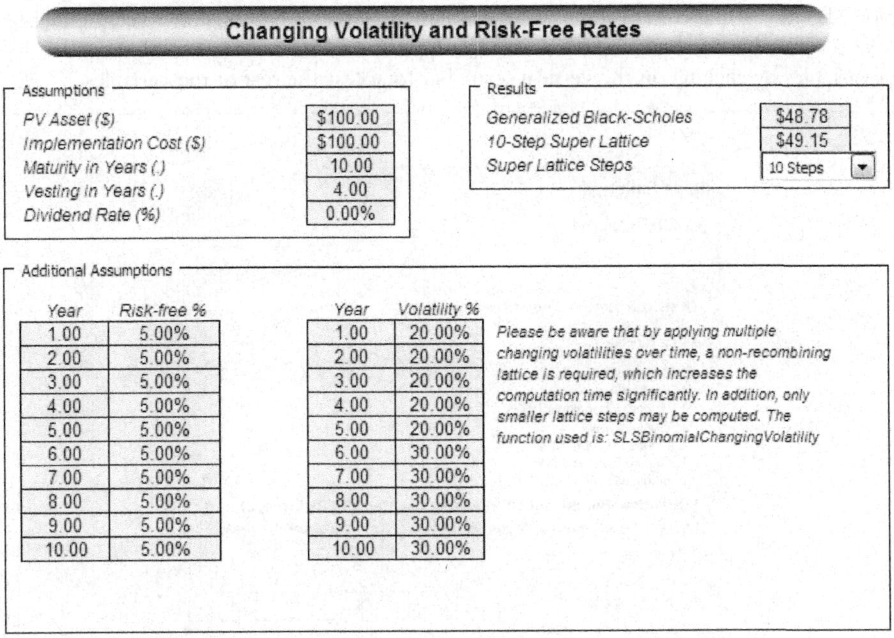

Changing Volatility and Risk-Free Rates

Assumptions

PV Asset ($)	$100.00
Implementation Cost ($)	$100.00
Maturity in Years (.)	10.00
Vesting in Years (.)	4.00
Dividend Rate (%)	0.00%

Results

Generalized Black-Scholes	$48.78
10-Step Super Lattice	$49.15
Super Lattice Steps	10 Steps ▾

Additional Assumptions

Year	Risk-free %		Year	Volatility %
1.00	5.00%		1.00	20.00%
2.00	5.00%		2.00	20.00%
3.00	5.00%		3.00	20.00%
4.00	5.00%		4.00	20.00%
5.00	5.00%		5.00	20.00%
6.00	5.00%		6.00	30.00%
7.00	5.00%		7.00	30.00%
8.00	5.00%		8.00	30.00%
9.00	5.00%		9.00	30.00%
10.00	5.00%		10.00	30.00%

Please be aware that by applying multiple changing volatilities over time, a non-recombining lattice is required, which increases the computation time significantly. In addition, only smaller lattice steps may be computed. The function used is: SLSBinomialChangingVolatility

Figure 11.16: Changing Volatility and Risk-free Rate Option

SLS FUNCTIONS

The software also provides a series of SLS functions that are directly accessible in Excel. To illustrate its use, start the SLS Functions by clicking on *Start | Programs | Real Options Valuation | Real Options SLS | SLS Functions*, or in Windows 8 and 10, click on the *Windows button + C*, select *Search* and enter *SLS Excel Function* as the search term, and click on the item found called SLS Excel Function and Excel will start. When in Excel, you can click on the function wizard icon or simply select an empty cell and click on *Insert | Function*. While in Excel's equation wizard, select the *ALL* category and scroll down to the functions starting with the SLS prefixes. Here you will see a list of SLS functions that are ready for use in Excel. Figure 11.17 shows the Excel equation wizard.

Start the Excel Functions module and select the ALL category when in Excel's function wizard, then scroll down to access the SLS functions. You may have to check your macro security settings before starting in Excel 2003 (click on Tools, Macro, Security, and make sure Security is set to Medium or below) as well as in Excel 2010 and 2013 (click on the large Office button on the top left corner of Excel, click on Excel Options, Trust Center, Trust Center Settings, Add-Ins, uncheck all three options, then click on Macro Settings, select Enable All Macros, check Trust Access to the VBA project, and click OK).

Suppose you select the first function, *SLSBinomialAmericanCall* and hit *OK*. Figure 11.17 shows how the function can be linked to an existing Excel model. The values in cells B1 to B7 can be linked from other models or spreadsheets, can be created using VBA macros, or can be dynamic and changing as in when running a simulation.

Note: Be aware that certain functions require many input variables, and Excel's equation wizard can only show five variables at a time. Therefore, remember to scroll down the list of variables by clicking on the vertical scroll bar to access the rest of the variables.

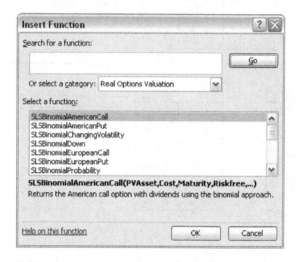

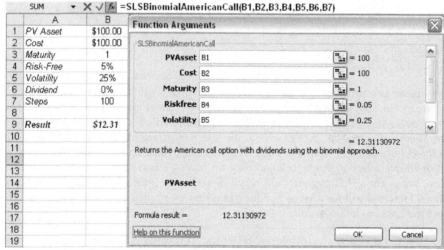

Figure 11.17: Excel's Equation Wizard

This concludes a quick overview and tour of the software. You are now equipped to start using the SLS software in building and solving real options, financial options, and employee stock options problems. However, it is highly recommended that you first review Dr. Johnathan Mun's *Real Options Analysis: Tools and Techniques,* Second Edition (Wiley, 2006) for details on the theory and application of real options. And if you are a new user of Real Options SLS or have upgraded from an older version, do spend some time reviewing the Key SLS Notes and Tips starting on the next few pages to familiarize yourself with the modeling intricacies of the software. Also, remember to spend some time watching some of the free getting started videos in the ROV website (*www.realoptionsvaluation.com*) to help you get a jump-start on using the software.

EXOTIC FINANCIAL OPTIONS VALUATOR

The Exotic Financial Options Valuator is a comprehensive calculator of more than 250 functions and models, from basic options to exotic options (e.g., from Black–Scholes and multinomial lattices to closed-form differential equations and analytical methods for valuing exotic options, as well as other options-related models such as bond options, volatility computations, delta-gamma hedging, etc.). Figure 11.18 illustrates the Valuator. You can click on the *Load Sample Values* button to load some samples to get started. Then, select the *Model Category* (left panel) as desired and select the *Model* (right panel) you wish to run. Click *Compute* to obtain the result. Note that this valuator complements the ROV Risk Modeler and ROV Valuator software tools, with more than 800 functions and models, also developed by Real Options Valuation, Inc. (ROV), which are capable of running at extremely fast speeds and handling large datasets and linking into existing ODBC-compliant databases (e.g., Oracle, SAP, Access, Excel, CSV, etc.). Finally, if you wish to access these 800 functions (including the ones in this Exotic Financial Options Valuator tool), use the ROV Modeling Toolkit software instead, where, in addition to having access to these functions and more, you can run Monte Carlo simulation on your models using ROV's Risk Simulator software.

Figure 11.18: Exotic Financial Options Valuator

PAYOFF CHARTS, TORNADO SENSITIVITY, SCENARIO, AND CONVERGENCE ANALYSIS

The main Single Asset SLS module also comes with payoff charts, sensitivity tables, scenario analysis, and convergence analysis (Figure 11.19). To run these analyses, first create a new model or open and run an existing model (e.g., from the first tab, *Options SLS*, click on *File*, *Examples*, and select *Plain Vanilla Call Option I*; then hit *Run* to compute the option value and click on any one of the tabs). To use these tools, you need to first have a model specified in the main *Options SLS* tab. Here are brief explanations of these tabs and how to use their corresponding controls as shown in Figure 11.19:

Payoff Chart. The *Payoff Chart* tab (A) allows you to generate a typical option payoff chart where you have the ability to choose the input variable to chart (B) by entering some minimum and maximum values (C) to chart, as well as its step size (e.g., setting minimum as 20 and maximum as 200 with a step of 10 means to run the analysis for the values 20, 30, 40, ..., 180, 190, 200) and lattice steps (the lower the lattice step number, the faster the analysis runs but the less precise the results—see the following discussion of *Lattice Step Convergence Analysis* for more details). Click *Update Chart* (D) to obtain a new payoff chart (E) each time. The default is to show a line chart (F), but you can opt to choose area or bar charts, and the generated chart and table can be copied and pasted into other applications or printed out as is (G). If you do not enter any minimum and maximum values, the software automatically picks some default test values for you, the PV Underlying Asset is chosen by default, and the typical hockey-stick payoff chart will be displayed. Finally, there will be a warning message if any of the original input is zero, requiring you to manually insert these minimum, maximum, and step size values in order to generate the payoff chart.

Tornado Sensitivity Analysis. The *Sensitivity* tab (H) runs a quick static sensitivity of each input variable of the model one at a time and lists the input variables with the highest impact to the lowest impact. You can control the option type, lattice steps, and sensitivity percentage to test (I). The results will be returned in the form of a tornado chart (J) and sensitivity analysis table (K). Tornado analysis captures the static impacts of each input variable on the outcome of the option value by automatically perturbing each input some preset ±% amount, captures the fluctuation on the option value's result, and lists the resulting perturbations ranked from the most significant to the least. The results are shown as a sensitivity table with the starting base case value, the perturbed input upside and downside, the resulting option value's upside and downside, and the absolute swing or impact. The precedent variables are ranked from the highest impact to the lowest impact. The tornado chart illustrates this data in graphic form. Green bars in the chart indicate a positive effect, while red bars indicate a negative effect on the option value. For example, Implementation Cost's red bar is on the right side, indicating a negative effect of investment cost—in other words, for a simple call option, implementation cost (option strike price) and option value are negatively correlated. The opposite is true for PV Underlying Asset (stock price) where the green bar is on the right side of the chart, indicating a positive correlation between the input and output.

Scenario Analysis. The *Scenario* tab runs a two-dimensional scenario of two input variables (L) based on the selected option type and lattice steps (M) and returns a scenario analysis table (N) of the resulting option values based on the various combinations of inputs.

Lattice Step Convergence Analysis. The *Convergence* tab shows the option results from 5 to 5,000 steps—the higher the number of steps, the higher the level of precision (granularity in lattices increases)—where at some point the results of the lattice converge and once convergence is achieved, no additional lattice steps are required. The number of steps is set by default from 5 to 5,000, but you can select the option type and number of decimals to show (O), and the convergence chart is displayed (Q) depending on your selection. You can also copy or print the table with the chart as required (P).

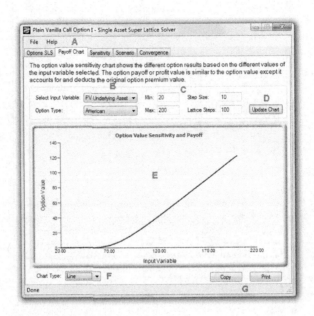

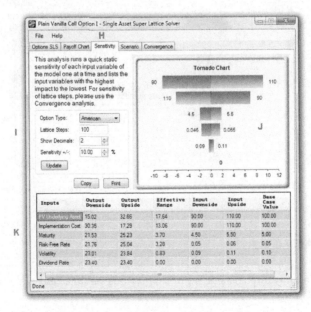

Figure 11.19: Payoff Charts, Sensitivity Analysis, Scenario Tables, and Convergence Analysis (continues)

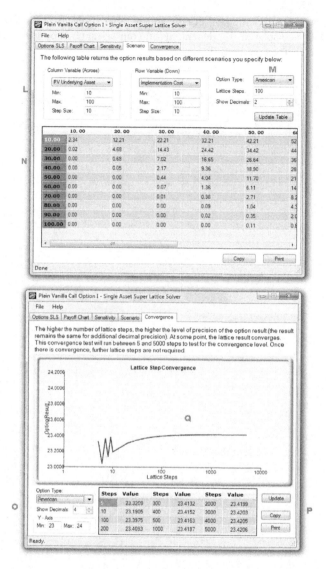

Figure 11.19: Payoff Charts, Sensitivity Analysis, Scenario Tables, and
Convergence Analysis (continued)

KEY SLS NOTES AND TIPS

Here are some noteworthy changes from the previous versions and tips on using the Real
Options SLS software:

- The *User Manual* is accessible within SLS, MSLS, or MNLS. For instance, simply start
  the Real Options SLS software and create a new model or open an existing SLS,
  MSLS, or MNLS model. Then click on *Help | User Manual*.

- *Example Files* are accessible directly in the SLS Main Screen; when in the SLS, MSLS,
  or MNLS models, you can access the example files at *File | Examples*.

- Current *License* information can be obtained in SLS, MSLS, or MNLS at *Help | About*.

- A *Variable List* is available in SLS, MSLS, and MNLS by going to *Help | Variable List*. Specifically, the following are allowed variables and operators in the *custom equations* boxes:

  - Asset   –value of the underlying asset at the current step (in currency)

  - Cost   –implementation cost (in currency)

  - Dividend   –value of dividend (in percent)

  - Maturity   –years to maturity (in years)

  - OptionOpen   –value of keeping the option open (formerly @@ in version 1.0)

  - RiskFree   –annualized risk-free rate (in percent)

  - Step   –integer representing the current step in the lattice

  - LatticeSteps   –the total number of lattice steps in the model

  - Volatility   –annualized volatility (in percent)

  - \-   – subtract

  - !   – not

  - !=, <>   – not equal

  - &   – and

  - *   – multiply

  - /   – divide

  - ^   – power

  - | – or

  - +   – add

  - <, >, <=, >=   – comparisons

  - =   – equal

- *OptionOpen at Terminal Nodes* in SLS or MSLS. If *OptionOpen* is specified as the Terminal Node equation, the value will always evaluate to *Not a Number* error (NaN). This is clearly a user error as *OptionOpen* cannot apply at the terminal nodes.

- *Unspecified interval of custom variables.* If a specified interval in which a custom variable has no value, the value is assumed zero. For example, suppose a model exists with 10 steps where a custom variable *"myVar"* of value 5 starts at step 6 exists. This specification means *myVar* will be substituted with the value 5 from step 6 onward. However, the model did not specify the value of *myVar* from steps 0 to 5. In this situation, the value of *myVar* is assumed to be 0 for steps 0 to 5.

- *Blackout Step Specifications.* To define the blackout steps, use the following examples as a guide:

- o 3   Step 3 is a blackout step.

- o 3, 5   Steps 3 and 5 are blackout steps.

- o 3, 5-7   Steps 3, 5, 6, 7 are blackout steps.

- o 1, 3, 5-6   Steps 1, 3, 5, 6 are blackout steps.

- o 5-7   Steps 5, 6, 7 are blackout steps.

- o 5-10|2   Steps 5, 7, 9 are blackout steps (symbol | is skip-size).

- o 5-14|3   Steps 5, 8, 11, 14 are blackout steps.

- o 5-6|3   Step 5 is a blackout step.

- o 5 - 6 | 3   Step 5 is a blackout step (white spaces are ignored).

- *Identifiers.* An identifier is a sequence of characters that begins with a-z, A-Z, _ or $. After the first character, a-z, A-Z, 0-9, _, $ are valid characters in the sequence. Note that space is not a valid character. However, it can be used if the variable is enclosed in a pair of curly braces { }. Identifiers are case sensitive, except for function names. The following are some examples of valid identifiers: myVariable, MYVARIABLE, _myVariable, _____myVariable, $myVariable, {This is a single variable}.

- *Numbers.* A number can be an *integer*, defined as one or more characters between 0 and 9. The following are some examples of integers: 0, 1, 00000, 12345. Another type of number is a *real number*. The following are some examples of real numbers: 0., 3., 0.0, 0.1, 3.9, .5, .934, .3E3, 3.5E-5, 0.2E-4, 3.2E+2, 3.5e-5,

- *Operator Precedence.* The operator precedence when evaluating the equations is shown in the following list. However, if there are two terms with two identical precedence operators, the expression is evaluated from left to right.

    - o ( )   – parenthesized expression has highest precedence

    - o !, -   – not, and unary minus. e.g. -3

    - o ^

    - o *, /

    - o +, -

    - o =, <>, !=, <, <=, >, >=

    - o &, |

- *Mathematical Expression.* The following shows some examples of valid equations usable in the *custom equations* boxes. Review the rest of the user manual, recommended texts, and example files for more illustrations of actual options equations and functions used in SLS 6.0.

    - o Max(Asset-Cost,0)

    - o Max(Asset-Cost,OptionOpen)

    - o 135

    - o 12 + 24 * 12 + 24 * 36 / 48

    - o 3 + ABS(-3)

    - o 3*MAX(1,2,3,4) - MIN(1,2,3,4)

- SQRT(3) + ROUND(3) * LOG(12)
- IF(a > 0, 3, 4)   – returns 3 if a > 0, else 4
- ABS+3
- MAX(a + b, c, MIN(d,e), a > b)
- IF(a > 0 | b < 0, 3, 4)
- IF(c <> 0, 3, 4)
- IF(IF(a <= 3, 4, 5) <> 4, a, a-b)
- MAX({My Cost 1} - {My Cost 2}, {Asset 2} + {Asset 3})

DYNAMIC SIMULATED DECISION TREES

One major misunderstanding that analysts tend to have about real options is that they can be solved using decision trees alone. This is untrue. Instead, decision trees are a great way of depicting strategic pathways that a firm can take, showing graphically a decision road map of management's strategic initiatives and opportunities over time. However, to solve a real options problem, it is better to combine decision-tree analytics with real options analytics, rather than solely relying on decision trees. When used in framing real options, these trees should be more appropriately called strategy trees (used to define optimal strategic pathways) as seen in *Modeling Risk's* Chapter 14's business cases.

Multiple other real options problems using more advanced techniques are required in certain circumstances. These models include the applications of stochastic optimization as well as other exotic types of options. In addition, as discussed, decision trees are insufficient when trying to solve real options problems because subjective probabilities with Bayesian updating are required as well as different discount rates at each node. The difficulties in forecasting the relevant discount rates and probabilities of occurrence are compounded over time, and the resulting values are oftentimes in error. However, decision trees by themselves are great as a depiction of management's strategic initiatives and opportunities over time. Decision trees should be used in conjunction with real options analytics in more complex cases.

Models used to solve decision tree problems range from a simple expected value to more sophisticated Bayesian probability updating approaches. Neither of these approaches alone is applicable when trying to solve a real options problem. In addition, as shown in Chapter 11, binomial lattices are a much better way to solve real options problems, and because these lattices can also ultimately be converted into decision trees, they are far superior to using decision trees as a stand-alone application for real options. Nonetheless, there is a common ground between decision trees and real options analytics, as seen in *Modeling Risk's* case studies.

For instance, if a decision-tree analysis is used (which by itself is insufficient for solving real options), then different discount rates have to be estimated at each decision node at different times because different projects at different times have different risk structures. Estimation errors will then be compounded on a large decision-tree analysis. Binomial lattices using risk-neutral probabilities avoid this error. In addition, risk-free rates are objective and easy to obtain, and because volatility is obtained from a robust Monte Carlo simulation approach, the imputed risk-neutral probability is more accurate, compared to guessing at the discount rate. Also, the discount rate requires a market benchmark that may or may not exist in the real options world (e.g., the beta coefficient is covariance divided by the variance of an external comparable market, to compute the CAPM discount rate).

One major conclusion that can be drawn using binomial lattices is that because risk-adjusting cash flows provides the same results as risk-adjusting the probabilities leading to those cash flows, the results stemming from a discounted cash flow analysis are identical to those generated using a binomial lattice. The only condition that is required is that the volatility of the cash flows be zero—in other words, the cash flows are assumed to be known with certainty. Because zero uncertainty exists, there is zero strategic option value, meaning that the net present value of a project is identical to its expanded net present value.

One of the fatal errors analysts tend to run into includes creating a decision tree and calculating the expected value using risk-neutral probabilities, akin to the risk-neutral probability used in Chapter 11. This approach is incorrect because risk-neutral probabilities are calculated based on a constant volatility. The risk structures of nodes on a decision tree (for instance, e-learning versus a dot.com strategy have very different risks and volatilities). In addition, for risk-neutral probabilities, a Martingale process is required. That is, in a binomial lattice, each node has two bifurcations, an up and a down. The up and down jump sizes are identical in magnitude for a recombining lattice. This characteristic has to hold before risk-neutral probabilities are valid. Clearly the return magnitudes of different events along the decision tree are different, and risk-neutralization does not work here. Because risk-neutral probabilities cannot be used, the risk-free rate, therefore, cannot be used here for discounting the cash flows. Also, because risks are different at each strategy node, the market risk-adjusted discount rate, such as a WACC, should also be different at every node. A correct single discount rate is difficult enough to calculate, let alone multiple discount rates on a complex tree, and the errors tend to compound by the time the NPV of the strategy is calculated.

In addition, chance nodes are usually added in decision-tree analysis, indicating that a certain event may occur given a specific probability. For instance, chance nodes may indicate a 30 percent chance of a great economy, a 45 percent chance of a nominal one, and a 25 percent chance of a downturn. Then events and payoffs are associated with these chances. Back-calculating these nodes using risk-neutral probabilities will be incorrect because these are chance nodes, not strategic options. Because these three events are complementary—that is, their respective probabilities add up to 100 percent—one of these events *must* occur, and given enough trials, all of these events must occur at one time or another. Real options analysis stipulates that one does not know what will occur, but only what the strategic alternatives are if a certain event occurs. If chance nodes are required in an analysis, the discounted cash flow model can accommodate them to calculate an expected value, which could then be simulated based on the probability and distributional assumptions. These simulated values can then be run in a real options modeling environment. The results can be shown on a strategy tree looking similar to a decision tree as depicted in Chapter 11. However, strategic decision pathways should be shown in the strategy tree environment, and each strategy node or combinations of strategy nodes can be evaluated in the context of real options analysis as described throughout this book. Then the results can be displayed in the strategy tree.

In summary, decision-tree analysis is incomplete as a stand-alone analysis in complex situations. Both the decision-tree and real options methodologies discussed approach the same problem from different perspectives. However, a common ground could be reached. Taking the advantages of both approaches and melding them into an overall valuation strategy, decision trees should be used to frame the problem, real options analytics should be used to solve any existing strategic optionalities (either by pruning the decision tree into subtrees or solving the entire strategy tree at once), and the results should be presented back on a decision tree. These so-called option strategy trees are useful for determining the optimal decision paths the firm should take.

ROV Decision Tree Module

Having made the preceding caveats on decision trees, know that they are still useful in a variety of settings, especially when advanced analytics such as Integrated Risk Management is integrated into decision trees as presented in this section. Selecting *Risk Simulator | ROV Decision Tree* runs the Decision Tree module (Figure 11.20). ROV Decision Tree is used to create and value decision tree models. Additional advanced methodologies and analytics are also included:

- Decision Tree Models
- Monte Carlo Risk Simulation
- Sensitivity Analysis
- Scenario Analysis
- Bayesian (Joint and Posterior Probability Updating)
- Expected Value of Information
- MINIMAX
- MAXIMIN
- Risk Profiles

Example Case Illustration

Figure 11.20, a sample oil and gas drilling project, illustrates the modeling of a risky decision on whether small drill bits or large drill bits should be used in an offshore oil exploration project on a secondary well. Start the *ROV Decision Tree* and click on *File | Example | 01 Basic Large or Small Development* to load this example to follow along. In the example, there is an expected 30% probability that this secondary well will become critical (if the primary well does not function properly or when oil prices start to skyrocket), or 70% probability (its complement) that it will not. If the large drill bits are used, it will cost more to set up (e.g., $20M as opposed to $10M). However, if things do become critical, the project can be completed with less of a delay if a large initial drill bit is user rather than a small drill bit. The event probabilities, weeks to completion or delays, and their respective probabilities of delays are mapped in the decision tree. This model can be then be run to show the decision path with the minimum cost, and a risk simulation can also be run and the results can be tabulated as a probability distribution (Figure 11.21). The following provides more details on how the decision is set up as well as what each of the nodes and values represents:

- Start by drawing the entire decision tree, then add the values after the tree has been constructed.

- Squares are decision nodes (i.e., a decision that has to be made) where in the example, we see that the decision is whether to use a small drill bit or a large drill bit.

- Circles are uncertainty nodes where various events can occur and each event carries with it some probability, and the sum of the probabilities in each circle uncertainty node must sum to 100%.

- Finally, the decision tree must always end on the right with the triangular terminal nodes. A decision tree cannot be modeled and solved unless every final node is a terminal node.

- The decision tree implementation pathway and sequence of events progress from the left to right. In the example, we see that the decision (the initial square decision node) is whether to implement the large drill bit or small drill bit. The decision takes two outcome paths: small or large drill bits.

- Regardless of which decision path is taken, there is uncertainty in terms of whether the secondary well will become critical (30% probability) or not critical (70% probability). This uncertainty is independent of and applies whether the large or small drills are implemented, which is why you see the two circular uncertainty nodes in the second step in the figure, denoted as "Critical?" The two identical nodes splits into two outcomes: "Yes" it is critical (30%) and "No" it is not critical (70%), as depicted as the third column of the decision tree.

- Next, the level of uncertainty is the secondary well completion time. Although the well will be completed faster with the larger drill bit and slower with the smaller drill bit, the completion time is still uncertain. With the large drill bit, regardless of whether the well is critical or not, the uncertainty in terms of completion time can be 12 days with a 30% probability, 14 days with a 50% probability, and 18 days with 20% probability. Note that this uncertainty node has three outcomes, and the sum of the probabilities for the uncertainty node must equal 100%. This Completion Time A node is replicated for Completion Time B node as the time to complete the wells, again, are independent of whether the well is critical or not, although it is dependent on the drill size. This is why in Completion Time C and D, which are identical, have 16 days, 18 days, and 23 days, indicating a delay in completion time when the small drill bit is used.

- Finally, each of the branches on the right must finish with triangular terminal nodes. These nodes will require user inputs in the payoff under each situation. In other words, if the large drill bit is executed and the well is critical, and if the well could somehow be completed in 12 days, the present value of the cost or payoff is a cost of $248M. Continue with the terminal nodes and complete the inputs for the cost structure.

- Note that you can enter the terminal values as either positive or negative, and terminal nodes are usually net present values or costs (although other variables can be used, of course, such as time or resources). Since we are modeling the cost, when we run the analysis, select the cost Minimization Option. If these payoffs are net present values, then by all means choose the Maximum Payoff option.

- As mentioned, finish drawing the decision tree from left to right first, then start entering the values in the nodes, either left to right or right to left, it really does not matter. The following are the required inputs in the sample decision tree:

  o All terminal node payoffs. As explained, in this example, the payoffs are the costs under each pathway, for example, $248M, $286M, $362M, and so forth. You can double-click on the each of the terminal nodes to enter the required inputs.

  o All probabilities of the event outcomes in the uncertainty nodes. For instance, double-click on the circle uncertainty nodes and enter the probabilities of each event branch. In the Critical node, enter 30% and 70%. In the Completion Time nodes, enter the 30%, 50%, and 20% probabilities. Again, all probabilities in the same node must sum to 100%.

- Then, click on the *Run* icon and select either *Minimize* or *Maximize*. In this example where we use cost as the positive payoff values, *Minimize* is the correct option. After running, you will see a few things:

  o The optimal path will be highlighted. In this case, the minimal cost is to execute the large drill, which will, given the cost structure and probability of various event outcomes, be the course of action that best minimizes the total cost to the company. Note that the highlighted path is short in this case as there is only one decision node, and the highlighted path shows which decision to take. The path will not continue past any uncertainty nodes because these are uncertain outcomes and, hence, the model will not be able to determine which event outcome or path will occur. In larger decision trees with additional decision nodes, you will see a longer highlighted optimal path.

o Additional values are now displayed on the decision tree.

- In the terminal node, you will see the percentages, such as 9.00% for the first terminal node. This is the expected probability given this pathway, assuming independence among the probabilistic outcomes. That is, 30% × 30% = 9.00%. The first 30% is the *Critical = Yes* path, and the second 30% is the *Fast Completion Time* path. As another example, the second terminal node is 15.00%, which is computed by multiplying 30% × 50% = 15.00% (the *Critical = Yes* and *Completion Time = Medium* path). All other percentages are computed in a similar fashion.

- Under each uncertainty node you will now see a computed number. These are the expectation values. For instance, the value $289.80 under the Completion Time A node is computed by 30% × $248 + 50% × $286 + 20% × $362 = $289.80. The same expected value calculation applies to the other uncertainty nodes.

- Finally, you see the initial square decision node shows a computed value of $120.82, which is the minimum value comparing $120.82 and $131.44. The highlighted path indicates the best decision to take, and in this case it is to go with the large drill bit, which will minimize the total expected cost of the project.

• Click on the *Summary of Values* tab to see a tabular outcome of the values above.

• In the *Simulation Modeling* tab, the decision node's simulated results will be seen (Figure 11.21):

o The simulated mean value is $118.39 for the cost, close to the single-point estimated cost of $120.82 in the decision tree. The simulated mean value includes all the assumptions that we set up in the model.

o Note that only user input values can be simulated, which means only the terminal payoff values and the uncertainty probability values can be set as input assumptions for the simulation to proceed.

o Figure 11.20 shows a sample user interface that opens when one of the uncertainty nodes is double-clicked. Here you see that the set input assumption icon can be clicked under the column named *Simulate*. In this column, users can set simple probability assumptions or create their own equations to simulate.

o The simulated result in Figure 11.21 shows that the 90% confidence interval (i.e., 5% on the left tail and 5% on the right tail with 90% in the middle of the distribution, which is the same as entering the *5th* and *95th Percentiles*) returns a value of $115.70M and $121.12M. In the 5% best-case scenario, the cost will be under $115M, whereas it will be over $121M in the worst-case scenario.

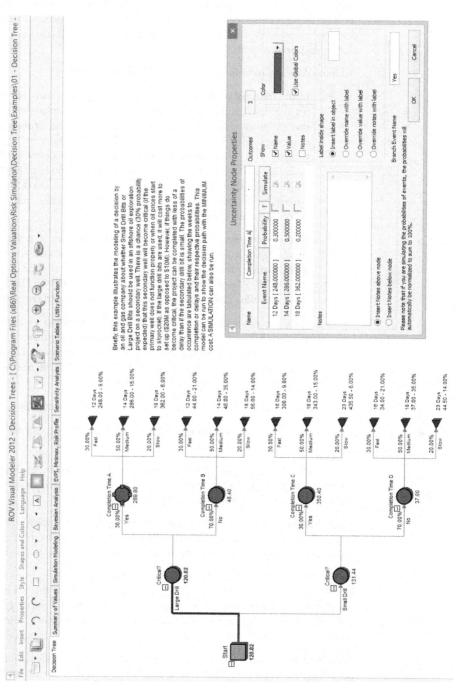

Figure 11.20: ROV Decision Tree

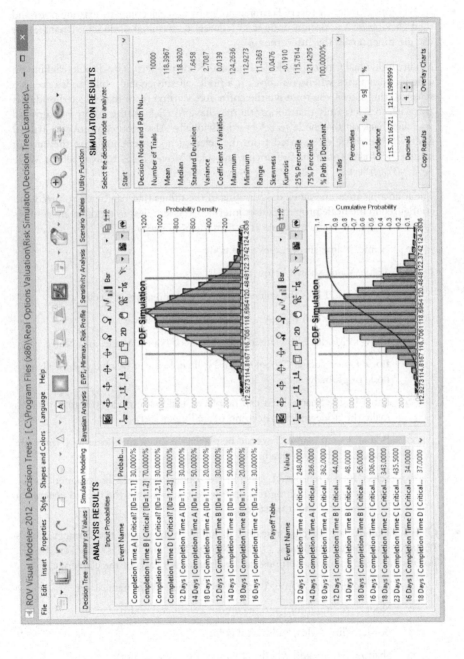

Figure 11.21: Decision Tree Simulation Results

The following are some key quick getting started tips and procedures:

- There are 11 localized languages available in this module and the current language can be changed through the Language menu. Select the language of your choice to begin; English is the default language selected.

- Insert Option nodes or Insert Terminal nodes by first selecting any existing node and then clicking on the option node icon (square) or terminal node icon (triangle), or use the functions in the Insert menu.

- Modify individual Option Node or Terminal Node properties by double-clicking on a node. Sometimes when you click on a node, all subsequent child nodes are also selected (this allows you to move the entire tree starting from that selected node). If you wish to select only that node, you may have to click on the empty background and click back on that node to select it individually. Also, you can move individual nodes or the entire tree started from the selected node depending on the current setting (right-click, or in the Edit menu, and select Move Nodes Individually or Move Nodes Together).

- The following are some quick descriptions of the things that can be customized and configured in the node properties user interface. It is simplest to try different settings for each of the following to see its effects in the Strategy Tree:

  o Name. Name shown above the node.

  o Value. Value shown below the node.

  o Excel Link. Links the value from an Excel spreadsheet's cell.

  o Notes. Notes can be inserted above or below a node.

  o Show in Model. Show any combinations of Name, Value, and Notes.

  o Local Color versus Global Color. Node colors can be changed locally to a node or globally.

  o Label Inside Shape. Text can be placed inside the node (you may need to make the node wider to accommodate longer text).

  o Branch Event Name. Text can be placed on the branch leading to the node to indicate the event leading to this node.

  o Select Real Options. A specific real option type can be assigned to the current node. Assigning real options to nodes allows the tool to generate a list of required input variables.

- Global Elements are all customizable, including elements of the Strategy Tree's Background, Connection Lines, Option Nodes, Terminal Nodes, and Text Boxes. For instance, the following settings can be changed for each of the elements:

  o Font settings on Name, Value, Notes, Label, Event names.

  o Node Size (minimum and maximum height and width).

  o Borders (line styles, width, and color).

  o Shadow (colors and whether to apply a shadow or not).

  o Global Color.

  o Global Shape.

- The Edit menu's View Data Requirements Window command opens a docked window on the right of the Strategy Tree such that when an option node or terminal node is selected, the properties of that node will be displayed and can be updated directly. This feature provides an alternative to double-clicking on a node each time.

- Example Files are available in the File menu to help you get started on building Decision Trees and Strategy Trees.

- Protect File from the File menu allows the Strategy Tree to be encrypted with up to a 256-bit password encryption. Be careful when a file is being encrypted because if the password is lost, the file can no longer be opened.

- Capturing the Screen or printing the existing model can be done through the File menu. The captured screen can then be pasted into other software applications.

- Add, Duplicate, Rename, and Delete a Strategy Tree can be performed through right-clicking the Strategy Tree tab or the Edit menu.

- You can also Insert File Link and Insert Comment on any option or terminal node, or Insert Text or Insert Picture anywhere in the background or drawing canvas area.

- You can Change Existing Styles, or Manage and Create Custom Styles of your Strategy Tree (this includes size, shape, color schemes, and font size/color specifications of the entire Strategy Tree).

- Insert Decision, Insert Uncertainty, or Insert Terminal nodes by selecting any existing node and then clicking on the decision node icon (square), uncertainty node icon (circle), or terminal node icon (triangle), or use the functionalities in the Insert menu.

- Modify individual Decision, Uncertainty, or Terminal nodes' properties by double-clicking on a node. The following are some additional unique items in the Decision Tree module that can be customized and configured in the node properties user interface:

  o Decision Nodes: Custom Override or Auto Compute the value on a node. The automatically compute option is set as default and when you click RUN on a completed Decision Tree model, the decision nodes will be updated with the results.

  o Uncertainty Nodes: Event Names, Probabilities, and Set Simulation Assumptions. You can add probability event names, probabilities, and simulation assumptions only after the uncertainty branches are created.

  o Terminal Nodes: Manual Input, Excel Link, and Set Simulation Assumptions. The terminal event payoffs can be entered manually or linked to an Excel cell (e.g., if you have a large Excel model that computes the payoff, you can link the model to this Excel model's output cell) or set probability distributional assumptions for running simulations.

- View Node Properties Window is available from the Edit menu and the selected node's properties will update when a node is selected.

- The Decision Tree module also comes with the following advanced analytics:

  o Monte Carlo Risk Simulation Modeling on Decision Trees

  o Bayes Analysis for obtaining posterior probabilities

    o   Expected Value of Perfect Information, MINIMAX and MAXIMIN Analysis, Risk Profiles, and Value of Imperfect Information

    o   Sensitivity Analysis

    o   Scenario Analysis

    o   Utility Function Analysis

Simulating a Decision Tree

This tool runs Monte Carlo risk simulation on the decision tree (Figure 11.21). It allows you to set probability distributions as input assumptions for running simulations. You can either set an assumption for the selected node or set a new assumption and use this new assumption (or use previously created assumptions) in a numerical equation or formula. For example, you can set a new assumption called Normal (e.g., normal distribution with a mean of 100 and standard deviation of 10) and run a simulation in the decision tree, or use this assumption in an equation such as (100*Normal+15.25).

Create your own model in the numerical expression box. You can use basic computations or add existing variables into your equation by double-clicking on the list of existing variables. New variables can be added to the list as required either as numerical expressions or assumptions.

Bayes Analysis on Decision Trees

This Bayesian analysis tool (Figure 11.22) can be used on any two uncertainty events that are linked along a path. For instance, in the example on the right in Figure 11.22, uncertainties A and B are linked, where event A occurs first in the timeline and event B occurs second. First Event A is Market Research with 2 outcomes (Favorable or Unfavorable). Second Event B is Market Conditions also with 2 outcomes (Strong and Weak). This tool is used to compute joint, marginal, and Bayesian posterior-updated probabilities by entering the prior probabilities and reliability conditional probabilities; or reliability probabilities can be computed when you have posterior-updated conditional probabilities. Select the relevant analysis desired and click on Load Example to see the sample inputs corresponding to the selected analysis and the results shown in the grid on the right, as well as which results are used as inputs in the decision tree in Figure 11.22.

Procedure

1.   Enter the names for the first and second uncertainty events and choose how many probability events (states of nature or outcomes) each event has.

2.   Enter the names of each probability event or outcome.

3.   Enter the second event's prior probabilities and the conditional probabilities for each event or outcome. The probabilities must sum to 100%.

Expected Value of Perfect Information, MINIMAX and MAXIMIN Analysis, Risk Profiles, and Value of Imperfect Information in Decision Trees

This tool (Figure 11.23) computes the Expected Value of Perfect Information (EVPI), and MINIMAX and MAXIMIN Analysis, as well as the Risk Profile and the Value of Imperfect Information. To get started, enter the number of decision branches or strategies under consideration (e.g., build a large, medium, or small facility), the number of uncertain events or states of nature outcomes (e.g., good market, bad market), and the expected payoffs under each scenario.

The Expected Value of Perfect Information (EVPI), that is, assuming you had perfect foresight and knew exactly what to do (through market research or other means to better discern the probabilistic outcomes), computes if there is added value in such information (i.e., if market research will add value) as compared to more naïve estimates of the probabilistic states of nature. To get started, enter the number of decision branches or strategies under consideration (e.g., build a large, medium, or small facility) and the number of uncertain events or states of nature outcomes (e.g., good market, bad market), and enter the expected payoffs under each scenario.

MINIMAX (minimizing the maximum regret) and MAXIMIN (maximizing the minimum payoff) are two alternate approaches to finding the optimal decision path. These two approaches are not used often but still provide added insight into the decision-making process. Enter the number of decision branches or paths that exist (e.g., build a large, medium, or small facility), as well as the uncertainty events or states of nature under each path (e.g., good economy vs. bad economy). Then, complete the payoff table for the various scenarios and Compute the MINIMAX and MAXIMIN results. You can also click on Load Example to see a sample calculation.

Sensitivity Analysis in Decision Trees

Sensitivity analysis (Figure 11.24) on the input probabilities is performed to determine the impact of inputs on the values of decision paths. First, select one Decision Node to analyze and then select one probability event to test from the list. If there are multiple uncertainty events with identical probabilities, they can be analyzed either independently or concurrently.

The sensitivity charts show the values of the decision paths under varying probability levels. The numerical values are shown in the results table. The location of crossover lines, if any, represents at what probabilistic events a certain decision path becomes dominant over another.

Scenario Tables in Decision Trees

Scenario tables (Figure 11.25) can be generated to determine the output values given some changes to the input. You can choose one or more Decision paths to analyze (the results of each path chosen will be represented as a separate table and chart) and one or two Uncertainty or Terminal nodes as input variables to the scenario table.

Procedure

1. Select one or more Decision paths to analyze from the list.

2. Select one or two Uncertainty Events or Terminal Payoffs to model.

3. Decide if you wish to change the event's probability on its own or all identical probability events at once.

4. Enter the input scenario range.

Utility Functions in Decision Trees

Utility functions (Figure 11.26), or U(x), are sometimes used in place of expected values of terminal payoffs in a decision tree. U(x) can be developed two ways: using tedious and detailed experimentation of every possible outcome or an exponential extrapolation method (used here). They can be modeled for a decision maker who is risk-averse (downsides are more disastrous or painful than an equal upside potential), risk-neutral (upsides and downsides have equal attractiveness), or risk-loving (upside potential is more attractive). Enter the minimum and maximum expected value of your terminal payoffs and the number of data points in between to compute the utility curve and table.

If you had a 50:50 gamble where you either earn $X or lose –$X/2 versus not playing and getting a $0 payoff, what would this $X be? For example, if you are indifferent between a bet where you can win $100 or lose –$50 with equal probability compared to not playing at all, then your X is $100. Enter the X in the Positive Earnings box. Note that the larger X is, the less risk-averse you are, and whereas a smaller X indicates that you are more risk-averse.

Enter the required inputs, select the U(x) type, and click Compute Utility to obtain the results. You can also apply the computed U(x) values to the decision tree to rerun it, or revert the tree back to using expected values of the payoffs.

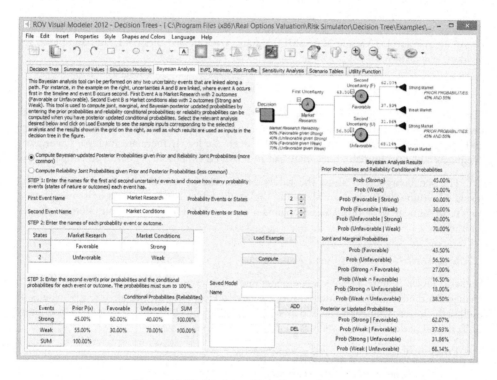

Figure 11.22: Decision Tree Bayes Analysis

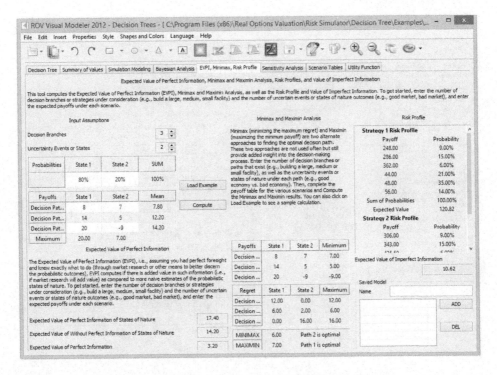

Figure 11.23: Decision Tree EVPI, MINIMAX, Risk Profile

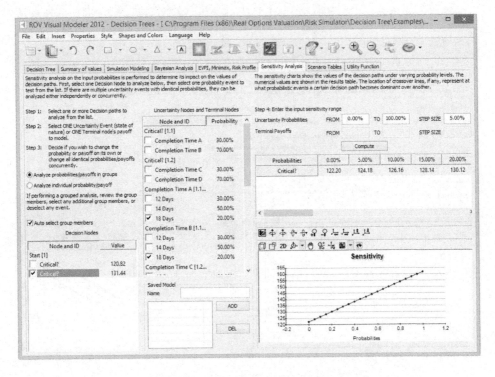

Figure 11.24: Decision Tree Sensitivity Analysis

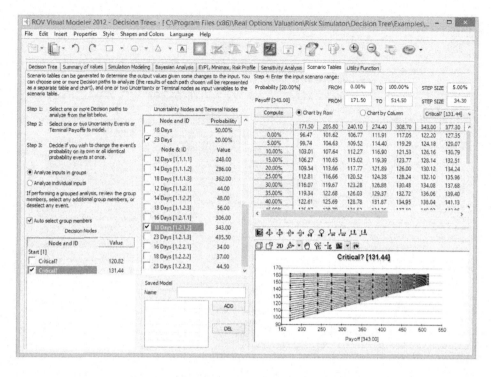

Figure 11.25: Decision Tree Scenario Tables

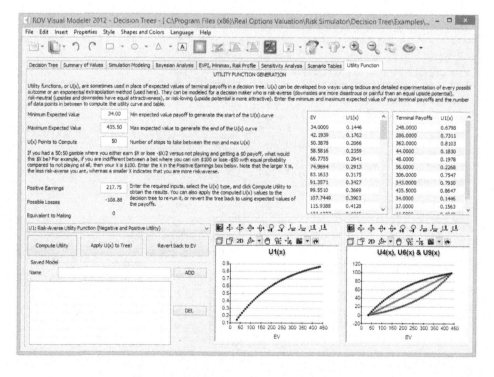

Figure 11.26: Decision Tree Utility Function

EXERCISE 1: BASIC AMERICAN, EUROPEAN, AND BERMUDAN CALL OPTIONS

The following are exercises on solving strategic real options problems using Real Options SLS software (the exercises here require version 2014 or later). It is assumed that you have already successfully reviewed Chapters 10 and 11, and have the software installed and ready to use. This first exercise illustrates how to use Real Options SLS for solving:

1. American Call Options

2. European Call Options

3. Bermudan Call Options

4. The Value Differential among American, European, and Bermudan Options

5. Custom Equations in Call and Put Options

6. Input Impacts on a Call and Put Option

Figure 11E1.A shows the computation of basic American, European, and Bermudan Options without dividends (example file used: *File | Examples | Basic American, European, versus Bermudan Call Options*), while Figure 11E1.B shows the computation of the same options but with a dividend yield. Of course, European Options can only be executed at termination and not before, while in American Options, early exercise is allowed, versus a Bermudan Option where early exercise is allowed except during blackout or vesting periods. Notice that the results for the three options without dividends are identical for simple call options, but they differ when dividends exist. When dividends are included, the simple call option values for American $\geq$ Bermudan $\geq$ European in most basic cases, as seen in Figure 11E1.B (insert a 5% dividend rate and blackout steps of 0-50). Of course this generality can be applied only to plain-vanilla call options and do not necessarily apply to other exotic options (e.g., Bermudan options with vesting and suboptimal exercise behavior multiples tend to sometimes carry a higher value when blackouts and vesting occur than regular American options with the same suboptimal exercise parameters).

Exercises

1. Using Real Options SLS, recreate the first call option without dividends.

   a. Prove that the binomial lattice method, when sufficient steps exist, converge to the closed-form Black–Scholes result in the benchmark section of the software. Use the *Convergence* analysis to assist you.

   b. Look at the *Payoff Chart* and explain what is on the x-axis and y-axis, and how you would replicate drawing the chart.

   c. Use *Sensitivity Analysis* to determine which input has the highest effect on the option value.

2. Re-create and solve the American, European, and Bermudan call options with a 5% dividend rate using Real Options SLS software as illustrated.

   a. Prove that the Bermudan call option value decreases as the blackout steps increase, until the point where the option value equals the European call option. Explain your findings.

b. What happens to the value differential among these three types of options as dividends increase? What does dividend represent in the real options context? (Hint: What are opportunity costs, cost of deferment, and cost outlay?)

c. Select the *Custom* option checkbox and replicate each of the results above using your own "Max(Asset-Cost)" and "OptionOpen" equations.

d. For each of the following inputs, determine whether an increase in its input value will increase or decrease the value of a plain-vanilla call option: asset value (stock), implementation cost (strike), maturity, risk-free rate, dividend, volatility.

3. Create a *put option* instead of a call option. How would the custom equations differ? For each of the following inputs, determine whether an increase in its input value will increase or decrease the value of a plain vanilla call option: asset value (stock), implementation cost (strike), maturity, risk-free rate, dividend, volatility.

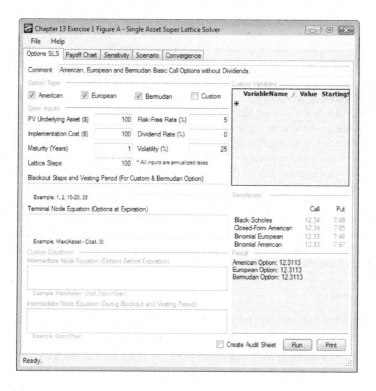

Figure 11E1.A: Simple American, Bermudan, and European Options without Dividends

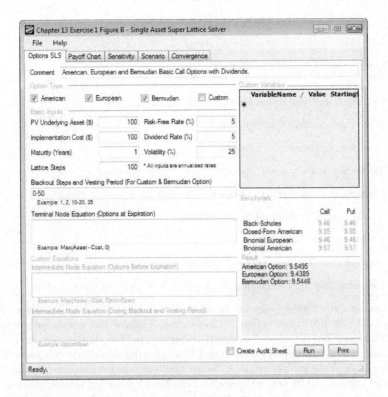

Figure 11E1.B: Simple American, Bermudan, and European Options with Dividends and Blackout Steps

EXERCISE 2: AMERICAN, EUROPEAN, BERMUDAN, AND CUSTOMIZED ABANDONMENT OPTIONS

This exercise illustrates how to use Real Options SLS for solving:

1. American Abandonment Options

2. European Abandonment Options

3. Bermudan Abandonment Options

4. Customized Abandonment Options

5. The Effects of Vesting and Blackout Periods

6. Optimal Trigger Values

7. The Effects of Opportunity Cost, Leakage, and Cost of Waiting

8. Risk Simulation on Lattice Models using Risk Simulator and Lattice Maker

The *Abandonment Option* looks at the value of a project's or asset's flexibility in being abandoned over the life of the option. As an example, suppose that a firm owns a project or asset and that based on traditional discounted cash flow (DCF) models, it estimates the present value of the asset (*PV Underlying Asset*) to be $120M (for the abandonment option this is the net present value of the project or asset). Monte Carlo simulation indicates that the *Volatility* of this asset value is significant, estimated at 25%. Under these conditions, there is a lot of uncertainty as to the success or failure of this project (the volatility calculated models the different sources of uncertainty and computes the risks in the discounted cash flow (DCF) model including price uncertainty, probability of success, competition, cannibalization, and so forth), and the value of the project might be significantly higher or significantly lower than the expected value of $120M. Suppose an abandonment option is created whereby a counterparty is found and a contract is signed that lasts 5 years (*Maturity*) such that for some monetary consideration now, the firm has the ability to sell the asset or project to the counterparty at any time within these 5 years (indicative of an American option) for a specified *Salvage* of $90M. The counterparty agrees to this $30M discount and signs the contract.

What has just occurred is that the firm bought itself a $90M insurance policy. That is, if the asset or project value increases above its current value, the firm may decide to continue funding the project, or sell it off in the market at the prevailing fair market value. Alternatively, if the value of the asset or project falls below the $90M threshold, the firm has the right to execute the option and sell off the asset to the counterparty at $90M. In other words, a safety net of sorts has been erected to prevent the value of the asset from falling below this salvage level. Thus, how much is this safety net or insurance policy worth? One can create competitive advantage in negotiation if the counterparty does not have the answer and you do. Further assume that the 5-year Treasury Note *Risk-Free Rate* (zero coupon) is 5% from the U.S. Department of Treasury (http://www.treasury.gov). The *American Abandonment Option* results in Figure 11E2.A show a value of $125.48M, indicating that the option value is $5.48M as the present value of the asset is $120M. Hence, the *maximum* value one should be willing to pay for the contract on *average* is $5.48M. This resulting expected value weights the continuous probabilities that the asset value exceeds $90M versus when it does not (where the option to abandon is valuable). Also, it weights when the timing of executing the abandonment is optimal such that the expected value is $5.48M.

In addition, some experimentation can be conducted. Changing the salvage value to $30M (this means a $90M discount from the starting asset value) yields a result of $120M, or $0M for the option. This result means that the option or contract is worthless because the safety net is set so low that it will never be utilized. Conversely, setting the salvage level to thrice the prevailing asset value or $360M would yield a result of $360M, which means that there is no option value, there is no value in waiting and having this option, or, simply, execute the option immediately and sell the asset if someone is willing to pay three times the value of the project right now. Thus, you can keep changing the salvage value until the option value disappears, indicating the *optimal trigger value* has been reached. For instance, if you enter $166.80 as the salvage value, the abandonment option analysis yields a result of $166.80, indicating that at this price and above, the optimal decision is to sell the asset immediately. At any lower salvage value, there is option value, and at any higher salvage value, there will be no option value. This breakeven salvage point is the optimal trigger value. Once the market price of this asset exceeds this value, it is optimal to abandon. Finally, adding a *Dividend Rate*, the *cost of waiting before abandoning the asset* (e.g., the annualized taxes and maintenance fees that have to be paid if you keep the asset and not sell it off, measured as a percentage of the present value of the asset) will decrease the option value. Hence, the breakeven trigger point, where the option becomes worthless, can be calculated by successively choosing higher dividend levels. This breakeven point again illustrates the trigger value at which the option should be optimally executed immediately, but this time with respect to a dividend yield. That is, if the *cost of carry* or holding on to the option, or the option's *leakage value* is high, that is, if the *cost of waiting* is too high, do not wait and execute the option immediately.

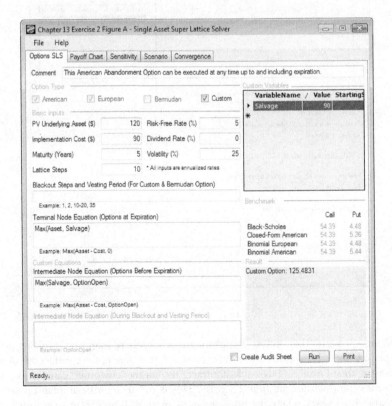

Figure 11E2.A: Simple American Abandonment Option

Figure 11E2.B shows the same abandonment option but with a 100-step lattice. To follow along, open the Single Asset SLS example file: *File | Examples | Abandonment American Option*. Notice that the 10-step lattice yields $125.48 while the 100-step lattice yields $125.45, indicating that the lattice results have achieved convergence. The Terminal Node Equation is *Max(Asset,Salvage)*, which means the decision at maturity is to decide if the option should be executed, selling the asset and receiving the salvage value, or not to execute, holding on to the asset. The Intermediate Node Equation used is *Max(Salvage,OptionOpen)* indicating that before maturity, the decision is either to execute early in this American option to abandon and receive the salvage value, or to hold on to the asset, and, hence, hold on to and keep the option open for potential future execution, denoted simply as *OptionOpen*. To run the European version of the abandonment option, the Intermediate Node Equation is set to *OptionOpen*, as early execution is prohibited before maturity. Of course, being only able to execute the option at maturity is worth less ($124.5054 compared to $125.4582) than being able to exercise earlier. The example files used are *File | Examples | Abandonment American Option* and *File | Examples | Abandonment European Option*. For example, the airline manufacturer in the previous case example can agree to a buy-back provision that can be exercised at any time by the airline customer versus only at a specific date at the end of 5 years—the former American option will clearly be worth more than the latter European option.

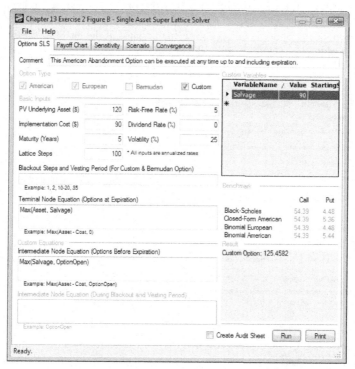

Figure 11E2.B: American Abandonment Option with 100-Step Lattice

Sometimes, a Bermudan option is appropriate, where there might be a vesting period or blackout period when the option cannot be executed. For instance, the contract stipulates that for the 5-year abandonment buy-back contract, the airline customer cannot execute the abandonment option within the first 2.5 years. This is run using a Bermudan option with a 100-step lattice on 5 years, where the blackout steps are 0-50. This means that during the first 50 steps (as well as right now or step 0), the option cannot be executed. This is modeled by inserting *OptionOpen* into the Intermediate Node Equation During Blackout and Vesting

Periods. This forces the option holder to only keep the option open during the vesting period, preventing execution during this blackout period. You can see that the American option is worth more than the Bermudan option, which is worth more than the European option, by virtue of each option type's ability to execute early and the frequency of execution possibilities.

Sometimes, the salvage value of the abandonment option may change over time. To illustrate, in the previous example of an acquisition of a start-up firm, the intellectual property will most probably increase over time because of continued research and development activities, thereby changing the salvage values over time. An example is seen in Figure 11E2.C, where there are five salvage values over the 5-year abandonment option. This can be modeled by using the Custom Variables. Type in the *Variable Name*, *Value*, and *Starting Step* and hit *ENTER* to input the variables one at a time as seen in Figure 11E2.C's Custom Variables list. Notice that the same variable name (*Salvage*) is used but the values change over time, and the starting steps represent when these different values become effective. For instance, the salvage value $90 applies at step 0 until the next salvage value of $95 takes over at step 21. This means that for a 5-year option with a 100-step lattice, the first year including the current period (steps 0 to 20) will have a salvage value of $90, which then increases to $95 in the second year (steps 21 to 40), and so forth. Notice that as the value of the firm's intellectual property increases over time, the option valuation results also increase, which makes logical sense. You can also model in blackout vesting periods for the first 6 months (steps 0-10 in the blackout area). The blackout period is very typical of contractual obligations of abandonment options where during specified periods, the option cannot be executed (a cooling-off period). Note that you may use *TAB* on the keyboard to move from the variable name column to the value column, and on to the starting step column. However, remember to hit *ENTER* on the keyboard to insert the variable and to create a new row so that you may enter a new variable.

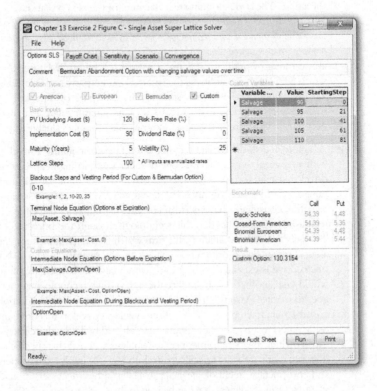

Figure 11E2.C: Customized Abandonment Option

Exercises

1. Replicate the abandonment options as illustrated above, solving for the American, European, Bermudan, and Custom types using Real Options SLS.

    a. Generate Audit Sheets in the analysis.

    b. Generate the live lattice using the Lattice Maker module and apply a Monte Carlo simulation on the real options lattice model using Risk Simulator.

2. Other applications of the abandonment option include buy-back lease provisions in a contract (guaranteeing a specified asset value); asset preservation flexibility; insurance policies; walking away from a project and selling off its intellectual property; and purchase price of an acquisition; and so forth. Solve the following abandonment options.

    a. An aircraft manufacturer sells its small private jets in the primary market for, say, $30M each to various airline companies. Airlines are usually risk-averse and may find it hard to justify buying an additional plane with all the uncertainties in the economy, demand, price competition, and fuel costs. When uncertainties become resolved over time, airline carriers may have to reallocate and reroute their existing portfolio of planes globally, and an excess plane on the tarmac is very costly. The airline can sell the excess plane in the secondary market where smaller regional carriers buy used planes, but the price uncertainty is very high and is subject to significant volatility, of, say, 45%, and may fluctuate wildly between $10M and $25M for this class of aircraft. The aircraft manufacturer can reduce the airline's risk by providing a buy-back provision or abandonment option, where at any time within the next 5 years, the manufacturer agrees to buy back the plane at a guaranteed residual salvage price of $20M, at the request of the airline. The corresponding risk-free rate for the next 5 years is 5%. *This reduces the downside risk of the airline, and hence reduces its risk, chopping off the left tail of the price fluctuation distribution, and shifting the expected value to the right. This abandonment option provides risk reduction and value enhancement to the airline.* Hint: Applying the abandonment option in SLS using a 100-step binomial lattice, this option is worth $3.52M. If the airline is the smarter counterparty and calculates this value and gets this buy-back provision for free as part of the deal, the aircraft manufacturer has just lost over 10% of its aircraft value that it left on the negotiation table. Information and knowledge is highly valuable in this case.

    b. A high-tech disk-drive manufacturer is thinking of acquiring a small startup firm with a new micro drive technology (a super-fast and high-capacity pocket hard drive) that may revolutionize the industry. The startup is for sale and its asking price is $50M based on an NPV fair market value analysis some third-party valuation consultants have performed. The manufacturer can either develop the technology itself or acquire this technology through the purchase of the firm. The question is, how much is this firm worth to the manufacturer, and is $50M a good price? Based on internal analysis by the manufacturer, the NPV of this micro drive is expected to be $45M, with a cash flow volatility of 40%, and it would take another 3 years before the micro drive technology is successful and goes to market. Assume that the 3-year risk-free rate is 5%. In addition, it would cost the manufacturer $45M in present value to develop this drive internally. If using an NPV analysis, the manufacturer should build the drive itself. However, if you include an abandonment option analysis where if this specific micro drive does not work, the start-up still has an abundance of intellectual property (patents and proprietary technologies) as well as physical assets (buildings and manufacturing facilities) that can be sold in the market at up to $40M. (Hint: The abandonment option together with the NPV yields $51.83, making buying the start-up worth more than developing the technology internally, and making the purchase price of $50M worth it). See the section on Expansion Option for more examples on how this startup's technology can be used as a platform to further develop newer technologies that can be worth much more than just the abandonment option.

EXERCISE 3: AMERICAN, EUROPEAN, BERMUDAN, AND CUSTOMIZED CONTRACTION OPTIONS

This exercise illustrates how to use Real Options SLS for solving:

1. American Contraction Options

2. European Contraction Options

3. Bermudan Contraction Options

4. Customized Contraction Options

A *Contraction Option* evaluates the flexibility value of being able to reduce production output or to contract the scale and scope of a project when conditions are not as amenable, thereby reducing the value of the asset or project by a *Contraction Factor*, but at the same time creating some cost *Savings*. As an example, suppose you work for a large aeronautical manufacturing firm that is unsure of the technological efficacy and market demand for its new fleet of long-range supersonic jets. The firm decides to hedge itself through the use of strategic options, specifically an option to contract 10% of its manufacturing facilities at any time within the next 5 years (i.e., the *Contraction Factor* is 0.9).

Suppose that the firm has a current operating structure whose static valuation of future profitability using a discounted cash flow model (in other words, the present value of the expected future cash flows discounted at an appropriate market risk-adjusted discount rate) is found to be $1,000M (*PV Asset*). Using Monte Carlo simulation, you calculate the implied volatility of the logarithmic returns of the asset value of the projected future cash flows to be 30%. The risk-free rate on a riskless asset (5-year U.S. Treasury Note with zero coupons) is found to be yielding 5%.

Further suppose the firm has the option to contract 10% of its current operations at any time over the next 5 years, thereby creating an additional $50 million in savings after this contraction. These terms are arranged through a legal contractual agreement with one of its vendors, who had agreed to take up the excess capacity and space of the firm. At the same time, the firm can scale back and lay off part of its existing workforce to obtain this level of savings (in present values).

The results indicate that the strategic value of the project is $1,001.71M (using a 10-step lattice as seen in Figure 11E3.A), which means that the NPV currently is $1,000M and the additional $1.71M comes from this contraction option. This result is obtained because contracting now yields 90% of $1,000M + $50M, or $950M, which is less than staying in business and not contracting and obtaining $1,000M. Therefore, the optimal decision is to not contract immediately but keep the ability to do so open for the future. Hence, in comparing this optimal decision of $1,000M to $1,001.71M of being able to contract, the option to contract is worth $1.71M. This should be the maximum amount the firm is willing to spend to obtain this option (contractual fees and payments to the vendor counterparty).

In contrast, if *Savings* were $200M instead, then the strategic project value becomes $1,100M, which means that starting at $1,000M and contracting 10% to $900M and keeping the $200M in savings, yields $1,100M in total value. Hence, the additional option value is $0M which means that it is optimal to execute the contraction option immediately as there is no option value and no value to wait to contract. So, the value of executing now is $1,100M as compared to the strategic project value of $1,100M; there is no additional option value, and the contraction should be executed immediately. That is, instead of asking the vendor to wait, the firm is better off executing the contraction option now and capturing the savings.

Other applications include shelving an R&D project by spending a little to keep it going but reserving the right to come back to it should conditions improve; the value of synergy in a merger and acquisition where some management personnel are let go to create the additional savings; reducing the scope and size of a production facility; reducing production rates; a joint venture or alliance, and so forth.

Figure 11E3.B illustrates a customized option where there is a blackout period and the savings from contracting change over time (example file used is *File | Examples | Contraction Customized Option*). These results are for the aeronautical manufacturing example.

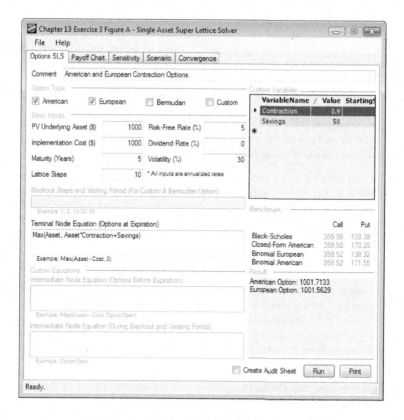

Figure 11E3.A: Contraction Option

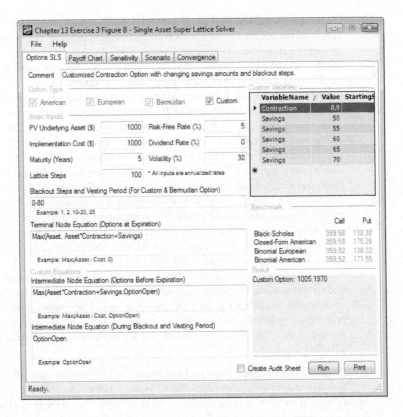

Figure 11E3.B: Customized Option to Contract with Changing Savings

Exercises

1. Replicate the two illustrations above for the basic contraction option and customized contraction option with changing savings, and answer the following questions:

   a. How would you run a simulation on a contraction option by simulating some of the inputs?

   b. How does simulating the input Savings compare analytically to the approach illustrated above with a changing Savings value at different lattice steps? Explain how each approach is doing something different.

2. Solve the following two cases:

   a. A large oil and gas company is embarking on a deep-sea drilling platform that will cost the company billions to implement. A DCF analysis is run and the NPV is found to be $500M over the next 10 years of economic life of the offshore rig. The 10-year risk-free rate is 5%, and the volatility of the project is found to be at an annualized 45% using historical oil prices as a proxy. If the expedition is highly successful (oil prices are high and production rates are soaring), then the company will continue its operations. However, if things are not looking too good (oil prices are low or moderate and production is only decent), it is very difficult for the company to abandon operations (why lose everything when net income is still positive although not as high as anticipated and not to mention the environmental and legal ramifications of simply abandoning an oil rig in the middle of the ocean). Hence, the oil company decides to hedge its downside risk through an American Contraction Option. The oil company was able to find a smaller oil and gas company (a former partner on other explorations) to be interested in a joint venture. The joint venture is structured such that the oil company pays this smaller counterparty a lump sum right now for a 10-year contract whereby at any time and at the oil company's request, the smaller counterparty will have to take over all operations of the offshore oil rig (i.e., taking over all operations and, hence, all relevant expenses) and keep 30% of the net revenues generated. The counterparty is in agreement because it does not have to partake in the billions of dollars required to implement the rig in the first place, and it actually obtains some cash up front for this contract to assume the downside risk. The oil company is also in agreement because it reduces its own risks if oil prices are low and production is not up to par, and it ends up saving over $75M in present value of total overhead expenses, which can then be reallocated and invested somewhere else. (Hint: In this example, the contraction option using a 100-step lattice is valued to be $14.24M using SLS. This means that the maximum amount that the counterparty should be paid should not exceed this amount. Of course the option analysis can be further complicated by analyzing the actual savings on a present value basis. For instance, if the option is exercised within the first 5 years, the savings is $75M but if exercised during the last 5 years, then the savings is only $50M. The revised option value is now $10.57M.)

b. A manufacturing firm is interested in outsourcing its manufacturing of children's toys to a small province in China. By doing so, it will produce overhead savings of more than $20M in present value over the economic life of the toys. However, outsourcing this internationally will mean lower quality control, delayed shipping problems, added importing costs, and assuming the added risks of unfamiliarity with the local business practices. In addition, the firm will consider outsourcing only if the quality of the workmanship in this Chinese firm is up to the stringent quality standards it requires. The NPV of this particular line of toys is $100M with 25% volatility. The firm's executives decide to purchase a contraction option by locating a small manufacturing firm in China, spending some resources to try out a small-scale proof of concept (thereby reducing the uncertainties of quality, knowledge, import-export issues, and so forth). If successful, the firm will agree to give this small Chinese manufacturer 20% of its net income as remuneration for its services, plus some start-up fees. The question is, how much is this option to contract worth; that is, how much should the firm be willing to pay, on average, to cover the initial start-up fees plus the costs of this proof of concept stage? (Hint: A contraction option valuation result using SLS shows that the option is worth $1.59M, assuming a 5% risk-free rate for the 1-year test period. So, as long as the total costs for a pilot test costs less than $1.59, it is optimal to obtain this option, especially if it means potentially being able to save more than $20M.)

EXERCISE 4: AMERICAN, EUROPEAN, BERMUDAN, AND CUSTOMIZED EXPANSION OPTIONS

This exercise illustrates how to use Real Options SLS for solving:

1. American Expansion Options

2. European Expansion Options

3. Bermudan Expansion Options

4. Customized Expansion Options

5. Optimal Trigger Values

6. Opportunity Cost of Waiting

The *Expansion Option* values the flexibility to expand from a current existing state to a larger or expanded state. Therefore, an existing state or condition must first be present in order to use the expansion option. That is, there must be a base case to expand upon. If there is no base case state, then the simple *Execution Option* (calculated using the simple *Call Option*) is more appropriate, where the issue at hand is whether or not to execute a project immediately or to defer execution.

As an example, suppose a growth firm has a static valuation of future profitability using a discounted cash flow model (in other words, the present value of the expected future cash flows discounted at an appropriate market risk-adjusted discount rate) that is found to be $400 million (*PV Asset*). Using Monte Carlo simulation, you calculate the implied *Volatility* of the logarithmic returns on the assets based on the projected future cash flows to be 35%. The *Risk-Free Rate* on a riskless asset (5-year U.S. Treasury Note with zero coupons) for the next 5 years is found to be 7%.

Further suppose that the firm has the option to expand and double its operations by acquiring its competitor for a sum of $250 million (*Implementation Cost*) at any time over the next 5 years (*Maturity*). What is the total value of this firm, assuming that you account for this expansion option? The results in Figure 11E4.A indicate that the strategic project value is $638.73 M (using a 100-step lattice), which means that the expansion option value is $88.73M. This result is obtained because the net present value of executing immediately is $400M x 2 – $250M, or $550M. Thus, $638.73 M less $550M is $88.73M, the value of the ability to *defer* and to wait and see before executing the expansion option. The example file used is *File | Examples | Expansion American and European Option*.

Exercises

1. Replicate the basic expansion option illustration above. Make sure you are able to obtain the same results.

2. We will now learn about *Optimal Trigger Values*. Using the same model as above, increase the dividend rate to, say, 2% and notice that both the American and European Expansion Options are now worth less, and that the American Expansion Option is worth more than the European Expansion Option by virtue of the American Option's ability for early execution. The dividend rate implies that the cost of waiting to expand, to defer and not execute, the *opportunity cost of waiting on executing the option*, and the cost of holding the option is high, then the ability to defer reduces. In addition, increase the Dividend Rate to 4.9% and see that the binomial lattice's Custom Option result reverts to $550 (the static, expand-

now scenario), indicating that the option is worthless. This result means if the *cost of waiting* as a proportion of the asset value (as measured by the dividend rate) is too high, then execute now and stop wasting time deferring the expansion decision! Of course this decision can be reversed if the volatility is significant enough to compensate for the cost of waiting. That is, it might be worth something to wait and see if the uncertainty is too high even if the cost to wait is high.

3. Using Real Options SLS, show how you can create a customized expansion option with changing expansion factors over time and changing execution cost over time, all the while with some vesting or blackout periods where the option cannot be executed.

4. Other applications of this option simply abound! To illustrate, here are some additional quick exercises of the expansion option:

    a. Suppose a pharmaceutical firm is thinking of developing a new type of insulin that can be inhaled and the drug will directly be absorbed into the bloodstream. A novel and honorable idea. Imagine what this means to diabetics who no longer need painful and frequent injections. The problem is, this new type of insulin requires a brand new development effort but if the uncertainties of the market, competition, drug development, and FDA approval are high, perhaps a base insulin drug that can be ingested is first developed. The ingestible version is a required precursor to the inhaled version. The pharmaceutical firm can decide to either take the risk and fast track development into the inhaled version or buy an option to defer, to first wait and see if the ingestible version works. If this precursor works, then the firm has the option to expand into the inhaled version. How much should the firm be willing to spend on performing additional tests on the precursor and under what circumstances should the inhaled version be implemented directly? Suppose the intermediate precursor development work yields an NPV of $100M, but at any time within the next 2 years, an additional $50M can be further invested into the precursor to develop it into the inhaled version, which will triple the NPV. However, after modeling the risk of technical success and uncertainties in the market (competitive threats, sales, and pricing structure), the annualized volatility of the cash flows using the logarithmic present value returns approach comes to 45%. Suppose the risk-free rate is 5% for the 2-year period. (Hint: Using the SLS, the analysis results yields $254.95M, indicating that the option value to wait and defer is worth more than $4.95M after accounting for the $250M NPV if executing now. In playing with several scenarios, the breakeven point is found when dividend yield is 1.34%. This means that if the cost of waiting [lost net revenues in sales by pursuing the smaller market rather than the larger market, and loss of market share by delaying] exceeds $1.34M per year, then it is not optimal to wait and the pharmaceutical firm should engage in the inhaled version immediately. The loss in returns generated each year does not sufficiently cover the risks incurred.)

    b. An oil and gas company is currently deciding on a deep-sea exploration and drilling project. The platform provides an expected NPV of $1,000M. This project is fraught with risks (price of oil and production rate are both uncertain) and the annualized volatility is computed to be 55%. The firm is thinking of purchasing an expansion option by spending an additional $10M to build a slightly larger platform that it does not currently need, but if the price of oil is high, or when production rate is low, the firm can execute this expansion option and execute additional drilling to obtain more oil to sell at the higher price, which will cost another $50M, thereby increasing the NPV by 20%. The economic life of this platform is 10 years and the risk-free rate for the corresponding term is

5%. Is obtaining this slightly larger platform worth it? (Hint: Using the SLS, the option value is worth $27.12M when applying a 100-step lattice. Therefore, the option cost of $10M is worth it. However, this expansion option will not be worth it if annual dividends exceed 0.75% or $7.5M a year—this is the annual net revenues lost by waiting and not drilling as a percentage of the base case NPV.)

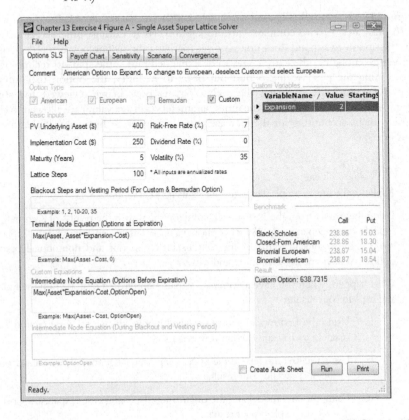

Figure 11E4.A: American and European Options to Expand with a 100-Step Lattice

EXERCISE 5: CONTRACTION, EXPANSION, AND ABANDONMENT OPTIONS

This exercise illustrates how to use Real Options SLS for solving:

1. · American, Bermudan, European, Customized Contraction, Expansion, and Abandonment Options

2. Competing and Mutually Exclusive Options

3. Dominant and Dominated Options

The *Contraction, Expansion, and Abandonment Option* applies when a firm has three *competing and mutually exclusive* options on a single project to choose from at different times up to the time of expiration. Be aware that this is a mutually exclusive set of options. That is, you cannot execute any combinations of expansion, contraction, or abandonment at the same time. Only one option can be executed at any time. That is, for mutually exclusive options, use a single model to compute the option value as seen in Figure 11E5.A (example file used is *File | Examples | Expand Contract Abandon American and European Option*). However, if the options are non-mutually exclusive, calculate them individually in different models and add up the values for the total value of the strategy (that is, solve the option to contract, then solve the option to expand, and then the option to abandon, each in its own model, and sum all of their option values).

Figure 11E5.B (example file used is *File | Examples | Expand Contract Abandon Customized Option II*) illustrates a more complex Custom Option where during some earlier period of vesting, the option to expand does not exist yet (perhaps the technology being developed is not yet mature enough in the early stages to be expanded into some spin-off technology). In addition, during the post-vesting period but prior to maturity, the option to contract or abandon does not exist (perhaps the technology is now being reviewed for spin-off opportunities), and so forth. Finally, the input parameters (salvage value) are allowed to change over time perhaps accounting for the increase in project, asset, or firm value if abandoned at different times.

Exercises

1. Replicate the first example illustrated above using Real Options SLS.

2. Using the results from the first model, compare them with the results of summing three models run independently. Which option value is larger and why? Hint: Explain the analysis and results in terms of mutually exclusive options and nonmutually exclusive options. Which one is worth more and why?

3. What happens when you have a dominant versus a dominated option? Run the following and explain your results:

   a. Using the first model and the original inputs, change the Contraction Savings from 25 to 100 and explain your results.

   b. Using the first model and the original inputs, change the Salvage value from 100 to 300 and explain your results.

   c. Using the first model and the original inputs, change the Expansion Cost from 25 to 1 and explain your results.

   d. Replicate the three exercises (a-c) above using the Lattice Solver and explain what you see in terms of the decision lattice. What do you observe as dominant and dominated options?

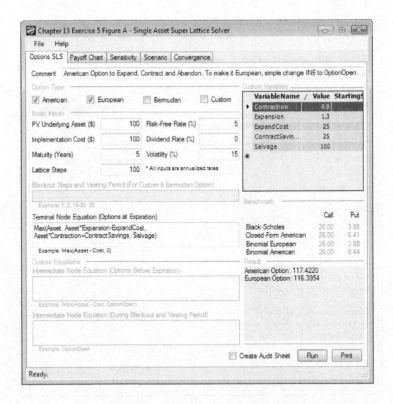

Figure 11E5.A: American, European, and Custom Options to Expand, Contract, and Abandon

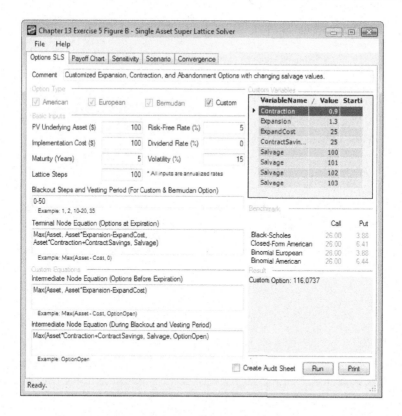

Figure 11E5.B: Custom Options with Mixed Expand, Contract, and Abandon Capabilities with Changing Input Parameters

EXERCISE 6: COMPLEX SEQUENTIAL COMPOUND OPTIONS

This exercise illustrates how to use Real Options SLS for solving:

1. Basic Two-Phased Sequential Compound Options

2. Multiple-Phased Sequential Compound Options (Stage-Gate Development)

3. Customized Complex Mixed Sequential Compound Options (Mixed-Gate Strategies)

4. The Expected Value of Information

Basic Two-Phased Sequential Compound Options

Sequential Compound Options are applicable for research and development investments or any other investments that have multiple stages. The Real Options SLS (multiple assets/phases module) is required for solving Sequential Compound Options. The easiest way to understand this option is to start with a two-phased example as seen in Figure 11E6.A. In the two-phased example, management has the ability to decide if Phase II (PII) should be implemented after obtaining the results from Phase I (PI). For example, a pilot project or market research in PI indicates that the market is not yet ready for the product, hence PII is not implemented. All that is lost is the PI sunk cost, not the entire investment cost of both PI and PII. An example below illustrates how the option is analyzed.

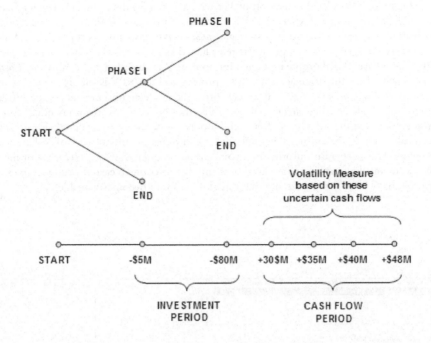

Figure 11E6.A: Graphical Representation of a Two-Phased Sequential Compound Option

The illustration in Figure 11E6.A is valuable in explaining and communicating to senior management the aspects of an American Sequential Compound Option and its inner workings. In the illustration, the *Phase I* investment of –$5M (in present value dollars) in Year 1 is followed by *Phase II* investment of –$80M (in present value dollars) in Year 2. Hopefully, positive net free cash flows (CF) will follow in Years 3 to 6, yielding a sum of *PV Asset* of $100M (CF discounted at, say, a 9.7% discount or hurdle rate), and the *Volatility* of these CFs is 30%. At a 5% risk-free rate, the strategic value is calculated at $27.67 as seen in Figure 11E6.B using a 100-step lattice, which means that the strategic option value of being able to *defer* investments and to *wait and see* until more information becomes available and uncertainties become resolved is worth $12.67M because the NPV is worth $15M ($100M – $5M – $85M). In other words, the *Expected Value of Perfect Information* is worth $12.67M, which indicates that assuming market research can be used to obtain credible information to decide if this project is a good one, the maximum the firm should be willing to spend in Phase I is *on average no more than* $17.67M (i.e., $12.67M + $5M) if PI is part of the market research initiative, or simply $12.67M otherwise. If the cost to obtain the credible information exceeds this value, then it is optimal to take the risk and execute the entire project immediately at $85M. The Multiple Asset module example file used is *File | Examples | Simple Two Phased Sequential Compound Option*.

In contrast, if the volatility decreases (uncertainty and risk are lower), the strategic option value decreases. In addition, when the cost of waiting (as described by the *Dividend Rate* as a percentage of the *Asset Value*) increases, it is better not to defer and wait that long. Therefore, the higher the dividend rate, the lower the strategic option value. For instance, at an 8% dividend rate and 15% volatility, the resulting value reverts to the NPV of $15M, which means that the option value is zero, and that it is better to execute immediately as the cost of waiting far outstrips the value of being able to wait given the level of volatility (uncertainty and risk). Finally, if risks and uncertainty increase significantly even with a high cost of waiting (e.g., 7% dividend rate at 30% volatility), it is still valuable to wait.

This model provides the decision-maker with a view into the optimal balancing between *waiting for more information* (Expected Value of Perfect Information) and the *cost of waiting*. You can analyze this balance by creating strategic *options to defer* investments through development stages where at every stage the project is reevaluated as to whether it is beneficial to proceed to the next phase. Based on the input assumptions used in this model, the *Sequential Compound Option* results show the strategic value of the project, and the NPV is simply the *PV Asset* less both phases' *Implementation Costs*. In other words, the strategic option value is the difference between the calculated strategic value minus the NPV. It is recommended for your consideration that the volatility and dividend inputs are varied to determine their interactions, specifically, where the breakeven points are for different combinations of volatilities and dividends. Thus, using this information, you can make better *go* or *no-go decisions* (for instance, breakeven volatility points can be traced back into the discounted cash flow model to estimate the probability of crossing over and that this ability to wait becomes valuable).

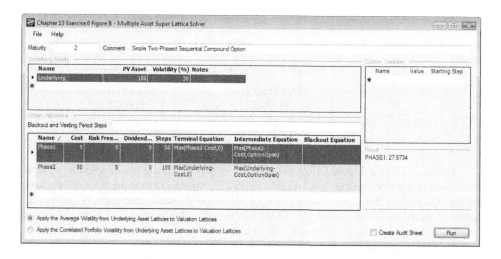

Figure 11E6.B: Solving a Two-Phased Sequential Compound Option

Multiple Phased Sequential Compound Options (Stage-Gate Development)

The Sequential Compound Option can similarly be extended to multiple phases with the use of MSLS. A graphical representation of a multi-phased or stage-gate investment is seen in Figure 11E6.C. The example illustrates a multi-phase project, where at every phase management has the option and flexibility to either continue to the next phase if everything goes well, or to terminate the project otherwise. Based on the input assumptions, the results in the Real Options SLS (multiple assets/phases module) indicate the calculated strategic value of the project, while the NPV of the project is simply the *PV Asset* less all *Implementation Costs* (in present values) if implementing all phases immediately. Therefore, with the strategic option value of being able to defer and wait before implementing future phases due to the volatility, there is a possibility that the asset value will be significantly higher. Hence, the ability to wait before making the investment decisions in the future is the option value or the strategic value of the project less the NPV.

Figure 11E6.D shows the results using Real Options SLS. Notice that due to the backward induction process used, the analytical convention is to start with the last phase and go all the way back to the first phase (the Multiple Asset module's example file used: *File | Examples |*

Sequential Compound Option for Multiple Phases). In NPV terms the project is worth –$500. However, the total strategic value of the stage-gate investment option is worth $41.78. This means that although on an NPV basis the investment looks bad, in reality, by hedging the risks and uncertainties through sequential investments, the option holder can pull out at any time and not have to keep investing unless things look promising. If after the first phase things look bad, pull out and stop investing and the maximum loss will be $100 (Figure 11E6.D) and not the entire $1,500 investment. If however, things look promising, the option holder can continue to invest in stages. The expected value of the investments in present values after accounting for the probabilities that things will look bad (and, hence, stop investing) versus things looking great (and, hence, continuing to invest), is worth an average of $41.78M.

Notice that the option valuation result will always be greater than or equal to zero (e.g., try reducing the volatility to 5% and increasing the dividend yield to 8% for all phases). When the option value is very low or zero, this means that it is not optimal to defer investments and that this stage-gate investment process is not optimal here. If the cost of waiting is too high (high dividend) or the uncertainties in the cash flows are low (low volatility), invest now if the NPV is positive. In such a case, although you obtain a zero value for the option, the analytical interpretation is significant! A zero or very low value is indicative of an optimal decision not to wait.

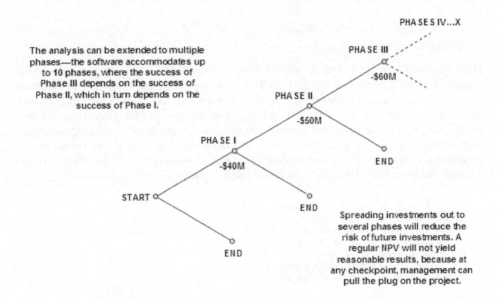

Figure 11E6.C: Graphical Representation of a Multi-Phased Sequential Compound Option

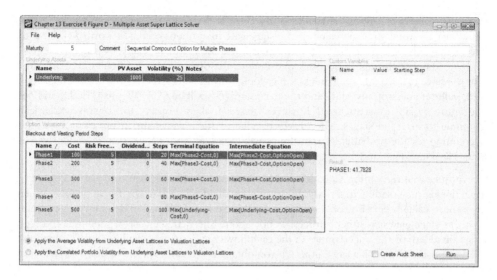

Figure 11E6.D: Solving a Multi-Phased Sequential Compound Option using MSLS

Customized Complex Mixed Sequential Compound Options (Mixed-Gate Strategies)

The Sequential Compound Option can be further complicated by adding customized options at each phase as illustrated in Figure 11E6.E, where at every phase, there may be different combinations of mutually exclusive options including the flexibility to stop investing, *abandon* and *salvage* the project in return for some value, *expand* the scope of the project into another project (e.g., spin-off projects and expand into different geographical locations), *contract* the scope of the project resulting in some savings, or continue on to the next phase. The seemingly complicated option can be very easily solved using Real Options SLS as seen in Figure 11E6.F (example file used: *File | Examples | Multiple Phased Complex Sequential Compound Option*).

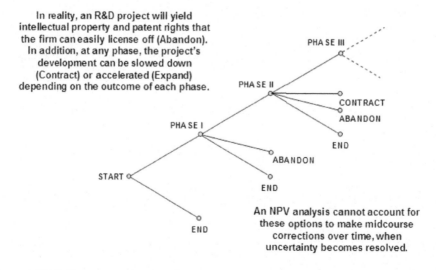

Figure 11E6.E: Representation of a Complex Multi-Phased Sequential Compound Option

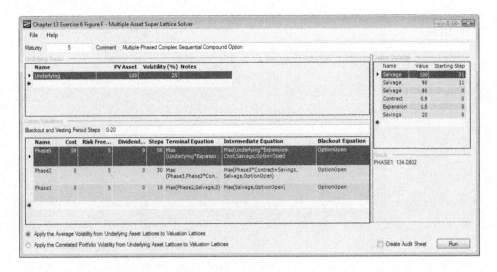

Figure 11E6.F: Solving a Complex Multi-Phased Sequential Compound Option using MSLS

To illustrate, Figure 11E6.F's MSLS path-dependent sequential option uses the following inputs and equations:

Phase 3:	Terminal:	Max(Underlying*Expansion-Cost,Underlying,Salvage)
	Intermediate:	Max(Underlying*Expansion-Cost,Salvage,OptionOpen)
	Steps:	50
Phase 2:	Terminal:	Max(Phase3,Phase3*Contract+Savings,Salvage,0)
	Intermediate:	Max(Phase3*Contract+Savings,Salvage,OptionOpen)
	Steps:	30
Phase 1:	Terminal:	Max(Phase2,Salvage,0)
	Intermediate:	Max(Salvage,OptionOpen)
	Steps:	10

SECTION SEVEN – RISK MANAGEMENT

CHAPTER 12 – THE WARNING SIGNS

The finding of absence is very different from an absence of findings. How does management appropriately evaluate the validity and applicability of analytical results? How should management challenge the assumptions used in the analysis? What are some of the questions that should be asked? This chapter deals with some of the more difficult questions that arise when evaluating the results of Monte Carlo risk simulation, stochastic forecasting, portfolio optimization, and strategic real options analysis.

THE PROBLEM OF NEGLIGENT ENTRUSTMENT

Power tools such as Risk Simulator and Real Options SLS took years to build and many more years to be perfected. It is extremely likely that a new user can simply pick up software products such as these and hit the ground running immediately. However, some knowledge of the theoretical underpinnings is required. In short, to create and perform sophisticated modeling, the analyst first needs to understand some of the underlying assumptions and approaches used in these analytics. Otherwise, it is akin to giving a 3-year-old child a loaded machine gun. The correct term for this situation might be *negligent entrustment*. In fact, when the rubber meets the road, more often than not, even so-called power users are perplexed and have a difficult time using these tools with respect to their models and business cases. These software tools despite their analytical power are just tools. They do not replace the analyst in any way. In fact, tools such as these only accouter the analyst with the appropriate analytics at their fingertips and do not by themselves make the relevant decisions, such tools only relieve the analyst from having facility with fancy mathematics in order to build sophisticated models. In most cases, 50 percent of the challenge in decision making is simply thinking about the problem, 25 percent being the actual modeling and analytics, and the remaining 25 percent of the value comes from being able to convince and explain the results to senior management, clients, colleagues, and yourself. These tools provide simple graphical methods to broach difficult analytical subjects to management while freeing the analysts' time to focus on the bulk of the value of a decision-making process: *thinking about and framing the problem*.

MANAGEMENT'S DUE DILIGENCE

It might be the job of the analyst to create the models and use the fancy analytics, but it is senior management's job to challenge the assumptions and results obtained from said analysis. For instance, Figure 12.1 lists some of the issues that may arise when running a multivariate regression analysis and time-series forecasting. Although it may not be senior management's job to understand the mathematical or theoretical implications of these issues, management must nonetheless have a good grasp of what they mean.

The following sections are written specifically for senior management who are recipients of different types of advanced analyses results. The next section starts off with a general set of warning signs and moves on to the specifics of each analytical methodology used throughout this book.

Warning Signs: Regression Analysis

- Out of Range Forecast
- Structural Breaks
- Specification Errors
- Omitted and Redundant Variables
- Heteroskedasticity vs. Homoskedasticity
- Multicollinearity
- Spurious Regression
- Time Dependencies
- Autocorrelation
- Serial Correlation
- Correlation vs. Causation
- Random Walks
- Stochastic Process
- Mean Reversion
- Jump Diffusion

Figure 12.1: Warning Signs in Regression Analysis

SINS OF AN ANALYST

In general, warning signs can be grouped into five categories:

- Model errors

- Assumption and input errors

- Analytical errors

- User errors

- Interpretation errors

Model errors are the errors an analyst would make while creating models. For instance, a financial model created in Excel may have errors stemming from broken links, incorrect functions and equations, poor modeling practices, or a break in the knowledge transfer between the originator of the model and subsequent users as well as successors of the model. This error can be eliminated through diligence on the part of the model creator.

Good model-building practices can assist in eliminating messy models. These good practices may include:

- Good documentation of the approaches used in the model as well as the integration and connectivity of the subparts that exist in the model.

- Creating a starting page that is linked through hyperlinks or macros with sufficient descriptions of each subpage or worksheet.

- Differentiating assumption input sheets from the models actually performing the number crunching, and from the results or reports page.

- Allowing changes to be made only on the input assumptions page and not directly in the model to prevent accidentally breaking the model.

For a detailed listing of good model building practices and modeling etiquette, please refer to Chapter 3, A Guide to Model-Building Etiquette of *Modeling Risk*.

Assumption and input errors are more difficult to tackle. These errors include the inputs required to make the model compute; for example, items such as levels of competitive threats, levels of technological success, revenue projections, income growth rates, market share determination, and so forth. Many of these determinant factors are almost impossible to determine. In fact, the old adage of *garbage in, garbage out* holds true here. The analyst can only do so much.

Multiple approaches exist to help clean up these so-called garbage assumptions. One way is simply to use expert knowledge and advice. For instance, the Delphi method requires the presence of a group of expert engineers in a room to discuss the levels of technological success rates. These engineers with intimate knowledge of the potential success rates are able to provide valuable insights that would otherwise be unavailable to a financial analyst sitting in front of a computer, far removed from the everyday technological challenges. Senior management, based on their many years of experience and expertise, can often provide valuable insights into what certain market outcomes may be. A double-blind experiment also can be conducted, where experts in a group are asked on anonymous questionnaires what their objective estimates of an outcome are. These quantitative outcomes are then tabulated and, on occasion, more experienced participants' comments will be weighted more heavily. The expected value is then used in the model. Here, Monte Carlo simulation can be applied on the distribution of the outcomes related to these expert testimonies. A custom distribution can be constructed using Risk Simulator, which relates back to the weights given to each outcome, or a simple nonparametric custom distribution simulation can also be applied on all possible outcomes obtained. Obviously, if there are ample historical data, then it is relatively easier to project the future, whether it is using some time-series forecast, regression analysis, or Monte Carlo simulation. That is, *when in doubt, simulate!* Instead of arguing and relying on a particular single-point input value of a particular variable, an analyst can just simulate it around the potential outcomes of that input, whether it is the worst-case scenario, nominal-case scenario, or best-case scenario using a triangular distribution or some other distribution through expert assumptions.

No matter the approach used to obtain the data, management must test and challenge these assumptions. One way is to create tornado and sensitivity charts. The variables that drive the bottom line the most (the variable of interest, e.g., net present value, net income, return on investment) that are unpredictable and subject to uncertain levels of fluctuations are the ones that management should focus on. These critical success factors are the ones that management should care about, not some random variable that has little to no effect on the bottom line no matter how attractive or important the variable may be in other instances.

The upshot being that the more expert knowledge and historical data that exist, the better the assumption estimates will be. A good test of the assumptions used is through the application of backcasting, as opposed to forecasting, which looks forward into the future. Backcasting uses historical data to test the validity of the assumptions. One approach is to take the historical data, fit them to a distribution using Risk Simulator's distributional-fitting routines, and test the assumption input. Observe where the assumption value falls within this historical distribution. If it falls outside of the distribution's normal set of parameters (e.g., 95 percent or 99 percent confidence intervals), then the analyst should be able to better describe why there will be a potential structural shift going forward (e.g., mergers and acquisition, divestiture, reallocation of resources, economic downturn, entry of formidable competition, and so forth). In forecasting, similar approaches can be used such as historical data-fitting of the forecast model and holdout approaches (i.e., some historical data are left out in the original forecast model but are used in the subsequent forecast-fitting to verify the model's accuracy).

READING THE WARNING SIGNS IN MONTE CARLO SIMULATION

Monte Carlo simulation is a very potent methodology. Statisticians, econometricians, and mathematicians sometimes dislike it because it solves difficult and often intractable problems with too much simplicity and ease. Instead, mathematical purists would prefer the more elegant approach: the old-fashioned way. Solving a fancy stochastic mathematical model provides a sense of accomplishment and completion as opposed to the brute force method. Monte Carlo creates artificial futures by generating thousands and even millions of sample paths of outcomes and looks at their prevalent characteristics. For analysts in a company, taking graduate-level advanced mathematics courses is neither logical nor practical. A brilliant analyst would use all available tools at his or her disposal to obtain the same answer the easiest way possible. One such tool is Monte Carlo simulation using Risk Simulator. The major benefit that Risk Simulator brings is its simplicity of use. The major downfall that Risk Simulator brings is also its simplicity of use!

Here are a few due-diligence issues management should evaluate when an analyst presents a report with a series of advanced analytics using simulation.

How Are the Distributions Obtained?

One thing is certain. If an analyst provides a report showing all the fancy analyses undertaken and one of these analyses is the application of Monte Carlo simulation of a few dozen variables, where each variable has the same distribution (e.g., triangular distribution), management should be very worried indeed and with good reason. One might be able to accept the fact that a few variables are triangularly distributed, but to assume that this holds true for several dozen other variables is ludicrous. One way to test the validity of distributional assumptions is to apply historical data to the distribution and see how far off one is.

Another approach is to take the distribution and test its alternate parameters. For instance, if a normal distribution is used on simulating market share, and the mean is set at 55 percent with a standard deviation of 45 percent, one should be extremely worried. Using Risk Simulator's alternate-parameter function, the 10th and 90th percentile levels indicate a value of −2.67 percent and 112.67 percent. Clearly these values cannot exist under actual conditions. How can a product have -2.67 or 112.67 percent of the market share? The alternate-parameters function is a very powerful tool to use in conditions such as these. Almost always, the first thing that should be done is the use of alternate parameters to ascertain the logical upper and lower values of an input parameter.

How Sensitive Are the Distributional Assumptions?

Obviously, not all variables under the sun should be simulated. For instance, a U.S.-based firm doing business within the 48 contiguous states should not have to worry about what happens to the foreign exchange market of the Zambian kwacha. Risk is something one bears and is the outcome of uncertainty. Just because there is uncertainty, there could very well be no risk. If the only thing that bothers a U.S.-based firm's CEO is the fluctuation of the Zambian kwacha, then I might suggest shorting some kwachas and shifting his or her portfolio to U.S.-based bonds.

In short, simulate when in doubt, but simulate the variables that actually have an impact on what you are trying to estimate. Two very powerful tools to decide which variables to analyze are tornado and sensitivity charts. Make sure the simulated variables are the critical success drivers—variables that have a significant impact on the bottom line being estimated while at the same time being highly uncertain and beyond the control of management.

What Are the Critical Success Drivers?

Critical success drivers are related to how sensitive the resulting bottom line is to the input variables and assumptions. The first step that should be performed before using Monte Carlo simulation is the application of tornado charts. Tornado charts help identify which variables are the most critical to analyze. Coupled with management's and the analyst's expertise, the relevant critical success drivers—the variables that drive the bottom line the most while being highly uncertain and beyond the control of management—can be determined and simulated. Obviously the most sensitive variables should receive the most amount of attention.

Are the Assumptions Related, and Have Their Relationships Been Considered?

Simply defining assumptions on variables that have significant impact without regard to their interrelationships is also a major error most analysts make. For instance, when an analyst simulates revenues, he or she could conceivably break the revenue figures into price and quantity, where the resulting revenue figure is simply the product of price and quantity. The problem is if both price and quantity are considered as independent variables occurring in isolation, a major error arises. Clearly, for most products, the law of demand in economics takes over, where the higher the price of a product, *ceteris paribus*, or holding everything else constant, the quantity demanded of the same product decreases. Ignoring this simple economic truth, where both price and quantity are assumed to occur independently of one another, means that the possibility of a high price and a high quantity demanded may occur simultaneously, or vice versa. Clearly this condition will never occur in real life, thus, the simulation results will most certainly be flawed. The revenue or price estimates can also be further disaggregated into several product categories, where each category is correlated to the rest of the group (competitive products, product life cycle, product substitutes, complements, and cannibalization). Other examples include the possibility of economies of scale (where a higher production level forces cost to decrease over time), product life cycles (sales tend to decrease over time and plateau at a saturation rate), average total costs (the average of fully allocated cost decreases initially and increases after it hits some levels of diminishing returns). Therefore, relationships, correlations, and causalities have to be modeled appropriately. If data are available, a simple correlation matrix can be generated through Excel, to capture these relationships.

Have You Considered Truncation?

Truncation is a major error Risk Simulator users commit, especially when using the infamous triangular distribution. The triangular distribution is very simple and intuitive. As a matter of fact, it is probably the most widely used distribution in Risk Simulator, apart from the normal and uniform distributions. Simplistically, the triangular distribution looks at the minimum value, the most probable value, and the maximum value. These three inputs are often confused with the worst-case, nominal-case, and best-case scenarios. This assumption is indeed incorrect.

In fact, a worst-case scenario can be translated as a highly unlikely condition that *will* still occur given a percentage of the time. For instance, one can model the economy as high, average, and low, analogous to the worst-case, nominal-case, and best-case scenarios. Thus, logic would dictate that the worst-case scenario might have, say, a 15 percent chance of occurrence, the nominal-case, a 50 percent chance of occurrence, and a 35 percent chance that a best-case scenario will occur. This approach is what is meant by using a best-, nominal-, and worst-case scenario analysis. However, compare that to the triangular distribution, where the minimum and maximum cases will almost never occur, with a probability of occurrence set at zero!

For instance, see Figure 12.2, where the worst-, nominal-, and best-case scenarios are set as 5, 10, and 15, respectively. Note that at the extreme values, the probability of 5 or 15 occurring is virtually zero, as the areas under the curve (the measure of probability) of these extreme points are zero. In other words, 5 and 15 will almost *never* occur. Compare that to the economic scenario where these extreme values have either a 15 percent or 35 percent chance of occurrence.

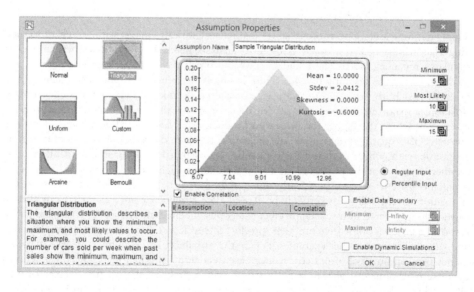

Figure 12.2: Sample Triangular Distribution

Instead, distributional truncation should be considered here. The same applies to any other distribution. Figure 12.3 illustrates a truncated normal distribution where the extreme values do not extend to both positive and negative infinities, but are truncated at 7 and 13.

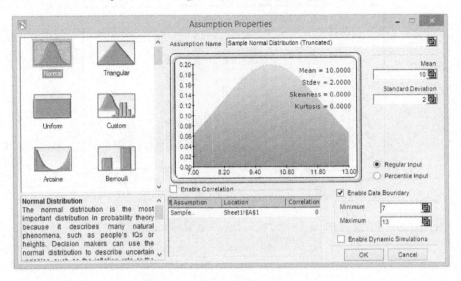

Figure 12.3: Truncating a Distribution

How Wide Are the Forecast Results?

I have seen models that are as large as 300MB with over 1,000 distributional assumptions. When you have a model that big with so many assumptions, there is a huge problem! For one, it takes an unnecessarily long time to run in Excel, and for another, the results generated are totally bogus. One thing is certain. The final forecast distribution of the results will most certainly be too large to make any definitive decision with. Besides, what is the use of generating results that are close to a range between negative and positive infinity?

The results that you obtain should fall within decent parameters and intervals. One good check is to simply look at the single-point estimates. In theory, the single-point estimate is based on all precedent variables at their respective expected values. Thus, if one perturbs these expected values by instituting distributions about their single-point estimates, then the resulting single-point bottom line estimate should also fall within this forecast interval.

What Are the Endpoints and Extreme Values?

Mistaking end points is both an error of interpretation and a user error. For instance, Figure 12.4 illustrates the results obtained from a financial analysis with extreme values between $7.16 million and $13.16 million. By making the leap that the worst possible outcome is $7.16 million and the best possible outcome is $13.16 million, the analyst has made a major error.

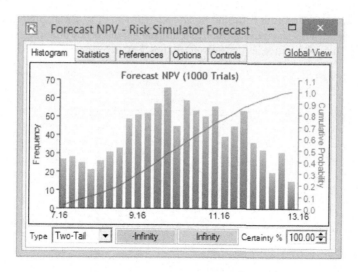

Figure 12.4: Truncated Extreme Values

Clicking on the *Options* menu and selecting *Display Range,* one can choose any display range (Figure 12.5). Clearly, if the *show data less than 2 standard deviation* option is chosen, the graph looks somewhat different (the endpoints are now 7.24 and 13.24 as compared to 7.16 and 13.16), indicating the actual worst and best cases (Figure 12.6). Of course, the interpretation would be quite different here than with the 2 standard deviations option chosen.

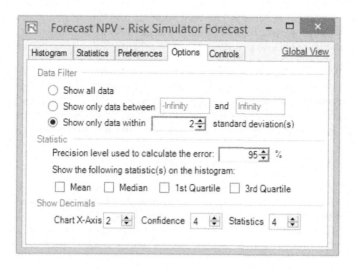

Figure 12.5: Display Range Options

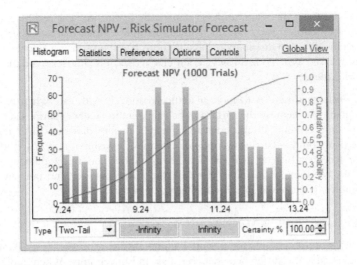

Figure 12.6: Display Range Using Fixed Endpoints

Are There Breaks Given Business Logic and Business Conditions?

Assumptions used in the simulation may be based on valid historical data, which means that the distributional outcomes would be valid if the firm indeed existed in the past. However, going forward, historical data may not be the best predictor of the future. In fact, past performance is no indicator of future ability to perform, especially when structural breaks in business conditions are predicted to occur. Structural breaks include situations where firms decide to go global, acquire other firms, divest part of their assets, enter into new markets, and so forth. The resulting distributional forecasts need to be revalidated based on these conditions. The results based on past performance could be deemed as the base-case scenario, with additional adjustments and add-ons as required. This situation is especially true in the research and development arena, where by definition of research and development, things that are yet to be developed are new and novel in nature; thus by definition, there exist no historical data on which to base the future forecasts. In situations such as these, it is best to rely on experience and expert opinions of future outcomes. Other approaches where historical data do not exist include using market proxies and project comparables—where current or historical projects and firms with similar functions, markets, and risks are used as benchmarks.

Do the Results Fall Within Expected Economic Conditions?

One of the most dangerous traps analysts fall into is the trap of data mining. Rather than relying on solid theoretical frameworks, analysts let the data sort things out by themselves. For instance, analysts who blindly use stepwise regression and distributional fitting fall directly into this data-mining trap. Instead of relying on theory *a priori*, or before the fact, analysts use the results to explain the way things look, *a posteriori*, or after the fact.

A simple example is the prediction of the stock market. Using tons of available historical data on the returns of the Standards & Poor's 500 index, an analyst runs a multivariate stepwise regression using over a hundred different variables ranging from economic growth, gross domestic product, and inflation rates, to the fluctuations of the Zambian kwacha, to who won the Super Bowl and the frequency of sunspots on particular days. Because the stock market by itself is unpredictable and random in nature, as are sunspots, there seems to be some relationship over time. Although this relationship is purely spurious and occurred out of happenstance, a stepwise regression and correlation matrix will still pick up this spurious relationship and register the relationship as statistically significant. The resulting analysis will show that sunspots do, in fact, explain fluctuations in the stock market. Therefore, is the analyst correct in setting up distributional assumptions based on sunspot activity in the hopes of beating the market? When one throws a computer at data, it is almost certain that a spurious connection will emerge.

The lesson learned here is to look at particular models with care when trying to find relationships that may seem on the surface to be valid, but in fact are spurious and accidental in nature, and that holding all else constant, the relationship dissipates over time. Merely correlating two randomly occurring events and seeing a relationship is nonsense and the results should not be accepted. Instead, analysis should be based on economic and financial rationale. In this case, the economic rationale is that the relationship between sunspots and the stock market is completely accidental and should thus be treated as such.

What Are the Values at Risk?

Remember the story about my friend and I going skydiving in the first chapter? Albeit fictitious, it illustrates the differences between risk and uncertainty. When applying Monte Carlo simulation, an analyst is looking at uncertainty. That is, distributions are applied to different variables that drive a bottom-line forecast. Figure 12.7 shows a very simple calculation, where on a deterministic basis, if revenue is $2 and cost is $1, the resulting net income is simply $1 (i.e., $2 – $1). However, in the dynamic model, where revenue is "around $2" and cost is "around $1," the net income is "around $1." This "around" comment signifies the uncertainty involved in each of these variables. The resulting variable will also be an "around" number. In fact, when Risk Simulator is applied, the resulting single-point estimate also ends up being $1. The only difference is that there is a forecast distribution surrounding this $1 value. By performing Monte Carlo simulation, a level of uncertainty surrounding this single-point estimate is obtained. Risk analysis has *not yet* been done. Only uncertainty analysis has been done thus far. By running simulations, only the levels of uncertainty have been quantified if the reports are shown but the results are not used to adjust for risk.

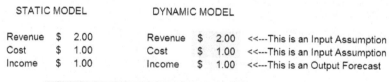

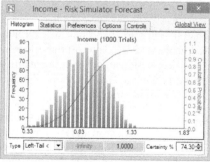

Figure 12.7: Illustrating the Differences between Risk and Uncertainty

For instance, one can, in theory, simulate everything under the sun, including the fluctuations of the Zambian kwacha, but if the Zambian kwacha has no impact on the project being analyzed, not to mention that capturing the uncertainty surrounding the currency does not mean one has managed, reduced, or analyzed the project's foreign exchange risks. It is only when the results are analyzed and used appropriately, will risk analysis have been done. For instance, if an analyst is evaluating three similar projects where each project has an expected value of $1 in net income but with different distributions, no new information is realized. However, only when the results are used appropriately, where we say the first project has a $0.30 value-at-risk at the 5th percentile, while the second and third projects have $0.20 and –$0.10 values-at-risk at the 5th percentile, has risk analysis been done. Holding everything else constant, the best project is clearly the first project, where in the worst-case scenario 5 percent of the time, the minimum amount to be gained is $0.30, the largest of the three. Obviously, other measures can be used, including the mean divided by the standard deviation (creating an inverse of the coefficient of variability or *bang-for-the-buck* measure), risk-adjusted return on capital (RAROC or median less the 5th percentile divided by the volatility), and so forth, as detailed in Chapter 2, From Risk to Riches. Suffice it to say, as long as the risk adjustment is applied appropriately across all projects for comparability purposes, the measurement will be valid. The upshot is that simply noting the uncertainty levels around a value is not risk analysis. It is only when this value is adjusted according to its risk levels has risk analysis actually been performed.

How Do the Assumptions Compare to Historical Data and Knowledge?

Suspect distributional assumptions should be tested through the use of backcasting, which uses historical data to test the validity of the assumptions. One approach is to take the historical data, fit them to a distribution using Risk Simulator's distributional-fitting routines, and test the assumption inputs. See if the distributional-assumption values fall within this historical distribution. If they fall outside of the distribution's normal set of parameters (e.g., 95 percent or 99 percent confidence intervals), then the analyst should better be able to describe and explain this apparent discontinuity, which can very well be because of changing business conditions and so forth.

How Do the Results Compare Against Traditional Analysis?

A very simple test of the analysis results is through its single-point estimates. For instance, remember the $1 net income example? If the single-point estimate shows $1 as the expected value of net income, then, in theory, the uncertainty surrounding this $1 should have the initial single-point estimate somewhere within its forecast distribution. If $1 is not within the resulting forecast distribution, something is amiss here. Either the model used to calculate the original $1 single-point estimate is flawed or the simulation assumptions are flawed. To recap, how can "around $2" minus "around $1" not be "around $1"?

Do the Statistics Confirm the Results?

Risk Simulator provides a wealth of statistics after performing a simulation. Figure 12.8 shows a sample listing of these statistics, which can be obtained through the *View | Statistics* menu in Risk Simulator. Some of these statistics when used in combination provide a solid foundation of the validity of the results. When in doubt as to what the *normal* looking statistics should be, simply run a simulation in Risk Simulator and set the distribution to normal with a mean of 0.00 and a standard deviation of 1.00. This condition would create a standard-normal distribution, one of the most basic statistical distributions. The resulting set of statistics is shown in Figure 12.8. See Chapter 2, From Risk to Riches for more details on some basic statistics and interpreting distributional moments.

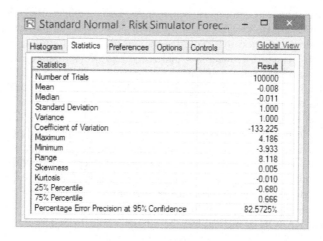

Figure 12.8: Standard-Normal Distribution Statistics

Clearly, after running 10,000 trials, the resulting mean is 0.00 with a standard deviation of 1.00, as specified in the assumption. Of particular interest are the skewness and kurtosis values. For a normally distributed result, the skewness is close to 0.00, and the excess kurtosis is close to 0.00. If the results from your analysis fall within these parameters, it is clear that the forecast values are symmetrically distributed with no excess areas in the tail. A highly positive or negative skew would indicate that something might be going on in terms of some distributional assumptions that are skewing the results either to the left or to the right. This skew may be intentional or something is amiss in terms of setting up the relevant distributions. Also, a significantly higher kurtosis value would indicate that there is a higher probability of occurrence in the tails of the distribution, which means extreme values or catastrophic events are prone to occur more frequently than predicted in most normal circumstances. This result may be expected or not. If not, then the distributional assumptions in the model should be revisited with greater care, especially the extreme values of the inputs.

Are the Correct Methodologies Applied?

The problem of whether the correct methodology is applied is where user error comes in. The analyst should be able to clearly justify why a lognormal distribution is used instead of a uniform distribution, and so forth. In addition, why distributional fitting is used instead of bootstrap simulation, or why a tornado chart is used instead of a sensitivity chart. All of these methodologies and approaches require some basic levels of understanding and questions such as these are most certainly required as part of management's due diligence when evaluating an analyst's results.

Warning signs to watch out for in Monte Carlo simulation and questions to ask include how the distributions are obtained, how sensitive are the distributional assumptions, how to identify the critical success drivers, how the distributional assumptions are related, if the distributions are truncated, how wide are the forecast values, what are the end points and extreme values, are there breaks in business logic and conditions, do the results follow economic rationale, what are the values-at-risk, how do the results compare with historical data and knowledge, how do the results compare with traditional analyses, do the statistics confirm expectations, and are the correct methodologies applied?

READING THE WARNING SIGNS IN TIME-SERIES FORECASTING AND REGRESSION

Another frequently used decision-analysis tool is forecasting. One thing is certain: You can never predict the future with perfect accuracy. The best that you can hope for is to get as close as possible. In addition, it is actually okay to be wrong on occasion. As a matter of fact, it is sometimes good to be wrong, as valuable lessons can be learned along the way. It is better to be wrong consistently than to be wrong on occasion because if you are wrong consistently in one direction, you can correct or reduce your expectations, or increase your expectations when you are consistently overoptimistic or underoptimistic. The problem arises when you are occasionally right and occasionally wrong, and you have no idea when or why it happens. Some of the issues that should be addressed when evaluating time-series or any other forecasting results include the following:

Out of Range Forecasts

Not all variables can be forecast using historical data. For instance, did you know that you can predict, rather reliably, the ambient temperature given the frequency of cricket chirps? Collect a bunch of crickets and change the ambient temperature, collect the data, and run a bivariate regression, and you would get a high level of confidence as seen in the coefficient of determination or R-squared value. Given this model, you could reasonably predict ambient temperature whenever crickets chirp, correct? Well, if you answered yes, you have just fallen into the trap of forecasting out of range.

Suppose your model holds up to statistical scrutiny, which it may very well do, assuming you do a good job with the experiment and data collection. Using the model, one finds that crickets chirp more frequently the higher the ambient temperature, and less frequently the colder if gets. What do you presume would happen if one were to toss a poor cricket in the oven and turn it up to 550 degrees? What happens when the cricket is thrown into the freezer instead? What would occur if a Malaysian cricket were used instead of the Arizona reticulated cricket? The quick answer is you can toss your fancy statistical regression model out the window if any of these things happened. As for the cricket in the oven, you would most probably hear the poor thing give out a very loud chirp and then complete silence. Regression and prediction models out of sample, that is, modeling events that are out of place and out of the range of the data collected in ordinary circumstances, on occasion will fail to work, as is clearly evident from the poor cricket.

Structural Breaks

Structural breaks in business conditions occur all the time. Some example instances include going public, going private, merger, acquisition, geographical expansion, adding new distribution channels, existence of new competitive threats, union strikes, change of senior management, change of company vision and long-term strategy, economic downturn, and so forth. Suppose you are an analyst at FedEx performing volume, revenue, and profitability metric forecasting of multiple break-bulk stations. These stations are located all around the United States and each station has its own seasonality factors complete with detailed historical data. Some advanced econometric models are applied, ranging from ARIMA (autoregressive integrated moving average) and ECM (error correction models) to GARCH (generalized autoregressive conditional heteroskedasticity) models; these time-series forecasting models usually provide relatively robust forecasts. However, within a single year, management reorganization, union strikes, pilot strikes, competitive threats (UPS, your main competitor, decided to enter a new submarket), revised accounting rules, and a plethora of other *coincidences* simply made all the forecasts invalid. The analyst must decide if these coincidences are just that, coincidences, or if they point to a fundamental structural change in the way global freight businesses are run. Obviously, certain incidences are planned or expected, whereas others are unplanned and unexpected. The planned incidences should thus be considered when performing forecasting.

Specification Errors

Sometimes, models are incorrectly specified. A nonlinear relationship can be very easily masked through the estimation of a linear model. In the forecasting chapters (Chapters 6-7), running a linear regression model on a clearly nonlinear dataset still resulted in statistically valid models and provided decent estimates. Another specification error that is fairly common has to do with autocorrelated and seasonal datasets. Estimating the demand of flowers in a floral chain without accounting for the holidays (Valentine's Day, Mother's Day, and so forth) is a blatant specification error. Failure to clearly use the correct model specification or first sanitizing the data may result in highly erroneous results.

Omitted and Redundant Variables

This type of model error in multivariate regression exists when regression is used to forecast the future. Suppose an analyst uses multivariate regression to obtain a statistical relationship between a dependent variable (e.g., sales, prices, revenues) and other regressors or independent variables (e.g., economic conditions, advertising levels, market competition) and he or she hopes to use this relationship to forecast the future. Unfortunately, the analyst may not have all the available information at his or her fingertips. If important information is unavailable, an important variable may be omitted (e.g., market saturation effects, price elasticity of demand, threats of emerging technology), or if too much data is available, redundant variables may be included in the analysis (e.g., inflation rate, interest rate, economic growth). It may be counterintuitive but the problem of redundant variables is more serious than omitted variables.[48] In a situation where redundant variables exist,[49] and if these redundant variables are perfectly correlated or collinear with each other, the regression equation does not exist and cannot be solved. In the case where slightly less severe collinearity exists, the estimated regression equation will be less accurate than without this collinearity. For instance, suppose both interest rates and inflation rates are used as explanatory variables in the regression analysis, where if there is a significant negative correlation between these variables with a time lag, then using both variables to explain sales revenues in the future is redundant. Only one variable is sufficient to explain the relationship with sales. If the analyst uses both variables, the errors in the regression analysis will increase. The prediction errors of an additional variable will increase the errors of the entire regression.

Heteroskedasticity

If the variance of the errors in a regression analysis increases over time, the regression equation is said to be flawed and suffers from heteroskedasticity. Although this may seem to be a technical matter, many regression practitioners fall into this heteroskedastic trap without even realizing it. See Chapter 7, Using the Past to Predict the Future, for details on heteroskedasticity, testing for its existence, and methods to fix the error.

Multicollinearity

One of the assumptions required for a regression to run is that the independent variables are noncorrelated or noncollinear. These independent variables are exactly collinear when a variable is an exact linear combination of the other variables. This error is most frequently encountered when dummy variables are used.[50] A quick check of multicollinearity is to run a correlation matrix of the independent variables.[51] In most instances, the multicollinearity problem will prevent the regression results from being computed. See Chapter 7's appendix on detecting and fixing multicollinearity for more details.

Spurious Regression, Data Mining, Time Dependency, and Survivorship Bias

Spurious regression is another danger that analysts often run into. This mistake is made through certain uses of data-mining activities. Data mining refers to using approaches such as a step-wise regression analysis, where analysts do not have some prior knowledge of the economic effects of what independent variables drive the dependent variable, and use all available data at their disposal. The analyst then runs a step-wise regression, where the methodology ranks the highest correlated variable to the least correlated variable.[52] Then the methodology automatically adds each successive independent variable in accordance with its correlation until some specified stopping statistical criteria. The resulting regression equation is then taken as the final and best result. The problem with this approach is that some independent variables may simply be randomly moving about while the dependent variable may also be randomly moving about, and their movements depend on time.[53] Suppose this randomness in motion is somehow related at certain points in time but the actual economic fundamentals or financial relationships do not exist. Data-mining activities will pick up the coincidental randomness and not the actual relationship, and the result is a spurious regression. That is, the relationship estimated is bogus and is purely a chance happentance. Multicollinearity effects may also unnecessarily eliminate highly significant variables from the step-wise regression. Finally, survivorship bias and self-selection bias are important, as only the best-performing realization will always show up and have the most amount of visibility. For instance, looking to the market to obtain proxy data can be dangerous for only successful firms will be around and have the data. Firms that have failed will most probably leave no trails of their existence, let alone credible market data for an analyst to collect. Self-selection occurs when the data that exist are biased and selective. For instance, pharmacology research on a new cancer treatment will attract cancer patients of all types, but the researchers will clearly only select those patients in the earlier stages of cancer, making the results look more promising than they actually are.

Autoregressive Processes, Lags, Seasonality and Serial Correlation

In time-series data, certain variables are autoregressive in nature. That is, future values of variables such as price, demand, interest rates, inflation rates, and so forth, depend on values that occurred in the past, or are autoregressive.[54] This reversion to the past occurs because of many reasons, including seasonality and cyclicality.[55] Because of these cyclical or seasonal and autoregressive effects, regression analysis using seasonal or cyclical independent variables as is will yield inexact results. In fact, some of these autoregressive, cyclical, or seasonal variables will affect the dependent variable differently over time. There may be a time lag between effects, for example, an increase in interest rates may take 1 to 3 months before the mortgage market feels the effects of this decline. Ignoring this time lag will downplay the relationships of highly significant variables.

Correlation and Causality

Regression analysis looks at correlation effects, not causality.[56] To say that there is a cause in X (independent variable) that drives the outcome of Y (dependent variable) through the use of regression analysis is flawed. For instance, there is a high correlation between the number of shark attacks and lunch hour around the world. Clearly, sharks cannot tell that it is time to have lunch. However, because lunchtime is the warmest time of the day, and this is also the hour that beaches around the world are most densely populated. With a higher population of swimmers, the chances of heightened shark attacks are almost predictable. Therefore, lunchtime does not *cause* sharks to go hungry and prompt them to search for food. Just because there is a correlation does not mean that there is causality. Making this leap will provide analysts and management an incorrect interpretation of the results.

Random Walks

Certain financial data (e.g., stock prices, interest rates, inflation rates) follow something called a random walk. Random walks can take on different characteristics, including random walks with certain jumps, random walks with a drift rate, or a random walk that centers or reverts to some long-term average value. Even the models used to estimate random walks are varied, from geometric to exponential, among other things. A simple regression equation will yield no appreciable relationship when random walks exist.[57]

Jump Processes

Jump processes are more difficult to grasp but are nonetheless important for management to understand and challenge the assumptions of an analyst's results. For instance, the price of oil in the global market may sometimes follow a jump process. When the United States goes to war with another country, or when OPEC decides to cut the production of oil by several billion barrels a year, oil prices will see a sudden jump. Forecasting revenues based on these oil prices over time using historical data may not be the best approach. These sudden probabilistic jumps should most certainly be accounted for in the analysis. In this case, a jump-diffusion stochastic model is more appropriate than simple time-series or regression analyses.

Stochastic Processes

Other stochastic processes are also important when analyzing and forecasting the future. Interest rates and inflation rates may follow a mean-reversion stochastic process. That is, interest rates and inflation rates cannot increase or decrease so violently that they fall beyond all economic rationale. In fact, economic factors and pressures will drive these rates to their long-run averages over time. Failure to account for these effects over the long run may yield statistically incorrect estimates, resulting in erroneous forecasts.

> Warning signs to watch out for in time-series forecasting and regression as well as questions to ask include whether the forecasts are out of range, are there structural and business breaks anticipated in the forecast period, are there any misspecifications in the model, are there omitted and redundant variables, are there heteroskedasticity effects, are there any spurious relationships and biases, are there autoregressive lags, are correlations confused with causality, and are there variables that follow a random walk, jump processes, or other stochastic processes?

READING THE WARNING SIGNS IN REAL OPTIONS ANALYSIS

Risk analysis is never complete without the analysis of real options. What are uncertainty and risk analyses good for if one cannot make use of them? Real options analysis looks at the flexibility of a project or management's ability to make midcourse corrections when uncertainty becomes resolved through the passage of time, actions, and events. At the outset, real options analysis looks like a very powerful analytical tool, but care should be taken when real options analysis is applied. For instance, consider the following statements.

Do Not Let Real Options Simply Overinflate the Value of a Project

One of the most significant criticisms of real options approaches is that of over-inflating the value of a project. This criticism, of course, is false. Real options are applicable if and only if the following requirements are met: traditional financial analysis can be performed and models can be built; uncertainty exists; the same uncertainty drives value; management or the project has strategic options or flexibility to either take advantage of these uncertainties or to hedge them; and management must be credible in executing the relevant strategic options when they become optimal to do so, otherwise all the options in the world would be useless. Thus, an analyst should not simply apply real options analysis to every project that comes across his or her desk, but only to those that are appropriate and ripe for analysis.

An option will always bear a value greater than or equal to zero. Hence, critics argue that by applying real options analysis, a project's value will be artificially inflated. In reality, real options may sometimes appear without cost, but in most cases, firms need to pay to acquire these options (e.g., spending money to retrofit a refinery to obtain a switching option to choose between input fuels) and although the value of an option may be positive, its value can be clouded by the cost to obtain the option, making the entire strategy unprofitable and reduce the value of a project. So, although the value of an option is positive, the entire strategy's value may be negative. The lesson here is well learned—do not apply real options analysis on everything in sight, just to those projects that actually do have strategic options. Without doing so may mean leaving money on the table.

How Is Volatility Obtained and How Do You Reconcile Its Value?

Fifty percent of the value of a real options analysis is simply thinking about it and realizing that management has the flexibility to make midcourse corrections when uncertainty becomes resolved over time. Twenty-five percent is crunching the numbers, and the remaining twenty-five percent of the value in applying real options comes from being able to convince and explain the results to management and to yourself. One of the toughest things to explain is the concept of where and how volatility is obtained. Volatility should be obtained from a project based on a project's level of uncertainty going forward. One major error is to use external market proxies for volatility. Using a firm's stock price to estimate volatility of a single project in a company with hundreds or even thousands of projects is not only incorrect, it is ludicrous. An analyst should hence be able to defend the choice of volatility estimates. See Johnathan Mun's *Real Options Analysis,* Second Edition (Wiley 2005) for details on converting volatility to probability, and explaining volatility to management in an easy to understand manner.

What About Competing Options or Options That Have Not Even Been Considered?

If a project has 10 strategic options, do you analyze all 10 options? What about projects in the distant future, where the options are not yet known for certain, that may be highly valuable? For a project with many options, the analyst has to determine which of these options are independent and which are interacting type options. If the options are interacting, dominant strategies will always dominate over less valuable options and the value of the project's total set of options will revert to these dominant options.[58] Thus, do not evaluate all the options in the world if only a few options capture a significant portion of the value. Focus instead on valuing those important or dominant options.

The Error of Interpretation of Option Results

Sometimes options come without a cost, while sometimes they do have a cost. On some occasions, option value is tangible or explicit, and sometimes option value is implicit or intangible. As an example, the land seller illustration used in Chapter 11, The Black Box Made Transparent: Real Options SLS looks at the value of having an abandonment option, where if the counterparty signs the contractual agreement, the maximum expected cost of the contract is the option value.[59] However, in the case of some of the illustrations in Chapter 10, What's So Real About Real Options, and Why Are They Optional? where a research and development outfit performing stage-gate development has the option to abandon at every stage, valuing these options does not automatically mean the IRS or a counterparty will show up at the door and give the company a check in that amount. In this situation, the option value is an intangible or implicit value, useful as a measure against other projects and alternate strategies with or without such a flexibility option value.[60]

Warning signs to watch out for in real options analysis and questions to ask include whether the real options analysis is applied inappropriately when there are no options such that the value of a project is inappropriately overinflated, how the volatility measure is obtained, are competing or omitted options appropriately considered, and are the results interpreted correctly.

READING THE WARNING SIGNS IN OPTIMIZATION UNDER UNCERTAINTY

Finally, uncertainty and risk analyses are irrelevant if these quantified risks cannot be diversified away. Optimization looks at the ability to diversify away risks to find the best combination of projects subject to some prespecified constraints.

Why Are the Decision Variables the Decision Variables?

Decision variables are the variables that management has control over (e.g., which projects to execute, which product to manufacture, which vendors to purchase from, which wells to drill). However, sometimes things that are seemingly decision variables at the outset may not exactly be decision variables. For instance, the CEO's pet project is definitely a "go" decision no matter what the analytical results. The internal politics involved in decision making is something that cannot be taken lightly. Decision variables in an optimization analysis should most certainly be decision variables, not decisions that have already been made with the façade that their existence still has to be justified. Finally, certain decision variables are related to other decision variables and this interaction must be considered. For instance, Project A is a precursor to Projects B, C, and D; however, Project C cannot be executed if project B is executed, and Project C is a precursor to Project D.[61]

How Certain Are the Optimization Results?

Has the analyst looked at enough combinations to obtain the optimal results? In static optimization without simulation, whether it is using Risk Simulator, Excel's goal seek, or Excel's Solver add-in, the optimal solution will be found, if there is one, rather quickly, as the computer can calculate all possible combinations and permutations of inputs to yield the optimal results. However, in optimization under uncertainty,[62] the process will take much longer and the results may not achieve optimality quickly. Even if the results do seem to be optimal, it is hard to tell, thus, it is safer to run the simulation much longer than required. An impatient analyst may fall into the trap of not running sufficient simulation trials to obtain robust stochastic or dynamic optimization results.

What Is the Analyst's Level of Training?

Little knowledge of probability will lead to more dangerous conclusions than no knowledge at all. Knowledge and experience together will prove to be an impressive combination, especially when dealing with advanced analytics. Almost always, the first step in getting more advanced analytics accepted and rolled out corporate wide is to have a group of in-house experts trained in both the art and science of advanced analytics. Without a solid foundation, plans on rolling out these analytics will fail miserably.

> Warning signs to watch out for in an optimization under uncertainty and questions to ask include whether the decision variables are indeed decisions to be made, what are the levels of certainty of the results, and what is the level of training of the analyst.

Questions

1. Define what is meant by negligent entrustment.

2. What are some of the general types of errors encountered by an analyst when creating a model?

3. Why is truncation in a model's assumption important? What would happen to the results if truncation is not applied when it should be?

4. What is a critical success driver?

5. What are some of the normal-looking statistics?

6. What are structural breaks and specification errors, and why are they important?

CHAPTER 13: ENTERPRISE RISK MANAGEMENT

Enterprise Risk Management (ERM) in an organization includes the business processes and methods used to identify and manage risks as well as seize upside opportunities to achieve its objectives. ERM, therefore, provides a methodological framework in risk management for identifying risky events or conditions relevant to the organization's objectives, risks, and opportunities, identifying and assessing these conditions in terms of *Likelihood* or frequency of occurrence as well as the risk condition's magnitude of *Impact*, determining risk mitigation and postrisk response strategy, and monitoring the progress of these risk controls. When organizations identify and proactively address risks and opportunities, organizations are able to protect and create value for their stakeholders (e.g., owners, employees, shareholders, executives, customers, regulators, nations, and society in general).

ERM is usually also described as a risk-based approach to strategic planning as well as for managing an organization by integrating internal risk controls and external risk-compliance requirements (e.g., COSO, ISO 31000:2009, Basel III, and Sarbanes–Oxley Act). It applies to a broad spectrum of risks facing an organization to ensure that these risks are properly identified and managed. Investors, government regulators, banks, and debt rating agencies, among others, tend to scrutinize the risk-management processes of an organization as a key metric to its potential success.

In addition, the reasons for an organization to implement ERM should, at the very least, include the following areas of concern:

- Alignment of Risk Appetite and Strategy. Senior management typically considers the organization's risk appetite when strategic investment alternatives are being evaluated, as well as when setting objectives and developing mechanisms to manage risks. This tactic helps the organization to align its risk objectives with its business processes.

- Enhanced Risk-Response Decisions. ERM provides both the qualitative and quantitative rigor to identify and select from among alternative risk responses, including strategic real options and analysis of alternatives for risk avoidance, risk reduction, risk sharing, risk mitigation, and risk acceptance.

- Reduction in Operational Surprises and Losses. Organizations will gain enhanced capabilities to Identify, Assess, Prioritize, Value, Diversify, and Mitigate potential risk events' losses using advanced quantitative risk analytics. Instead of just qualitatively identifying risks, organizations can now translate these qualitative elements into quantitative risk models where Monte Carlo Risk Simulations, Stochastic Modeling, Portfolio Optimization, Predictive Forecasting, Business Intelligence, and Capital Investment Valuation and Modeling can be performed.

- Identify and Manage Multiple Cross-Enterprise Correlated Risks within a Corporate Portfolio Environment. Every enterprise faces a myriad of risks affecting different parts of the organization. ERM facilitates effective response to these interrelated and correlated impacts and integrates responses to multiple risks. Financial risks and risks in capital investment projects can also be handled within the environment of a correlated portfolio of projects where risks are hedged and diversified.

- Seizing Opportunities. Risks imply uncertainties, and uncertainties carry with them downside risks as well as upside potential. By considering a full range of potential events and risks, and creating Strategic Investment Flexibility or Strategic Real Options, management will be positioned to proactively realize upside opportunities, while at the same time mitigate downside risks.

- Improved Capital Deployment. Robust Quantitative Risk Metrics and Key Performance Indicators (KPI) generated through a comprehensive ERM process will allow management to effectively assess overall capital needs and enhance its capital allocation (e.g., creating an Efficient Investment Portfolio subject to Budgetary, Schedule, Strategic, and other Constraints).

THE TYPICAL TRADITIONAL ERM PROCESS

Traditionally, the ERM process involves *qualitative* risk assessment and documentation. The following lists the standard approach and traditional ERM process, which of course, can be modified and adapted to fit the organization under analysis. Throughout the rest of the chapter, we will revisit some of these steps to incorporate Integrated Risk Management (IRM)® methods and overlay *quantitative* risk management techniques onto the process.

- Establish senior management buy-in and risk-management culture.

- Seek the board of directors and senior management involvement and oversight to discuss a risk-management framework and its benefits and to obtain agreement on high-level objectives and expectations with resources and target dates regarding risk management in line with the organization's strategic plan.

- Review existing ERM practices in the organization and identify the areas for improvement.

- Facilitate initial training and working sessions to ensure buy-in and establish risk-management culture with key personnel involved with ERM implementation.

- Conduct working group discussions with stakeholders and key personnel to identify sources of risks.

- Provide input for implementation in the strategic business planning process.

- Coordinate the development, implementation, and monitoring of identified risk metrics.

- Document risk inventories and mitigations within Risk Registers in the organization.

- Develop risk dashboards for presentation to senior decision makers and the board of directors.

- Assess exposure to the risk, assess adequacy of existing risk mitigation or monitoring, and identify opportunities to enhance mitigation or monitoring activities, then suggest and build best practices for enhanced risk-adjusted returns.

- Create reports that effectively and concisely deliver the business intelligence based on risk measures that management needs to make cost-effective financial decisions.

- Establish a reporting process for management and the board.

- Establish a management working group to support the resources identified and drive the effort across the organization.

RISK REGISTERS AND BASIC ENTERPRISE RISK MANAGEMENT

The typical traditional ERM method uses *Risk Registers*, which simply involves recording all risks present or anticipated. Each *Risk Element* (i.e., each risk item that is recorded in the Risk Register) may include information on the name of the risk, the category or type of the risk, who reported it, who is responsible or is assigned the risk, what if any risk mitigation or risk control is required, contact person, documentation, and so forth. Sometimes additional information such as frequency, or *Likelihood,* and severity, or *Impact,* that risk may have on the organization is included. These Likelihood and Impact measures are usually qualitative estimates (high, medium, low) or can be assigned numerical values (1 to 5 or 1 to 10, where the higher the frequency or severity, the higher the value assigned). Alternate methods of using *Vulnerability* (or the inverse of amount of risk mitigation completed) with multiple risk controls are also supported. Clearly the amount of information and detail required varies depending on the organization. One way to think of Risk Registers is akin to a check register. For example, if you have a checking account, you can write a check to pay a specific bill; on that single check, you write the recipient's name, date, and amount. You can, of course, write multiple checks to different recipients. And every time a check is written, you would record said checks in a check register (whether electronically in an accounting software or manually in a physical check register). Continuing with this analogy, each check represents a different risk element, and multiple risk elements make up the Risk Register. You may also own multiple bank accounts, each with its own check register, or, in other words, an organization may have multiple Risk Registers set up, one for each division or business unit or project, and so forth.

However, the use of only Risk Registers by themselves often leads to ritualistic decision making, an illusion of control, and the fallacy of misplaced concreteness and reliance on purely qualitative risks. While the use of Risk Registers is a good starting point, Integrated Risk Management takes this qualitative assessment to the next level with more powerful quantitative risk management approaches.

CASE EXAMPLE: HOSPITAL
RISK MANAGEMENT

A simple example of a Risk Register in a hospital is shown in Figure 13.1, where certain types of risk events (e.g., wrong dosage given, equipment failure, etc.) that have occurred within specific departments (e.g., surgery, intensive care) and the number of events that happened within a specific time period are recorded, as well as other qualitative notes and associated details. Reports are then typically generated. Figure 13.2 shows a sample periodic (e.g., monthly) report of another organization showing the number of risk events that occurred in the past.

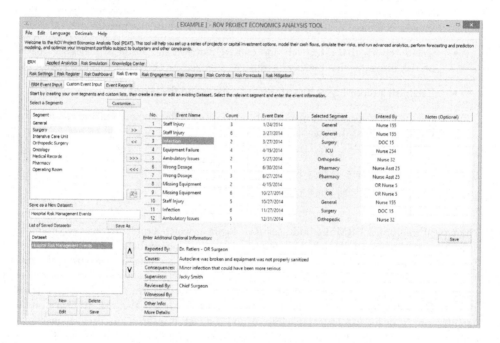

Figure 13.1: Example Risk Events in a Hospital

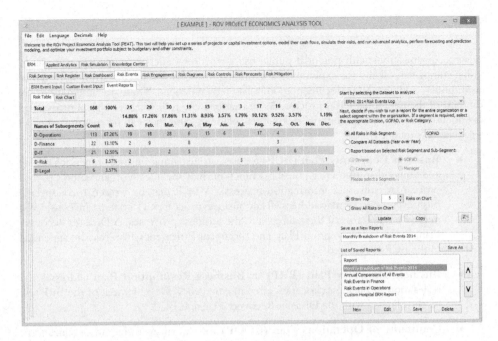

Figure 13.2: Example Risk Event Reports

RISK MATRIXES

In other types of Risk Registers, *Likelihood* (L) and *Impact* (I) values can be used and entered for each risk element, and the product of these two variables is termed the *Key Risk Indicator* (*KRI*), where $KRI = L \times I$. These KRI values can be color coded into various regions based on their respective values. For instance, Figure 13.3 shows a 10×10 matrix where the columns going from left to right represent Likelihood from 1 to 10 (low to high), and the rows from bottom to top represent the Impact from 1 to 10 (low to high). The values inside each of the cells represent the KRI, and the color coding depends on the computed KRI (typically, lower KRI values are green, medium KRI values are yellow, and high KRI values are red). In a later section, we showcase examples of how these KRI values can be incorporated into the ERM Risk Register. As will be seen later, the color coding, matrix size, and category labels can be customized as required.

10	10	20	30	40	50	60	70	80	90	100
9	9	18	27	36	45	54	63	72	81	90
8	8	16	24	32	40	48	56	64	72	80
7	7	14	21	28	35	42	49	56	63	70
6	6	12	18	24	30	36	42	48	54	60
5	5	10	15	20	25	30	35	40	45	50
4	4	8	12	16	20	24	28	32	36	40
3	3	6	9	12	15	18	21	24	27	30
2	2	4	6	8	10	12	14	16	18	20
1	1	2	3	4	5	6	7	8	9	10

Risk Impact (Severity) / Risk Likelihood (Frequency)

Figure 13.3: Risk Matrix

BUSINESS CONTINUITY PLANNING

In some organizations with potential public risk exposures—such as nuclear power plants, airline companies, oil and gas exploration and drilling firms, banks, and government or public institutions—additional risk documentation is also recommended. These documentations are also part of the traditional ERM process. As an example, the following are typical procedures and documentation arising from operational risk planning, and they can be customized to an organization's unique needs:

- **Business Continuity Plan (BCP)** focuses on sustaining business functions during and after a disruption (e.g., business functions may include an organization's payroll process or consumer information process). A BCP may be written for a specific business process or may address all key business processes. IT systems are considered in the BCP in terms of their support to the business processes. A Disaster Recovery Plan, Business Resumption Plan, and Occupant Emergency Plan may be appended to the BCP as required.

- **Business Recovery Plan (BRP)** or **Business Resumption Plan** addresses the restoration of business processes after an emergency. Development of the BRP will be coordinated with the Disaster Recovery Plan and BCP.

- **Continuity of Operations Plan (COOP)** focuses on restoring an organization's main essential functions at an alternate site and performing those functions for up to 4 weeks before returning to normal operations. COOP addresses headquarters-level issues; it is developed and executed independently from the BCP. The document can include Delegation of Authority, Orders of Succession, and Procedures for Vital Records and Databases.

- **Continuity of Support Plan** and **IT Contingency Plan (Recovery Strategy)** includes the development and maintenance of continuity of support plans for general support systems and contingency plans for major applications.

- **Cyber Incident Response Plan (CIRP)** establishes procedures to address cyber-attacks against an organization's IT system. It is designed to enable security personnel to identify, mitigate, and recover from malicious computer incidents, such as unauthorized access to a system or data, denial of service, or unauthorized changes to system hardware, software, or data (e.g., malicious logic, such as a virus, worm, or Trojan horse).

- **Disaster Recovery Plan (DRP)** becomes applicable after catastrophic events that deny access to the normal facility for an extended period. Depending on the organization's needs, several DRPs may be appended to the BCP.

- **Crisis Management Plan (CMP)** and **Crisis Communications Plan (CCP)** detail how organizations prepare their internal and external procedures prior to and during a disaster. A crisis communications plan is often developed by the organization responsible for public outreach. Plan procedures are included as an appendix to the BCP. The communications plan includes designation of specific individuals as the only authority for answering questions from the public regarding disaster response.

COMPREHENSIVE ERM WITH QUANTITATIVE RISK MANAGEMENT

A true next-generation comprehensive ERM process should include, at a minimum, the qualitative methods and steps previously outlined plus quantitative IRM methodologies. Instead of continuing the chapter by outlining additional items and bullet lists of methods and steps, we illustrate the quantitative ERM methods through the use of the PEAT software.

PEAT: PROJECT ECONOMICS ANALYSIS TOOL

The Project Economics Analysis Tool (PEAT) software was developed to perform a comprehensive Integrated Risk Management analysis on capital investments, discounted cash flow, cost and schedule risk project management, oil and gas applications, healthcare analytics, and Enterprise Risk Management. This tool will help you to set up a series of projects or capital investment options, model their cash flows, simulate their risks, run advanced risk simulations, perform business intelligence analytics, run forecasting and prediction modeling, optimize your investment portfolio subject to budgetary and other resource and qualitative constraints, and generate automated reports and charts, all within a single easy-to-use integrated software suite. The following modules are available in PEAT (Figure 13.4), and this chapter focuses on the ERM module:

- Enterprise Risk Management (ERM)

- Corporate Investments (Dynamic Discounted Cash Flow)

- Corporate Investments (Lease versus Buy)

- Goals Analytics (Sales Force Automation)

- Healthcare Economics (HEAT and REJ)

- Oil and Gas (Oil Field Reserves, Oil Recovery Analysis, Well-Type Curves)

- Project Management (Cost and Schedule Risk)

- Public Sector Analysis (Knowledge Value Added)

- ROV Compiled Models

- Customized company-specific modules and applications

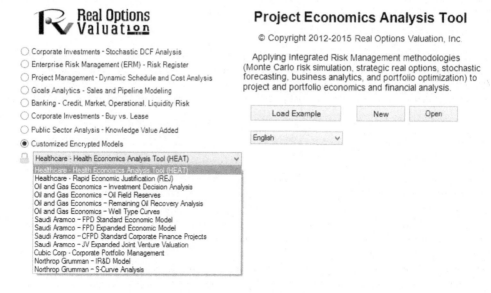

Figure 13.4: Project Economics Analysis Tool (PEAT) by ROV

ROV's PEAT incorporates all of the advanced risk and decision analytical methodologies covered in this book into a simple-to-use and step-by-step integrated software application suite. It simplifies the risk-based decision analysis process and empowers the decision maker with insights from powerful analytics. If you already perform discounted cash flow modeling or Enterprise Risk Management in Excel, why do you still need PEAT? Because PEAT's integrated advanced analytical techniques extend the analysis you have already performed, and do so in a simple-to-use, simple-to-understand, and automated format, thus generating valuable insights that would be impossible without such advanced methods. PEAT allows you to scale and replicate your analysis, archive and encrypt your models and data, create automated reports, and customize your own PEAT modules.

- *Enterprise Risk Management (ERM)*: Perform traditional qualitative ERM with Risk Registers but also enhance the analysis with more quantitative analysis. This ERM module comes with an online Web version as well as a module within PEAT, where you can enter and save multiple Risk Registers to generate Key Risk Indicators (KRI) by Risk Divisions and Risk Taxonomy (Geographic, Operations, Products, Activity or Process, and Department); assign risk items to different Risk Managers by performing Risk Mapping of Risk Categories to different Risk Divisions; create Risk Dashboards of the results; enter Risk Elements within multiple customizable Risk Engagements; draw Risk Diagrams; perform and run Risk Controls on KRIs to see if certain risks are within control or out of control; perform Risk Forecasts; check if certain Risk Mitigation projects do, indeed, work or are statistically ineffective; perform Risk Sensitivity on KRIs; perform Risk Scenarios on quantitative risk metrics; run Risk Simulations on risk metrics; generate Risk Reports; and encrypt your data and files for the purposes of Risk Security. See Chapter 14's case study on Eletrobrás in Brazil on how The PEAT ERM was employed at this multinational company in the *Modeling Risk* book.

- *Corporate Investments (Dynamic Discounted Cash Flow)*: With a few simple assumptions, you can auto-generate cash flow statements of multiple projects; obtain key performance indicators and financial metrics (NPV, IRR, MIRR, PP, DPP, ROI);

run risk simulations on uncertainty inputs; generate static tornado sensitivity analysis; run dynamic sensitivities; simultaneously compare multiple projects within a portfolio; perform forecasts of future revenues and cash flow; draw multiple strategic investment pathways and options, and model and value these strategic paths; compute and optimize the best projects within a portfolio subject to multiple constraints and restrictions; view results in management dashboards; encrypt your model and data; and auto-generate analysis reports. See Chapter 15 for more details on using PEAT's stochastic discounted cash flow module.

- *Corporate Investments (Lease versus Buy)*: Run a lease versus buy analysis, compare capital and operating leases with interest payments and tax advantages, value the lease contract from the point of view of the lessee and lessor, and generate the complete cash flow analysis to obtain the net advantage to leasing.

- *Goals Analytics (Sales Force Automation)*: Develop and maintain corporate sales goals. A Web-based SaaS and desktop-based PEAT module, it focuses on the creation and use of goals that help make goal-setting more accurate and sustainable by any company seeking to improve its sales performance (sales goal forecasting, probability of hitting corporate revenues, sales pipeline analysis, and other sales-based metrics analysis). See Chapter 14 for a case study on using PEAT's business plan forecasting module in *Modeling Risk*.

- *Healthcare Economics (HEAT and REJ)*: Run the economics of various options available under the U.S. Affordable Care Act (Obamacare) for corporations providing employer-sponsored healthcare by loading employee-census data (healthcare economics analysis tool, HEAT), or perform rapid economic justification (REJ) of each option by simulating its high-level inputs. See Chapter 14 for a case study on using PEAT's healthcare economics module in *Modeling Risk*.

- *Oil and Gas (Oil Field Reserves, Oil Recovery, and Well-Type Curves)*: Perform oil and gas industry models on analyzing the economics of oil field reserves and available oil recovery based on uncertainty and risks, as well as generate oil-well–specific type curves and economics.

- *Project Management (Cost and Schedule Risk)*: Draw your own project pathways (simple linear project tasks versus complex parallel and recombining projects), then click a button to auto-generate the model. Enter the cost and schedule estimates as well as their spreads, then run a risk simulation on the model to determine the probability of cost-schedule overruns, cost-schedule buffers at various probabilities of completion, critical path identification, and sensitivity analysis. See Technical Note 6 for a case study on using PEAT's project management (cost and schedule risk) module.

- *Public Sector Analysis (Knowledge Value Added)*: Model government and nonprofit organizations' value, value to society, or intangible value via Knowledge Value Added utilizing market comparables to identify and monetize such projects and assets.

- *ROV Compiled Models*: With the compiler software, users can compile their existing Excel models into license-controlled executable EXE files. ROV's patented methods can be used to encrypt and lock up the intellectual property and mathematical algorithms of the model, and issue hardware-controlled and timed licenses to the purchaser's own users or customers.

CRITICAL ERM RISK CHARACTERISTICS
AND MODELING CRITERIA

PEAT ERM is both a desktop software and online Web-based application, with over 20 related U.S. and worldwide patents and patents pending. The desktop PEAT version is for internal risk department personnel to manage the results and dataset, keep the data encrypted and safe, and run analyses such as simulations, scenarios, tornado analysis, and so forth. Not everyone needs these advanced analytics. Therefore, in a large corporation, there can be multiple end users who should have the ability to enter data, and a few local administrators with access to control everything from granting access to and creating end users, to setting up the risk profile of the company. End users (e.g., plant managers, supervisors, secretaries, etc.) can only enter in data and information. These end users have limited access and limited knowledge, making training simple, and they enter in values only pertaining to their areas of responsibilities. Local administrators then have a database that rolls up to the corporate level and they can see results, generate reports, perform more advanced quantitative risk analytics, and so on.

- **Risk Settings and Risk Classifications**

Users typically start by setting up how Key Risk Indicators (KRI) should be set up, any E-Alerts that need to be triggered and sent if KRIs exceed certain values for any Risk Element, etc. Such global settings should also allow users to set Risk Indicator Categories (1–5 or 1–10) with Customizable Color Coding of KRI (Key Risk Indicators) via a Risk Matrix (Figure 13.5).

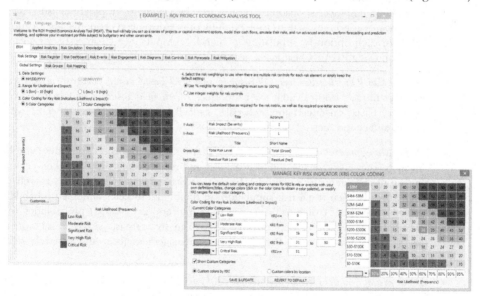

Figure 13.5: Risk Settings

- **Risk Groups and Risk Taxonomy**

Typically, ERM implementation also requires the ability to create various divisions, departments, risk categories, and other segmentation within an organization. Such segregation is required because data entered for the Risk Elements can be sliced and diced every which way, as well as being in compliance with COSO Integrated Risk Framework.

Figure 13.6 shows the PEAT set up of various Risk Divisions, Risk G.O.P.A.D., Risk Category, and Risk Managers. Cumulatively, these categories represent the Risk Taxonomy of the ERM system. For example, multiple business or operational Divisions within a Company can be created, such that the company can manage multiple risk profiles for each division. Users can also create and assign various G.O.P.A.D. categories (geographic, operations, products, activity or process, and department) such that analysts can analyze the company's risk profile from multiple points of view, select from and create queries of specific G.O.P.A.D. categories to analyze, and so on. Users can create customized Risk Categories or use PEAT's library of predefined risk categories, and lists of persons in charge of certain risks and their contact information can be set up.

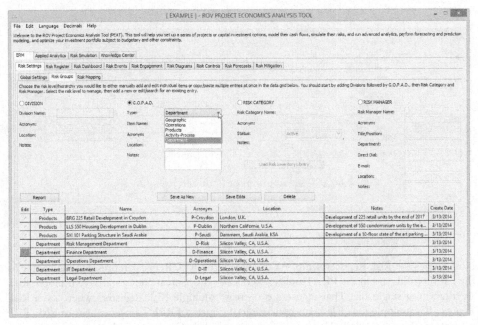

Figure 13.6: Risk Groupings in an Organization

- **Risk Mapping**

Based on previously created Risk Groups and Risk Taxonomy, we can now map and link these hierarchies on one or more dimensions. This process will allow putting various projects with related risks into the various groups and segments for analysis and the ability to view how a certain risk permeates through the organization as well as how a specific risk element may touch multiple departments, divisions, processes, and so forth. The previously completed segments can then be mapped as shown in Figure 13.7. For example, a Risk Category can be mapped to one or multiple G.O.P.A.D. categories, which can then be mapped to one or more Divisions. All Divisions roll up to the Corporation. This way, when a risk element is entered in the Risk Register, users can choose the Risk Category and the remaining connection routes will be determined. Using these mapped connections, the software can slice-and-dice and look at different Divisions, or G.O.P.A.D. categories and see the risk profile from various points of view.

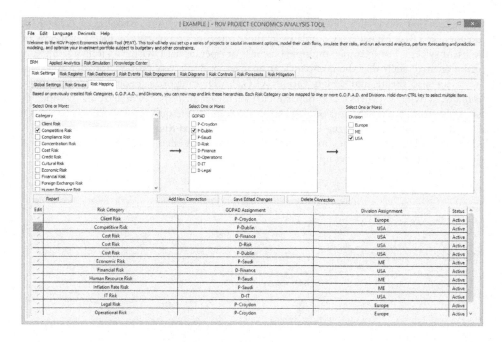

Figure 13.7: Risk Mapping or Grouped Relationships

- **Risk Register**

Now comes the Risk Register setup. As discussed, the Risk Register represents the center of the ERM world, and in the PEAT utility, users can set up, create new, and save multiple Risk Registers in a single file. That is, users can create multiple Risk Registers where each Risk Register has multiple Risk Elements consisting of Causes of Risk, Consequences of Risk, Risk Mitigation Response, Risk Manager Assignments, Risk Category, Risk Status, Likelihood, Impact, Key Risk Indicators, Risk Dates (Creation, Edit, and Due Dates), Total Risk Levels ($), Residual Risk Levels ($), Mitigation Cost, Multiple Risk Controls, and so forth, as illustrated in Figure 13.8.

Informational Inputs

Multiple Risk Registers (e.g., different projects, business units, investment initiatives, plants, facilities, etc.) can be saved and archived as required, where each Risk Register contains multiple Risk Elements (e.g., the individual risks such as fire, fraud, IT downtime, human errors, accidents, and so forth, within each project, business unit, initiative, facility, etc.), shown as rows in the data grid (Figure 13.8). The typical qualitative informational inputs include the name of the risk, a short name or acronym, causes of the specific risk, consequences of the risk, any risk mitigation responses, action plans to execute, current status (active or inactive), risk manager it is assigned to, and the Likelihood and Impact levels of the current Risk Element. Risk Category is also a required input and based on the Risk Mapping performed, selecting a specific Risk Category will automatically insert the inputted risk into all mapped relationships, as will be used later in the Risk Dashboards.

IMPACT AND LIKELIHOOD

As mentioned, the Risk Register entries require a two-dimensional input of Likelihood (L) or frequency of a risk event occurring and Impact (I) or the severity in terms of financial, economic, and noneconomic effects of the risk. These L and I concepts are industry standard and used even in regulatory environments such as the Basel II and Basel III Accords (initiated by the Bank of International Settlements in Switzerland and accepted by most Central Banks around the world as regulatory reporting standards for operational risks). Alternate measures such as Vulnerability (V), Velocity (υ), and other measures can be used as well. The case study in Chapter 14 on applying PEAT ERM at Eletrobrás in Brazil showcases one example of how Vulnerability measures are used in the *Modeling Risk* book.

The uncertainties of repetitive events observed in enterprises' operations over long periods of time can become predictable but usually not with absolute certainty. Such observances can be associated with mathematical functions that reflect the statistical properties of something likely to occur at a future time. The risk of an event occurring is connected to two parameters: the Impact (I) caused by an uncertain event and the probability, or Likelihood (L), of an event occurring. Given some known probability of a risk event occurring, the higher the impact, the greater the risk. If the impact is zero, the risk will be zero even though the event has a high probability of occurring. The reverse argument is also true. If the probability of a risk event occurring is equal to zero, the risk is zero (this is an environment of pure certainty), regardless of the magnitude of the impact.

RISK MITIGATION AND TOTAL VERSUS RESIDUAL RISK

Risk Mitigation, Total Risk, and Residual Risk are the optional monetary inputs in each Risk Element in the Risk Register. Total Risk means the total amount of risk impact this specific Risk Element may cost the organization. The inputs are the projected minimum impact, most likely impact, and maximum impact it might cause. For instance, the risks of a counterparty violating an existing contract may have financial impacts, where the minimal impact might be, say, $0 if the contract is still in force through the end of its term, to a most likely impact of $100,000 in anticipated delays and cost overruns by the counterparty, to a maximum of $300,000 if the counterparty becomes insolvent and subsequent lost business opportunities due to nonperformance of the counterparty. The Mitigation Cost is the amount of money used to reduce the risk exposure of the specific Risk Element, for instance, the cost of obtaining a secondary subcontractor with prenegotiated terms whose contract becomes live only if the original contractor is not performing. Such risk mitigation methods tend to have a financial cost, and the Residual Risk Level as seen in Figure 13.8 reflects the remaining risk exposure after these risk mitigation strategies have been employed. That is, by having a secondary contract, the risk exposure is a lot less but may still remain.

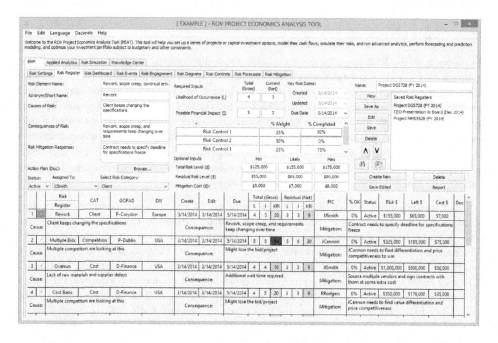

Figure 13.8: Risk Register

- ### Risk Dashboard

Users of the PEAT ERM system can create multiple types of customized Risk Dashboard views complete with reports, data grids, charts, and visuals, where analysts can select from a specific G.O.P.A.D. category, Division, Risk Category, or Risk Dates. The Risk Dashboard is used to slice and dice the Risk Register elements into various drill down views. Following are some sample Risk Dashboard views.

- ### Risk Dashboard – Risk Elements

Here KRIs can be viewed using Pareto charts, that is, visual charts on KRI scores across different selected segments, division, or G.O.P.A.D. category of the organization over a specified time span, as shown in Figure 13.9.

The Risk Elements View allows users to see the color-coded KRI for each risk element and a pie chart showcasing the percentage allocation of each KRI color code. The Pareto Chart View shows the same results using a Pareto chart where the KRIs are ranked from the highest to the lowest and the cumulative contributions to variance are computed (e.g., we can determine that the top 5 risk elements contributes to 80% of the risk portfolio).

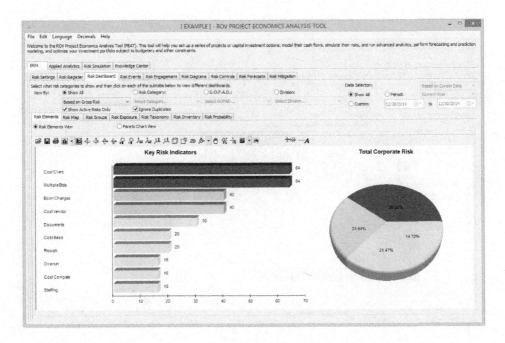

Figure 13.9: Risk Dashboard's Risk Elements

- **Risk Dashboard – Risk Heat Maps**

Risk Heat Maps of KRI counts with relevant customizable risk-based color codes across various risk categories, divisions, and segments over specified time periods can also be generated (Figure 13.10). Each value in the matrix's cells represents the total number of Risk Elements falling within that specific cross section of Likelihood and Impact levels.

The color settings (green to red), number of color categories (3 colors or 5 colors), and the granularity of the risk matrix (5 × 5 or 10 × 10) are based on the inputs in the Risk Settings tab. The axis labels are also customizable in the Risk Settings tab (Risk Likelihood, Risk Impact, and the category labels).

- **Risk Dashboard – Risk Groups**

Risk accumulation by G.O.P.A.D. category or other risk groups can be shown as bar charts indicating the Risk Element counts within these selected groups (Figure 13.11). The ability to slice and dice the data to generate customized reports comes from the previously set up various G.O.P.A.D. components and their mapped relationships to risk types and risk categories.

In the example shown in Figure 13.11, the x-axis shows the 5 risk levels aggregated by Risk Groups. The y-axis of the bar charts can be set as the total KRI for each Risk Group or by Risk Element counts.

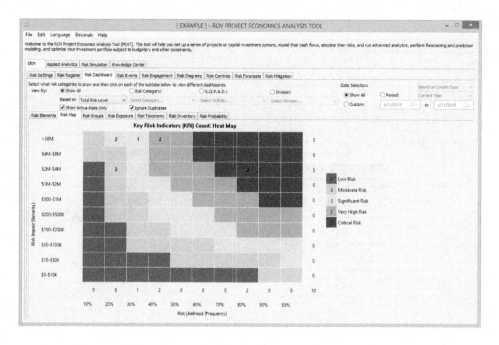

Figure 13.10: Risk Dashboard's Risk Heat Map

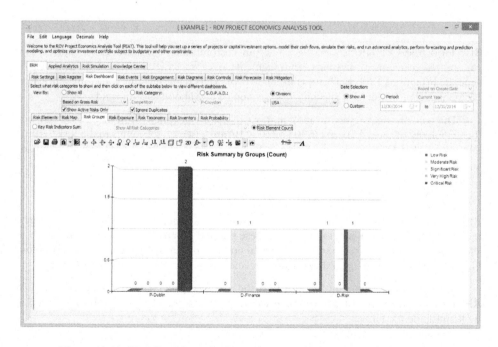

Figure 13.11: Risk Dashboard's Risk Groups (Element Count by Division)

- **Risk Dashboard – Risk Exposure**

The Risk Exposure of a selected segment is shown as risk dials and charts and is compared against the entire Company (Figure 13.12). These dials and charts represent the Total Risk Exposure and Total Residual Risk Exposure for the selected category and time period, by summing all the relevant Risk Elements' dollar or monetary exposures in the active Risk Register. The default terms of Total Gross Risk (also known as Inherent Risk or Total Risk) and Residual Risk (also known as Active Risk, Remaining Risk, or Current Risk) can all be user-defined in the Risk Settings tab.

- **Risk Dashboard – Risk Taxonomy**

This report provides top-down (drill-down) visual representation of the structure of the corporation and its risk associations or Risk Taxonomy, as well as a bottom-up view of how a specific risk permeates throughout the corporation (Figure 13.13).

- **Risk Dashboard – Risk Inventory**

SQL queries are used to obtain the customized risk profiles and risk reports by Division, G.O.P.A.D. category, Risk Category, Risk Dates, and so forth. The queries will search the active Risk Register for all the relevant Risk Elements that fall within the search parameters and return an inventory of all the risks identified (Figure 13.14). This report allows for the Risk Monitoring of project management, tasks, completion, and assignments, and it also provides for Risk Governance; provides a Risk Effectiveness Summary, Risk Audit Trail, and Compliance; and complies with International Standards Organization (ISO) Standards. See the sections at the end of this chapter on how PEAT and ROV technology is in compliance with multiple global risk standards such as COSO, BASEL III, NIST, ISO 31000:2009, and others.

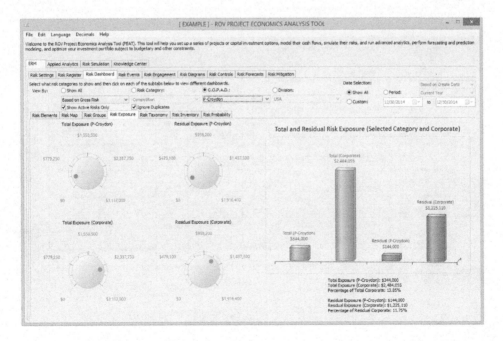

Figure 13.12: Risk Dashboard's Risk Exposure Levels (by GOPAD and Corporate)

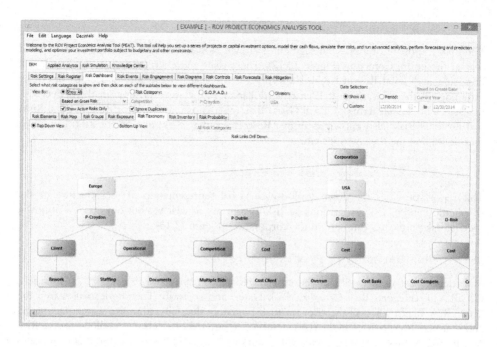

Figure 13.13: Risk Dashboard's Risk Taxonomy (Top-Down View)

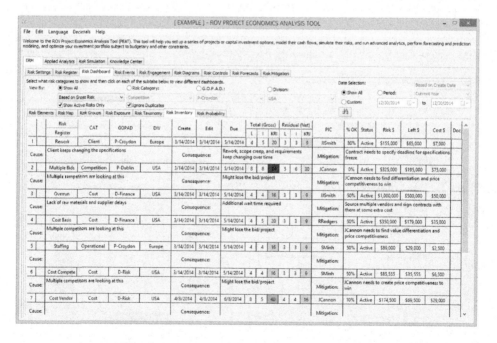

Figure 13.14: Risk Dashboard's Risk Inventory

- ### Risk Dashboard – Risk Probability

This dashboard provides users the ability to compute the PDF/CDF probability of a discrete risk event occurring or continuous risk amounts using historical experience. The analysis is similar to that in Risk Simulator's Distributional Analysis tool, where after a probability distribution is selected and its required input parameters are entered, the PDF and CDF values are returned as a probability table. Figure 13.15 shows an example situation where a discrete Poisson distribution is selected and the Lambda (mean) value entered is 1.5 (e.g., data was collected for 3 months on the number of errors in bank check deposits per work week at a specific branch of a national bank, and the data shows that there is, on average, 1.5 errors per work week). By setting some starting and ending range and step size, the computed table shows the PDF probability and CDF cumulative probability of a specific risk category's number of events per work week (check deposit errors). The probability that within any work week there will be no check deposit errors is 22.31%, exactly one error is 33.47%, exactly two errors is 25.10%, and so forth. Cumulatively, we can also state that we are 93.44% sure that within any work week, there will be three or fewer risk event errors of the same risk category, assuming history is the best indicator of future performance.

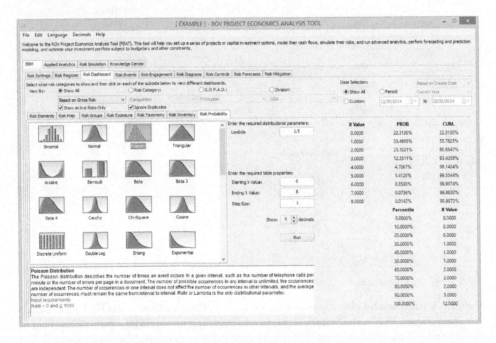

Figure 13.15: Risk Dashboard's Exact Probability Analysis (CDF and PDF)

- **Risk Diagrams**

Users can create Risk Diagrams with ready-made templates on Bowtie Hazard Diagrams, Cause and Effect Ishikawa Fishbone Diagrams, Drill-Down Diagrams, Influence Diagrams, Mind Maps, and Node Diagrams. Sometimes, customized risk diagrams such as those shown in Figure 13.16 can be used to better illustrate the risk process, risk mitigation, risk cause and effect, and risk impact of the Risk Register. Right-click on the Risk Diagram tab to add additional diagrams or to delete and rename existing diagrams. In addition, various pre-configured diagram templates are available in the droplist to help users get started in generating their own risk diagrams.

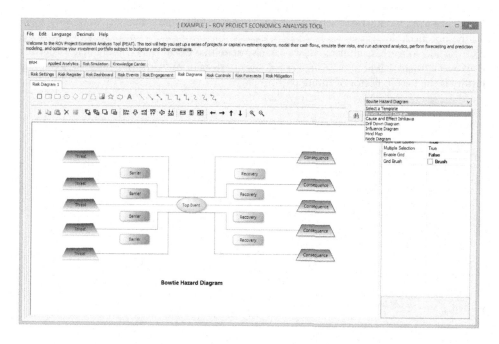

Figure 13.16: Risk Diagrams

- **Risk Controls**

The PEAT ERM system also allows for the creation of Control Charts and KRI Risk Trends over time (Figure 13.17), and statistical process controls can be applied. Control charts help to visually and statistically determine if a specific risk event is in-control or out-of-control. For instance, if the number of risk events such as a plant accident spikes within a certain time period, was that set of events considered expected under statistically normal circumstances or was it an outlier requiring more detailed analysis?

The charts' statistical control limits are computed based on the actual data collected (e.g., the number of risks in a manufacturing factory floor). The number of risk events is taken over time and the upper control limit (UCL) and lower control limit (LCL) are computed, as are the central line (CL) and other sigma levels. The resulting chart is called a control chart, and if the process if out-of-control, the actual defect line will be outside of the UCL and LCL lines. Typically, when the LCL is a negative value, we set the floor as zero. The ERM software presents several control chart types, and each type is used under different circumstances.

- X-chart: used when the variable has raw data values and there are multiple measurements in a sample experiment, and multiple experiments are run, and the average of the collected data is of interest.

- R-chart: used when the variable has raw data values and there are multiple measurements in a sample experiment, and multiple experiments are run, and the range of the collected data is of interest.

- XmR-chart: used when the variable has raw data values and is a single measurement taken in each sample experiment, and multiple experiments are run, and the actual value of the collected data is of interest.

- P-chart: used when the variable of interest is an attribute (e.g., defective or non-defective) and the data collected are in proportions of defects (or number of defects in a specific sample) and there are multiple measurements in a sample experiment, and multiple experiments are run, and the average proportion of defects of the collected data is of interest; also, the number of samples collected in each experiment differs.

- NP-chart: used when the variable of interest is an attribute (e.g., defective or non-defective) and the data collected are in proportions of defects (or number of defects in a specific sample) and there are multiple measurements in a sample experiment, and multiple experiments are run, and the average proportion of defects of the collected data is of interest; also, the number of samples collected in each experiment is constant for all experiments.

- C-chart: used when the variable of interest is an attribute (e.g., defective or non-defective) and the data collected are in total number of defects (actual count in units) and there are multiple measurements in a sample experiment, and multiple experiments are run, and the average number of defects of the collected data is of interest, also, the number of samples collected in each experiment are the same.

- U-chart: used when the variable of interest is an attribute (e.g., defective or non-defective) and the data collected are in total number of defects (actual count in units) and there are multiple measurements in a sample experiment, and multiple experiments are run, and the average number of defects of the collected data is of interest, also, the number of samples collected in each experiment differs.

- **Risk Forecast**

As part of the IRM process, historical risk data can be used to apply predictive modeling to forecast future states of risk, as well as Risk Tracking, Time-Series Risk Forecasts, PDF/CDF Likelihood of Occurrence, and Snapshots per period and over time (Figure 13.18). Using historical data or subject matter estimates, you can run forecast models on time-series or cross-sectional data by applying advanced forecast analytics such as ARIMA, Auto ARIMA, Auto Econometrics, Basic Econometrics, Cubic Splines, Fuzzy Logic, GARCH (8 variations), Exponential J-Curves, Logistic S-Curves, Markov Chains, Generalized Linear Models (Logit, Probit, and Tobit), Multivariate Regressions (Linear and Nonlinear), Neural Network, Stochastic Processes (Brownian Motion, Mean-Reversion, Jump-Diffusion), Time-Series Analysis, and Trendlines.

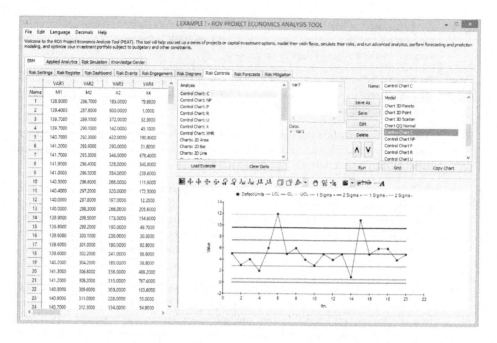

Figure 13.17: Risk Controls Charts (Sample C-Chart)

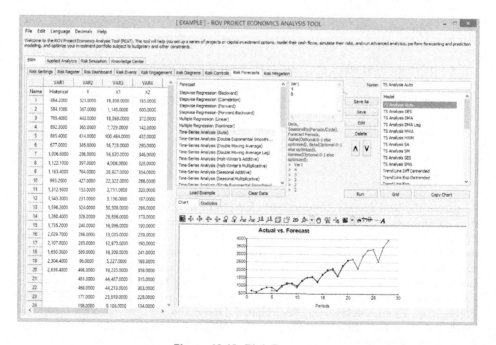

Figure 13.18: Risk Forecast

- **Risk Mitigation**

The Risk Mitigation analysis in PEAT's ERM helps determine if a specific risk mitigation strategy or technique is working, at least statistically speaking. Risk managers can collect data from *before* and *after* a risk mitigation strategy is implemented and determine if there is a statistically significant difference between the two. The utility allows for the valuation and statistical computation of the effectiveness of risk mitigation programs through various hypothesis testing methods. For example, in the risk event of check deposit errors, the bank could potentially invest in high-resolution check scanners with smart optical character recognition software with embedded algorithms to check for any potential human errors. If the number of check errors is tracked before the new scanner system was implemented and compared with after the implementation, risk analysts can determine the efficacy and effectiveness of said scanner, if it was worth the money invested, and if additional scanners should be implemented across other bank branches.

- **Risk Knowledge**

Any good ERM system should always include quick getting started guides and training videos. The Knowledge Center in PEAT's ERM module has slides, training materials, and videos that are all fully customizable for an organization (Figure 13.19).

Figure 13.19: Risk Knowledge Center

Archiving Risk Events and Risk Engagements

Sometimes Risk Registers can be simplified to not require any Likelihood, Impact, Risk Exposure amounts, Mitigation Costs, or Residual Risk Exposure amounts. That is, only qualitative information and details are required by the organization. Figure 13.20 shows an illustration of a simplified Risk Register of items in the PEAT ERM system. The risk maps can still be used but only simple risk event counts, event names, and dates are used and captured.

Sometimes, qualitative risk event information needs to be saved and archived. This is where the PEAT ERM's Risk Engagement sections come in handy. Multiple Risk Engagements can be created in a single file where each of the following subsections has multiple Risk Elements: Pre-Engagement Risks, Engagement Risks, and Lessons Learned (Post-Engagement) as seen in Figure 13.21. By archiving these qualitative risk aspects, a Risk Library can be generated and historical risks can be analyzed over time.

Bridging the Gap between Qualitative and Quantitative Risk Management

ERM historically has been a qualitative risk management technique. However, in this chapter, IRM methods have been applied and interjected into this traditional ERM process. For instance, Likelihood and Impact measures, Total Risk Levels, Residual Risk Levels, and Mitigation Costs are all numerical values. These variables are applicable to each Risk Element in the Risk Register and are Risk Mapped throughout various Risk Segments in the organization. By doing this, we are now able to apply quantitative IRM risk analytics to these values such as tornado analysis, Monte Carlo Risk Simulations, scenario analysis, heat maps, and other analytics.

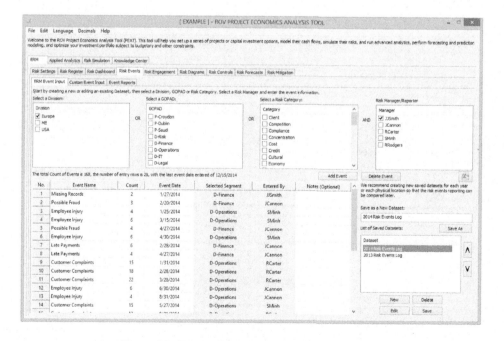

Figure 13.20: Risk Events Data Entry and Archive

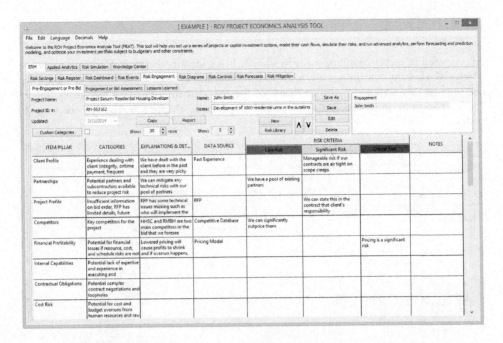

Figure 13.21: Risk Engagement: Pre-Engagement, Engagement Assessment, and
Lessons Learned

ERM TORNADO ANALYSIS

As discussed in earlier chapters, tornado analysis helps identify the critical success factors or which risk element contributes the most to the bottom-line risk profile of the company (or risk segment) by statically perturbing each of the risk element's financial risk levels (Figure 13.22). The same interpretation as discussed in previous chapters holds true for tornado analysis.

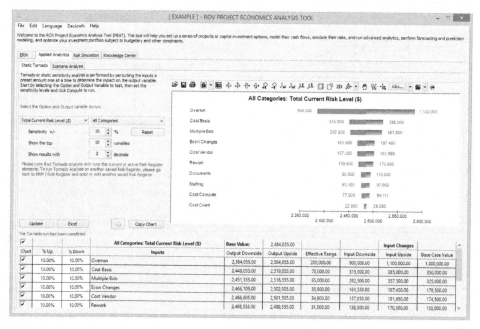

Figure 13.22: Tornado Analysis on ERM Risk Register Elements

ERM SCENARIO ANALYSIS

Scenario Analysis helps create multiple risk scenarios of your current or total risk amounts of individual risk elements to determine the impact on the corporate risk profile and to create scenario heat maps.

ERM MONTE CARLO
RISK SIMULATIONS

The PEAT ERM system also allows for the creation of Risk Simulations of the user's risk register element input assumptions via ranges (e.g., minimum, most likely, maximum, average, standard deviation, location, scale, range, percentiles) and returns probabilistic distributions of the individual risk elements or rolled-up risks by categories (output metrics include risk element count, KRI sum, sum and count of risk register elements within a risk category, total risk dollars, total risk mitigation cost, etc.). These probability distributions are automatically generated based on the user's total and residual risk inputs and can be modified and updated as required in the *Set Input Assumptions* tab (Figure 13.23). The simulated results can be interpreted as usual (Figure 13.24).

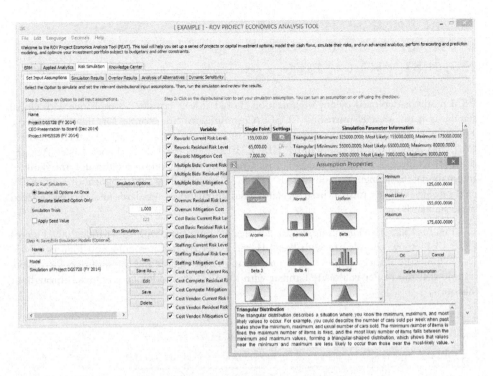

Figure 13.23: Risk Simulation Assumptions

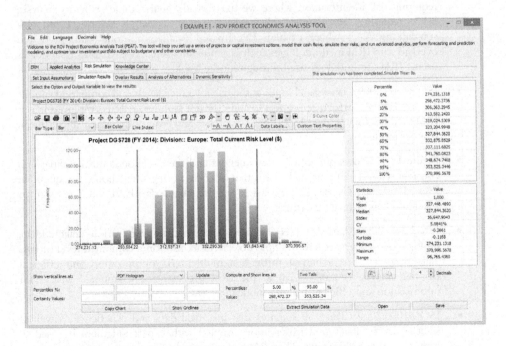

Figure 13.24: Risk Simulation Results

COMPLIANCE WITH GLOBAL STANDARDS: BASEL, COSO, ISO, NIST, AND SARBOX

ERM methods deployed by any organization should at least consider compliance with global standards if not exactly mirroring COSO (Committee of Sponsoring Organizations of the Treadway Commission, with respect to their organizing committees at AAA, AICPA, FEI, IMA, and IIA), International Standards ISO 31000:2009, the U.S. Sarbanes–Oxley Act, the Basel III requirements for Operational Risk (from the Basel Committee through the Bank of International Settlements), and NIST 800-37. The parallels and applications of ROV methodologies closely mirror these regulatory and international standards and, at times, exceed these standards.

Figures 13.25-13.34 illustrate some examples of compliance with ISO 31000:2009, Figures 13.35-13.44 show compliance with Basel II and Basel III requirements, and Figures 13.45-13.53 show compliance with COSO requirements. These figures and the summary lists below assume that the reader is already familiar with the IRM methodology employed throughout this book.

COMPLIANCE WITH INTERNATIONAL STANDARDS ORGANIZATION ISO 31000:2009

- The IRM methodology we employ is in line with ISO 31000:2009 Clauses 2.3 and 2.8 requiring a risk management process (Figure 13.25), as well as Clause 5 (5.4.2 requiring risk identification where we use tornado analysis and scenario analysis; 5.4.3. requiring quantitative risk analysis where we apply Monte Carlo risk simulations; 5.4.4 where existing Excel-based evaluation models are used and overlaid with IRM methodologies such as simulations; etc.). See Chapter 1 for details on the IRM methodology used throughout the book.

- ISO 31000:2009 Clause 5.4.4 looks at the risk tolerance levels and comparing various risk levels in a portfolio optimization and efficient frontier analysis employed in our IRM methodology (Figure 13.26). See Chapters 8 and 9 for optimization and efficient frontier modeling.

- Figure 13.27 shows quantified consequences and the likelihoods (probabilities and confidence levels) of potential events that can occur using simulations, as required in ISO 31000:2009 Clauses 2.1 and 5.4.3. See this chapter's PEAT ERM section for Likelihood and Impact measures.

- ISO 31000:2009 Clause 5.4.3 requires viewing the analysis from various stakeholders, multiple consequences, and multiple objectives to develop a combined level of risk. This perspective is achieved through a multicriteria optimization and efficient frontier analysis (Figure 13.28) in the IRM process. See Chapters 8 and 9 for optimization and efficient frontier modeling.

- ISO 31000:2009 Clause 3F requires that historical data and experience as well as stakeholder feedback and observation coupled with expert judgment be used to forecast future risk events. The IRM process employs a family of 16 forecasting methods (Figure 13.29 shows an example of the ARIMA model) coupled with risk simulations with high fidelity to determine the best goodness-of-fit when historical data exists, or using subject matter expert estimates and stakeholder assumptions, we can apply the Delphi method and custom distribution to run risk simulations on the forecasts. See Chapters 6 and 7 for forecast methods and analytical details.

- ISO 31000:2009 Clauses 3C, 5.4.3, 5.5, and 5.5.2 require risk evaluations on risk treatments, options to execute when there are different types of risks, and selecting and implementing various risk treatment strategic options that are not solely reliant on economics. The IRM's strategic real options methodology allows users to model multiple path-independent and path-dependent implementation strategies or alternate courses of action that are generated to mitigate downside risks and take advantage of upside potentials (Figure 13.30). See Chapters 10 and 11 for details on real options analysis modeling techniques.

- Figure 13.31 illustrates how ISO 31000:2009 Clauses 3D, 3E, and 5.4.3 are satisfied using the IRM process of probability distribution fitting of uncertain variables and how their interdependencies (correlations) are executed. See Chapter 4 on how such simulation assumptions can be correlated and run in Risk Simulator.

- Risk controls are required in ISO 31000:2009 Clauses 2.26, 4.43, and 5.4.3 (Figure 13.32). The control charts and Risk Effectiveness calculations in PEAT ERM help decision makers identify if a particular risk mitigation strategy and response that was enacted had sufficiently and statistically significantly affected the outcomes of future risk states.

- Scenarios, cascading, and cumulative effects (consequences) are also the focus of ISO 31000:2009 Clause 5.4.2. The IRM method employs tornado analysis, scenario analysis, dynamic sensitivity analysis, and risk simulations (Figure 13.33) to identify which input(s) have the highest impact on the organization's risks and model their impacts on the total risks of the organization.

- ISO 31000:2009 Clause 5.2 requires proper communication of risk exposures and consequences, and an understanding of the basis and reasons of each risk. The PEAT ERM Risk Dashboards provide details and insights for a better understanding of the issues governing each of the risk issues in an organization (Figure 13.34).

(Text continues on page 577.)

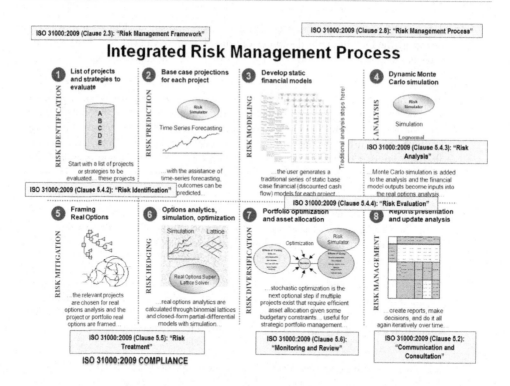

Figure 13.25: ISO 31000:2009—IRM

Investment Efficient Frontiers analysis provides for a variety of budget scenarios when considering portfolios of options

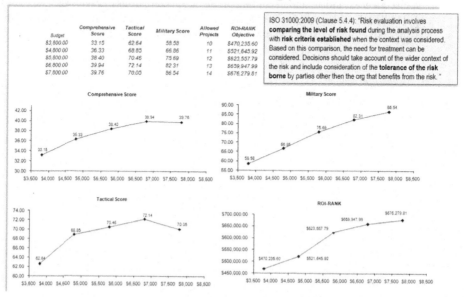

Figure 13.26: ISO 31000:2009—Risk Tolerance

Risk Simulation provides the decision maker with additional data

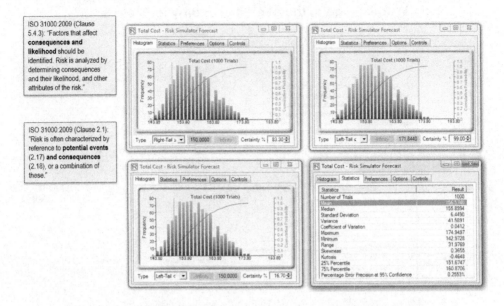

Figure 13.27: ISO 31000:2009—Consequences and Likelihood

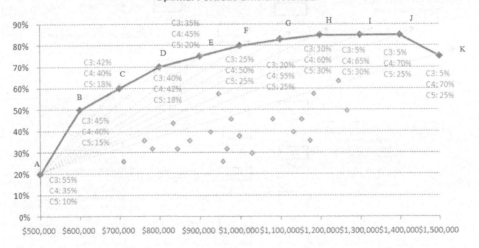

Figure 13.28: ISO 31000:2009—Multiple Stakeholder Objectives and Consequences

ACTUAL SALES VS. ECONOMETRIC FORECAST
With linkage to the overall economy indicators

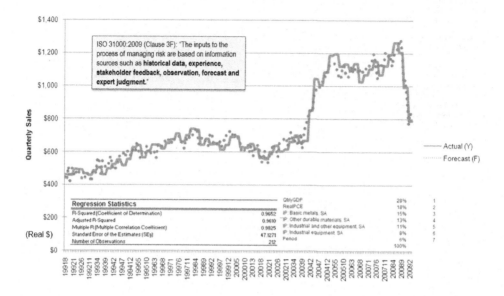

Figure 13.29: ISO 31000:2009—Historical Data and Future Forward Forecast

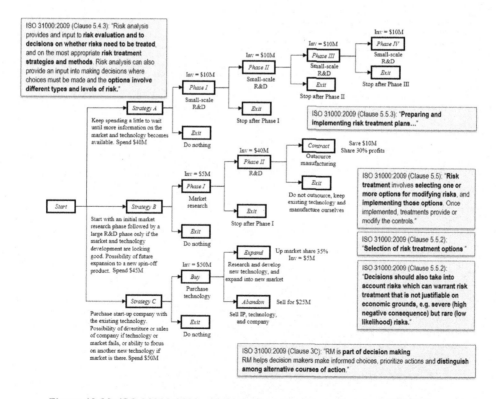

Figure 13.30: ISO 31000:2009—Multiple Options, Strategies, and Alternatives

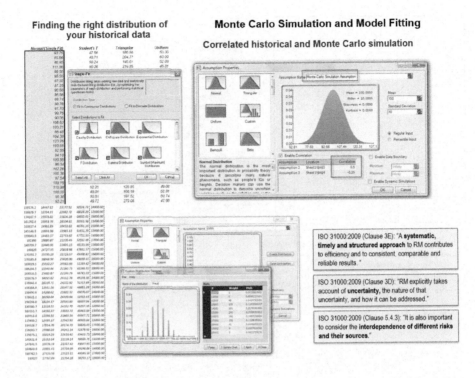

Figure 13.31: ISO 31000:2009 Structured Approach, Probability Fitting, and Correlations

Operational Risk Controls

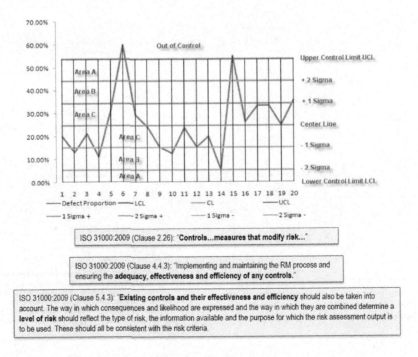

ISO 31000:2009 (Clause 2.26): "**Controls...measures that modify risk...**"

ISO 31000:2009 (Clause 4.4.3): "Implementing and maintaining the RM process and ensuring the **adequacy, effectiveness and efficiency of any controls.**"

ISO 31000:2009 (Clause 5.4.3): "**Existing controls and their effectiveness and efficiency** should also be taken into account. The way in which consequences and likelihood are expressed and the way in which they are combined determine a **level of risk** should reflect the type of risk, the information available and the purpose for which the risk assessment output is to be used. These should all be consistent with the risk criteria."

Figure 13.32: ISO 31000:2009—Risk Control Efficiency and Effectiveness

ISO 31000:2009 (Clause 5.4.2): "Risk Identification: Risk identification should include examination of the knock-on effect of particular consequences, including cascade and cumulative effects. It is necessary to consider possible causes and scenario that show what consequence can occur."
Tornado Chart
Single Variable Distributional Fitting
Statistical Summary
Theoretical vs. Empirical Distribution

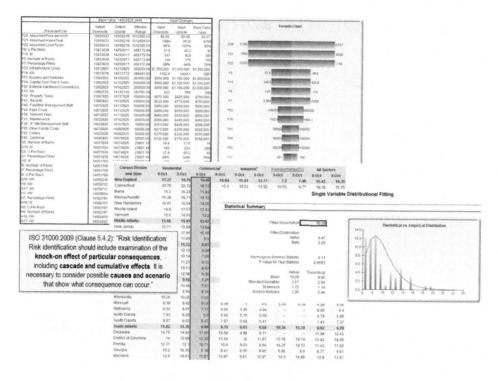

Figure 13.33: ISO 31000:2009—Consequences, Cascades, and Scenarios

Management Dashboards

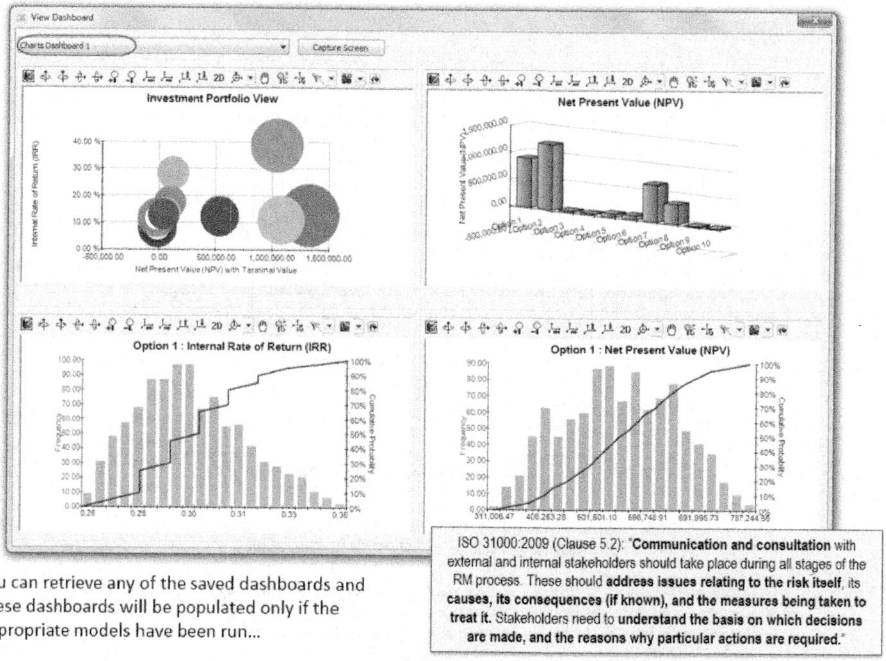

View Dashboard
Charts Dashboard 1
Capture Screen
Investment Portfolio View
Internal Rate of Return (IRR)
Net Present Value (NPV) with Terminal Value
Net Present Value (NPV)
Option 1 : Internal Rate of Return (IRR)
Option 1 : Net Present Value (NPV)
Frequency
Cumulative Probability
ISO 31000:2009 (Clause 5.2): "Communication and consultation with external and internal stakeholders should take place during all stages of the RM process. These should address issues relating to the risk itself, its causes, its consequences (if known), and the measures being taken to treat it. Stakeholders need to understand the basis on which decisions are made, and the reasons why particular actions are required."
You can retrieve any of the saved dashboards and these dashboards will be populated only if the appropriate models have been run...

Figure 13.34: ISO 31000:2009—Communication and Consultation

COMPLIANCE WITH BASEL II AND BASEL III FRAMEWORK

The following provides a quick summary of Basel II and Basel III compliance when using the IRM methodology:

- Figure 13.35 shows Monte Carlo risk simulations applied to determine confidence levels, percentiles, and probabilities of occurrence using historically fitted data or forecast expectations. These methods are in line with Basel II and Basel III requirements Sections 16 and 161 concerning the use of historical simulations, Monte Carlo simulations, and 99th percentile confidence intervals. See Chapters 4 and 5 for more details on simulations and data fitting techniques.

- Figure 13.36 shows a correlated simulation of a portfolio of assets and liabilities, where asset returns are correlated against one another in a portfolio and optimization routines were run on the simulated results. These processes provide compliance with Basel II and Basel III requirements Sections 178, 232, and 527(f) involving correlations, Value at Risk (VaR) models, portfolios of segments, and pooled exposures (assets and liabilities). See Chapter 4 for correlated simulations and *Modeling Risk's* Chapter 7's case study on Basel II and Basel III Credit, Market, Operational, and Liquidity Risks with Asset Liability Management for details on how VaR models are computed based on historical simulation results.

- Figure 13.37 shows Value at Risk percentile and confidence calculations using structural models and simulation results that are in line with Basel II and Basel III requirements Sections 179, 527(c), and 527(f). As noted above, see *Modeling Risk's* Chapter 7's case study for details on how VaR models are computed based on historical simulation results.

- Figure 13.38 shows the computations of probability of default (PD) as required in the Basel Accords, specifically Basel II and Basel III Section 733 and Annex 2's Section 16. PD can be computed using structural models or based on historical data through running basic ratios to more advanced binary logistic models. Chapter 7's case study as well as Chapter 14's Credit and Market Risk case study in *Modeling Risk* provide more insights into how PD can be computed using these various methods.

- Figure 13.39 shows the simulation and generation of interest rate yield curves using Risk Simulator and Modeling Toolkit models. These methods are in line with Basel II and Basel III requirements Section 763 requiring the analysis of interest rate fluctuations and interest rate shocks.

- Figure 13.40 shows additional models for volatile interest rates, financial markets, and other liquid instruments' instantaneous shocks using Risk Simulator's stochastic process models. These analyses conform to Basel II and Basel III requirements Sections 155, 527(a), and 527(b).

- Figure 13.41 shows several forecast models with high predictive and analytical power, which is a part of the Risk Simulator family of forecast methods. Such modeling provides compliance with Basel II and Basel III requirements Section 417 requiring models of good predictive power.

- Figure 13.42 shows the list of financial and credit models available in the ROV Modeling Toolkit and ROV Real Options SLS software applications. These models conform to Basel II and Basel III requirements Sections 112, 203, and 527(e) requiring the ability to value and model over-the-counter (OTC) derivatives, nonlinear equity derivatives and convertibles, hedges, and embedded options.

- Figure 13.43 shows the modeling of foreign exchange instruments and hedges to determine the efficacy and effectiveness of foreign exchange hedging vehicles and their impact on valuation, portfolio profitability, and VaR, in line with Basel II and Basel III Sections 131 and 155 requiring the analysis of different currencies, correlations, volatility, and hedges.

- Figure 13.44 shows the option-adjusted spread (OAS), credit default swaps (CDS), and credit spread options (CSO) models in ROV Modeling Toolkit. These models provide compliance with Basel II and Basel III requirements Sections 140 and 713 pertaining to modeling and valuing credit derivatives and credit hedges.

(*Text continues on page 584.*)

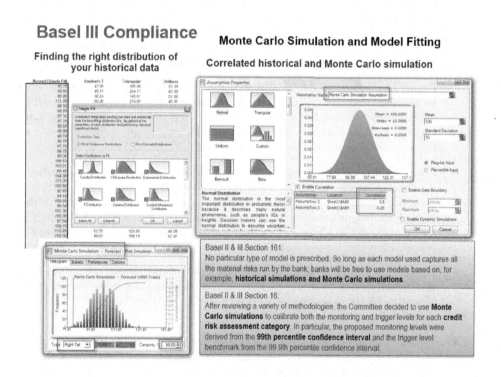

Figure 13.35: Basel II and Basel III Confidence Levels, Monte Carlo Simulations, and Credit Risk

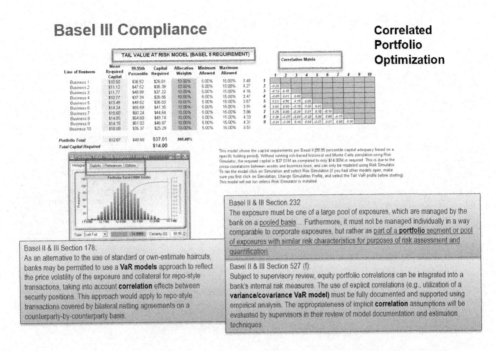

Figure 13.36: Basel II and Basel III Correlated Portfolios and Correlated Simulations

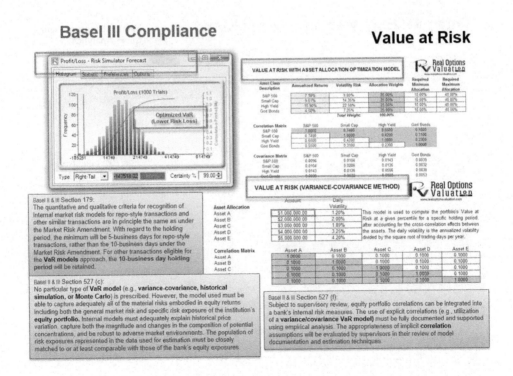

Figure 13.37: Basel II and Basel III Value at Risk and Percentiles

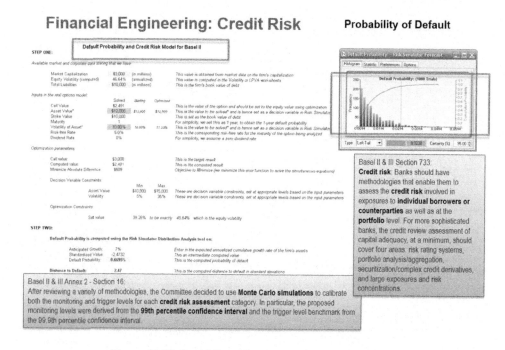

Figure 13.38: Basel II and Basel III Credit Risk Analysis

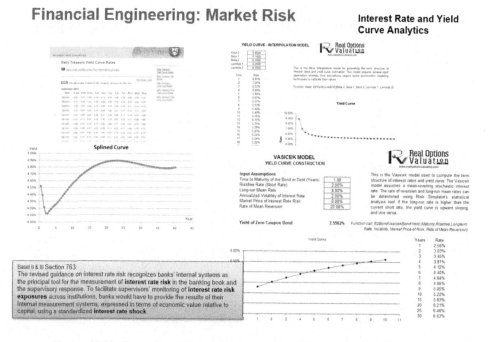

Figure 13.39: Basel II and Basel III Interest Rate Risk and Market Shocks

Financial Engineering: Market Risk

- ARIMA
- GARCH Volatility
- Brownian Motion Random Walk
- Cubic Spline Yield Curves
- Implied Yield Curves from Debt
- Mean-Reverting Interest Rates
- Jump-Diffusion Prices
- Mixed Stochastic Processes
- Time-Series Decomposition

Stochastic Forecasting

Basel II & III Section 527 (a) and (b):
The capital charge is equivalent to the **potential loss** on the institution's equity portfolio arising from an assumed **instantaneous shock** equivalent to the 99th percentile, one-tailed confidence interval of the difference between quarterly returns and an appropriate risk-free rate computed over a long-term sample period. The **estimated losses** should be robust to **adverse market movements** relevant to the long-term risk profile of the institution's specific holdings.

Basel II & III Section 155:
Banks must **estimate the volatility** of the collateral instrument or foreign exchange mismatch individually: estimated volatilities for each transaction must not take into account the **correlations** between unsecured exposure, collateral and **exchange rates.**

Figure 13.40: Basel II and Basel III Volatility and Adverse Instantaneous Shocks

Data and Relationship Modeling

Econometric Analysis –
ARIMA, Regressions, GARCH

Modeling and forecasting cross-sectional, time-series, and mixed panel data, and applications of volatility forecasts

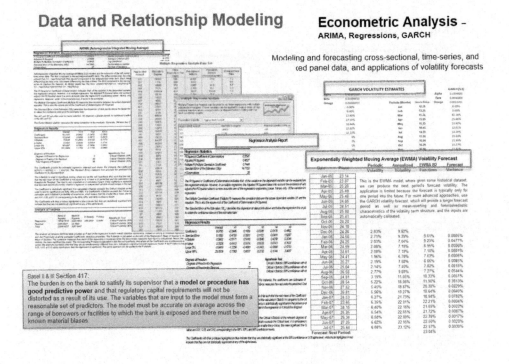

Basel II & III Section 417:
The burden is on the bank to satisfy its supervisor that a **model or procedure has good predictive power** and that regulatory capital requirements will not be distorted as a result of its use. The variables that are input to the model must form a reasonable set of predictors. The model must be accurate on average across the range of borrowers or facilities to which the bank is exposed and there must be no known material biases.

Figure 13.41: Basel II and Basel III Forecast Models with Strong Predictive Power

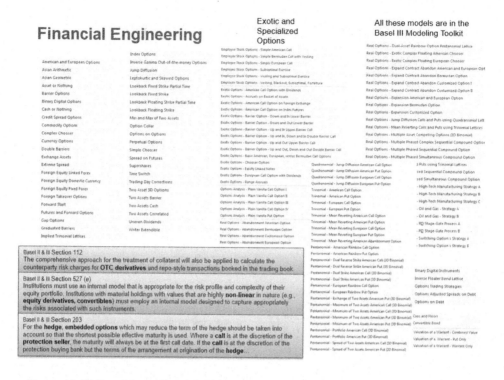

Figure 13.42: Basel II and Basel III Modeling OTC Derivatives and Exotic Convertibles

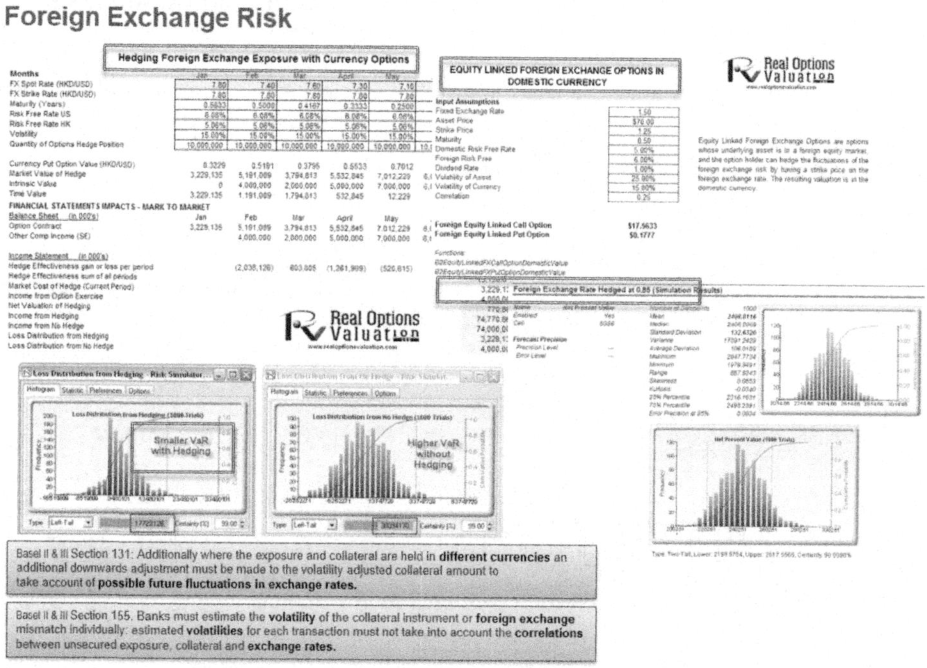

Foreign Exchange Risk

Figure 13.43: Basel II and Basel III Modeling Foreign Exchange Fluctuations

Credit Derivatives

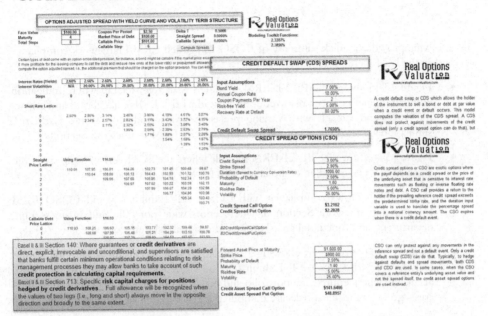

Figure 13.44: Basel II and Basel III Credit Derivatives and Hedging

COMPLIANCE WITH COSO
INTEGRATED RISK FRAMEWORK

The following provides a quick summary of COSO Integrated ERM Framework compliance when using the IRM methodology:

- Figure 13.45 shows the PEAT ERM module's Risk Register tab where mitigation costs and benefits (gross risks reduced to residual risk levels), likelihood and impact measures, and spreads with varying precision levels ready for Monte Carlo risk simulation are situated, in compliance with COSO ERM Framework Sections 5 & 6.

- Figure 13.46 shows the PEAT ERM module where the likelihood and impact within a risk map is generated, in compliance with COSO AT/Exhibit 5.13.

- Figure 13.47 shows compliance with COSO AT/Exhibit 6.5 and COSO ERM Integrated Framework Section 6, where entity-wide portfolio and business unit, department, and functional areas' gross and residual risks are computed.

- Figure 13.48 continues by showing a sample of the Risk Dashboard reports also in compliance with COSO AT/Exhibit 6.5 and COSO ERM Integrated Framework Section 6, where entity-wide portfolio and business unit, department, and functional areas' gross and residual risks are computed and compared against each other.

- Figure 13.49 shows the PEAT DCF module's efficient frontier model, consistent with COSO AT/Exhibit 3.7 requiring an analysis of the capital investment in relation to the returns within a diversified (optimized) portfolio.

- Figure 13.50 shows the PEAT ERM and DCF module's simulated results, where Value at Risk, percentiles, and statistical probabilities can be obtained, in compliance with COSO AT/Exhibit 5.5 requiring a range of outcomes based on distributional assumptions, and COSO ERM Integrated Framework Exhibit 5.2 requiring historical or simulated outcomes of future behaviors under probabilistic models.

- Figure 13.51 shows compliance with COSO AT/Exhibit 3.1 requiring the use of scenario modeling and stress testing.

- Figure 13.52 shows the CMOL module in PEAT where scenario analysis, stress testing, and gap analysis are performed, in compliance with COSO AT/Exhibit 5.10, to complement probabilistic models.

- Figure 13.53 shows compliance with COSO AT/Exhibits 5.8 & 5.9 requiring the modeling of operational and credit loss distributions with back-testing or historical simulation, sensitivity analysis, and Value at Risk calculations.

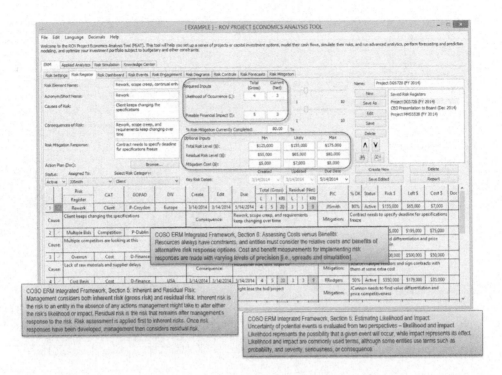

Figure 13.45: PEAT ERM and COSO Integrated Framework

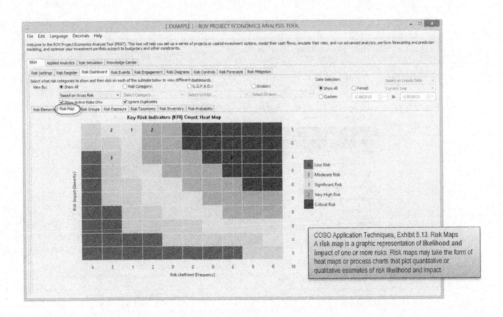

Figure 13.46: PEAT ERM Heat Map and Risk Matrix

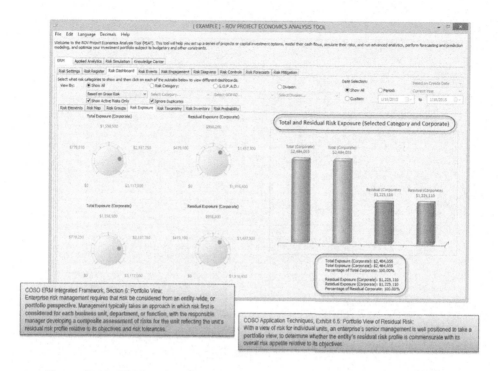

Figure 13.47: PEAT ERM Corporate Portfolio View of Gross and Residual Risk

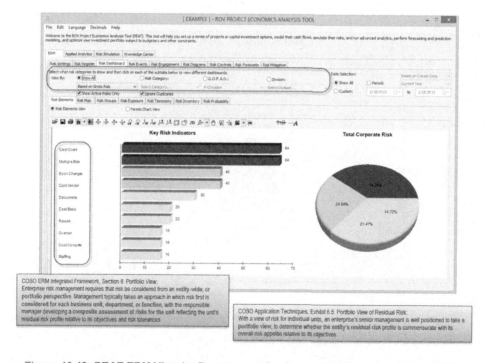

Figure 13.48: PEAT ERM View by Department, Business Unit, Function, and Portfolio

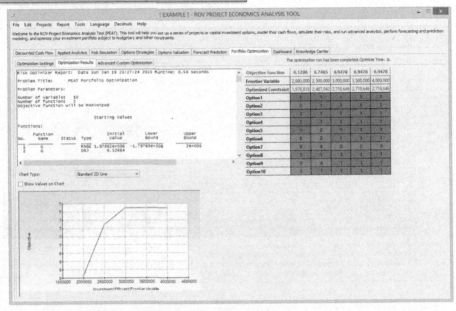

Figure 13.49: PEAT DCF Module's Portfolio Optimization and Efficient Frontier

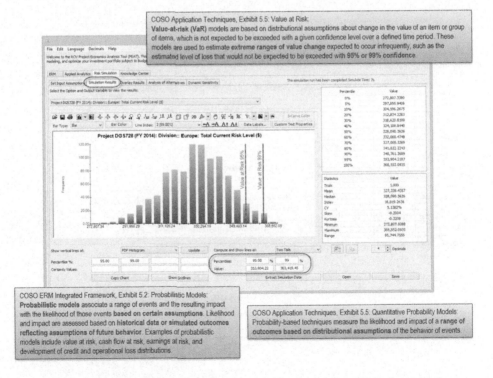

Figure 13.50: PEAT ERM & DCF Module's Risk Simulation and Value at Risk

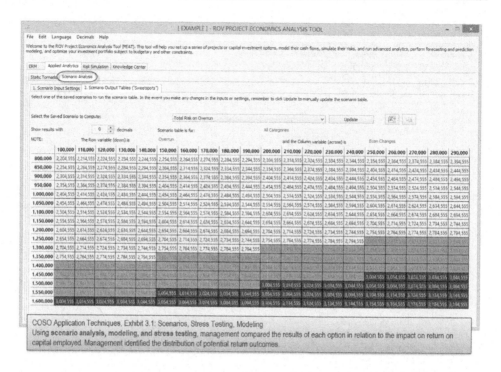

Figure 13.51: PEAT ERM & DCF Module's Scenario Analysis and Heat Map Regions

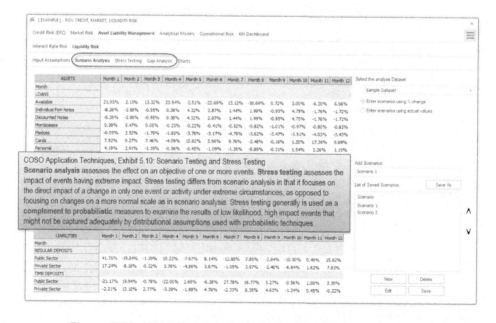

Figure 13.52: CMOL Module's Scenario Analysis and Stress Testing

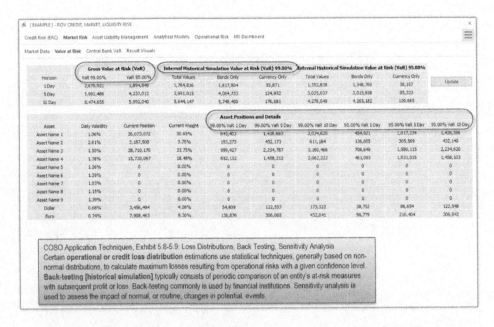

Figure 13.53: CMOL Module's Value at Risk and Back-Testing Historical Simulations

CHAPTER 14 – CHANGING A CORPORATE CULTURE

HOW TO GET RISK ANALYSIS ACCEPTED IN AN ORGANIZATION

Advanced analytics are hard to explain to management.[63] So, how do you get risk analysis accepted as the norm in a corporation, especially if your industry is highly conservative? It is almost a guarantee in conservative companies that an analyst showing senior management a series of fancy, mathematically complex, and computationally sophisticated models will be thrown out of the office together with his or her results and have the door slammed in his or her face. Changing management's thinking is the topic of discussion in this chapter. Explaining results and convincing management appropriately go hand in hand with the characteristics of the advanced analytical tools, which if they satisfy certain change-management requisites, the level and chances of acceptance become easier.

CHANGE-MANAGEMENT ISSUES AND PARADIGM SHIFTS

Change-management specialists have found that there are several criteria to be met before a paradigm shift in thinking is found to be acceptable in a corporation. For example, in order for senior management to accept a new and novel set of advanced analytical approaches—simulation, forecasting, real options, and portfolio optimization—the models and processes themselves must have applicability to the problem at hand and not merely be an academic exercise.[64] Figure 14.1 lists the criteria required for change.

As we saw previously, it is certainly true that large multinationals have embraced the concept of risk analysis with significant fervor and that risk analysis is here to stay.[65] It is not simply an academic exercise, nor is it the latest financial analysis fad that is here today and gone tomorrow. In addition, the process and methodology have to be consistent, accurate, and replicable, that is, they pass the scientific process. Given similar assumptions, historical data and assertions, one can replicate the results with ease and predictability. This replicability is especially true with the use of software programs described in this book.

Changing a Corporate Culture
"No change of paradigm comes quickly"

Criteria for instituting change:

- Method Applicability
  - Not just an academic exercise
- Accurate, Consistent, and Replicable
  - Creates a standard for decision making
- Value-added Propositions
  - Competitive advantage over competitors
  - Provide valuable insights otherwise unavailable
- Exposition
  - Making the black box transparent
  - Explaining the value to senior management
- Comparative Advantage
  - Better method than the old
  - It takes a good theory to kill an old one
- Compatibility With Old Approach
  - Based on the old with significant improvements
- Flexibility
  - Able to be tweaked
  - Covers a multitude of problems
- External Influences
- From "Main Street" to "Wall Street"
- Communicating to the investment community the value created internally

Figure 14.1: Changing a Corporate Culture

Next, the new method must provide a compelling value-added proposition. Otherwise, it is nothing but a fruitless and time-consuming exercise. The time, resources, and effort spent must be met and even surpassed by the method's added value. This added value is certainly the case in larger capital investment initiatives, where a firm's future or the future of a business unit may be at stake—incorrect and insufficient results may be obtained, and disastrous decisions made if risk analysis is not undertaken.

Other major criteria include the ability to provide the user a comparative advantage over its competitors, which is certainly the case when the additional valuable insights generated through advanced risk analysis will help management identify options, value, prioritize, and select strategic and less risky alternatives that may otherwise be overlooked.

Finally, in order to accept a change in mind-set, the new methodology, analysis, process, or model must be easy to explain and understand. In addition, there has to be a link to previously accepted methods, whether the new methodology is an extension of the old or a replacement of the old due to some clear superior attributes. These last two points are the most difficult to tackle for an analyst. The sets of criteria prior to this are direct and easy to define.

The new set of risk analytics is nothing but an extension of existing methodologies.[66] For instance, Monte Carlo simulation can be explained simply as scenario analysis applied to the nth degree. Simulation is nothing but scenario analysis done thousands of times but not just on a single variable (e.g., the three common scenarios: good economy, average economy, and bad economy complete with their associated probabilities of occurrence and payoffs at each state), but on multiple variables interacting simultaneously, where multiple variables are changing independently or dependently, in a correlated or uncorrelated fashion (e.g., competition, economy, market share, technological efficacy, and so forth). In fact, the results stemming from new analytics is simply a logical extension of the traditional approaches. For instance, Figure 14.2 illustrates this logical extension.

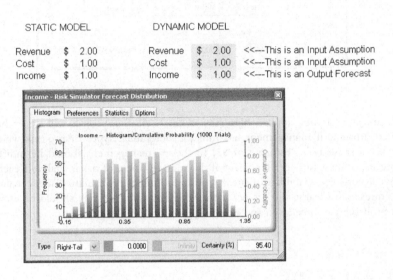

Figure 14.2: Monte Carlo Simulation as a Logical Extension of Traditional Analysis

The static model in the illustration shows a revenue value of $2, cost of $1, and the resulting income value, calculated as the difference between the two, is $1. Compare that to the dynamic model, where the same inputs are used but the revenue and cost variables have been subjected to Monte Carlo simulation. Once simulation has been completed, the dynamic model still shows the same single-point estimate of $1 as in the static model. In other words, adding in the more advanced analytics, namely Monte Carlo simulation, the model or results have not changed. If management still wants the single-point estimate of $1 reported, then so be it. However, by logical extension, if both revenues and costs are uncertain, then by definition, the resulting income will also be uncertain. The forecast chart for the income variable shows this uncertainty of the resulting income with fluctuations around $1. In fact, additional valuable information is obtained using simulation, where the probability or certainty of breakeven or exceeding $0 in income is shown as 95.40 percent in Figure 14.2. In addition, rather than relying on the single-point estimate of $1, simulation reveals that the business only has 8.90 percent probability of exceeding the single-point estimate of $1 in income (Figure 14.3).

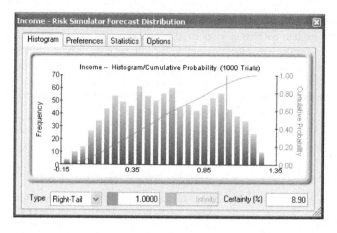

Figure 14.3: Probability of Exceeding the Original $1 Income

If simulation is not applied here, the riskiness of this project will never be clearly elucidated. Imagine if management has multiple but similar types of projects where every project has a single-point estimate of $1. In theory, management should be indifferent in choosing any of these projects. However, if the added element of risk is analyzed, each project may have different probabilities of breakeven and different probabilities of exceeding the $1 income threshold. Clearly, the project with the least amount of risk should be chosen (i.e., highest probability of breakeven and exceeding the threshold value).

MAKING TOMORROW'S FORECAST TODAY

Firms that are initially skeptical about applying advanced analytics in their decision-making activities should always consider first applying these new rules to smaller projects. Instead of biting off too much immediately, a small-scale project is always preferable. Companies new to advanced risk analytics should first learn to crawl before they start running and head straight for the wall. If management can be eased into the new analytical paradigm slowly, the transition will be more palatable.

Having a vision to change the entire organization's decision-making processes overnight is very admirable but will be very short-lived and bound for disaster. Before an organization can learn to make tomorrow's forecast today, it has to learn from the lessons of yesterday. One approach is to look at high-profile projects in the past. Instead of starting with forecasting, perform some backcasting first. Instead of waiting for years to verify if the results from the analysis were actually correct or valuable, the results from a backcasting analysis is almost immediate. If the analyst is true to himself or herself, using the actual data coupled with the assumptions used in the past (without the advantage of hindsight), the new analytical results can then be compared to the decisions that were made to see if different strategies and decisions would have been undertaken instead. However, care should be taken as corporate politics come into play because the individuals who made the decisions in the past may not take it too kindly when their decisions are negatively scrutinized.

No matter the strategy moving forward, one thing is certain. If senior management buys into the techniques, acceptance would be imminent. Otherwise, a few junior analysts in a cubicle somewhere trying to get management's attention will fail miserably. In retrospect, a midlevel manager trying to impress his or her superiors without the adequate knowledge and support from analysts will not work either.

The approach for successful implementation has to be comprehensive and three pronged. Senior management must keep an open mind to alternatives. Middle management must keep championing the approach and not let minor setbacks be permanent, while attempting to be the conduit of information between the junior analysts and senior management. Finally, analysts should attempt to acquire as much knowledge about the techniques and applications as possible. The worst possible outcome is where extreme expectations are set from high above and the powers that be, while the lower rungs cannot deliver the goods as required.

> In order to facilitate adoption of a new set of analytical methods in an organization, several criteria must first be met. To judge the level of potential adoption, the following questions should be asked, including whether the method is applicable to the problem at hand, how accurate, consistent and replicable are the methods, what are the value-added propositions, what is the level of expositional ease, what are the comparative advantages, how compatible is the new method to the old models, how flexible is the new method, and what are some of the external influences in using the methods.

PARTING SHOTS AND A WORD OF CAUTION FROM THE AUTHOR

I sincerely hope that you have enjoyed this book. Modeling risk is clearly a hard and sometimes dry and difficult subject, but I hope that I was successful in making the concepts clearer and simpler to understand. As a professor, my ultimate goal is knowledge transmission, and as a consultant, it is to show and teach you things that are applicable so you can hit the ground running. And as a software developer, it is to create a tool that is super-powerful yet super-simple to use and completely applicable across multiple domains and industries. I hope that I am successful on all counts.

So what now? You spent weeks going through this book, had a few laughs along the way, and learned a new thing or two. How do you take this experience back to your workplace? How do you present this risk analysis approach to someone new to the topic or, worse, to senior management? Here are some suggestions based on some things that the author has been successful with in past consulting engagements and teaching activities, especially if it concerns senior-level management:

- **Practice Makes Perfect**. This adage is true of almost everything in life. Make sure you understand the theory and practice of these risk analysis methods. You really do not want to demonstrate the software, methodology, and applications and be questioned beyond your ability to answer intelligently. Be well-versed and be well-prepared before you broach this topic at work.

- **Low Hanging Fruits**. The proverbial advice to "not bite off more than you can chew" is apropos here. Do not hit the ground running by analyzing the highest priority, largest, and most cumbersome project in the entire company. Do so only if you are truly well-trained and well-versed in all of the risk concepts. Rather, look for some low-hanging fruits: projects that are simple to tackle, less convoluted, and having clear risks, clear portfolio optimization requirements, sufficient data to run distributional fitting on, well-behaved to run forecast approaches on, very clear strategic options, and so forth.

- **Executive Summary**. Using the low-hanging fruits approach, create a two-page executive summary—executives are super busy or get distracted easily, while some are just scared of learning new things, and when reviewing technical stuff they do not really understand, have the attention span of a two-year-old—which just means a single sheet of paper on both sides. Start with the basics such as an introduction to the problem being solved, some basic traditional single-point analysis, and then jump into basic risk analysis methodologies such as a tornado analysis (it is easy enough to run and to describe), a scenario analysis table, perhaps a few three-point high-medium-low triangular distributions (clearly avoid the beta, gamma, or hypergeometric world for now). Then run a simulation and show the forecast chart, with some basic things such as probability of exceeding a certain value, or worst-case scenario Value at Risk, and so forth. You get the idea. By following this approach, you slowly but concretely show the applicability of risk analysis, without all the jargon and at the same time using the company's own projects and terminology. This sort of a summary will go a long way. Do several of these, and preferably across different divisions and departments, showing that these methods are not confined and limited to the finance and strategy department, but are also applicable to the quality control Six Sigma guys down the hall, to marketing strategy and pricing, to research and development, and so forth. And being that it is only two pages (and half of that is occupied by Risk Simulator generated charts and tables anyway), it is simple to do and more likely that senior management will actually review it.

- **Senior Level Buy-In: Elevator Pitch and Keep It Simple, Stupid**. You get the idea. Create your own elevator pitch. What I mean is that you go back to work tomorrow and you run into the chairman of the board, the big cheese himself, walking into the elevator. He says hello and pretends to know your name, but he's a really nice guy, or so you hope. He looks over and asks what you are currently working on. You hastily answer, "modeling risk." There is a moment of silence and you are kicking yourself for saying that. Then the big guy asks you for more specific details, and, of course, the elevator door closes. You have exactly 30 seconds to explain to him what Integrated Risk Management is and why he should care. Remember, this is the chairman of the board, not a mathematician or financial analyst. The moment you use words such as stochastic, heteroskedasticity, multicollinearity, mean-reversion with jump-diffusion, or kurtosis, he will press the emergency button and toss you out of the elevator! So, what should you say? You should say something like, "Risk is a very important issue that our firm has not really spent too much time on, especially in the current economic situation… in fact, our competitors, X and Y are doing these types of analysis, and it can potentially save us millions of dollars by seeing how to better forecast and allocate our resources to generate a better portfolio of products and services that will reduce our risks, identify optimal pricing points, increase our bottom line," and so forth. He will probably be excited and interested as you have hit enough key points of interest, and you may find yourself riding the elevator to the top floor much more often!

- **Knowledge Is Power**. And just like riding a bicycle, practice makes perfect. Try taking some seminars and training classes on quantitative risk analysis. A highly recommended seminar would be the weeklong CQRM, or Certified Quantitative Risk Management, certification program. See *www.realoptionsvaluation.com* for more details on this program. Participating in the program allows you to interact with the instructors and other participants as well as forces you to spend an entire week in a classroom and computer lab working on projects, problems, and exercises, and listening to real-life case studies and applications. Having read the book, you would be very well prepared, and hedged your risks, for the class and the certification exam if you choose to do so. Also, visit aforementioned website for additional free training videos, case studies, white papers, and applications of risk analysis.

The following are best practices in risk management for organizations from multinational corporations and banks to the U.S. military, and are based on many years of experience consulting for these firms and implementing risk analysis within these organizations:

- **Senior Management Support.** This is vital for success of any Integrated Risk Management implementation within a firm, as without senior management support, this effort will not take root and will fail before it even starts.

- **Senior Management's High-Level Training.** Senior management needs to be trained in at least a half-day session in terms of understanding the key elements of risk management, how it works within organizations, and what it can do, and to explore multiple business cases at various multinational organizations, both successes and failures. The outcome of this training is the ability to quickly identify what projects might be a best fit for these types of advanced risk management techniques, as well as how to interpret the results and make strategic decisions based on the results.

- **Mandate from Senior Management.** Mandates and standardized rules for certain decision processes in the company are required. For instance, any projects over US$10 million will need a business case justification, and within that business case, certain elements must always exist, such as a tornado sensitivity analysis (which identifies the critical and key success factors within a project, the bottlenecks, and the risks), and each of these identified critical factors will need to be subject to some basic simulation by using ranges as inputs instead of single-point estimates.

- **Middle Management Training.** Typically, when the author performs this training, it is a two-day hands-on computer-based training with business cases illustrating how decisions are made under uncertainty and risk. Middle management needs to understand more than senior management, as their job is to interpret the results for senior management while at the same time be able to take charge and manage the more junior analysts.

- **Analyst Detailed Training.** This is typically a five-day weeklong detailed computer-based hands-on **CQRM** training where analysts are subject to a barrage of hands-on modeling and case study analysis.

- **A Culture of Learning.** The most successful organizations are those interested in change and willing to learn and adapt. The Integrated Risk Management techniques are detailed, vast, and varied, and certainly there are aspects that are useful to all organizations and other aspects that may be less useful to one organization but more useful to another. Without the exposure and culture of embracing learning and change, it would be very difficult to make these risk management techniques successful in a company.

- **A Standardized Language of Risk.** By implementing training sessions for all three levels (senior management, middle management, and junior staff), everyone will have a standardized language or lingo. For example, when the term simulation is used, everyone will understand what it means, what it is used for, and why it is required.

- **Standardized Toolset.** To support the decision process, standardized toolsets such as Risk Simulator are a required software application for each person in the organization. This allows interchangeable and group collaboration on strategic decisions, where one staff member can replicate and run another's models and come to the same conclusions.

- **A Centralized Strategic Risk Team.** This team ideally reports indirectly or directly to the chief financial officer or president of the company so that it has exposure and credibility, and the members of the team are hand-picked from the entire organization for their thought leadership and analytical capabilities. These individuals need to be properly trained in Integrated Risk Management, have experience implementing at least several projects, and make up the core of the strategic risk team. The purpose of this team is to provide advice to all analysts in the organization, a gatekeeper or guardian of decision risk analytics, the go-to persons in the organization, and the people who will approve the business cases submitted over a certain threshold based on the mandate from senior management. In other words, they are the gatekeepers in a stage-gate development and investment process, whereby a business case justification or proposal and request for investment will never reach senior management's offices without first passing through this centralized team.

- **Work Cross-Functionally.** Strategic risk management should never be confined to one department or business unit. That is, risk management is not the responsibility of just a financial or sales and marketing department. Instead, most projects within an organization are cross-functional and involve multiple staff members from various departments and divisions. This cross-functional team provides better subject matter experts and creates a diverse and rich view of the decisions and risks.

- **Nothing Beats Hands-On Experience.** Never fully rely on consultants alone. Analysts and staff in an organization need to learn how certain risk management projects are executed, analyzed, and modeled. This provides the organization better control over the decisions and reliability of the inputs, and allows the process to be repeated.

- **Portfolio View.** The entire organization should be viewed as a portfolio and each project or major decision should be viewed in the same way, on how it impacts the organization as a whole. For instance, certain projects that may seem unprofitable may actually be very profitable and strategic if viewed in a portfolio sense (e.g., options to expand, platform technology that can be used to springboard into other more profitable areas later on, sequential stage-gate options of a multiple phased investment or development).

A Word on Closed-form Partial Differential Equations: They Do Not Work!

It would be a major disservice to the reader if I do not include something about my consulting experience and to point out some potential landmines in the road ahead in terms of actual applications and consulting implementations. At the time of writing, I have had successfully trained and consulted more than 300 corporations around the world these past two decades in terms of applying advanced analytics and real options analysis, but this was not always the case. The key takeaway and advice I can offer any reader is how you would approach these methods in a company:

- Avoid showing or using advanced equations, models and functions

- Avoid any references to advanced terminology

- Show how simple things are to understand

Let us face it, C-level executives and senior management of large corporations are usually not mathematical or technical and showing them a series of advanced closed-form partial differential equations will scare them off, piss them off, or turn them off. Regardless of how accurate and well thought out the models might be, or even how correct they are, showing a series of fancy equations and models is not appropriate, and asking executives for buy-in into the results is a battle not worth fighting for because you will never win. There are several reasons for this:

- First, *you* would have a hard time *explaining* and using these advanced models correctly. Take a look at some sample *basic* closed-form and partial differential equations in the next few pages. How many people actually know what a *Sup* function means or how to solve a recursive model using the Newton–Raphson algorithm? If you write these things out and show them to a senior decision maker, his or her eyes will glaze over and completely and immediately marginalize all your efforts as purely academic and not applicable to the business at hand.

- Second, speaking of iterative processes, you would have a hard time *solving* these equations. Again, look at some of the sample basic equations in the next few pages. The first set is for a closed-form American call option approximation, and the second is a closed-form equation for a basic European chooser option. Neither of these basic option models can be solved using an Excel spreadsheet. More advanced programming knowledge and mathematics are required. Therefore, how sure are you that you can obtain a solution, and if so, is it correct?

- Third, the models are never always perfect or appropriate and always require customization. Okay, that's putting it in a politically correct way. In reality, most of these fancy closed-form partial differential equations are completely useless in any real-life context. For example, take a look at the next few pages and review the part on optimal trigger values. From an initial inspection, this looks like a great idea, and in fact, it really is, to identify when it might be appropriate to invest in a risky project. But if you start looking at the assumptions and inputs that go into the model, you will see that it is theoretically elegant but practically useless. The creators will get these models published in academic journal articles and get the requisite points for promotion and tenure at a university but the circle of influence is limited to academics, researchers, and professors. Notice that in the entire equation development, deciding on whether to invest in a multimillion dollar project depends only on two things, profits and cost. What about competition, uncertainty, risks, market reaction, co-opetition strategies, product and market success, geographical location, related product types, contractual structures, negotiated terms, and a million other assumptions? All these have been assumed away, and this generic model is then presented for use in all cases. This is complete garbage. Every company is unique, and every project in a company is unique. Using a single generic model and applying it to every situation will mean that you are taking the company's constraints and decisions and squeezing them into a black-box. Any analyst presenting such an analysis and any decision-maker accepting such analysis should be terminated immediately. Instead, a model should take on its namesake, to model real-life, and not the other way around by changing real-life and assuming things away in order to stick the real-life into a predetermined or canned model.

- In order to replicate and model a company's real-life situations using closed-form equations, well, you will need a double doctorate in mathematics and finance in order to properly *customize* the model for use. For example, in the simple closed-form American option model illustrated in the following pages, if you wish to change any of the inputs (e.g., making it variable in time by taking a derivative with respect to time, for example, $\delta X/\delta t$) or adding a new variable, and so forth, you will need to re-solve the equation from scratch, and the mathematics is fairly daunting. In fact, regular calculus is insufficient, as these models incorporate a stochastic property (e.g., the phi Φ function is a standard-normal cumulative distribution function, and solving it requires facility with stochastic calculus such as using Ito's Lemma, and so forth). No wonder Myron Scholes and Robert Merton won the Nobel Prize for their work in developing the Black–Scholes–Merton model, and the Black–Scholes–Merton model is pretty much the most basic closed-form European call and put option model there is. Good luck to the general analyst in trying to do this.

Another key takeaway is how you would introduce these advanced analytics at your company or client site. Whenever I broach the subject of advanced analytics contained in this book, I use *simple* terminologies, avoiding big words like real options, differential equations, autoregressive integrated moving average forecasts, generalized autoregressive conditional heteroskedasticity models, and the like. Instead, I use terms like uncertainty and risk, things can go up or down, or basic words like forecasts or seasonality. It really does not matter what method you use when you close your office door and do the number crunching, but the moment you use terminology foreign to the decision maker, you might very well get thrown out of the board room and have the door slammed in your face so fast your head will spin! Are you saying that a board room filled with seasoned senior management types with decades of experience, who are quite brilliant and successful at what they do (at least we assume so, otherwise they would not hold the position they do), cannot make a decision and you, a young whippersnapper analyst/consultant, with very little exposure in the specific industry, comes in with some black-box advanced analytical models and tell them how they should run their business? You get the picture, and it is not pretty. So, my advice is to keep it simple! Use strategy trees to visualize and draw the solutions, use terms like strategic options or courses of action instead of real options, and do not show fancy equations but use things like binomial lattices with up and down branches. Now, you might think I am biased toward lattices, and you are indeed correct, because I have found them to work... Analytically, in Risk Simulator, PEAT, Real Options SLS, ROV Modeling Toolkit and other software applications I created, there are more than 1,000 models and functions, and most of them are advanced closed-form partial differential equations, and I would not have bothered doing them unless there is value, but for the purposes of consulting and presentations, avoid them like the plague!

Sample Closed-Form Differential Equations

The following is a sample portion of an American closed-form approximation model using an iterative algorithm:

$$C(S,X,T) = Sup(C + \psi (S/S')^q, S - X)^+$$

$$\psi = (1 - e^{(b-r)T})\Phi\left[\frac{\ln(S/X) + (b + \sigma^2/2)T}{\sigma\sqrt{T}}\right](S'))(S'/q)$$

$$q = \frac{N + 1 + \sqrt{(N^2 + N + 8r/(1 - e^{-rT})\sigma^2 + 1}}{2}$$

S' is solved using the Newton-Raphson algorithm

The following is a sample closed-form model for a European chooser option. First, solve recursively for the critical I value as below:

$$0 = Ie^{-q(T_C-t)}\Phi\left[\frac{\ln(I/X_C)+(r-q+\sigma^2/2)(T_C-t)}{\sigma\sqrt{T_C-t}}\right]$$

$$-X_C e^{-r(T_C-t)}\Phi\left[\frac{\ln(I/X_C)+(r-q+\sigma^2/2)(T_C-t)}{\sigma\sqrt{T_C-t}}-\sigma\sqrt{T_C-t}\right]$$

$$+Ie^{-q(T_P-t)}\Phi\left[\frac{-\ln(I/X_P)+(q-r-\sigma^2/2)(T_P-t)}{\sigma\sqrt{T_P-t}}\right]$$

$$-X_P e^{-r(T_P-t)}\Phi\left[\frac{-\ln(I/X_P)+(q-r-\sigma^2/2)(T_P-t)}{\sigma\sqrt{T_P-t}}+\sigma\sqrt{T_P-t}\right]$$

Then using the I value, calculate

$$d_1 = \frac{\ln(S/I)+(r-q+\sigma^2/2)t}{\sigma\sqrt{t}} \quad \text{and} \quad d_2 = d_1-\sigma\sqrt{t}$$

$$y_1 = \frac{\ln(S/X_C)+(r-q+\sigma^2/2)T_C}{\sigma\sqrt{T_C}} \quad \text{and} \quad y_2 = \frac{\ln(S/X_P)+(r-q+\sigma^2/2)T_P}{\sigma\sqrt{T_P}}$$

$$\rho_1 = \sqrt{t/T_C} \quad \text{and} \quad \rho_2 = \sqrt{t/T_P}$$

$$Option\ Value = Se^{-qT_C}\Omega(d_1;y_1;\rho_1) - X_C e^{-rT_C}\Omega(d_2;y_1-\sigma\sqrt{T_C};\rho_1)$$

$$-Se^{-qT_P}\Omega(-d_1;-y_2;\rho_2) + X_P e^{-rT_P}\Omega(-d_2;-y_2+\sigma\sqrt{T_P};\rho_2)$$

A related analysis is that of *optimal trigger values*. This analysis is adapted from Chapter 7's appendix in *Real Options Analysis*, Second Edition (Wiley Finance 2005) by Dr. Johnathan Mun. Suppose we create a generic valuation structure for an option value and add a level of complexity, the total implementation cost of an option should be discounted at a risk-free rate (r_f), as we segregate the market risk (Π_G) and private risk (TC), and the structure could be represented as

$$\Pi_{CALL} = \max\left\{[\Pi_0 - TC], \frac{p^G\left(\Pi_1^G\right)}{1+r} - \frac{TC}{1+r_f}\right\}$$

$$= \max\left\{\left[\pi_0 + \frac{E(\pi_1)}{r} - TC\right]^+, \left[\frac{p^G \pi_1^G\left(\frac{r+1}{r}\right)}{1+r} - \frac{TC}{1+r_f}\right]^+\right\}$$

This simply is to calculate the maximum value of either starting now which is represented by $[\Pi_0 - TC]$ or starting later, which is represented as $\dfrac{p^G\left(\pi_1^G\right)}{1+r} - \dfrac{TC}{1+r_f}$. Because the future starting point has been collapsed into a single static state, any starting points in the future can be approximated by the valuation of a single period in the future. Looking at the formulation for the call valuation price structure, if there is a change in total cost, i.e., the initial capital outlay, something interesting occurs. The total cost in starting now is not discounted because the outlay occurs immediately. However, if the outlay occurs in the future, the total cost will have to be discounted at the risk-free rate. Therefore, the higher the initial cost outlay, the discounting effect of starting in the future decreases the effective cost in today's dollar, hence making it more efficient to wait and defer the cost until a later time. If the cost is lower and the firm becomes more operationally efficient, it is beneficial to begin now as the value of starting now is greater than waiting. The total cost break-even point can be obtained by solving the call valuation equation above for total cost and can be represented as

$$TC^* = \left[1 - \frac{1}{(1+r_f)^n}\right]^{-1} \left[\pi_0 + \frac{E[\pi_1]}{r} - \frac{p^G \pi_1^G \left(\frac{r+1}{r}\right)}{(1+r)^n}\right]$$

If total cost of implementation exceeds TC^* above, it is optimal to wait, and if total cost does not exceed TC^*, it is beneficial to execute the option now. Remember that the optimal trigger value depends on the operational efficiency of the firm as well, because it is a dynamic equation given that the optimal trigger value depends on how much money can be saved with implementation of the Cryogenic modifications. Refer to Chapters 8 and 9 of *Real Options Analysis*, Second Edition (Wiley Finance 2005) by Dr. Johnathan Mun for details on optimal timing and optimal trigger values computed using binomial lattices.

Conclusion

You probably have no idea what was just said these past few pages, nor should you, and that is precisely the point. The bottom line: In order to get risk analytics to stick in an organization, the right approach is not to intimidate others by showing how smart you are, but to show applicability and how simple it is to apply and understand the analytics, as well as showing the added value and insights obtained in the results.

Now that you are well versed in the theory and application of Integrated Risk Management, we conclude this book with the next chapter, Chapter 15, which brings it all together in a unified modeling approach, where you can see how the process works from start to finish using the PEAT software application.

CHAPTER 15—PUTTING IT ALL TOGETHER: INTEGRATED RISK MANAGEMENT WITH PEAT

This final chapter completes a full circle and showcases a capstone analysis of a portfolio of projects that applies all of the Integrated Risk Management® (IRM) steps introduced throughout the book, starting in Chapter 1.

Before diving into the details of the portfolio project analysis, let's first review the IRM process and recap how these different techniques are related in a risk analysis and risk management context in a seamless analytical framework. The IRM framework comprises eight distinct phases of a successful and comprehensive risk analysis implementation, going from a qualitative management screening process to creating clear and concise reports for management. The process was developed by the author based on previous successful implementations of risk analysis, forecasting, real options, valuation, and optimization projects both in the consulting arena and in industry-specific problems. These phases can be performed either in isolation or together in any combinatorial sequence for a more robust integrated analysis. Although the steps presented below represent the most usual implementation path, modifications can be applied as required based on the uniqueness in the projects under analysis.

Figure 15.1 reviews the Integrated Risk Management process up close. The IRM process can be divided into the following eight simple steps:

1. *Qualitative Management Screening.* Management has to decide which projects, assets, investments, initiatives, or strategies are viable for further analysis, in accordance with the firm's mission, vision, goal, or overall business strategy. These business requirements may include market penetration strategies, competitive advantage, technical, mergers and acquisition, growth, synergistic, or globalization issues.

2. *Forecast Prediction.* Risk always pertain to the unknown future; hence, to perform IRM, future values are forecasted using time-series analysis, econometric modeling, fuzzy logic, neural networks, nonlinear extrapolation, stochastic processes, ARIMA, GARCH, multivariate regression forecasts, and others.

3. *Base Case (Net Present Value Modeling).* For each project that passes the initial qualitative screens a static base case model is created. Typically, a discounted cash flow model is used

and serves as the base case analysis where a net present value is calculated for each project, using the forecasted values in the previous step. This net present value is calculated by the traditional approach of using the forecast revenues and costs, and discounting the net of these revenues and costs at an appropriate risk-adjusted rate.

4. *Monte Carlo Risk Simulation and Risk Analytics.* Usually, a tornado sensitivity analysis is first performed on the discounted cash flow model; that is, setting the net present value as the resulting variable, we can change each of its precedent variables and note the change in the results. The uncertain key variables that drive the net present value and, hence, the decision are called critical success drivers. These critical success drivers are prime candidates for Monte Carlo risk simulation where thousands of trials of each input assumption are generated to account for all possible outcomes and scenarios that are modeled.

5. *Real Options Problem Framing.* The risk information obtained somehow needs to be converted into actionable intelligence. The first step in real options is to generate a strategic map through the process of framing the problem.

6. *Real Options Modeling and Analysis.* The present value of future cash flows for the base case discounted cash flow model is used as the initial underlying asset value in real options modeling, and risk simulation generates the required volatility inputs. Using these inputs, real options analysis is performed to obtain the projects' strategic option values.

7. *Portfolio and Resource Optimization.* If the analysis is performed on multiple projects, management should view the results as a portfolio of rolled-up projects because the projects are, in most cases, correlated with one another, and viewing them individually will not present the true picture. As firms do not only have single projects, portfolio optimization based on budgetary, resource, and schedule constraints is crucial.

8. *Reporting, Presentation, and Update Analysis.* The analysis is not complete until reports can be generated. The process should also be shown along with presentation of the results. Clear, concise, and precise explanations transform a difficult black-box set of analytics into transparent steps.

PROJECT ECONOMICS ANALYSIS TOOL (PEAT)

The remaining sections illustrate how the IRM process can be run seamlessly to provide a comprehensive risk-based decision analytics framework through the use of the *Project Economics Analysis Tool* (PEAT) software. PEAT has over 20 related registered patents and patent-pending technologies and incorporates all the elements of IRM in a simple-to-use software. See the *Software Download and Install* for more details on obtaining a trial version of the software and see the ROV website for additional getting started videos and PEAT documentation.

Figure 15.2 illustrates the PEAT software utility. This software was designed to apply IRM methodologies (Monte Carlo risk simulation, strategic real options, stochastic and predictive forecasting, business analytics, business statistics, business intelligence, decision analysis, and portfolio optimization) to project and portfolio economics and financial analysis. The PEAT utility can house multiple industry-specific or application-specific modules such as oil and gas industry models (industry specific) or discounted cash flow model (application specific). The utility can house multiple additional types of models (industry or application specific) as required. The user can choose the module desired and create a new model from scratch, open a previously saved model, load a predefined example, or exit the utility.

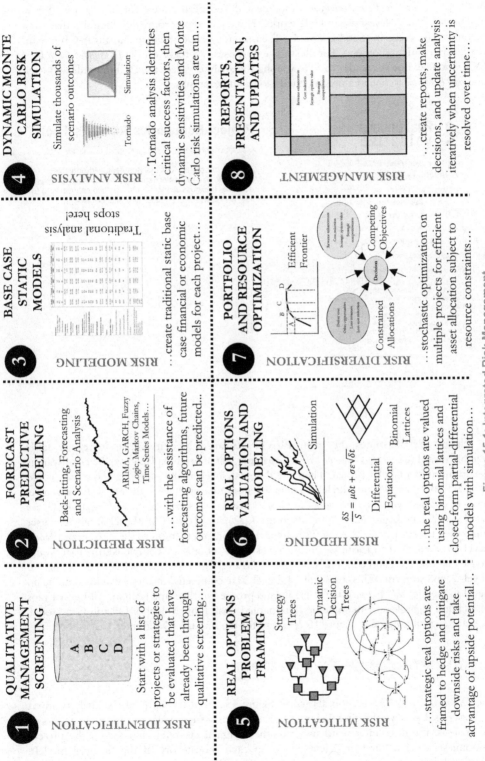

1 RISK IDENTIFICATION

QUALITATIVE MANAGEMENT SCREENING

A
B
C
D

Start with a list of projects or strategies to be evaluated that have already been through qualitative screening...

2 RISK PREDICTION

FORECAST PREDICTIVE MODELING

Back-fitting, Forecasting and Scenario Analysis

ARIMA, GARCH, Fuzzy Logic, Markov Chains, Time Series Models...

...with the assistance of forecasting algorithms, future outcomes can be predicted...

3 RISK MODELING

BASE CASE STATIC MODELS

Traditional analysis stops here!

...create traditional static base case financial or economic models for each project...

4 RISK ANALYSIS

DYNAMIC MONTE CARLO RISK SIMULATION

Simulate thousands of scenario outcomes

Tornado   Simulation

...Tornado analysis identifies critical success factors, then dynamic sensitivities and Monte Carlo risk simulations are run...

5 RISK MITIGATION

REAL OPTIONS PROBLEM FRAMING

Strategy Trees

Dynamic Decision Trees

...strategic real options are framed to hedge and mitigate downside risks and take advantage of upside potential...

6 RISK HEDGING

REAL OPTIONS VALUATION AND MODELING

Simulation

$$\frac{\delta S}{S} = \mu \delta t + \sigma \varepsilon \sqrt{\delta t}$$

Differential Equations

Binomial Lattices

...the real options are valued using binomial lattices and closed-form partial-differential models with simulation...

7 RISK DIVERSIFICATION

PORTFOLIO AND RESOURCE OPTIMIZATION

Efficient Frontier

Competing Objectives

Constrained Allocations

Decision

...stochastic optimization on multiple projects for efficient asset allocation subject to resource constraints...

8 RISK MANAGEMENT

REPORTS, PRESENTATION, AND UPDATES

...create reports, make decisions, and update analysis iteratively when uncertainty is resolved over time...

Figure 15.1: Integrated Risk Management

As shown in Figure 15.2, multiple modules exist in PEAT, and you can see Chapter 13 for PEAT's *Enterprise Risk Management* module and Technical Note 6 for an example of how the *Dynamic Project Management* module works. There are some proprietary modules that were customized for companies and will not be discussed (e.g., Saudi Aramco, Northrop Grumman, Cubic, Arco, 3M, and others). For illustrative purposes, we focus on the *Discounted Cash Flow (DCF)* module. For the reader to follow along the analysis, select the DCF module and click the *Load Example* to obtain a pregenerated model and example.

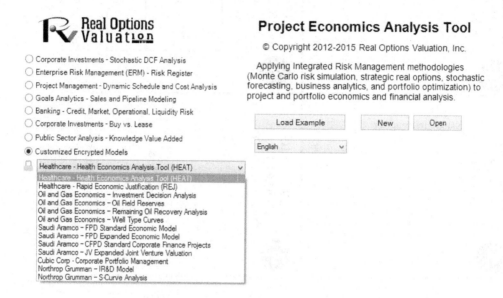

Figure 15.2: Project Economics Analysis Tool (PEAT) Splash Screen

Figure 15.3 illustrates the main PEAT software where its menu items are fairly straightforward (e.g., *File | New or File | Save* items that are self-explanatory). The software is also arranged in a tabular format. There are three tab levels in the software, and a user would proceed from top to bottom and left to right when running analyses in the utility. For instance, a user would start with the *Discounted Cash Flow* (Level 1) tab, select *Custom Calculations* or *Option 1* in (Level 2), and begin entering inputs in the *1. Discounted Cash Flow* (Level 3) tab. The user would then proceed to the *2. Cash Flow Ratios* (Level 3), and then on to the *3. Economic Results* (Level 3) subtab, and so forth. When the lowest level subtabs are completed, the user would proceed up one level and continue with *Option 2* (Level 2), *Option 3* (Level 2), *Portfolio Analysis* (Level 2), and so forth. When these tabs at Level 2 are completed, the user would continue up a level to the *Applied Analytics* (Level 1) tab, and proceed in the same fashion. All Level 1 tabs are identical regardless of the module (Discounted Cash Flow Model or Oil and Gas Model, etc.) chosen as illustrated in Figure 15.2, except for the first tab (Discounted Cash Flow).

DISCOUNTED CASH FLOW MODEL

The *Discounted Cash Flow* section shown in Figure 15.3 is at the heart of the analysis' input assumptions. Users would enter their input assumptions—such as starting and ending years of the analysis, the discount rate to use, and the marginal tax rate—and set up the project economics model (adding or deleting rows in each subcategory of the financial model). Additional time-series inputs are entered in the data grid as required, while some elements of this grid are intermediate computed values. The entire grid can be copied and pasted into another software application such as Microsoft Excel, Microsoft Word, or other third-party software applications, or can be viewed in its entirety as a full screen pop-up.

Users can also identify and create the various options, and compute the economic and financial results such as net present value (NPV), internal rate of return (IRR), modified internal rate of return (MIRR), profitability index (PI), return on investment (ROI), payback period (PP), and discounted payback (DPP). This section will also auto-generate various charts, cash flow ratios and models, intermediate calculations, and comparisons of the options within a portfolio view, as illustrated in the next few figures. As a side note, the term *Project* is used in PEAT's DCF module to represent a generic analysis option, where each project can be a different asset, project, acquisition, investment, research and development, or simply variations of the same investment (e.g., different financing methods when acquiring the same firm, different market conditions and outcomes, or different scenarios or implementation paths). Therefore, the more flexible terminology of *Project* is adopted instead.

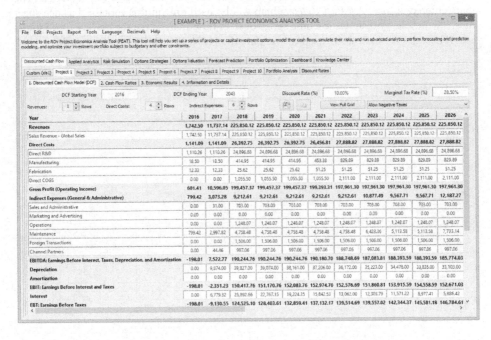

Figure 15.3: PEAT Discounted Cash Flow Module

Procedure

When the user is in any of the *Project* tabs, the *Projects* menu will become available, ready for users to add, delete, duplicate, or rename a project or rearrange the order of the *Project* tabs by first clicking on any *Project* tab and then selecting *Add, Delete, Duplicate, Rearrange,* or *Rename* from the menu. All of the required functionalities such as input assumptions, adding or reducing the number of rows, selecting discount rate type, or copying the grid are available within each *Project* tab. The input assumptions entered in these individual *Project* tabs are localized and used only within each tab, whereas input assumptions entered in the *Global Settings* (to be discussed later) tab apply to all *Project* tabs simultaneously. Typically, the user will need to enter all the required inputs, and if certain cells are irrelevant, users will have to enter zeros. Users can also increase or decrease the number of rows for each category as required.

The *DCF Starting Year* input is the discounting base year, where all cash flows will be present valued to this year. The main categories are in boldface, and the input boxes under the categories are for entering in the line item name/label. Users can click on *Copy Grid* icon to copy the results into the Microsoft Windows clipboard in order to paste into another software application such as Microsoft Excel or Microsoft Word. Finally, the *View Full Grid* button pops up the data grid to a full screen to facilitate the viewing of the model in its entirety without the need to scroll to the left/right or up/down. The grid will be maximized to full view, which facilitates the taking of screen shots.

Figure 15.4 illustrates the *Cash Flow Ratios* that are automatically calculated. This tab is where additional balance sheet data can be entered (current asset, shares outstanding, common equity, total debt, etc.) and the relevant financial ratios will be computed (EBIT, Net Income, Net Cash Flow, Operating Cash Flow, Economic Value Added, Return on Invested Capital, Net Profit Margin, etc.). Computed results or intermediate calculations are shown as data grids. Data grid rows are color coded by alternate rows for easy viewing. Users can enter the input assumptions as best they can, or they can guess at some of these figures to get started. The inputs entered in this *Cash Flow Ratios* subtab will be used only in this subtab's balance sheet ratios. The results grid shows the time series of cash flow analysis for the project for multiple years. These are the cash flows used to compute the NPV, IRR, MIRR, and so forth.

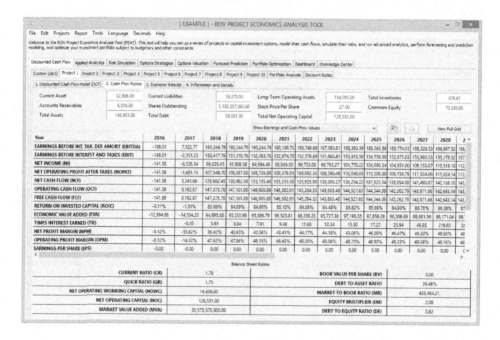

Figure 15.4: Cash Flow Ratios

Figure 15.5 illustrates the *Economic Results* of each project. This Level 3 subtab shows the results from the chosen project and returns the NPV, IRR, MIRR, PI, ROI, PP, and DPP. These computed results are based on the user's selection of the discounting convention, if there is a constant terminal growth rate, and the cash flow to use (e.g., net cash flow versus net income or operating cash flow). An *NPV Profile* table and chart are also provided, where different discount rates and their respective NPV results are shown and charted. Users can change the range of the discount rates to show/compute by entering the *From/To* percent, copy the results, copy the profile chart, as well as use any of the chart icons to manipulate the chart's look and feel (e.g., change the chart's line/background color, chart type, chart view, or add/remove gridlines, show/hide labels, and show/hide legend). Users can also change the variable to display in the chart. For instance, users can change the chart from displaying the NPV profile to the time-series charts of net cash flows, taxable income, operating cash flows, cumulative final cash flows, present value of the final cash flows, and so forth. Users can then click on the *Copy Results* icon or *Copy Chart* buttons to take a screen shot of the modified chart that can then be pasted into another software application such as Microsoft Excel or Microsoft PowerPoint.

The *Economic Results* subtabs are for each individual project, whereas the *Portfolio Analysis* tab (which is shown later as Figure 15.7) compares the economic results of all projects at once. The *Terminal Value Annualized Growth Rate* is applied to the last year's cash flow to account for a perpetual constant growth rate cash flow model, and these future cash flows, depending on which cash flow type chosen, are discounted back to the base year and added to the NPV to arrive at the perpetual valuation.

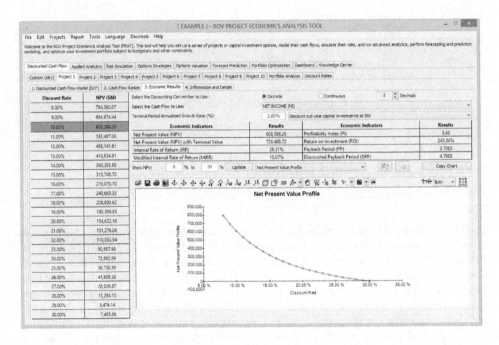

Figure 15.5: Economic Results

Figure 15.6 illustrates the *Information and Details* tab. Users would select this tab for entering justifications for the input assumptions used as well as any notes on each of the projects. For numerical calculations and notes, use the *Custom* calculation tab (discussed later; see Figure 15.8) instead. Users can also change the labels and *Categories* of the *Information and Details* tab by clicking on *Categories* and editing the default labels. The formatting of entered text can be performed in the *Description* box by clicking on the various text formatting icons.

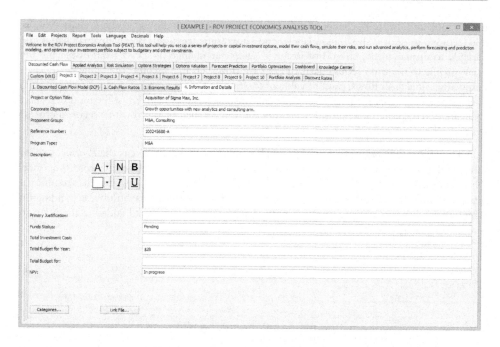

Figure 15.6: Information and Details

STATIC PORTFOLIO ANALYSIS AND COMPARISONS OF MULTIPLE PROJECTS

Figure 15.7 illustrates the *Portfolio Analysis* of multiple *Projects*. This Portfolio Analysis tab returns the computed economic and financial indicators such as NPV, IRR, MIRR, PI, ROI, PP, and DPP for all the projects combined into a portfolio view (these results can be stand-alone with no base case or computed as incremental values above and beyond the chosen base case). The *Economic Results* (Level 3) subtabs show the individual project's economic and financial indicators, whereas this Level 2 *Portfolio Analysis* view shows the results of all projects' indicators and compares them side by side. There are also two charts available for comparing these individual projects' results. The *Portfolio Analysis* tab is used to obtain a side-by-side comparison of all the main economic and financial indicators of all the projects at once. For instance, users can compare all the NPVs from each project in a single results grid. The bubble chart on the left provides a visual representation of up to three chosen variables at once (e.g., the y-axis shows the IRR, the x-axis represents the NPV, and the size of the bubble may represent the capital investment; in such a situation, one would prefer a smaller bubble that is in the top right quadrant of the chart). These charts have associated icons that can be used to modify their settings (chart type, color, legend, etc.).

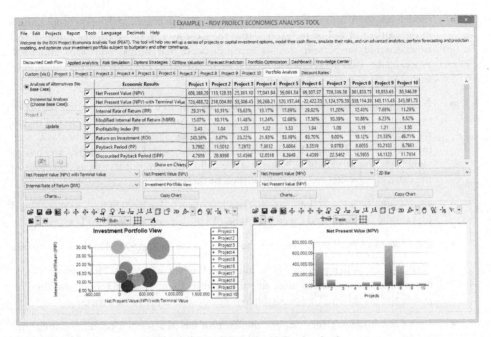

Figure 15.7: Static Portfolio Analysis

CUSTOM MODELING

Figure 15.8 illustrates the *Custom* calculation tab also available for making the user's own custom calculations just as they would in a Microsoft Excel spreadsheet. Clicking on the *Function F(x)* button will provide users with a list of the supported functions that can be used in this tab. A manual *Calculate* can be clicked to update the worksheet's calculations. Other basic mathematical functions are also supported, such as =, +, -, /, *, ^. If users use this *Custom* calculations tab and wish to link some cells to the other project input tabs (e.g., Project 1), they can select the cells in the *Custom* calculations tab, right-click, and select *Link To*. Then they would proceed to the location in the project tabs and highlight the location of the input cells they wish to link to, right-click, and select *Link From*. Any subsequent changes users make in the *Custom* calculations tab will be updated in the linked input assumption cells.

Procedures

The following are some additional procedural notes on using the Custom tab:

- *Simple Paste.* Copy information from Microsoft Excel or other software into the Custom tab's data grid, then paste into the Custom tab and the values and text will be pasted. Only values will be pasted into the grid and cell formatting is not supported in the Custom tab. Users can click *Ctrl+V* to paste or right-click and select the various paste options (simple paste, pasting absolute values, pasting reversed signed values, etc.).

- *CTRL~.* If the actual model and equations in Excel need to be pasted into the Custom tab data grid, when in Excel, first hit Ctrl~ (control button with the tilde, ~, button) to change the Excel worksheet into an equation view mode. Then select the model and paste into the data grid. This way the existing models and computations in the worksheet will be transferred into the Custom tab. Be aware that not all Excel functions are supported, so it is recommended that simple equations and basic functions be used and equation linking be restricted to the current worksheet (links across worksheet are not supported).

- *Naming Cells.* Select one or multiple cells, then type in a cell name (top left corner of the Custom tab) and hit enter. The cells will be named (multiple cells selected means the names will be indexed: Name 1, Name 2, Name 3, etc.) and the names will come in handy when *Tornado, Set Simulation Assumptions,* and *Scenario Analysis* are run to identify the input variables. Note that the cell names are not usable as equations in the Custom tabs themselves, only outside of these tabs.

- *Excel Links.* Live Excel links can also be created such that any changes to these Excel files can be modified and saved, and when PEAT opens, the links will be updated.

- *Insert Function F(x).* The icon shows the list of functions supported in the Custom tab.

- *Auto Calculate.* When pasting a large live model (while using the CTRL~ mode), users can temporarily uncheck and disable this feature, then paste the model, and then re-enable the checkbox. This procedure speeds up the copy/paste process.

- *Right-Click Linking.* Users can use the Custom tab as a scratch calculation area, and model outcomes can be selected and linked to the other project tabs. This way, any changes to the Custom tab or simulations run on any values in the Custom tab can be computed and linked to the project tabs.

- *Right-Click Set Simulation Assumption.* Non-equation numerical input values can be set as simulation assumptions. These assumptions will be visible in the *Set Input Assumptions* tab later to create simulation inputs.

- *Right-Click Custom Headers.* Users can add multiple additional Custom tabs and delete, rename, or move existing Custom tabs.

- *Refresh Links.* Allows users to manually update the external Excel links.

As an illustrative example, in the *Custom* calculations tab, a user may enter the following: *1, 2, 3* into cells A1, B1, C1, respectively. Then in cell D1, enter =*A1+B1+C1* and click on any other cell and it will update the cell and return the value *6.* Similarly, users type in =*SUM(A1:C1)* to obtain the same results. A list of preset functions can be seen by clicking on the *F(x)* the button.

As another example, in the *Custom* calculations tab, a user may enter the following: *1, 2, 3* into cells A1, B1, C1, respectively. Then, select these three cells, right-click, and select *Link To.* Proceed to any one of the project tabs, and in the *Discounted Cash Flow* or *Input Assumptions* subtabs, select three cells across (e.g., on the Revenue line item), right-click, and select *Link From.* The values of cells A1, B1, C1 in the *Custom Calculations* tab will be linked to this location. Users can go back to the *Custom Calculations* tab to change the values in the original three cells and they will see the linked cells in the *Discounted Cash Flow* or *Input Assumptions* subtabs change and update to reflect the new values.

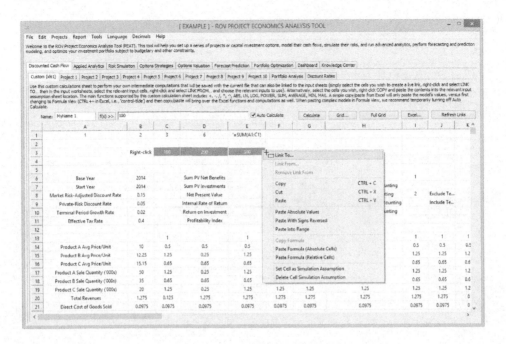

Figure 15.8: Custom Tab

WEIGHTED AVERAGE COST OF CAPITAL

Figure 15.9 illustrates the *Discount Rate* tab where the *Weighted Average Cost of Capital,* or WACC, calculations are housed. This is an optional set of analytics whereby users can compute the firm's WACC to use as a discount rate. Users start by selecting either the *Simple WACC* or *Detailed WACC Cost Elements.* Then, they can either enter the required inputs or click on the *Load Example* button to load a sample set of inputs that can then be used as a guide to entering their own set of assumptions and additional settings.

Figure 15.10 illustrates the *Beta* calculations. This is another optional subtab used for computing the beta risk coefficient by pasting in historical stock prices or stock returns to compute the beta, and a time-series chart provides a visual for the data entered. The resulting beta is used in the Capital Asset Pricing Model (CAPM), one of the main inputs into the WACC model. Users start by selecting whether they have historical *Stock Prices* or *Stock Returns,* then enter the number of rows or periods of historical data they have, and paste the data into the relevant columns and click *Compute.* Users can also click on *Load Example* to open a sample dataset. The beta coefficient result will update and users can use this beta as an input into the WACC model.

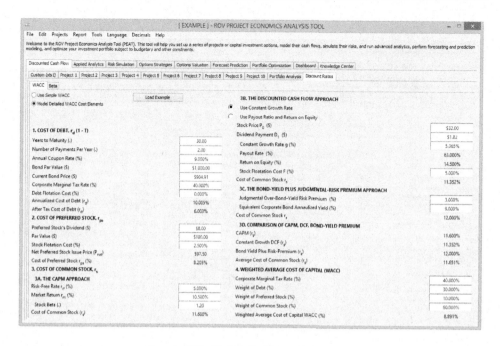

Figure 15.9: Global Settings and WACC

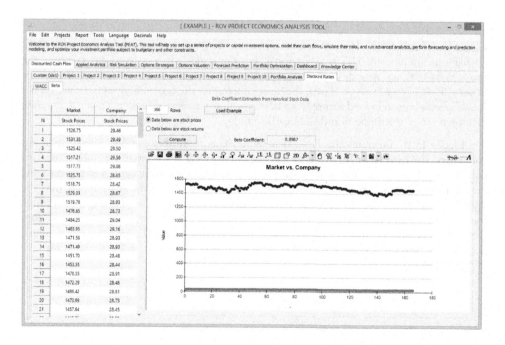

Figure 15.10: CAPM Beta

APPLIED ANALYTICS: TORNADO AND SCENARIO

Figure 15.11 illustrates the *Applied Analytics* section, which allows users to run *Tornado Analysis* and *Scenario Analysis* on any one of the projects previously modeled—this analytics tab is on Level 1, which means it covers all of the various projects on Level 2. Users can, therefore, run tornado or scenario analyses on any one of the projects. Tornado analysis, as we already know, is a static sensitivity analysis of the selected model's output to each input assumption, performed one at a time, and ranked from most impactful to the least. Users start the analysis by first choosing the output variable to test from the droplist.

Procedure

Users can change the default sensitivity settings of each input assumption to test and decide how many input variables to chart (large models with many inputs may generate unsightly and less useful charts, whereas showing just the top variables reveals more information through a more elegant chart). Users can also choose to run the input assumptions as unique inputs, group them as a line item (all individual inputs on a single line item are assumed to be one variable), or run as variable groups (e.g., all line items under Revenue will be assumed to be a single variable). Users will need to remember to click *Update* to run the analysis if they make any changes to any of the settings. The sensitivity results are also shown as a table grid at the bottom of the screen (e.g., the initial base value of the chosen output variable, the input assumption changes, and the resulting output variable's sensitivity results). The following summarizes the tornado analysis chart's main characteristics:

- Each horizontal bar indicates a unique input assumption that constitutes a precedent to the selected output variable.

- The x-axis represents the values of the selected output variable. The wider the bar chart, the greater the impact/swing the input assumption has on the output.

- A green bar on the right indicates that the input assumption has a positive effect on the selected output (conversely, a red bar on the right indicates a negative effect).

- Each of the precedent or input assumptions that directly affect the NPV with *Terminal Value* is tested ±10% by default (this setting can be changed); the top 10 variables are shown on the chart by default (this setting can be changed), with a 2-decimal precision setting; and each unique input is tested individually.

- The default sensitivity is globally ±10% of each input variable but each of these inputs can be individually modified in the data grid. Note that a larger percentage variation will test for nonlinear effects as well.

- The model's granularity can be set (e.g., *Variable Groups* look at an entire variable group such as all revenues or direct costs will be modified at once; *Line Items* change the entire row for multiple years at once; and *Individual Unique Inputs* look at modifying each input cell).

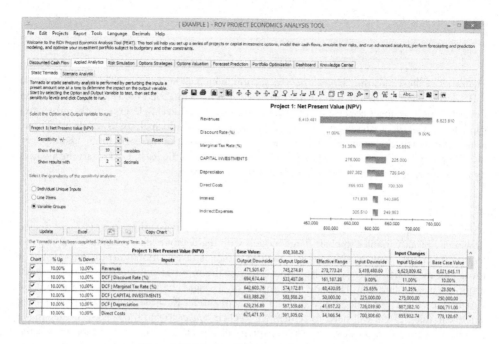

Figure 15.11: Applied Analytics: Tornado

Figure 15.12 illustrates the *Scenario Analysis* tab, where the scenario analysis can be easily performed through a two-step process: identify the model input settings and run the model to obtain scenario output tables. In the *Scenario Input Settings* subtab, users start by selecting the output variable they wish to test from the droplist. Then, based on the selection, the precedents of the output will be listed under two categories (*Line Item*, which will change all input assumptions in the entire line item in the model simultaneously, and *Single Item*, which will change individual input assumption items). Users select one or two checkboxes at a time and the inputs they wish to run scenarios on, and enter the plus/minus percentage and the number of steps between these two values to test. Users can also add color coding of sweetspots or hotspots in the scenario analysis (values falling within different ranges have unique colors). Users can create multiple scenarios and *Save As* each one (enter a name and model notes for each saved scenario).

Scenario analysis can sometimes be used as heat maps to identify the combinations of input parameter conditions whereby the calculated outputs will be above or below certain thresholds. A visual heat map can be created by adding color thresholds in the scenario results table.

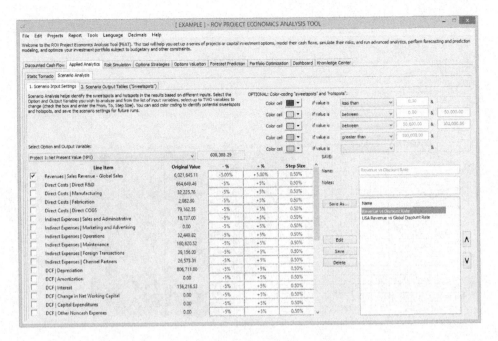

Figure 15.12: Applied Analytics: Scenario Analysis Input

Figure 15.13 illustrates the *Scenario Output Tables* to run the saved *Scenario Analysis* models. Users click on the droplist to select the previously saved scenarios to *Update* and run. The selected scenario table complete with sweetspot/hotspot color coding will be generated. Decimals can be increased or decreased as required, and users can *Copy Grid* or *View Full Grid* as needed. The following are some notes on using the scenario analysis methodology:

- Create and run scenario analysis on either one or two input variables at once.

- The scenario settings can be saved for retrieval in the future, which means users can modify any input assumptions in the options models and come back to rerun the saved scenarios.

- Increase/decrease decimals in the scenario results tables, as well as change colors in the tables for easier visual interpretation (especially when trying to identify scenario combinations, or so-called sweetspots and hotspots).

- Additional input variables are available by scrolling down the form.

- Line Items can be changed using $\pm X\%$ where all inputs in the line are changed multiple times within this specific range all at once. Individual Items can be changed $\pm Y$ units where each input is changed multiple times within this specific range.

- Sweetspots and hotspots refer to specific combinations of two input variables that will drive the output up or down. For instance, suppose investments are below a certain threshold and revenues are above a certain barrier. The NPV will then be in excess of the expected budget (the sweetspots, perhaps highlighted in green). Or if investments are above a certain value, NPV will turn negative if revenues fall below a certain threshold (the hotspots, perhaps highlighted in red).

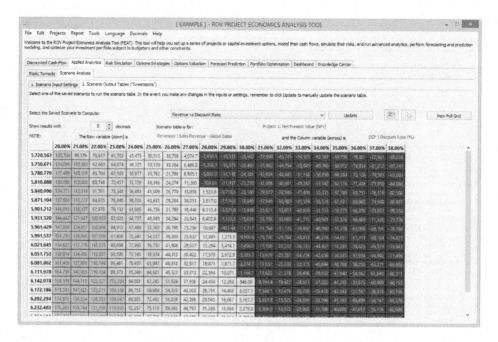

Figure 15.13: Applied Analytics: Scenario Tables

MONTE CARLO RISK SIMULATION

Figure 15.14 illustrates the *Risk Simulation* section, where Monte Carlo risk simulations can be set up and run. Users can set up probability distribution assumptions on any combinations of inputs, run a risk simulation tens to hundreds of thousands of trials, and retrieve the simulated forecast outputs as charts, statistics, probabilities, and confidence intervals in order to develop comprehensive risk profiles of the projects.

Procedure

In the *Set Input Assumptions* subtab, users start the simulation analysis by first setting simulation distributional inputs here (assumptions can be set to individual input assumptions in the model or as an entire line item). Users click on and choose one project at a time to list the available input assumptions. Users then click on the probability distribution icon under the *Settings* header for the relevant input assumption row, select the probability distribution to use, and enter the relevant input parameters. Users continue setting as many simulation inputs as required (users can check/uncheck the inputs to simulate). Users then enter the simulation trials to run (it is suggested to start with 1,000 as initial test runs and use 10,000 for the final run as a rule of thumb for most models). Users can also *Save As* the model (remembering to provide it a name). Then they click on *Run Simulation*. Finally, in this tab, users can set simulation assumptions across multiple projects and *Simulate All Options at Once*, apply a *Seed Value* to replicate the exact simulation results each time it is run, and *Edit* or *Delete* a previously saved simulation model.

Although the software supports up to 50 probability distributions, in general, the most commonly used and applied distributions include Triangular, Normal, and Uniform. If the user has historical data available, he or she can use the *Forecast Prediction* (discussed in a later section) tab to perform a Distributional Fitting to determine the best-fitting distribution to use as well as to estimate the selected distribution's input parameters. Multiple simulation settings can be saved such that they can be retrieved, edited, and modified as required in the future. Users can select either *Simulate All Options at Once* or *Simulate Selected Option Only*, depending on whether they wish to run a risk simulation on all the projects that have predefined simulation assumptions or to run a simulation only on the current project that is selected.

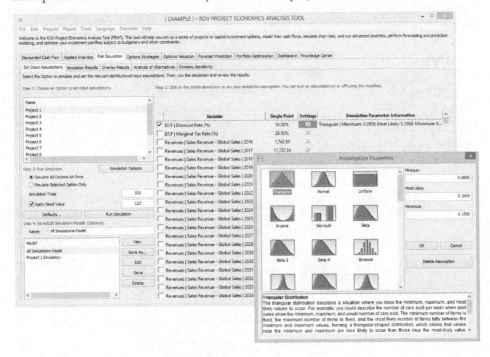

Figure 15.14: Risk Simulation Input Assumptions

SIMULATION RESULTS, CONFIDENCE INTERVALS, AND PROBABILITIES

Figure 15.15 illustrates the Risk Simulation results. After the simulation completes its run, the utility will automatically take the user to the *Simulation Results* tab. The user selects the output variable to display using the droplist. The simulation forecast chart is shown on the left, while percentiles and simulation statistics are presented on the right.

Procedure

Users can change and update the chart type (e.g., PDF, CDF), enter *Percentiles* (in %) or *Certainty Values* (in output units) on the bottom left of the screen (remembering to click *Update* when done) to show their vertical lines on the chart, or compute/show the *Percentiles/Confidence* levels on the bottom right of the screen (selecting the type: *Two Tail, Left Tail, Right Tail*, then either entering the percentile values to auto-compute the confidence interval or entering the confidence desired to obtain the relevant percentiles). Users can also *Save* the simulated results and *Open* them at a later session, *Extract Simulation Data* to paste into Microsoft Excel for additional analysis, modify the chart using the chart icons, and so forth. The simulation forecast chart is highly flexible in the sense that users can modify its look and feel (color, chart type, background, gridlines, rotation, chart view, data labels, etc.) using the chart icons.

If users entered either a percentile or certainty value at the bottom left of the screen and clicked *Update*, they can then click on custom text properties in the chart icon, select the *Vertical Line*, type in some custom texts, click on the *Properties* button to change the font size/color/type, or use the icons to move the custom text's location. Users can also enter in custom percentile or numerical values to show in the chart. As a side note, this *Simulation Results* forecast chart shows one output variable at a time, whereas the *Overlay Results* compares multiple simulated output forecasts at once.

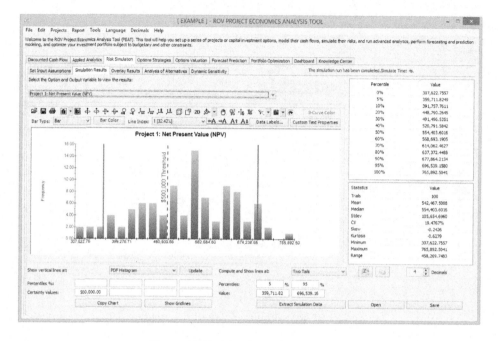

Figure 15.15: Risk Simulation Results

PROBABILITY DISTRIBUTION
OVERLAY CHARTS

Figure 15.16 illustrates the *Overlay Results* tab. Multiple simulation output variables can be compared at once using the overlay charts. Users simply check/uncheck the simulated outputs they wish to compare and select the chart type to show (e.g., S-Curves, CDF, PDF). Users can also add percentile or certainty lines by first selecting the output chart, entering the relevant values, and clicking the *Update* button. As usual, the generated charts are highly flexible in that users can modify them using the included chart icons (as well as whether to show or hide gridlines) and the chart can be copied into the Microsoft Windows clipboard for pasting into another software application. Typically, S-curves of CDF curves are used in overlay analysis when comparing the risk profile of multiple simulated forecast results.

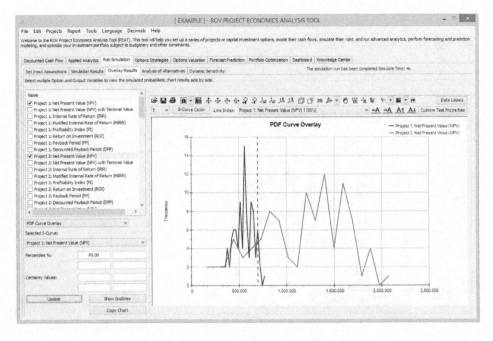

Figure 15.16: Simulated Overlay Results

ANALYSIS OF ALTERNATIVES

Figure 15.17 illustrates the *Analysis of Alternatives* subtab. Whereas the *Overlay Results* subtab shows the simulated results as charts (PDF/CDF), the *Analysis of Alternatives* subtab shows the results of the simulation statistics in a table format as well as a chart of the statistics such that one project can be compared against another. The default is to run an analysis of alternatives to compare one project versus another, but users can also choose the *Incremental Analysis* project (remembering to choose the desired economic metric to show, its precision in terms of decimals, the *Base Case* project to compare the results to, and the chart display type).

DYNAMIC SENSITIVITY ANALYSIS

Figure 15.18 illustrates the *Dynamic Sensitivity Analysis* computations. Tornado analysis and scenario analysis are both static calculations. Dynamic sensitivity, in contrast, is a dynamic analysis, which can only be performed after a simulation is run. Users start by selecting the desired project's economic output. Red bars on the *Rank Correlation* chart indicate negative correlations and green bars indicate positive correlations for the left chart. The correlations' absolute values are used to rank the variables with the highest relationship to the lowest, for all simulation input assumptions. The *Contribution to Variance* computations and chart indicate the percentage fluctuation in the output variable that can be statistically explained by the fluctuations in each of the input variables. As usual, these charts can be copied and pasted into another software application.

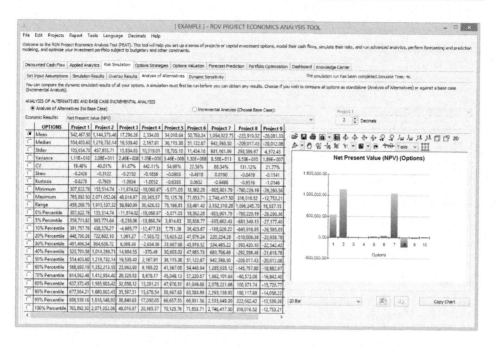

Figure 15.17: Simulated Analysis of Alternatives

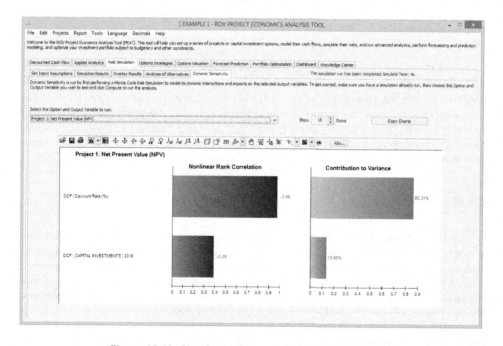

Figure 15.18: Simulated Dynamic Sensitivity Analysis

STRATEGIC REAL OPTIONS ANALYSIS

Figure 15.19 illustrates the *Options Strategies* tab. Options Strategies is where users can draw their own custom strategic maps, and each map can have multiple strategic real options paths. This section allows users to draw and visualize these strategic pathways and does not perform any computations. (The next section, *Options Valuation*, actually performs the computations.) Users can explore this section's capabilities, but viewing the *Video on Options Strategies* (see Figure 15.30 for the Knowledge Center videos) to quickly get started on using this very powerful tool is recommended.

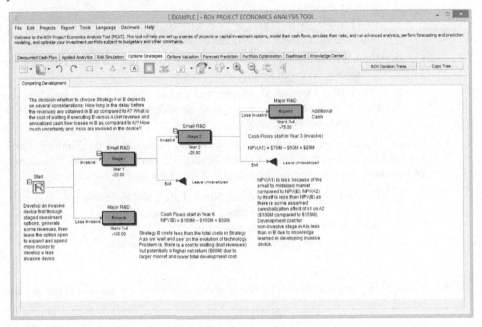

Figure 15.19: Options Strategies

Procedure

Users can also explore some preset options strategies by clicking on the first icon and selecting any one of the examples (click on the first icon and select *Examples*). Below are details on this *Options Strategies* tab:

- Users can Insert Option nodes or Insert Terminal nodes by first selecting any existing node and then clicking on the Option Node icon (square) or Terminal Node icon (triangle).

- Users can modify individual Option Node or Terminal Node properties by double-clicking on a node. Sometimes when users click on a node, all subsequent child nodes are also selected (this allows users to move the entire tree starting from that selected node). If users wish to select only that node, they may have to click on the empty background and click back on that node to select it individually. Also, users can move individual nodes or the entire tree starting from the selected node depending on the current setting (right-click, or in the Edit menu, select Move Nodes Individually or Move Nodes Together).

- The following are some quick descriptions of the things that can be customized and configured in the node properties user interface. It is simplest for the user to try different settings for each of the following to see its effects in the Strategy Tree.

  o Name. Name shown above the node.

  o Value. Value shown below the node.

  o Excel Link. Links the value from an Excel spreadsheet's cell.

  o Notes. Notes can be inserted above or below a node.

  o Show in Model. Show any combinations of Name, Value, and Notes.

  o Local Color versus Global Color. Node colors can be changed locally to a node or globally.

  o Label Inside Shape. Text can be placed inside the node (users may need to make the node wider to accommodate longer text).

  o Branch Event Name. Text can be placed on the branch leading to the node to indicate the event leading to this node.

  o Select Real Options. A specific real option type can be assigned to the current node. Assigning real options to nodes allows the tool to generate a list of required input variables.

- Global Elements are all customizable, including elements of the Strategy Tree's Background, Connection Lines, Option Nodes, Terminal Nodes, and Text Boxes. For instance, the following settings can be changed for each of the elements:

  o Font settings on Name, Value, Notes, Label, and Event names.
  o Node Size (minimum and maximum height and width).
  o Borders (line styles, width, and color).
  o Shadow (colors and whether to apply a shadow or not).
  o Global Color.
  o Global Shape.

- Example Files are available in the first icon menu to help users get started on building Strategy Trees.

- Protect File from the first icon menu allows the Strategy Tree and the entire PEAT model to be encrypted with up to a 256-bit password encryption. Care must be taken when a file is being encrypted because if the password is lost, the file can no longer be opened.

- Capturing the screen or printing the existing model can be done through the first icon menu. The captured screen can then be pasted into other software applications.

- Add, Duplicate, Rename, and Delete a Strategy Tree can be performed through right-clicking the Strategy Tree tab or the Edit menu.

- Users can also Insert File Link and Insert Comment on any option or terminal node, or Insert Text or Insert Picture anywhere in the background or canvas area.

- Users can Change Existing Styles or Manage and Create Custom Styles of their Strategy Tree (this includes size, shape, color schemes, and font size/color specifications of the entire Strategy Tree).

REAL OPTIONS VALUATION MODELING

Figure 15.20 illustrates the *Options Valuation* tab and the *Strategy View*. This section performs the calculations of real options valuation models. Users must understand the basic concepts of real options before proceeding. This *Options Valuation* tab internalizes the more sophisticated Real Options SLS software as described and explained in Chapter 11. Instead of requiring more advanced knowledge of real options analysis and modeling, users can simply choose the real option types, and the required inputs will be displayed for entry. Users can compute and obtain the real options value quickly and efficiently, as well as run the subsequent tornado, sensitivity, and scenario analyses.

Procedure

Users start by choosing the option execution type (e.g., American, Bermudan, or European), selecting an option to model (e.g., single phased and single asset or multiple phased sequential options), and, based on the option types selected, entering the required inputs and clicking *Compute* to obtain the results. Users can also click on the *Load Example* to load preset input assumptions based on the selected option type and option model. Some basic information and a sample strategic path are shown on the right under the Strategy View. Also, a tornado analysis and scenario analysis can be performed on the option model and users can *Save As, Delete,* or *Edit* existing saved models. The *Sensitivity* subtab runs a static sensitivity table of the real options model based on updated user inputs and settings. The *Tornado* subtab develops the tornado chart of the real options model. The interpretation of this tornado chart is identical to those previously described. The *Scenario* subtab runs a scenario table of the real options model based on updated user settings (input variables to analyze as well as the range and amount to perturb).

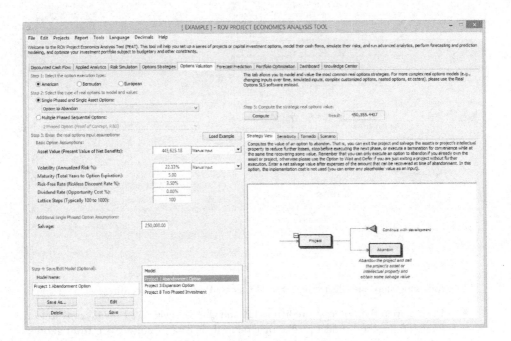

Figure 15.20: Options Valuation

STOCHASTIC FORECASTING
AND PREDICTION MODELING

Figure 15.21 illustrates the *Forecast Prediction* module. This is a sophisticated business analytics and business statistics module with over 150 functionalities. The user starts by entering the data in Step 1's data grid (user can copy and paste from Microsoft Excel or other ODBC-compliant data source, manually type in data, or click on the *Options | Load Example* button to load a sample dataset complete with previously saved models). The user then chooses the analysis to perform in Step 2 and, using the variables list provided, enters the desired variables to model given the chosen analysis (if users previously clicked *Example*, users can double-click to use and run the saved models in Step 4 to see how variables are entered in Step 2, and use that as an example for their analysis). The user then clicks *Run* in Step 3 when ready to obtain the results, charts, and statistics of the analysis that can be copied and pasted to another software application. Users can alternatively *Save* or *Edit/Delete* their models in Step 4 by giving them a name for future retrieval from a list of saved models, which can be sorted or rearranged accordingly. Users may also explore the power of this forecasting module by loading the preset *Options | Load Example*, or they can watch the *Getting Started Videos* (see Figure 15.30) to quickly get started using the module and review the user manual for more details on the 150 analytical methods.

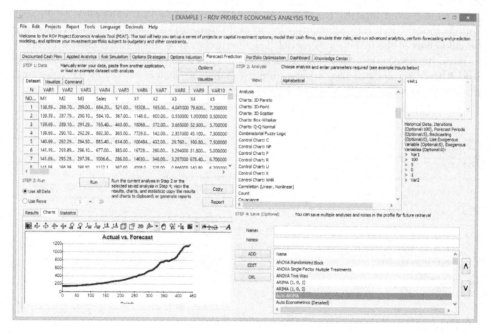

Figure 15.21: Forecast Prediction

Procedure

The following steps are illustrative of the Forecast Prediction procedures:

- Users start at the Forecast Prediction tab and click on *Options | Load Example* to load a sample data and model profile or type in their data or copy/paste from another software application such as Microsoft Excel or Microsoft Word/text file into the data grid in Step 1. Users can add their own notes or variable names in the first *Notes* row.

- Users then select the relevant model to run in Step 2 and using the example data input settings, enter in the relevant variables. Users must separate variables for the same parameter using semicolons and use a new line (hit *Enter* to create a new line) for different parameters.

- Clicking *Run* will compute the results. Users can view any relevant analytical results, charts, or statistics from the various tabs in Step 3.

- If required, users can provide a model name to save into the profile in Step 4. Multiple models can be saved in the same profile. Existing models can be edited or deleted and rearranged in order of appearance, and all the changes can be saved.

- The data grid size can be set in the *Options | Data Grid Configure* button, where the grid can accommodate up to 1,000 variable columns with 1 million rows of data per variable. The pop-up menu also allows users to change the language and decimal settings for their data.

- In getting started, it is always a good idea to load the example file that comes complete with some data and precreated models. Users can double-click on any of these models to run them, and the results are shown in the report area, which sometimes can be a chart or model statistics. Using this example file, users can now see how the input parameters are entered based on the model description, and users can proceed to create their own custom models.

- Users can click on the variable headers to select one or multiple variables at once, and then right-click to add, delete, copy, paste, or visualize the variables selected.

- Users can click on the data grid's column header(s) to select the entire column(s) or variable(s), and once selected, users can right-click on the header to *Auto Fit* the column, or to cut, copy, delete, or paste data. Users can also click on and select multiple column headers to select multiple variables, and then right-click to select *Visualize* in order to chart the data.

- If a cell has a large value that is not completely displayed, the user can click on and hover the mouse over that cell to see a pop-up comment showing the entire value, or simply resize the variable column (drag the column to make it wider, double-click on the column's edge to auto-fit the column, or right-click on the column header and select *Auto Fit*).

- Users can use the up, down, left, and right keys to move around the grid, or use the *Home* and *End* keys on the keyboard to move to the far left and far right of a row. Users can also use combination keys such as *Ctrl+Home* to jump to the top left cell, *Ctrl+End* to the bottom right cell, *Shift+Up/Down* to select a specific area, and so forth.

- Users can enter short, simple notes for each variable on the Notes row.

- Users can try out the various chart icons on the *Visualize* tab to change the look and feel of the charts (rotate, shift, zoom, change colors, add legend, etc.).

- The Copy button is used to copy the results, charts, and statistics tabs in Step 3 after a model is run. If no models are run, then the copy function will only copy a blank page.

- The *Report* button will only run if there are saved models in Step 4 or if there are data in the grid; otherwise the report generated will be empty. Users will also need

Microsoft Excel to be installed to run the data extraction and results reports, and have Microsoft PowerPoint available to run the chart reports.

- When in doubt about how to run a specific model or statistical method, the user should start the *Options | Load Example* profile and review how the data are set up in Step 1 or how the input parameters are entered in Step 2. Users can use these examples as getting started guides and templates for their own data and models.

- Users can click the *Options | Load Example* button to load a sample set of previously saved data and models. Then double-click on one of the *Saved Models* in Step 4. Users can see the saved model that is selected and the input variables used in Step 2. The results will be computed and shown in the Step 3 results area, and users can view the results, charts, or statistics depending on what is available based on the model they chose and ran.

- Users can select a variable in the data grid by clicking on the header(s). For instance, users can click on VAR1 and it will select the entire variable.

Figure 15.22 illustrates the forecast prediction's *Visualize* and *Charts* subtabs. Depending on the model run, sometimes the results will return a chart (e.g., a stochastic process forecast was created and the results are presented both in the results and charts subtabs). The charts subtab has multiple chart icons users can use to change the appearance of the chart (modify the chart type, chart line colors, chart view, etc.). Also, when a variable header in the data grid is selected, users can click on the *Visualize* button or right-click and select *Visualize*, and the data will be collapsed into a time-series chart.

Figure 15.23 illustrates the forecast prediction's *Command Console*. Users can also quickly run multiple models using direct commands here. It is recommended that new users set up the models using the user interface, starting from Step 1 through to Step 4. To start using the console, users create the models they need, then click on the *Command* subtab, copy/edit/replicate the command syntax (e.g., users can replicate a model multiple times and change some of its input parameters very quickly using the command approach), and when ready, click on the *Run Command* button. Alternatively, models can also be entered using a console. To see how this works, users can double-click to run a model and go to the console. Users can replicate the model or create their own and click *Run Command* when ready. Each line in the console represents a model and its relevant parameters. The figure also shows a sample set of results in the *Statistics* subtab.

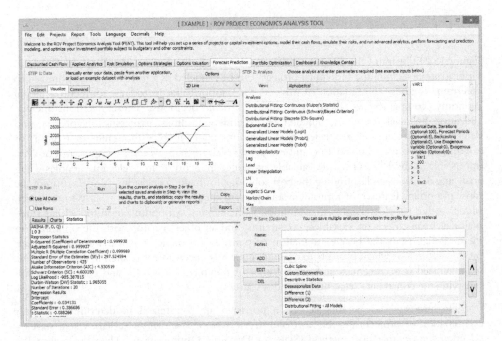

Figure 15.22: Forecast Prediction: Visualize and Charts

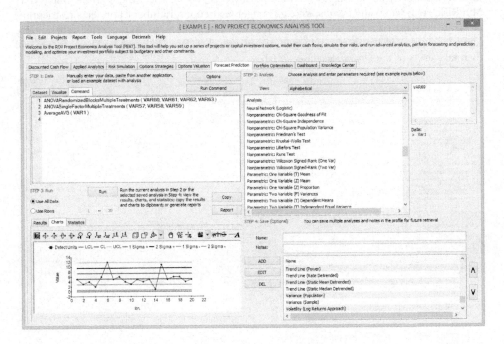

Figure 15.23: Forecast Prediction: Command Console

PORTFOLIO OPTIMIZATION

Figure 15.24 illustrates the *Portfolio Optimization's Optimization Settings* subtab. In the Portfolio Optimization section, the individual projects can be modeled as a portfolio and optimized to determine the best combination of projects for the portfolio. In today's competitive global economy, companies are faced with many difficult decisions. These decisions include allocating financial resources, building or expanding facilities, managing inventories, and determining product-mix strategies. Such decisions might involve thousands or millions of potential alternatives. Considering and evaluating each of them would be impractical or even impossible. A model can provide valuable assistance in incorporating relevant variables when analyzing decisions and in finding the best solutions for making decisions. Models capture the most important features of a problem and present them in a form that is easy to interpret. Models often provide insights that intuition alone cannot. An optimization model has three major elements: decision variables, constraints, and an objective. In short, the optimization methodology finds the best combination or permutation of decision variables (e.g., which products to sell or which projects to execute) in every conceivable way such that the objective is maximized (e.g., revenues and net income) or minimized (e.g., risk and costs) while still satisfying the constraints (e.g., budget and resources).

The projects can be modeled as a portfolio and optimized to determine the best combination of projects for the portfolio in the *Optimization Settings* subtab. Users start by selecting the optimization method (Static or Dynamic Optimization). Then they select the decision variable type of *Discrete Binary* (choose which Project or Options to execute with a Go/No-Go Binary 1/0 decision) or *Continuous Budget Allocation* (returns % of budget to allocate to each *option* or *project* as long as the total portfolio is 100%); select the *Objective* (Max NPV, Min Risk, etc.); set up any *Constraints* (e.g., budget restrictions, number of projects restrictions, or create customized restrictions); select the options or projects to optimize/allocate/choose (default selection is *all options*); and when completed, click *Run Optimization*. The software will then take users to the *Optimization Results* tab.

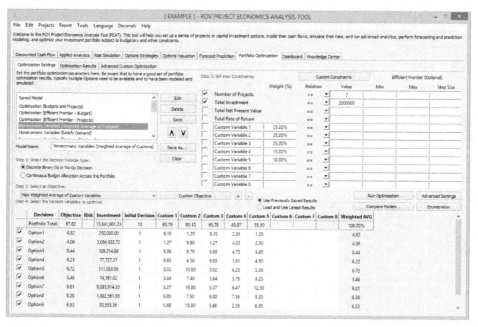

Figure 15.24: Portfolio Optimization Settings

Figure 15.25 illustrates the *Optimization Results* tab, which returns the results from the portfolio optimization analysis. The main results are provided in the data grid, showing the final *Objective Function* results, final *Optimized Constraints*, and the allocation, selection, or optimization across all individual options or projects within this optimized portfolio. The top left portion of the screen shows the textual details and results of the optimization algorithms applied, and the chart illustrates the final objective function. The chart will only show a single point for regular optimizations, whereas it will return an investment efficient frontier curve if the optional *Efficient Frontier* settings are set (min, max, step size) in the tab.

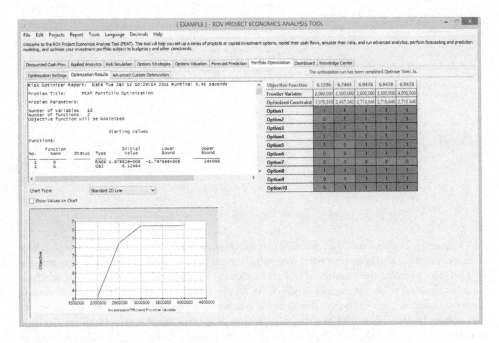

Figure 15.25: Portfolio Optimization Results

CUSTOMIZED
OPTIMIZATION MODELING

Figure 15.26 illustrates the *Advanced Custom Optimization* tab's *Optimization Method* routines, where users can create and solve their own optimization models. Knowledge of optimization modeling is required to set up models, but users can click on *Load Example* and select a sample model to run. Users can use these sample models to learn how the optimization routines can be set up. Users click *Run* when done to execute the optimization routines and algorithms. The calculated results and charts will be presented on completion. When users set up their own optimization model, it is recommended that they go from one tab to another, starting with the *Method* (Static, Dynamic, or Stochastic Optimization) and based on the selected method, input the simulation seeds or simulation trials, or the number of stochastic optimization iterations to perform. The *Optimized Results* will be shown after the model is run, where the resulting optimized decision variables are presented as a data grid. Perhaps the best way to get started for a new user is to load an existing set of example models to run. The user's own custom model can be checked using the *Verify* process to determine if the model is set up correctly.

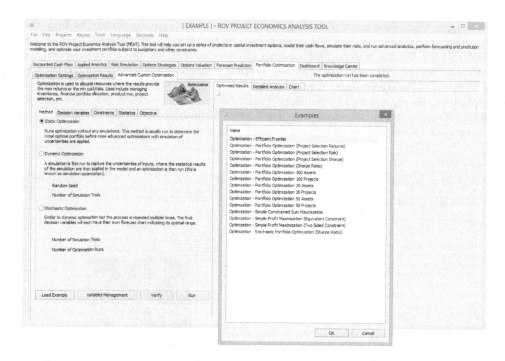

Figure 15.26: Custom Portfolio Optimization Methods

Figure 15.27 illustrates the *Advanced Custom Optimization's Decision Variables* setup, where decision variables are those quantities over which users have control; for example, the amount of a product to make, the number of dollars to allocate among different investments, or which projects to select from among a limited set. As an illustrative example, portfolio optimization analysis includes a go or no-go decision on particular projects. In addition, the dollar or percentage budget allocation across multiple projects also can be structured as decision variables. Users can click *Add* to add a new Decision Variable. Users can also *Change, Delete,* or *Duplicate* an existing decision variable. The Decision Variables can be set as *Continuous* (with lower and upper bounds), *Integers* (with lower and upper bounds), *Binary* (0 or 1), or a *Discrete Range*. The list of available variables is shown in the data grid, complete with their assumptions (rules, types, starting values). Users can view the *Detailed Analysis* of the optimization results.

Figure 15.28 illustrates the *Advanced Custom Optimization's Constraints* setup, which describes relationships among decision variables that restrict the values of the decision variables. For example, a constraint might ensure that the total amount of money allocated among various investments cannot exceed a specified amount or, at most, one project from a certain group can be selected; budget constraints; timing restrictions; minimum returns; or risk tolerance levels. Users can add a new constraint, and change or delete existing constraints. When adding a new constraint, the list of available Variables will be shown. Users can simply double-click on a desired variable and its variable syntax will be added to the *Expression* window. For example, double-clicking on a variable named "Return1" will create a syntax variable "$(Return1)$" in the window. Users can enter their own constraint equation(s). For example, the following is a constraint: *$(Asset1)$+$(Asset2)$+$(Asset3)$+$(Asset4)$=1* where the sum of all four decision variables must add up to 1. Users can keep adding as many constraints as needed without any upper limit. The optimization results on occasion will also return a chart, for example, when an investment efficient frontier (Modern Portfolio Theory) is modeled in the optimization routines. Additional chart functionalities are available in the charts.

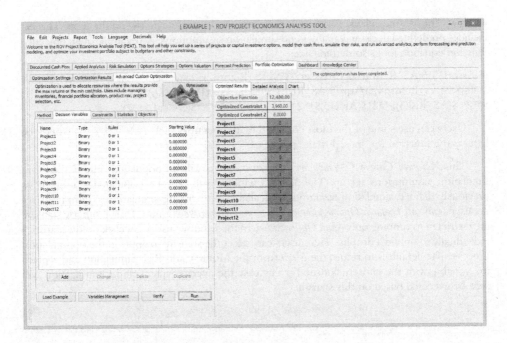

Figure 15.27: Custom Portfolio Optimization Decision Variables

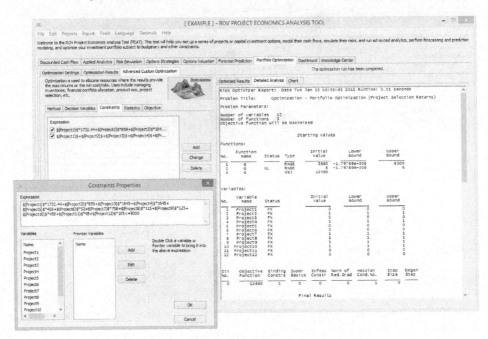

Figure 15.28: Custom Portfolio Optimization Constraints

Figure 15.29 illustrates the *Advanced Custom Optimization's Objective*, which provides a mathematical representation of the model's desired outcome, such as maximizing profit or minimizing cost, in terms of the decision variables. In financial analysis, for example, the objective may be to maximize returns while minimizing risks (maximizing the Sharpe's ratio or returns-to-risk ratio). Users can enter their own customized objective in the function window. The list of available variables is shown in the *Variables* window on the right. This list includes predefined decision variables and simulation assumptions. An example of an objective function equation looks something like:

($(Asset1)$*$(AS_Return1)$+$(Asset2)$*$(AS_Return2)$+$(Asset3)$*$(AS_Return3)$+$(Asset4)$*$(AS_Return4)$)/sqrt((AS_Risk1)**2*$(Asset1)$**2+(AS_Risk2)**2*$(Asset2)$**2+(AS_Risk3)**2*$(Asset3)$**2+(AS_Risk4)**2*$(Asset4)$**2)

Users can use some of the most common math operators such as +, -, *, /, **, where the latter is the function for "raised to the power of."

The *Advanced Custom Optimization's Statistics* subtab will be populated only if there are simulation assumptions set up. The *Statistics* window will only be populated if users have previously defined simulation assumptions available. If there are simulation assumptions set up, users can run *Dynamic Optimization* or *Stochastic Optimization* (Figure 15.26); otherwise users are restricted to running only *Static Optimization*. In the window, users can click on the statistics individually to obtain a droplist. Here users can select the statistic to apply in the optimization process. The default is to return the *Mean* from the Monte Carlo Risk Simulation and replace the variable with the chosen statistic (in this case the average value), and Optimization will then be executed based on this statistic.

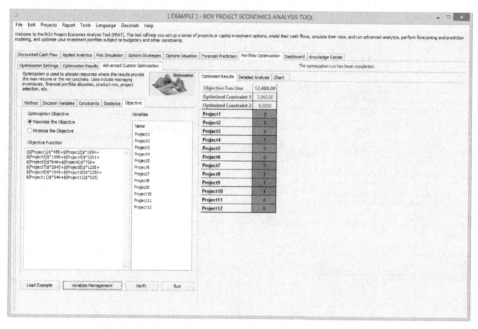

Figure 15.29: Custom Portfolio Optimization Objective

KNOWLEDGE CENTER

Figure 15.30 illustrates the *Knowledge Center's Step-by-Step Procedures*, where users will find quick getting started guides and sample procedures that are straight to the point to assist them in quickly getting up to speed in using the software. Users click on the *Previous* and *Next* buttons to navigate from slide to slide or to view the *Getting Started Videos*. These sessions are meant to provide a quick overview to help users get started with using PEAT and do not substitute for years of experience or the technical knowledge required in the Certified in Risk Management

(CRM) and Certified in Quantitative Risk Management (CQRM) programs. The *Step-by-Step Procedures* section highlights some quick getting started steps in a self-paced learning environment that is incorporated within the PEAT software. There are short descriptions above each slide, and key elements of the slide are highlighted in the figures for quick identification.

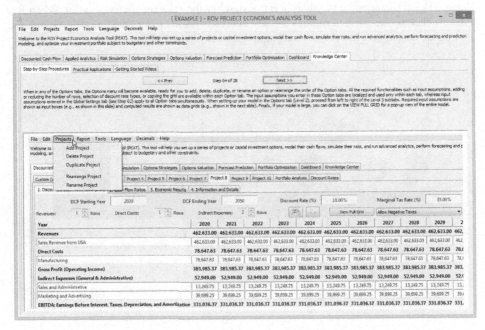

Figure 15.30: Knowledge Center

The Knowledge Center's *Basic Project Economics Lessons* section provides an overview tour of some common concepts involved with cash flow analysis and project economic analysis such as the computations of NPV, IRR, MIRR, PI, ROI, PP, DPP, and so forth. In addition, the Knowledge Center's *Getting Started Videos* subtab is where users can watch a short description and hands-on examples of how to run one of the sections within this PEAT software. The first quick getting started video is preinstalled with the software while the rest of the videos may be downloaded at first viewing. Before downloading any materials, users should ensure they have a good Internet connection to view the online videos. The videos may be entirely preinstalled or entirely downloadable.

The Knowledge Center has additional functionalities that users can customize. The Knowledge Center files (videos, slides, and figures) may be available in the installation path's three subfolders: *Lessons*, *Videos*, and *Procedures*. Users can access the raw files directly or modify/update these files and the updated files will show in the software tool's Knowledge Center the next time the software utility tool is started. Users can utilize the existing files (e.g., file type such as *.BMP or *.WMV as well as pixel size of figures) as a guide to the relevant file specifications they can use when replacing any of these original Knowledge Center files. If users wish to edit the text shown in the Knowledge Center, they can edit the *.XML files in the three subfolders, and the next time the software tool is started, the updated text will be shown. This file format is small in size and, hence, more portable when implementing it in the PEAT software tool installation build, such that users can still e-mail the installation build without the need for uploading to an FTP site. There are no minimum or maximum size limitations to this file format.

Figure 15.31 illustrates the PEAT Dashboard. After all the models are run (simulations, tornado, scenarios, etc.), users can access the *Dashboard* to create the settings required to generate the dashboard. Multiple dashboards can be saved and rerun as required for presentation to senior management. Figure 15.32 illustrates the Excel report generated in PEAT. After running all the models (simulations, tornado, scenario, etc.), users can click on *Report | Report Configuration* and then select or deselect the relevant analyses to run. When *Run Report* is clicked, the selected models will run and their results (data grids, models, charts, and results) are pasted into Microsoft Excel and Microsoft PowerPoint.

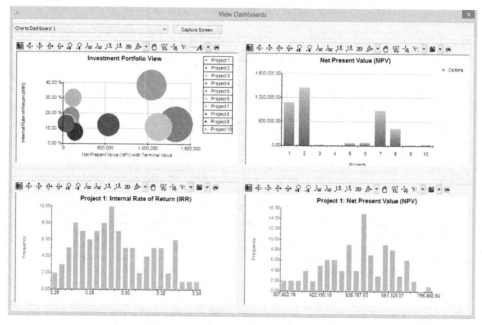

Figure 15.31: Dashboard

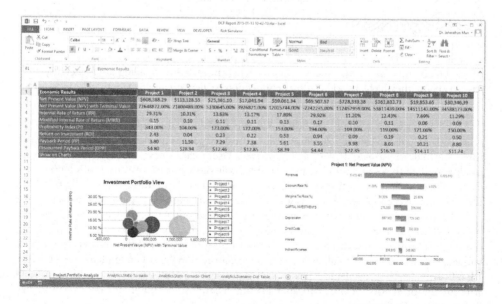

Figure 15.32: Reports

SECTION EIGHT – TECHNICAL NOTES

TECHNICAL NOTE 1: THE BASICS OF INTERPRETING PDF, CDF, AND ICDF

This technical note briefly explains the probability density function (PDF) for continuous distributions, which is also called the probability mass function (PMF) for discrete distributions (we use these terms interchangeably), where given some distribution and its parameters, we can determine the probability of occurrence given some outcome or random variable x. In addition, the cumulative distribution function (CDF) can also be computed, which is the sum of the PDF values up to this x value. Finally, the inverse cumulative distribution function (ICDF) is used to compute the value x given the cumulative probability of occurrence.

In mathematics and Monte Carlo risk simulation, a probability density function (PDF) represents a continuous probability distribution in terms of integrals. If a probability distribution has a density of $f(x)$, then, intuitively, the infinitesimal interval of $[x, x + dx]$ has a probability of $f(x)dx$. The PDF, therefore, can be seen as a smoothed version of a probability histogram; that is, by providing an empirically large sample of a continuous random variable repeatedly, the histogram using very narrow ranges will resemble the random variable's PDF.

The probability of the interval between $[a, b]$ is given by $\int_a^b f(x)dx$, which means that the total integral of the function f must be 1.0.

It is a common mistake to incorrectly think of $f(a)$ as the probability of a. In fact, $f(a)$ can sometimes be larger than 1 (consider a uniform distribution between 0.0 and 0.5). The random variable x within this distribution will have $f(x)$ greater than 1. The probability, in reality, is the function $f(x)dx$ discussed previously, where dx is an infinitesimal amount.

The cumulative distribution function (CDF) is denoted as $F(x) = P(X \leq x)$, indicating the probability of X taking on a less than or equal value to x. Every CDF is monotonically increasing, is continuous from the right, and at the limits has the following properties: $\lim_{x \to -\infty} F(x) = 0$ and $\lim_{x \to +\infty} F(x) = 1$.

Further, the CDF is related to the PDF by $F(b) - F(a) = P(a \leq X \leq b) = \int_a^b f(x)dx$, where the PDF function f is the derivative of the CDF function F. In probability theory, a probability mass function, or PMF, gives the probability that a discrete random variable is exactly equal to some value. The PMF differs from the PDF in that the values of the latter, defined only for continuous random variables, are not probabilities; rather, its integral over a set of possible values of the random variable is a probability. A random variable is discrete if its probability distribution is discrete and can be characterized by a PMF.

Therefore, X is a discrete random variable if

$$\sum_u P(X = u) = 1$$

as u runs through all possible values of the random variable X.

INTERPRETING PROBABILITY CHARTS

Here are some tips to help decipher the characteristics of a distribution when looking at different PDF and CDF charts:

- For each distribution, a continuous distribution's PDF is shown as an area chart (Figure TN.1) whereas a discrete distribution's PMF is shown as a bar chart (Figure TN.2).

- If the distribution can only take a single shape (e.g., normal distributions are always bell shaped, with the only difference being the central tendency measured by the mean and the spread measured by the standard deviation), then typically only one PDF area chart will be shown with an overlay PDF line chart (Figure TN.3) showing the effects of various parameters on the distribution.

- The CDF charts, or S-Curves, are shown as line charts (Figure TN.4), and sometimes as bar graphs.

- The central tendency of a distribution (e.g., the mean of a normal distribution) is its central location (Figure TN.3).

- Multiple area charts and line charts will be shown (e.g., beta distribution) if the distribution can take on multiple shapes (e.g., the beta distribution is a uniform distribution when alpha = beta = 1; a parabolic distribution when alpha = beta = 2; a triangular distribution when alpha = 1 and beta = 2, or vice versa; a positively skewed distribution when alpha = 2 and beta = 5, and so forth). In this case, you will see multiple area charts and line charts (Figure TN.5).

- The starting point of the distribution is sometimes its minimum parameter (e.g., parabolic, triangular, uniform, arcsine, etc.) or its location parameter (e.g., the beta distribution's starting location is 0, but a beta 4 distribution's starting point is the location parameter; Figure TN.5 shows a beta 4 distribution with location = 10, its starting point on the x-axis).

- The ending point of the distribution is sometimes its maximum parameter (e.g., parabolic, triangular, uniform, arcsine, etc.) or its natural maximum multiplied by the factor parameter shifted by a location parameter (e.g., the original beta distribution has a minimum of 0 and maximum value of 1, but a beta 4 distribution with location = 10 and factor = 2 indicates that the shifted starting point is 10 and ending point is 11, and its width of 1 is multiplied by a factor of 2, which means that the beta 4 distribution now will have an ending value of 12, as shown in Figure TN.5).

- Interactions between parameters are sometimes evident. For example, in the beta 4 distribution, if the alpha = beta, the distribution is symmetrical, whereas it is more positively skewed the greater the difference between beta and alpha, and the more negatively skewed, the greater the difference between alpha and beta (Figure TN.6).

- Sometimes a distribution's PDF is shaped by two or three parameters called *shape* and *scale*. For instance, the Laplace distribution has two input parameters, alpha location and beta scale, where alpha indicates the central tendency of the distribution (like the mean in a normal distribution) and beta indicates the spread from the mean (like the standard deviation in a normal distribution).

- The narrower the PDF (Figure TN.3's normal distribution with a mean of 10 and standard deviation of 2), the steeper the CDF S-Curve looks (Figure TN.4), and the smaller the width on the CDF curve.

- A 45-degree straight line CDF (an imaginary straight line connecting the starting and ending points of the CDF) indicates a uniform distribution; an S-Curve CDF with equal amounts above and below the 45-degree straight line indicates a symmetrical and somewhat bell- or mound-shaped curve; a CDF completely curved above the 45-degree line indicates a positively skewed distribution (Figure TN.7), while a CDF completely curved below the 45-degree line indicates a negatively skewed distribution (Figure TN.8).

- A CDF line that looks identical in shape but shifted to the right or left indicates the same distribution but shifted by some location, and a CDF line that starts from the same point but is pulled both to the left and right indicates a multiplicative effect on the distribution such as a factor multiplication, as shown in Figures TN.9 and TN.10.

- An almost vertical CDF indicates a high kurtosis distribution with fat tails, and where the center of the distribution is pulled up (e.g., see the Cauchy distribution) versus a relatively flat CDF, a very wide and perhaps flat-tailed distribution is indicated.

- Some discrete distributions can be approximated by a continuous distribution if its number of trials is sufficiently large and its probability of success and failure is fairly symmetrical (e.g., see the binomial and negative binomial distributions). For instance, with a small number of trials and a low probability of success, the binomial distribution is positively skewed, whereas it approaches a symmetrical normal distribution when the number of trials is high and the probability of success is around 0.50.

- Many distributions are both flexible and interchangeable—refer to the details of each distribution in Chapter 4's appendices and Technical Note 2—e.g., binomial is Bernoulli repeated multiple times; arcsine and parabolic are special cases of beta; Pascal is a shifted negative binomial; binomial and Poisson approach normal at the limit; chi-square is the squared sum of multiple normal; Erlang is a special case of gamma; exponential is the inverse of the Poisson but on a continuous basis; F is the ratio of two chi-squares; gamma is related to the lognormal, exponential, Pascal, Erlang, Poisson, and chi-square distributions; Laplace comprises two exponential distributions in one; the log of a lognormal approaches normal; the sum of multiple discrete uniforms approach normal; Pearson V is the inverse of gamma; Pearson VI is the ratio of two gammas; PERT is a modified beta; a large degree of freedom T approaches normal; Rayleigh is a modified Weibull; and so forth.

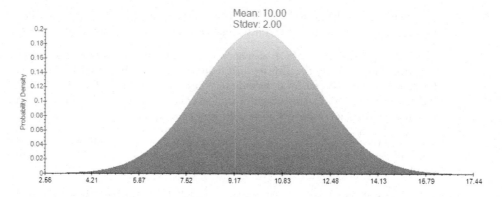

Figure TN.1: Continuous PDF (Area Chart)

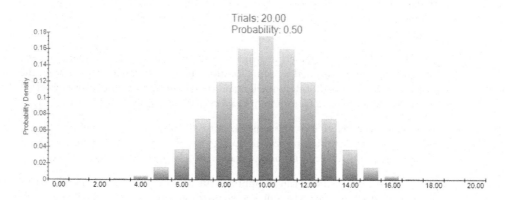

Figure TN.2: Discrete PMF (Bar Chart)

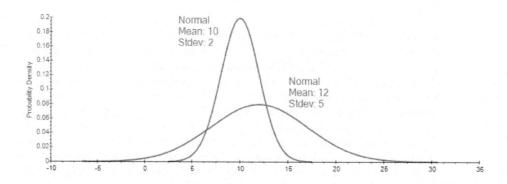

Figure TN.3: Multiple Continuous PDF Overlay Charts

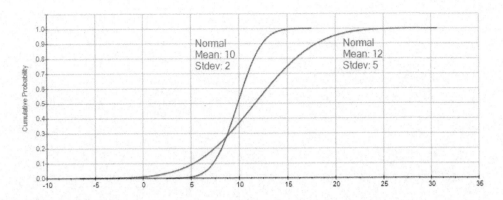

Figure TN.4: CDF Overlay Charts

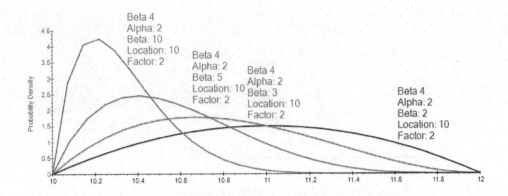

Figure TN.5: PDF Characteristics of the Beta Distribution

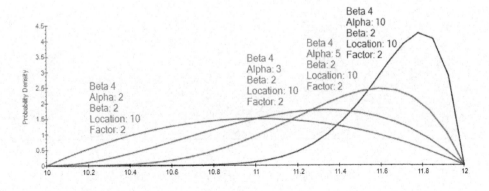

Figure TN.6: PDF of a Negatively Skewed Beta Distribution

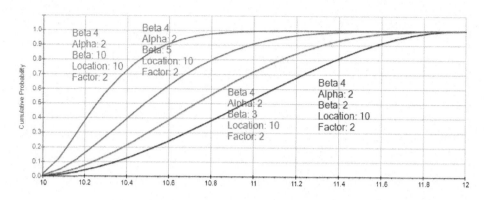

Figure TN.7: CDF of a Positively Skewed Distribution

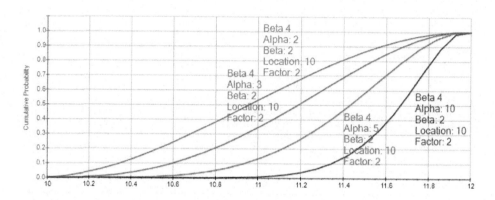

Figure TN.8: CDF of a Negatively Skewed Distribution

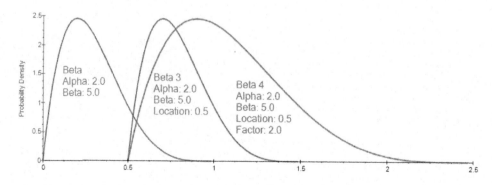

Figure TN.9: PDF Characteristics of a Shift

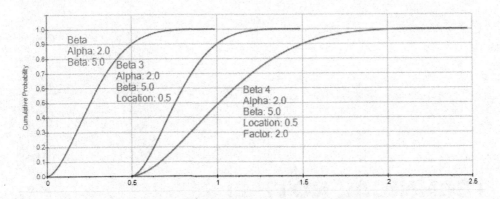

Figure TN.10: CDF Characteristics of a Shift

TECHNICAL NOTE 2: CONVOLUTION AND COPULAS—THEORY VERSUS PRACTICE

This technical note explains the basics of Convolution Theory and Copula Theory as they apply to probability distributions and stochastic modeling, both in theory and practice. It attempts to show that, in theory, convolution and copulas are elegant and critical in solving basic distributional moments but when it comes to practical applications, these theories are unwieldy and mathematically intractable. Consequently, it is necessary to run empirical Monte Carlo simulations, where the results of said empirical simulations approach the theoretically predicted results at the limit, allowing practitioners a powerful practical toolkit for modeling.

Many probability distributions are both flexible and interchangeable. For example:

- Arcsine and Parabolic distributions are special cases of the Beta distribution.

- Binomial and Poisson distributions approach the Normal distribution at the limit.

- Binomial distribution is a Bernoulli distribution with multiple trials.

- Chi-Square distribution is the squared sum of multiple Normal distributions.

- Discrete Uniform distributions' sum (12 or more) approaches the Normal distribution.

- Erlang distribution is a special case of the Gamma distribution when the alpha shape parameter is positive.

- Exponential distribution is the inverse of the Poisson distribution on a continuous basis.

- F-distribution is the ratio of two Chi-Square distributions.

- Gamma distribution is related to the Lognormal, Exponential, Pascal, Erlang, Poisson, and Chi-Square distributions.

- Laplace distribution comprises two Exponential distributions in one.

- Lognormal distribution's logarithmic values approach the Normal distribution.

- Pascal distribution is a shifted Negative Binomial distribution.

- Pearson V distribution is the inverse of the Gamma distribution.

- Pearson VI distribution is the ratio of two Gamma distributions.

- PERT distribution is a modified Beta distribution.

- Rayleigh distribution is a modified Weibull distribution.

- T-distribution with high degrees of freedom (>30) approaches the Normal distribution.

CONVOLUTION

Mathematicians came up with the distributions listed above through the use of convolution, among other methods. As a quick introduction, if there are two independent and identically distributed (*i.i.d.*) random variables, X and Y, and where their respectively known probability density functions (PDF) are $f_X(x)$ and $f_Y(y)$, we can then generate a new probability distribution by combining X and Y using basic summation, multiplication, and division. Some examples are listed above, e.g., the F-distribution is a division of two Chi-Square distributions, the normal distribution is a sum of multiple uniform distributions, etc. To illustrate how this works, consider the cumulative distribution function (CDF) of a joint probability distribution between the two random variables X and Y:

$$F_{X+Y}(u) = \iint\limits_{x+y \leq u} f(x,y)\,dx\,dy = \int_{-\infty}^{\infty} \left(\int_{y=-\infty}^{u-x} f(x,y)\,dy \right) dx$$

Differentiating the CDF equation above yields the PDF:

$$f_{X+Y}(u) = \int_{-\infty}^{\infty} f(x, u-x)\,dx$$

Example 1: The convolution of the simple sum of two identical and independent uniform distributions approaches the triangular distribution.

As a simple example, if we take the sum of two *i.i.d.* uniform distributions with a minimum of 0 and maximum of 1, we have:

$$f_{X+Y}(u) = \int_{-\infty}^{\infty} f(x)f(u-x)\,dx$$

where for a Uniform [0, 1] distribution, $f(x) = 1$ *when* $0 \leq x \leq 1$, we have:

$$f_{X+Y}(u) = \int_{0}^{1} f(u-x)\,dx = \int_{u-1}^{u} f(t)\,dt = \begin{cases} u & u \leq 1 \\ 2-u & 1 < u \leq 2 \end{cases}$$

which approaches a simple triangular distribution.

Figure TN.11 shows an empirical approach where two Uniform [0, 1] distributions are simulated for 20,000 trials and their sums added. The computed empirical sums are then extracted and the raw data fitted using the Kolmogorov–Smirnov fitting algorithm in Risk Simulator. The triangular distribution appears as the best-fitting distribution with a 74% goodness-of-fit. As seen in the convolution of only two uniform distributions, the result is a simple triangular distribution.

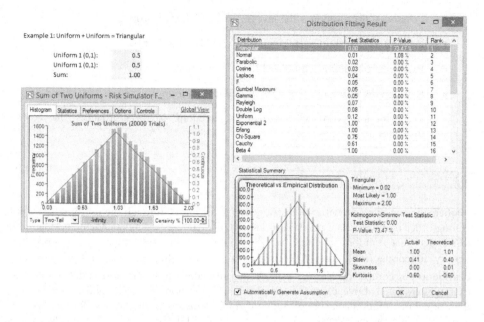

Figure TN.11: Convolution of Two Uniform Distributions via Simulation

Example 2: The convolution simple sum of 12 identical and independent uniform distributions approaches the normal distribution.

If we take the same approach and simulate 12 *i.i.d.* Uniform [0, 1] distributions and sum them, we would obtain a very close to perfect normal distribution as shown in Figure TN.12, with a goodness-of-fit at 99.3% after running 20,000 simulation trials.

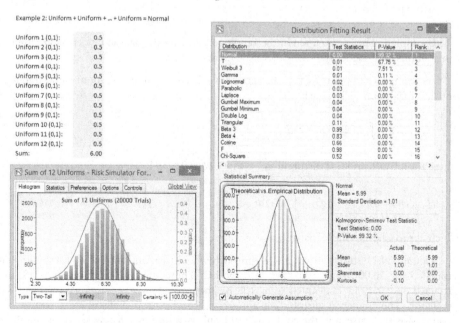

Figure TN.12: Convolution of 12 Uniform Distributions to Create a Normal

Example 3: The convolution simple sum of multiple identical and independent exponential distributions approaches the gamma (Erlang) distribution.

In this example, we sum two *i.i.d.* exponential distributions and generalize it to multiple distributions. To get started, we use two identical Exponential $[\lambda = 2]$ distributions:

$$f_{X+Y}(z) = \int_0^z f_X(x) f_Y(z-x) dx = \int_0^z \lambda e^{-\lambda x} \lambda e^{-\lambda(z-x)} dx = \lambda^2 z e^{-\lambda z}$$

where $f(x) = \lambda e^{-\lambda x}$ is the PDF for the exponential distribution for all $x \geq 0; \lambda \geq 0$, and the distribution's mean is $\beta = 1/\lambda$.

If we generalize to n random *i.i.d.* exponential distributions and apply mathematical induction:

$$f_{X_1+X_2+\ldots+X_n}(x) = \frac{x^{n-1} e^{-x/\beta}}{(n-1)!\beta^n} = \Gamma[0,n,1/\lambda]$$

$$f(x) = \frac{x^{\alpha-1} e^{-x/\beta}}{\Gamma(\alpha)\beta^\alpha} \quad \text{with any value of } \alpha > 0 \text{ and } \beta > 0$$

This is, of course, the generalized gamma distribution with α and β for the shape and scale parameters:

$$f_{X_1+X_2+\ldots+X_n}(x) = \Gamma[0,n,1/\lambda] = \Gamma[0,\alpha,\beta]$$

When the β parameter is a positive integer, the gamma distribution is called the Erlang distribution, used to predict waiting times in queuing systems, where the Erlang distribution is the sum of random variables each having a memoryless exponential distribution. Setting n as the number of these random variables, the mathematical construct of the Erlang distribution is:

$$f(x) = \frac{x^{\alpha-1} e^{-x}}{(\alpha-1)!} \quad \text{for all } x > 0 \text{ and all positive integers of } \alpha$$

The empirical approach is shown in Figure TN.13, where we have two exponential distributions with $\lambda = 2$ (this means that the mean $\beta = 1/\lambda = 0.5$). The sum of these two distributions, after running 20,000 Monte Carlo simulation trials and extracting and fitting the raw simulated sum data (Figure TN.13), shows a 99.4% goodness-of-fit when fitted to the gamma distribution where the $\alpha = 2$ and $\beta = 0.5$ (rounded), corresponding to $n = 2$ and $\lambda = 2$.

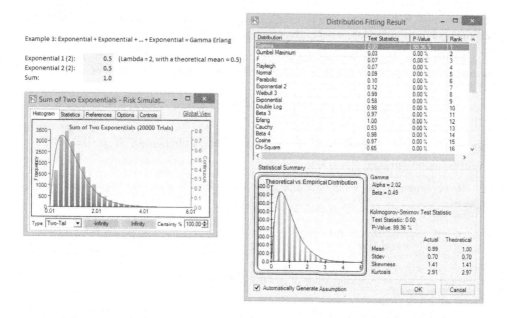

Figure TN.13: Convolution of Exponentials to Create a Gamma Erlang

COPULA

A copula is a multivariate probability distribution for which the marginal probability distribution of each variable is uniform. Copulas are used to describe the dependence between random variables and are typically used to model distributions that are correlated with one another.

The standard definition of copulas is based on Sklar's Theorem, which states that an m-dimensional copula (or m-copula) is a function C from the unit m-cube $[0, 1]^m$ to the unit interval $[0, 1]$ that satisfies the following conditions:

$C(1,...,1,a_n,1,...,1) = a_n$ for $n \leq m$ and all a_n in $[0,1]$

$C(a_1,...,a_m) = 0$ if $a_n = 0$ for any $n \leq m$ where C is m − increasing

Consider a continuous m-variate distribution function $F(y_1,...,y_m)$ with univariate marginal distributions $F_1(y_1),...,F_m(y_m)$ and inverse quantile functions $F_1^{-1},...,F_m^{-1}$. Then we have $y_1 = F_1^{-1}(u_1) \sim F_1,...,y_m = F_m^{-1}(u_m) \sim F_m$ where $u_1,...,u_m$ are uniformly distributed variates. Therefore, the transforms of uniform variates are distributed as $F_i(i=1,...,m)$. This means we have:

$$F(y_1,...,y_m) = F[F_1^{-1}(u_1),...,F_m^{-1}(u_m)]$$
$$F(y_1,...,y_m) = P[U_1 \leq u_1,...,U_m \leq u_m]$$
$$F(y_1,...,y_m) = C[u_1,...,u_m]$$

where C is the unique copula associated with the distribution function. That is, $y \sim F$, and F is continuous, then $F_1(y_1),...,F_m(y_m) \sim C$, and if $U \sim C$, then we have $F_1^{-1}(u_1),..,F_m^{-1}(u_m) \sim F$. Mathematical algorithms using Iman-Conover and Cholesky decomposition matrices are used to compute the joint marginal distributions. Copulas are parametrically specified joint distributions generated from given marginals. Therefore, properties of copulas are analogous to properties of joint distributions.

PROS AND CONS OF CONVOLUTION AND COPULA

Convolution theory is applicable and elegant for theoretical constructs of probability distributions. With basic addition, multiplication, and division of known *i.i.d.* distributions, we can determine its theoretical outputs. The issue with convolution theory is that there are no correlations (independently distributed) between the random variables and their distributions, and the individual distributions have to be exactly the same (identically distributed) and commonly known.

Therefore, if one modifies the distributions, uses exotic distributions, mixes and matches different non–*i.i.d.* distributions, adds correlations, creates large Excel models (beyond the simple addition, multiplication, or division as shown above, such as when there are exotic financial models and computations), and uses truncation, empirical nonparametric distributions, historical simulation, and other combinations of such issues, convolution will not work and cannot predict the outcomes. In addition, both convolution and copula theorems can only be used to compute correlations of joint distributions but would be limited to only a few distributions before the mathematics become intractable due to the large matrix inversions, multiple integrals, and differential equations that need to be solved. Therefore, users are restricted to using Monte Carlo risk simulations.

TECHNICAL NOTE 3: CONVOLUTION OF MULTIPLICATION OF FREQUENCY AND SEVERITY DISTRIBUTIONS IN OPERATIONAL RISK CAPITAL MODEL IN BASEL III

In October 2014, the Basel Committee on Banking Supervision released a Basel Consultative Document entitled, "Operational Risk: Revisions to the Simpler Approaches," and in it describes the concepts of operational risk as the sum product of frequency and severity of risk events within a one-year time frame and defines the Operational Capital at Risk (OPCAR) as the tail-end 99.9% Value at Risk. The Basel Consultative Document describes a Single Loss Approximation (SLA) model defined as $F_S^{-1}(p) = F_X^{-1}\left[1 - \frac{1-p}{\lambda}\right] + (\lambda - 1)E[X]$, where the inverse of the compound distribution F_S^{-1} is the summation of the unexpected losses $UL = F_X^{-1}\left[1 - \frac{1-p}{\lambda}\right]$ and expected losses $EL = (\lambda - 1)E[X]$; λ is the Poisson distribution's input parameter (average frequency per period; in this case, 12 months); and X represents one of several types of continuous probability distributions representing the severity of the losses (e.g., Pareto, Log Logistic, etc.). The Document further states that this is an approximation model limited to subexponential-type distributions only and is fairly difficult to compute. The X distribution's cumulative distribution function (CDF) will need to be inverted using Fourier transform methods, and the results are only approximations based on a limited set of inputs and their requisite constraints. Also, as discussed below, the SLA model proposed in the Basel Consultative Document significantly underestimates OPCAR.

This current technical note provides a new and alternative convolution methodology to compute OPCAR that is applicable across a large variety of continuous probability distributions for risk severity and includes a comparison of their results with Monte Carlo risk simulation methods. As will be shown, both the new algorithm using numerical methods to model OPCAR and the Monte Carlo risk simulation approach tend to the same results, and seeing that simulation can be readily and easily applied in the CMOL software and Risk Simulator software (source: www.realoptionsvaluation.com), we recommend using simulation methodologies for the sake of simplicity. While the Basel Committee has, throughout its Basel II-III requirements and recommendations, sought after simplicity so as not to burden banks with added complexity, it still requires sufficient rigor and substantiated theory. Monte Carlo risk simulation methods pass the test on both fronts and are, hence, the recommended path when modeling OPCAR.

PROBLEM WITH BASEL OPCAR

We submit that the SLA estimation model proposed in the Basel Consultative Document is insufficient and significantly underestimates an actual OPCAR value. A cursory examination shows that with various λ values, such as $\lambda = 1$, $\lambda = 10$, $\lambda = 100$, $\lambda = 1000$, the $UL = F_X^{-1}\left[1 - \frac{1-p}{\lambda}\right]$ will yield $\left[1 - \frac{1-p}{\lambda}\right]$ probability values (η) of 0.999, 0.9999, 0.99999, and 0.999999. $UL = F_X^{-1}[\eta]$ for any severity distribution X will only yield the severity distribution's values, and not the total unexpected losses. For instance, suppose the severity distribution (X) of a single risk event on average ranges from \$1M (minimum) to \$2M (maximum), and, for simplicity, assume it is a Uniformly distributed severity of losses. Further suppose that the average frequency of events is 1,000 times per year. Based on back of the envelop calculation, one could then conclude that the absolute highest operational risk capital losses will never exceed \$2B per year (this assumes the absolute worst case scenario of \$2M loss per event multiplied by 1,000 events in that entire year). Nonetheless, using the inverse of the X distribution at $\eta = 0.999999$ will yield a value close to \$2M only, and adding that to the adjusted expected value of EL (let's just assume somewhere close to \$1.5B based on the Uniform distribution) is still a far cry from the upper end of \$2B.

Figure TN.14 shows a more detailed calculation that proves the Basel Consultative Document's SLA approximation method significantly understates the true distributional operational Value at Risk amount. In the figure, we test four examples of a Poisson–Weibull convolution. The Poisson distribution with Lambda risk event frequency $\lambda = 10$, $\lambda = 25$, $\lambda = 50$, and $\lambda = 100$ are tested, together with a Weibull risk severity distribution: $\alpha = 1.5$ and $\beta = 2.5$. These values are shown as highlighted cells in the figure. Using the Basel OPCAR model, we compute the UL and EL. In the UL computation, we use $UL = F_X^{-1}\left[1 - \frac{1-p}{\lambda}\right] = F_X^{-1}[\eta]$. The column labeled PROB is η. The ICDF X column denotes the $UL = F_X^{-1}[\eta]$. By applying the inverse of the Weibull CDF on the probability, we obtain the UL values. Next, the EL calculations are simply $EL = (\lambda - 1)E[X]$ with $E[X]$ being the expected value of the Weibull distribution X, where $E[X] = \beta\Gamma[1 + 1/\alpha]$. The OPCAR is simply $UL + EL$. The four OPCAR results obtained are 31.30, 65.87, 122.82, and 236.18.

We then tested the results using Monte Carlo risk simulation using the Risk Simulator software (source: www.realoptionsvaluation.com) by setting four Poisson distributions with their respective λ values and a single Weibull distribution with $\alpha = 1.5$ and $\beta = 2.5$. Then, the Weibull distribution is multiplied by each of the Poisson distributions to obtain the four Total Loss Distributions. The simulation was run for 100,000 trials and the results are shown in Figure TN.14 as forecast charts at the bottom. The Left Tail $\leq 99.9\%$ quantile values were obtained and can be seen in the charts (116.38, 258.00, 476.31, and 935.25). These are significantly higher than the four OPCAR results.

Next, we ran a third approach using the newly revised convolution algorithm we propose in this technical note. The convolution model shows the same values as the Monte Carlo risk simulation results: 116.38, 258.00, 476.31, and 935.25, when rounded to two decimals. The inverse of the convolution function computes the corresponding CDF percentiles and they are all 99.9% (rounded to one decimal; see the Convolution and Percentile columns in Figure TN.14). Using the same inverse of the convolution function and applied to the Basel Consultative Document's SLA model results, we found that the four SLA results were at the following OPCAR percentiles: 75.75%, 66.94%, 62.78%, and 60.38%, again significantly different than the requisite 99.9% Value at Risk level for operational risk capital required by the Basel Committee.

Therefore, due to this significant understatement of operational capital at risk, the remainder of this technical note focuses on explaining the theoretical details of the newly revised convolution model we developed that provides exact OPCAR results under certain conditions. We then compare the results using Monte Carlo risk simulation methods using Risk Simulator software as well as the Credit, Market, Operational, and Liquidity (CMOL) Risk software (source: www.realoptionsvaluation.com). Finally, the caveats and limitations of this new approach as well as conclusions and recommendations are presented.

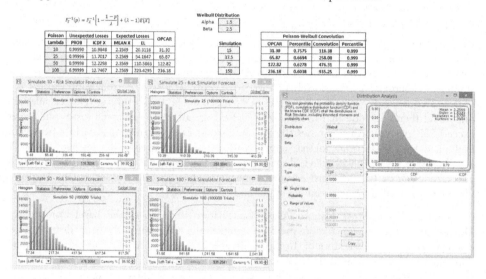

Figure TN.14: Comparing Basel OPCAR, Monte Carlo Risk Simulation, and the Convolution Algorithm

Theory

Let X, Y, and Z be real-valued random variables whereby X and Y are independently distributed with no correlations. Further, we define F_X, F_Y, and F_Z as their corresponding CDFs, and f_X, f_Y, and f_Z are their corresponding PDFs. Next, we assume that X is a random variable denoting the Frequency of a certain type of operational risk occurring and is further assumed to have a discrete Poisson distribution. Y is a random variable denoting the Severity of the risk (e.g., monetary value or some other economic value) and can be distributed from among a group of continuous distributions (e.g., Fréchet, Gamma, Log Logistic, Lognormal, Pareto, Weibull, etc.). Therefore, *Frequency* × *Severity* equals the *Total Risk Losses*, which we define as Z, where $Z = X \times Y$.

Then the Total Loss formula, which is also sometimes known as the Single Loss Approximation (SLA) model, yields:

$$F_Z(t) = P(Z < t) = \sum_k P(XY < t \mid X = k) \times P(X = k)$$

$$F_Z(t) = P(Z < t) = \sum_k P(kY < t) \times P(X = k)$$

where the term with $X = 0$ is treated separately:

$F_Z(t) = P(0 < t | X = 0) \times P(X = 0) + \sum_{k \neq 0} P(Y < t/k) \times P(X = k)$

$F_Z(t) = \sum_{k \neq 0} f_X(k) F_Y(t/k) + P(X = 0)$ (Equation 1)

The next step is the selection of the number of summands in Equation 1. As previously assumed, $f_X(k) = P(X = k)$ is a Poisson distribution where $P(X = k) = \frac{\lambda^k e^{-\lambda}}{k!}$ and the rate of convergence in the series depends solely on the rate of convergence to 0 of $\frac{\lambda^k}{k!}$ and does not depend on t, whereas the second multiplier $P(Y < t/k) \leq 1!$ Therefore, for all values of t and an arbitrary $\delta > 0$ there is value of n such that:

$\sum_{k>n} \frac{\lambda^k e^{-\lambda}}{k!} F_Y(t/k) < \delta$ (Equation 2)

In our case, δ can be set, for example, to $1/1000$. Thus, instead of solving the quantile equation for t_p with an infinite series, on the left-hand side of the equation we have:

$F_Z(t) = P(Z < t) = \sum_k P\left(Y < \frac{t}{k}\right) \frac{\lambda^k e^{-\lambda}}{k!} = p$ (Equation 3)

We can then solve the equation:

$F_Z(t, n) = \sum_{k \leq n} \frac{\lambda^k e^{-\lambda}}{k!} F_Y(t/k) = p$ (Equation 4)

with only n summands.

For example, if we choose $p = 0.95$, $\delta = 1/1000$, and n such that Equation 2 takes place, then the solution $t_p(n)$ of Equation 4 is such that:

$|F_Z(t_p(n)) - F_Z(t_p(n), n)| < 1/1000$ (Equation 5)

In other words, a quantile found from Equation 4 is almost the true value, with a resulting error precision in probability of less than 0.1%.

The only outstanding issue that remains is to find an estimate for n given any level of δ. We have:

$\sum_{k>n} \frac{\lambda^k e^{-\lambda}}{k!} F_Y(t/k) < e^{-\lambda} \sum_{k>n} \frac{\lambda^k}{k!}$ (Equation 6)

The exponential series $R_n(\lambda) = \sum_{k>n} \frac{\lambda^k}{k!}$ in Equation 6 is bounded by $\frac{\lambda^{n+1} e^{\lambda}}{(n+1)!}$ by applying the Taylor's Expansion Theorem, with the remainder of the function left for higher exponential function expansions. By substituting the upper bound for $R_n(\lambda)$ in Equation 6, we have:

$\sum_{k>n} \frac{\lambda^k e^{-\lambda}}{k!} F_Y(t/k) < \frac{\lambda^{n+1}}{(n+1)!}$ (Equation 7)

Now we need to find the lower bound in n for the solution of the inequality:

$\frac{\lambda^{n+1}}{(n+1)!} < \delta$ (Equation 8)

Consider the following two cases:

1. If $\lambda \leq 1$, then $\frac{\lambda^{n+1}}{(n+1)!} \leq \frac{1}{(n+1)!} \leq (n+1)^{-(n+1)}e^n$. Consequently, we can solve the inequality $(n+1)^{-(n+1)}e^n < \delta$. Since n^n grows quickly, we can simply take $n > -\ln \delta$. For example, for $\delta = 1/1000$ it is sufficient to set $n = 7$ to satisfy Equation 8.

2. If $\lambda > 1$, then, in this case, using the same bounds for the factorial, we can choose n such that:

$$(n+1)(\ln(n+1) - \ln\lambda - 1) > -\ln\delta - 1 \tag{Equation 9}$$

To make the second multiplier greater than 1, we will need to choose $n > e^{2+\ln\lambda} - 1$.

Approximation to the solution of the equation $F_Z(t) = p$ for a quantile value

From the previous considerations we found that instead of solving $F_Z(t) = p$ for t, we can solve $F_Z(t,n) = \sum_{k \leq n} \frac{\lambda^k e^{-\lambda}}{k!} F_Y(t/k) = p$ with n set at the level indicated above. The value for t_p resulting from such a substitution will satisfy the inequality $|F_Z(t_p(n)) - F_Z(t_p(n),n)| < \delta$.

Solution of the equation $F_Z(t,n) = p$ given n and δ

By moving t to the left one unit at a time, we can find the first occurrence of the event $t = a$ such that $F_Z(a,n) \leq p$. Similarly, moving t to the right we can find b such that $F_Z(b,n) \geq p$. Now we can use a simple Bisection Method or other search algorithms to find the optimal solution to $F_Z(t,n) = p$.

EMPIRICAL RESULTS: CONVOLUTION VERSUS MONTE CARLO RISK SIMULATION FOR OPCAR

Based on the explanations and algorithms outlined above, the convolution approximation models are run and results compared with Monte Carlo risk simulation results. These comparisons will serve as empirical evidence of the applicability of both approaches.

Figure TN.15 shows the 10 most commonly used Severity distributions, namely, Exponential, Fréchet, Gamma, Logistic, Log Logistic, Lognormal (Arithmetic and Logarithmic inputs), Gumbel, Pareto, and Weibull. The Frequency of risk occurrences is set as Poisson, with Lambda (λ) or average frequency rate per period as its input. The input parameters for the 10 Severity distributions are typically Alpha (α) and Beta (β), except for the Exponential distribution that uses a rate parameter, Rho (ϱ), and Lognormal distribution that requires the mean (μ) and standard deviation (σ) as inputs. For the first empirical test, we set $\lambda = 10$, $\alpha = 1.5$, $\beta = 2.5$, $\varrho = 0.01$, $\mu = 1.8$, and $\sigma = 0.5$ for the Poisson frequency and 10 severity distributions. The Convolution Model row in Figure TN.15 was computed using the algorithms outlined above, and a set of Monte Carlo risk simulation assumptions were set with the same input parameters and simulated 100,000 trials with a prespecified seed value. The results from the simulation were pasted back into the model under the Simulated Results row and the Convolution Model was calculated based on these simulated outputs. Figure TN.15 shows 5 sets of simulation percentiles: 99.9%, 99.0%, 95.0%, 90.0%, and 50.0%. As can be seen, all of the simulation results and the convolution results on average agree to approximately within ±0.2%.

Figure TN.16 shows another empirical test whereby we select one specific distribution; in the illustration, we used the Poisson–Weibull compound function. The alpha and beta parameters in Weibull were changed, in concert with the Poisson's lambda input. The first four columns show alpha and beta being held steady while changing the lambda parameter, whereas the last six columns show the same lambda with different alpha and beta input values (increasing alpha with beta constant, and increasing beta with alpha constant). When the simulation results and the convolution results were compared, on average, they agree to approximately within ±0.2%.

Figure TN.17 shows the Credit, Market, Operational, and Liquidity (CMOL) risk software's operational risk module and how the simulation results agree with the convolution model. The CMOL software uses the algorithms as described above. The CMOL software settings are 100,000 Simulation Trials with a Seed Value of 1 with an OPCAR set to 99.90%.

Figures TN.18-TN.21 show additional empirical tests where all 10 severity distributions were perturbed, convoluted, and compared with the simulation results. The results agree on average around ±0.3%.

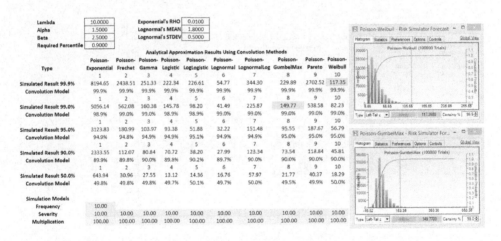

Figure TN.15: Comparing Convolution to Simulation Results I

Lambda	10.00	25.00	75.00	100.00	50.00	50.00	50.00	50.00	50.00	50.00
Alpha	1.50	1.50	1.50	1.50	1.50	15.00	45.00	1.50	45.00	1.50
Beta	2.50	2.50	2.50	2.50	2.50	2.50	2.50	15.00	50.00	75.00

Analytical Approximation Results Using Convolution Methods: Weibull Distribution

Type	Poisson-Weibull 1	Poisson-Weibull 2	Poisson-Weibull 3	Poisson-Weibull 4	Poisson-Weibull 5	Poisson-Weibull 6	Poisson-Weibull 7	Poisson-Weibull 8	Poisson-Weibull 9	Poisson-Weibull 10
Simulated Result	117.35	251.52	716.62	943.55	488.72	186.23	183.36	2919.98	3651.15	14629.3
Convolution Model	99.9%	99.9%	99.9%	99.9%	99.9%	99.9%	99.9%	99.9%	99.9%	99.9%
Simulated Result	82.23	185.40	531.75	708.24	362.16	169.24	167.17	2159.08	3339.56	10750.8
Convolution Model	99.0%	98.9%	99.0%	99.0%	99.0%	99.0%	99.0%	99.0%	99.0%	99.0%
Simulated Result	56.79	134.72	393.66	522.88	264.25	154.15	153.77	1589.67	3071.24	7909.56
Convolution Model	95.0%	95.0%	94.9%	94.9%	94.9%	95.0%	95.1%	95.0%	95.0%	94.9%
Simulated Result	45.81	110.63	327.60	437.82	219.00	146.39	146.76	1323.64	2932.39	6579.73
Convolution Model	90.0%	89.8%	89.8%	90.0%	89.8%	90.0%	90.2%	90.1%	90.0%	89.9%
Simulated Result	18.27	47.35	145.21	193.97	96.33	120.06	122.99	578.52	2461.52	2895.14
Convolution Model	50.0%	49.8%	49.9%	49.9%	49.9%	49.8%	50.0%	50.0%	50.2%	50.0%

Simulation Models

Frequency	10.00	25.00	75.00	100.00	50.00	50.00	50.00	50.00	50.00	50.00
Severity	2.26	2.26	2.26	2.26	2.26	2.41	2.47	13.54	49.38	67.71
Multiplication	22.57	56.42	169.26	225.69	112.84	120.71	123.46	677.06	2469.13	3385.29

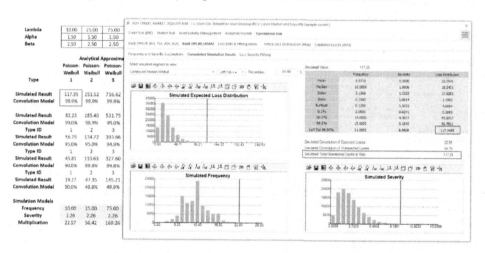

Figure TN.16: Comparing Convolution to Simulation Results II

Figure TN.17: Comparing Convolution to Simulation Results III

Frequency: Poisson (λ=10) and Severity: 10 Distributions (α=1.5, β=2.5, ρ=0.01, μ=1.8, σ=0.5)

SIMULATION RESULTS (APPROXIMATE PERCENTILE FROM SIMULATION GIVEN THE LEFT TAIL VALUE)

Exponential	Frechet	Gamma	Logistic	Log Logistic	Lognormal	Lognormal	Gumbel	Pareto	Weibull
99.8%	99.8%	99.8%	99.9%	99.9%	99.8%	99.9%	99.9%	99.8%	99.8%
0.06%	0.08%	0.07%	0.03%	0.04%	0.09%	0.04%	0.03%	0.10%	0.08%
98.9%	99.0%	99.4%	99.0%	98.9%	98.9%	99.0%	98.9%	98.9%	98.9%
0.10%	0.03%	-0.38%	0.00%	0.07%	0.08%	0.05%	0.06%	0.10%	0.10%
94.9%	95.1%	94.7%	95.0%	95.2%	95.0%	94.8%	95.0%	94.9%	95.0%
0.06%	-0.06%	0.35%	0.03%	-0.15%	0.00%	0.21%	0.00%	0.10%	0.01%
90.0%	90.2%	90.1%	90.1%	90.2%	90.0%	90.1%	90.0%	89.9%	90.1%
0.00%	-0.17%	-0.08%	-0.08%	-0.17%	-0.02%	-0.07%	-0.01%	0.10%	-0.12%
50.0%	50.2%	50.1%	50.1%	50.1%	50.1%	50.1%	50.1%	50.0%	50.1%
0.05%	-0.15%	-0.05%	-0.08%	-0.13%	-0.10%	-0.05%	-0.06%	0.01%	-0.11%

Figure TN.18: Empirical Results 1: Small Value Inputs

Frequency: Poisson (λ=50) and Severity: 10 Distributions (α=3, β=5, ρ=0.10, μ=5, σ=1)

SIMULATION RESULTS (APPROXIMATE PERCENTILE FROM SIMULATION GIVEN THE LEFT TAIL VALUE)

Exponential	Frechet	Gamma	Logistic	Log Logistic	Lognormal	Lognormal	Gumbel	Pareto	Weibull
99.9%	99.8%	99.9%	99.8%	99.8%	99.8%	99.8%	99.8%	99.8%	99.8%
0.04%	0.05%	-0.01%	0.06%	0.06%	0.07%	0.06%	0.09%	0.08%	0.09%
98.9%	99.0%	99.0%	99.0%	98.9%	98.9%	99.0%	98.9%	98.9%	98.9%
0.08%	-0.01%	-0.05%	-0.04%	0.08%	0.08%	0.03%	0.06%	0.06%	0.08%
95.0%	95.0%	95.1%	94.9%	95.1%	94.9%	95.0%	94.9%	94.9%	95.1%
-0.02%	-0.02%	-0.05%	0.06%	-0.10%	0.10%	0.03%	0.05%	0.09%	-0.07%
90.2%	90.0%	90.0%	90.0%	90.2%	90.0%	89.9%	90.0%	89.8%	90.1%
-0.15%	-0.03%	0.00%	0.04%	-0.20%	0.00%	0.07%	0.03%	0.16%	-0.05%
49.8%	50.0%	50.0%	50.1%	49.4%	50.0%	50.1%	50.0%	50.0%	50.1%
0.18%	0.00%	0.00%	-0.10%	0.65%	0.00%	-0.10%	0.00%	0.00%	-0.10%

Figure TN.19: Empirical Results 2: Average Value Inputs

Frequency: Poisson (λ=100) and Severity: 10 Distributions (α=25, β=35, ρ=0.025, μ=2.5, σ=0.9)

SIMULATION RESULTS (APPROXIMATE PERCENTILE FROM SIMULATION GIVEN THE LEFT TAIL VALUE)

Exponential	Frechet	Gamma	Logistic	Log Logistic	Lognormal	Lognormal	Gumbel	Pareto	Weibull
99.9%	99.9%	99.8%	99.9%	99.8%	99.8%	99.8%	99.8%	99.9%	99.8%
-0.05%	0.04%	0.06%	0.04%	0.07%	0.07%	0.05%	0.07%	0.03%	0.08%
99.5%	99.0%	99.0%	99.0%	99.0%	99.0%	98.9%	98.9%	98.9%	99.0%
-0.54%	0.03%	0.01%	-0.02%	-0.02%	0.05%	0.10%	0.11%	0.06%	0.01%
97.2%	95.0%	95.2%	95.0%	95.1%	95.0%	95.0%	94.9%	94.9%	95.0%
-2.20%	0.00%	-0.17%	0.00%	-0.10%	0.05%	0.00%	0.15%	0.13%	0.00%
93.7%	90.0%	90.0%	90.0%	90.0%	90.1%	89.9%	90.0%	90.0%	90.3%
-3.70%	0.00%	0.05%	0.00%	0.00%	-0.05%	0.15%	0.00%	0.00%	-0.25%
56.2%	50.0%	50.1%	50.0%	50.0%	50.0%	50.0%	50.1%	50.0%	50.0%
-6.21%	0.00%	-0.05%	-0.01%	-0.01%	0.00%	-0.01%	-0.06%	0.05%	0.00%

Figure TN.20: Empirical Results 3: Medium Value Inputs

Frequency: Poisson (λ=15) and Severity: 10 Distributions (α=80, β=25, ρ=5, μ=25, σ=3)

SIMULATION RESULTS (APPROXIMATE PERCENTILE FROM SIMULATION GIVEN THE LEFT TAIL VALUE)

Exponential	Frechet	Gamma	Logistic	Log Logistic	Lognormal	Lognormal	Gumbel	Pareto	Weibull
99.9%	99.8%	99.9%	99.9%	99.9%	99.8%	99.8%	99.8%	99.9%	99.8%
0.05%	0.06%	0.04%	0.05%	0.03%	0.12%	0.12%	0.08%	0.05%	0.06%
98.9%	98.9%	99.0%	99.0%	99.0%	99.0%	99.0%	98.9%	99.1%	99.0%
0.07%	0.06%	-0.02%	0.03%	0.04%	0.01%	0.01%	0.08%	-0.07%	0.04%
95.0%	95.0%	95.0%	95.1%	95.0%	95.0%	95.0%	95.0%	95.0%	95.0%
0.04%	0.00%	0.01%	-0.06%	0.00%	0.02%	0.02%	0.02%	0.00%	0.05%
90.0%	90.0%	90.2%	90.0%	90.2%	90.0%	90.0%	89.9%	90.0%	90.1%
0.00%	0.00%	-0.16%	0.01%	-0.17%	0.01%	0.01%	0.09%	0.00%	-0.10%
49.9%	50.1%	50.1%	50.0%	49.9%	50.0%	50.0%	50.1%	50.0%	50.0%
0.08%	-0.05%	-0.05%	0.05%	0.10%	0.00%	0.00%	-0.10%	0.00%	0.00%

Figure TN.21: Empirical Results 4: High Value Inputs

HIGH LAMBDA AND LOW
LAMBDA LIMITATIONS

As seen in Equation 4, we have the $F_Z(t, n) = \sum_{k \leq n} \frac{\lambda^k e^{-\lambda}}{k!} F_Y(t/k) = p$ convolution model. The results are accurate to as many decimal-points precision as desired as long as n is sufficiently large, but this would mean that the convolution model is potentially mathematically intractable. When λ and k are high (the value k depends on the Poisson rate λ), such as $\lambda = 10{,}000$, the summand cannot be easily computed. For instance, Microsoft Excel 2013 can only compute up to a factorial of 170! where 171! and above returns the #NUM! error. Banks whose operational risks have large λ rate values (extremely high frequency of risk events when all risk types are lumped together into a comprehensive frequency count) have several options: Create a breakdown of the various risk types (broken down by risk categories, by department, by division, etc.) such that the λ is more manageable; use a continuous distribution approximation as shown below; or use Monte Carlo risk simulation techniques, where large λ values will not pose a problem whatsoever.

Poisson distributions with large λ values approach the Normal distribution, and we can use this fact to generate an approximation model for the convolution method. The actual deviation between Poisson and Normal approximation can be estimated by the Berry–Esseen inequality. For a more accurate and order of magnitude tighter estimation we can use the Wilson–Hilferty approximation instead. For the large lambda situation, we can compute the CDF of the compound of two continuous distributions whose PDFs are defined as $f(x)$ defined on the positive interval of (a, b) for the random variable X, and $g(y)$ defined on the positive interval of (c, d), for the random variable Y. In other words, we have $0 < a < b < \infty$ and $0 < c < d < \infty$. The joint distribution $Z = XY$ has the following characteristics:

$$f(v) = \int_i^j f(x)g(v/x)\frac{1}{x}dx$$

$$F(v) = \int_m^n f(v) = \iint\limits_{m\ i}^{n\ j} f(x)g(v/x)\frac{1}{x}dx$$

The integration can be applied analytically using numerical integration methods but the results will critically depend on the integration range of x and v. The values of a, b, c, d can be computed by taking the inverse CDF of the distributions at 0.01% and 99.99% respectively (e.g., in the Normal distribution, this allows us to obtain real values instead of relying on the theoretical tails of $-\infty$ and $+\infty$). The following table summarizes the integration ranges:

When $AD < BC$:	When $AD = BC$:	When $AD > BC$:
$j = v/c$ if $ac < v < ad$	$j = v/c$ if $ac < v < ad$	$j = v/c$ if $ac < v < bc$
$j = v/c$ if $ad < v < bc$	$j = b$ if $ad < v < bd$	$j = b$ if $bc < v < ad$
$j = b$ if $bc < v < bd$	$i = a$ if $ac < v < ad$	$j = b$ if $ad < v < bd$
$i = a$ if $ac < v < ad$	$i = v/d$ if $ad < v < bd$	$i = a$ if $ac < v < bc$
$i = v/d$ if $ad < v < bc$		$i = a$ if $bc < v < ad$
$i = v/d$ if $bc < v < bd$		$i = v/d$ if $ad < v < bd$

To obtain the values of m and n, we can first run a Monte Carlo Risk Simulation of the two independent distributions, then multiply them to obtain the joint distribution, and from this joint distribution, we obtain the left tail 0.01% value, and set this as m. The value of n is the left tail VaR% (e.g., 99.95%) value. The second integral when run based on this range, will return the CDF percentile of the OPCAR VaR. Alternatively, as previously described, the Bisection Method can be used to obtain the lowest value of m by performing iterative searches such that the CDF returns valid results at 0.01% and then a second search is performed to identify the upper range or n, where the resulting n that makes the integral equal to the user specified VaR%, i.e., the OPCAR value.

Finally, for low lambda values, the algorithm still runs but will be a lot less accurate. Recall in Equation 2 that $\sum_{k>n} \frac{\lambda^k e^{-\lambda}}{k!} F_Y(t/k) < \delta$ where δ signifies the level of error precision (the lower the value, the higher the precision and accuracy of the results). The problem is, with low λ values, both k and n, which depend on λ, will also be low. This means that in the summand there would be an insufficient number of integer intervals, making the summation function less accurate. For best results, λ should be between 5 and 100.

CAVEATS, CONCLUSIONS, AND RECOMMENDATIONS

Based on the theory, application, and empirical evidence above, one can conclude that the convolution of *Frequency × Severity* independent stochastic random probability distributions can be modeled using the algorithms outlined above as well as using Monte Carlo simulation methods. On average, the results from these two methods tend to converge with some slight percentage variation due to randomness in the simulation process and the precision depending on the number of intervals in the summand or numerical integration techniques employed.

However, as noted, the algorithms described above are only applicable when the lambda parameter $5 \leq \lambda \leq 100$, else the approximation using numerical integration approach is required.

In contrast, Monte Carlo risk simulation methods are applicable in any realistic lambda situation (in simulation, a high lambda condition can be treated by using a Normal distribution). As both the numerical method and simulation approach tend to the same results, and seeing that simulation can be readily and easily applied in CMOL and using Risk Simulator, we recommend using simulation methodologies for the sake of simplicity. The Basel Committee has, throughout its Basel II-III requirements and recommendations, sought for simplicity so as not to burden the banks with added complexity, and yet it still requires sufficient rigor and substantiated theory. Therefore, Monte Carlo risk simulation methods are the recommended path when it comes to modeling OPCAR.

TECHNICAL NOTE 4: PARETO AND SENSITIVITY CHARTS

A Pareto chart contains both a bar chart and a line graph. Individual values are represented in descending order by the bars, and the cumulative total is represented by the ascending line as shown in Figure TN.22. The following sample dataset is used to generate the chart:

Name	Value
Weld LOF	9.8
Porosity	18.5
Shrink	69.5
Shell	8.2
Hard Alpha	5.6
Tungsten	3.2

As can be seen in Figure TN.22, the variables are listed from high to low, and the cumulative percentage (%) is computed. The cumulative percentage goes to 100% and is shown on the right vertical axis, whereas the values are shown on the left vertical axis.

The Pareto chart is also known as the "80-20" chart, whereby you see that by focusing on the top three variables, we are already accounting for more than 80% of the cumulative effects of the total.

COMPARING PARETO WITH SENSITIVITY

A related feature is sensitivity analysis. While tornado analysis (tornado charts and spider charts) applies static perturbations before a simulation run, sensitivity analysis applies dynamic perturbations created after the simulation run. Tornado and spider charts are the results of static perturbations, meaning that each precedent or assumption variable is perturbed a preset amount one at a time, and the fluctuations in the results are tabulated. In contrast, sensitivity charts are the results of dynamic perturbations in the sense that multiple assumptions are perturbed simultaneously and their interactions in the model and correlations among variables are captured in the fluctuations of the results. Tornado charts, therefore, identify which variables drive the results the most and, hence, are suitable for simulation, whereas sensitivity charts identify the impact on the results when multiple interacting variables are simulated together in the model. This effect is clearly illustrated in Figure TN.23. Notice that the rankings of critical success drivers are similar to the Pareto chart in the previous example. Sensitivity charts are typically shown as horizontal bars whereas Pareto charts are shown as vertical bars (you can think of sensitivity charts as Pareto analysis "on its side").

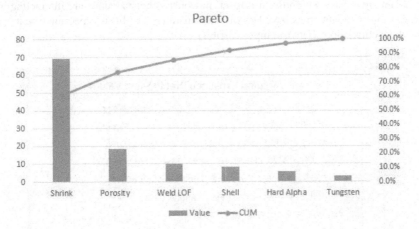

Figure TN.22: Pareto Chart

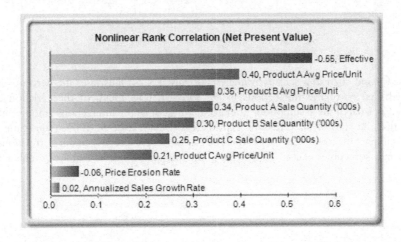

Figure TN.23: Dynamic Sensitivity Chart

If correlations are added between the simulation assumptions, sensitivity analysis will return a very different chart. Note that neither tornado analysis nor Pareto charts can capture these correlated dynamic simulated relationships. Only after a simulation is run will such relationships become evident in a sensitivity analysis. A tornado chart's pre-simulation critical success factors and a Pareto chart's cumulative effects charts will, therefore, sometimes be different from a sensitivity chart's postsimulation dynamic critical success factor. The postsimulation critical success factors should be the ones that are of interest as these more readily capture the model precedents' interactions.

In addition, the results of the sensitivity analysis include a report and two key charts. The first is a nonlinear rank correlation chart, as seen in Figure TN.23, that ranks from highest to lowest the assumption-forecast correlation pairs. These correlations are nonlinear and nonparametric, making them free of any distributional requirements (i.e., an assumption with a Weibull distribution can be compared to another with a beta distribution). The results from this chart are sometimes similar to that of the tornado analysis and Pareto charts, but sometimes the rankings might be different. This difference occurs because by itself, a certain input variable may have a significant impact, but once other variables are interacting in the model, this initial variable may have less of a dominant effect (this is especially true in a large model where correlations between input variables exist).

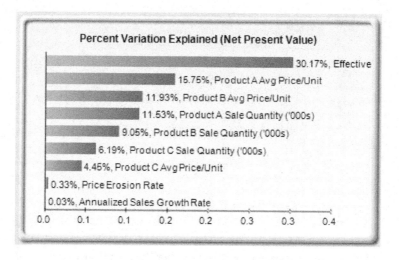

Figure TN.24: Percent Variation Explained in Dynamic Sensitivity Analysis

The second chart in a sensitivity analysis (Figure TN.24) illustrates the percent variation explained; that is, of the fluctuations in the forecast, how much of the variation can be explained by each of the assumptions after accounting for all the interactions among variables? Notice that the sum of all variations explained is usually close to 100% (sometimes other elements impact the model but they cannot be captured here directly), and if correlations exist, the sum may sometimes exceed 100% (due to the interaction effects that are cumulative).

TECHNICAL NOTE 5: DISTRIBUTION CHARTS AND TABLES USING THE PROBABILITY DISTRIBUTION TOOL

Distributional Charts and Tables is a new Probability Distribution tool that is a very powerful and fast module used for generating distribution charts and tables. Note that there are three similar tools in Risk Simulator but each does very different things:

1. Distributional Analysis: Used to quickly compute the PDF, CDF, and ICDF of the 50 probability distributions available in Risk Simulator, and to return a probability table of these values.

2. Distributional Charts and Tables: The Probability Distribution tool described here used to compare different parameters of the same distribution (e.g., the shapes and PDF, CDF, ICDF values of a Weibull distribution with Alpha and Beta of [2, 2], [3, 5], and [3.5, 8], and overlays them on top of one another).

3. Overlay Charts: Used to compare different distributions (theoretical input assumptions and empirically simulated output forecasts) and to overlay them on top of one another for a visual comparison.

SHAPES OF DISTRIBUTIONS

The following illustrates how multiple probability distribution charts can be developed and compared against each other.

- Run *Risk Simulator | Analytical Tools | Distributional Charts and Tables*, click on the *Apply Global Inputs* button to load a sample set of input parameters or enter your own inputs, and click *Run* to compute the results. The resulting four moments and CDF, ICDF, PDF are computed for each of the 50 probability distributions (Figure TN.25).

- Click on the *Charts and Tables* tab (Figure TN.26), select a distribution (e.g., Beta 4), then choose if you wish to run the CDF, ICDF, or PDF, enter the relevant inputs, and click *Run Chart*. You can switch between the *Chart* and *Table* tab to view the results as well as try out some of the chart icons to see the effects on the chart.

- You can also change two parameters to generate multiple charts and distribution tables by entering the *From | To | Step* input after selecting the relevant *Change First* and *Second Parameter* droplists; then hit *Run*. For example, as illustrated in Figure TN.26, run the Beta 4 distribution and select PDF, select *Alpha* and *Beta* to change using the custom droplists and enter the relevant input parameters: 3; 5; 2 for the Alpha inputs and 2; 4; 2 for the Beta inputs, and click *Run Chart*. This will generate four Beta 4 distributions: Beta 4 (3, 2, 10, 2), Beta 4 (3, 4, 10, 2), Beta 4 (5, 2, 10, 2), and Beta 4 (5, 4, 10, 2). Explore various chart types, gridlines, language, and decimal settings, and try rerunning the distribution using theoretical versus empirically simulated values.

- Figure TN.27 is the same set of distributions viewed under the CDF selection with gridlines turned on. Notice that the decimal has been set to 1 and the labels have been moved to different locations for the sake of clarity of the charts. Use the *Index* number droplist (default is 1) and +A, –A, ←A, →A, A↑, and A↓ icons (located immediately above the chart) to resize and move the labels. The index droplist is for you to select which chart line's labels you wish to manipulate.

- Figure TN.28 illustrates the probability tables generated for a binomial distribution where the probability of success and number of successful trials (random variable X) are selected to vary using the *From | To | Step* option. Try to replicate the calculation as shown and click on the *Table* tab to view the created CDF results. This example uses a binomial distribution with a starting input set of *Trials* = 20, *Probability* (i.e., the probability of success for each trial) = 0.5, and *Random X* (the number of successful trials) = 10, where the *Probability* is allowed to change from 0.1, 0.2, …, 0.9 and is shown as the row variable, and the *Number of Successful Trials* is also allowed to change from 0, 1, 2, …, 20, and is shown as the column variable. CDF is chosen and, hence, the results in the table show the cumulative probability given that the number of successful events occurs under various probabilities of success.

- Finally, Figure TN.29 shows the *Compare Charts* subtab where PDF and CDF curves from different probability distributions can be overlaid on top of one another to compare their characteristics. The example shown has the PDFs of the gamma and Weibull distributions. Start by going to the *Charts and Tables | Compare Charts* subtab, and select the *Weibull* distribution. Enter *Alpha* = 2 and *Beta* = 5 and click *Add*. Then, select the *Gamma* distribution and enter the same alpha and beta values, and click *Add*. Finally, click *Run Chart* to see the resulting distributions.

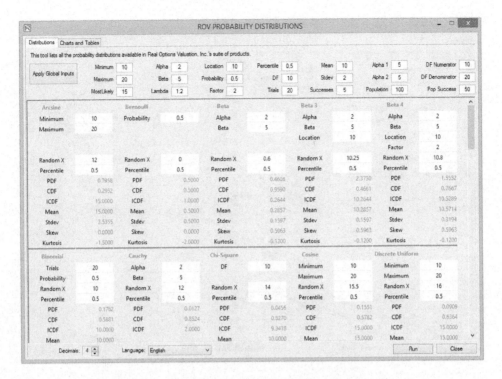

Figure TN.25: Distributional Charts and Tables Tool

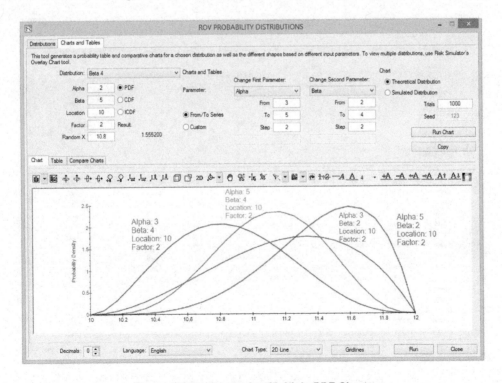

Figure TN.26: Overlaying Multiple PDF Charts

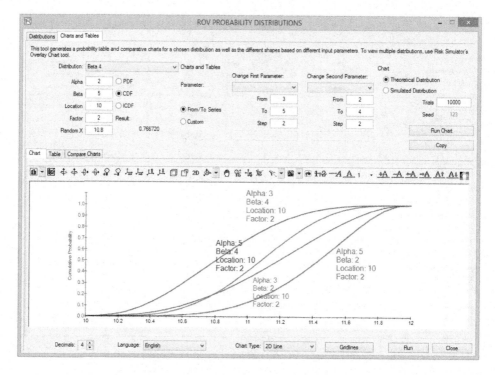

Figure TN.27: Overlay CDF Charts with Gridlines

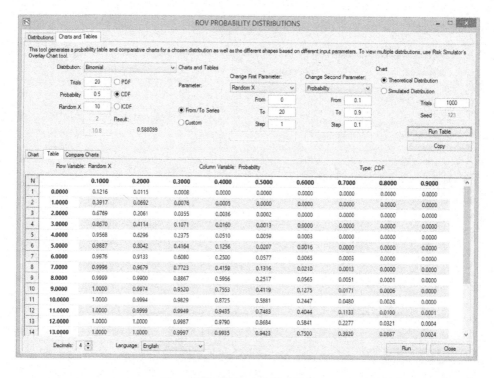

Figure TN.28: Probability Tables

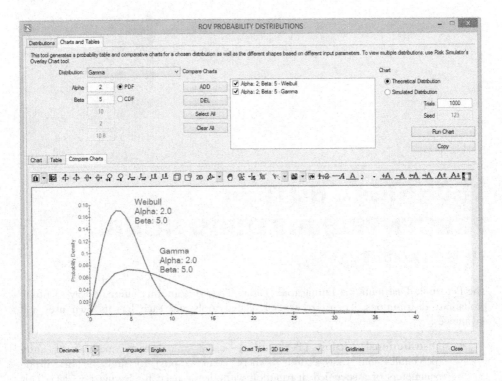

Figure TN.29: Overlay and Compare Different Distributions

TECHNICAL NOTE 6: PERCENTILE DISTRIBUTIONAL FITTING TOOL

The Percentile Distributional Fitting tool (Figure TN.30) is another alternate way of fitting probability distributions. There are several related tools and each has its own uses and advantages:

- **Distributional Fitting (Percentiles)**—using an alternate method of entry (percentiles and first/second moment combinations) to find the best-fitting parameters of a specified distribution without the need for having raw data. This method is suitable for use when there are insufficient data, only when percentiles and moments are available, or as a means to recover the entire distribution with only two or three data points but the distribution type needs to be assumed or known.

- **Distributional Fitting (Single Variable)**—using statistical methods to fit your raw data to all 45 distributions to find the best-fitting distribution and its input parameters. Multiple data points are required for a good fit, and the distribution type may or may not be known ahead of time.

- **Distributional Fitting (Multiple Variables)**—using statistical methods to fit your raw data on multiple variables at the same time. This method uses the same algorithms as the single variable fitting, but incorporates a pairwise correlation matrix between the variables. Multiple data points are required for a good fit, and the distribution type may or may not be known ahead of time.

- **Custom Distribution (Set Assumption)**—using nonparametric resampling techniques to generate a custom distribution with the existing raw data and to simulate the distribution based on this empirical distribution. Fewer data points are required, and the distribution type is not known ahead of time.

Procedure

Click on *Risk Simulator | Analytical Tools | Distributional Fitting (Percentiles)*, choose the probability distribution and types of inputs you wish to use, enter the parameters, and click *Run* to obtain the results. Review the fitted R-square results and compare the empirical versus theoretical fitting results to determine if your distribution is a good fit.

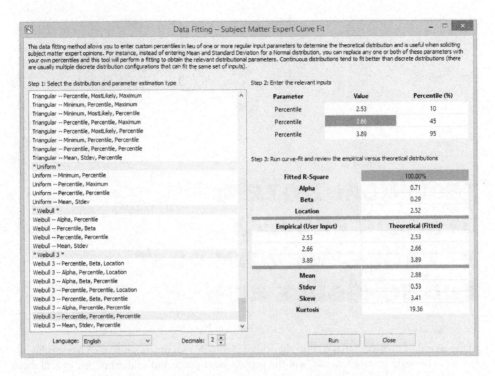

Figure TN.30: Percentile Distributional Fitting Tool

TECHNICAL NOTE 7: DYNAMIC PROJECT MANAGEMENT WITH COST AND SCHEDULE RISK

In the world of project management, there are essentially two major sources of risks: schedule risk and cost risk. In other words, will the project be on time and under budget, or will there be a schedule crash and budget overrun, and, if so, how bad can they be? To illustrate how quantitative risk management can be applied to project management, we use ROV PEAT to model these two sources of risks.

To follow along, start the PEAT software, select the *Project Management—Dynamic Cost and Schedule Risk* module, and *Load Example*. We begin by illustrating a simple linear path project in the *Simple Linear Path 1* tab (Figure TN.31). Note that users can click on the *Projects* menu to add additional projects, or delete and rename existing projects. The example loaded has 5 sample predefined projects. In this simple linear path project, there are 11 sample tasks in this project and each task is linked to its subsequent tasks linearly (i.e., Task 2 can only start after Task 1 is done, and so forth). For each project, a user has a set of controls and inputs:

- *Sequential Path* versus *Complex Network Path*. The first example illustrated uses the sequential path, which means there is a simple linear progression of tasks. In the next example, we will explore the complex network path where tasks can be executed linearly, simultaneously, and recombined at any point in time.

- *Fixed Costs*. The fixed costs and their ranges suitable for risk simulation (minimum, most likely, maximum) are required inputs. These fixed costs are costs that will be incurred regardless if there is an overrun in schedule (the project can be completed early or late but the fixed costs will be the same regardless).

- *Time Schedule*. Period-specific time schedule (minimum, most likely, maximum) in days, weeks, or months. Users will first select the periodicity (e.g., days, weeks, months, or unitless) from the droplist and enter the projected time schedule per task. This schedule will be used in conjunction with the variable cost elements (see next bullet item), and will only be available if *Include Schedule-Based Cost Analysis* is checked.

- *Variable Cost*. This is the variable cost that is incurred based on the time schedule for each task. This variable cost is per period and will be multiplied by the number of periods to obtain the total variable cost for each task. The sum of all fixed costs and variable costs for all tasks will of course be the total cost for the project (denoted as *Project Total Cost*).

- *Overrun Assumption.* This is a percent budget buffer or cushion to include in each task. This column is only available and used if *Include Budget Overruns and Buffers* checkbox is selected.

- *Probability of Success.* This allows users to enter the probability of each task being successful. If a task fails, then all subsequent tasks will be canceled and the costs will not be incurred, as the project stops and is abandoned. This column is available and will be used in the risk simulation only if *Include Probabilities of Success* checkbox is selected.

- *Run.* The run button will perform the relevant computations based on the settings and inputs, and also run risk simulations if the *Perform Risk Simulation* checkbox is selected (as well as the requisite simulation settings such as distribution type, number of trials, and seed value settings are entered appropriately). This will run the current project's model. If multiple projects need to be run, you can first proceed to the *Portfolio Analysis* tab and click on the *Run All Projects* button instead.

To see which of these input assumptions drive total cost and schedule the most, a tornado analysis can be executed (Figure TN.32). The model can then be risk simulated and the results show probability distributions of cost and schedule (Figure TN.33). For instance, the sample results show that for Project 1, there is a 95% probability that the project can be completed at a cost of $398,594. The expected median or most likely value was originally $377,408 (Figure TN.31). With simulation, it shows that to be 95% sure that there are sufficient funds to complete the project, an additional buffer of $21,186 is warranted.

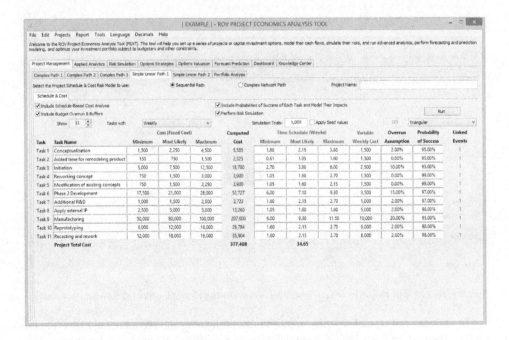

Figure TN.31: Simple Linear Path Project Management with Cost and Schedule Risk

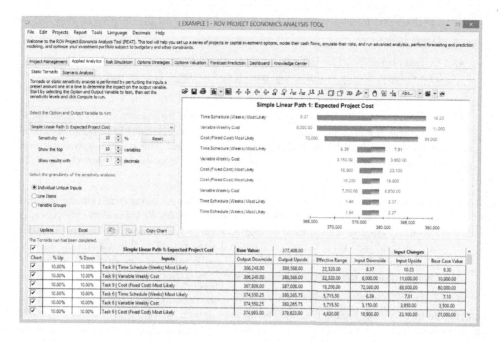

Figure TN.32: Simple Linear Path Tornado Analysis

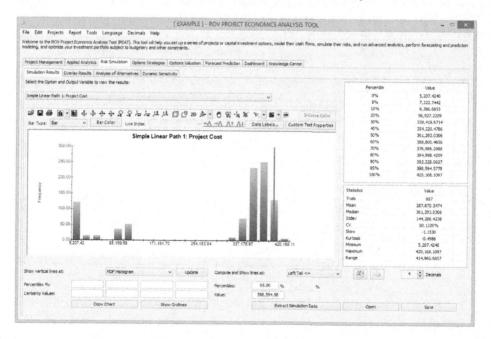

Figure TN.33: Monte Carlo Risk Simulated Results for Risky Cost and Schedule Values

In complex projects where there are nonlinear bifurcating and recombining paths (Figure TN.34), the cost and schedule risk modeling is more difficult to model and compute. For instance, in the *Complex Path 1* tab, we can see that after Task 1, future tasks can be run in parallel (Tasks 2, 3, and 4). Then, Tasks 3 and 4 recombine into Task 8. Such complex path models can be created by the user simply by adding tasks and combining them in the visual map as shown. The software will automatically create the analytical financial model when *Create Model* is clicked. That is, you will be taken to the *Schedule & Cost* tab and the same setup as shown previously is now available for data entry for this complex model (Figure TN.35). The complex mathematical connections will automatically be created behind the scenes to run the calculations so that the user will only need to perform very simple tasks of drawing the complex network path connections. Below are some tips on getting started:

- Start by adding a new project from the *Projects* menu. Then, click on the *Complex Network Path* radio selection to access the *Network Diagram* tab.

- Use the icons to assist in drawing your network path. Hover your mouse over the icons to see their descriptions. You can start by clicking on the third icon to *Create a Task*, and then click anywhere in the drawing canvas to insert said task.

- With an existing task clicked on and selected, click on the fourth icon to *Add a Subtask*. This will automatically create the adjoining next task and next task number. You then need to move this newly inserted task to its new position. Continue with this process as required to create your network diagram. You can create multiple subtasks off a single existing task if simultaneous implementations occur.

- You can also recombine different tasks by clicking on one task, then holding down the Ctrl key, click on the second task you wish to join. Then click on the fifth icon to *Link Tasks* to join then. Similarly, you can click on the sixth icon to *Delete Link* between any two tasks.

- When the network diagram is complete, click on *Create Model* to generate the computational algorithms where you can then enter the requisite data in the *Schedule & Cost* tab as described previously.

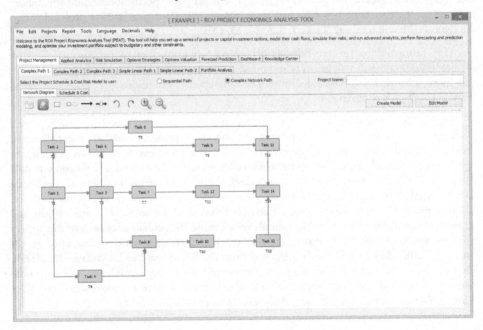

Figure TN.34: Complex Path Project Management

Figure TN.35: Complex Project Simulated Cost and Duration Model with Critical Path

After running the model, the complex path map shows the highlighted critical path (Figure TN.36) of the project, that is, the path that has the highest potential for bottlenecks and delays in completing the project on time. The exact path specifications and probabilities of being on the critical path is seen in Figure TN.35 (e.g., there is a 56.30% probability that the critical path will be along Tasks 1, 3, 8, 10, 13, 14).

If there are multiple projects or potential project path implementations, the portfolio view (Figure TN.37) compares all projects and implementation paths for the user to make a better and more informed risk-based decision. The simulated distributions can also be overlaid (Figure TN.38) for comparison.

Figure TN.37 allows users to see all projects that were modeled at a glance. Each project modeled can actually be different projects or the same project modeled under different assumptions and implementation options (i.e., different ways of executing the project), to see which project or implementation option path makes more sense in terms of cost and schedule risks. The *Analysis of Alternatives* radio selected allows users to see each project as standalone (as compared to *Incremental Analysis* where one of the projects is selected as the base case and all other projects' results show their differences from the base case), in terms of cost and schedule: single-point estimate values, simulated averages, the probabilities each of the project will have a cost or schedule overrun, and the 90th percentile value of cost and schedule. Of course more detailed analysis can be obtained from the *Risk Simulation | Simulation Results* tab, where users can view all the simulation statistics and select any confidence and percentile values to show. This *Portfolio Analysis* tab also charts the simulated cost and schedule values using bubble and bar charts for a visual representation of the key results.

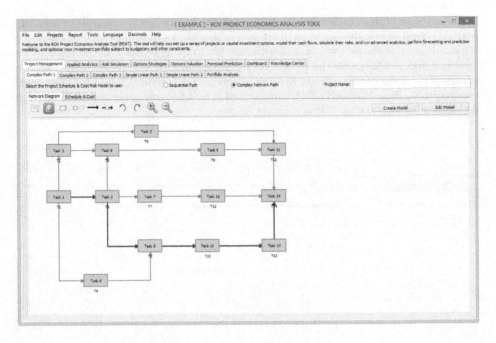

Figure TN.36: Complex Project Critical Path

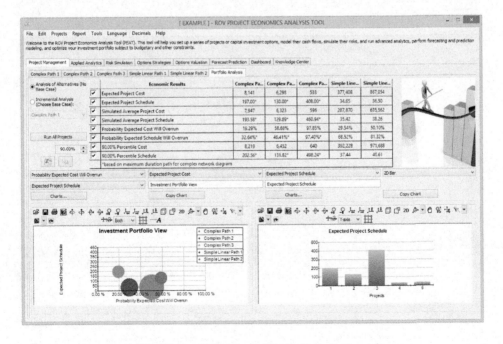

Figure TN.37: Portfolio View of Multiple Projects at Once

The *Overlay* chart in Figure TN.38 shows multiple projects' simulated costs or schedules overlaid on top of one another to see their relative spreads, location, and skew of the results. We clearly see that the project whose distribution lies to the right has a much higher cost to complete than the left, with the project on the right also having a slightly higher level of uncertainty in terms of cost spreads. Refer to Chapter 4 and Technical Note 1 for more details on interpreting these PDF and CDF charts, as well as how to make better and more informed decisions using their results.

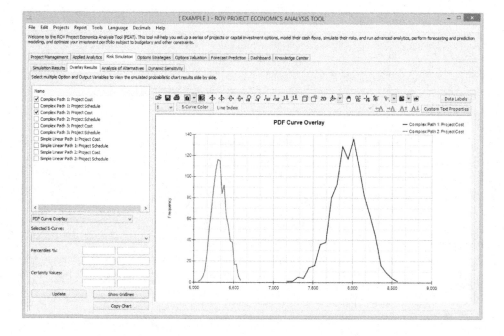

Figure TN.38: Overlay Charts of Multiple Projects' Cost or Schedule

N8

TECHNICAL NOTE 8: ROV BIZSTATS

This new ROV BizStats tool is a very powerful and fast module in Risk Simulator that is used for running business statistics and analytical models on your data. It covers more than 130 business statistics and analytical models (Figures TN.39 through TN.42). The following provides a few quick getting started steps on running the module and details on each of the elements in the software.

Procedure

- Run ROV BizStats at *Risk Simulator | ROV BizStats* and click on *Example* to load a sample data and model profile [A] or type in your data or *copy/paste* into the data grid [D] (Figure TN.39). You can add your own notes or variable names in the first *Notes* row [C].

- Select the relevant model [F] to run in *Step 2* and using the example data input settings [G], enter in the relevant variables [H]. Separate variables for the same parameter using semicolons and use a new line (hit *Enter* to create a new line) for different parameters.

- Click *Run* [I] to compute the results [J]. You can view any relevant analytical results, charts, or statistics from the various tabs in *Step 3*.

- If required, you can provide a model name to save into the profile in *Step 4* [L]. Multiple models can be saved in the same profile. Existing models can be edited or deleted [M] and rearranged in order of appearance [N], and all the changes can be saved [O] into a single profile with the file name extension *.bizstats.

Notes

- The data grid size can be set in the menu, where the grid can accommodate up to 1,000 variable columns with 1 million rows of data per variable. The menu also allows you to change the language settings and decimal settings for your data.

- To get started, it is always a good idea to load the example file [A] that comes complete with some data and precreated models [S] (Figure TN.40). You can double-click on any of these models to run them and the results are shown in the report area [J], which sometimes can be a chart or model statistics [T/U]. Using this example file, you can now see how the input parameters [H] are entered based on the model description [G], and you can proceed to create your own custom models.

- Click on the variable headers [D] to select one or multiple variables at once, and then right-click to add, delete, copy, paste, or visualize [P] the variables selected.

- Models can also be entered using a *Command* console [V/W/X] (Figure TN.41). To see how this works, double-click to run a model [S] and go to the *Command* console [V]. You can replicate the model or create your own and click *Run Command* [X] when ready. Each line in the console represents a model and its relevant parameters.

- The entire *.bizstats profile (where data and multiple models are created and saved) can be edited directly in XML [Z] by opening the *XML Editor* from the File menu (Figure TN.42). Changes to the profile can be programmatically made here and take effect once the file is saved.

- Click on the data grid's column header(s) to select the entire column(s) or variable(s), and once selected, you can right-click on the header to *Auto Fit* the column, *Cut*, *Copy*, *Delete*, or *Paste* data. You can also click on and select multiple column headers to select multiple variables and right-click and select *Visualize* to chart the data.

- If a cell has a large value that is not completely displayed, click on and hover your mouse over that cell and you will see a pop-up comment showing the entire value, or simply resize the variable column (drag the column to make it wider, double click on the column's edge to auto fit the column, or right click on the column header and select auto fit).

- Use the up, down, left, right keys to move around the grid, or use the *Home* and *End* keys on the keyboard to move to the far left and far right of a row. You can also use combination keys such as *Ctrl+Home* to jump to the top left cell, *Ctrl+End* to the bottom right cell, *Shift+Up/Down* to select a specific area, and so forth.

- You can enter short notes for each variable on the *Notes* row. Remember to make your notes short and simple.

- Try out the various chart icons on the *Visualize* tab to change the look and feel of the charts (e.g., rotate, shift, zoom, change colors, add legend, and so forth).

- The *Copy* button is used to copy the *Results*, *Charts*, and *Statistics* tabs in *Step 3* after a model is run. If no models are run, then the copy function will only copy a blank page.

- The *Report* button will only run if there are saved models in *Step 4* or if there is data in the grid, else the report generated will be empty. You will also need Microsoft Excel to be installed to run the data extraction and results reports, and Microsoft PowerPoint available to run the chart reports.

- When in doubt about how to run a specific model or statistical method, start the *Example* profile and review how the data is set up in *Step 1* or how the input parameters are entered in *Step 2*. You can use these as getting started guides and templates for your own data and models.

- The language can be changed in the *Language* menu. Note that currently there are 12 languages available in the software with more to be added later. However, sometimes certain limited results will still be shown in English.

- You can change how the list of models in *Step 2* is shown by changing the *View* droplist. You can list the models alphabetically, categorically, and by data input requirements—note that in certain Unicode languages (e.g., Chinese, Japanese, and Korean), there is no alphabetical arrangement and, therefore, the first option will be unavailable.

- The software can handle different regional decimal and numerical settings (e.g., one thousand dollars and fifty cents can be written as 1,000.50 or 1.000,50 or 1'000,50 and so forth). The decimal settings can be set in ROV BizStats' menu *Data | Decimal Settings*. However, when in doubt, please change the computer's regional settings to English USA and keep the default North America 1,000.50 in ROV BizStats (this setting is guaranteed to work with ROV BizStats and the default examples).

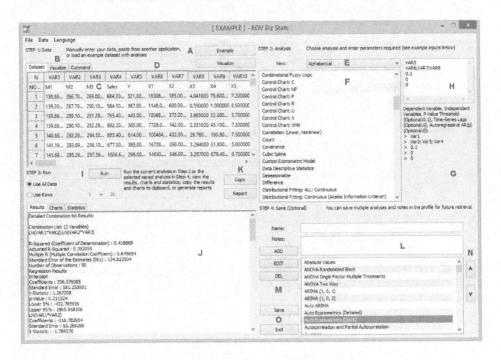

Figure TN.39: ROV BizStats (Statistical Analysis)

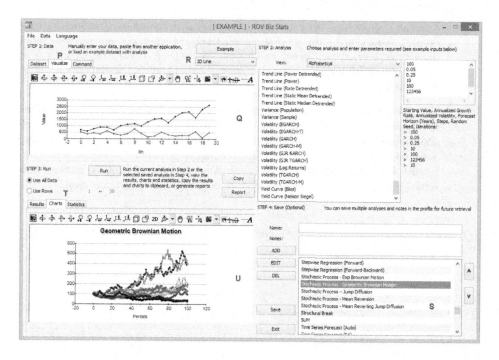

Figure TN.40: Data Visualization and Results Charts

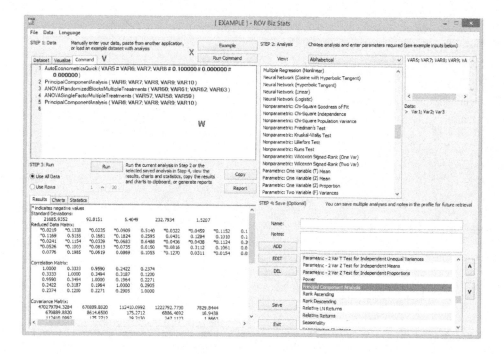

Figure TN.41: Command Console

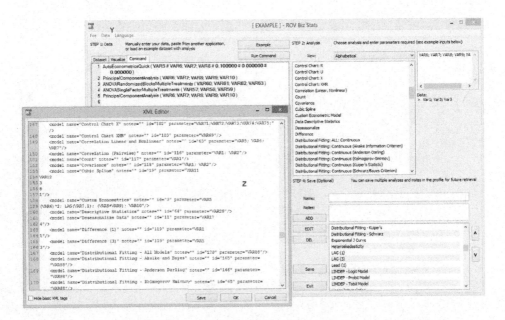

Figure TN.42: XML Editor

SECTION NINE – VISUAL GUIDES AND SUMMARIES

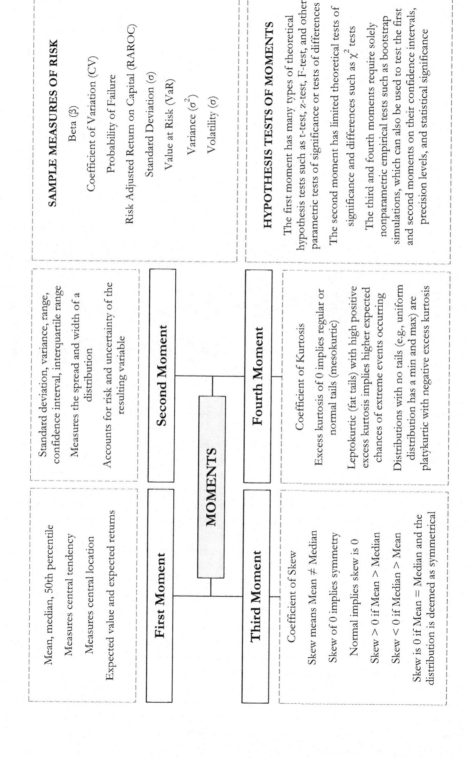

First Moment

- Mean, median, 50th percentile
- Measures central tendency
- Measures central location
- Expected value and expected returns

Second Moment

- Standard deviation, variance, range, confidence interval, interquartile range
- Measures the spread and width of a distribution
- Accounts for risk and uncertainty of the resulting variable

MOMENTS

Third Moment

- Coefficient of Skew
- Skew means Mean ≠ Median
- Skew of 0 implies symmetry
- Normal implies skew is 0
- Skew > 0 if Mean > Median
- Skew < 0 if Median > Mean
- Skew is 0 if Mean = Median and the distribution is deemed as symmetrical

Fourth Moment

- Coefficient of Kurtosis
- Excess kurtosis of 0 implies regular or normal tails (mesokurtic)
- Leptokurtic (fat tails) with high positive excess kurtosis implies higher expected chances of extreme events occurring
- Distributions with no tails (e.g., uniform distribution has a min and max) are platykurtic with negative excess kurtosis

SAMPLE MEASURES OF RISK

Beta (β)

Coefficient of Variation (CV)

Probability of Failure

Risk Adjusted Return on Capital (RAROC)

Standard Deviation (σ)

Value at Risk (VaR)

Variance (σ^2)

Volatility (σ)

HYPOTHESIS TESTS OF MOMENTS

The first moment has many types of theoretical hypothesis tests such as t-test, z-test, F-test, and other parametric tests of significance or tests of differences

The second moment has limited theoretical tests of significance and differences such as χ^2 tests

The third and fourth moments require solely nonparametric empirical tests such as bootstrap simulations, which can also be used to test the first and second moments on their confidence intervals, precision levels, and statistical significance

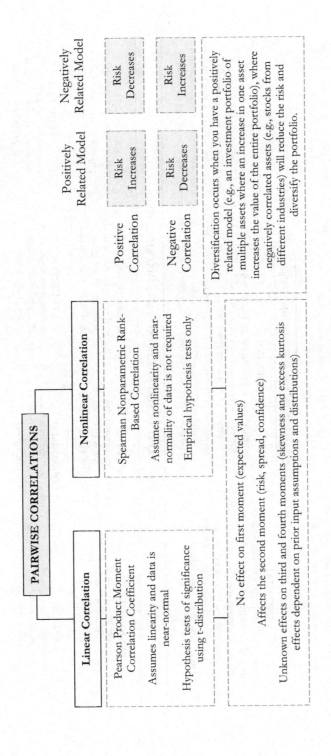

PAIRWISE CORRELATIONS

Linear Correlation

Pearson Product Moment Correlation Coefficient

Assumes linearity and data is near-normal

Hypothesis tests of significance using t-distribution

Nonlinear Correlation

Spearman Nonparametric Rank-Based Correlation

Assumes nonlinearity and near-normality of data is not required

Empirical hypothesis tests only

No effect on first moment (expected values)

Affects the second moment (risk, spread, confidence)

Unknown effects on third and fourth moments (skewness and excess kurtosis effects dependent on prior input assumptions and distributions)

	Positively Related Model	Negatively Related Model
Positive Correlation	Risk Increases	Risk Decreases
Negative Correlation	Risk Decreases	Risk Increases

Diversification occurs when you have a positively related model (e.g., an investment portfolio of multiple assets where an increase in one asset increases the value of the entire portfolio), where negatively correlated assets (e.g., stocks from different industries) will reduce the risk and diversify the portfolio.

TRIANGULAR

Looks like a triangle, continuous values, tails end at min and max with most likely as its peak. Can be skewed or symmetrical, with negative excess kurtosis (truncated tails). Examples: sales forecasts, subject matter estimates, management assumptions.

NORMAL

Continuous bell curve, a.k.a. Gaussian distribution, infinite tails on both ends, requires mean and standard deviation as inputs. Symmetrical with zero skew and zero excess kurtosis. Examples: stock returns, height, weight, IQ (most are truncated normal with limits).

UNIFORM

Flat continuous area with equal probability of occurrence at any point between the minimum and maximum. Symmetrical with zero skew and negative excess kurtosis (fixed end points). Examples: business forecasts and economic forecasts.

COMMONLY USED DISTRIBUTIONS

BINOMIAL

Discrete events with two mutually exclusive and independent outcomes with fixed probability of success at each successive trial. Symmetrical and approaches normal distribution with high number of trials. Example: tossing a coin multiple times.

POISSON

Discrete events occurring independently with the same average rate of repetition, and measured in time or space (area). Examples: sales forecasts, subject matter estimates, management assumptions. Approaches normal with high average rates.

CUSTOM

Empirically-fitted discrete distribution when little data is available or when other theoretical distributions fail. Suitable for Delphi methods, can be multimodal or irregular. Examples: subject matter estimates, management assumptions, and qualitative estimates that are converted numerically.

LESS COMMONLY USED BUT IMPORTANT DISTRIBUTIONS

BERNOULLI

Single discrete trial version of Binomial (e.g., simulating success or failure of projects).

GUMBEL

Tail-end extreme value simulations of continuous outcomes (e.g., market crashes).

BETA 4

Highly flexible continuous distribution capable of taking on multiple shapes and scales.

LOGNORMAL

Variables with continuous non-negative and non-zero values (e.g., stock prices).

DISCRETE UNIFORM

Range of discrete events with equal probability of occurrence (e.g., rolling a six-sided die).

STUDENT'S T

Continuous-normal with fat tails or higher probability of extremes (e.g., risky returns).

EXPONENTIAL 2

High probably of low values, low probability of continuous high values (e.g., wait time).

WEIBULL 3

Continuous mean time before failure and reliability estimates (e.g., MTBF of an engine).

OTHER DISTRIBUTIONS: Arcsine, Beta, Beta 3, Cauchy, Chi-square, Cosine, Double Log, Erlang, Exponential, F, Fréchet, Gamma, Geometric, Gumbel Min, Gumbel Max, Hypergeometric, Laplace, Logistic, Lognormal 3, Negative Binomial, Parabolic, Generalized Pareto, Pareto, Pascal, Pearson V, Pearson VI, Pert, Power, Power 3, Rayleigh, Standard-Normal, Standard-T, Weibull

DISTRIBUTIONAL FITTING

What distribution and distributional parameters do you use? This technique fits historical empirical data to probability distributions using Akaike Information Criterion (AIC), Anderson–Darling (AD), Chi-Square, Kolmogorov–Smirnov (KS), Kuiper's Statistic, and Schwarz/Bayes Information Criterion (SC/BIC).

DATA DIAGNOSTICS

Executes multiple tests on existing dataset to determine its characteristics prior to running forecast models: autocorrelation, heteroskedasticity, lags, micronumerosity, multicollinearity, nonlinearity, and seasonality. Certain tests are relevant only for time-series, cross-sectional, or panel data types.

DYNAMIC SENSITIVITY

Applies dynamic perturbations created after simulations and calculates contribution to variance.

DISTRIBUTIONAL ANALYSIS

Distributional Analysis (PDF, CDF, ICDF of 50 distributions), Distributional Charts and Tables (compares PDF & CDF shapes and characteristics). Overlay Charts (overlays empirically simulated output forecasts for a visual comparison of the moments).

ANALYTICAL TOOLS

SCENARIO ANALYSIS

Runs multiple scenarios quickly and effortlessly by changing one or two input parameters a prespecified range for a heat map of the output variable.

HYPOTHESIS TESTS

Determines if two variables are statistically identical or different from one another.

CORRELATED SIMULATION

Runs correlated simulations by setting pairwise nonlinear correlations among multiple input assumptions. Normal, T, and Quasi-Normal Copulas are used in the convolution simulation. Correlations affect the second moment or risk of an output forecast distribution.

TORNADO ANALYSIS

Static impacts of each variable on the outcome of the model by perturbing each input variable a preset amount, captures the final result, lists the pre-simulation perturbations ranked from most significant to least. Performed to identify critical factors to set as simulation assumptions to run.

OVERLAY CHARTS

Overlays multiple assumptions and simulated forecast charts to compare their characteristics.

BOOSTRAP SIMULATION

Estimates reliability or accuracy of forecast statistics, answers confidence/precision questions.

OTHER ANALYTICAL TOOLS: Check Model, Data Deseasonalization, Data Diagnostics, Data Open & Import, Distributional Fitting (Single, Multiple, Percentile), Principal Component Analysis, Seasonality Test, Segmentation Clustering, Statistical Tests, and Structural Break

WAYS OF SAVING A MODEL AND RESULTS: Generate live Excel charts after simulation runs, Tornado, and Sensitivity analyses, as well as:

COPY/PASTE CHARTS

Copy and paste the simulation and forecast charts into PowerPoint/Word.

REPORT GENERATION

Run simulation, forecasting, analytical methods, and optimization reports.

CUSTOM DISTRIBUTION

Create and save nonparametric custom distributions based on actual empirical data.

RISK SIMULATOR PROFILE

Create multiple profiles and scenarios of simulation and optimization variable settings.

DATA EXTRACTION

Simulated assumptions and forecasts' raw data can be extracted into Excel or text files.

RISK SIM FILE

Save live Risk Simulator charts for future retrieval without having to re-run simulations.

EXCEL FILE

One file saves all assumptions, forecasts, decisions, constraints, objectives, and profiles.

STATISTICS TABLE

Generate reports of statistical results as tables in Excel for archiving.

Akaike Information Criterion (AIC)

Rewards goodness-of-fit but also includes a penalty that is an increasing function of the number of estimated parameters (although AIC penalizes the number of parameters less strongly than other methods).

Anderson–Darling (AD)

When applied to testing if a normal distribution adequately describes a set of data, it is one of the most powerful statistical tools for detecting departures from normality and is powerful for testing normal tails. However, in non-normal distributions with skew and kurtosis, this test lacks power compared to other methods.

Chi-Square (CS)

Used to exclusively test discrete distributions where data are statistically categorized into various groups. The CS approach cannot be readily used to fit continuous distributions.

DISTRIBUTIONAL FITTING

Kolmogorov–Smirnov (KS)

A nonparametric test for the equality of continuous probability distributions that can be used to compare a sample with a reference probability distribution, making it useful for testing abnormally shaped distributions and non-normal distributions. Use the KS by default if the underlying distribution is unknown.

Kuiper's Statistic (K)

Related to the KS test making it as sensitive in the tails as at the median and also making it invariant under cyclic transformations of the independent variable, rendering it invaluable when testing for cyclic variations over time. In comparison, the AD test provides equal sensitivity at the tails as the median, but it does not provide the cyclic invariance.

Schwarz/Bayes Information Criterion (SC/BIC)

The SC/BIC test introduces a penalty term for the number of parameters in the model with a larger penalty than AIC.

HYPOTHESIS TEST

The null hypothesis being tested is such that the fitted distribution is the same distribution as the population from which the sample data to be fitted comes. Thus, if the computed p-value is lower than a critical alpha level (typically 0.10 or 0.05), then the distribution is the wrong distribution (reject the null hypothesis). Conversely, the higher the p-value, the better the distribution fits the data (do not reject the null hypothesis, which means the fitted distribution is the correct distribution, or null hypothesis of H_0: Error = 0, where error is defined as the difference between the empirical data and the theoretical distribution). Roughly, you can think of p-value as a percentage explained. The higher the p-value, the better the data fits the selected probability distribution.

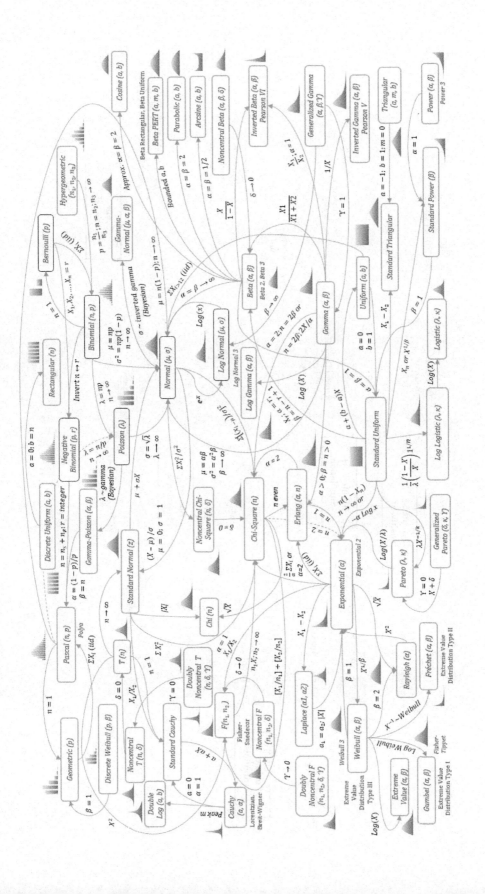

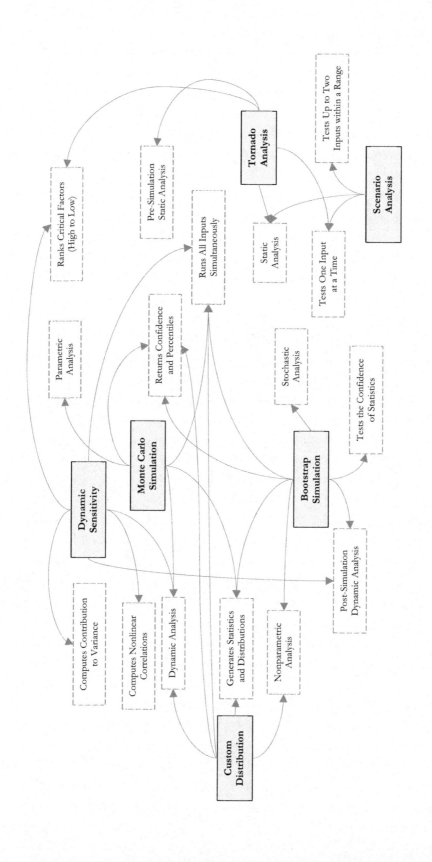

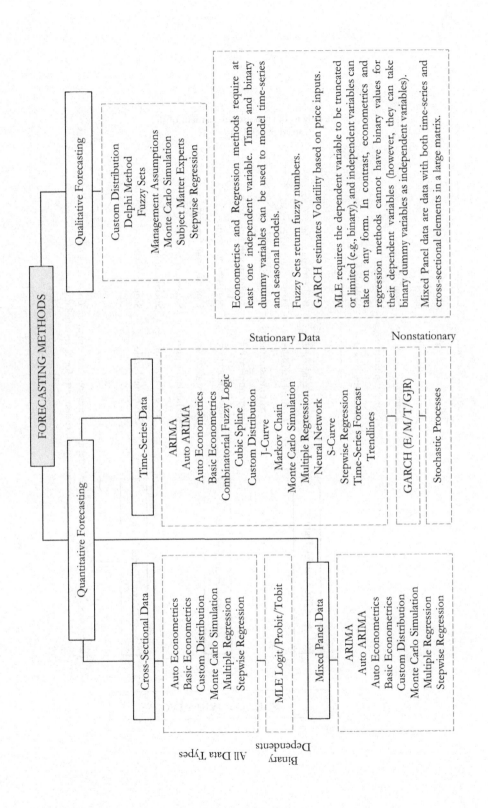

FORECASTING METHODS

Qualitative Forecasting

Custom Distribution
Delphi Method
Fuzzy Sets
Management Assumptions
Monte Carlo Simulation
Subject Matter Experts
Stepwise Regression

Quantitative Forecasting

Time-Series Data

Stationary Data

ARIMA
Auto ARIMA
Auto Econometrics
Basic Econometrics
Combinatorial Fuzzy Logic
Cubic Spline
Custom Distribution
J-Curve
Markov Chain
Monte Carlo Simulation
Multiple Regression
Neural Network
S-Curve
Stepwise Regression
Time-Series Forecast
Trendlines

Nonstationary

GARCH (E/M/T/GJR)

Stochastic Processes

Cross-Sectional Data

Auto Econometrics
Basic Econometrics
Custom Distribution
Monte Carlo Simulation
Multiple Regression
Stepwise Regression

MLE Logit/Probit/Tobit

Mixed Panel Data

ARIMA
Auto ARIMA
Auto Econometrics
Basic Econometrics
Custom Distribution
Monte Carlo Simulation
Multiple Regression
Stepwise Regression

All Data Types

Binary Dependents

Econometrics and Regression methods require at least one independent variable. Time and binary dummy variables can be used to model time-series and seasonal models.

Fuzzy Sets return fuzzy numbers.

GARCH estimates Volatility based on price inputs.

MLE requires the dependent variable to be truncated or limited (e.g., binary), and independent variables can take on any form. In contrast, econometrics and regression methods cannot have binary values for their dependent variables (however, they can take binary dummy variables as independent variables).

Mixed Panel data are data with both time-series and cross-sectional elements in a large matrix.

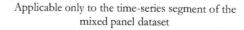

Applicable only to the time-series segment of the mixed panel dataset

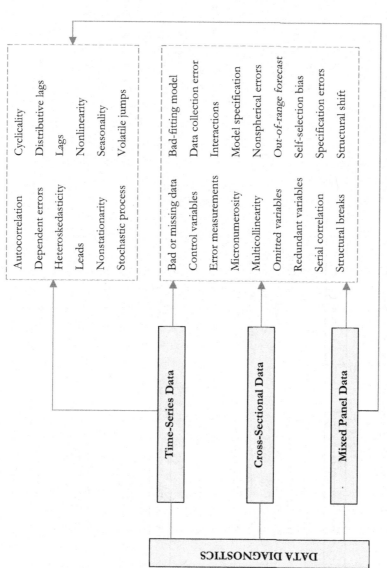

Time-series data is more prevalent in real life, and, therefore, there are more time-series forecast methods as well as error and specification tests for time-series data.

DATA DIAGNOSTICS

Time-Series Data

Cross-Sectional Data

Mixed Panel Data

Autocorrelation
Cyclicality
Dependent errors
Distributive lags
Heteroskedasticity
Lags
Leads
Nonlinearity
Nonstationarity
Seasonality
Stochastic process
Volatile jumps

Bad or missing data
Bad-fitting model
Control variables
Data collection error
Error measurements
Interactions
Micronumerosity
Model specification
Multicollinearity
Nonspherical errors
Omitted variables
Out-of-range forecast
Redundant variables
Self-selection bias
Serial correlation
Specification errors
Structural breaks
Structural shift

OPTIMIZATION METHODS

STATIC
Runs optimization by iteratively changing the decision variables based on their allowed ranges to maximize or minimize the objective, while satisfying the constraints and restrictions imposed in the model. Optimization without simulation.

DYNAMIC
Runs a Monte Carlo risk simulation, and the selected statistic (e.g., mean, percentile, Value at Risk) is inserted into the model before optimization is run. This statistic accounts for uncertainties and variability in the inputs and model. Also known as the simulation-optimization approach.

STOCHASTIC
Replicates dynamic optimization multiple times (i.e., simulate thousands of trials, statistics used in lieu of single-point-estimates, optimization run with multiple iterations, and the process is repeated multiple times). Distributions of decision variables are obtained as the result.

OPTIMIZATION INPUTS

OBJECTIVE
The outcome that is to be minimized (e.g., cost, schedule, error) or maximized (e.g., net income, revenues, profitability).

CONSTRAINT
Limitations or restrictions in the model (e.g., resource, budget, schedule, competing needs, risk, management constraints).

DECISION
Variables or decisions you have control over (e.g., go or no-go decisions, % budget portfolio allocations, quantities to build).

ASSUMPTION
Uncertain variables to be simulated in dynamic and stochastic optimization (e.g., profits, returns, demand).

EFFICIENT FRONTIER

Running multiple optimizations where each successive run perturbs and changes the constraints by some set amount to maximize or minimize the objective outcome while still satisfying the constraints and restrictions. The outcome is a set of multiple points that are the most optimal and efficient, and, when connected by a line, constitutes the efficient investment frontier, representing the best bang-for-the-buck, where given the requisite constraints and restrictions, each point along the frontier is a portfolio of the best that can be achieved given the set of decision variables. The steep part of the frontier indicates it is better to pursue the higher constraint portfolio whereas, conversely, flat frontiers indicate diminishing marginal returns, and any additional resources provided to the portfolio will not significantly increase its overall portfolio objective.

ABANDONMENT

Exit and salvage or sell the assets to cut losses, stop before executing the next phase after completing the current phase, contractual Termination for Convenience, downside guaranteed price and value protection. To have an abandonment option, the holder must first own the asset.

EXPANSION

Platform technologies, mergers and acquisitions (new technologies, market, clients, or vertical solution), reusability, scalability, pre-investments, and pre-building facilities (faster and cheaper to pre-invest now then restart development in the future). To have an expansion option, the holder must first own the asset.

SWITCHING

Switching among multiple vendors, modular designs, multiple inputs or raw materials. This option allows production risk mitigation through multiple vendors and a strong industrial base, and takes advantage of market-based cost fluctuations. Negatively correlated assets tend to generate greater option values (portfolio diversification effects).

BARRIER

The option comes in-the-money or out-of-the-money if the underlying asset value exceeds or does not exceed some prespecified fixed or fluctuating contractual barrier. This option typically has lower value to the holder than a similarly specified option without the barriers. Any combinations of single, double, upper, lower, knock-in, and knock-out barriers can be constructed.

STRATEGIC REAL OPTIONS

SEQUENTIAL

Stage-gate implementation of high-risk project development, prototyping, drug development phases, technology demonstration, contracts with multiple stages with the option to exit at any time, built-in flexibility to execute different courses of action at specific stages of development, milestones, R&D, and phased investments.

EXECUTION TYPES

American Options: Any time up to and including maturity date.

Asian Options: Backward-looking, time-specific.

Bermudan Options: Any time except during blackouts and vesting.

European Options: One time at maturity only.

American ≥ Bermudan ≥ European except for plain-vanilla call options with zero dividends, where all values are identical.

CONTRACTION

Outsourcing, alliances, co-marketing, subcontractors, joint ventures, foreign partnerships, and other strategic relationships whereby cost is reduced and part of the asset's profits is shared with the partner. To have a contraction option, the holder must first own the asset prior to contracting.

SIMULTANEOUS

Multiple assets or investments are executed simultaneously to reduce risks that one of these assets or projects fails. This is the same computation as a combination into a single asset for an option to wait and defer or execute. The result for Simultaneous options is typically less than Sequential options given the same parameters and asset valuation.

WAIT & DEFER/EXECUTE

Proof of concept to better determine the costs, profitability, and schedule risks of a project. Holding on to the opportunity with contract in place while reducing large-scale implementation risks, low rate initial production, R&D, prototyping, and right of first refusal. Ability to wait and see for valuable information to arrive before deciding to execute the option if optimal.

Abandonment, Contraction, Expansion, and Switching options imply that the option holder currently owns the asset and, therefore, can sell it (abandon), reduce output and save on expenses (contract), expand upon it (expand), or change it out to an alternative (switch). Further, Switching options imply that the option holder can sequentially switch back and forth the underlying assets with some predetermined switching cost. Abandonment, Barrier, Contraction, Expansion, and Wait & Defer options typically have a single underlying asset, and can be executed in a single phase or multiple-phased Sequential option. Sequential options usually imply multiple phases (more than one) and a single underlying asset, and can be combined with the other types of real options. Finally, Switching and Simultaneous options imply more than one underlying asset exists and can be executed in a single or multiple-phased Sequential option.

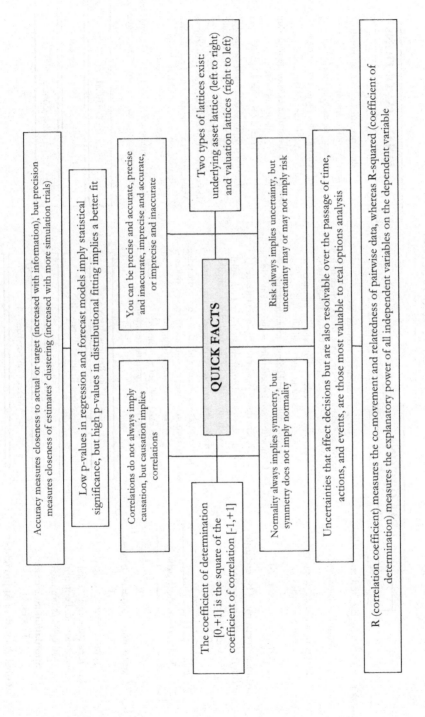

QUICK FACTS

Accuracy measures closeness to actual or target (increased with information), but precision measures closeness of estimates' clustering (increased with more simulation trials)

Low p-values in regression and forecast models imply statistical significance, but high p-values in distributional fitting implies a better fit

You can be precise and accurate, precise and inaccurate, imprecise and accurate, or imprecise and inaccurate

Two types of lattices exist: underlying asset lattice (left to right) and valuation lattices (right to left)

Correlations do not always imply causation, but causation implies correlations

Risk always implies uncertainty, but uncertainty may or may not imply risk

The coefficient of determination [0,+1] is the square of the coefficient of correlation [-1,+1]

Normality always implies symmetry, but symmetry does not imply normality

Uncertainties that affect decisions but are also resolvable over the passage of time, actions, and events, are those most valuable to real options analysis

R (correlation coefficient) measures the co-movement and relatedness of pairwise data, whereas R-squared (coefficient of determination) measures the explanatory power of all independent variables on the dependent variable

OPTIONS THEORY

REAL OPTIONS

- A model can be created and valued
- Uncertainties must exist
- Decisions are affected by uncertainties
- Options must exist
- Management must be credible enough to execute options when they are optimal

- Longer maturity, usually in years
- Underlying variables are free cash flows, which in turn are driven by competition, demand, management
- Can increase strategic option value by management decisions and flexibility
- Major million and billion dollar decisions
- Competition and market drives the option value
- A recent development in corporate finance
- Solved using closed-form equations and binomial lattices with simulation of the underlying variables
- Not traded, proprietary, no market comparables
- Management assumptions and actions drive the value of a real option—institute options to reduce risk and take advantage of upsides
- Strategies exist only for real options (expansion, switching, sequential compound)

- Log Cash Flow Returns Approach
- Log Stock Returns Approach
- Management Assumptions
- Market Comparables
- Simulated CV of NPV

Valuation Methods

Closed-Form Models (Black-Scholes, American Approximation Models)
Lattices (Binomial, Trinomial, Quadranomial, Pentanomial, Other Multinomials)
Simulation (Stochastic Processes)
Other Analytical Approaches

FINANCIAL OPTIONS

- Short maturity, usually in months
- Underlying variable driving value is equity price of financial asset or stock price
- Cannot control value by manipulating stock prices
- Values are usually small
- Competitive or market effects are irrelevant to its value and pricing
- Traded for over 40 years
- Usually solved using closed-form partial differential equations and simulation/variance reduction techniques for exotic options
- Marketable and traded security with comparables
- Management assumptions and actions have no bearing on valuation although used for hedging/speculation
- Strategies of creating new vehicles by buying/selling combinations (butterflies, straddles, strangles)

- GARCH
- Log Stock Returns Approach
- Market Comparables

QUICK REFERENCE GUIDE: ANALYTICS SUMMARY

List of Analytical Methods

The following is a quick reference guide to all the analytics presented in this book in one convenient list.

- **ARIMA.** Autoregressive Integrated Moving Average is used for forecasting time-series data using its own historical data by itself or with exogenous/other variables. The first segment is the autoregressive (AR) term corresponding to the number of lagged value of the residual in the unconditional forecast model. In essence, the model captures the historical variation of actual data to a forecasting model and uses this variation or residual to create a better predicting model. The second segment is the integration order (I) term corresponding to the number of differencing the time series to be forecasted goes through to make the data stationary. This element accounts for any nonlinear growth rates existing in the data. The third segment is the moving average (MA) term, which is essentially the moving average of lagged forecast errors. By incorporating this lagged forecast errors term, the model in essence learns from its forecast errors or mistakes and corrects for them through a moving average calculation. The ARIMA model follows the Box–Jenkins methodology with each term representing steps taken in the model construction until only random noise remains.

- **ARIMA (Auto).** Runs some common combinations of ARIMA models (low-order PDQ) and returns the best models.

- **Autocorrelation and Partial Autocorrelation.** One very simple approach to test for autocorrelation is to graph the time series of a regression equation's residuals. If these residuals exhibit some cyclicality, then autocorrelation exists. Another more robust approach to detect autocorrelation is the use of the Durbin–Watson statistic, which estimates the potential for a first-order autocorrelation. The Durbin–Watson test employed also identifies model misspecification, that is, if a particular time-series variable is correlated to itself one period prior. Many time-series data tend to be autocorrelated to their historical occurrences, and applicable only to time-series data. This relationship can exist for multiple reasons, including the variables' spatial relationships (similar time and space), prolonged economic shocks and events, psychological inertia, smoothing, seasonal adjustments of the data, and so forth.

- **Auto Econometrics.** Runs some common combinations of Basic Econometrics and returns the best models.

- **Basic Econometrics/Custom Econometrics.** Applicable for forecasting time-series and cross-sectional data and for modeling relationships among variables, and allows you to create custom multiple regression models. Econometrics refers to a branch of business analytics, modeling, and forecasting techniques for modeling the behavior of or forecasting certain business, financial, economic, physical science, and other variables. Running the Basic Econometrics models is similar to regular regression analysis except that the dependent and independent variables are allowed to be modified before a regression is run.

- **Charts.**

  - **Box-Whisker Chart.** Box plots or box-and-whisker plots graphically depict numerical data using their descriptive statistics: the smallest observation (Minimum), First Quartile or 25th Percentile (Q1), Median or Second Quartile or 50th Percentile (Q2), Third Quartile (Q3), and largest observation (Maximum). A box plot may also indicate which observations, if any, might be considered outliers.

  - **Pareto Chart.** A Pareto chart contains both a bar chart and a line graph. Individual values are represented in descending order by the bars and the cumulative total is represented by the ascending line. Also known as the "80-20" chart, whereby you see that by focusing on the top few variables, we are already accounting for more than 80% of the cumulative effects of the total.

  - **Q-Q Normal Chart.** This Quantile-Quantile chart is a normal probability plot, which is a graphical method for comparing a probability distribution with the normal distribution by plotting their quantiles against each other.

  - **Combinatorial Fuzzy Logic.** Applies fuzzy logic algorithms for forecasting time-series data by combining forecast methods to create an optimized model. Fuzzy logic is a probabilistic logic dealing with reasoning that is approximate rather than fixed and exact where fuzzy logic variables may have a truth value that ranges in degree between 0 and 1.

  - **Control Charts: C, NP, P, R, U, XMR.** Sometimes specification limits of a process are not set; instead, statistical control limits are computed based on the actual data collected (e.g., the number of defects in a manufacturing line). The upper control limit (UCL) and lower control limit (LCL) are computed, as are the central line (CL) and other sigma levels. The resulting chart is called a control chart, and if the process is out of control, the actual defect line will be outside of the UCL and LCL lines for a certain number of times.

  - **C Chart:** variable is an attribute (e.g., defective or nondefective), the data collected are in total number of defects (actual count in units), and there are multiple measurements in a sample experiment; when multiple experiments are run and the average number of defects of the collected data is of interest; and constant number of samples collected in each experiment.

  - **NP Chart:** variable is an attribute (e.g., defective or nondefective), the data collected are in proportions of defects (or number of defects in a specific sample), and there are multiple measurements in a sample experiment; when multiple experiments are run and the average proportion of defects of the collected data is of interest; and constant number of samples collected in each experiment.

o **P Chart:** variable is an attribute (e.g., defective or nondefective), the data collected are in proportions of defects (or number of defects in a specific sample), and there are multiple measurements in a sample experiment; when multiple experiments are run and the average proportion of defects of the collected data is of interest; and with different number of samples collected in each experiment.

o **R Chart:** variable has raw data values, there are multiple measurements in a sample experiment, multiple experiments are run, and the range of the collected data is of interest.

o **U Chart:** variable is an attribute (e.g., defective or nondefective), the data collected are in total number of defects (actual count in units), and there are multiple measurements in a sample experiment; when multiple experiments are run and the average number of defects of the collected data is of interest; and with different number of samples collected in each experiment.

o **XMR Chart:** raw data values, single measurement taken in each sample experiment, multiple experiments are run, and the actual value of the collected data is of interest.

- **Correlation (Linear and Nonlinear).** Computes the Pearson's linear product moment correlations (commonly referred to as the Pearson's R) as well as the nonlinear Spearman rank-based correlation between variable pairs and returns them as a correlation matrix. The correlation coefficient ranges between –1.0 and +1.0, inclusive. The sign indicates the direction of association between the variables, while the coefficient indicates the magnitude or strength of association.

- **Cubic Spline.** Interpolates missing values of a time-series dataset and extrapolates values of future forecast periods using nonlinear curves. Spline curves can also be used to forecast or extrapolate values of future time periods beyond the time period of available data and the data can be linear or nonlinear.

- **Descriptive Statistics.** Almost all distributions can be described within four moments (some distributions require one moment, while others require two moments, and so forth). This tool computes the four moments and associated descriptive statistics.

- **Deseasonalizing.** This model deseasonalizes and detrends your original data to take out any seasonal and trending components. In forecasting models, the process eliminates the effects of accumulating datasets from seasonality and trend to show only the absolute changes in values and to allow potential cyclical patterns to be identified by removing the general drift, tendency, twists, bends, and effects of seasonal cycles of a set of time-series data.

- **Distributional Fitting.** Which distribution does an analyst or engineer use for a particular input variable in a model? What are the relevant distributional parameters? The null hypothesis tested is that the fitted distribution is the same distribution as the population from which the sample data to be fitted comes.

o **Akaike Information Criterion (AIC).** Rewards goodness-of-fit but also includes a penalty that is an increasing function of the number of estimated parameters (although AIC penalizes the number of parameters less strongly than other methods).

o **Anderson–Darling (AD).** When applied to testing if a normal distribution adequately describes a set of data, it is one of the most powerful statistical tools for detecting departures from normality, and is powerful for testing normal tails. However, in non-normal distributions, this test lacks power compared to others.

    ○ **Kolmogorov–Smirnov (KS).** A nonparametric test for the equality of continuous probability distributions that can be used to compare a sample with a reference probability distribution, making it useful for testing abnormally shaped distributions and non-normal distributions.

    ○ **Kuiper's Statistic (K).** Related to the KS test making it as sensitive in the tails as at the median and also makes it invariant under cyclic transformations of the independent variable, making it invaluable when testing for cyclic variations over time. The AD provides equal sensitivity at the tails as the median, but it does not provide the cyclic invariance.

    ○ **Schwarz/Bayes Information Criterion (SC/BIC).** The SC/BIC introduces a penalty term for the number of parameters in the model with a larger penalty than AIC.

- **Exponential J-Curve.** This function models exponential growth where value of the next period depends on the current period's level and the increase is exponential. Over time, the values will increase significantly from one period to another. This model is typically used in forecasting biological growth and chemical reactions over time.

- **Generalized Linear Models/Limited Dependent Variables: Logit.** Limited dependent variables techniques are used to forecast the probability of something occurring given some independent variables (e.g., predicting if a credit line will default given the obligor's characteristics such as age, salary, credit card debt levels; or the probability a patient will have lung cancer based on age and number of cigarettes smoked monthly, and so forth). The dependent variable is limited (i.e., binary 1 and 0 for default/cancer, or limited to integer values 1, 2, 3, etc.). Traditional regression analysis will not work as the predicted probability is usually less than zero or greater than one, and many of the required regression assumptions are violated (e.g., independence and normality of the errors). We also have a vector of independent variable regressors, X, which are assumed to influence the outcome, Y. A typical ordinary least squares regression approach is invalid because the regression errors are heteroskedastic and non-normal, and the resulting estimated probability estimates will return nonsensical values of above 1 or below 0. This analysis handles these problems using an iterative optimization routine to maximize a log likelihood function when the dependent variables are limited.

- **Generalized Linear Models/Limited Dependent Variables: Probit.** A Probit model (sometimes also known as a Normit model) is a popular alternative specification for a binary response model. It employs a Probit function estimated using maximum likelihood estimation and is called Probit regression. The Probit and logistic regression models tend to produce very similar predictions where the parameter estimates in a logistic regression tend to be 1.6 to 1.8 times higher than they are in a corresponding Probit model. The choice of using a Probit or Logit is entirely up to convenience, and the main distinction is that the logistic distribution has a higher kurtosis (fatter tails) to account for extreme values. For example, suppose that house ownership is the decision to be modeled, and this response variable is binary (home purchase or no home purchase) and depends on a series of independent variables X_i such as income, age, and so forth, such that $I_i = \beta_0 + \beta_1 X_1 + \ldots + \beta_n X_n$, where the larger the value of I_i, the higher the probability of home ownership. For each family, a critical I^* threshold exists, where if exceeded, the house is purchased, otherwise, no home is purchased, and the outcome probability (P) is assumed to be normally distributed, such that $P_i = CDF(I)$ using a standard-normal cumulative distribution function (CDF). Therefore, use the estimated coefficients exactly like that of a regression model and, using the estimated Y, apply a standard-normal distribution to compute the probability.

- **Generalized Linear Models/Limited Dependent Variables: Tobit.** The Tobit model (Censored Tobit) is an econometric and biometric modeling method used to describe the relationship between a non-negative dependent variable Y_i and one or more independent variables X_i. A Tobit model is an econometric model in which the dependent variable is censored; that is, the dependent variable is censored because values below zero are not observed. The Tobit model assumes that there is a latent unobservable variable Y^*. This variable is linearly dependent on the X_i variables via a vector of β_i coefficients that determine their interrelationships. In addition, there is a normally distributed error term U_i to capture random influences on this relationship. The observable variable Y_i is defined to be equal to the latent variables whenever the latent variables are above zero, and Y_i is assumed to be zero otherwise. That is, $Y_i = Y^*$ if $Y^* > 0$ and $Y_i = 0$ if $Y^* = 0$. If the relationship parameter β_i is estimated by using ordinary least squares regression of the observed Y_i on X_i, the resulting regression estimators are inconsistent and yield downward-biased slope coefficients and an upward-biased intercept.

- **Heteroskedasticity.** Several tests exist to test for the presence of heteroskedasticity, that is, where the volatilities or uncertainties (standard deviation or variance of a variable is nonconstant over time). These tests also are applicable for testing misspecifications and nonlinearities, and applicable only to time-series data. The test is based on the null hypothesis of no heteroskedasticity.

- **Linear Interpolation.** Sometimes interest rates or any type of time-dependent rates may have missing values. For instance, the Treasury rates for Years 1, 2, and 3 exist, and then jump to Year 5, skipping Year 4. We can, using linear interpolation (i.e., we assume the rates during the missing periods are linearly related), determine and "fill in" or interpolate their values.

- **Logistic S-Curve.** The S-curve, or logistic growth curve, starts off like a J-curve, with exponential growth rates. Over time, the environment becomes saturated (e.g., market saturation, competition, overcrowding), the growth slows, and the forecast value eventually ends up at a saturation or maximum level. The S-curve model is typically used in forecasting market share or sales growth of a new product from market introduction until maturity and decline, population dynamics, growth of bacterial cultures, and other naturally occurring variables.

- **Markov Chain.** The Markov Chain models the probability of a future state that depends on a previous state (a mathematical system that undergoes transitions from one state to another), forming a chain when linked together (a random process characterized as memoryless: the next state depends only on the current state and not on the sequence of events that preceded it) that reverts to a long-run steady state level. Used to forecast the market share of two competitors.

- **Multiple Regression (Linear and Nonlinear).** Multivariate regression is used to model the relationship structure and characteristics of a certain dependent variable as it depends on other independent exogenous variables. Using the modeled relationship, we can forecast the future values of the dependent variable. The accuracy and goodness-of-fit for this model can also be determined. Linear and nonlinear models can be fitted in the multiple regression analysis.

- **Neural Network.** Commonly used to refer to a network or circuit of biological neurons, modern usage of the term neural network often refers to artificial neural networks that consist of artificial neurons, or nodes, recreated in a software environment. Such networks attempt to mimic the neurons in the human brain in ways of thinking and identifying patterns and, in our situation, identifying patterns for the purposes of forecasting time-series data.

    o **Linear.** Applies a linear function.

    o **Nonlinear Logistic.** Applies a nonlinear logistic function.

    o **Nonlinear Cosine-Hyper Tangent.** Applies a nonlinear cosine with hyperbolic tangent function.

    o **Nonlinear Hyper Tangent.** Applies a nonlinear hyperbolic tangent function.

Nonparametric Hypothesis Tests

Nonparametric techniques make no assumptions about the specific shape or distribution from which the sample is drawn. This lack of assumptions is different from the other hypotheses tests such as ANOVA or t-tests (parametric tests) where the sample is assumed to be drawn from a population that is normally or approximately normally distributed. If normality is assumed, the power of the test is higher due this normality restriction. However, if flexibility on distributional requirements is needed, then nonparametric techniques are superior. In general, nonparametric methodologies provide the following advantages over other parametric tests:

    o Normality or approximate normality does not have to be assumed.

    o Fewer assumptions about the population are required; that is, nonparametric tests do not require that the population assume any specific distribution.

    o Smaller sample sizes can be analyzed.

    o Compared to parametric tests, nonparametric tests use data less efficiently.

    o The power of the test is lower than that of the parametric tests.

    o Samples with nominal and ordinal scales of measurement can be tested.

    o Sample variances do not have to be equal, which is required in parametric tests.

The following are some sample nonparametric tests:

- **Nonparametric Chi-Square Goodness-of-Fit.** The Chi-Square test for goodness-of-fit is used to examine if a sample dataset could have been drawn from a population having a specified probability distribution. The probability distribution tested here is the normal distribution. The null hypothesis tested is such that the sample is randomly drawn from the normal distribution.

- **Nonparametric Chi-Square Independence.** The Chi-Square test for independence examines two variables to see if there is some statistical relationship between them. This test is not used to find the exact nature of the relationship between the two variables, but to simply test if the variables could be independent of each other. The null hypothesis tested is such that the variables are independent of each other.

- **Nonparametric Chi-Square Population Variance.** The Chi-Square test for population variance is used for hypothesis testing and confidence interval estimation for a population variance. The population variance of a sample is typically unknown, and hence the need for quantifying this confidence interval. The population is assumed to be normally distributed.

- **Nonparametric Friedman's Test.** The Friedman test is the extension of the Wilcoxon Signed-Rank test for paired samples. The corresponding parametric test is the Randomized Block Multiple Treatment ANOVA, but unlike the ANOVA, the Friedman test does not require that the dataset be randomly sampled from normally distributed populations with equal variances. The Friedman test uses a two-tailed hypothesis test where the null hypothesis is such that the population medians of each treatment are statistically identical to the rest of the group; that is, there is no effect among the different treatment groups.

- **Nonparametric Kruskal–Wallis Test.** The Kruskal–Wallis test is the extension of the Wilcoxon Signed-Rank test by comparing more than two independent samples. The corresponding parametric test is the One-Way ANOVA, but unlike the ANOVA, the Kruskal–Wallis does not require that the dataset be randomly sampled from normally distributed populations with equal variances. The Kruskal–Wallis test is a two-tailed hypothesis test where the null hypothesis is such that the population medians of each treatment are statistically identical to the rest of the group; that is, there is no effect among the different treatment groups.

- **Nonparametric Lilliefors Test.** The Lilliefors test evaluates the null hypothesis of whether the data sample was drawn from a normally distributed population, versus an alternate hypothesis that the data sample is not normally distributed. If the calculated p-value is less than or equal to the alpha significance value, then reject the null hypothesis and accept the alternate hypothesis. Otherwise, if the p-value is higher than the alpha significance value, do not reject the null hypothesis. This test relies on two cumulative frequencies: one derived from the sample dataset and one from a theoretical distribution based on the mean and standard deviation of the sample data. An alternative to this test is the Chi-Square test for normality. The Chi-Square test requires more data points to run compared to the Lilliefors test.

- **Nonparametric Runs Test.** The Runs test evaluates the randomness of a series of observations by analyzing the number of runs it contains. A run is a consecutive appearance of one or more observations that are similar. The null hypothesis tested is whether the data sequence is random, versus the alternate hypothesis that the data sequence is not random.

- **Nonparametric Wilcoxon Signed-Rank (One Var).** The single-variable Wilcoxon Signed-Rank test looks at whether a sample dataset could have been randomly drawn from a particular population whose median is being hypothesized. The corresponding parametric test is the one-sample t-test, which should be used if the underlying population is assumed to be normal, providing a higher power on the test.

- **Nonparametric Wilcoxon Signed-Rank (Two Var).** The Wilcoxon Signed-Rank test for paired variables looks at whether the median of the differences between the two paired variables are equal. This test is specifically formulated for testing the same or similar samples before and after an event (e.g., measurements taken before a medical treatment are compared against those measurements taken after the treatment to see if there is a difference). The corresponding parametric test is the two-sample t-test with dependent means, which should be used if the underlying population is assumed to be normal, providing a higher power on the test.

Parametric Hypothesis Tests

The following are some sample parametric tests:

- **Parametric ANOVA: One-Way Single Factor with Multiple Treatments.** An extension of the two-variable t-test, looking at multiple variables simultaneously and when the sampling distribution is assumed to be approximately normal. A two-tailed hypothesis tests the null hypothesis such that the population means of each treatment is statistically identical to the rest of the group, indicating that there is no effect among the different treatment groups.

- **Parametric ANOVA: One-Way Randomized Block.** The sampling distribution is assumed to be approximately normal and when there exists a block variable for which ANOVA will control (i.e., block the effects of this variable by controlling it in the experiment). This analysis can test for the effects of both the treatments as well as the effectiveness of the control or block variable. If the calculated p-value for the treatment or block is less than or equal to the significance level used in the test, then reject the null hypothesis and conclude that there is a significant difference among the different treatments or blocks.

- **Parametric ANOVA: Two-Way.** An extension of the Single Factor and Randomized Block ANOVAs by simultaneously examining the effects of two factors on the dependent variable, along with the effects of interactions between the different levels of these two factors. Unlike the randomized block design, this model examines the interactions between different levels of the factors or independent variables. In a two-factor experiment, interaction exists when the effect of a level for one factor depends on which level of the other factor is present. There are three sets of null and alternate hypotheses to be tested.

- **Parametric One Variable (T).** The one-variable t-test of means is appropriate when the population standard deviation is not known but the sampling distribution is assumed to be approximately normal (the t-test is used when the sample size is less than 30). This t-test can be applied to three types of hypothesis tests—a two-tailed test, a right-tailed test, and a left-tailed test—to examine if the population mean is equal to, less than, or greater than the hypothesized mean based on the sample dataset.

- **Parametric One Variable (Z).** The one-variable Z-test is appropriate when the population standard deviation is known and the sampling distribution is assumed to be approximately normal (this applies when the number of data points exceeds 30).

- **Parametric One-Variable (Z) Proportion.** The one-variable Z-test for proportions is appropriate when the sampling distribution is assumed to be approximately normal (this applies when the number of data points exceeds 30, and when the number of data points, N, multiplied by the hypothesized population proportion mean, P, is greater than or equal to 5, $NP \geq 5$). The data used in the analysis have to be proportions and be between 0 and 1.

- **Parametric Two-Variable (T) Dependent.** The two-variable dependent t-test is appropriate when the population standard deviation is not known but the sampling distribution is assumed to be approximately normal (the t-test is used when the sample size is less than 30). In addition, this test is specifically formulated for testing the same or similar samples before and after an event (e.g., measurements taken before a medical treatment are compared against those measurements taken after the treatment to see if there is a difference).

- **Parametric Two-Variable (T) Independent Equal Variance.** The two-variable t-test with equal variances is appropriate when the population standard deviation is not known but the sampling distribution is assumed to be approximately normal (the t-test is used when the sample size is less than 30). In addition, the two independent samples are assumed to have similar variances.

- **Parametric Two-Variable (T) Independent Unequal Variance.** The two-variable t-test with unequal variances (the population variance of sample 1 is expected to be different from the population variance of sample 2) is appropriate when the population standard deviation is not known but the sampling distribution is assumed to be approximately normal (the t-test is used when the sample size is less than 30). In addition, the two independent samples are assumed to have similar variances.

- **Parametric Two-Variable (Z) Independent Means.** The two-variable Z-test is appropriate when the population standard deviations are known for the two samples, and the sampling distribution of each variable is assumed to be approximately normal (this applies when the number of data points of each variable exceeds 30).

- **Parametric Two-Variable (Z) Independent Proportions.** The two-variable Z-test on proportions is appropriate when the sampling distribution is assumed to be approximately normal (this applies when the number of data points of both samples exceeds 30). Further, the data should all be proportions and be between 0 and 1.

- **Parametric Two-Variable (F) Variances.** The two-variable F-test analyzes the variances from two samples (the population variance of Sample 1 is tested with the population variance of Sample 2 to see if they are equal) and is appropriate when the population standard deviation is not known but the sampling distribution is assumed to be approximately normal.

List of Analytical Methods (Continued)

The following is a continuation of the quick reference guide.

- **Principal Component Analysis.** Principal component analysis, or PCA, makes multivariate data easier to model and summarize. To understand PCA, suppose we start with N variables that are unlikely to be independent of one another, such that changing the value of one variable will change another variable. PCA modeling will replace the original N variables with a new set of M variables that are less than N but are uncorrelated to one another, while at the same time, each of these M variables is a linear combination of the original N variables, so that most of the variation can be accounted for just using fewer explanatory variables.

- **Seasonality.** Many time-series data exhibit seasonality where certain events repeat themselves after some time period or seasonality period (e.g., ski resorts' revenues are higher in winter than in summer, and this cycle will repeat itself every winter).

- **Segmentation Clustering.** Taking the original dataset, we run some internal algorithms (a combination or k-means hierarchical clustering and other method of moments in order to find the best-fitting groups or natural statistical clusters) to statistically divide or segment the original dataset into multiple groups.

- **Stepwise Regression (Backward).** In the backward method, we run a regression with Y on all X variables and reviewing each variable's p-value, systematically eliminate the variable with the largest p-value. Then run a regression again, repeating each time until all p-values are statistically significant.

- **Stepwise Regression (Correlation).** In the correlation method, the dependent variable Y is correlated to all the independent variables X, and starting with the X variable with the highest absolute correlation value, a regression is run. Then subsequent X variables are added until the p-values indicate that the new X variable is no longer statistically significant. This approach is quick and simple but does not account for interactions among variables, and an X variable, when added, will statistically overshadow other variables.

- **Stepwise Regression (Forward).** In the forward method, we first correlate Y with all X variables, run a regression for Y on the highest absolute value correlation of X, and obtain the fitting errors. Then, correlate these errors with the remaining X variables and choose the highest absolute value correlation among this remaining set and run another regression. Repeat the process until the p-value for the latest X variable coefficient is no longer statistically significant and then stop the process.

- **Stepwise Regression (Forward-Backward).** In the forward and backward method, apply the forward method to obtain three X variables, and then apply the backward approach to see if one of them needs to be eliminated because it is statistically insignificant. Repeat the forward method and then the backward method until all remaining X variables are considered.

- **Stochastic Processes.** Sometimes variables cannot be readily predicted using traditional means, and these variables are said to be stochastic. Nonetheless, most financial, economic, and naturally occurring phenomena (e.g., motion of molecules through the air) follow a known mathematical law or relationship. Although the resulting values are uncertain, the underlying mathematical structure is known and can be simulated using Monte Carlo risk simulation.

    o **Brownian Motion Random Walk Process.** The Brownian motion random walk process takes the form of $\frac{\delta S}{S} = \mu(\delta t) + \sigma \varepsilon \sqrt{\delta t}$ for regular options simulation, or a more generic version takes the form of $\frac{\delta S}{S} = (\mu - \sigma^2 / 2)\delta t + \sigma \varepsilon \sqrt{\delta t}$ for a geometric process. For an exponential version, we simply take the exponentials, and, as an example, we have $\frac{\delta S}{S} = \exp\left[\mu(\delta t) + \sigma \varepsilon \sqrt{\delta t}\right]$, where we define S as the variable's previous value, δS as the change in the variable's value from one step to the next, μ as the annualized growth or drift rate, and σ as the annualized volatility

    o **Mean-Reversion Process.** The following describes the mathematical structure of a mean-reverting process with drift: $\frac{\delta S}{S} = \eta(\bar{S}e^{\mu(\delta t)} - S)\delta t + \mu(\delta t) + \sigma \varepsilon \sqrt{\delta t}$. Here we define η as the rate of reversion to the mean and $\bar{S}$ as the long-term value the process reverts to.

    o **Jump-Diffusion Process.** A jump-diffusion process is similar to a random walk process but includes a probability of a jump at any point in time. The occurrences of such jumps are completely random but their probability and magnitude are governed by the process itself. We have the structure

$$\frac{\delta S}{S} = \eta(\bar{S}e^{\mu(\delta t)} - S)\delta t + \mu(\delta t) + \sigma\varepsilon\sqrt{\delta t} + \theta F(\lambda)(\delta t)$$ for a jump diffusion process and we define θ as the jump size of S, $F(\lambda)$ as the inverse of the Poisson cumulative probability distribution, and λ as the jump rate of S.

- o **Jump-Diffusion Process with Mean Reversion.** This model is essentially a combination of all three models discussed above (geometric Brownian motion with mean-reversion process and a jump-diffusion process).

- **Structural Break.** Tests if the coefficients in different datasets are equal, and is most commonly used in time-series analysis to test for the presence of a structural break. A time-series dataset can be divided into two subsets and each subset is tested on the other and on the entire dataset to statistically determine if, indeed, there is a break starting at a particular time period. A one-tailed hypothesis test is performed on the null hypothesis such that the two data subsets are statistically similar to one another; that is, there is no statistically significant structural break.

- **Time-Series Analysis.** In well-behaved time-series data (e.g., sales revenues and cost structures of large corporations), the values tend to have up to three elements: a base value, trend, and seasonality. Time-series analysis uses these historical data and decomposes them into these three elements, and recomposes them into future forecasts. In other words, this forecasting method, like some of the others described, first performs a backfitting (backcast) of historical data before it provides estimates of future values (forecasts).

  - o **Time-Series Analysis (Auto).** Selecting this automatic approach will allow the user to initiate an automated process in methodically selecting the best input parameters in each model and ranking the forecast models from best to worst by looking at their goodness-of-fit results and error measurements.

  - o **Time-Series Analysis (DES).** The double exponential-smoothing (DES) approach is used when the data exhibit a trend but no seasonality.

  - o **Time-Series Analysis (DMA).** The double moving average (DMA) method is used when the data exhibit a trend but no seasonality.

  - o **Time-Series Analysis (HWA).** The Holt–Winters Additive (HWA) approach is used when the data exhibit both seasonality and trend.

  - o **Time-Series Analysis (HWM).** The Holt–Winters Multiplicative (HWM) approach is used when the data exhibit both seasonality and trend.

  - o **Time-Series Analysis (SA).** The Seasonal Additive (SA) approach is used when the data exhibit seasonality but no trend.

  - o **Time-Series Analysis (SM).** The Seasonal Multiplicative (SM) approach is used when the data exhibit seasonality but no trend.

  - o **Time-Series Analysis (SES).** The Single Exponential Smoothing (SES) approach is used when the data exhibit no trend and no seasonality.

  - o **Time-Series Analysis (SMA).** The Single Moving Average (SMA) approach is used when the data exhibit no trend and no seasonality.

- **Trending and Detrending:** The following are typical methods for trending and detrending data: Difference, Exponential, Linear, Logarithmic, Moving Average, Polynomial, Power, Rate, Static Mean, and Static Median. Detrends your original data to take out any trending components. In forecasting models, the process removes the effects of accumulating datasets from seasonality and trend to show only the absolute changes in values and to allow potential cyclical patterns to be identified after removing the general drift, tendency, twists, bends, and effects of seasonal cycles of a set of time-series data. For example, a detrended dataset may be necessary to discover a company's true financial health—one may detrend increased sales around Christmas time to see a more accurate account of a company's sales in a given year more clearly by shifting the entire dataset from a slope to a flat surface to better see the underlying cycles and fluctuations. The resulting charts show the effects of the detrended data against the original dataset, and the statistics reports show the percentage of the trend that was removed based on each detrending method employed, as well as the actual detrended dataset.

- **Volatility: GARCH Models.** The Generalized Autoregressive Conditional Heteroskedasticity model is used to model historical and forecast future volatility levels of a time-series of raw price levels of a marketable security (e.g., stock prices, commodity prices, and oil prices). GARCH first converts the prices into relative returns, and then runs an internal optimization to fit the historical data to a mean-reverting volatility term structure, while assuming that the volatility is heteroskedastic in nature (changes over time according to some econometric characteristics). Several variations of this methodology are available in Risk Simulator, including EGARCH, EGARCH-T, GARCH-M, GJR-GARCH, GJR-GARCH-T, IGARCH, and T-GARCH. The dataset has to be a time series of raw price levels.

- **Volatility: Log Returns Approach.** Calculates the volatility using the individual future cash flow estimates, comparable cash flow estimates, or historical prices, computing the annualized standard deviation of the corresponding logarithmic relative returns.

- **Yield Curve (Bliss).** Used for generating the term structure of interest rates and yield curve estimation with five estimated parameters. Some econometric modeling techniques are required to calibrate the values of several input parameters in this model. Virtually any yield curve shape can be interpolated using these models, which are widely used at banks around the world.

- **Yield Curve (Nelson–Siegel).** An interpolation model with four estimated parameters for generating the term structure of interest rates and yield curve estimation. Some econometric modeling techniques are required to calibrate the values of several input parameters in this model.

ENDNOTES

Chapter 1

1. Peter L. Bernstein, *Against the Gods: The Remarkable Story of Risk.* (Wiley, 1996).

2. Save the potentiality of a plane crash, in which case I would have very much regretted not taking the parachute.

3. The concepts of high risk and high return are nothing new and are central to the development of the *capital asset pricing model* (*CAPM*) used to estimate the required rate of return on a project based on its *systematic risk*. In the *CAPM* model, the higher the risk, the higher the expected rate of return (*ceteris paribus,* or holding everything else constant).

4. Risk can be measured in different ways. In this example, it is measured using the standard deviation of the distribution of returns.

5. This selection is because Project X bears a positive net return (positive net present value) above its implementation cost, making it profitable. Thus, the cheapest project is selected.

6. Independence means that the projects themselves are uncorrelated, thus it is assumed that there are no risk-diversification effects. Mutually exclusive means that the manager cannot mix and match among the different projects (e.g., 2 Project Xs with 3 Project Ys).

7. This choice, of course, is based purely on financial analysis alone by holding everything else constant (management's taste and preferences, or other strategic values inherent in different projects).

8. On a continuous basis, the probability of hitting exactly $30 (i.e., $30.0000000000 and so forth) is very close to zero. The probability in a distribution is measured as the area under the curve, which means two values are required, for example, the probability of net revenues being between $29 and $31 is 25 percent. Thus, the area under the curve for a single-point estimate (a single line in a distribution) is close to zero.

9. The *Law of Demand* in economics requires that, in most cases, price and quantity demanded are negatively correlated, in accordance with a downward-sloping demand curve. The exception being Giffen or status goods where a higher price may yield a higher quantity demanded (e.g., Porsches are desirable and have a higher status because they are expensive, among other things).

10. A firm's average variable cost curve is U shaped, with an initial downward slope at lower quantities (economies of scale), hits a global minimum value where marginal cost equals average variable cost, and then continues to slope upward (diseconomies of scale).

11. The weighted average cost of capital (WACC) is a commonly used approach to compute the discount rate used in a discounted cash flow model, comprising the weighted average of three cost of capital elements: common equity, preferred equity, and debt (bonds).

12. See Chapter 7 for details on time-series and regression models.

13. DCF means discounted cash flow model, a typical financial analysis model used to evaluate the profitability of projects.

14. The simulated actual values depicted graphically are based on a geometric Brownian motion with a volatility of 20 percent calculated as the standard deviation of the simulated natural logarithms of historical returns.

15. See Chapter 2 for details of other measures of risk and uncertainty.

Chapter 2

16. Ron Denbo and Andrew Freeman, *Seeing Tomorrow: Rewriting the Rules of Risk* (John Wiley & Sons, 1998). This book provides an interesting nonmathematical review of risk management.

17. That is, the standard deviation of the population (σ) and the standard deviation of a sample (s) are

$$\sigma = \sqrt{\frac{\sum_{i=1}^{N}(x_i - \mu)^2}{N}} \qquad s = \sqrt{\frac{\sum_{i=1}^{n}(x_i - \overline{x})^2}{n-1}}$$ where the standard deviation is the square root

of the sum of the deviation of each data point (x_i) from the population mean (μ) or sample mean ($\overline{x}$) squared, and then divided into the population size (N) or sample size (n) less one. For the sample statistic, the division is into n less one to correct for the degrees of freedom in a smaller sample size. The variance is simply the square of the standard deviation.

18. Johnathan Mun, *Real Options Analysis,* Second Edition (Wiley 2005) or Johnathan Mun, *Real Options Analysis Course* (Wiley 2003). Refer to these books for details on estimating volatility in a real options context.

19. For instance, the height distribution's mean is 10 m with a standard deviation of 1 m, which yields a coefficient variation of 0.1, versus the weight distribution's mean of 100 kg and a standard deviation of 20 kg, which yields a coefficient of variation of 0.2. Clearly, the weight distribution carries with it more variability.

Chapter 3

20. This example is an adaptation from papers and lectures provided by Professor Sam Savage of Stanford University.

21. In this example, the median is a better measure of central tendency.

22. The same nonparametric simulation can also be applied using Risk Simulator's custom distribution where each occurrence has an equal chance of being selected.

23. The approach used here is the application of a geometric Brownian motion stochastic process for forecasting and simulating potential outcomes.

Chapter 4

24. This approach is valid because in typical simulations, thousands of trials are being simulated and the assumption of normality can be applied.

Chapter 7

25. An arbitrary 3-month moving average is chosen. For modeling purposes, different n-length moving averages should be computed and the one with the least amount of errors should be chosen.

26. To start Excel's Data Analysis, first click on *File | Options | Add-Ins | Excel Add-Ins | Go.* Then make sure the checkbox beside *Analysis Tool Pak* is selected and hit *OK.* Then return to the *Data* tab and select *Data Analysis.* The *Regression* functionality should now exist.

27. See Chapter 6, Tomorrow's Forecast Today, for specifics on using Risk Simulator.

28. The critical t-statistic can be found in the t-distribution table at the end of this book, by looking down the two-tailed alpha 0.025 (alpha 0.05 for two tails means that each tail has an area of 0.025) and cross-referencing it to 6 degrees of freedom. The degrees-of-freedom is calculated as the number of data points, n (7), used in the regression, less the number of independent regressors, k (1).

29. As this is a two-tailed hypothesis test, the alpha should be halved, which means that as long as the p-value calculated is less than 0.025 (half of 0.05), then the null hypothesis should be rejected.

30. The adjusted R-squared is used here as this is a multivariate regression, and the adjustment in the coefficient of determination accounts for the added independent variable.

31. The two most notable and challenging econometric models include the ARCH (Autoregressive Conditional Heteroskedasticity) as well as the GARCH (Generalized Autoregressive Conditional Heteroskedasticity) models.

Chapter 8

32. For a total cost of $550 for the entire trip.

33. The number of possible itineraries is simply the factorial of the number of cities, that is, $3! = 3 \times 2 \times 1 = 6$.

34. A total of five cities means $5! = 5 \times 4 \times 3 \times 2 \times 1 = 120$.

35. A triangular distribution can be applied here, with the minimum level set at $300, most likely value of $325, and a maximum level set at $500.

36. The straight lines in Figure 8.6 would now be nonlinear and the problem would be difficult to solve graphically.

37. To access Solver, start Excel, click on *File | Options | Add-Ins | Excel Add-Ins | Go.* Then make sure the checkbox beside *Solver* is selected and hit *OK.* Solver can then be accessed by clicking on *Data* tab and selecting *Solver.*

38. A two-decision variable optimization problem requires a two-dimensional graph, which means an n-decision variable problem requires the use of an n-dimensional graph, making the problem manually intractable using the graphical method.

39. Chapter 9, Optimization under Uncertainty, illustrates a similar portfolio-optimization process but under uncertainty using Risk Simulator.

Chapter 12

40. The problem of omitted variables is less vital as an analyst will simply have to work with all available data. If everything about the future is known, then why bother forecasting? If there is no uncertainty, then the future is known with certainty.

41. The problem of redundant variables is also known as multicollinearity.

42. For instance, if a dummy variable on sex is used (i.e., "0" for male and "1" for female), then a regression equation with *both* dummy variables will be perfectly collinear. In such a situation, simply drop one of the dummy variables as they are mutually exclusive of each other.

43. Make sure there are no independent variables that are perfectly or almost perfectly correlated to each other. In addition, correlation analysis can be performed to test the linear relationships among the independent variables.

44. If Y is the dependent variable and X_i are the independent variables, then the correlation pairs are between all possible combinations of Y and X_i.

45. Interest rates tend to be time dependent (mean-reverting over longer periods of time) and demand for a product that is not related to interest rate movements may also be time dependent (exhibiting cyclicality and seasonality effects).

46. The term "auto" means self and "regressive" means reverting to the past. Hence, the term autoregressive means to revert back to one's own past history.

47. Seasonality effects are usually due to periodicities in time (12-month seasonality in a year, 4-quarter seasonality in a year, 7-day seasonality in a week, etc.), while cyclical effects are due to larger influences without regard to periodicities (e.g., business cycle movements and technological innovation cycles).

48. However, there are other approaches used to estimate causality, for example, Granger causality approaches look at statistical causalities.

49. More advanced econometric models are required to estimate random walks, including methods using differences and unit root models.

50. See *Real Options Analysis*, 2nd Edition (Wiley, 2005) and *Real Options Analysis Course* (Wiley, 2003) for details on interacting options and chooser options.

51. In this case, the option value is explicit, or something that is tangible and the seller of the option can actually acquire this value.

52. Management's compensation should not be tied to actualizing this implicit option.

53. This means the decision strategies are: A-B, A-C, and A-C-D.

54. Optimization under uncertainty means to run a set of simulations for a certain number of trials (e.g., 1,000 trials), pause, estimate the forecast distributions, test a set of combinations of decision variables, and rerun the entire analysis again, for hundreds to thousands of times.

Chapter 14

55. Advanced analytics are all the applications discussed in this book, including simulation, time-series forecasting, regression, optimization, and real options.

56. Examples of an academic exercise that has little pragmatic application for general consumption in the areas of advanced analytics include sensitivity simulation, variance reduction, closed-form partial-differential models, and so forth. These are mathematically elegant approaches, but they require analysts with advanced degrees in finance and mathematics to apply, making the methodology and results very difficult to explain to management.

57. The case is made through the actual business cases and examples in this book.

58. This is particularly true for Monte Carlo simulation where simulation cannot be applied unless there already is a spreadsheet model.

ANSWERS TO END OF CHAPTER QUESTIONS

Chapter 1

1. Why is risk important in making decisions?

Risk is important in decision making as it provides an added element of insight into the project being evaluated. Projects with higher returns usually carry with them higher risks, and neglecting the element of risk means that the decision maker may unnecessarily select the riskiest projects.

2. Describe the concept of bang for the buck.

Bang for the buck implies selecting the best project or combination of projects that yields the highest returns subject to the minimum amount of risk. That is, given some set of risk, what is the best project or combination of projects that provides the best returns? Conversely, it also answers what the minimum level of risk is, subject to some prespecified return. This concept is the Markowitz efficient frontier in portfolio optimization discussed later in the book.

3. Compare and contrast between risk and uncertainty.

Uncertainty implies an event's outcome in which no one knows for sure what may occur. Uncertainties can range from the fluctuation in the stock market to the occurrences of sunspots. In contrast, uncertainties that affect the outcome of a project's or asset's value directly or indirectly are termed risks.

Chapter 2

1. What is the efficient frontier and when is it used?

The efficient frontier was first introduced by Nobel laureate Harry Markowitz and it captures the concept of bang for the buck where projects or assets are first grouped into portfolios. Then, the combinations of projects or assets that provide the highest returns subject to the varying degrees of risk are calculated. The best and most efficient combinations of projects or assets are graphically represented and termed the efficient frontier.

2. What are inferential statistics and what steps are required in making inferences?

Inferential statistics refers to the branch of statistics that performs statistical analysis on smaller-sized samples to infer the true nature of the population. The steps undertaken include designing the experiment, collecting the data, analyzing the data, estimating or predicting alternate conditions, testing of the hypothesis, testing of goodness-of-fit, and making decisions based on the results.

3. When is using standard deviation less desirable than using semi-standard deviation as a measure of risk?

Standard deviation measures the average deviation of each data point from the mean, which implies that both upside and downside deviations are captured in a standard deviation calculation. In contrast, only the downside deviations are captured in the semi-standard deviation measure. The semi-standard deviation when used as a measure of risk is more appropriate if only downsides are deemed as risky.

4. If comparing three projects' net profitability or returns with similar first, second, and fourth moments, would you prefer a project that has no skew, a positive skew, or a negative skew?

Holding everything else constant, projects with negative skew are preferred as the higher probability of occurrences are weighted more on the higher net returns.

5. If comparing three projects with similar first to third moments, would you prefer a project that is leptokurtic (high kurtosis), mesokurtic (average kurtosis), or platykurtic (low kurtosis)? Explain your reasoning with respect to a distribution's tail area. Under what conditions would your answer change?

The answer depends on the type of project. For instance, for financial assets such as stocks, clearly a lower kurtosis stock implies a lower probability of occurrence in the extreme areas, or that catastrophic losses are less likely to occur. However, the disadvantage is that the probability of an extreme upside is also lessened.

6. What are the differences and similarities between Value at Risk and worst-case scenario as a measure of risk?

Value at Risk (VaR) measures the worst-case outcome for a particular holding period with respect to a given probability. For instance, the worst-case 5 percent probability VaR of a particular project is $1 million for a 10-year economic life with a 90 percent statistical confidence. Compare that to a simplistic worst-case scenario, which in most cases are single-point estimates, for example, the worst-case scenario for the project is a $10,000 loss. Worst-case scenarios can be added to probabilistic results as in the VaR approach but are usually single-point estimates (usually just a management assumption or guesstimate).

Chapter 3

1. Compare and contrast parametric and nonparametric simulation.

Parametric simulation is an approach that requires distributional parameters to be first assigned before it can begin. For instance, a Monte Carlo simulation of 1,000 trials using input assumptions in a normal distribution with an average of 10 and standard deviation of 2 is a parametric simulation. In contrast, nonparametric simulation uses historical or comparable data to run the simulation, where specific distributional assumptions (i.e., size and shape of the distribution, type of distribution and its related inputs such as average or standard deviation, and so forth) are not required. Nonparametric simulation is used when the data are "left alone to tell the story."

2. What is a stochastic process (e.g., Brownian motion)?

The term stochastic means the opposite of deterministic. Stochastic variables are characterized by their randomness, for example, a stock's price movement over time. A stochastic process is a mathematical relationship that captures this random characteristic over time. The most common stochastic process is the Brownian motion random walk used to simulate stock prices.

3. What does the "RAND()" function do in Excel?

The RAND( ) function in Excel creates a random number from the uniform distribution between 0 and 1. Hitting *F9* repeatedly on the keyboard will generate additional random numbers from the same distribution.

4. What does the "NORMSINV()" function do in Excel?

The NORMSINV() function in Excel calculates the inverse of the standard cumulative normal distribution with a mean of zero and a standard deviation of one or Normal (0,1).

5. What happens when both functions are used together, that is, "NORMSINV(RAND())"?

When used in conjunction, the function NORMSINV(RAND()) simulates a standard-normal distribution random variable.

Chapter 4

1. Why do you need to have profiles in a simulation?

Starting a new profile is like starting a new file in Excel, but a profile is part of the Excel file and holds all the information on the simulation parameters. That is, you can perform scenario analysis on simulation by creating multiple similar profiles and changing each profile's distributional assumptions and parameters and see what the resulting differences are.

2. Explain the differences between Pearson's product moment correlation coefficient and Spearman's rank-based correlation.

Pearson's product moment correlation coefficient is a linear parametric correlation where the two variables being correlated are assumed to be linearly related and the underlying assumption is that the correlation's distribution is normal. Spearman's rank-based correlation is a nonparametric correlation that can account for nonlinearities between variables and is, hence, more robust and better suited for use in simulation where different distributions can be correlated to one another due to its nonparametric properties that do not rely on the normal assumption.

3. Will more or fewer trials be required to obtain: higher error levels, higher precision levels, and wider confidence interval?

More simulation trials are required to obtain a lower error level, a higher precision level, and a narrower confidence interval.

4. Explain the differences between error and precision, and how these two concepts are linked.

Error and precision are related but they are not the same thing. Error relates to how far off a particular value is, that is, its forecast interval. For example, the mean is 10 with an error of 1, which means that the forecast interval is between 9 and 11. However, precision indicates the level of confidence of this forecast interval. For example, this error has a 90% precision, which means that 90% of the time, the error will be between 9 and 11.

5. If you know that two simulated variables are correlated but do not have the relevant correlation value, should you still go ahead and correlate them in a simulation?

Yes. Even using rough rules of thumb such as ±0.25 (low correlation), ±0.50 (moderate correlation), and ±0.75 (strong correlation) when, in fact, there are correlations among the variables, although their exact values are unknown, will provide better estimates than not applying these correlations.

Chapter 5

1. Name the key similarities and differences between a tornado chart and a spider chart. Then, compare tornado and spider charts with sensitivity analysis.

Tornado and spider charts are used to obtain the static sensitivities of a variable to its precedents by perturbing each of the precedent variables one at a time at a prespecified range. They are typically applied before a simulation is run and no simulation assumptions are required in the analysis. In contrast, sensitivity analysis is applied after a simulation run and requires both assumptions and forecasts. The assumptions are applied in a dynamic environment (with the relevant correlations and truncations) and the sensitivities of the forecast to each of the assumptions are then computed.

2. In distributional fitting, sometimes you may not get the distribution you thought is the right fit as the best choice. Why is this so? Also, why does the beta distribution usually come up as one of the top few candidates as the best-fitting distribution?

Some of the distributions are fairly closely related to one another (for instance, the Poisson and binomial distributions become normally distributed when their rates and number of trials increase) and it will be no surprise that some other distribution may be a better fit. In addition, distributions like the beta are highly flexible and can assume multiple shapes and forms, and hence can be used to fit multiple distributions and datasets.

3. Briefly explain what a hypothesis test is.

A hypothesis test is used to test if a certain value or parameter is similar to or different from another hypothesized value—for example, whether two means from two different distributions are statistically similar or different.

4. How is bootstrap simulation related to precision and error control in simulation?

Bootstrap simulation is used to obtain a forecast statistic's confidence interval and, hence, can be used to determine a statistic's precision and error level.

5. In sensitivity analysis, how is percent variation explained linked to rank correlation?

The square of the nonlinear rank correlation coefficient is an approximation of the percent variation in a sensitivity analysis.

Chapter 6

1. What are the differences between time-series forecasting techniques and nonlinear extrapolation?

Time-series forecasting can be used to incorporate linear trends and seasonality in the forecasts, while nonlinear extrapolation can only incorporate a nonlinear trend in its forecast. The former cannot include a nonlinear trend, while the latter cannot have a seasonality component in its forecasts.

2. Which forecasting method requires existing data and which method does not?

All forecasting methods require data except for stochastic process forecasts, which does not require any historical or comparable data, albeit the existence of data can be exploited by using these data to compute the relevant growth rate, volatility, reversion rate, jump rates, and so forth used in generating these stochastic processes.

3. How do you use the software to perform qualitative forecasts?

A Delphi survey method can be applied and the results of the survey can be used to generate a custom distribution. Simulation can, hence, be applied on this custom distribution.

4. Time-series data that exhibit seasonality are easier to forecast than data that exhibit cyclicality. Is this statement true and why or why not?

This statement is true. Seasonality is, in most cases, easy to forecast, but cyclicality is more difficult if not impossible to forecast. Examples of seasonality effects include the sales levels of ski passes (peaks during winter and troughs during summer and, hence, are fairly easy to predict year after year) versus cyclicality effects like the business cycle or stock price cycles (extremely hard to predict as the timing, frequency, and magnitude of peaks and troughs are highly unpredictable).

Chapter 7

1. Explain what each of the following terms means:

   o Time-series analysis

The application of forecasting methodology on data that depends on time.

   o Ordinary least squares

A type of regression analysis that minimizes the sum of the square of errors.

   o Regression analysis

The estimation of the best-fitting line through a series of historical data used to predict a statistical relationship or to forecast the future based on this relationship.

   o Heteroskedasticity

The variance of the errors of a regression analysis is unstable over time.

   o Autocorrelation

The historical data of a variable depends on or is correlated to itself over time.

   o Multicollinearity

The independent variables are highly correlated to each other or there exists an exact linear relationship between the independent variables

   o ARIMA

Autoregressive Integrated Moving Average—a type of forecasting methodology.

2. What is the difference between the R-squared versus the adjusted R-squared measure in a regression analysis? When is each applicable and why?

The R-squared or coefficient of determination is used on bivariate regressions whereas the adjusted R-squared is used on multivariate regressions. The latter penalizes the excessive use of independent variables through a degree of freedom correction, making it a more conservative measure useful in multivariate regressions.

3. Explain why if each of the following is not detected properly or corrected for in the model, the estimated regression model will be flawed:

a. Heteroskedasticity

In the event of heteroskedasticity, the estimated R-squared is fairly low and the regression equation is both insufficient and incomplete, leading to potentially large estimation errors.

b. Autocorrelation

If autocorrelated dependent variable values exist, the estimates of the slope and intercept will be unbiased, but the estimates of their variances will not be reliable and, hence, the validity of certain statistical goodness-of-fit tests will be flawed.

c. Multicollinearity

In perfect multicollinearity, the regression equation cannot be estimated at all. In near-perfect collinearity, the estimated regression equation will be inefficient and inaccurate. The corresponding R-squared is inflated and the t-statistics are lower than actual.

4. For the answers to Question 4's Exercises, please refer to the ROV website. The files are freely downloadable.

5. Explain briefly how to fix the problem of nonlinearity in the dataset.

Nonlinear independent variables can be transformed into linear variables by taking the logarithm, square (or higher powers), square root, or multiplicative combinations of the independent variables. A new regression is then run based on these newly transformed variables.

Chapter 8

1. What is the difference between deterministic optimization and optimization under uncertainty?

Deterministic optimization means that the input variables are single-point deterministic values, whereas optimization under uncertainty means that the input variables are uncertain and simulated while the optimization process is occurring.

2. Define then compare and contrast each of the following:

o Objective

An objective is the forecast output value that is to be maximized or minimized in an optimization (e.g., profits).

o Constraint

A constraint is a restriction that is observed in an optimization (e.g., budget constraint).

o Decision variable

The variables that can be changed based on management decisions such that the objective is achieved. These variables are usually subject to the constraints in the model.

3. Explain what some of the problems are in a graphical linear programming approach and if they can be easily solved.

Some problems arising from a graphical linear programming approach include nonlinear constraints, unbounded solutions, no feasible solutions, multiple solutions, and too many constraints. These problems cannot be solved graphically.

4. What are some of the approaches to solve an optimization problem? List each approach as well as their corresponding pros and cons.

The graphical approach is simple to implement but may sometimes be too tedious if too many constraints or nonlinear constraints exist. Optimization can also be solved mathematically by taking first and second derivatives but is more difficult to do. Excel's Solver add-in can be used to systematically search by brute force through a series of input combinations to find the optimal solution but the results may be local minimums or local maximums, providing false answers. Risk Simulator can also be used to solve an optimization problem under uncertainty when the input assumptions are unknown and simulated.

Chapter 9

1. Compare and contrast between a discrete versus continuous decision variable when used in an optimization under uncertainty.

Discrete decision variables are typically integers such as 0, 1, 2, 3, and so forth, whereas continuous variables can vary between any two values (e.g., between 0 and 1, we can have an infinite number of values such as 0.113354, 0.00012546, and so forth).

Chapter 10

1. Create your own definition of real options analysis.

Real options analysis is a critical part of the Integrated Risk Management methodology that is used to hedge risks and to take advantage of upside uncertainties, where management has flexibility in making midcourse corrections on decisions when uncertainties become resolved through the passage of time, actions, and events; and strategic real options is used for identifying and valuing the optimal strategic decision pathways to execute.

2. What are some of the possible approaches used to solve a real options analysis problem?

Real options can be solved using closed-form models, simulation approaches, binomial and multinomial lattices, as well as other more advanced numerical approaches such as variance reduction and partial differential equations.

3. In choosing the right methodology to be used in a real options analysis, what are some of the key requirements that should be considered?

The method must be valid, accurate, replicable, tractable, robust, explainable, and, most importantly, flexible enough to handle various inputs and able to mirror real-life conditions.

4. What are the necessary conditions that must exist before real options analysis can be applied on a project?

A model must exist or can be built; there must exist uncertainties and risks in the decision; these uncertainties and risks must affect the outcomes and, hence, the decisions in the project; there must be strategic flexibility or options in the project; and the decision makers or senior management must be credible enough to execute the options when they become optimal to do so.

5. What is the major limitation of only using Monte Carlo simulation to perform risk analysis?

The risks and uncertainties are not hedged or taken advantage of. That is, simulation can be used to forecast, predict and quantify risks, but only real options analysis can be applied to hedge these risks or to take advantage of the upside.

Chapter 12

1. Define what is meant by negligent entrustment.

Negligent entrustment simply means that management takes the results from some fancy analytics generated by an analyst as is, without any due diligence performed on them. This situation usually occurs because management does not understand the approach used or know the relevant questions to ask.

2. What are some of the general types of errors encountered by an analyst when creating a model?

Some general types of errors encountered when creating a model include model errors, assumption and input errors, analytical errors, user errors, and interpretation errors.

3. Why is truncation in a model's assumption important? What would happen to the results if truncation is not applied when it should be?

If truncation is not applied when it should be, then the resulting forecast distribution will be too wide and the errors of estimations too large. Therefore, truncation is important as it provides results that are more accurate with lower errors.

4. What is a critical success driver?

A critical success driver is an input variable that has significant impact on the output result. By itself, the input variable is also highly uncertain and should be simulated.

5. What are some of the normal-looking statistics?

A skewness of 0 and a kurtosis of 3 or excess kurtosis of 0 are considered normal-looking statistics.

6. What are structural breaks and specification errors, and why are they important?

Structural breaks occur when the underlying variable undergoes certain economic, business or financial shifts (e.g., merger or divestiture). Specification errors occur when the underlying variable follows some nonlinearities (e.g., growth curves, exponential, or cyclical curves) but the regression is estimated based on a strict linear model.

SOFTWARE
DOWNLOAD & INSTALL

As current versions of the software are updated all the time, we highly recommend that you visit the Real Options Valuation, Inc., website and follow the instructions below to install the latest software applications.

- **Step 1**: Visit **www.realoptionsvaluation.com** and click on **Downloads** and **Download Software** (Figure A). You will be prompted to log in. Please first register if you are a first-time user (Figure B) and an automated e-mail will be sent to you within several minutes. (If you do not receive a registration e-mail after you register, then please send a note to support@realoptionsvaluation.com.) While waiting for the automated e-mail, browse this page and see the free getting started videos, case studies, and sample models you can download.

- **Step 2**: Return to this site and LOGIN using the login credentials you received via e-mail. Download and install the latest versions of **Risk Simulator** and **Real Options SLS** on this Web page. The download links, installation instructions, and Hardware ID information are also presented on this page (Figure C).

- **Step 3**: After installing the software, start Excel and you will see a Risk Simulator ribbon. Follow the instructions provided on the Web page to obtain and e-mail support@realoptionsvaluation.com your Hardware ID and mention the code **"MR3E 30 Days"** and you will be sent a free extended 30-day license to use both the Risk Simulator and Real Options SLS software.

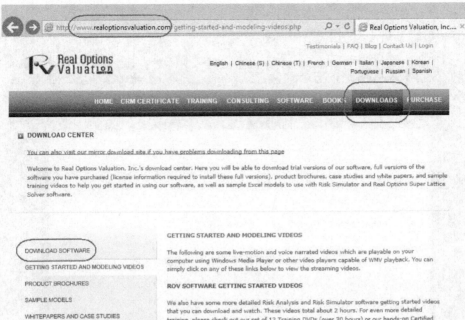

Figure A: Step 1 – Software download site

Figure B: Register if you are a first-time visitor

English | Chinese (S) | Chinese (T) | French | German | Italian | Japanese | Korean | Portuguese | Russian | Spanish

HOME   CRM CERTIFICATE   TRAINING   CONSULTING   SOFTWARE   BOOKS   **DOWNLOADS**   PURCHASE

DOWNLOAD CENTER

You can also visit our mirror download site if you have problems downloading from this page

Welcome to Real Options Valuation, Inc.'s download center. Here you will be able to download trial versions of our software, full versions of the software you have purchased (license information required to install these full versions), product brochures, case studies and white papers, and sample training videos to help you get started in using our software, as well as sample Excel models to use with Risk Simulator and Real Options Super Lattice Solver software.

DOWNLOAD SOFTWARE

GETTING STARTED AND MODELING VIDEOS

PRODUCT BROCHURES

SAMPLE MODELS

WHITEPAPERS AND CASE STUDIES

SOFTWARE DOWNLOADS

Risk Simulator

SOFTWARE DOWNLOADS SOFTWARE DOWNLOAD: RISK SIMULATOR 2014
(ENGLISH, FRENCH, GERMAN, ITALIAN, JAPANESE, KOREAN, PORTUGUESE, SIMPLIFIED CHINESE, TRADITIONAL CHINESE, SPANISH, RUSSIAN)

FULL & TRIAL VERSION DOWNLOAD:

Download Risk Simulator 2014 [WIN x32/x64 and Excel x32 most common edition]
Download Risk Simulator 2014 [WIN x32/x64 and Excel x32 most common edition] (mirror site)

Download Risk Simulator 2014 [WIN x64 and Excel x64 special edition]
Download Risk Simulator 2014 [WIN x64 and Excel x64 special edition] (mirror site)

This is a full version of the software but will expire in 15 days, during which time you can purchase a license to permanently unlock the software. Please first **uninstall all previous versions** of Risk Simulator before installing this newer version.

To permanently unlock the software, purchase a license and e-mail us your Hardware ID (after installing the software, start **Excel**, click on **Risk Simulator, License**, and e-mail admin@realoptionsvaluation.com the 16 to 20 digit **Hardware ID** located on the bottom left of the splash screen). We will then e-mail you a permanent license file. **Save** this file to your hard drive, start **Excel**, click on **Risk Simulator, License, Install License** and point to the location of this license file, restart Excel and you are now permanently licensed. Installing the license only takes a few seconds.

System requirements, FAQ, and additional resources:

. Windows XP, Vista (32 and 64 bit), Windows 7 (32 and 64 bit), or Windows 8 (32 and 64 bit)
. Microsoft Excel XP, 2003, 2007, 2010, or 2013
. 1GB RAM Minimum (2 GB minimum recommended)
. 350 MB Hard Drive
. Administrative Rights to install software
. Microsoft .NET Framework 2.0, 3.0, 3.5 or later
. MAC OS users will require either Virtual Machine or Parallels running Microsoft Excel

Figure C: Download links and hardware ID instructions

INDEX

BOOKS BY DR. JOHNATHAN MUN

See: www.amazon.com/author/johnathanmun for any newer books and updates

Real Options Analysis:
Tools and Techniques for
Valuing Strategic
Investments & Decisions,
3rd Edition
680 Pages (2016)
ROV Press

Certified Quantitative
Risk Management
(CQRM): Readings
736 Pages (2015)
IIPER Press

Modeling Risk: Applying
Monte Carlo Risk
Simulation, Strategic Real
Options Analysis,
Stochastic Forecasting,
and Portfolio
Optimization, 3rd Edition
1112 Pages (2015)
ISBN: 978-0470592212
Thomson–Shore

Certified Quantitative
Risk Management
(CQRM): Case Studies
352 Pages (2015)
IIPER Press

Advanced Analytical
Models in ROV Modeling
Toolkit: Over 800 Models
and 300 Applications from
the Basel Accords to Wall
Street and Beyond
760 Pages (2016)
ROV Press

Risk Simulator Guide
216 Pages (2015)
ISBN: 978-1515273639
ROV Press

Credit Engineering
for Bankers
(with Morton Glantz)
529 Pages (2010)
ISBN: 978-0123785855
Elsevier Academic Press

PEAT: Project
Economics Analysis Tool
348 Pages (2015)
ISBN: 978-1515273530
ROV Press

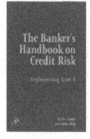

The Banker's Handbook
on Credit Risk
(with Morton Glantz)
420 Pages (2008)
ISBN: 978-0123736666
Elsevier Science

Real Options SLS Guide
152 Pages (2015)
ISBN: 978-1515273677
ROV Press

 CQRM Training
250 Pages (2015)
ISBN: Restricted
ROV Press

 Modeling Risk:
Applying Monte Carlo
Simulation, Real
Options Analysis,
Stochastic Forecasting,
and Optimization
610 Pages (2006)
ISBN: 0-471-78900-3
Wiley Finance

 Modeling Risk: Applying
Monte Carlo Risk
Simulation, Strategic Real
Options, Stochastic
Forecasting, Portfolio
Optimization, 2nd Ed.
1112 Pages (2005)
ISBN: 978-1943290000
Wiley Finance

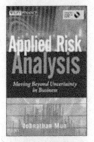 Applied Risk Analysis:
Moving Beyond
Uncertainty
460 Pages (2003)
ISBN: 0-471-47885-7
Wiley Finance

 Real Options Analysis:
Tools and Techniques for
Valuing Strategic
Investments & Decisions,
2nd Edition
670 Pages (2005)
ISBN: 978-0471747483
Wiley Finance

 Real Options Analysis
Course: Business Cases
and Software
Applications
360 Pages (2003)
ISBN: 0-471-43001-3
Wiley Finance

 Advanced Analytical
Models: Over 800 Models
and 300 Applications from
the Basel Accords to Wall
Street and Beyond
1002 Pages (2008)
ISBN: 978-0470179215
Wiley Finance

 Real Options Analysis:
Tools and Techniques
for Valuing Strategic
Investments &
Decisions
416 Pages (2002)
ISBN: 0-471-25696-X
Wiley Finance

 Valuing Employee Stock
Options: Under 2004
FAS 123
320 Pages (2004)
ISBN: 0-471-70512-8
Wiley Finance

 Managing Your
Finances God's Way
128 Pages (2015)
ISBN: 978-1515212362
ROV Press

Made in the USA
Columbia, SC
26 September 2024

43077773R00402